Index of Sample Documents

Index of Sample Documents

Messages

Proposals

External Proposals

Internal Proposals

Research

Index of Sample Documents

Reports

Formal Reports

Informal Reports

Résumés

Parts of Résumés

Sample Résumés

Visuals

Data

Images

Presentations

Writing That Works

Communicating Effectively on the Job

TWELFTH EDITION

Writing That Works

Communicating Effectively on the Job

Walter E. Oliu

Charles T. Brusaw

Gerald J. Alred

bedford/st.martin's
Macmillan Learning
Boston | New York

For Bedford/St. Martin's

Vice President, Editorial, Macmillan Higher Education Humanities: Edwin Hill
Editorial Director, English: Karen S. Henry
Senior Publisher for Composition and Business and Technical Writing: Leasa Burton
Executive Editor: Molly Parke
Developmental Editor: Rachel C. Childs
Media Producer: Melissa Skepko-Masi
Publishing Services Manager: Andrea Cava
Production Supervisor: Robert Cherry
Marketing Manager: Sophia LaTorre-Zengierski
Project Management: Cenveo Publisher Services
Director of Rights and Permissions: Hilary Newman
Photo Research Manager: Martha Friedman
Permissions Researcher: Pablo D'Stair
Senior Art Director: Anna Palchik
Text Design: Books By Design, Inc.
Cover Design: William Boardman
Cover Photo: Fuse / Getty Images
Composition: Cenveo Publisher Services
Printing and Binding: RR Donnelley and Sons

Copyright © 2016, 2013, 2010, 2007 by Bedford/St. Martin's.

All rights reserved. No part of this book may be reproduced, stored in a retrieval system, or transmitted in any form or by any means, electronic, mechanical, photocopying, recording, or otherwise, except as may be expressly permitted by the applicable copyright statutes or in writing by the Publisher.

Manufactured in the United States of America.

1 0 9 8 7 6
f e d c b a

For information, write: Bedford/St. Martin's, 75 Arlington Street, Boston, MA 02116
(617-399-4000)

ISBN 978-1-319-01948-8

Acknowledgments

Text acknowledgments, art acknowledgments, and copyrights appear on the same page as the text and art selections they cover. It is a violation of the law to reproduce these selections by any means whatsoever without the written permission of the copyright holder.

At the time of publication, all Internet URLs published in this text were found to accurately link to their intended website. If you do find a broken link, please forward the information to rachel.childs@macmillan.com so that it can be corrected for the next printing.

With sorrow we mark the passing of our esteemed coauthor, Charles "Ted" Brusaw, and dedicate this edition of *Writing That Works* to honor his memory. Ted began his professional career as a freelance writer and moved on to a variety of positions in business and industry as a technical writer and corporate trainer, and for many years was manager of technical publications at the NCR Corporation. Ted coauthored *Practical Writing, The Business Writer's Handbook, Handbook of Technical Writing, The Professional Writer, The Business Writer's Companion*, and *Writing That Works.* He also independently authored a well-reviewed book of World War II military history (a Book of the Month Club selection), a Civil War novel, and an upcoming biography on Benedict Arnold. Ted was the consummate professional writer, teacher, and mentor (most especially to both of us) with whom we had the good fortune to work. He also was our friend. His standards were simply the highest.

Gerald J. Alred and Walter E. Oliu
August 2015

About the Authors

Walter E. Oliu served as Chief of the Publishing Services Branch at the U.S. Nuclear Regulatory Commission, where he managed the agency's printing, graphics, editing, and publishing programs as well as daily operations of the agency's public website. He has taught at Miami University of Ohio, Slippery Rock State University, Montgomery College, and George Mason University.

Charles T. Brusaw served as a faculty member at NCR Corporation's Management College, where he developed and taught courses in professional writing, editing, and presentation skills for the corporation worldwide. He worked in advertising, technical writing, public relations, and curriculum development and was a communications consultant, an invited speaker at academic conferences, and a teacher of business writing at Sinclair Community College. He passed away in 2015.

Gerald J. Alred is Professor Emeritus of English at the University of Wisconsin–Milwaukee, where he is a teaching award recipient and an adviser to the Professional Writing Program. He is the author of numerous scholarly articles and several standard bibliographies on business and technical communication, and he is a founding member of the editorial board of the *Journal of Business Communication*. He is a recipient of the prestigious Jay R. Gould Award for "profound scholarly and textbook contributions to the teaching of business and technical writing."

Workplace Technology Adviser

Richard C. Hay is owner and manager of Twenty Six Design, LLC, a company that provides computer hosting, programming, and design solutions for organizations, including thousands of college writing, advising, and academic support centers across the United States. He is publisher of the peer-reviewed *Writing Lab Newsletter*, has taught business and technical writing at the University of Wisconsin–Milwaukee, sits on the boards of two nonprofits, and is president of Quest Theater Ensemble in Chicago.

Preface

Writing That Works has been successful through eleven editions because it effectively prepares students to apply the writing process to the documents and situations they will encounter in the workplace — regardless of their academic background or occupational interest. Informed by the decades of professional and academic experience we have between us, the book integrates practical coverage of the writing process with clear guidelines for specific types of workplace writing — correspondence, reports, proposals, instructions, presentations, blogs, wikis, and more — supported by a wealth of sample documents, hundreds of exercises and projects, and the most current advice for using technology in today's workplace.

The twelfth edition continues to offer the structure and features that instructors have told us time and again prove effective. Workplace communications, however, is not a static field. Tools, sources of information, and practices continue to evolve, in both the classroom and the workplace. In preparing this edition, we looked critically at every facet of the book and added and updated material to keep it current. We enlisted workplace technology adviser Richard Hay to guide these updates, lending his real-world expertise to the situations and technologies facing students today and providing practical advice based on professional experience. As we have added new or altered existing material, model documents, and visuals throughout, our focus continues to be on helping students prepare for and adapt to today's digital workflow, an economy that has vastly altered the way we look for and land jobs, and the critical professional and ethical concerns of workplace writing. (For a detailed description of what's new to this edition, see page xi.)

About This Book

Rhetorically Focused Guidance on the Writing Process at Work

The advice, assignments, and features in *Writing That Works* all draw on our workplace and classroom experiences and have been honed by the suggestions and contributions of hundreds of teachers and writers over the years. They take as their premise the belief that strong workplace writing comes from an understanding of the rhetorical framework of audience and purpose.

Divided into four parts, the book is structured so that it begins with an overview of the writing process and then applies that process to the specific tasks and types of workplace writing, all of them illustrated by an impressive number of samples that are annotated to clarify what they demonstrate.

- **Part One: The Writing Process at Work** Chapters 1 through 4 guide students through the steps of planning, organizing, drafting, and revising, with a focus on the contexts and practices distinctive to workplace writing. Students are taught to consider audience, purpose, and the medium through which they'll communicate as they draft and revise.
- **Part Two: Methods and Design** Chapters 5 through 7 help students develop additional communication skills essential to workplace writing. The collaborative writing chapter includes advice on how to peer-review and edit shared documents, as well as how to effectively resolve problems that may arise while collaborating; the research chapter covers primary, print, and online research, with updated guidelines for documenting sources; and the design chapter offers concrete advice and examples for creating effective visuals and integrating them into documents and presentations.
- **Part Three: Messages and Models** Chapters 8 through 15 help students apply the skills learned in Parts One and Two, guiding them through the many types of writing and communications they will face in any workplace. They provide detailed advice on routine correspondence — e-mail and instant messages, letters, and memos — informal and formal reports; instructions; and internal, sales, and grant proposals. These chapters also cover creating and delivering presentations, conducting meetings, and finding a job.
- **Part Four: Appendixes** Appendix A provides expert guidance on how to write and organize online content for optimal speed and accessibility, whereas Appendix B is a self-contained handbook providing help with sentence errors, punctuation, and mechanics.

Practical Skills for Workplace Success

Almost 250 diverse, annotated sample documents and visuals model successful workplace writing. Helpful annotations on real-world correspondence, proposals, presentations, formal reports, and résumés illustrate the characteristics of each document type.

Consistent focus on key rhetorical concepts as the foundation for workplace writing. Emphasizing process, Part One of the book applies seasoned advice on audience and purpose to guide students through planning, organizing, drafting, and revising professional messaging.

Succinct checklists for considering audience and purpose, drafting, and designing documents summarize for students the nuts and bolts of ethical, effective communication.

Flexible, thorough apparatus for student learning — in the classroom and online. Streamlined end-of-chapter exercises, collaborative projects, and research projects provide starting points for engaging students in live, online, or hybrid courses and in their community.

Practical help for approaching time-sensitive correspondence, proposals, and presentations. Recognizing the often demanding schedules of professional life, Meeting the Deadline sections offer advice for writing successfully, even under the pressure of a tight deadline.

New to This Edition

As with each edition of *Writing That Works*, this revision has been guided by the thoughtful reviews and recommendations of business- and technical-writing instructors across the country. In response to their feedback and to better address the demands of the contemporary workplace, we have made several improvements.

Greater emphasis on the use of digital technology in the workplace. Chapter 1 now features savvy advice in convenient table format on selecting the appropriate medium for a given communication, weaving effective guidelines for considering audience and purpose together with fresh recommendations for choosing the method of communication that best suits both.

New content in Chapter 7 covering infographics and a table defining and illustrating techniques for showing the illusion of motion in static, two-dimensional drawings.

A heavily revised Chapter 8 highlights the greatest pitfalls of e-mail—today's primary form of business communication.

Updated models in progress and side-by-side comparisons help students visualize how rhetorical and design principles affect the success of workplace documents.

Expanded and updated advice on social media, document management, and online presentation tools recognizes the growing importance of composing, collaborating, and constructing an identity in digital environments for a digital audience.

Integrated coverage of language acknowledges our increasingly global economy and helps all students communicate effectively across cultures.

Updated guidance on library research and documentation styles continues to provide the latest information on finding, evaluating, and documenting primary and secondary source material. Chapter 6 has been updated to include relevant links to a variety of Web sources across the disciplines, conforming to the latest guidelines of both the American Psychological Association (APA) and the Modern Language Association (MLA). Extensive up-to-date citation models offer examples for dozens of source types, including a variety of online and multimedia sources.

Augmented intellectual property coverage includes an overview of patent and trademark law, and a new section in Chapter 15 explains important changes to federal law concerning the difference between paid and unpaid internships.

Get the Most Out of Your Course with *Writing That Works*, Twelfth Edition

Bedford/St. Martin's offers resources and format choices that help you and your students get even more out of your book and course. To learn more about or to order any of the following products, contact your Bedford/St. Martin's sales representative, e-mail sales support (sales_support@bfwpub.com), or visit the website at macmillanhighered.com/writingthatworks/catalog.

Choose from Alternative Formats of Writing That Works

Bedford/St. Martin's offers a range of affordable formats, allowing students to choose the one that works best for them. For details, visit macmillanhighered.com/writingthatworks/catalog.

- *Paperback.* To order the paperback edition, use ISBN 978-1-319-01948-8.
- *Popular e-book formats.* For details, visit macmillanhighered.com/ebooks.

Select Value Packages

Add value to your text by packaging one of the following resources with *Writing That Works.* To learn more about package options for any of the following products, contact your Bedford/St. Martin's sales representative or visit macmillanhighered.com/writingthatworks/catalog.

LaunchPad Solo for Professional Writing
macmillanhighered.com/professionalwriting1e

LaunchPad Solo for Professional Writing offers online tutorials on today's most relevant digital writing topics, from content management to personal branding, and allows students to work on whatever they need help with the most. Students develop the professional writing and communication skills they need to succeed both in the classroom and in the workplace and can explore today's technologies in clickable, assignable learning sequences organized by popular professional writing topics.

LaunchPad Solo for Professional Writing features:

Digital tips. Step-by-step instruction for using technology to support workplace writing includes guidance for synchronizing data, assessing software and hardware, creating templates, and organizing productive online meetings.

Sample documents. A wide range of effective professional writing models provides students with e-mail, résumés, cover letters, reports, proposals, brochures, and questionnaires (and more) to emulate.

Tutorials. Screen captures walk students through maximizing free online tools to access projects across platforms, design dynamic presentations, develop podcasts, manage their personal brand, and build common citations in APA and MLA styles.

Adaptive quizzing for targeted learning, skills practice, and grammar help. LearningCurve, a game-like adaptive quizzing program, helps students focus on the writing and grammar skills for which they need the most help.

The ability to monitor student progress. Use our Gradebook to see which students are on track and which need additional help with specific topics.

LaunchPad Solo for Professional Writing can be packaged with *Writing That Works* at **a significant discount**. Order ISBN 978-1-319-06788-5 to ensure your students can take full advantage. Visit macmillanhighered.com/professionalwriting/catalog for more information.

For technical support, visit macmillanhighered.com/getsupport.

Team Writing by Joanna Wolfe, University of Louisville

Team Writing is a print supplement with online videos that provides guidelines and examples of collaborating to manage written projects by documenting tasks, deadlines, and team goals. Two- to five-minute videos corresponding with the chapters in *Team Writing* give students the opportunity to analyze team interactions and learn about communication styles. Practical troubleshooting tips show students how best to handle various types of conflicts within peer groups.

Instructor Resources

macmillanhighered.com/writingthatworks/catalog

You have a lot to do in your course. Bedford/St. Martin's wants to make it easy for you to find the support you need—and to get it quickly.

The instructor resources for *Writing That Works* can be downloaded from the Bedford/St. Martin's online catalog at the URL above. In addition to chapter overviews and teaching tips, the instructor's manual includes sample syllabi, suggested assignment responses, presentation slides, and additional classroom activities.

Join Our Community! The Macmillan English Community is now Bedford/St. Martin's home for professional resources, featuring Bedford *Bits*, our popular blog site offering new ideas for the composition classroom and composition teachers. Connect and converse with a growing team of Bedford authors and top scholars who blog on *Bits*: Andrea Lunsford, Nancy Sommers, Steve Bernhardt, Traci Gardner, Barclay Barrios, Jack Solomon, Susan Bernstein, Elizabeth Wardle, Doug Downs, Liz Losh, Jonathan Alexander, and Donna Winchell.

In addition, you'll find an expanding collection of resources that support your teaching:

- Sign up for webinars.
- Download resources from our professional resource series that support your teaching.
- Start a discussion.
- Ask a question.
- Follow your favorite members.
- Review projects in the pipeline.

Visit community.macmillan.com to join the conversation with your fellow teachers.

Acknowledgments

We wish to thank the following instructors who have substantially strengthened the twelfth edition by generously sharing their helpful comments and recommendations: Shazia Ali, Easfield College; Erin O'Neill Armendarez, New Mexico State University Alamogordo; Isabel Baca, University of Texas at El Paso; Gwendolyn Blume, University of Wisconsin–Marathon County; Sonya Brown, Fayetteville State University; Shani Bruce, Nova Southeastern University; Daniel Emery, University of Oklahoma;

Kendra Gaines, Pima Community College; William Garland, University of South Carolina; Natalie Gerber, State University of New York at Fredonia; Robert Holderer, Edinboro University of Pennsylvania; Marjorie Justice, University of Missouri; Sonja Khatchadourian, University of Wisconsin–Milwuakee; Steve Krause, Eastern Michigan University; Tamara Kuzmenkov, Tacoma Community College; Elizabeth Lagenfeld, Crafton Hills College; Jessica Ludders, University of Maine at Augusta; Jennifer Mahoney, Indiana University–Purdue University Indianapolis; Julie Mengert, Virginia Tech University; Renee Rallo, St. Joseph College; Angela Rogers, Clemson University; Amy Rubens, Francis Marion University; Anne Scarlett, Columbia College; Marilyn Sequin, Kent State University; Christina Seymour, Maryville College; Charla Stosser, Southern Utah University; Katherine Tirabassi, Keene State College; Gary Valcana, Athens State University; Sharon Van Sluijs, University of Wisconsin–Madison; Star Vanguri, Nova Southeastern University; Charles F. Warren, Salem State University; Concetta Williams, Chicago State University; Erin Williams, University of Saint Francis; Will Zhang, Des Moines Area Community College; and Pinfan Zhu, Texas State University. We also gratefully acknowledge the ongoing contributions and help of the students and faculty at the University of Wisconsin–Milwaukee, as well as our colleagues in the United States and abroad.

We are indebted to Richard Hay, who assessed and provided specific advice relative to each chapter's coverage and models to ensure they reflect the current use of workplace technology and business practice. We wish to thank Kate Mayhew for her detailed eye in updating the documenting sources material in the research chapter.

We are also greatly indebted to the leadership of Bedford/St. Martin's for helping us reimagine our approach to this edition and for their unstinting support throughout the revision process. We thank Andrea Cava, who, with the help of Yashmita Hota at Cenveo Publisher Services, oversaw the difficult task of producing this book, and we are grateful to Sharon O'Donnell for her careful copyediting. Finally, we are most grateful to Rachel Childs, our developmental editor at Bedford/St. Martin's, for her astute editorial judgment, expertise, and effectiveness in coordinating the myriad of tasks essential to the publication of this edition.

Walter E. Oliu
Gerald J. Alred

Brief Contents

Contents

PART 1

The Writing Process at Work

In Part 1, you will learn techniques for developing, drafting, and revising memos, e-mails, and a wide array of other on-the-job writing tasks. These techniques will help you produce clearly written, well-organized documents because effective on-the-job writing always reflects the writer's attention to the work that goes on before the document is finished.

- **Determining Audience and Purpose.** Chapters 1 through 3 provide discussion and exercises to help you clearly define your reader's needs for the message you intend for your document.
- **Brainstorming and Gathering Information.** Chapter 1 includes a detailed case study to illustrate methods you can use to generate ideas, to select only those that are relevant, and to begin organizing them clearly for your audience.
- **Assessing and Selecting the Medium.** Chapter 1 also describes the broad and diverse range of workplace media currently in widespread use and provides guidelines for selecting from among them the best for your audience, purpose, and dissemination requirements.
- **Outlining.** Chapter 2 describes in detail how you can organize your information into an outline that is appropriate to your purpose and audience. It also offers examples in a wide range of outline styles.
- **Drafting.** Chapter 3 discusses and offers examples of the process by which writers turn an outline into a workable rough draft.
- **Revising.** Chapter 4 describes the kinds of problems you need to evaluate when you revise your draft. You will learn to review your draft to see how well it communicates to its intended audience, to be sure it is complete and coherent, to look for ways to emphasize key ideas, to check information for accuracy, to consider the ethical implications of your writing, and to proofread for correctness.

1 Understanding the Workplace Writing Context: A Case Study

Contents

This chapter describes how one employee successfully completed an important on-the-job writing task from first thought to final product. The process she used can be divided into a series of steps applicable to all workplace writing:

Christine Thomas was aware of a potential opportunity at HVS Accounting Services, where she worked as the company's system administrator. The company was prospering. In just the past year, Harriet Sullivan, the president and founder of the small company, hired five new employees to handle the increasing workload of tax preparation, financial planning, and investment services. HVS now had 12 full-time employees, about half of whom commuted more than an hour each way. Christine was also aware that the company recently had lost several promising job applicants because they did not wish to spend two or more hours a day driving to and from work.

With this information in mind, Christine reviewed online case studies about the benefits of telecommuting for companies and their employees and experimented with various software programs designed to allow remote employee access to company systems. She learned that companies offering

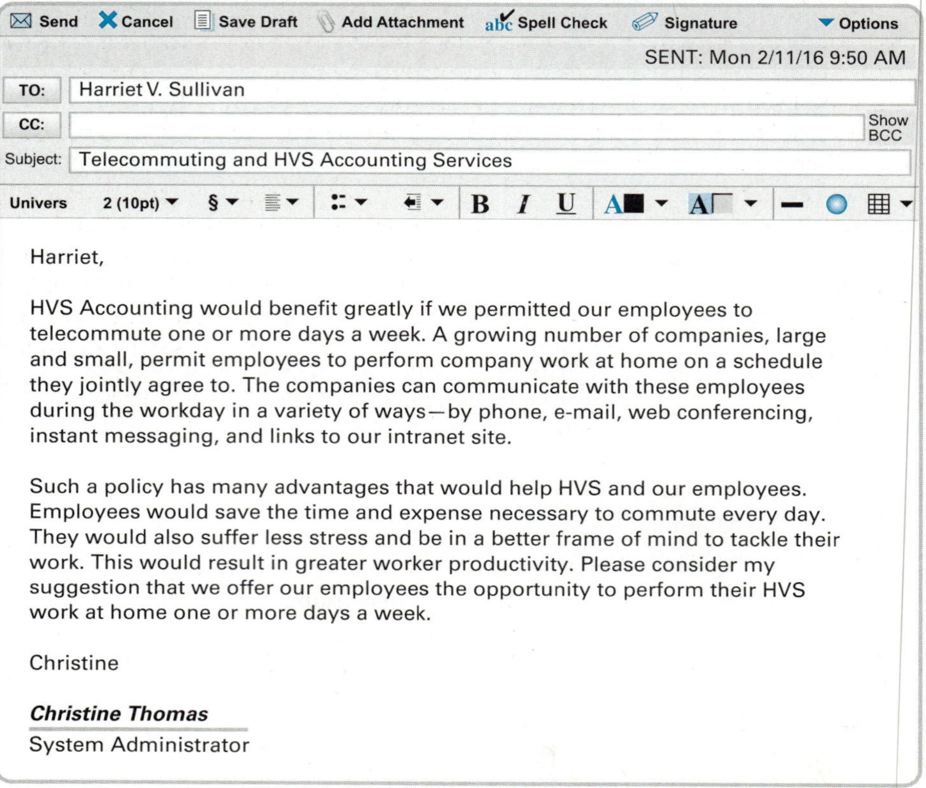
Send Cancel Save Draft Add Attachment Spell Check Signature Options

SENT: Mon 2/11/16 9:50 AM

TO: Harriet V. Sullivan

CC:

Subject: Telecommuting and HVS Accounting Services

Harriet,

HVS Accounting would benefit greatly if we permitted our employees to telecommute one or more days a week. A growing number of companies, large and small, permit employees to perform company work at home on a schedule they jointly agree to. The companies can communicate with these employees during the workday in a variety of ways—by phone, e-mail, web conferencing, instant messaging, and links to our intranet site.

Such a policy has many advantages that would help HVS and our employees. Employees would save the time and expense necessary to commute every day. They would also suffer less stress and be in a better frame of mind to tackle their work. This would result in greater worker productivity. Please consider my suggestion that we offer our employees the opportunity to perform their HVS work at home one or more days a week.

Christine

Christine Thomas
System Administrator

Figure 1–1 First Proposal (E-mail)

a telecommuting option to their employees had a more satisfied workforce, less absenteeism, and greater productivity per employee.

So, with all the information in hand and confident of the value of her suggestion, Christine wrote an e-mail message to Harriet Sullivan (Figure 1–1). Two days later, Christine received the following terse e-mail reply from Harriet: "Not right for HVS." Christine was not only disappointed but also puzzled. She knew that her suggestion was timely and reasonable because she had checked all the facts before writing the e-mail. Yet she had failed to convince Harriet Sullivan.

Writing Systematically

In writing her e-mail message, Christine Thomas committed the most common mistake made by people who write on the job: She lost sight of the purpose of her message and overlooked the needs of her audience. Convinced of the value of her suggestion, she did not consider that Harriet might not be familiar with the results of her research and she did not look at the situation from Harriet's perspective.

Had she kept her primary purpose and her reader clearly in mind, Christine would have been better focused in gathering her facts and ideas, selecting which to use, and organizing them to achieve her objective: convincing Harriet. The last three steps are important: Even with her reader and her purpose clearly in mind, Christine was not ready to write her e-mail to Harriet. She simply established a framework in which to develop her message.

A systematic approach helps writers over this hurdle. Before beginning to write, careful writers not only identify their purpose (why they are writing) and audience (to whom they are writing) but also think seriously about the context of their writing (its setting). This process involves listing all the ideas and facts the writer might include, refining that list by examining each item from the perspectives of audience and purpose, organizing what's left in a way that satisfies both the writer's purpose and the audience's needs, and, finally, deciding on the best medium in which to send it — e-mail, letter, memorandum, or other means.

WRITER'S CHECKLIST

Planning Your Document

- ✔ Determine your purpose.
- ✔ Assess your audience's needs.
- ✔ Consider the context of your writing.
- ✔ Generate, gather, and record ideas and facts.
- ✔ Establish the scope of coverage for your topic.
- ✔ Organize your ideas.
- ✔ Select the appropriate medium.

Determining Your Purpose

Everything you write in the workplace has a purpose. You want your readers to know, to believe, or to be able to do something when they have finished reading what you have written. Determining your purpose is the first step in preparing to write; unless you know what you hope to accomplish, you cannot know what information you should present.

Purpose gives direction to your writing. The more precisely you can state your primary purpose at the outset, the more successful your writing is likely to be. (You may also have a secondary purpose, such as to motivate or to reassure.) Christine Thomas might have said that her purpose was "to allow HVS employees to telecommute" — but permitting employees to telecommute was the *result* she wanted; it was not the precise purpose of her e-mail message. Further thought would have led Christine to recognize the specific goals of the e-mail itself. To ensure that your purpose is precise, put it in writing. In most cases, you can use the following pattern to guide you:

> My primary purpose is to __________ so that my audience ___________.

By filling in the blanks, Christine Thomas might have developed the following statement of purpose:

> My primary purpose is to explain the advantages of telecommuting to Harriet Sullivan so that she agrees to permit it at HVS Accounting for a trial period.

With this statement, Christine would have recognized that her purpose was more complicated than it first appeared and that she would have to present persuasive evidence to be effective. She would also need to consider how she sent her message — the medium she used. Was a brief e-mail appropriate for the major workplace change she proposed?

Assessing Your Audience's Needs

Your job as a writer is to express your ideas so clearly that your audience cannot misinterpret them. An important element of the purpose statement is the phrase "so that my audience . . . ." Simply identifying the response you would like is very different from actually achieving it. Although a purpose statement addresses a problem from the writer's point of view, it must also take into account the audience's needs if it is to be persuasive. Yet many writers often forget that they have an audience and focus solely on their own purposes.

After stating your purpose, ask yourself, "Who is my audience?" Often you will know the answer. If you are writing a memo to persuade your manager to fund a project, your reader is obvious to you. However, if you write an e-mail or a letter to someone you do not know in another company, first consider what you know about that company, your reader's position in the company or department, and his or her responsibilities regarding the topic you are writing about. Without at least that much information, you cannot know your reader's needs.

Even if you know your audience very well, a little reflection is necessary. Without careful thought, Christine Thomas might have answered the question "Who is my reader?" from only one point of view:

> My reader is Harriet Sullivan, and she's been my manager for ten years. We've worked together since she founded the company, so she'll no doubt understand that I have her best interests in mind.

With more careful thought, Christine would have considered Harriet's role in the company, her lack of familiarity with the topic, and her anxiety about taking such a step. Bearing these concerns in mind, Christine might have defined her reader differently.

> My reader is Harriet Sullivan, president of HVS Accounting Services. Harriet founded HVS ten years ago with modest savings and a substantial loan. Cautious, industrious, and a stickler for detail, Harriet has built HVS into a sound business and is now beginning to see some return on her investment. Harriet is also a hands-on executive. She puts in long hours at the office and is in frequent contact with the staff by telephone; face-to-face conversations; and, less often, by e-mail. In addition to a regularly scheduled staff meeting every Wednesday, she holds informal meetings several times a week. She may strongly resist the loss of

CONSIDERING AUDIENCE AND PURPOSE

Writing for Your Reader

Try to answer each of the following questions in as much detail as possible to help focus on your reader's needs in relation to your subject. This process is helpful for all types of writing, but it will be especially important for longer, more complex tasks.

- Who is your audience?
- What do you want your audience to know, to believe, or to be able to do after reading your content?
- Have you narrowed your topic to best focus on what you want your audience to know?
- What are your audience's needs in relation to the subject?
- What does your audience know about the subject?
- Do you have more than one audience?
- If you have multiple audiences, do they have different levels of knowledge about your subject?
- What are your audience's feelings about your subject—sympathetic? hostile? neutral?
- Does your writing acknowledge other or contrary points of view about the subject?
- Is your tone respectful?
- Have you selected the right medium—e-mail, memo, letter, brochure, social-media posting, and so on—for your subject and audience?
- Does your format enhance audience understanding?

> hands-on access to her staff when they work at home. She values computer technology and purchased laptop computers for the accountants and financial analysts to help them as they visit clients throughout the metropolitan area. However, although she uses e-mail, she does so reluctantly and prefers memos. She is also unfamiliar with many of the new tools available to help telecommuting employees remain accessible as active members of the workplace — such as collaborative work software, virtual private networks, videoconferencing, and Webinars.

Based on this analysis, Christine would have been better prepared to select the information that Harriet needed to understand, to agree with, and to act on Christine's proposal.

Considering the Context

In the workplace, everything is written in a context. The environment, or situation, in which you write a document (such as responding to a customer complaint when the customer was wrong or drafting safety instructions after an accident) will affect how your audience interprets its meaning. Even a good idea will fail to get support if the writer does not take into account the circumstances — both inside and outside the organization — that could influence its acceptance. Context includes your medium, as well. Are you writing a brochure, a blog entry, website content, or a report? Each is better suited to some audiences and content than the others. Table 1–1 on page 14 describes the variety, purpose, and pros and cons of workplace media.

Christine Thomas, for example, had to consider her manager's style and the company's infrastructure. Aware of Harriet's hands-on approach to management, Christine needed to address Harriet's potential anxiety about the staff being away from the office one or more days a week. Christine also had to consider the larger context of how telecommuting might affect the company as a whole. For example, she needed to think about each staff member's personal situation and commuting habits, equipment requirements, communications technologies, customer confidentiality and convenience, jobs most and least suitable for telecommuting, and any expenses her suggestions might incur. Without addressing these issues, she could not adequately develop a proposal that would merit Harriet's serious consideration.

WRITER'S CHECKLIST

Assessing Context

Use the following questions as a starting point as you assess the context for your topic:

✔ What is your professional relationship with your readers, and how might that affect the tone, style, and scope of your writing?

✔ What is "the story" behind the immediate reason you are writing; that is, what series of events or previous communications led to your need to write?

✔ What specific factors or values, such as business competition, financing, and regulatory environment, are important to your readers' organization or department?

✔ What is the corporate culture in which your readers work?

✔ What recent or current events within or outside an organization or a department may influence how readers interpret your writing?

✔ What national or cultural differences might affect your readers' expectations for or interpretations of a document?

✔ What medium do your readers prefer—e-mail, memo, letter, report, or other?

Generating, Gathering, and Recording Ideas and Facts

When you have determined your purpose, assessed your reader's needs, and considered the context for your writing, you must decide what information will satisfy these demands. Several techniques are available for gathering and recording information.

Brainstorming

The easiest way to generate ideas is to tap into your own knowledge and experience. You may already know enough information to get started. The technique of interviewing yourself, commonly known as *brainstorming,* may also suggest ways to obtain additional information.

Unlock Your Imagination. To begin, jot down as many ideas as you can think of about the general subject and, if possible, where you learned them, using a computer, note cards, or other medium you prefer. Keep the ideas flowing by being open-minded. Don't stop to analyze whether you think an idea is important. Keep the ideas coming until you can think of no more. After the stream of ideas slows to a trickle and stops, you can step back to sort out the useful from the irrelevant. (This type of research also works well with a group of writers or project team members.)

Think Like a Journalist. Journalists and other writers have long used the following questions as a guide to ensure that they have answered the questions their audience is most likely to have about a particular story: *What* happened? *Why* did it happen? *When* did it happen? *How* did it happen? *Where* did it happen? *Who* was involved? Rarely will you be able to apply all these questions to any single on-the-job writing situation, but the range of information they cover can help to start your thinking.

Test Your Ideas. Once you have assembled a list of ideas, examine each item and decide whether it contributes to your purpose or satisfies your audience's needs. The items relating clearly to both your purpose and the needs of your audience are easiest to work with. Items that your audience might need but that would get in the way of your purpose are trickier. Harriet Sullivan, for example, needs to know that after the program begins, she will have less direct access to employees working from home. Because she's a hands-on manager, this break with her customary practice will be difficult for Harriet to accept. Christine, however, might be reluctant to mention this fact because it appears to undermine her purpose, which is to persuade Harriet to support telecommuting. To reconcile Harriet's interests and her own, Christine would have to point out this aspect of the program. To have credibility, you need to acknowledge opposing points of view when they are relevant; doing so allows you to respond to your audience's objections rather than leaving them unanswered. After such a review, Christine Thomas might have generated the well-balanced list shown in Figure 1–2.

Note that she has marked each item with a *P* for purpose or an *A* for audience. When you generate such a list, some items will satisfy both your purpose and your audience, others will appear to satisfy only one, and still others will appear to have nothing to do with either. When you have finished marking your list, cross out any item not marked with a *P* or an *A*. But before crossing out an idea, make certain that it fits neither your purpose nor your audience. Ideally, you will have a comprehensive list of items beside which you have placed both a *P* and an *A*. The more common ground your purpose and your audience's needs share, the more effective your writing will be.

ETHICS NOTE: Anticipate Objections Be honest in acknowledging any real or potential conflicting opinions. Doing so not only is ethical but also allows you to anticipate and overcome possible objections. It helps build your credibility by showing readers that your coverage is balanced.

Turning a writer's list of ideas into a reader's list of information should be neither difficult nor mysterious; thoroughness is the key. Such a list will give you an idea of the content of the project. The list will probably be sketchy or have missing information, but that's actually helpful in showing where additional research is needed. It will also give you a framework for where to integrate the details of the additional research.

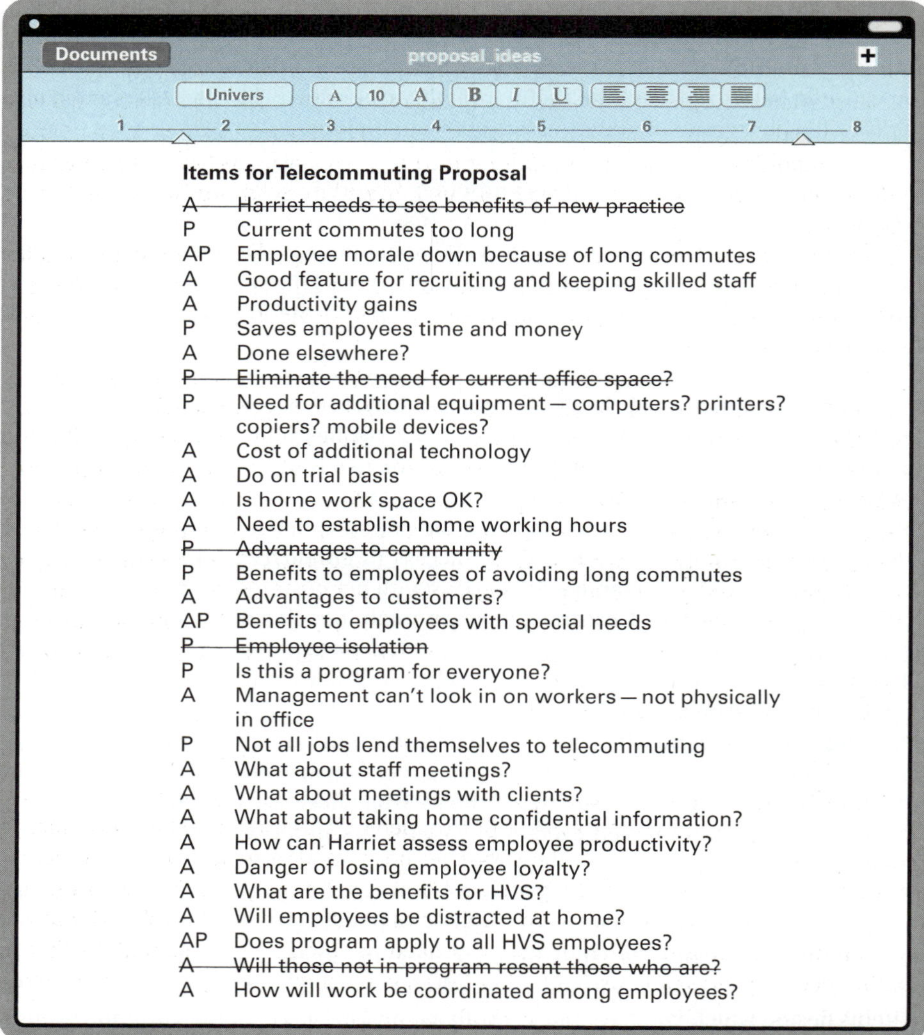

Documents
proposal_ideas
Univers
A 10 A B I U
Items for Telecommuting Proposal
A ~~Harriet needs to see benefits of new practice~~
P Current commutes too long
AP Employee morale down because of long commutes
A Good feature for recruiting and keeping skilled staff
A Productivity gains
P Saves employees time and money
A Done elsewhere?
P ~~Eliminate the need for current office space?~~
P Need for additional equipment — computers? printers? copiers? mobile devices?
A Cost of additional technology
A Do on trial basis
A Is home work space OK?
A Need to establish home working hours
P ~~Advantages to community~~
P Benefits to employees of avoiding long commutes
A Advantages to customers?
AP Benefits to employees with special needs
P ~~Employee isolation~~
P Is this a program for everyone?
A Management can't look in on workers — not physically in office
P Not all jobs lend themselves to telecommuting
A What about staff meetings?
A What about meetings with clients?
A What about taking home confidential information?
A How can Harriet assess employee productivity?
A Danger of losing employee loyalty?
A What are the benefits for HVS?
A Will employees be distracted at home?
AP Does program apply to all HVS employees?
A ~~Will those not in program resent those who are?~~
A How will work be coordinated among employees?

Figure 1–2 Brainstorming List for a Proposal

◆ *These different sources of information are discussed in detail in Chapter 6, Conducting Research for a Document.*

Using Other Sources of Information

Brainstorming may not produce all the information you need. Christine, for example, read telecommuting case studies and experimented with software on the Web. To gather enough information to meet the needs of your audience, you may have to conduct formal, systematic research. In such cases, consider how thoroughly you need to cover your subject. If you know what you are looking for and where to find it, research presents few problems.

Before you begin, however, consider using content created in your own organization. In the workplace, you often merely need to phone or e-mail a colleague to obtain the facts, data, or proper source for your information needs. The right colleague may lead you to text, tables, visuals, and other content that can be repurposed for your needs. *Repurposing* is the copying or converting of existing content from one document into another for a different purpose. This process saves time because content that often requires substantial effort to develop need not be re-created for each new use.

◆ *For more on repurposing, see Chapter 6, Conducting Research for a Document, and Chapter 13, Writing Proposals.*

Note, however, that content can be repurposed exactly as it is written only if it fits the scope, audience, and purpose of the new document. If it does not, adapt the content to fit its new context. You also may need to adapt the verb tense, voice, tone, and point of view for the new setting.

When you need additional information, consider the following rich and varied sources: The Internet, used carefully, provides access to programs, demonstrations, applications, and content from commercial, educational, governmental, and other sources. And do not overlook the library's wealth of books, articles, and reference works. To save time, describe your project to a reference librarian. He or she can help narrow your search and provide access to search tools and online databases not available on the Internet. Beyond these sources, consider interviewing an expert or conducting a survey. An expert can provide you with up-to-date information not readily available in printed material. A questionnaire permits you to obtain the views of a group of people and requires less time and money than numerous personal interviews.

Establishing Your Scope

Having refined your list of ideas and facts, you must review it once again to establish the scope of coverage for your topic. Your scope is the degree of detail necessary to cover each item in your list based on your purpose and the needs of your audience. As you think about each item, ask yourself, "How much information should I include to support my purpose and satisfy my audience's needs?" Often you will find that you have omitted important points or that you need to research your subject further to obtain necessary facts or figures. At other times, you will find that your list is cluttered with unnecessary detail.

Had Christine drawn up the list shown in Figure 1–2 and then reviewed it to establish her scope, she would have discovered that some of the items on her list needed detailed information to satisfy Harriet Sullivan's concerns. Entries such as "Cost of additional technology" would tell her that she had to either provide detailed figures for the cost of this equipment or explain why no additional expense is necessary. However, other items requiring more detail might be more difficult to identify: "How can Harriet assess employee productivity?" indicates Christine's sense that evaluating productivity would present a cost-conscious person like Harriet with a challenge. She would want to know how this could be done effectively. Given these gaps in Christine's first attempt to convince Harriet, Christine realized that she needed to turn her brief e-mail message into a fully developed internal proposal.

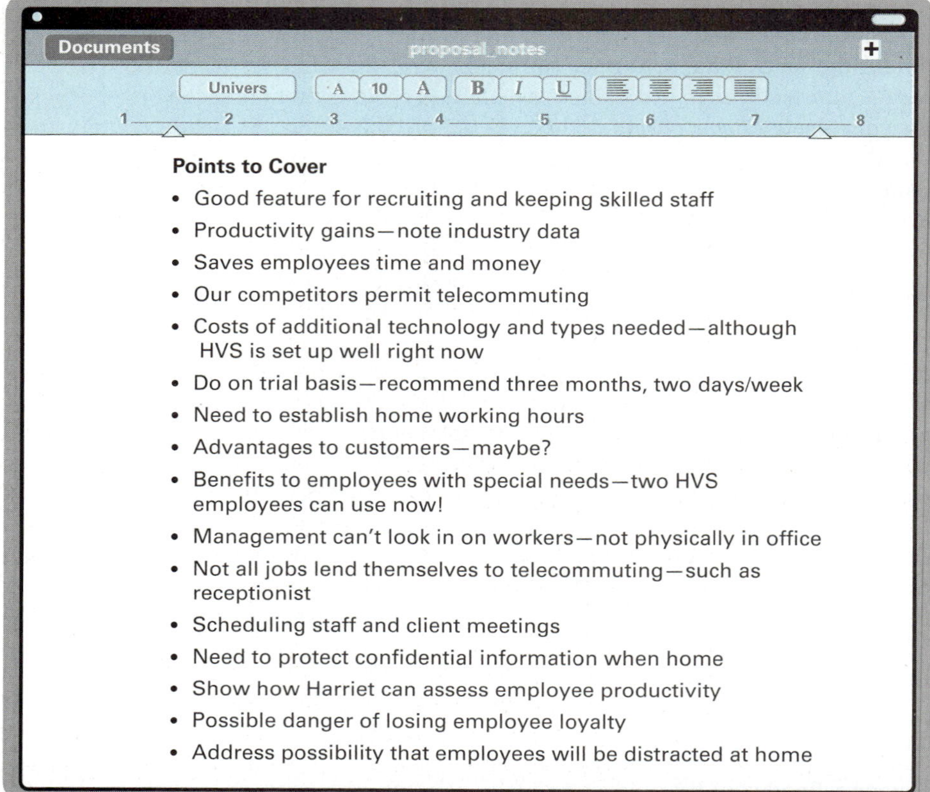

Figure 1–3 Notes for Proposal

Figure 1–3 shows the list in Figure 1–2 after the scope has been established. Christine eliminated the ideas outside the scope of her purpose, such as concerns about employee morale and office space. She crossed out the first item, too. It's unnecessary because Harriet's need to see the benefits of telecommuting is the overall topic of her proposal, not a separate topic within it.

Be careful when deciding how much detail to include. Writers who know a lot about a subject tend to overwhelm their audiences with more information than they have time for or need. Understand, too, that establishing your scope in the classroom may be different from doing so on the job. Classroom assignments must often be limited because of accessibility of information, the goals of the course, or other learning objectives. Consider these limitations as part of the purpose of an assignment. Whether in class or the workplace, however, be guided by your purpose and your audience's needs in establishing your scope of coverage.

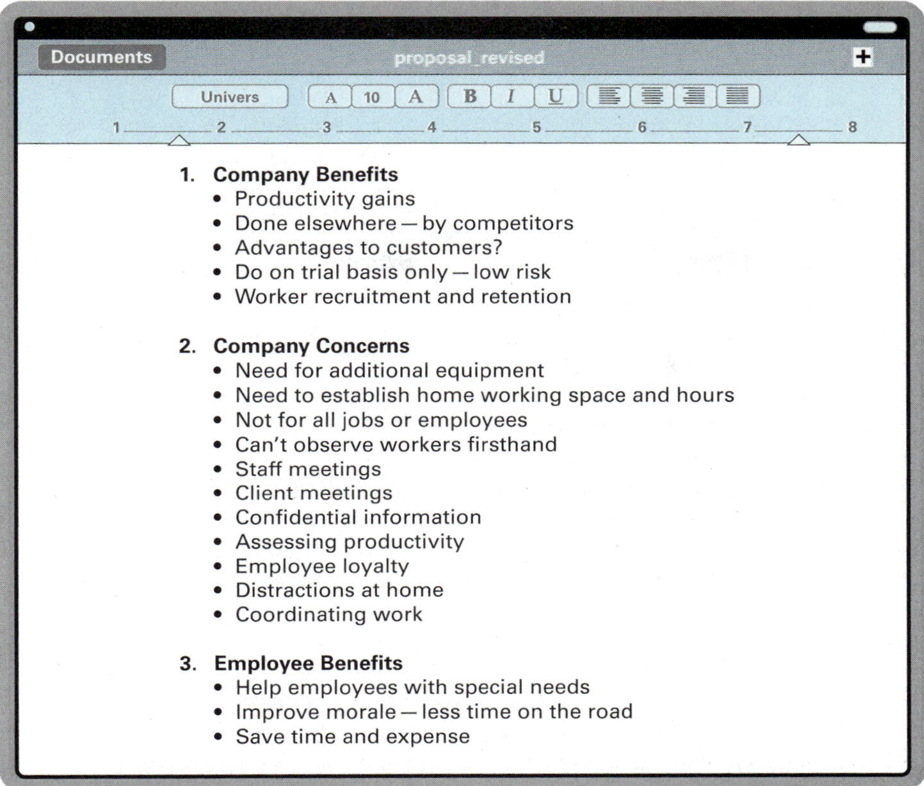

Documents
proposal_revised
Univers
A 10 A B I U
1 2 3 4 5 6 7 8
1. Company Benefits
• Productivity gains
• Done elsewhere — by competitors
• Advantages to customers?
• Do on trial basis only — low risk
• Worker recruitment and retention
2. Company Concerns
• Need for additional equipment
• Need to establish home working space and hours
• Not for all jobs or employees
• Can't observe workers firsthand
• Staff meetings
• Client meetings
• Confidential information
• Assessing productivity
• Employee loyalty
• Distractions at home
• Coordinating work
3. Employee Benefits
• Help employees with special needs
• Improve morale — less time on the road
• Save time and expense

Figure 1–4 Revised Notes for Proposal

Organizing Your Ideas

Once you have established your scope, you should have a list of the ideas and facts to be included in your writing. Examine this list and look for relationships among the items in it. Group the related ideas and arrange them under headings, using short phrases that identify the kind of items in each group. As you group the related ideas, consider the following questions: Is the time sequence among items important? If so, organize them chronologically. Do you need to compare the features of one item with those of one or more other items? Organize accordingly. Should you present the most important information first or, instead, build a case that ends with the most important information? In other words, should you organize items by decreasing order of importance or by increasing order of importance? As you assemble and arrange the groups of ideas, add, delete, and move ideas around until you feel that you have the best possible organization. For example, Christine turned her brainstorming list of thoughts, shown in Figure 1–2, into the list of points to cover in Figure 1–3 after narrowing the topic. She then organized these points into the three major subtopics covered in Figure 1–4.

◆ *For a detailed discussion of organizing techniques or for guidance on outlining more complex topics, see Chapter 2, Planning a Document.*

DIGITAL TIP: Creating Drafts

- Do not write your first draft without any planning. Use your word processor's outline feature to organize the ideas from your brainstorming and research, using the cut-and-paste feature to test alternative ways to organize your outline.
- Use the spell-check and grammar-check features carefully. Did you mean "here" or "hear"? A spell checker cannot tell. And be wary of grammar-check recommendations—the software cannot interpret the context of your writing.
- Create effective document design. Specify styles for headings and other repeated text elements using the Page Layout feature and allow extra white space to set off examples and illustrations.

◆ *For more document design information, see Chapter 7, Designing Documents and Visuals.*

Selecting the Medium

With so many media and forms of communication available, selecting the most appropriate can be challenging. Keep in mind that many of the following media and forms of communication, found in Table 1–1, evolve and overlap as technology develops. Understanding their basic functions will help you select the most appropriate medium for your needs, whether you work for a large organization, small business, or as a private consultant. Make your choice based on answers to the following types of questions:

- What are your audience's preferences and expectations?
- What are current organizational policies and practices for workplace communications?
- What technological resources are available?
- Is the message brief or long and complex?
- Is communicating "on the go" necessary?
- Do you wish to encourage an online dialogue with customers?
- Is the communication time sensitive? confidential?

TABLE 1–1 Selecting the Medium

MEDIA	PURPOSE	BENEFITS	CAVEATS
E-mail *(or email)*	Best for sending messages, sharing files, and providing links to websites.	• Can be sent to one or more recipients at the same time. • Saves time with near-instant delivery of messages. • Reduces the need for phone calls and meetings.	• Requires that writers review messages carefully before clicking the Send button: — Can be sent to wrong recipient and reveal information intended for another recipient.

(continued)

TABLE 1–1 Selecting the Medium *(continued)*

MEDIA	PURPOSE	BENEFITS	CAVEATS
E-mail *(or email)*		• Allows recipients to forward messages and attachments to others. • Is a mobile medium for business travelers. • Provides a record of all messages — content, dates, times, etc.	— Is subject to legal disclosure.
Instant and text messaging	Best for sending brief messages in real time through cellular and wired networks.	• Allows communications between people on the move or at work sites without access to e-mail. • Retains records of conversations that can be referenced or replied to at a later time.	• Screen space is limited — best for short messages only. • Slang and such shortened spellings as "u" for *you* to save time and screen space can cause confusion. • Recipients must be ready and willing to participate in an online conversation. • Not recommended for secure or proprietary information because less secure than other media.
Printed memo	Best for when electronic communications are not practical or when the information requires a more formal appearance.	• Essential in manufacturing and services workplaces where employees do not have e-mail. • Can be posted in common work areas for enhanced visibility. • Permits the use of logos and official signatures to denote importance of content.	• More expensive to create and distribute and slower to reach staff than e-mail.
Letter	Best when it is necessary to send official communications on organizational stationary with signatures to customers, clients, suppliers, and others.	• Especially useful for first contacts with customers, clients, etc. • Effective for high-profile communications like legal documents and notices, job applications, and recommendation letters.	• More expensive to create and distribute and slower to reach recipients than e-mail.

(continued)

TABLE 1–1 Selecting the Medium (*continued*)

MEDIA	PURPOSE	BENEFITS	CAVEATS
Letter		• Can be effective for reaching recipients who receive a high volume of electronic correspondence. • Easier to reach international recipients in countries with inefficient electronic infrastructures.	
Phone call	Best for exchanges that require extended conversations and the ability of participants to interpret each other's tone of voice.	• Useful for discussing sensitive issues and resolving misunderstandings, although they do not provide the visual cues possible during face-to-face meetings. • Cell (or *mobile*) phones are useful for communicating away from the workplace.	• Participants must be available to participate in the call.
Voicemail	Best for leaving messages when the call recipient does not answer your call.	• Provides recipient with your name and contact information. • Leaves a record that a call was made at a given time and date. • Lets the recipient know the subject of the call so that he or she can prepare a response before returning your call.	• If the message is complicated or contains numerous details, use another medium, such as e-mail.
Conference call	Best for calls among three or more participants separated geographically.	• Allows participants to use the Web during calls to share and view common documents. • Less expensive alternative to face-to-face meetings that require travel.	• Requires planning to ensure all participants are present for the call. • More efficient when the person coordinating the call works from an agenda shared by all the participants and directs the discussion as if chairing a meeting. • Requires written confirmation of decisions that have been reached following the call. • Requires coordination for participants in different time zones.

(*continued*)

TABLE 1–1 Selecting the Medium *(continued)*

MEDIA	PURPOSE	BENEFITS	CAVEATS
Video conference	Best for meetings among geographically separated attendees.	• Useful when travel is impractical or costly. • Permits live demonstrations and training. • Allows sharing of charts, graphs, and other visuals. • Allows participants to see as well as to hear one another.	• For enterprise-level conferencing, requires special setting with sophisticated audio, visual, and telecommunications equipment and connections. • Requires coordination for participants in different time zones.
Web conference	Best for disseminating information, conducting training, promoting a product, and the like for geographically separated participants who access a conference site on their workplace computers to "attend" the conference.	• Can incorporate video, voice, and instant message capabilities. • Allows participants to interact in real time. • Saves on travel costs.	• Requires attendees to have appropriate program software and webcams. • Requires that conference be coordinated by a moderator. • Requires coordination for participants in different time zones.
Website posting	*Internal* Best for posting, sharing, and exchanging documents, policies and procedures, and other organization-specific information as well as for hosting active networking sites among employees. *External* Best for posting promotional and informational content about a company's products and services, offering online sales, hosting social-networking sites (blogs and forums, Facebook, Twitter, and others) to foster contacts with customers and clients, and many other functions.	*Internal* • Permits the exchange of company-confidential e-mails and other information behind a security firewall. • Facilitates employee communications through blogs, discussion boards, forums, and wiki. *External* • Provides companies a way to conduct business; inform others of its plans; solicit customer feedback; post FAQs; and announce its mission, goals, locations, contact information, and more. • Affords a forum for interactions with its customers, clients, and others. • Allows organizations to control how they wish to be perceived by the public.	

(continued)

TABLE 1–1 Selecting the Medium *(continued)*

MEDIA	PURPOSE	BENEFITS	CAVEATS
Social-media tools	*Social media* refers to websites — such as Facebook, LinkedIn, Twitter, and YouTube — that allow the creation of online communities through which individuals and organizations with common interests can create content, interact, and share information.	*LinkedIn* • Offers individuals opportunities to connect with others and to create a professional network or community. • Provides a profile page that acts much like a résumé by highlighting an individual's work, education, skills, and experiences. • Allows community members to participate in profession-specific discussion boards, as well as post and respond to employment ads. • Allows people to "follow" specific businesses and organizations. • Circulates job-opening announcements to members based on their profiles. *Facebook* • Enables businesses to broaden their brand recognition and to interact with current and new customers. • Provides insight about potential employees, vendors, and business associates. • Assigns each individual or business a "wall" that can be used to post status updates, pictures, videos, or links to other websites. • Allows users to "friend" or "like" other users, connecting the accounts and allowing interaction among users. *Twitter* • Allows users to "follow" a company or individual who can keep clients and others aware of an organization's or individual's activities.	Note that these sites require care in setting up and administering, such as: • Establishing corporate policy and best practices guidelines. • Ensuring compliance with laws governing privacy, freedom of speech, and employment. • Ensuring that information sent or posted is accurate and in line with company policies. • Controlling risks of employee use: — Disclosure of protected information. — Use of offensive or inflammatory language. — Damage to company or organization brand, image, or reputation.

(continued)

TABLE 1–1 Selecting the Medium (*continued*)

MEDIA	PURPOSE	BENEFITS	CAVEATS
Social-media tools		• Limits every message or "status update" to 140 characters; allows businesses and individuals to post timely updates or critical announcements. • Allows organizations to enter near-synchronous conversations with their clients and customers.	

DIGITAL TIP: Synchronizing Information

If you use multiple computers (for instance, one at your office and one at home) to work on the same files, synchronizing the data on all your computers can save you time and eliminate the hassle of e-mailing or copying files from one computer to another. You can also synchronize data between your computer(s) and your mobile devices, which allows you access to your e-mails, contacts, and calendars when you are away from your computer. Numerous "cloud computing" (or off-site) applications offer free or inexpensive accounts for keeping your most important data synchronized.

Writing for Results

Soon after she received the disappointing response to her e-mail, Christine found the courage to step into Harriet's office. Christine explained, "I've really investigated the situation, and I'm sure my proposal would be in our best interest. Perhaps if I gave you more information, you'd reconsider it." Harriet thought for a moment and then said, "All right. Give me the major benefits and any associated disadvantages and costs by next Monday. If they are convincing, I'll meet with you and Fred Sadowski as soon as I get the chance. And, by the way, an e-mail is too informal—attach the information as a PDF memo to an e-mail." Christine Thomas left Harriet Sullivan's office both relieved and determined that this time she would convince Harriet.

Christine realized that she would have to summon all of her thinking about the proposal and shape it into a persuasive memo. She wrote the statement of purpose; determined the general needs of her reader; generated, gathered, and recorded the key ideas and facts; and established her scope of coverage. After organizing her notes (see Figure 1–4 on page 13), Christine wrote a draft and put it aside, planning to reread her work the next morning. Note that a first draft is less concerned with creating a coherent, correct, and persuasive memo than it is with getting all the needed information down in a reasonably organized manner. She also e-mailed the draft to a trusted colleague and instant-messaged her directly to ask for suggestions (Figure 1–5).

◆ *For a discussion of specific revision techniques and strategies, see Chapter 4, Revising a Document.*

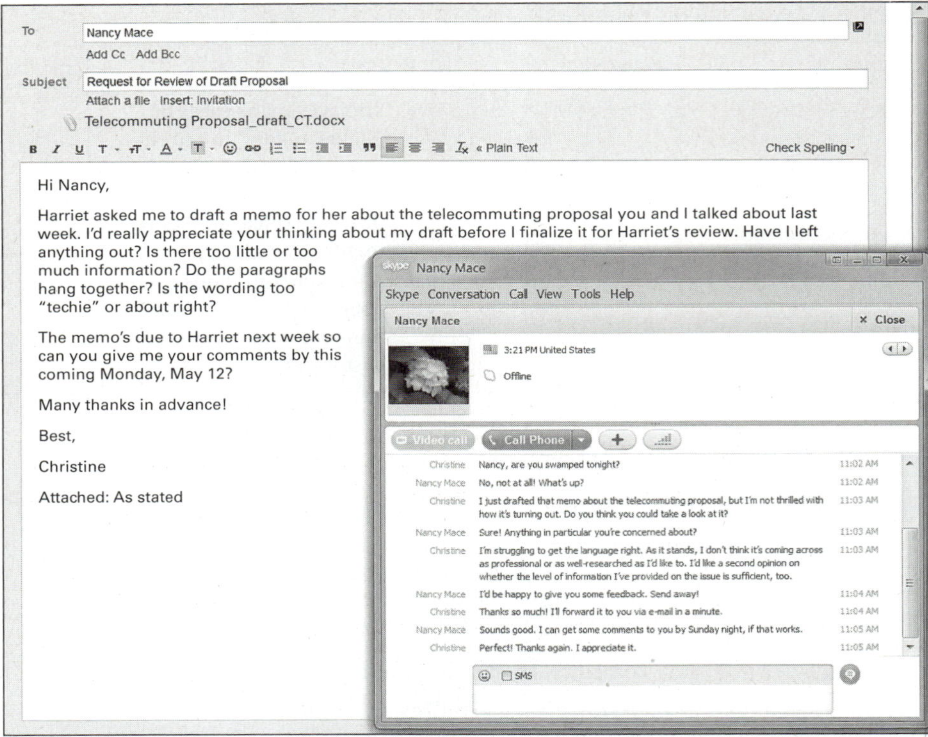

Figure 1–5 Instant Message Requesting Comments on Draft Memo

Her coworker, Nancy Mace, reviewed the draft and replied that Christine had obviously researched her subject with care and that she presented the appropriate information about starting the new program but that she needed to do a better job of anticipating some of Harriet's questions. She also noted that the memo would benefit from headings to introduce each topic and commented that Harriet would need the details of how the new program would benefit both the company and its employees. Finally, she told Christine that the writing was too choppy and needed better transitions to connect her ideas. She e-mailed Christine a copy of the draft with her suggestions (Figure 1–6).

◆ *For detailed guidance on memo format, see pages 285–287 in Chapter 8, Writing E-mails, Memos, and Letters.*

Christine considered her coworker's suggestions and reviewed the brainstorming lists she'd written earlier. She added an introduction and a conclusion and reworked the body of the memo. The extra attention she gave to Harriet's needs provided a helpful focal point she used to restructure and polish her writing. Using the heading and organization tools in her word processor, she also heeded the format advice to add topic headings to guide Harriet through the proposal. When she finished her revisions, Christine proofread her work for grammatical and mechanical errors and sent the final version of the memo to Harriet Sullivan (Figure 1–7). Note the content and style of the finished memo, which reflect the suggestions made by Christine's coworker, as well as her decision to send the proposal as a memo attached to an e-mail, as Harriet requested. Christine's story had a happy ending: Harriet was persuaded by Christine's final memo and started the work-at-home program on a trial basis that September.

◆ *For help in locating and correcting sentence-level errors, see Appendix B, Revision Guide.*

◆ *Handwritten initials on printed memos are based on organizational practice. See page 285 in Chapter 8, Writing E-mails, Memos, and Letters.*

**** **DRAFT** ****

Memo

Date: May 9, 2016
To: Harriet V. Sullivan, President
From: Christine Thomas
Subject: Telecommuting and HVS Accounting Services

Comment [NM01]: Make subject line more descriptive?

HVS Accounting Services and its employees would benefit if we permit our professional staff to telecommute two days a week. Telecommuting is becoming increasingly common throughout the United States. I suggest that we try the program for three months. That would give us a trial basis. I suggest that we begin on September 2. That would be before our busy end-of-year and winter tax-preparation period.

Comment [NM02]: Sentences too choppy—smooth out.

Comment [NM03]: Add topic headings for readability.

Such a program offers a lot of advantages to HVS. The biggest advantage is that employee productivity could increase. I read several online telecommuting articles and case studies and they show average gains of from 15 to 30 percent. I spoke with other financial-services companies at monthly Accounting Society meetings. They mention gains in the 20–30 percent range. We need to pull even with the competition.

Comment [NM04]: Include sources of information?

This would also benefit our employees. They save time and money on the days they work at home. They also wind up being less frazzled. Employees say that the time savings and better frame of mind are two reasons why they can better focus on their jobs. Also, the competition is doing it. They say they have an easier time recruiting and keeping employees. This is an important option that we can offer to our employees.

Comment [NM05]: Name one or two competitors?

The program would also be good for Bill Mayhue and Mabel Chong. Bill is having a hip replacement next month. He will be away from work for up to six weeks. Part of this time away could be used productively if he's allowed to work at home. Mabel's baby is due in September. She plans to spend three months at home after the birth and wants to keep up with her projects. Instead of losing their services, we would all mutually benefit. This would be a great boost for employee morale, too.

Comment [NM06]: Note that staff has well-defined tasks.

Figure 1–6 Draft Proposal (with Notes from Coworker)

page 2

Will the program work in practice? One key issue is keeping track of employees working away from the office. HVS currently has details on staff productivity by billable hours. This system would apply to work-at-home employees. I will work with our business consultant, Fred Sadowski, to set up and maintain measurable goals for those in the program. We would then review these goals in the middle and at the end of the three-month trial period with you. Mondays and Fridays would be ideal work-at-home days. That would leave Tuesday through Thursday as core business days.

Comment [NM07]: I wouldn't approach Fred w/o Harriet's permission.

Comment [NM08]: OK for all jobs at HVS?

Can they work effectively from home? Everyone I have spoken with already maintains a home office, so they have access to private work space already. In addition to home desktop computers with high-speed broadband access, most staff have laptop or notebook computers, as well as mobile devices with phone, e-mail, and text-messaging capabilities. They also have associated peripheral equipment (multifunction printers that can also scan and copy) and telephones. HVS has several tools for secure electronic information exchanges, including an employee virtual private network. That's how we send and receive confidential client information electronically. Those in the program can be given password access to this information with their current remote-access software. In other words, they can log into and work on their office computers from their home computers. Finally, we can put home e-mail addresses and phone and fax numbers on our internal website. We can give that information to clients, also. If the pilot program is successful, I will research an integrated system that permits our clients and suppliers to call only one number to access employees and voice-mail messages.

Comment [NM09]: Who pays for paper and other supplies?

Comment [NM10]: International calls?

Comment [NM11]: Any costs to HVS?

Can we keep in touch with employees at their homes? Keeping in touch with employees at home will not be difficult with our upgraded communications technology. They also believe that they would not lose touch with everyone else at HVS if they're gone for only a day or two a week. Our staff has a proven record of getting the job done. This makes them well-suited to a work-at-home program.

Comment [NM12]: Any evidence?

Comment [NM13]: Maybe auditors?

Figure 1–6 Draft Proposal (with Notes from Coworker) *(continued)*

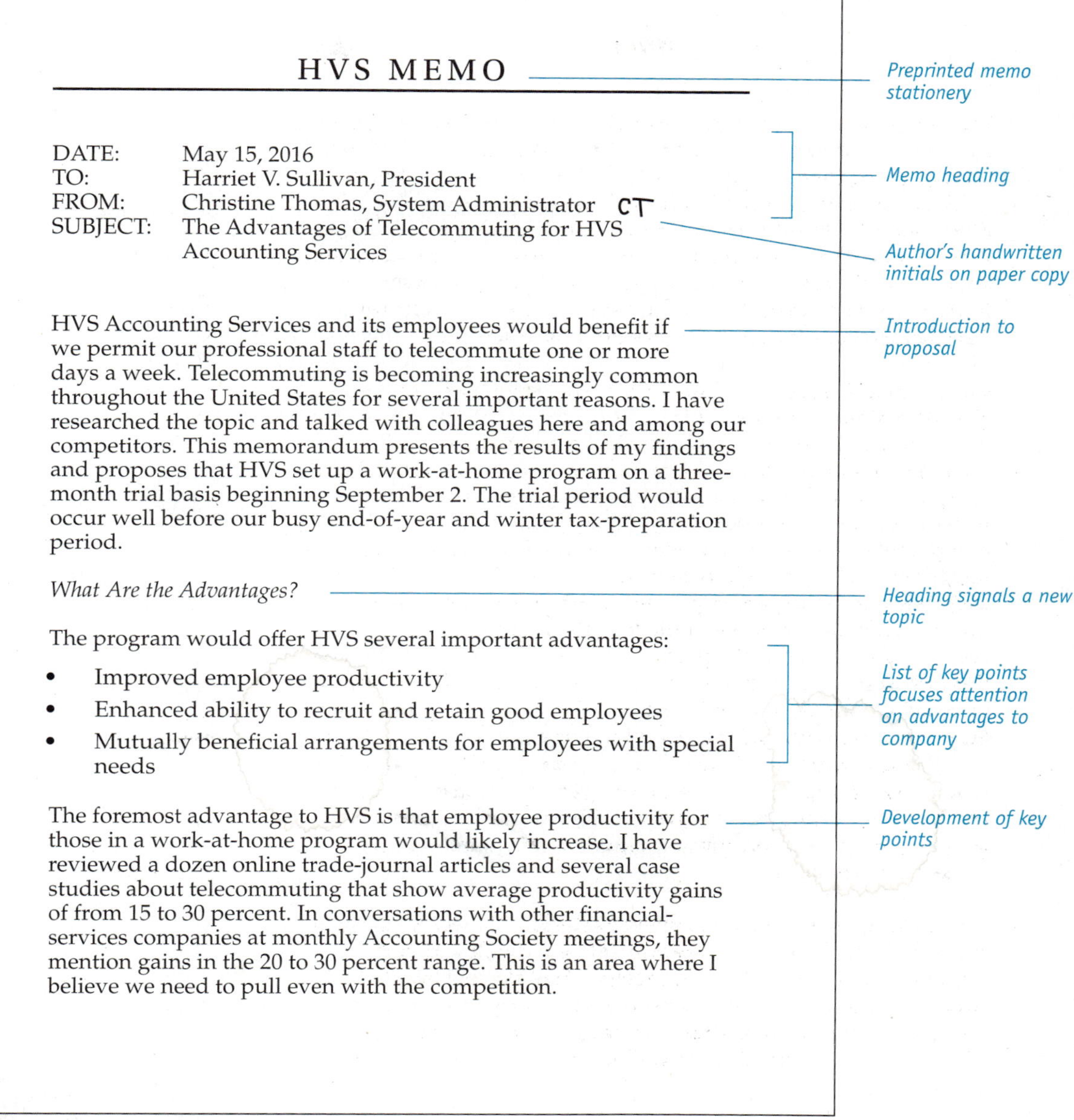

HVS MEMO

DATE: May 15, 2016
TO: Harriet V. Sullivan, President
FROM: Christine Thomas, System Administrator CT
SUBJECT: The Advantages of Telecommuting for HVS Accounting Services

HVS Accounting Services and its employees would benefit if we permit our professional staff to telecommute one or more days a week. Telecommuting is becoming increasingly common throughout the United States for several important reasons. I have researched the topic and talked with colleagues here and among our competitors. This memorandum presents the results of my findings and proposes that HVS set up a work-at-home program on a three-month trial basis beginning September 2. The trial period would occur well before our busy end-of-year and winter tax-preparation period.

What Are the Advantages?

The program would offer HVS several important advantages:

- Improved employee productivity
- Enhanced ability to recruit and retain good employees
- Mutually beneficial arrangements for employees with special needs

The foremost advantage to HVS is that employee productivity for those in a work-at-home program would likely increase. I have reviewed a dozen online trade-journal articles and several case studies about telecommuting that show average productivity gains of from 15 to 30 percent. In conversations with other financial-services companies at monthly Accounting Society meetings, they mention gains in the 20 to 30 percent range. This is an area where I believe we need to pull even with the competition.

Figure 1–7 Final Proposal

Harriet V. Sullivan 2 May 15, 2016

Advantages to employees

Telecommuting would provide important advantages to the staff that would help us to recruit and retain qualified employees. Several of our employees commute over an hour each way daily. Telecommuting would permit them to save time and money on the days they work at home. They would also be less frazzled on those days. Employees who telecommute report that the time saved and better frame of mind are two reasons they can better focus on their jobs. As you are aware, we have lost qualified job candidates because of their objections to long commutes. Other firms note that they have an easier time recruiting and retaining valuable employees when they offer telecommuting as an option. This is an important benefit that we can offer to our employees, especially in a competitive job market.

The program would also be strongly beneficial to HVS and two employees in particular: Bill Mayhue and Mabel Chong. Bill is scheduled for a hip replacement in late summer and will be away from work for up to six weeks. Part of this time away could be used productively if he's allowed to work at home. Mabel's baby is due in September. She plans to spend three months at home after the birth and would also be a good candidate for this program. Instead of losing their services for extended periods—and their ongoing contacts with their clients—we would all benefit. This would be a great boost for employee morale, too.

How Would Telecommuting Work at HVS?

Any new program of this kind raises questions about how well it will work in practice. I believe that the key questions are the following:

List focuses attention on company concerns

- How can we track the work of those in the program?
- Should everyone participate?
- Which days of the week would work best?
- Are there startup or ongoing costs to HVS?

Figure 1–7 Final Proposal *(continued)*

Harriet V. Sullivan 3 May 15, 2016

HVS Accounting Services is in an ideal position to be able to keep track of employees working away from the office. Each member of the professional staff has well-defined tasks in financial and estate planning for families, and in tax preparation and auditing for both families and small businesses. As you know from our monthly reports, HVS currently maintains detailed information that quantifies staff productivity by billable hours. This system would apply equally well to work-at-home employees. Also, with your approval, I will work with our business consultant, Fred Sadowski, to set up and maintain measurable goals for those in the program. We would then review these goals in the middle and at the end of the three-month trial period with you. Not all jobs at HVS would be suitable for the program. The receptionist, several of our temporary employees, and I need to be at the office during business hours, so we would not participate.

Development of key points

Mondays and Fridays would be ideal work-at-home days. That would leave Tuesday through Thursday as core business days for staff meetings, client conferences, and other activities better done at the office. Even on Mondays and Fridays, keeping in touch with employees at home will not be difficult in this electronic era. Everyone I have spoken with maintains a home office, so they have access to a telephone and private work space already. In addition to home desktop computers with high-speed broadband access, staff in the proposed pilot program have HVS-supplied laptop or notebook computers, as well as mobile devices with phone, e-mail, and text-messaging capabilities. They also have multifunction printers that provide fax and copy capabilities.

If the pilot program is successful, I will research an integrated system that permits our clients and suppliers to call only one number to access employees and voice-mail messages. Essentially, no startup or ongoing expenses for HVS are associated with the program, as several Internet-based programs widely used by other companies provide free Internet-based calling and videoconferencing. And, as the company's system administrator, I am uniquely positioned to provide and support these technologies, as well as provide the tools necessary for secure, private, remote access to our intranet.

Figure 1–7 Final Proposal *(continued)*

Harriet V. Sullivan 4 May 15, 2016

Heading signals shift in topic

Can We Protect Customer Confidentiality?

Customer confidentiality would also be protected. HVS has secure electronic information-exchange software that allows us to send and receive client confidential information electronically. HVS staff in the program can be given password access to confidential and other client information at home using a "virtual private network" (vpn) program. The software allows employees to connect to and work on the office network from their home computers.

Will Our Staff Be Distracted at Home?

Because everyone I have spoken with already maintains a home office, having access to private work space at home is not a hindrance. Having this space also minimizes the possibility of interruptions or other disturbances during the day while still permitting employees to schedule home-repair visits rather than having to leave work to meet a repair person, as happens now. Staff members also believe that they would not lose touch with everyone else at HVS if they're gone for only a day or two a week. As you know, the auditing staff is periodically away from the office for a week or two at a time at client sites until an audit is completed. Working away from the office is customary to them and causes few disruptions. Finally, everyone in the program would keep the same business hours, minus the commute, of course. Another indirect benefit of telecommuting is that it allows us to help do our part to reduce air pollution and traffic congestion in the area.

Can We Make It Happen?

Closing

Members of our staff have a proven record of getting the job done regardless of where they are working, which I believe makes them well suited to a work-at-home program. I look forward to discussing this option with you at your convenience.

Figure 1–7 Final Proposal *(continued)*

WRITER'S CHECKLIST

Drafting with Ethical Considerations in Mind

On the job, ethical dilemmas do not always present themselves as clear-cut choices. To help avoid ethical problems in your writing, ask the following questions as you plan and review your draft:

- ✔ Is the communication honest and truthful?
- ✔ Am I ethically consistent in my communications?
- ✔ Am I acting in the best interest of my employer? the public? myself?
- ✔ What would happen if everybody acted or communicated in this way?
- ✔ Does the action or communication violate anyone's rights?
- ✔ Am I willing to take responsibility for the communication, publicly and privately?

CHAPTER 1 SUMMARY: UNDERSTANDING THE WORKPLACE WRITING CONTEXT: A CASE STUDY

Successful writing on the job is the result of careful preparation. Review the following checklist to ensure that your writing assignments—in the classroom and on the job—are adequately planned.

- Have I determined the purpose of my writing?
- Have I considered my audience's needs and perspectives?
- Have I considered the context in which my audience will evaluate the document?
- Have I gathered and recorded all the ideas and facts necessary to fulfill my purpose and to address my audience's needs?
- Have I established the appropriate scope of coverage?
- Have I organized my ideas into related groups and determined the best sequence to link these groups for my audience?
- Have I revised the draft to emphasize the points most important to my audience?
- Have I reviewed my draft for clarity, coherence, and correctness?
- Have I formatted the final draft to highlight key ideas?
- Have I selected the right medium—e-mail, memo, letter, press release, or other—for my target audience?

Exercises

1. For three of the following topics, or three topics of your own choosing, list the topic, the audience, one possible purpose for a document, and the information needed to achieve that purpose. (List types of information, not sources of information.) Because the following topics are broad, you will need to select some particular aspect of each topic that you choose.

   Banking
   Computer programming
   Digital photography
   E-commerce
   Health care
   Highway construction
   Marketing
   Medical electronics
   Music
   Occupations
   Office procedures
   Real estate
   Small businesses
   Smartphones
   Social media
   Sports
   Tablet computers
   Television
   Welding

The following is a sample list:

Topic	The Track Changes feature of a word-processing program
Audience	A high school student
Purpose	To instruct the student how to actuate and use the Track Changes feature to comment on the classroom written assignments of his or her classmates
Kinds of information	Required hardware, word-processing software, student Internet access, and e-mail address

◆ *See Chapter 8, Writing E-mails, Memos, and Letters for memo-format examples.*

2. Using the techniques described in this chapter, write a memo explaining how to perform your job (or a job you've had) for an employee who will be replacing you while you are on vacation. Write two versions of this memo: Write one to a temporary employee hired through a temporary job agency and write a second to an employee who works in your department but not in the same job.
3. Write a memo to your manager asking for tuition reimbursement to enroll in this or another course. Assume that you work for a large organization that does not have a regular procedure for such a request and thus requires approval beyond your department. Therefore, you will need adequate background information and detail for someone who may not be familiar with your job duties or this type of request. Use the course, text descriptions, and the syllabus to prepare your memo. This memo will be most successful if you help your audience see the value of this course. You may wish to attach supporting material (such as the course syllabus).
4. Your company is experiencing financial difficulties, which has resulted in a hiring freeze. Because of limited support-staff positions and internships, upper-management personnel will now have to do more of their own office tasks, such as photocopying and typing correspondence. First, consider the possible reactions and feelings regarding the change in responsibilities. Then write a memo from the human-resources department to upper management, describing the situation and explaining the new policy.
5. Your company's human-resources manager has asked you to create an employee manual that details how to use the following office machines: the fax, the digital photocopier, and the phone and electronic filing systems. Brainstorm about the amount of detail (the scope) that you would have to provide in this manual for the following groups of employees: interns with no office work experience; administrative assistants with one to two years of office experience; and senior-management personnel who have more than ten years of office experience but who have relied on staff to complete copying and file retrieval tasks. Write a brief e-mail to the human-resources manager suggesting the number of manuals needed and for whom. Briefly discuss the various options for publishing these manuals, including the advantages and disadvantages of each. Who might benefit from a printed manual? What might be the advantages of a digital manual posted to the company's intranet? Support your claims.

Collaborative Classroom Projects

1. Divide into groups as directed by your instructor. Discuss similarities and differences between writing for the audience in Exercise 2 and writing for the audience in Exercise 3. Make a list that you can share with the class.
2. The manager of your company's publications department believes that sharing a production printer among four employees is slowing down their productivity on company

manuals, brochures, and other communications pieces. In the long run, this slowdown might cause his department to miss publication deadlines. The manager of the information technology (IT) department, however, doesn't want to purchase a new printer because it is near the end of the fiscal year and an equipment purchase could push her department over budget, making IT look bad to upper management. Part *c* may be completed outside of class.

a. Divide into two groups, one that represents the publications department and the other the IT department. Each group should brainstorm separately a list of reasons that support your manager's concerns and needs.
b. Debate your position with the other group. Acknowledge each other's concerns and address them. At the end of the debate, discuss what you have learned and research possibilities that would benefit both sides. (For example, would a used or refurbished printer be a possible solution?)
c. The publications-department group should now draft a memo to send to the IT-department manager. The IT-department group should draft a memo to send to the publications-department manager. For either memo, state your group's needs, acknowledge the other side's concerns, and suggest possible compromises or solutions that could resolve this issue amicably.

3. Divide into groups of four to six students. For 20 to 25 minutes, brainstorm and develop a list of problems that make studying on campus difficult. Then take 15 minutes to revise the list into two versions: (1) a list for the dean's office committee whose assignment it is to make studying on campus easier and (2) a list for the residence-hall planning committee in charge of designing a new dormitory on campus. Discuss how the different purposes and audiences affected your lists.

Research Projects

1. Find an article on a subject of interest to you in two different types of publications—for example, a newspaper or a general-interest magazine (such as *The Economist*) and a technical journal (such as the *Journal of the American Medical Association*). After you have read the two articles, do the following:
   a. Identify the target audience of each publication. Compare the approaches taken in each article toward the intended audience. Look specifically for indicators of the audience's knowledge of the subject, such as the presence or absence of technical terms and the kind and number of illustrations used.
   b. Create statements of purpose for each article, as if you had been the writer.
   c. Discuss or report on how well the writers met the needs of their audiences. (Respond only after you have completed *a* and *b*.)
2. Interview at least three current or former instructors about how they prepare their class lectures for different groups of students. For example, you might ask them how their style of teaching first-year students differs from teaching juniors or seniors (or graduate students). Or you might ask how the style of their exams or essay questions varies, depending on the class for which they are written. Write your findings and present them to the class. (*Note:* Before you begin, read pages 150–151 about interviewing for information in Chapter 6, Conducting Research for a Document.)
3. Suppose the company you work for provides a week's paid vacation package as a reward to the Employee of the Year and his or her immediate family. Your manager has

asked you to select this year's vacation package at a location that has educational value. You have a budget of $6,000. Using the Web, compare and contrast different vacation packages and then outline the reasons for your recommendation. Keep the checklists Planning Your Document on page 5 and Writing for Your Reader on page 7 in mind as you write an e-mail to your manager.

4. Imagine that you volunteer several hours a week at an adult community learning center where you teach basic computer skills to people over the age of 65. They usually are interested in learning how to use e-mail or how to set up a social-networking account in order to keep in touch with their grandchildren. However, their lack of experience with the Internet leaves them vulnerable to scams, particularly ones that require them to send e-mails to receive free things or that ask them to verify bank-account or credit-card information. Go to sites that debunk online scams and sites that offer advice on how to spot scams. Write a single-sided illustrated handout to your students warning them about these scams and how to avoid them. Be sure to give examples.

2 Planning a Document

Contents

How do business and technical writers arrange facts and ideas to serve their purposes and meet the needs of different audiences? This chapter reviews proven organizing techniques and describes a wide range of organizing strategies that you can apply to your own writing.

When a motion picture is being filmed, the scenes are usually shot out of sequence. Different locations, actors' schedules, weather conditions, and many other circumstances make working out of sequence necessary. If it were not for a skilled film editor, the completed film would be a jumble of random scenes. The editor, following the script, carefully assembles the scenes so that the story moves smoothly and logically from one event to the next, as the screenwriter and the director planned. Without a plan, no such order would be possible because the editor would have no guide for organizing the jigsaw puzzle of hundreds of separate scenes and shots.

Organizing a movie and organizing a written document are obviously different tasks, but they have one element in common — both must be planned ahead of time. For a film, planning means creating a script. For a written document, it means organizing information into a sequence appropriate to the subject, the purpose, and the audience.

Outlining

Organizing your information before you write has two important advantages. First, it forces you to reexamine the information you plan to include to be sure that you have sufficient facts and details to satisfy your audience's needs and achieve the purpose of your writing. Second, it forces you to order the information in a sequence that your audience will understand as clearly as you do.

The importance of these advantages has been confirmed by research studies of workplace writing. According to one study in a corporate setting, more than three times the number of good writers as compared with poor writers create a written outline. In fact, 36 percent of the poor writers said they never use an outline or plan, either written or mental.[1]

◆ *For an example of informal organizational notes for a memo, see Figure 1–4 on page 13.*

Not all writing benefits from a full-scale outline, of course. For relatively short documents, such as memos, letters, and important e-mails, you may need only to jot down a few notes to make sure that you haven't left out any important information and that you have arranged the information in a logical order. These notes then guide you as you write the draft.

Longer documents, such as formal reports or large proposals, and documents that have a wider audience, such as blog entries or content for publicly available websites, require outlines to provide the content with a coherent structure. In addition to guiding your first draft, an outline can be circulated for review by your colleagues and superiors. They can easily see in the outline the scope of information you plan to include and the sequence in which it is organized. Their reviews can help you find and fix major problems before you've committed a great deal of time to writing your draft. An outline is preliminary by its nature — a means to an end, not an end in itself. Don't view it as a final product. If you suddenly see a better way to organize your material while you are writing the draft, depart from your outline and follow the better approach. The main purpose of the outline is to bring order and shape to your information before you begin to write. This chapter introduces conventions for creating simple and complex outlines and provides techniques for verifying that your outline is sound.

Traditional Roman Numeral Outline

The most common type of outline emphasizes topics and subtopics by means of Roman numerals, letters, and Arabic numbers in the following sequence of subdivisions:

I. Major section
  A. First-level subsection
    1. Second-level subsection
      a. Third-level subsection
        1) Fourth-level subsection

---

[1]Christine Barabas, *Technical Writing in a Corporate Culture: A Study of the Nature of Information* (Norwood, NJ: Ablex Publishing Corp., 1991), p. 188. "Good" and "poor" writers were so classified by their readers within the corporation.

Your subject will seldom require four subdivisions, but dividing it this way allows for a highly detailed outline if one is necessary. Stop at the level at which you can no longer subdivide into at least two items.

Begin your outline by typing or writing down its major sections. For example, if you are writing an article about the development of the Internet for a company magazine, you might start with the following major sections:

I. History of the Internet
II. Growth of Internet technology and societal issues for the Internet

After a moment's reflection, you decide that the first-level heading is actually the overall topic of the article. After reviewing your research notes, you realize that the topic of the first section should be the background and developments that led to Internet technology, so you revise the outline accordingly:

I. Background of Internet technology
II. Growth of Internet technology and societal issues for the Internet

You quickly decide, however, that you have put too many topics in your second major section, so you make another effort:

I. Background of Internet technology
II. Growth of Internet technology
III. Development and evolution of web technology

Once you establish your major sections, look for minor divisions within each section. For example, you might first arrive at the following minor divisions within your major sections:

I. Background of Internet technology
  A. Pioneers
  B. Later developments
II. Growth of Internet technology
  A. Network technology
  B. Improvements in network technology
III. Development and evolution of web technology
  A. Invention of web and hyperlinking
  B. Launch of Mosaic browser

This outline is a start, but the second-level divisions (A and B) are too vague to be useful. After considering Growth of Internet technology, for example, you might produce the following revision:

II. Growth of Internet technology
  A. Competing network techniques and protocols throughout the mid-1970s and early 1980s
  B. Improvements and standardization of techniques and protocols with increased users in the mid-1980s

C. Transition from a community of scholars, scientists, and defense contractors to widespread infrastructure in the late 1980s and early 1990s
D. Expansion of Internet in business, academic, and government institutions from the late 1990s and beyond
E. Growth of Internet technology to encompass all aspects of personal interactions in the early 2000s.

After evaluating the whole outline, you are ready to insert the information you compiled during your research under the appropriate major and minor divisions, as shown in Figure 2–1. When you have finished, you should have a complete outline. However, although the outline looks final at this point, you still may need to revise it. Make sure that corresponding divisions present material of equal importance (that is, that major and subordinate divisions are equal to one another in importance). Likewise, ensure that every heading is divided into at least two parts if it is to be divided at all: For every *1* there should be a *2*, for every *A* there should be a *B*, although doing so may not always be possible.

NOT

A. Pioneering communications technology
    1. Morse and telegraph, calculating machines, silicon chip, and remote-access computers

BUT

A. Pioneering communications technology
    1. Morse and telegraph
    2. Calculating machines
    3. Silicon chip
    4. Remote-access computers

Finally, review your outline for completeness, determining whether you need additional information. If you find that your research is not really complete, return to your sources and locate the missing material.

Decimal Numbering System Outline

Many science and technology authors use a decimal numbering system instead of the Roman numeral system to develop their outlines, such as the following:

1. FIRST MAJOR IDEA
    1.1 Supporting idea for 1
    1.2 Supporting idea for 1
        1.2.1 Example or illustration of 1.2
        1.2.2 Example or illustration of 1.2
            1.2.2.1 Detail for 1.2.2
            1.2.2.2 Detail for 1.2.2
    1.3 Supporting idea for 1
2. SECOND MAJOR IDEA

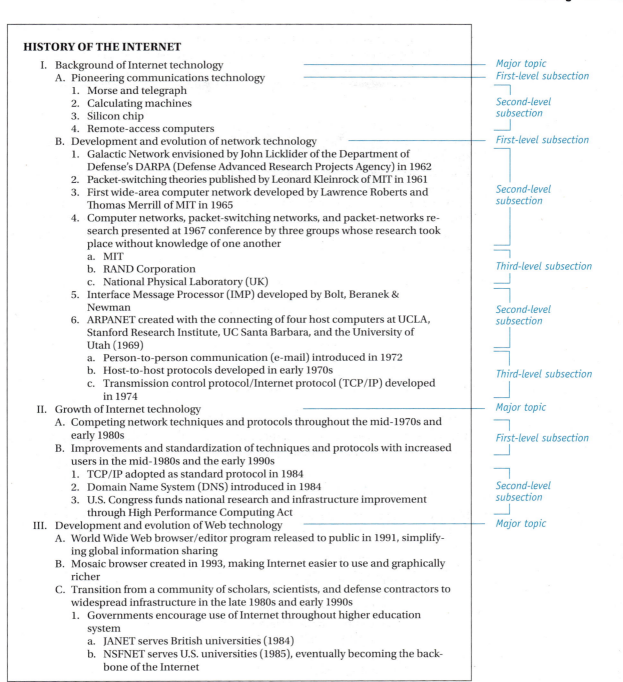

HISTORY OF THE INTERNET

I. Background of Internet technology
   A. Pioneering communications technology
      1. Morse and telegraph
      2. Calculating machines
      3. Silicon chip
      4. Remote-access computers
   B. Development and evolution of network technology
      1. Galactic Network envisioned by John Licklider of the Department of Defense's DARPA (Defense Advanced Research Projects Agency) in 1962
      2. Packet-switching theories published by Leonard Kleinrock of MIT in 1961
      3. First wide-area computer network developed by Lawrence Roberts and Thomas Merrill of MIT in 1965
      4. Computer networks, packet-switching networks, and packet-networks research presented at 1967 conference by three groups whose research took place without knowledge of one another
         a. MIT
         b. RAND Corporation
         c. National Physical Laboratory (UK)
      5. Interface Message Processor (IMP) developed by Bolt, Beranek & Newman
      6. ARPANET created with the connecting of four host computers at UCLA, Stanford Research Institute, UC Santa Barbara, and the University of Utah (1969)
         a. Person-to-person communication (e-mail) introduced in 1972
         b. Host-to-host protocols developed in early 1970s
         c. Transmission control protocol/Internet protocol (TCP/IP) developed in 1974

II. Growth of Internet technology
   A. Competing network techniques and protocols throughout the mid-1970s and early 1980s
   B. Improvements and standardization of techniques and protocols with increased users in the mid-1980s and the early 1990s
      1. TCP/IP adopted as standard protocol in 1984
      2. Domain Name System (DNS) introduced in 1984
      3. U.S. Congress funds national research and infrastructure improvement through High Performance Computing Act

III. Development and evolution of Web technology
   A. World Wide Web browser/editor program released to public in 1991, simplifying global information sharing
   B. Mosaic browser created in 1993, making Internet easier to use and graphically richer
   C. Transition from a community of scholars, scientists, and defense contractors to widespread infrastructure in the late 1980s and early 1990s
      1. Governments encourage use of Internet throughout higher education system
         a. JANET serves British universities (1984)
         b. NSFNET serves U.S. universities (1985), eventually becoming the backbone of the Internet

Figure 2–1 Sample Outline

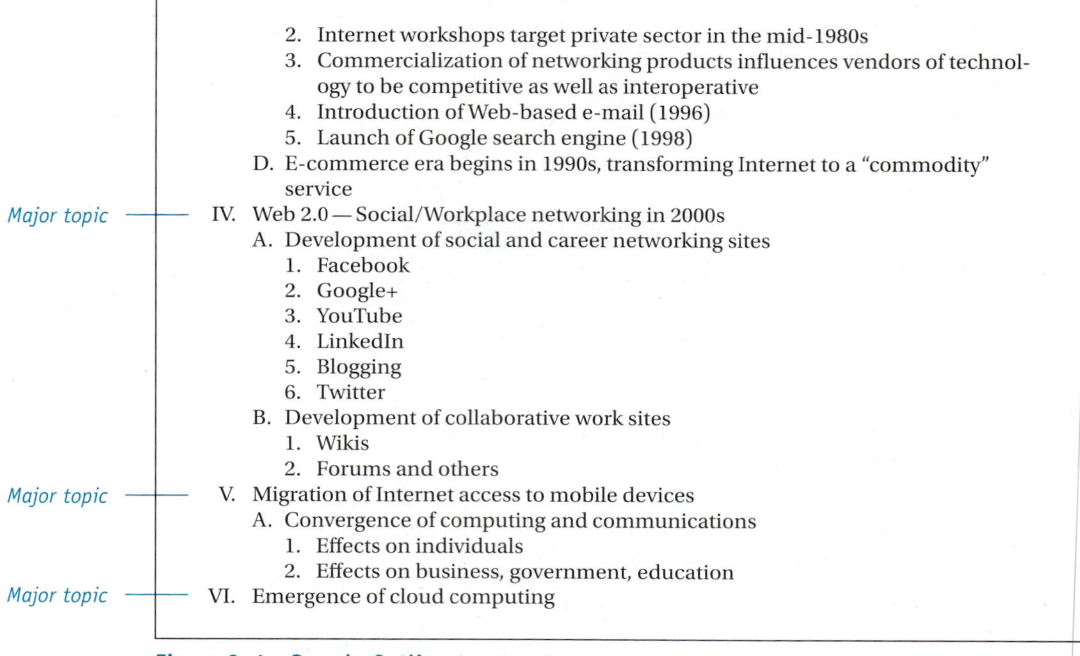

2. Internet workshops target private sector in the mid-1980s
3. Commercialization of networking products influences vendors of technology to be competitive as well as interoperative
4. Introduction of Web-based e-mail (1996)
5. Launch of Google search engine (1998)

D. E-commerce era begins in 1990s, transforming Internet to a "commodity" service

IV. Web 2.0 — Social/Workplace networking in 2000s
- A. Development of social and career networking sites
  1. Facebook
  2. Google+
  3. YouTube
  4. LinkedIn
  5. Blogging
  6. Twitter
- B. Development of collaborative work sites
  1. Wikis
  2. Forums and others

V. Migration of Internet access to mobile devices
- A. Convergence of computing and communications
  1. Effects on individuals
  2. Effects on business, government, education

VI. Emergence of cloud computing

Figure 2–1 Sample Outline *(continued)*

◆ *For a discussion of decimal numbering in formal reports, see page 382 in Chapter 11, Writing Formal Reports.*

◆ *For detailed information on researching information, see Chapter 6, Conducting Research for a Document.*

This system should not go beyond the fourth level because the numbers get too cumbersome past that point. In many technical articles and reports, the decimal numbering system is carried over from the outline to the final version of the document for ease of cross-referencing sections. Typical uses for the decimal outline include procedural manuals, technical reports and specifications, mathematical texts, and scientific and technical material of many kinds.

WRITER'S CHECKLIST
Creating an Outline

✔ Break a large topic into its major divisions and type or write them down. Does the sequence fit your organizing pattern? (See pages 40–63 for organizing patterns.) If not, reorganize and label the topics with Roman numerals (I, II, III, and so on).

✔ Repeat the process for each major topic. Break each into its logical subtopics and list them under each major topic. Then sequence the subtopics to fit your pattern of development and label them with capital letters (A, B, C, and so on).

✔ If necessary, repeat the process for each third-level topic and label the topics with Arabic numbers (1, 2, 3, and so on).

✔ Key each of your notes to the appropriate place in your outline (for example, placing II-C beside any note that fits the portion of your outline labeled II-C).

- ✔ Merge your notes and your outline, placing every note under the appropriate head, subhead, or sub-subhead in your outline. Then organize the notes under each head in the most logical sequence.
- ✔ To convert your detailed outline into your first draft, put the first head on your computer screen and expand the notes listed under it into sentences and paragraphs.

DIGITAL TIP: Formatting Your Outline

Using the outline feature of your word-processing software enables you to do the following:

- Format your outline automatically.
- Fill in, rearrange, and update your outline.
- Experiment with the organization and scope of information while retaining the outline format.
- Rearrange sections and subsections easily.
- Create Roman numeral or decimal numbering outline styles.

Experiment with the default settings of the outline feature to make the best use of this software.

How Audience and Purpose Shape Organization: A Case Study

The kinds of information and organization that shape your outline will vary according to your purposes for writing and your audience's specific needs. Let us say, for example, that a writer needs to prepare two separate documents about the Lifemaker System, a home gym that combines the features of ten separate resistance machines into a compact weight-and-cable exercise system. The first document will be a sales brochure directed at potential purchasers of the Lifemaker; the second document will be a maintenance manual written for customers who have already purchased the system. Both will be offered by the manufacturer online and in print.

◆ *For an explanation of written statements of purpose, see pages 5–6 in Chapter 1, Understanding the Workplace Writing Context: A Case Study.*

ETHICS NOTE: Write Credibly Readers are persuaded in part if they believe the source is credible. Therefore, be careful not to overstate the claims you make. And although comparing your product or service with that of a competitor is an effective persuasive strategy, speaking negatively or disparagingly about a competitor is not.

The sales brochure and the maintenance manual both need to describe the design and structure of the Lifemaker System, although they will do so in different ways and for different reasons. The audience for each document is composed of nonspecialists, so each document should contain minimal technical language and avoid terms that would be familiar only to technicians, engineers, and sales representatives. Whether they are potential or current customers of Lifemaker, readers will likely be familiar with exercise systems, so descriptions of the exercise equipment for either document need not be too detailed. Much of the information gathered and used for brainstorming and outlining will be useful for both the sales brochure and the maintenance manual.

However, these documents reflect different purposes in two important ways. Consider how a statement of purpose might look for each.

SALES BROCHURE	My primary purpose is to describe the benefits and features of the Lifemaker System so that my readers will be motivated to purchase it.
MAINTENANCE MANUAL	My primary purpose is to explain the assembly and maintenance requirements of the Lifemaker System so that the customer knows exactly how to put it together and take care of it.

The brochure's outline, then, should highlight the benefits of buying the system and offer more general comments about the design and structural features of the system.

The maintenance manual will be directed at readers who have already purchased the system, so the writer will not be concerned with organizing information to form a persuasive argument. Instead, the writer will want to create an outline that will lead to clearly written, step-by-step instructions on how to assemble and maintain the Lifemaker. References to structural features will be very specific and more technical than they would be for the sales brochure. (The audience is still made up of nonspecialists, so the writer needs to keep the use of technical terms to a minimum and should leave places in the outline for diagrams that will eventually appear in the manual to clarify the instructions.)

The outline for the sales brochure (Figure 2–2) notes specific design details (cast-iron plates, adjustable cables, 4-by-7-foot size), but the information is organized to support the brochure's persuasive purpose. Although the purpose of the maintenance manual is to instruct rather than to persuade the audience, its organization differs from that used for the sales brochure. The maintenance manual outline (Figure 2–3) follows a *sequential* (*step-by-step*) organization of information (see pages 40–42), an ideal pattern to use when instruction, rather than persuasion, is the primary purpose for writing. In contrast, the outline for the sales brochure uses a *general-to-specific* sequence of information (see pages 53), which is more appropriate when the purpose for writing is to persuade the audience with a general argument supported with specific details. Within the major topic divisions, the sales brochure also uses two other types of organization: *comparison* (see pages 56–63) to emphasize its features against those of its competitors and *division* (see pages 48–50) to illustrate how its features (weights and cables) function in the system. These differences are summarized as follows:

	Lifemaker Sales Brochure	**Lifemaker Maintenance Manual**
Purpose	Describe benefits and features to attract purchasers	Explain maintenance requirements for system customers
Audience	Nonspecialists who are potential Lifemaker customers	Nonspecialists who have purchased the Lifemaker System
Organizing patterns	General to specific; comparison; division	Sequential (step by step)

LIFEMAKER: The Compact, Affordable Home Gym

I. General benefits of owning Lifemaker
   A. More compact than other systems
   B. Provides better training programs than other systems
   C. Lower priced and easier to assemble and maintain than other systems

II. Design benefits/features
   A. Multiple stations, so two people can work out at the same time
   B. Takes up minimal space (measures only 4 feet by 7 feet)
   C. Designed to work all muscle groups (40 different combinations of exercises)

III. Structural benefits/features: Weights
   A. Dual weight stacks that total 200 pounds of cast-iron plates
   B. Adjustable weight stacks with resistance range of 10 to 150 pounds
   C. Varied individual weights with resistance adjustable in 5-, 10-, and 15-pound increments

IV. Structural benefits/features: Cables
   A. Adjustable cables that increase tension at stations working strongest muscle groups
   B. Reconfigurable weight stacks (cables permit reconfiguring of weights without dismantling entire system)
   C. Reversible tension (cables can increase/decrease tension mid-set)

V. Financial and maintenance benefits
   A. More reasonably priced than leading system: $999.99
   B. Two-year guarantee for all parts
   C. Easy maintenance (no oiling or solvents necessary)

Organized to compare benefits with other systems (I)

Organized by division of features, according to function in system (II–IV)

Organized to compare benefits with other systems (V)

Figure 2–2 Outline for a Sales Brochure

MAINTAINING YOUR LIFEMAKER

I. Maintenance and troubleshooting
   A. Inspect and safeguard all parts each time you do the following:
      1. Inspect parts for wear.
         a. Check cables for fraying.
         b. Check weights for cracks.
         c. Replace worn parts immediately.
      2. Tighten tension on cable #1.
         a. Find end of 125″ cable (#43 on diagram).
         b. Turn end of cable clockwise.
         c. Thread cable farther into weight tube (#35 on diagram).
      3. Tighten tension on cable #2.
         a. Find end of 265″ cable (#46 on diagram).
         b. Turn end of cable clockwise.
         c. Thread cable farther into weight tube (#35 on diagram).
      4. Clean parts.
         a. Clean with damp cloth.
         b. Use nonabrasive detergent.
         c. Do not use solvents or oils.

Maintenance steps organized sequentially

Figure 2–3 Outline for Instructions for a Maintenance Manual (Excerpt)

◆ *For drafts and revisions of this sales brochure, see Chapter 3, Drafting a Document, and Chapter 4, Revising a Document.*

Thus, although both documents are drawn from the same source and speak to nontechnical audiences, their different purposes call for different patterns of organization.

Essential Organizing Patterns

The choice of a pattern for organizing information comes naturally for some types of writing. Instructions for how to process an invoice or operate a piece of equipment are arranged step by step. A trip report usually follows a chronological sequence. When a subject does not lend itself to one particular pattern, you can choose the best sequence or combination of sequences by considering your purpose and your audience's needs. Suppose, for example, that you report on a trip to several companies that fabricate industrial drainage systems. You wish to gather information on the most efficient way to arrange equipment for improved workflow through the shop where you work.

- **Visits**
  You would organize information about the visits *chronologically*.
- **Layouts**
  Your description of the various shop layouts, emphasizing the physical locations of the equipment, would be organized *spatially*.
- **Recommendations**
  Your recommendations about the most workable arrangement for your shop likely would be organized according to *decreasing order of importance* by presenting the most efficient arrangement first, the second most efficient arrangement next, and so on.

As this example illustrates, the method used will be determined by the topic and your purpose in writing about it. Organize your writing from the perspective of your audience. Keep in mind that some types of writing lend themselves logically to only one kind of organization and will best convey information to your reader by that pattern. Be consistent when using the method that most effectively communicates the material. If you begin presenting conclusions in most-to-least order of importance, maintain that order throughout the conclusions section. Likewise, if you present conclusions in that order, do the same for the recommendations. Once you establish a pattern of organizing information, retain it. Doing so satisfies your audience's expectations of consistency and predictability. Table 2–1 lists and describes the most common ways to organize, or sequence, information in on-the-job writing.

Sequential

In the sequential pattern, you divide your subject into steps and then present the steps in the order in which they occur. This arrangement is the most effective way to explain a process, such as how a digital photocopier works, or to explain how to perform a procedure, such as cardiopulmonary resuscitation (CPR). Sequencing is the logical

TABLE 2–1 Patterns of Organization

PATTERN	DESCRIPTION	USES
Sequential	Consecutive order of steps, not connected to a specific time	Takes your reader step by step through the stages of a process in the order in which the process occurs (*example:* description of an order processing system in a product warehouse)
Chronological	Sequence of steps or events as they occur in clock or date time	Takes your reader step by step through the stages of an activity or event as it occurs in time from beginning to end and denotes the time frame for each step (*example:* a trip report)
Spatial	Description of an object, area, or phenomenon according to the physical arrangement of its features	Describes the topic at the level of detail necessary for your reader to envision its appearance or how it occurred (*example:* a vehicle accident report)
Division	Division of a complex subject into its relevant parts, with a discussion of each part and how it is related to the whole	Describes a complex whole by breaking it into smaller units to make it easier to understand (*examples:* [1] a description of online social-networking resources available for job searches or [2] the contents of this table, which describes each pattern and its function as part of the overall topic of organizing information)
Classification	Grouping of disparate units of a whole into related categories	Organizes information by grouping the topic into its largest number of equivalent parts and, as needed, subdividing each of those into its relevant components (*example:* grouping exchange-traded funds by their investment sector)
Decreasing Order of Importance	Order beginning with the most important item and leading to the least important item	Introduces your reader to your main, or most important, points at the beginning of your writing, followed by background information that supports your main points (*examples:* [1] a press release or [2] the executive summary of a formal report)
Increasing Order of Importance	Order beginning with the least important item and leading to the most important item	Leads your reader through the thought process and details that support conclusions you reach at the end of your writing (*example:* a sales presentation)
General to Specific	Order leading from an overview or general statement to a detailed explanation that develops or supports it	Introduces your reader to the main, or general, point you wish to make at the beginning of your writing and leads your reader through the facts and other supporting information that describes how you reached your general point (*example:* a memo or proposal that begins with a recommendation)
Specific to General	Order leading from the details of a topic to a broad overview or conclusion	Leads your reader through the facts and other supporting information you use to build your case for reaching the conclusion you state at the end of your writing (*example:* a report that begins by using the details of an industrial accident to demonstrate how they lead to the root cause of the accident)

pattern for writing instructions—how to do it. For example, basic care for treating a minor burn follows a step-by-step sequence.

▶ Basic Care for Minor Burns

1. Cool the burned area using cool—not cold or icy—water.
2. Then wash the area with soap and water and apply an antibiotic ointment to prevent infection.
3. Finally, cover the burned area using dry sterile dressings.

To treat deeper, more serious burns, more detailed instructions are necessary, but they, too, would be organized in sequential order. The greatest advantage of presenting your information in sequential order is that it is easy for a reader to understand and follow the process because the sequence of steps in your writing corresponds to the order of the process being described. If you were to write instructions for submitting a workplace request, you would present the information in a step-by-step sequence (Figures 2–4 and 2–5). When you present your information in steps, do not assume that your readers are as familiar with your subject as you are; if they were, they wouldn't need your instructions. Even for a simple process, be sure that you list all steps and explain in adequate detail how each step is performed. Sometimes you must also indicate the purpose or function of each step.

Chronological

Sequential and chronological patterns overlap because each describes steps in a process. In a chronological sequence, however, you focus on the order in which the steps or events occur in time, beginning with the first event, going on to the next event, and so on, until you have reached the last event. Trip reports, work schedules, minutes of meetings, laboratory test procedures, and certain accident reports are among the types

Flextime Eligibility and Requests

I. Memo to outline eligibility and procedure for requesting a flextime work schedule
    A. Eligibility requirements:
        1. Not required to answer phone or be available to the public between 8 a.m. and 5 p.m.
        2. Must meet with department manager about other duties during those hours.
    B. If eligible, submit Form FT-32 to Human Resources:
        1. Must be signed by department manager.
        2. Human Resources will send form to division manager for review.
    C. Human Resources will notify you whether the request is approved or denied:
        1. If approved, begin flextime schedule the following Monday.
        2. Department manager will submit an evaluation after three weeks about the arrangement's impact on the department.
        3. If denied, meet with the department manager for an explanation.

Figure 2–4 Outline for Sequential Instructions

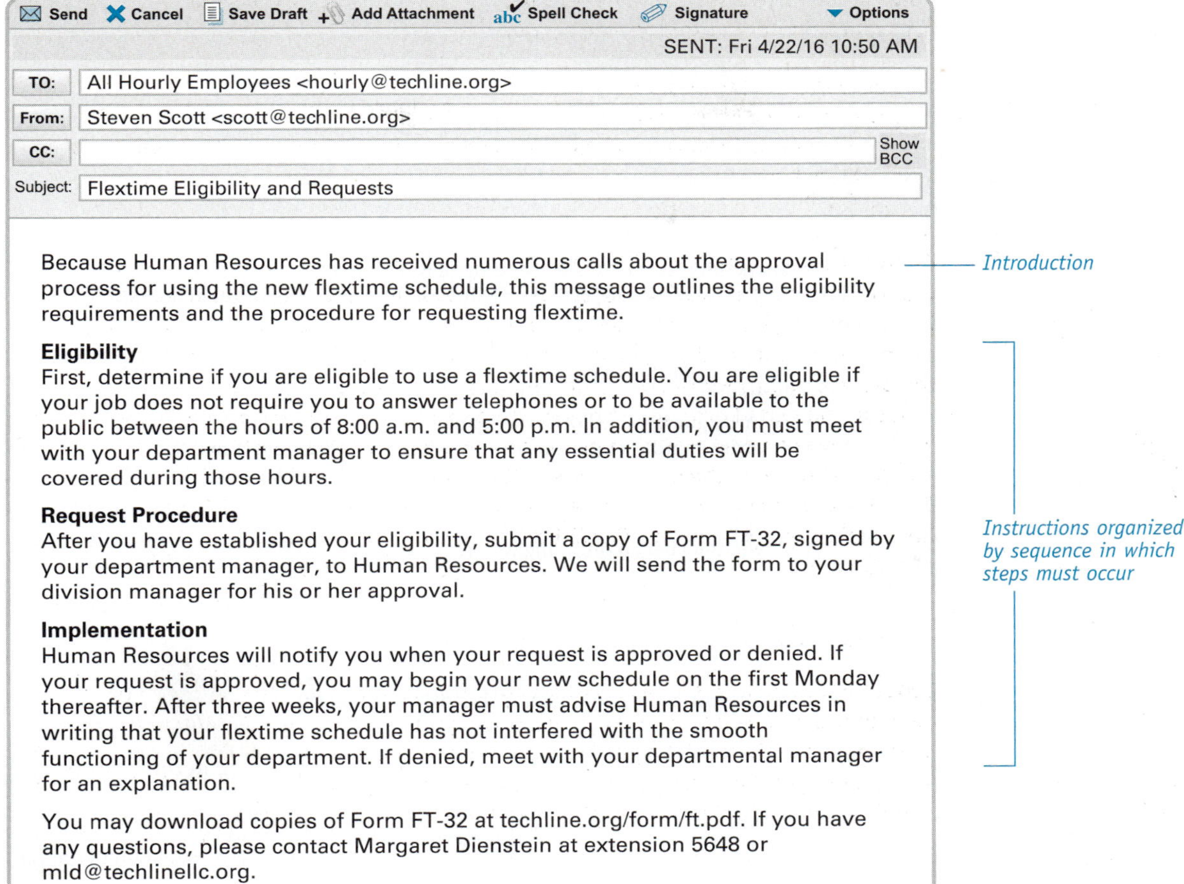

Send | Cancel | Save Draft | Add Attachment | Spell Check | Signature | Options

SENT: Fri 4/22/16 10:50 AM

TO: All Hourly Employees <hourly@techline.org>

From: Steven Scott <scott@techline.org>

CC:

Show BCC

Subject: Flextime Eligibility and Requests

Because Human Resources has received numerous calls about the approval process for using the new flextime schedule, this message outlines the eligibility requirements and the procedure for requesting flextime.

Eligibility
First, determine if you are eligible to use a flextime schedule. You are eligible if your job does not require you to answer telephones or to be available to the public between the hours of 8:00 a.m. and 5:00 p.m. In addition, you must meet with your department manager to ensure that any essential duties will be covered during those hours.

Request Procedure
After you have established your eligibility, submit a copy of Form FT-32, signed by your department manager, to Human Resources. We will send the form to your division manager for his or her approval.

Implementation
Human Resources will notify you when your request is approved or denied. If your request is approved, you may begin your new schedule on the first Monday thereafter. After three weeks, your manager must advise Human Resources in writing that your flextime schedule has not interfered with the smooth functioning of your department. If denied, meet with your departmental manager for an explanation.

You may download copies of Form FT-32 at techline.org/form/ft.pdf. If you have any questions, please contact Margaret Dienstein at extension 5648 or mld@techlinellc.org.

FIGURE 2–5 Sequential Method of Development

of writing in which information may be organized chronologically. These documents refer to clock times or dates to denote the time frames for each step. In the outline and memo shown in Figure 2–6 on page 44 and 2–7 on page 45, respectively, a plant superintendent reports the course of an accidental fire at a chemical plant.

Spatial

In a spatial sequence, you describe an object according to the physical arrangement of its features. Depending on the subject, you may describe the features from top to bottom, from side to side, from east to west (or west to east), from inside to outside, and so on. Descriptions of this kind rely mainly on dimension (*height, width, length*); direction (*up, down, north, south*); shape (*rectangular, square, semicircular*); proportion

OUTLINE

I. Conditions before fire
   A. Building A
      1. Three piles of scrap paper 100 feet outside building
      2. Six pallets of Class I flammable liquids along west wall
   B. Building B approximately 150 feet from scrap paper outside Building A

II. Chronology of fire
   A. 6:00 a.m.
      1. Spark initiated fire in electric shop of Building A
      2. Night security guard called Ardville Volunteer Fire Department and the plant superintendent
      3. Fire spread to drums of flammable liquid, engulfing Building A
      4. Fire spread to scrap paper
   B. 6:15 a.m.
      1. Security guard hosed down scrap paper
      2. Security guard set up lawn sprinklers between Buildings A and B
      3. Security guard noticed smoke coming from Building B
   C. 6:57 a.m. (approx.)
      1. Volunteer fire department arrived
      2. Firefighters began pumping water

III. Results of fire
   A. Building A destroyed
   B. Building B suffered $250K damage to roof

Figure 2–6 Outline for a Chronological Description (Excerpt)

(*one-half, two-thirds*); and other features, such as color, building materials, fabric, and the like. Features are described in relation to one another:

▶ One end is raised six to eight inches higher than the other end to permit the rain to run off.

Features are also described in relation to their surroundings:

▶ The lot is located on the east bank of the Kingman River.

The spatial pattern of organization is also commonly used in descriptions of building layouts; emergency evacuation plans; proposals for landscape work; fashion design; construction-site progress reports; and, in combination with a step-by-step sequence, many types of instructions. These descriptions commonly include drawings, diagrams, or photographs to further clarify the features being described, as in Figure 2–8, a guide to ergonomic workstation posture.

Contrast the description in Figure 2–8 with the installation requirements (in English and SI units)[2] for facility-construction compliance with the Americans with Disabilities Act (ADA) in Figure 2–9. The posture instructions use directional descriptions

[2]SI units refer to the International System of Units, or metric system.

Memorandum

To: Charles Artmier, Chair, Safety Committee
From: Willard Ricke, Plant Superintendent, Sequoia Chemical Plant WR
Date: November 19, 2017
Subject: Fire at the Sequoia Chemical Plant in Ardville on November 14, 2017

The following description provides an account of the conditions and development of the fire at our Sequoia Chemical Plant in Ardville on November 14, 2017. Because this description will be incorporated into the report that the Safety Committee will prepare, please let me know if I should add or clarify any details.

Conditions Before Fire

Clear headings allow readers to see major steps at a glance

Three piles of scrap paper were located about 100 feet south of Building A and 150 feet west of Building B at our Sequoia Chemical Plant in Ardville. Building A, which consisted of one story and a partial attic, was used in part as an electric shop and in part for equipment storage. Six pallets of Class I flammable liquids in 55-gallon drums were temporarily stored just outside Building A, along its west wall.

Cause of and Response to Fire

A spark created in the electric shop in Building A started a fire. The night security guard first noticed the fire in the electric shop at about 6:00 a.m. and immediately called the Ardville Volunteer Fire Department and the plant superintendent. Before the fire department arrived, the fire spread to the drums of flammable liquid just outside the west wall and quickly engulfed Building A in flames. The fire then spread to the scrap paper outside, with a 40-mph wind blowing it in the direction of Building B.

During this time, the security guard began to hose down the piles of scrap paper between the buildings to try to keep the fire from reaching Building B. He also set up lawn sprinklers between the fire and Building B to protect Building B from the fire. However, he saw smoke coming from Building B at 6:15 a.m., in spite of his best efforts to protect the building.

The volunteer fire department, which was 20 miles away, reached the scene at 6:57 a.m., nearly an hour after the fire was discovered. It is estimated that the fire department's pumps were started after the fire had been burning in Building B for at least 20 minutes.

All steps are timed to inform the audience of the sequence of events

Results of the Fire

Building A was destroyed, along with its contents, and the fire burned into the hollow-joisted roof of Building B, which sustained a $250,000 loss.

Figure 2–7 A Chronological Description (Excerpt)

Good Working Positions

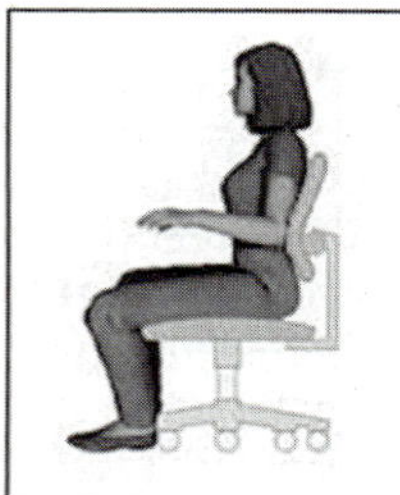

To understand the best way to set up a computer workstation, it is helpful to understand the concept of neutral body positioning. This is a comfortable working posture in which your joints are naturally aligned. Working with the body in a neutral position reduces stress and strain on the muscles, tendons, and skeletal system and reduces your risk of developing a musculoskeletal discorder (MSD). The following are important considerations when attempting to maintain neutral body postures while working at the computer workstation:

- *Hands, wrists,* and *forearms* are straight, in-line and roughly parallel to the floor.
- *Head* is level, or bent slightly forward, forward facing, and balanced. Generally it is in-line with the *torso.*
- *Shoulders* are relaxed and *upper arms* hang normally at the side of the body.
- *Elbows* stay in close to the body and are bent between 90 and 120 degrees.
- *Feet* are fully supported by the floor or a footrest may be used if the desk height is not adjustable.
- *Back* is fully supported with appropriate lumbar support when sitting vertical or leaning back slightly.
- *Thighs* and *hips* are supported by a well-padded seat and generally parallel to the floor.
- *Knees* are about the same height as the hips with the *feet* slightly forward.

Regardless of how good your working posture is, working in the same posture or sitting still for prolonged periods is not healthy. You should change your working position frequently throughout the day in the following ways:

- Make small adjustments to your chair or backrest.
- Stretch your fingers, hands, arms, and torso.
- Stand up and walk around for a few minutes periodically.

Figure 2–8 Spatial Description (Computer Workstation Posture) *Source:* www.osha.gov/SLTC/etools /computerworkstations/positions.html.

like "forward" and "roughly parallel" to indicate how employees should properly position themselves at a desk; the writer of the installation requirements uses precise measurements and a scaled illustration.

On a larger scale, spatial descriptions are also important for characterizing the configurations of construction, architectural, and other building sites and locations. Figure 2–10 presents an outline and Figure 2–11 presents a detailed description of tilt-up construction, a technique widely used in building construction. The description is accompanied by a step-by-step drawing of the process, shown in Figure 2–12. Note that this description combines both spatial and sequential organizing patterns.

Division and Classification

An effective way to organize information about a complex subject is to divide it into manageable parts and then discuss each part separately. You might use this approach, called *division*, to describe a physical object, such as the parts of a home backup generator; to examine an organization, such as a company; or to explain a system, such as the channels of communication that make up the Internet. The emphasis in division is on breaking down a complex whole into a number of like units — because it is easier for an audience to consider smaller units and to examine the relationship of each to the other.

If you were a financial planner describing the types of mutual funds available to your investors, you could divide the options into three broad categories: money-market funds, bond funds, and stock funds. Although this division is accurate, it is only

Drinking Fountains and Water Coolers — Spout Height and Knee Clearance

In addition to clearances discussed in the text, the following knee clearance is required underneath the fountain: 27 inches (685 mm) minimum from the floor to the underside of the fountain, which extends 8 inches (205 mm) minimum measured from the front edge underneath the fountain back toward the wall; if a minimum 9 inches (230 mm) of toe clearance is provided, a maximum of 6 inches (150 mm) of the 48 inches (1,220 mm) of clear floor space required at the fixture may extend into the top space.

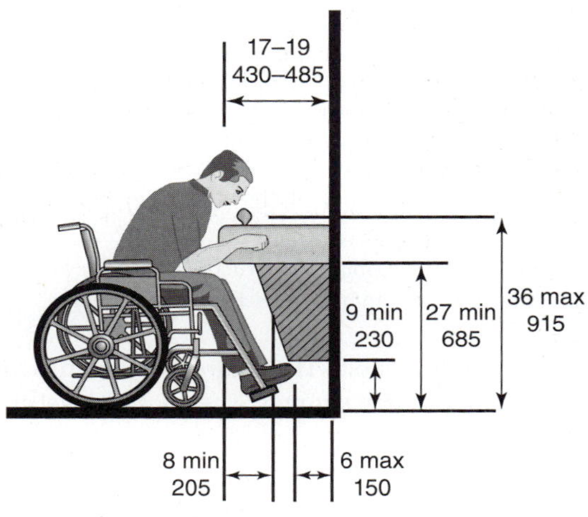

Figure 27a. Drinking Fountains and Water Coolers — Spout Height and Knee Clearance

Figure 2–9 Spatial Description with Precise Measurements *Source:* www.adaag.com/ada-accessibility-guidelines/fig27a.html; United States Dept. of Justice: Civil Rights Division - ADA.

TILT-UP CONSTRUCTION FOR CONCRETE BUILDING

I. Preparing the Concrete Panel Forms
   A. Plan and build the forms.
   B. Place the steel reinforcing bars, embeds, and inserts into the forms.
II. Pouring the Concrete Panels
   A. Pour the concrete into the forms and smooth the surface.
   B. Once the concrete sets, remove the forms.
III. Standing the Panels
   A. Lift the panel with a crane, stand it up, and place it into position.
   B. Brace the panel safely in place.
   C. Connect the panel to the slab.
   D. Move to the next panel and repeat the process.

Figure 2–10 Outline of a Spatial Description

HOW TILT-UP CONCRETE BUILDINGS ARE CONSTRUCTED

A tilt-up construction project begins with job site preparation and pouring the slab. During this phase of the project, workers install footings around the slab in preparation for the panels. The crew then assembles the panel forms on the slab. Normally, the form is created with wooden pieces that are joined together. The forms act like a mold for the cement panels. They provide the panels' exact shape and size, doorways and window openings, and ensure the panels meet the design specifications and fit together properly. Next, workers tie in the steel grid of reinforcing bars into the form. They install inserts and embeds for lifting the panels and attaching them to the footing, the roof system, and to each other. The slab beneath the forms is then cleaned of any debris or standing water, and workers pour concrete into the forms to create the panels.

Now comes the point where tilt-up construction gets its name. Once the concrete panels have solidified and the forms have been removed, the crew connects the first panel to a large crane with cables that hook into the inserts. The size of the crane depends on the height and weight of the cement panels, but it is typically two to three times the size of the largest panel. The crew also attaches braces to the tilt-up panel. The crane lifts, or "tilts up," the panel from the slab into a vertical position above the footings. Workers help to guide the concrete panel into position, and the crane sets it into place. They connect the braces from the tilt-up panel to the slab, attach the panel's embeds to the footing, and disconnect the cables from the crane. The crew then moves to the next panel and repeats this process.

Figure 2–11 A Spatial Description (Excerpt) Copyright © Bob Moore Construction. All rights Reserved. (www.tiltup.com/commercial-construction-articles/concrete-panel-building/). Reprinted by permission of Jeff Schaefer.

a first-level grouping of a complex whole. These three can, in turn, be subdivided into additional groups based on investment strategy. The second-level grouping could lead to the following categories:

Money-Market Funds

- Taxable money-market funds
- Tax-exempt money-market funds

Bond Funds

- Taxable bond funds
- Tax-exempt bond funds
- Balanced funds — mix of stocks and bonds

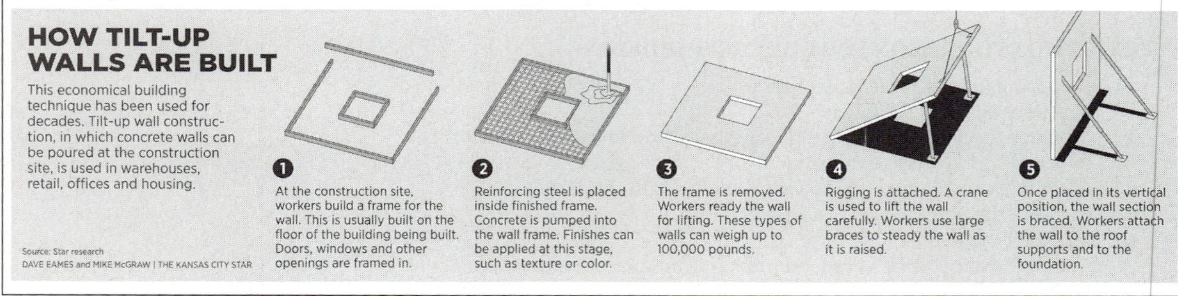

Figure 2–12 Step-by-Step Illustration Supporting a Spatial Description From Kansas City Star, April 9 © 2012 McClatchy. All rights reserved. Used by permission and protected by the Copyright Laws of the United States. The printing, copying, redistribution, or retransmission of this Content without express written permission is prohibited.

Stock Funds

- Balanced funds — mix of stocks and bonds
- Equity-income funds
- Growth and income funds
- Aggressive growth funds
- International growth funds
- Domestic growth funds
- Small capitalization funds
- Specialized funds

Specialized funds can be further subdivided as follows:

Specialized Funds

- Telecommunications
- Real estate
- Energy
- Financial services
- Technology
- Environmental services
- Metals and materials
- International
- Health services
- Utilities

After you have divided the variety of mutual funds into accurate categories, or parts, you could classify them by their degree of relative risk to investors. To do so, you would reorganize your original categories based on the criterion of risk. Depending on how risk is defined, this classification might look as follows:

Low-Risk Funds

- Taxable money-market funds
- Tax-exempt money-market funds

Low- to Moderate-Risk Funds

- Taxable bond funds
- Tax-exempt bond funds
- Balanced funds
- Equity-income funds
- Growth and income funds

High-Risk Funds

- Domestic growth stock funds
- Aggressive growth funds
- International funds
- Small capitalization funds

High- to Very High-Risk Funds

- Specialized stock funds

The process by which a subject is classified is similar to the process by which a subject is divided. *Division* is the separation of a whole into its parts (such as the components of a table-top centrifuge, a company's organization, a county's annual budget); *classification* is the grouping of a number of units into related categories (such as herbicides for weed control, allergens affecting people in Hawaii, or types of virus-checking software for desktop computers).

When dividing or classifying a subject, you must observe some basic rules of logic. First, divide the subject into its largest number of equal units. The *basis* for division depends, of course, on your subject and your purpose. If you are describing the *structure* of a four-cycle combustion engine, for example, you might begin by dividing the subject into its major parts — the pistons, the crankshaft, and the housing that contains them. If a more detailed explanation were needed, each of these parts, in turn, might be subdivided into its components. A discussion of the *function* of the same engine, however, would require a different logical basis for the division; such a breakdown would focus on the way combustion engines operate: (1) intake, (2) compression, (3) combustion and expansion, and (4) exhaust.

Once you have established the basis for the division, you must apply and express it consistently. Put each item into only one category so that items do not overlap categories. An examination of the structure of the combustion engine that listed the battery as a major part would be illogical. Although it is part of a vehicle's ignition system (which starts the engine), the battery is not a part of the engine itself. A discussion of the parts of the ignition system in which the battery is not mentioned would be just as illogical.

An outline provides a clear expression of classification and is especially useful in preparing a breakdown of any subject at several levels. In Figures 2–13 and 2–14, two Canadian park rangers classify typical park users according to four categories; the rangers then discuss how to deal with potential rule-breaking by members of each group. The rangers could have classified the visitors in a variety of other ways, of course: as city and country residents, backpackers and drivers of recreational vehicles, U.S. and Canadian citizens, and so on. However, for law-enforcement agents in public parklands, the size of a group and the relationships among its members (the bases of the comparison) were the most significant factors.

Decreasing Order of Importance

◆ *For an example of this way of organizing information, see page 602 in Appendix A.*

When you organize your information in decreasing order of importance, you begin with the most important fact or point, then go on to the next most important, and so on, ending with less important but related information. Readers of online and print news sources are familiar with this sequence of information. The most significant information usually appears first, with related but secondary information completing the narrative.

OUTLINE

I. Types of campers
    A. Family groups
    B. Small groups
    C. Large groups
    D. Hostile groups
II. Dealing with groups of campers
    A. Groups A and B
        1. One on one
        2. Courses of action
    B. Groups C and D
        1. Large groups
            a. Make the leader responsible
            b. Course of action
        2. Hostile groups
            a. Make the leader responsible (once determined)
            b. Course of action

Figure 2–13 Outline for a Memo Organized by Division and Classification

Decreasing order of importance is an especially appropriate pattern of organization for a report addressed to a busy decision maker, who may be able to reach a decision after considering only the most important points — and who may not have time to read the entire report. This sequence of information is useful, too, for a report written for a variety of audiences, some of whom may be interested in only the major points and others in all the points. The outline and memo shown in Figures 2–15 on page 53 and 2–16 on page 54, respectively, present an example of such an approach.

Increasing Order of Importance

When you want the most important of several ideas to be freshest in your readers' minds, organize your information by increasing order of importance. This sequence is useful in argumentative or persuasive writing when you wish to save your strongest points until the end. The sequence begins with the least important point or fact, then moves to the next least important, and builds to the most important point at the end.

Writing organized by increasing order of importance has the disadvantage of beginning weakly, with the least important information. Your readers may become impatient or distracted before reaching your main point. However, for writing in which the ideas lead, point by point, to an important conclusion, increasing order of importance is an effective pattern of organization. Reports on production or personnel goals are often arranged by this pattern, as are oral presentations. Figures 2–17 and 2–18 on page 55 present an outline and a memo, respectively, that show the use of increasing order of importance as a pattern of organization.

Memo

To: All Employees
From: Canadian National Park Service, Office of Rangers
Date: June 14, 2017
Subject: Dealing with Campers in Violation of National Park Rules

To respond to campers breaking National Park Rules and Codes for Safety and Conduct, first recognize the various types of campers. They can be categorized as follows:

Groups divided into major categories

A. Family groups
B. Small groups (up to six well-acquainted members)
C. Large groups or conventions (organized, but not always well-acquainted)
D. Hostile groups (may not have an evident leader)

Each group is then classified according to specific criteria

Groups A and B

Persons in groups A and B can often be dealt with on a one-on-one basis. For example, suppose a member of the group is picking wildflowers, which is an offense in most of our park areas. Two courses of action are open. You could either issue a warning or charge the person with the offense. In this situation, a warning is preferable to a charge. First, advise the person that this action is an offense, but, more important, explain why. Point out that the flowers are for all to enjoy and that most wildflowers are delicate and die quickly when picked.

Group C

For large groups, other approaches may be necessary. Every group has a leader. For a large group or convention, find out who the event organizer is (this is likely to be the person who reserved the campsite). Hold the group's leader responsible for the group's behavior and take action — issue a warning or charge the leader with the offense — according to the guidelines of the National Park Rules and Codes for Safety and Conduct.

Group D

For hostile groups without an obvious leader, observe the group's behavior to learn which person (or persons) assumes control of the group's actions, and try to deal with that person. Ultimately, it is best to regain control over a group through one or two individuals within the group. In a potentially hostile environment, always request backup of at least one other ranger on duty. Issue a warning or charge the leader of the group with the offense, according to the guidelines of the National Park Rules and Codes for Safety and Conduct. If necessary, eject the group from the premises, as outlined in the Codes.

Figure 2–14 Memo Organized by Division and Classification

OUTLINE

- I. Most qualified candidate: April Jackson, Acting Chief
  - A. Positive factors
    1. Twelve years of experience in claims processing
    2. Thoroughly familiar with section's operations
    3. Strong production record
    4. Continually ranked "outstanding" on job appraisals
  - B. Negative factors
    1. Supervisory experience limited to present tenure as Acting Chief
    2. Lacks college degree required by job description
- II. Second most qualified candidate: Michael Bastick, Claims Coordinator
  - A. Positive factors
    1. Able administrator
    2. Seven years of experience in section's operations
    3. Currently enrolled in management-training course
  - B. Negative factors
    1. Lacks supervisory experience
    2. Most recent work indirectly related to claims processing
- III. Third most qualified candidate: Jane Fine, Administrative Assistant
  - A. Positive factors
    1. Skilled administrator
    2. Three years of experience in claims processing
  - B. Negative factors
    1. Lacks broad knowledge of claims procedures
    2. Lacks supervisory experience

Figure 2–15 Outline for a Memo Organized by Decreasing Order of Importance

General to Specific

In a general-to-specific sequence, you begin your writing with a general statement and then provide facts or examples to develop and support that statement. For example, if you begin a report with the general statement "Companies that diversify their products or services are more successful than those that do not," the remainder of the report would offer examples and statistics that prove to your reader that companies that diversify are, in fact, more successful than companies that do not. Conversely, you could begin with such a statement and demonstrate with examples and supporting data why the idea was not valid. In either case, the organizing *pattern* would apply.

A memo or report organized in a general-to-specific sequence discusses only one point. All other information in the memo or report supports the general statement (Figures 2–19 and 2–20 on page 56). Examples and data that support the general statements are frequently accompanied by charts and graphs, providing further data to support your general point.

◆ *For guidelines for creating and presenting charts, tables, and other visuals, see pages 220–257 in Chapter 7, Designing Documents and Visuals.*

Memo

To: Tawana Shaw, Director, Human Resources Department
From: Frank W. Russo, Chief, Claims Department FWR
Date: November 12, 2017
Subject: Selection of Chief of the Claims Processing Section

This memorandum summarizes my assessments of three candidates for the position of chief of the Claims Processing Section. The assessments are based on an evaluation of each candidate's application for the position, work history, and a personal interview.

Memo begins with most important infor-mation (strongest candidate) and includes reasons why

The most qualified candidate for chief of the Claims Processing Section is April Jackson, who is at present acting chief of the Claims Processing Section. In her 12 years in the Claims Department, Ms. Jackson has gained wide experience in all facets of the department's operations. She has maintained a consistently high production record and has demonstrated the skills and knowledge that are required for the supervisory duties she is now handling in an acting capacity. Another consideration is that she has continually been rated "outstanding" in all categories of her job-performance appraisals. However, her supervisory experience is limited to her present three-month tenure as acting chief of the section, and she lacks the college degree required by the job description.

Third and fourth para-graphs rank and eval-uate other candidates

Michael Bastick, claims coordinator, my second choice, also has strong potential for the position. An able administrator, he has been with the company for 7 years. Further, he is currently enrolled in a management-training course at Belmont University. He is ranked second because he lacks supervisory experience and because his most recent work has been with the department's maintenance and supply components. He would be the best person to take over many of April Jackson's responsibilities if she should be made chief of the Claims Processing Section.

Jane Fine, my third-ranked candidate, has shown herself to be a skilled administrator in her 3 years with the Claims Processing Section. Despite her obvious potential, she doesn't yet have the breadth of experience in claims processing that would be required of someone responsible for managing the Claims Processing Section. Jane Fine also lacks on-the-job supervisory experience.

Figure 2–16 Memo Organized by Decreasing Order of Importance

OUTLINE

I. Staffing problem
   A. Too few qualified electronics technicians
   B. New recruiting program necessary
II. Apprentice program
   A. Providing insufficient numbers
   B. Enlistment bonuses are attracting the attention of high school graduates
III. Technical school
   A. Enrollment at area and regional technical schools up, but fewer students studying electronics
   B. Keen competition from the military for technical school graduates
IV. Military veterans
   A. Relied heavily on veterans in the past
   B. Military reenlistment incentives and extended active-duty assignments have affected this source
V. Strategy to compete with the military

Figure 2–17 Outline for Information Organized by Increasing Order of Importance

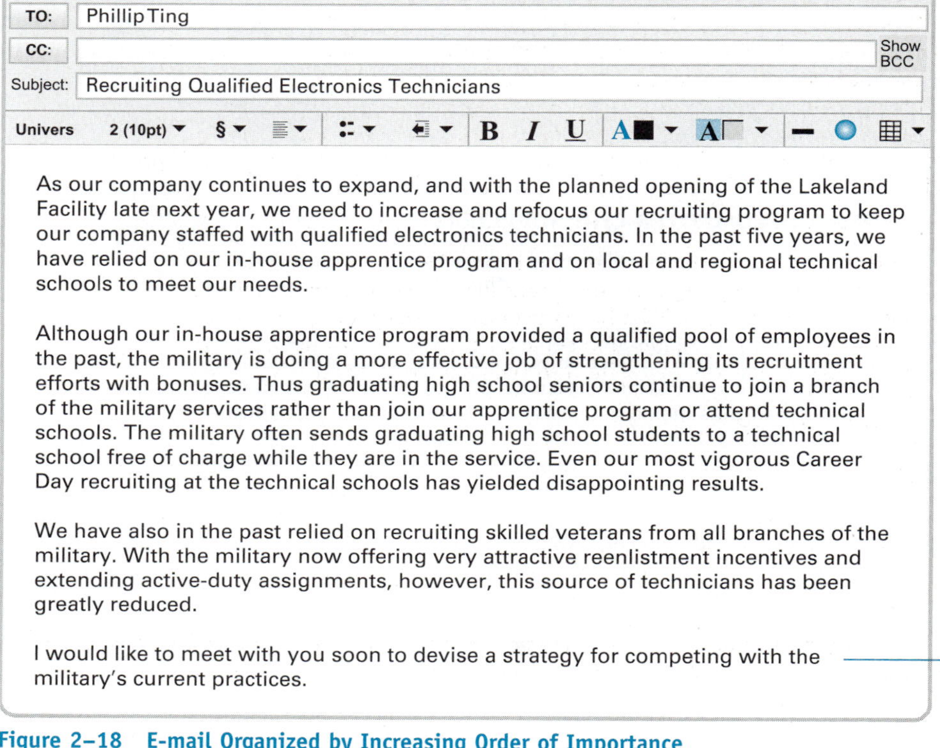

Send
Cancel
Save Draft
Add Attachment
Spell Check
Signature
Options
SENT: Wed 3/16/16 11:50 AM
TO: Phillip Ting
CC:
Show BCC
Subject: Recruiting Qualified Electronics Technicians
Univers
2 (10pt)
As our company continues to expand, and with the planned opening of the Lakeland Facility late next year, we need to increase and refocus our recruiting program to keep our company staffed with qualified electronics technicians. In the past five years, we have relied on our in-house apprentice program and on local and regional technical schools to meet our needs.
Although our in-house apprentice program provided a qualified pool of employees in the past, the military is doing a more effective job of strengthening its recruitment efforts with bonuses. Thus graduating high school seniors continue to join a branch of the military services rather than join our apprentice program or attend technical schools. The military often sends graduating high school students to a technical school free of charge while they are in the service. Even our most vigorous Career Day recruiting at the technical schools has yielded disappointing results.
We have also in the past relied on recruiting skilled veterans from all branches of the military. With the military now offering very attractive reenlistment incentives and extending active-duty assignments, however, this source of technicians has been greatly reduced.
I would like to meet with you soon to devise a strategy for competing with the military's current practices.

The point-by-point description of the dilemma leads the reader to the urgency of the conclusion

Final paragraph states the e-mail's most important message

Figure 2–18 E-mail Organized by Increasing Order of Importance

OUTLINE

The company needs to locate additional suppliers of computer chips because of several related events.

I. The current supplier is reducing output.
II. Domestic demand for our tablet computers continues to increase.
III. We are expanding into the international market.

Figure 2–19 Outline for Information Organized from General to Specific (Excerpt)

Specific to General

When you organize information in a specific-to-general pattern, you begin with specific information and build to a general conclusion. The examples, facts, and statistics that you present in your writing support the conclusion that comes at the end. For example, if your subject were highway safety, you might begin with details of a specific highway accident, go on to generalize about how that accident was similar to many others, and then present recommendations for reducing the probability of such accidents. If your purpose is to persuade a skeptical audience by providing specific details, this pattern is useful because it suspends the general point until your case has been made. This pattern of organization is somewhat like increasing order of importance in that you carefully build your case and reach your conclusion at the end, as shown in Figures 2–21 and 2–22.

LOCATING COMPUTER-CHIP SUPPLIERS

General statement

On the basis of information presented at the supply meeting on April 15, we recommend that the company locate additional suppliers of computer chips. Several related events make such action necessary.

Supporting information includes specific details

Our current supplier, ABC Electronics, is reducing its output. Specifically, we can expect a reduction of between 800 and 1,000 units per month for the remainder of this fiscal year. The number of units should stabilize at 15,000 units per month thereafter.

Domestic demand for our computers continues to grow. Demand during the current fiscal year is up 25,000 units over the last fiscal year. Sales Department projections for the next five years show that demand should peak next year at 50,000 units and then remain at that figure for at least the following four years.

Finally, our expansion into Eastern Europe will require additional shipments of 5,000 units per quarter to each country for the remainder of this fiscal year. Sales Department projections put computer sales for each country at double this rate, or 40,000 units in a fiscal year, for the next five years.

Figure 2–20 Document Organized from General to Specific (Excerpt)

Distracted Driving Among Teenagers

I. Age group is strongest user of cell phones:
   A. These devices pose higher risk for teens than for experienced drivers:
      1. Inexperience as drivers makes them less able to focus on driving while using these devices.
      2. Loss of focus causes distractions.
   B. Distractions increase cognitive load:
      1. They impair ability to recognize changes in driving environment.
      2. They lower the threshold of impairment.
   C. Teen brains are not fully developed:
      1. Affects ability to form judgments.
      2. Affects ability to make timely decisions.

II. Thus, teen drivers have more difficulty managing distracting behaviors and situations than experienced drivers.

Figure 2–21 Outline for Information Organized from Specific to General

Comparison

When you use comparison as a pattern of development, you evaluate the relative merits of the items you are considering. Comparison works well in determining which of two or more items is most suitable for some specific purpose, such as selecting the best color printer for digital photographs, determining the most cost-effective cyber security service for your company, or choosing the most qualified applicant for your job opening. Showing such information in tables often facilitates item-to-item

DISTRACTED DRIVING AMONG TEENAGERS

There are several reasons to be concerned about distracted driving and teenagers. Young drivers are among the strongest users of cell phones and tend to be early adopters of new technology (Lee, 2007). Moreover, distractions likely entail greater risk for novices than more experienced drivers. Driving is less automated for novices, so they may be more susceptible to a distraction-related crash (Lee, 2007). Distractions can impair the driver's ability to detect changes in the driving environment (Lamble et al, 1999) and for novices the threshold for "impairment" may be lower. Finally, key areas of the brain are still developing during adolescence, which has important implications for driving. For these reasons, teenage drivers may have greater difficulty than experienced adult drivers in managing potential distractions while driving.

Research findings to support general conclusion.

General conclusion.

Figure 2–22 Document Organized from Specific to General (Excerpt) Information from Distracted Driving Among Newly Licensed Teen Drivers. March 2012. AAA Foundation for Traffic Safety, Washington, DC.

TABLE 2–2 Table Layout for a Comparison

Types of sunscreens

Protection characteristics

	PROTECTION VALUES AND LABELING REQUIREMENTS FOR OVER-THE-COUNTER SUNSCREENS			
	BROAD SPECTRUM (SPF 15 OR HIGHER)[a]	**BROAD SPECTRUM (SPF 2-14)**	**SPF 15 OR HIGHER**	**SPF 2-14**
Blocks	Ultraviolet (UV) A and B radiation	UVB radiation	UVB radiation	UVB radiation
Protects against	Sunburn, premature skin aging, skin cancer	Sunburn	Sunburn	Sunburn
Required warning labels	None required	Skin cancer/ skin aging alert	Skin cancer/ skin aging alert	Skin cancer/ skin aging alert

[a]Sun protection factor (SPF) value indicates the level of UVB protection only.
Data from "FDA Sheds Light on Sunscreens," Food and Drug Administration, www.fda.gov/ForConsumers/ConsumerUpdates/ucm258416.htm. Accessed June 22, 2012.

◆ *For a discussion of tables, see pages 224–227 in Chapter 7, Designing Documents and Visuals.*

comparisons when you have more than a few options to consider, as in Table 2–2. The advantage of a table is that it provides a quick reference, allowing readers to see and compare all the information at once. The disadvantage is that a table cannot convey as much related detailed information as a narrative description.

To be sure that your choice will be the best one, you must determine the basis (or bases) for making your comparison. For example, if you were comparing recent labeling requirements for over-the-counter sunscreens for a health-care newsletter, you could organize them as shown in Table 2–2. Your newsletter readers are primarily concerned about skin protection, so you need not necessarily compare how sunscreens are applied (lotion, cream, spray, stick) or their price.

Once you decide on the bases important to your comparison, you can determine the most effective way to structure your comparison: whole-by-whole or part-by-part.

- In the *whole-by-whole pattern*, all the relevant characteristics of one item are discussed before those of the next item are considered.
- In the *part-by-part pattern*, the relevant features of each item are compared one by one.

Hearing aids, for example, may be compared in a variety of ways: style, size, correction range, control features, and more. To help consumers comparing hearing-aid options, the whole-by-whole pattern would allow them to consider each type in turn. The outline shown in Figure 2–23 and the detailed information in Figure 2–24, comparing types of hearing aids, are organized according to the whole-by-whole pattern. The writer describes each type according to its size and placement, features, and drawbacks before going on to the next type.

As is often the case when the whole-by-whole pattern is used, the purpose of this comparison is to weigh the advantages and disadvantages of each type of device against the others. However, if your purpose were to compare, one at a time, the major *functions* of hearing aids, the information might be arranged according to the part-by-part pattern. Note that this pattern emphasizes the specific characteristics of the hearing aids (size, hearing range, cosmetic appeal) rather than the different types of hearing aids (in the ear canal, behind the ear, etc.). The features being compared can be further highlighted by word order and by mechanical highlighting (*italic*, **boldface**, underlining, or font color).

Common Types of Hearing Aids

- I. Completely in the canal
  - A. Size and placement
  - B. Special considerations
    - 1. Correction range
    - 2. Volume control . . .
  - C. Potential problems
    - 1. Acoustic feedback
    - 2. Ear-wax maintenance . . .
- II. In the canal (partial)
  - A. Size and placement
  - B. Special considerations
    - 1. Correction range
    - 2. Volume control . . .
  - C. Potential problems
    - 1. Acoustic feedback
    - 2. Wind noise . . .
- III. In the ear
  - A. Size and placement
  - B. Special considerations
    - 1. Correction range
    - 2. Amplification range . . .
  - C. Potential problems
    - 1. Acoustic feedback
    - 2. Ear-wax maintenance . . .
- IV. Behind the ear
  - A. Size and placement
  - B. Special considerations
    - 1. Correction range
    - 2. Volume control . . .
  - C. Potential problems
    - 1. Cosmetic appeal
    - 2. Acoustic feedback . . .
- V. In the Canal or Ear

Figure 2–23 Outline for a Whole-by-Whole Comparison (Excerpt)

Types being compared

Detailed descriptions of advantages and disadvantages provide basis for comparison

ADVISING PATIENTS ON SELECTING HEARING AIDS

All hearing aids use similar parts to carry sounds from the environment into your ear and make them louder. Hearing aids vary a great deal in price, size, special features, and the way they're placed in your ear.

The following are common hearing-aid styles, beginning with the smallest, least visible in the ear. Hearing-aid designers keep making smaller hearing aids to meet the demand for a hearing aid that is not very noticeable. But the smaller aids may not have the power to give you the improved hearing you expect.

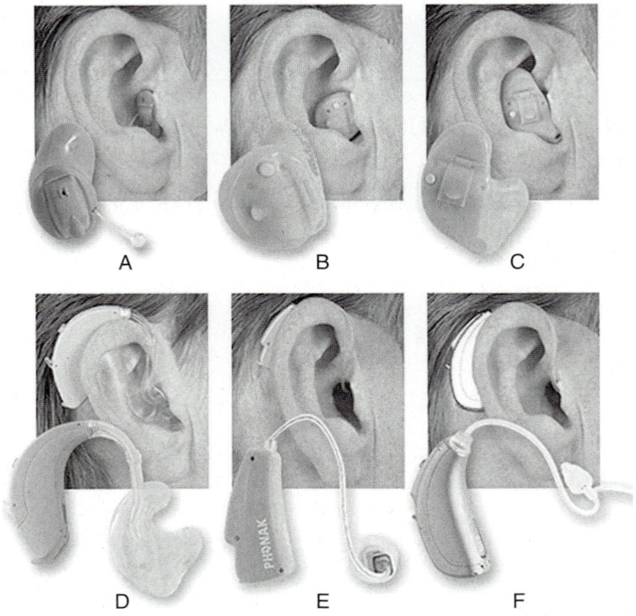

A B C

D E F

© MAYO FOUNDATION FOR MEDICAL EDUCATION AND RESEARCH. ALL RIGHTS RESERVED.

A. *Completely in the Canal (CIC) or Mini CIC*

A completely in the canal (CIC) hearing aid is molded to fit inside your ear canal. It improves mild to moderate hearing loss in adults.

A CIC hearing aid

- Is the smallest and least visible type
- Is less likely to pick up wind noise
- Uses very small batteries, which have shorter life and can be difficult to handle
- Doesn't contain extra features, such as volume control or a directional microphone
- Is susceptible to ear-wax clogging

Figure 2–24 Whole-by-Whole Comparison (Excerpt) Used by permission of Mayo Foundation for Medical Education and Research. All rights reserved.

B. *In the Canal (ITC)*

An in the canal (ITC) hearing aid is custom molded and fits partly in the ear canal. This style can improve mild to moderate hearing loss in adults.

An ITC hearing aid

- Is less visible in the ear than larger styles
- Includes features that won't fit on completely in the canal aids, but may be difficult to adjust due to its small size
- Is susceptible to ear-wax clogging

C. *In the Ear (ITE)*

An in the ear (ITE) hearing aid is custom made in two styles—one that fills most of the bowl-shaped area of your outer ear (full shell) and one that fills only the lower part (half shell). Both are helpful for people with mild to severe hearing loss.

An ITE hearing aid

- Includes features such as volume control and directional microphones that are easier to adjust
- Is generally easier to insert
- Uses larger batteries, which are easier to handle and last longer
- Is susceptible to ear-wax clogging
- May pick up more wind noise than smaller devices
- Is more visible in the ear than smaller devices

D. *Behind the Ear (BTE)*

A behind the ear (BTE) hearing aid hooks over the top of your ear and rests behind the ear. A tube connects the hearing aid to a custom earpiece called an earmold that fits in your ear canal. This type is appropriate for people of all ages and those with almost any type of hearing loss.

A BTE hearing aid

- Traditionally has been the largest type of hearing aid, though some newer mini designs are streamlined and barely visible
- Is capable of more amplification than are other styles
- May pick up more wind noise than other styles

E. *Receiver in Canal (RIC) and Receiver in the Ear (RITE)*

The receiver in canal (RIC) and receiver in the ear (RITE) styles are similar to a behind the ear hearing aid with the speaker or receiver in the canal or in the ear. A tiny wire, rather than tubing, connects the pieces.

An RIC hearing aid

- Has a less visible behind-the-ear portion
- Is susceptible to ear-wax clogging

Figure 2–24 Whole-by-Whole Comparison (Excerpt) *(continued)*

F. *Open Fit*

An open fit hearing aid is a variation of the behind the ear hearing aid. This style keeps the ear canal very open, allowing for low-frequency sounds to enter the ear naturally and for high-frequency sounds to be amplified through the hearing aid. This makes the style a good choice for people with mild to profound hearing loss.

The open fit behind the ear style has become the most popular. An open fit hearing aid

- Is less visible
- Doesn't plug the ear like the small in the canal hearing aids do, making your own speech sound better to you
- Is difficult to handle due to small parts and batteries
- Often lacks manual adjustments due to its small size

Figure 2–24 Whole-by-Whole Comparison (Excerpt) *(continued)*

Evaluating Hearing-Aid Characteristics

I. Size and Placement
   A. Completely in the canal
   B. In the canal (partial)
   C. In the ear
   D. Behind the ear
   E. In the canal or ear
II. Special Considerations
   A. Hearing-correction range
      1. Mild to moderate
      2. Moderate to severe
      3. Severe to profound
   B. Special features
      1. Volume control
      2. Telecoil for phone use
      3. Connection to external sound source
      4. Amplification range . . .
III. Potential Problems
   A. Acoustic feedback
   B. Ear-wax maintenance
   C. Wind noise
   D. Cosmetic appeal

Figure 2–25 Outline for a Part-by-Part Comparison (Excerpt)

EVALUATING HEARING-AID OPTIONS

The following comparison describes the features that consumers in need of hearing aids should evaluate in selecting the model most appropriate to their hearing loss and ease of use.

Size and Placement

The most common types of hearing aids are classified according to their size and location in or behind the ear. *Completely in the canal* (CIC) hearing aids, the smallest type manufactured, are worn deep inside the ear canal, next to the eardrum. *In the canal* (*partial*) (ITC) hearing aids, although larger than the CIC devices, are small and discreet. *In the ear* (ITE) hearing aids are worn in the contour of the outer ear, just outside the opening to the ear canal. *Behind the ear* (BTE) models fit snugly behind the ear and are the largest of the common models.

Correction Range and Special Features

Hearing loss is categorized from mild to profound. Mild-to-severe hearing loss can be helped with CIC, ITC, and ITE hearing aids. Severe-to-profound hearing loss can be helped with BTE hearing aids.

Hearing aids provide a variety of features to improve the user's quality of hearing. All models offer on/off capability, volume control, and circuitry to limit maximum volume of sound to tolerable levels. The ITC and ITE models can hold a telecoil. The BTE model can be connected to external sound sources, such as TV sets, radios, and infrared listening devices. . . .

Potential Problems

Acoustic feedback (whistling) is most often a problem for the smallest models because of the close proximity of the microphone to the speaker. Except for the BTE model, the others can be damaged by ear wax. The BTE hearing aid is the least cosmetically appealing because of its size. . . .

Figure 2–26 Part-by-Part Comparison (Excerpt)

CHAPTER 2 SUMMARY: PLANNING A DOCUMENT

Before you begin to write, consider the following questions as you organize your information into a logical sequence:

- Will I need a brief list or a full-scale outline to organize my information?
- Will I need to circulate the outline to colleagues or superiors?
- Is the outline divided into parts and subparts that reflect the logical divisions of the topic?
- Will my word-processing software structure the outline automatically?

- Does the topic lend itself naturally to one of the following patterns of development?
  - Sequential
  - Chronological
  - Spatial
  - Division and classification
  - Decreasing order of importance
  - Increasing order of importance
  - General to specific
  - Specific to general
  - Comparison
- Does the topic need to be organized by more than one pattern of development?

Exercises

1. Determine for ten of the following topics the best organizational method — sequential, chronological, spatial, division and classification, decreasing order of importance, increasing order of importance, general to specific, specific to general, or comparison. Then explain how consideration of audience and purpose might affect your decision.
   - Explaining how to register for classes at your school
   - Supporting an argument against e-cigarette smoking
   - Determining the job that is right for you
   - Explaining how to get the job you want
   - Announcing the winners of a contest
   - Describing the emergency exit for a building
   - Determining the best tablet computer to buy
   - Explaining the changing K–12 educational system in your state
   - Supporting an argument for or against specific environmental-protection laws
   - Giving instructions for performing CPR
   - Reporting the results of a police stakeout or other police activity
   - Reporting on the different kinds of news, drama, and comedy programs on prime-time network television
   - Giving instructions for preparing a five-course meal, including recipes
   - Reporting on the different types of media coverage of a world event (radio, television, Internet — including social media — etc.)
   - Reporting on the results of a local or state governmental election and its importance
   - Giving instructions for buying or selling a house
2. Make a list of topics and create an outline for one of the following writing projects, organizing each *sequentially*. As your instructor directs, use the outline to write a document of assigned length.
   - Preparing a household budget for clients of a financial planner
   - Tuning an acoustic guitar for customers new to the instrument
   - Setting up a personal computer for use in a home office: parts, peripherals, and desktop configuration

- Applying for a personal loan for customers of a local bank
- Finding an apartment to rent: a guide for international students
- Maturing of a monarch butterfly egg to an adult for a display at a nature center
- Hosting a social event for members of a networking group
- Purchasing a product on the Internet

3. Make a list of topics and create an outline for one of the following descriptions, organizing each *spatially*. As your instructor directs, use the outline to write a description of assigned length. Without relying on illustrations, describe the topic clearly enough so that a classmate, if asked, could create an accurate drawing or diagram based on your description.
   - The layout of your apartment or of a floor in your home (as it is, or as you would like it to be)
   - The dimensions and most significant features of a public park or building
   - The layout of a garden for a home-improvement website
   - The layout of the shop, office, or laboratory where you work (for new employees)
   - The physical process for disinfecting a hospital room or for painting a room
4. Make a list of topics and create an outline for one of the following writing projects, organizing each by a *decreasing-order-of-importance* sequence. As your instructor directs, use the outline to write a document of assigned length.
   - Your job qualifications and career goal to be used in future application cover letters and résumés
   - The advantages of living in a particular city or area of the country for an employee relocation guide
   - The importance of preventive care in one health-related area (diet, exercise, dental care, and so on)
   - The advantages of having paychecks directly deposited into checking accounts, of having savings automatically deducted from paychecks, or of using online banking for credit union members
   - The advantages of recycling for a city-council booklet
   - The advantages of owning life insurance for an agent training manual
   - The advantages of carpooling for an employee intranet website
5. Make a list of topics and create an outline for one of the following writing projects, organizing each by an *increasing-order-of-importance* sequence. As your instructor directs, use the outline to write a document of assigned length.
   - The advantages of learning to pilot a small airplane for prospective students of a flying school
   - The reasons you deserve a pay raise for a possible meeting with or a memo to your manager
   - The advantages of alternatively fueled vehicles for an environmental-resource organization
   - A proposal to change a procedure where you work for your management
6. For this exercise, use a *general-to-specific* sequence. Choose one of the following statements, then support it with pertinent facts, examples, anecdotes, and so on. As your instructor directs, outline the information to write a document of assigned length.
   - Volunteer jobs and internships provide valuable experience in the working world.
   - For families living within limited means, budgeting is essential.
   - Capable managers are willing to delegate authority.

- Post-high school education or vocational training is essential in today's job market.
- A sound human resources training program pays off for companies.

7. Create a topic outline for one of the following subjects, organizing it by *division and classification*. Using the outline, write a document of assigned length as instructed.
   - Tablet computers
   - Conventional and alternative medical therapies
   - Weight-loss strategies and programs
   - Home exercise equipment
   - Bicycles (for example, racing, mountain)
   - Cameras (for example, quality, convenience, price ranges)
   - Cable TV channels (select a single category: for example, news, information, public access, shopping, special interest)
8. Create a topic outline for one of the following subjects, organizing it by the *comparison* method of development. Using the outline, write a document of assigned length appropriate to the topic or as your instructor directs.
   - The features of two or more social-networking website (Facebook, Google+, etc.)
   - U.S. intellectual property laws (for example, copyright law, trademark law, and patent law)
   - Features of at least five specialized library databases (for example, InfoTrac, Clearinghouse, Health AtoZ, Thomas Legislative Information, ZIP Code Lookup)

Collaborative Classroom Projects

1. Following is an example of a poorly developed outline. In small groups and within the allotted time frame, revise this outline, using the guidelines provided in this chapter. Select a spokesperson from your group to present your outline to the class.

   Company Sports

   I. Intercompany sports
      A. Advantages to the company
         1. Publicity
         2. Intercompany relations
      B. Disadvantages
         1. Misplaced emphasis
         2. Athletic participation not available to all employees
   II. Intracompany sports
      A. Wide participation
      B. Physical fitness
      C. Detracts from work
      D. Risks injuries
2. Bring five common tools to class (a can opener, a pencil sharpener, and so on). In small groups, outline a narrative description of one or more of the tools, keeping in mind the particular function of the tool(s). When finished, exchange papers and critique one another's outlines based on whether the outline effectively describes the tool.

3. Long-term project: In small groups, create an outline for a guide for new students who need to learn how to sign up for classes. First, consider the obvious things students have to do, like learn their student identification numbers, meet with their advisers, and go over the course catalog and class schedules. Then, evaluate the scope of signing up for classes. (Review page 11 in Chapter 1, Understanding the Workplace Writing Context: A Case Study, for advice on considering scope in your writing.) Would it help to start at the very beginning—with enrollment at the university, required immunizations, and learning the locations of classroom buildings, for example? Determine the amount of information necessary before creating the outline; be prepared to defend your choices.

Research Projects

1. Locate a government, a business, or an industry report or an article in a professional journal. Analyze the organization of information in the report or article, and write an outline that mirrors the organization. Develop the outline to the level of detail of the outline shown in Figure 2–1 on pages 35–36 or to the level of detail specified by your instructor. Then assess the report or article for its use of the methods of organization described in this chapter, citing specific sections or paragraphs in which each method is demonstrated. Finally, describe how the organization of the report or article made it easier or more difficult to understand its content.
2. Material that will be read quickly is often organized by decreasing order of importance. Newspaper articles and news releases (announcements of upcoming events or company news created by public relations writers) are two such types of material. At a university or college, the university relations or advancement office often sends news releases about campus events to local newspapers and news stations, hoping to persuade reporters or camera crews to attend an event and write an article or present a film segment about it. Newspaper editors and television producers get many news releases a day, so they don't spend much time reading each one.
   a. Go to your university public relations office (or its link on your school's website) and ask for several examples of news releases about major events on your campus. You can also go to PR Newswire at www.prnewswire.com and look for news releases about your school. Then, in groups, analyze the order of the information in these releases. Create an outline of a news release based on your analysis.
   b. Ask someone in your university public relations office for copies of articles that were published by local newspapers based on the news releases they received. (You can also find articles in the LexisNexis database at your school's library.) In the same groups, analyze how these newspaper articles were written. Then create an outline of a newspaper article based on your analysis. Present your findings to the class.
3. Visit five or more government websites (.gov) and analyze the variety of ways that information is organized at each site; use specific examples to support your analysis. Write one to three paragraphs that detail the effectiveness or ineffectiveness of how information is presented at each site. Compare the sites. Write another analysis of the same length explaining how other methods of organization and the use of outlining (as discussed in this chapter) could improve each of these sites.

4. As noted in this chapter, writers should not overstate claims they make about a product or service, nor should they speak negatively or disparagingly about a competitor. Search the Web for products that are usually marketed with a large degree of hype, like diet products, sports drinks, weight-loss products, or home electronics.
   a. Print out several examples of online advertisements or Web pages for a particular type of product. First look at the visual persuasive strategies that the graphics and Web designers have chosen to use. (*Note:* Before you begin, read about graphics and design in Chapter 7, Designing Documents and Visuals.) Describe the pictures on the pages, the colors used, and the fonts and blinking images used. What do the visuals say about these products?
   b. Examine the sites' persuasive writing strategies. Do they include action words? repetitive use of certain words? lots of exclamation points?
   c. Write your findings in a memo to the class. How have the visual and rhetorical strategies added to or subtracted from the designers' and writers' persuasiveness?

3 Drafting a Document

Contents

Once you have gathered and organized your information, you are ready to write. But how do you turn an outline into a workable document? This chapter describes and illustrates several well-established strategies for preparing a first draft.

This chapter describes proven techniques for successfully writing your draft, staying focused on your audience, and developing your topic as you do so. It also guides you through the process of writing effective openings and closings and continues the development of the Lifemaker brochure introduced in Chapter 2, Planning a Document.

Beginning Your Rough Draft

The most effective way to start and to keep going is to use an outline—brief or detailed—as a springboard and a map for your writing. The outline also serves to group related facts and details. Once these facts are grouped, you are ready to construct unified and coherent paragraphs—the major building blocks of any piece of writing. Keep in mind, however, that first drafts are necessarily rough and unpolished. Writing and revising are two very different tasks. Trying to write something perfectly the first time puts undue pressure on you that can become self-defeating. In fact, any attempt to correct or polish your writing as you create the first draft only stimulates your internal critic and undermines your ability to complete your draft. To quell that critical voice, use positive motivation: Remember that your goal at this point is to write a draft, not a polished final product. Transcribe and expand the notes from your outline into paragraphs without worrying about grammar, refinements of language, or spelling. Experienced writers use the tactics described in this chapter to start, keep moving, and get the job done; you will discover which ones are the most helpful to you.

◆ *For detailed advice on outlining ideas before drafting, review Chapter 2, Planning a Document.*

◆ *For a detailed explanation of the revision process, see Chapter 4, Revising a Document.*

Start with the easiest or most interesting part to get moving and build some momentum. You may find that just writing a statement of your purpose will help you get started. Once you are rolling, keep going. You may wish to write comments to yourself while you are composing the rough draft if that tactic keeps you moving. When you reach landmarks or feel powerfully tempted to start revising, you may need to take a break. When you do, leave a signpost, such as a printout of an unfinished section or a note in red font in the outline recording the date and time you stopped so you will not waste time searching for your place when you resume work. If possible, avoid immersing yourself in another mental activity while you are on your break. If you are not under mental pressure, you may discover a solution to a nagging writing problem.

◆ *For editing guidelines, see Appendix B, Revision Guide.*

WRITER'S CHECKLIST

Developing Confidence

- ✔ Nothing builds a writer's confidence more than adequate preparation.
- ✔ Remember past writing projects — you have completed something before, and you will this time.
- ✔ Don't wait for inspiration to write the rough draft — treat writing the draft as you would any on-the-job task.
- ✔ Think of writing a rough draft as simply transcribing and expanding the notes from your outline into paragraphs.
- ✔ Don't worry about creating a good opening — that can wait until you've constructed your paragraphs.
- ✔ Concentrate on ideas without attempting to polish or revise. Don't worry about precise word choices, usage, syntax, grammar, or spelling. If you are using a computer to write your first draft, ignore the grammar and spelling suggestions until you have completed the draft.
- ✔ Keep writing quickly to achieve unity, coherence, and proportion.
- ✔ Don't criticize yourself for not being able to write a smooth, readable sentence the first time; it is natural for first drafts to be clumsy and long-winded.
- ✔ Remind yourself that you are beginning a draft that no one else will read.

◆ *For tips on practicing freewriting to get your ideas down quickly, see page 71, Digital Tip: Drafting on Your Computer.*

◆ *For guidelines on writing three types of time-sensitive documents, see*

- *Meeting the Deadline: The Time-Sensitive Message on pages 291–293 of Chapter 8, Writing E-mails, Memos, and Letters.*
- *Meeting the Deadline: The Time-Sensitive Proposal on pages 464–465 of Chapter 13, Writing Proposals.*
- *Meeting the Deadline: The Time-Sensitive Presentation on pages 491–495 of Chapter 14, Giving Presentations and Conducting Meetings.*

DIGITAL TIP: Drafting on Your Computer

- Try freewriting to overcome writer's block. Turn off the monitor or dim your laptop screen and write your thoughts as quickly as possible without stopping to correct mistakes, to complete sentences, or to polish your writing. After you finish, you can turn the monitor back on to review, revise, and reorganize as appropriate.
- If a difficult section hinders your progress, use the highlighting or comment feature to make note of it and move on.
- Name and save each draft separately so that you can return to earlier versions if necessary, but do not create separate drafts for minor corrections.
- Use a consistent naming pattern for multiple drafts, such as course abbreviation, assignment number, and draft number or date.
- When you resume, reread what you have written so that you can recall your frame of mind.

◆ *For more on 5–6 in Chapter 1, Understanding the Workplace Writing Context: A Case Study.*

WRITER'S CHECKLIST
Writing a Rough Draft

- ✔ Set up a quiet writing area with the necessary equipment and materials; then close the door or hang the "Do Not Disturb" sign.
- ✔ Start with the section that seems easiest or most interesting to you.
- ✔ The first rule of good writing is to help your audience by communicating clearly. Write in a plain and direct style that is comfortable and natural for both you and your audience.
- ✔ To make your writing more direct and conversational, imagine a typical reader sitting across the desk from you as you explain your topic.
- ✔ If you are writing instructions or procedures, visualize your readers actually performing the actions you are describing. This will help you envision the necessary steps and ensure that you provide adequate information in the right sequence and level of detail.
- ✔ If you are writing a sales letter, think of your arguments from the reader's point of view. Imagine how the features you describe can best be translated into benefits for a prospective customer.
- ✔ Give yourself a 10- or 15-minute time limit in which you write continuously, regardless of how good or bad your writing seems to you. The point is to keep writing during this period.
- ✔ Stop writing when you've finished a section (or before you're continuously, exhausted).
- ✔ Reread what you have written when you return to your writing. Often, seeing what you have written will trigger the frame of mind that was productive.

Keeping Your Audience in Mind

◆ *For an overview of selecting the right medium, see pages 14–18 in Chapter 1, Understanding the Workplace Writing Context: A Case Study.*

◆ *For detailed advice on analyzing an audience, see pages 6–7 in Chapter 1, Understanding the Workplace Writing Context: A Case Study.*

When writing the draft, focus on connecting with your readers. Think of your subject from their perspective. Ask: "What does my reader probably know?" and "What are my reader's feelings about the subject—sympathetic? hostile? neutral?" These questions will help to improve your draft by the effort required to think about them. When writing for international readers, consult someone from the target audience for guidance on language and cultural differences, if possible. For persuasive writing, support your ideas convincingly, acknowledge opposing points of view, and use the appropriate medium for your message. In all your writing, adopt the tone of voice—formal, authoritative, conversational—appropriate to your audience and purpose.

Writing from the Audience's Point of View

Whether your reader is a coworker, customer, or company president, he or she is interested in the problem you are addressing more from his or her point of view than from yours. Imagine yourself in your reader's position, perhaps by visualizing your reader performing a set of activities or making decisions based on your writing. Taken together with what you know about your reader's background, this picture will help you predict your reader's needs and reactions and ensure that you clearly provide all the information your reader needs.

For instance, suppose you work for a bicycle manufacturer and you need to write assembly instructions so that people who buy a new 21-speed all-terrain model can get from opening the carton to riding the bicycle with a minimum of frustration. You would break down the assembly process into a sensible series of easy-to-follow steps. You would avoid technical language and anticipate questions that your audience would likely have, making it unnecessary for them to consult other sources to follow your directions. You would also include assembly diagrams, a list of parts, and a list of the tools necessary for assembly. You would not explain the engineering theory that is responsible for the bicycle's unique design. Assembly instructions for a bicycle dealer would be different. You could use standard technical terms without defining them and could combine related steps because the dealer would be familiar with bicycle assembly and able to follow a set of instructions with fewer steps. A dealer would not need a list of tools required for assembly; the shop would no doubt have all the necessary tools, and the dealer would know which ones to use. You might well, in a separate section, include some theoretical detail, too. The dealer could possibly use this information to explain to customers the advantages of your bicycle over a competitor's.

Accommodating Multiple Audiences

When you write for readers similar in background and knowledge—all sales associates, for example, or all security officers—picture a typical representative of that group and write directly to that person. When you write for readers from widely different work environments, technical backgrounds, or professional positions, you must use a different approach. For example, to write a technical report that would be read by company executives, field-service engineers, and sales associates, you could address each audience separately in clearly identified sections of your document: an executive summary for the executives, the body of the document for the sales associates, and an appendix of technical details for the service engineers. If the document is posted on the company website for public availability, you could include notes and links to related information. When you cannot segment your writing this way, determine who your primary audience is, and make certain that you meet all of that audience's needs. Then try to meet the needs of other readers — only if you can do so without placing a burden on your primary audience.

Figures 3–1 and 3–2 are from a technical-assessment report that describes to an organization the advantages of acquiring media-streaming technology. The first part of the report (Figure 3–1) provides an overview of the topic for policy makers who may be unfamiliar with this technology and its uses. The second part (Figure 3–2) is targeted at technical experts who must understand the hardware and software requirements for the system.

◆ ***For an explanation of how the different parts of a formal report address the needs of different audiences, see Chapter 11, Writing Formal Reports.***

INTRODUCTION

This report demonstrates how the Office of the Chief Information Officer can improve the distribution of agency information and enhance communications with the staff, the nuclear industry, other federal agencies, the media, and the public by using media-streaming technology (MST). This report explains this technology and its advantages to our organization, details the resources necessary to deploy it, and recommends a course of action to achieve these goals.

Overview and purpose of report

Media streaming is the receipt of audio and video broadcast media over the Internet at one's computer or mobile device. The advantages of providing this capability to the agency are threefold:

Definition of a key term

- It enhances the agency's ability to collaborate with the nuclear industry, the states, other federal agencies, the public, and other agency stakeholders.
- It provides mobile delivery of training, commission meetings, public meetings at remote locations, staff safety programs, nuclear industry standards, and much else.
- It builds partnerships with government and private-sector organizations.

List of high-level advantages to organization

This report provides no single solution to deploying MST. Agency requirements are not static and will require alternative configurations over time at headquarters and the regional offices. Accordingly, the coverage includes necessary background information for decision makers in the following areas:

Statement defines intended audience (decision makers)

- Business requirements for and cost of supporting MST
- Technology cost alternatives based on a variety of agency program requirements as well as data security concerns based on each alternative solution
- A new internal website focusing on MST to assist management and staff in determining how the technology can be used to improve agency programs and customer relations

Statement of scope of report

Figure 3–1 Introduction to a Report (for a General Audience)

ARCHITECTURE OF THE REAL SYSTEM

Real System G2 is a client-server application that delivers live and on-demand MST content across TCP/IP networks. The Real System architecture has three main components: Real Server, Real Player Cloud, and content publishing tools.

- Real Server streams live and on-demand Real Audio, Real Video, Real Flash animation, Real Pix (GIF and JPEG images), and Real Text content across the Internet and NGN. Real System G2 supports most other existing media file formats, such as ASF, AVI, JPEG, MPEG, VIV, and WAV.
- The Real Player Cloud is used on client workstations to play the MST content.
- Real System publishing tools, such as the Real Producer and Real System G2 Authoring Tool, are used to create MST content.

Technical vocabulary and abbreviations for expert audience

Figure 3–2 Subsection of a Report (for a Technical Audience)

Writing for an International Audience

The prevalence of global communication technology, international trade agreements, and the emergence of Europe as a single market have made communicating with audiences from different countries and varied cultural backgrounds an essential skill. Language differences, of course, create the biggest obstacle to writing for readers whose primary language is not English.

The communications habits and expectations of audiences whose primary language is not English often will differ from those common in the United States and Canada. Organizational patterns, forms of courtesy, and ideas about efficiency can vary significantly from culture to culture. What might seem direct and efficient in the United States, for example, could be seen as blunt and even impolite in other cultures. To get a sense of these and other communications differences, consult with someone from your intended reader's culture before writing a draft or preparing a presentation for an international audience.

◆ *For a fuller discussion of cultural differences, see pages 251–257 in Chapter 7, Designing Documents and Visuals, and pages 320–326 in Chapter 9, Writing Routine and Sensitive Messages; and, for presentations, see pages 490–491 in Chapter 14, Giving Presentations and Conducting Meetings.*

Persuading Your Audience

Suppose you and a friend are arguing over whether the capital of Maine is Portland or Augusta. The issue is a simple question of fact that easily can be checked in an online atlas. (It's Augusta.) Now suppose you are trying to convince management at your company that it ought to adopt flexible working hours for its employees or develop a social-media strategy to improve communications with its customers. A quick look in a reference book will not settle the issue. You will have to persuade management that your idea is a good one. In all on-the-job writing, strive to keep your reader's needs, as well as your own, clearly in mind. Doing so is especially important in persuasive writing, in which your purpose may often be to ask your reader to change working procedures or habits. You may think that most people would automatically accept a recommendation for an improvement in the workplace, but people tend to resist change. To overcome resistance, you'll have to establish the need for your recommendation and then support it with convincing, objective evidence, just as Christine Thomas did in persuading a reluctant boss to try telecommuting at her business (see Chapter 1).

The memo in Figure 3–3 was written by an IT (information technology) administrator to persuade her staff to accept and participate in a change to a new computer system. Notice that not everything in this memo is presented in a positive light. Change brings disruption, and the writer acknowledges that fact.

For persuasive communications outside the company, you must take equal if not greater care in the way you present information. In the letter in Figure 3–4 on page 77, the writer is disappointed with the response to a request, but she attempts to persuade her audience to reconsider. Instead of responding with anger or sarcasm ("Your fee is highway robbery!"), the writer thanks the publisher and gets quickly to the point: her concern for the high fee and her wish to have it reduced. Throughout, her tone and language are courteous and respectful.

ETHICS NOTE: Acknowledge Opposing Points of View When writing to persuade your audience, do not overlook opposing points of view. Most issues have more than one side, and you should acknowledge them, as does the writer proposing a disruptive change in Figure 3–3. By anticipating and bringing up opposing views before your readers do, you gain several advantages:

- You show that you are honest enough to recognize opposing views when they exist.
- You can demonstrate the advantage of your viewpoint over those of others.
- You may be able to anticipate some or all of your readers' objections.

Finally, use the appropriate medium for communicating with your audience. The writer of the memo in Figure 3–3 recognized that a brief e-mail message was not the appropriate means to present her call for cooperation in the face of disruptive change. Her staff needed the formality and expanded scope offered by a memo. As you plan your writing and prepare the draft, consider how you want to package your finished communication.

◆ *For more on persuasive writing, see pages 427–428 in Chapter 13, Writing Proposals.*

◆ *For a description of media options available to help you make this decision, see pages 14–18 in Chapter 1, Understanding the Workplace Writing Context: A Case Study.*

Establishing Your Role and Voice as the Writer

Writers must also assume roles. As an on-the-job writer, for example, you may need to assume the role of a teacher who guides the audience through the process of learning a new task. In this case, you must do more than explain or persuade—you must also anticipate your audience's reactions and growing understanding of the subject. You must be alert to questions that readers might ask, such as "Why do I need to read this document?" "How much time must I spend to learn this subject?" and "Where can I find a quick answer to my problem?" By anticipating such questions, you will be more likely to answer them in your draft.

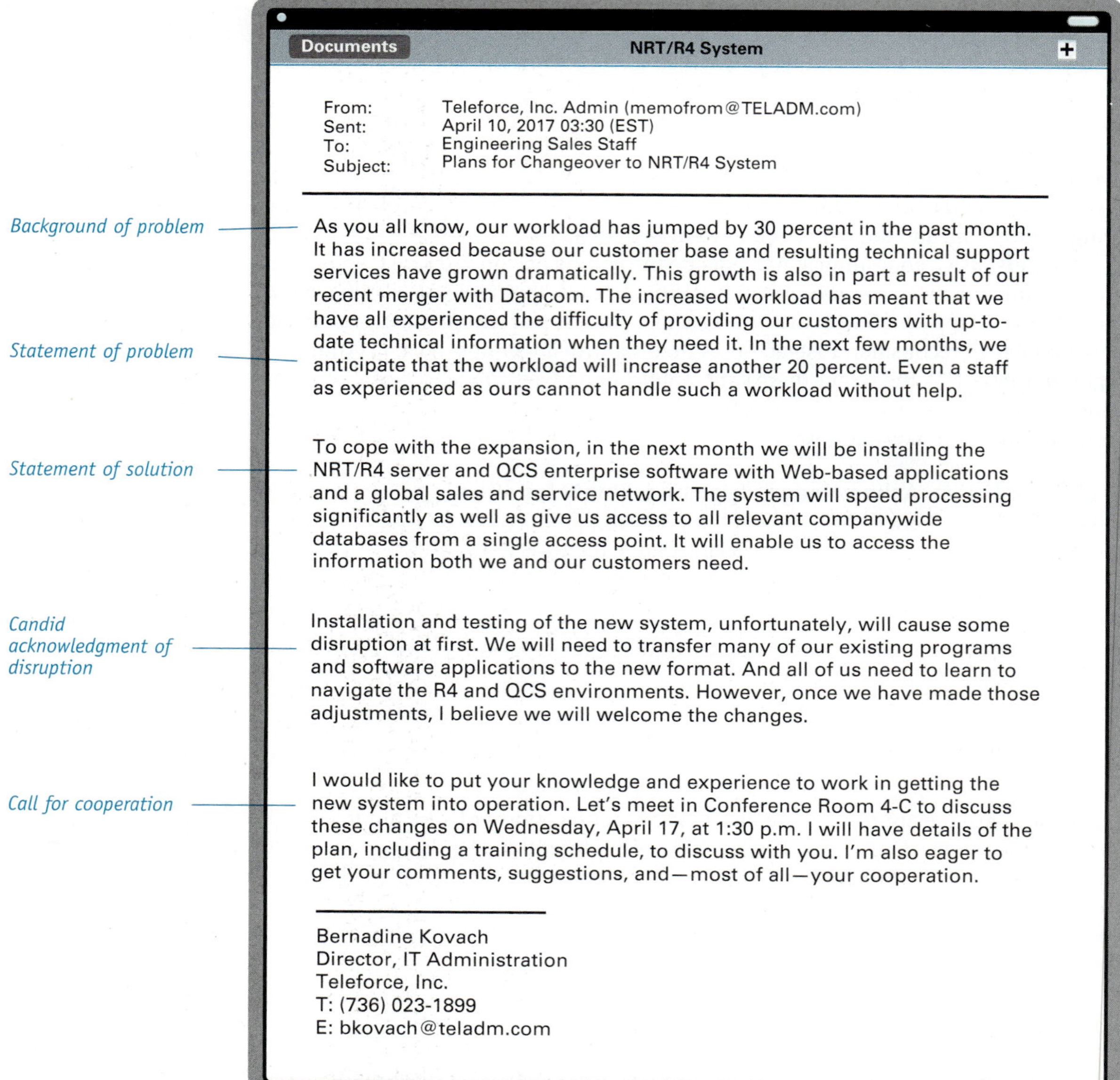

Documents NRT/R4 System

From: Teleforce, Inc. Admin (memofrom@TELADM.com)
Sent: April 10, 2017 03:30 (EST)
To: Engineering Sales Staff
Subject: Plans for Changeover to NRT/R4 System

Background of problem — As you all know, our workload has jumped by 30 percent in the past month. It has increased because our customer base and resulting technical support services have grown dramatically. This growth is also in part a result of our recent merger with Datacom. The increased workload has meant that we have all experienced the difficulty of providing our customers with up-to-date technical information when they need it. *Statement of problem* — In the next few months, we anticipate that the workload will increase another 20 percent. Even a staff as experienced as ours cannot handle such a workload without help.

Statement of solution — To cope with the expansion, in the next month we will be installing the NRT/R4 server and QCS enterprise software with Web-based applications and a global sales and service network. The system will speed processing significantly as well as give us access to all relevant companywide databases from a single access point. It will enable us to access the information both we and our customers need.

Candid acknowledgment of disruption — Installation and testing of the new system, unfortunately, will cause some disruption at first. We will need to transfer many of our existing programs and software applications to the new format. And all of us need to learn to navigate the R4 and QCS environments. However, once we have made those adjustments, I believe we will welcome the changes.

Call for cooperation — I would like to put your knowledge and experience to work in getting the new system into operation. Let's meet in Conference Room 4-C to discuss these changes on Wednesday, April 17, at 1:30 p.m. I will have details of the plan, including a training schedule, to discuss with you. I'm also eager to get your comments, suggestions, and—most of all—your cooperation.

Bernadine Kovach
Director, IT Administration
Teleforce, Inc.
T: (736) 023-1899
E: bkovach@teladm.com

Figure 3–3 Persuasive Memo

Commuter Aircraft Corporation
7328 Wellington Drive
Partridge, OH 45424
commair.com

March 8, 2017

Adele Chu, Permissions Editor
Poet's Press, Inc.
One Plaza Way, Suite 3
Boston, MA 02116

Dear Ms. Chu:

Thank you for responding so quickly to my request for permission to reprint the poem "Flight" in the pilot's manual for our new Aerosoar 100 Commuter.

Complimentary and courteous opening

I am writing to express concern about the fee you have requested for the use of this selection. It is much higher than we expected. Because the manual is an instructional booklet distributed to pilots free of charge, the budget for this project is strictly limited, particularly for nontechnical, ancillary materials such as poetry. We continue to feel that the poem would interest and even inspire our readers, however, and we would like to ask you to consider lowering your fee to make this possible. To meet the demands of our budget, we are able to pay no more than $300 for each selection in the manual—considerably less than the $900 you have requested.

Statement of problem, its basis, and counteroffer

I hope you understand our position and that you will consider reducing your fee for the use of this material. Thank you for considering my request. I look forward to hearing from you.

Restatement of request and respectful closing

Sincerely,

J. T. Walters

J. T. Walters
Publications Manager

cc: Legal Department

(890) 321-1231
Fax (890) 321-5116
jtw@commair.com

Figure 3–4 Persuasive Letter

Authoritative voice instructs, yet reassures

RESPIRATORY-CARE PLAN

1. Let the patient know exactly what is being done.
2. Maintain a good rapport; answer questions the patient may ask to allay fear.
3. Maintain the privacy and dignity of the patient at all times.
4. Be prepared. Depending on your work environment, a stethoscope, a watch with a sweep second hand or a stopwatch, and a pen or knowledge of the digital vital signs equipment and computer logging system are essential to this process.
5. Document your findings as soon as time permits; otherwise, you may forget important points.

Figure 3–5 Formal Voice (in Medical Instructions)

◆ ***For guidance on writing for users averse to reading instructions, see Chapter 12, Writing Instructions.***

◆ ***For guidance on whether to use the first or third person in your writing, see pages 107–108 in Chapter 4, Revising a Document.***

Your audience's interests may not always coincide with its needs. Some readers, for example, would prefer not to read your document at all; however, they also are interested in completing a task or solving a problem as quickly as possible. You must demonstrate how your document links the readers' interests with their need to read the document.

As you write the draft, consider which voice your audience should hear. Should that voice be authoritative or friendly, formal or accessible, provocative or reassuring — or some combination? Determine the voice you adopt by considering what is appropriate to your specific purpose. The guidelines shown in Figure 3–5 are intended for respiratory-care therapists who assess patients to develop a plan of care. The writer's voice is slightly formal (the guidance is in the imperative mood) yet caring in tone, as befits the subject.

By contrast, newsletter readers may expect a voice that is friendly, fast-paced, and conversational. Consider the attention-getting approach used in the opening of an article in a professional association newsletter (Figure 3–6).

Conversational voice directly engages audience

OVERCOMING WRITER'S BLOCK

Um, er, I would have delivered this article earlier, perhaps even on time, but, er, you see, I had writer's block!

Has this ever happened to you? Hah! Of course it has. It happens when you're writing to your Aunt Hattie to thank her for the butterfly book she gave you for your birthday as easily as when you're writing a crucial report to your boss or looking for a different way of presenting a procedure. Nobody is immune; it happens to us all at various times. November's meeting . . . dealt with how three successful writers cope with this near universal problem.

Figure 3–6 Conversational Voice (in a Professional Association Newsletter) *Source: Capital Letter*, Society for Technical Communications (December 1999).

CONSIDERING AUDIENCE AND PURPOSE

Preparing to Write a Draft

When preparing to write a draft, ask yourself the following questions:

- What is my purpose in writing this document?
- What do I want my readers to do after reading it? Do I want them to perform a task? obtain basic information? investigate a problem? make a decision?
- Who are my primary readers? Is there a secondary audience? What do my readers know and how do they feel about the subject I'm addressing or the idea I'm proposing?
- Does my audience include international clients or colleagues?
- How much information will my readers need to understand the subject or to be persuaded or informed by my idea? What is the best way to clearly present this material?
- What objections might my readers have to the subject or proposed idea?
- What medium would be most appropriate? (Should I use e-mail? a memo? a blog or Web posting? more than one?)
- What voice would best convey my message? (Should it be authoritative? friendly? provocative? reassuring?)

PROFESSIONALISM NOTE: Mind Your Manners Keep in mind that the way you present your ideas is as important as the ideas themselves. Respect your audience's needs and feelings by applying some basic manners in your writing. Avoid sarcasm or any other hostile tone that may offend your audience. Also avoid exaggerating or being overly enthusiastic. Your audience may interpret such an attitude as insincere or presumptuous. Of course, you should not conceal genuine enthusiasm; just be careful not to overdo it.

Development Strategies

The following strategies are frequently used for developing ideas in workplace writing:

- **Explaining a process:** tells how something works or how something happened
- **Describing information:** explains how something looks or is planned to look
- **Defining terms and concepts:** clarifies the meanings of ideas crucial to your topic
- **Explaining cause and effect:** analyzes why something happened

Although this section focuses on each method separately, the methods are often used in combination. For investigative and accident reports, for example, the writer must state exactly what happened (explaining a process), which may also require the writer to describe the physical appearance of people, places, or equipment (describing information) and to explain terminology or ideas that the audience may not understand (defining terms and concepts). Finally, the writer must try to explain why the event or accident happened (analyzing cause and effect). A skillful integration of these methods to present evidence will do much to convince your audience that your findings and recommendations are accurate and appropriate.

Explaining a Process

When you explain a process, you tell your audience how something works, how it happened, or how it is done. It may be an event that occurs in nature (the life cycle of a parasite), a function that requires human effort (conducting a marketing survey), or an activity in which people maintain machinery to produce goods or services (robotic assembly-line production).

The steps in explaining a process may also include illustrations that show the process from beginning to end. As in all on-the-job writing, aim your writing at a level appropriate to your audience's background and be as clear, accurate, and complete as possible. Remember that beginners require more basic information and less technical vocabulary than do experienced workers.

In your opening paragraph, tell your readers why it is important for them to become familiar with the process you are explaining. Before you explain the steps necessary to form a corporation, for example, you could cite the tax savings that incorporation would permit. To give your audience a framework for the details that will follow, you might present a brief overview of the process. Finally, you might describe how the process works in relation to a larger whole of which it is a part. In explaining the air-brake system of a large dump truck, for example, you might note that the braking system is one part of the vehicle's air system, which also controls the throttle and transmission-shifting mechanisms.

A process explanation can be long or short, depending on how much detail is necessary. The passage in Figure 3–7 explains the process by which drinking water is purified. It provides essential background information in the context of a discussion of how drinking water, which may be contaminated, is then treated before being distributed to homes. The information is intended for the average homeowner, but the vocabulary does assume an elementary familiarity with biological and chemical terms. The explanation is enhanced by a step-by-step illustration that complements the pattern of the writing by providing an overview image (first panel in Figure 3–8) and then three more detailed drawings of the water-treatment process (remaining three panels of Figure 3–8).

Describing Information

When you give your audience information about an object's size, shape, construction, or other features of its appearance, you are describing it. The kinds of description you write will vary — engineers must describe products they design according to technical specifications, marketing professionals must describe the products they are marketing to potential customers, software developers face the daunting task of describing something the audience cannot see, police must describe accident scenes, and so on.

DRINKING WATER TREATMENT PROCESS

After it has been transported from its source to a local water system, most surface water must be processed in a treatment plant before it can be used. Some groundwater, on the other hand, is considered chemically and biologically pure enough to pass directly from a well into the distribution system that carries it to the home.

Background to process

Although there are innumerable variations, surface water is usually treated as follows: First, it enters a storage lagoon (A) where a chemical, usually copper sulfate, is added to control algae growth. From there, water passes through one or more screens that remove large debris. Next, a coagulant, such as alum, is mixed into the water to encourage the settling of suspended particles. The water flows slowly through one or more sedimentation basins (B) so that larger particles settle to the bottom and can be removed. Water then passes through a filtration basin partially filled with sand and gravel (C) where yet more suspended particles are removed. (See Drinking Water Treatment Process illustration [Figure 3–8].)

Overview of steps in the process

At that point in the process, the Safe Drinking Water Act has mandated an additional step for communities using surface water. . . . Water is to be filtered through activated carbon to remove any microscopic organic material and chemicals that have escaped the other processes. Activated carbon is extremely porous — one pound of the material can have a surface area of one acre. This honeycomb of minute pores attracts and traps pollutants through a process called adsorption. . . .

Definition of key term

The final stage of water treatment is disinfection, where an agent capable of killing most biological pathogens is added to the water. Until the chlorination process was developed, devastating epidemics — such as the outbreak of typhoid and cholera that took 90,000 lives in Chicago in 1885. . . .

Basis for importance of the process

Figure 3–7 Explanation of a Process Excerpt(s) from INDOOR POLLUTION by Steve Coffel and Karyn Feiden, copyright © 1990 by Steve Coffel and Karyn Feiden. Used by permission of Ballantine Books, an imprint of Random House, a division of Penguin Random House LLC and by permission of Lowenstein Associates, Inc. All Rights Reserved.

Your description may be of something concrete, such as a machine, or of something abstract, such as computer software. The key to writing an effective description is to present details accurately. To select appropriate details, determine how your audience will use the description — to identify something? to assemble or repair the object being described? to use in marketing a product?

Descriptions can be brief and simple or they can be highly complex, but they should always be clear and specific. Simple descriptions usually require only a listing of key features. A purchase order, shown in Figure 3–9, is a typical example of simple descriptive writing. Notice that even an order for something as ordinary as trash-compactor bags needs (in addition to the part number) four specific descriptive details to ensure accuracy.

Complex descriptions, of course, require more detail than simple ones. The details you select should accurately and vividly convey what you are describing. If it is useful for your audience to visualize an object, for instance, include details, such as color and shape. To describe the physical characteristics of an object as a whole and go on to itemize the parts that go into its makeup, you would use the *whole-to-parts method.* To describe a piece of machinery, for example, you would probably find this approach the most useful for your purpose. First present a general description of the device as a

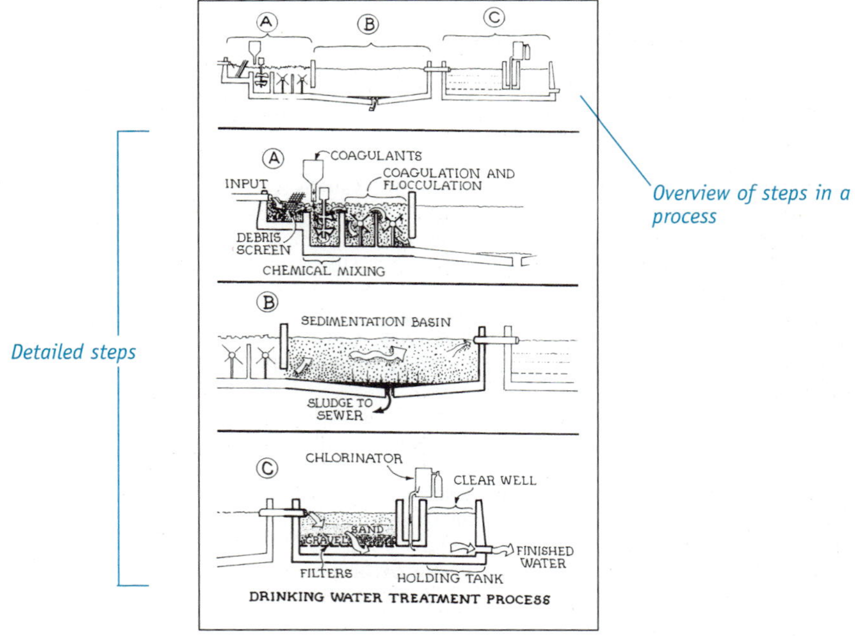

Figure 3–8 Illustration for Explanation of a Process Excerpted from the book, INDOOR POLLUTION (Fawcett Columbine) Copyright © 1990 by Steve Coffel and Karen Feiden Permission granted by Lowenstein Associates, Inc.

frame of reference for the more specific details that follow—physical description of the various parts and the location and function of each in relation to the whole. Conclude the description with an explanation of how the parts work together.

Illustrations can be powerful aids in descriptive writing, especially when they show details too difficult to explain completely in words. Do not hesitate to use an illustration with a complex description if doing so creates a clearer image. Figure 3–10 illustrates a storm-shutter installation that small businesses can use to protect windows from windborne debris damage. The illustration, with callouts highlighting important features, largely eliminates the need for extensive written details to describe their relationship to one another and their function.

◆ *For detailed instructions on the use of illustrations, see Chapter 7, Designing Documents and Visuals.*

Product specifications

PURCHASE ORDER		
Part No.	Description	Quantity
GL/020	Trash-compactor bags, 31″ × 50″ tubular, nontransparent, 5-mil thickness, including 100 tie wraps per carton	5 cartons @ 100 per carton

Figure 3–9 Simple Description

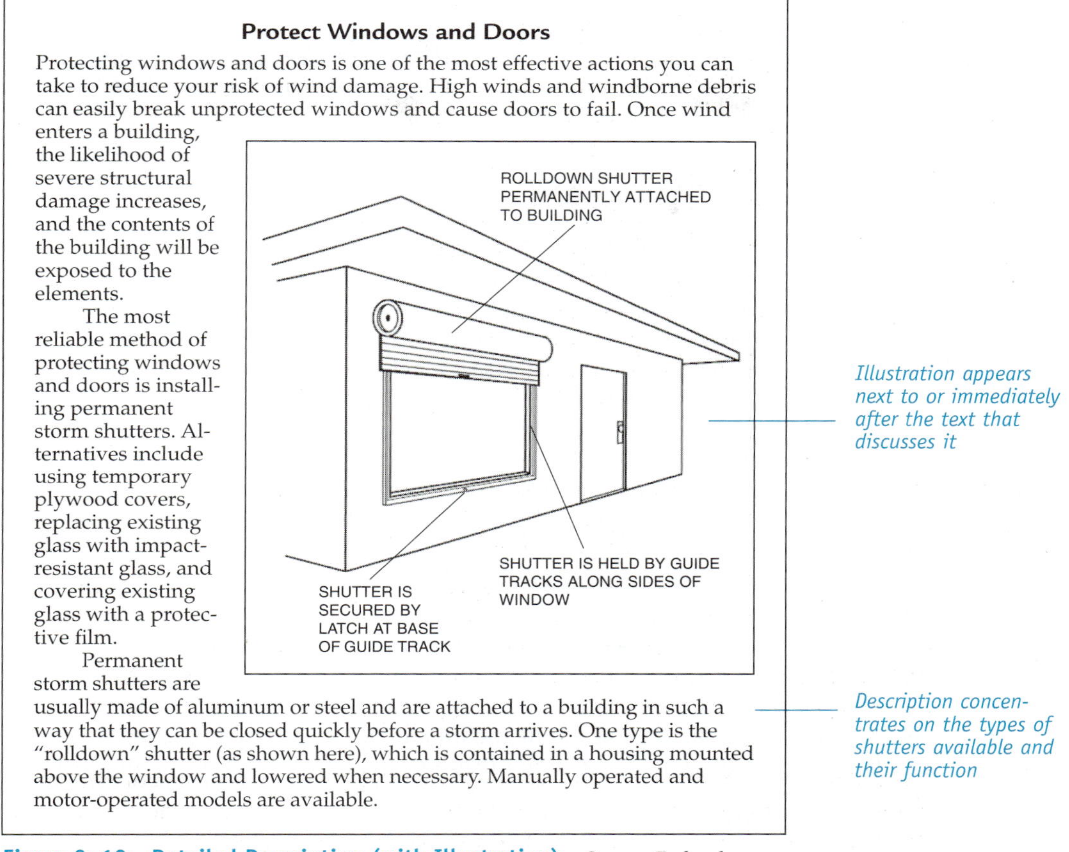

Protect Windows and Doors

Protecting windows and doors is one of the most effective actions you can take to reduce your risk of wind damage. High winds and windborne debris can easily break unprotected windows and cause doors to fail. Once wind enters a building, the likelihood of severe structural damage increases, and the contents of the building will be exposed to the elements.

The most reliable method of protecting windows and doors is installing permanent storm shutters. Alternatives include using temporary plywood covers, replacing existing glass with impact-resistant glass, and covering existing glass with a protective film.

Permanent storm shutters are usually made of aluminum or steel and are attached to a building in such a way that they can be closed quickly before a storm arrives. One type is the "rolldown" shutter (as shown here), which is contained in a housing mounted above the window and lowered when necessary. Manually operated and motor-operated models are available.

Illustration appears next to or immediately after the text that discusses it

Description concentrates on the types of shutters available and their function

Figure 3–10 Detailed Description (with Illustration) *Source:* Federal Emergency Management Agency (www.fema.gov).

Defining Terms and Concepts

Accurate definitions are crucial to many kinds of writing, especially for an audience unfamiliar with your subject. Depending on your audience's needs, your definition can be formal, informal, or extended.

A *formal definition* places a term in a class of related objects or ideas and shows how it differs from other members of the same class. (An auction is a public sale in which property passes to the highest bidder through successive increased offers.) An *informal definition* uses a familiar word or phrase as a synonym for an unfamiliar word or phrase. (Plants live in a symbiotic, or mutually beneficial, relationship with certain kinds of bacteria.) Informal definitions permit you to explain the meaning of a term with a minimum of interruption in the flow of your writing.

When more than a phrase or a sentence is needed to explain an idea, use an *extended definition,* which explores a number of qualities of the item being defined.

Metadata. Literally, "data about data." Examples of metadata include the author's name, creation date, content category, content type, intended audience, and access control properties. Metadata can be used to generate automated content directories, drive dynamic behavior, and support site measurement. . . .

Figure 3–11 Extended Definition, Using Examples *Source:* Gartner, Inc., Dealing in Web Currency (2001).

How an extended definition is developed depends on your readers' needs and on the complexity of the subject. Readers familiar with a topic might be able to handle a long, fairly complex definition, whereas readers less familiar with a topic might require simpler language and more basic information.

Perhaps the easiest way to define a term is to give specific examples of it. Listing examples gives readers easy-to-picture details that help them see and thus understand the term being defined. To clarify the abstract term *metadata,* the definition in Figure 3–11 provides specific examples of how metadata is used to identify subject matter on websites. Keep in mind when preparing documents for Web posting that you can integrate user-support tools as you create your document. For example, Web-based documents can be programmed to link words or concepts to their definitions. Readers not familiar with a term or concept can point and click to the term for the pop-up definition while readers familiar with the term or concept can ignore the explanation.

Another way to define a difficult concept, especially when you are writing for nonspecialists, is to use an analogy to link the unfamiliar concept with a simpler or more familiar one. In Figure 3–12, the writer uses the analogy of a golf game to clarify the concept of *management by objective.*

Sometimes it is useful to point out what something is *not* to clarify what it *is.* A what-it-is-not definition is effective only when the reader is familiar with the item with which the defined item is contrasted. If you say *x* is not *y,* your audience must

Management by objective has been quite popular, but it is important to remember that carefully selecting objectives is the key to successfully applying this principle. Think, for example, of a golfer who wishes to improve by hitting the ball farther. The golfer sets a goal of hitting every drive as far as possible. Every decision the golfer makes is governed by that goal — hitting the ball as far as possible. The golfer would then be managing his or her game by objective. However, the golfer is shortsighted because golf is as much a game of accuracy as it is of hitting balls for distance. Some of the decisions the golfer makes to hit the ball farther, therefore, might well be counterproductive to achieving the larger goal of obtaining the lowest possible score. In the same way, when a company decides to use a management-by-objective strategy, it must be certain that the objective is appropriate for achieving the desired results.

Figure 3–12 Extended Definition, Using Analogy

> A hydraulic crane is not like a lattice boom crane [a friction machine] in one very important way. In most cases, the safe lifting capacity of a lattice boom crane is based on the weight needed to tip the machine. Therefore, operators of friction machines sometimes depend on signs that the machine might tip to warn them of impending danger. This practice is very dangerous with a hydraulic crane. . . .

Figure 3–13 Negative Definition *Source: Operator's Manual* (Model W-180), Harnischfeger Corporation.

understand the meaning of *y* for the explanation to make sense. In a crane operator's manual, for instance, a "negative definition" is used to show that, for safety reasons, a hydraulic crane cannot be operated in the same manner as a lattice boom crane (Figure 3–13).

Explaining Cause and Effect

When your purpose is to explain why something happened or why you think something will happen, cause-and-effect analysis is a useful writing strategy. For instance, if you were asked to report on why the accident rate for the company truck fleet rose by 30 percent, you would use cause-and-effect analysis to work from an effect (higher accident rate) to its cause (bad driving weather, inexperienced drivers, poor truck maintenance, and so on). If you were to report on the possible effects that switching to a four-day workweek (ten hours per day) would have on the office staff, you would also use cause-and-effect analysis — but this time you would start with cause (the new work schedule) and look for possible effects (changes in morale, in productivity, in absenteeism, and the like).

The goal of cause-and-effect analysis is to make as plausible as possible the relationship between a situation and either its cause or its effect. The conclusions you draw about the relationship should be based on the evidence you have gathered. Because not all facts and arguments will be of equal value to you as you draw conclusions, it's a good idea to keep the following guidelines in mind.

- *Evidence should be relevant to your topic.* Be careful not to draw a conclusion that your evidence does not lead to or support. You may have researched some statistics, for example, that show that an increasing number of Americans are licensed to fly small airplanes. You cannot use that information as evidence for a decrease in new car sales in the United States — the evidence does not plausibly lead to that conclusion.
- *Evidence should be adequate.* Incomplete evidence can lead to false conclusions. If, for example, you know two people who completed driver-training classes but were later involved in traffic accidents, you do not have sufficient evidence to conclude that driver-training classes do not help prevent automobile accidents. A thorough investigation of the usefulness of driver-training

classes in keeping down the accident rate would require more than one or two examples; it would also require a sample comparison of the driving records of those who had completed training with the driving records of those who had not.

- *Evidence should be representative.* If you conduct a survey to obtain your evidence, do not solicit responses only from individuals or groups whose views are one-sided; be sure you obtain a representative sampling. A survey of backpackers in a national park on whether the park ought to be open to off-road vehicles would more than likely show them overwhelmingly against the idea. Such a survey should include opinions from more than one interested group.
- *Evidence should be demonstrable.* Two events that occur close to each other in time or place may or may not be causally related. For example, that new traffic signs were placed at an intersection and the next day an accident occurred does not necessarily prove that the signs caused the accident. You must demonstrate the relationship with pertinent facts about traffic for a specific period of time before and after installation of the signage.
- *Evidence should be up to date.* Up-to-date evidence is important in fields where research is ongoing, like medicine, engineering, ecology, information technology, and the physical and social sciences. Because evidence in these areas is dynamic and evolving, findings about them must take into account the most recent evidence available. A study of current trends in home cyber security, for example, that failed to note the hacking vulnerability of modern automobiles, would be judged incomplete.

To show a true relationship between a cause and an effect, you must demonstrate that the existence of the one *requires* the existence of the other. It is often difficult to establish beyond any doubt that one event was the cause of another event. More often, a result will have more than one cause. As you research your subject, your task is to determine which cause or causes are most plausible. When several probable causes are equally valid, report your findings accordingly, as in Figure 3–14. The paragraph is an excerpt from an article on the use of a furnace-vent damper, an energy-saving device that can be dangerous if it fails to work properly. The investigator located more than one cause of damper malfunctions and reported on them. Without such a thorough account, recommendations to prevent similar malfunctions would be based on incomplete evidence.

> One damper was sold without proper installation instructions, and another was wired incorrectly. Two of the units had slow-opening dampers (15 seconds) that prevented the [furnace] burner from firing. And one damper jammed when exposed to a simulated fuel temperature of more than 700 degrees. Accordingly, our investigation cannot single out a specific cause. . . .

Figure 3–14 Paragraph Linking Cause and Effect *Source:* Don DeBat, "Save Energy But Save Your Life, Too," *Family Safety,* n.d.

Writing an Opening

As discussed earlier in this chapter, you do not need to begin your draft by writing the opening; however, understanding the purposes of an opening and the strategies for writing one can help you start the draft. The opening statement of your writing should (1) identify your subject, (2) provide any necessary context for the subject, and (3) focus the audience's attention.

The title of your report, the first line of your blog posting or social-media content, or the subject line of the memo or e-mail message will announce the subject. The first paragraph of the opening should describe the context for why you are writing—the "story" behind the document. It should state what series of events led to your need to write: to answer a request for information, to recommend a new process to accomplish a goal, to propose that a new employee be hired, or to pass on information to someone.

Most audiences of on-the-job writing are preoccupied with other business when they begin to read a memo, a report, or even an e-mail. To focus your audience's attention, you first must know their needs. An awareness of those needs will help you determine which details your audience will find important and thus of interest to them. Consider the opening from a memo written by a human resources manager to her supervisor (Figure 3–15). The opening not only states the subject of the report (its context) but also promises that the writer will offer solutions to a specific problem. Solutions to problems are always of interest to audiences.

Memo

To: Paul Route, Corporate Relations Director
From: Sondra L. Rivera, Human Resources Manager SLR
Date: November 1, 2017
Subject: Decreasing Applications from Local College Graduates

This year, only 12 local college graduates have applied for jobs at Securex. Last year, more than 30 graduates applied; the year before, 50 applied. This decline in applications is occurring despite increasing enrollments at local schools. After talking with several college counselors, I am confident that we can solve the problem of decreasing applications from local colleges.

First, we could resume our advertisements in local student newspapers. . . .

Concise statement of a problem sets the stage for a proposed solution

Figure 3–15 Opening of a Memo

◆ *For a discussion of assessing audience needs, see pages 6–7 in Chapter 1, Understanding the Workplace Writing Context: A Case Study.*

◆ *For examples of openings for special types of writing, such as application letters, complaint letters, and formal reports, refer to specific entries in the Index.*

For most types of writing done in offices, shops, and laboratories, openings that simply get to the point are more effective than those that provide detailed background information. Furthermore, the subject line of a memo or the title of a report is often, by itself, enough to inform the audience whether they need to read it. The openings in Figures 3–16 and 3–17 on page 88 are typical; however, do not feel that you must slavishly follow these patterns. Rather, tailor your opening to the purpose of your writing and the needs of your audience. Notice that these openings do not introduce irrelevant subjects or include unnecessary details. They give the audience exactly what they need to focus their attention on what is to follow. As direct as they are, they establish context by noting the background for the communication (an error was made, a solution is proposed, a rewiring program is under way).

Writing a Closing

A good closing is concise and ends your writing emphatically. It can tie your points together in a number of ways: recommending a course of action, offering a value judgment, speculating on the implications of your ideas, making a prediction, or summarizing your main points. Even if your closing only states, "If I can be of further help, please call me" or "I would appreciate your comments," you end in a cooperative spirit.

PENROSE FIRST INVESTOR'S BANK
12 Powell Square
Penrose, ME 04291
penrosefib.com

March 4, 2017

Mr. George Whittier
12 Nautical Drive
Penrose, ME 04291

Dear Mr. Whittier:

Please note that we have corrected the error in your bank balance. The new balance shows . . .

Figure 3–16 Opening of a Letter

MEMO

To: David Diehl, Director of Athletics
From: Marylynn Scott, Project Engineer
Subject: Progress Report on Rewiring the Sports Arena
Date: August 23, 2017

The rewiring program at the Sports Arena is continuing ahead of schedule. Although the cost of certain equipment is higher than our original bid had indicated, we expect to complete the project without exceeding our budget because the speed with which the project is being completed will save labor costs.

Work Completed
As of August 13, we have . . .

Opens with a prediction

Figure 3–17 Opening of a Progress Report

The way you close depends on the purpose of your writing and the needs of your audience. For example, a committee report about possible locations for a new production facility might end with a recommendation that is realistic given the options available; a lengthy sales proposal might conclude persuasively with a summary of the proposal's salient points and the company's success at similar proposals; or the closing of a company's annual report might offer a judgment about why sales are up (or down). A report for a retail department store about consumer buying trends could end by speculating on the implications of these trends, perhaps even suggesting new product lines that the store might carry in the future or a change in its marketing strategy. Figures 3–18 and 3–19 illustrate typical closings.

Although my original estimate on equipment ($80,000) has been exceeded by $7,300, my original labor estimate ($120,000) has been reduced by $13,000. Therefore, I will easily stay within the limits of my original bid. In addition, I see no difficulty in having the arena finished in time for the December 23 Christmas program.

Ends with a summary of costs and a final prediction

Figure 3–18 Closing of a Progress Report

Ends with a recommendation and an offer to discuss the proposal in more detail

I recommend that ABO, Inc., participate in the corporate membership program at Aero Fitness Clubs, Inc., by subsidizing employee memberships. Implementing this program will help ABO reduce its health-care costs while building stronger employee relations by offering employees a desirable benefit. If this proposal is adopted, I have some additional thoughts about publicizing the program to encourage employee participation. I look forward to discussing the details of this proposal with you and answering any questions you may have.

Figure 3–19 Closing of a Company Internal Proposal

Importantly, do not introduce a new topic in your closing. A closing should always relate to and reinforce the ideas presented in the opening and body of your writing. Closings with recommendations or predictions, in particular, must grow out of the discussion that preceded them.

Case Study: Drafting the Lifemaker Brochure

◆ *For an outline of this brochure, see Figure 2–2 on page 39.*

◆ *For a marked-up version of a later draft of this memo, along with the final version and the full brochure, see Figures 4–2, 4–3, and 4–4 on pages 118–121.*

The techniques for drafting discussed in this chapter can be applied to any kind of workplace document. Figure 3–20 shows the rough draft of a sales brochure meant to persuade consumers to purchase the Lifemaker home gym. It follows the gist of the writer's initial outline and uses many of the drafting skills and development strategies discussed in this chapter.

The draft is quite rough—loosely organized, lacking in transitions and punctuation, ungrammatical, inconsistent in uppercase and lowercase letters and point of view, and cluttered with jargon and unnecessary phrases. Still, as drafts go, this one reflects a strong start for the writer. Not only has she followed the basic organization of her outline, but she has managed also to work through so-called writer's block and to jot down the new idea of emphasizing financial incentives.

She can now go on to write a second draft, develop an opening and a closing that will help her tighten her focus, and then revise the entire document by using the techniques covered in Chapter 4, Revising a Document.

****DRAFT****

LIFEMAKER: The Compact Exercise System You Can Afford

For opening ~~— say something about how owning a Lifemaker will give you healthy bones and teeth, straighten your hair, improve your love life . . . no . . .~~ Whether you are young or young at heart, male or female, developing well-conditioned muscles will help your body perform better, look better, and help you maintain an ideal level of fitness (Needs work! Keep going, go back to it later. Get to the muscle of the matter.)

Tentative cause-and-effect linkage

(*Description*) The Lifemaker design more compact than leading competitor's, eliminates hassle and expense of going to health club to work out. The Life-maker fits easily into small space — 4-by-7-foot living room can accommodate the Lifemaker with more ease than many home gym systems, offers more stations and more exercises because of its multiple stations. What's the point I'm making? More compact than many fancy systems, offers 40+ exercises, more than most systems priced at a comparable level — comparably priced and sized systems. OK OK, don't compromise your exercise needs with an overpriced or ineffective system. The integration of an exercise program to suit your lifestyle and budget is possible with Lifemaker. (I'm writing all over the place — too loose and unfocused. Needs headings like you used in outline.)

Tentative description of system compared with competitors' systems

Cast-Iron Weight Stack

Dual weight stacks total 200 pounds of cast-iron plates. You can arrange stacks to offer a resistance range of 10 to 150 pounds and they are adjustable in 10-pound increments.

Physical description

Adjustable Cables

~~Resistance can be increased — no —~~ The unique cable system is engineered to increase resistance at the stations that work the strongest muscle groups. The cables can quickly be redesigned — restructured — reconfigured without taking apart the entire system. Just pulling the center rod permits adding or removing as many plates as needed.

Combined process and physical description

The cable tension is also adjustable within sets to make sure that your muscles get the most resistance from each exercise for maximum efficiency and results.

Process description

(*Closing*) Heading? Low Maintenance — Easily Affordable

~~Best of all, no it's not best of all,~~ (Think later about transition. . . .) The Lifemaker is easy to assemble and requires little maintenance. And at $999.99, it is priced lower than the leading competitor.

***Need to emphasize financial perks — mention low-interest monthly payment plan. Lifemaker will fit your back and your budget.

Figure 3–20 Draft of a Sales Brochure (with Writer's Notes)

CHAPTER 3 SUMMARY: DRAFTING A DOCUMENT

Gathering the details you need (see Chapter 1, Understanding the Workplace Writing Context: A Case Study) and grouping them in an outline (see Chapter 2, Planning a Document) will enable you to write a good rough draft. When drafting, remember that your task is to produce only a working document, not a polished piece of writing. Polish will come with revision (see Chapter 4, Revising a Document). Use the following guidelines as you write the draft:

- Concentrate solely on getting your draft written.
- Do not confuse writing with revising; they are different tasks, and each requires a different frame of mind.
- Avoid revising as you write — do not worry about perfection at this point in the writing process. Focus on what you are writing, not on how you are writing.
- Sustain momentum once you begin writing.
- Take brief breaks after reaching milestones.
- Keep your intended readers actively in mind, visualizing them if possible, and address your topic from their point of view.
- Consider the voice your readers should hear — concerned, neutral, or authoritative.
- Be persuasive.
    - Take your readers' feelings into account.
    - Appeal to your readers' good sense.
    - Acknowledge other points of view where an issue is controversial.

Consider the following workplace strategies for your draft:

- Explain a process.
    - Introduce the process with information about its purpose and significance.
    - Divide the process into steps.
    - Present each step in its proper sequence.
    - Illustrate steps and procedures when doing so aids clarity.
    - Present the information at a language level appropriate to your readers' background.
    - Select details carefully, based on what use your readers will make of the description.
    - Provide a brief explanation of the function of any physical objects you describe, such as equipment.
    - Include only necessary details.
- Describe information.
    - Select details based on how your readers will use the description.
    - Provide a brief explanation of the function of any physical objects you describe, such as equipment.
    - Include only essential details based on your readers' needs.
    - Include illustrations where they add clarity.
- Define terms and concepts.
- Explain cause and effect.

- Establish a plausible relationship between an event and its cause.
- Evaluate evidence for the relationship carefully: Is it pertinent? sufficient? representative? plausible?
- Do not overstate conclusions — adhere to what is plausible based on the evidence that led to your findings.

■ Write an opening that identifies your subject to focus your readers' attention.

- Get to the point first, even when providing essential background information in the opening.
- Use the title of the report, subject line of an e-mail or memo, or the first line of a blog or social-media content to announce your subject.
- Use the opening to state why the information is important to your reader.

■ Create closings that reinforce, summarize, or tie together the ideas in the body of your writing.

- Base the type of closing you use — summary, recommendation, sales pitch, speculation — on the topic and audience.
- Do not introduce ideas in the closing that have not been discussed elsewhere in your writing.

Exercises

1. Write an opening paragraph for one or two of the following purposes and the audiences specified, as directed by your instructor:
   - Ways to improve employee participation in a blood, platelet, or similar donation program (to the president or head of the organization that employs you)
   - Ways to improve student use of the career-counseling office at your school (to the dean of students or someone in an equivalent position)
   - What to look for in housing in your area (for a guide for transferred employees)
   - Important features to consider when purchasing an all-terrain bicycle, smartphone, tablet computer, or line of women's fitness clothing (for a consumer guide)
   - The advantages of setting up an online budget or checking account (for an informational handout at a senior center or for students seeking help at your college mentoring center)
   - The high school teacher whose course best prepared you for college-level academic work (for a letter nominating him or her for a teaching award)
2. Building on Exercise 1, write a closing for the same topics and audiences.
3. Write a letter to a high school guidance counselor who wants to inform students about your chosen course of study. With your audience and purpose in mind, draft a letter that includes an effective opening, specifies important elements of the program and other relevant details in the body, and uses an appropriate closing. Use correct business-letter format when preparing your letter. For guidelines on format, see Chapter 8, Writing E-mails, Memos, and Letters.
4. Assume that the administration of your college or university is contemplating creating a learning center that will offer math and English tutoring. To implement this program, offices will need to be created from classroom space, tutors will need to be paid from the Student Services program, and a director will need to be hired. Reaction to this

center is mixed. As the president of a student organization, you have been asked to write a letter to the administration about your organization's position on the creation of the center.

a. Make a list of several possible points of view on this center. (Consider, for example, the perspectives of the admissions office, IT services, maintenance, faculty, and students.) Be aware that different audiences may share both supportive and unsupportive views on the same topic for different reasons.
b. Based on the points of view you have listed, draft an outline of a letter that supports creating the center, supports it with conditions, or opposes it.
c. Write a letter to the administration, explaining your organization's point of view on the creation of the learning center. Be sure you have addressed the potential multiple points of view in your letter. If you are for the center, offer strategies to address the concerns of those who are unsupportive; if you are against the center, address the concerns of those who believe such a center is needed.
d. Understanding the administration's growing interest in serving distance students, respond to their concerns about how a "brick and mortar" learning center will serve the diverse student body, regardless of location.

Collaborative Classroom Projects

1. Building on Exercise 4, form a small group and read each other's letters. Choose a spokesperson from your group to contact the director of your school's real learning center (if your school has one) for an interview. Select two or three people from your group to interview this person about the creation of the center. Ask questions about the many points of view and concerns that had to be addressed regarding funding, staffing, location, and so on. You can also interview faculty and staff about their experiences related to the creation of the center. (You should read the section on interviewing in Chapter 6, Conducting Research for a Document, first.) Are there similarities between your letters in Exercise 4 and what happened in the creation of a real center? If your school does not have a learning center, interview someone in the administration about creating one. What concerns does the administration have about such a project? In either case, write a memo to the class about your group's findings. If the school does not have a learning center, the group can brainstorm the possible need for a center, the academic areas it would cover, and whom they would interview about the feasibility of establishing one for on-campus and distance students. Relevant faculty members should be interviewed, too.
2. In small groups, design a draft of a brochure that helps volunteer relief workers put together a personal supplies kit. (You might refer to Chapter 7, Designing Documents and Visuals.) This brochure should detail items the workers should bring with them when they travel to the site of an earthquake, a hurricane, or a similar natural disaster—for example, alcohol-based hand sanitizer, toilet paper, sunblock, insect repellent, soap, shampoo, lightweight clothing, boots, rain gear, rubber gloves, flashlights, and a cell phone. What kinds of images would you use to represent different categories of supplies? Contact local organizations likely to respond to such disasters about their needs for a brochure. These could include support for organizations helping individuals who are homeless, animal welfare groups, religious charities, and local fire and rescue services departments. Be ready to share your ideas with the class.

probably put into revising it. Revising requires a different frame of mind than writing the draft does. Immediately after you write a rough draft, ideas are so fresh in your mind that you cannot read the words, sentences, and paragraphs objectively. You must detach yourself from them to be able to look at the writing critically. Do not allow yourself to think, "Because my ideas are good, the way I've expressed them must also be good." The first step of revision is to develop a critical frame of mind — to become objective.

During revision, be hard on yourself for the benefit of your readers. Read and evaluate the draft as if you were a reader seeing it for the first time. The techniques used by experienced writers — and listed in the following Writer's Checklist (Revision Strategies) — can help you achieve this mindset. Adopt the techniques most effective for you as you revise your draft.

WRITER'S CHECKLIST
Revision Strategies

✔ Allow for a cooling period. Wait a day or two (or even a few hours) between writing a rough draft and revising it — you will be able to be more objective then.

✔ Pretend that a stranger has written your draft. When you can look at your writing and ask, "How could I have written that?" you are in the right frame of mind to revise.

✔ Revise your draft in multiple passes, particularly if it is lengthy and complex. Don't try to improve everything all at once. Concentrate first on larger issues, such as content and organization; then turn to improving emphasis and polishing your language. Save mechanical corrections, like spelling and punctuation, for later proofreading.

✔ Be alert for the errors you typically make and correct them as you revise.

✔ Print your draft and read it aloud. Listening to sentences aloud often enables you to more easily detect flawed word order or other problems; reviewing the printed draft also makes formatting errors more obvious.

✔ Ask someone else to read and critique your draft. Someone unfamiliar with your draft can see it objectively and identify problems that you may overlook as you revise.

Content and Organization

Once you have put yourself in an objective frame of mind, begin with the whole-text tasks of purpose and organization. Then look for the accuracy of your content. Do you need to clarify meaning or delete redundant information? Are your recommendations adequately supported by your conclusions? Ensure, too, that topics mentioned in the introduction are not left out of the summary or conclusion.

Whether or not you created an outline for your first draft, you can test the soundness of your organization by outlining your rough draft. This technique is most useful for longer drafts but is helpful with shorter ones, too. Outlining your draft breaks the text into its essential ideas and makes their sequence easy to evaluate; you can then experiment with different sequences for laying out the most direct route to achieving your purpose. The new outline may differ from your original outline because you rethought some ideas or added or deleted information as you wrote. If you find a problem with the logic of the sequence or with the amount or type of information included or omitted, revise the outline—and then your draft—to reflect the solution.

Now is the time to insert any missing facts or ideas. If the information will help satisfy your audience's need and accomplish your purpose, by all means add it now. However, if the information—no matter how interesting—does not serve these ends, it has no place in your document. In workplace writing, readers expect your arguments, opinions, recommendations, and conclusions to be supported with relevant facts and examples.

WRITER'S CHECKLIST

Evaluating Your Draft

- ✔ Is the purpose of the document clear?
- ✔ Have you tailored your content to the right medium (e-mail, memo, letter, blog entry, or other)?
- ✔ Is the information organized in the most effective sequence?
- ✔ Does each section follow logically from the one that precedes it?
- ✔ Is the scope of coverage adequate? Is there too little or too much information?
- ✔ Are all the facts, details, and examples relevant to the stated purpose?
- ✔ Is the language appropriate for the reader?
- ✔ Are the main points obvious? Are subordinate points related to main points?
- ✔ Are contradictory statements resolved or eliminated?
- ✔ Do the descriptions and illustrations aid clarity? Are there enough illustrations?
- ✔ Are any recommendations adequately supported by the conclusions?
- ✔ Are all topics mentioned in the introduction and text also addressed in the conclusions?

A review of the relevant information in Chapters 1, 2, and 3 will be especially helpful as you reassess the effectiveness of your draft when it comes to these larger issues. In Chapter 1, Understanding the Workplace Writing Context: A Case Study, review the sections titled Establishing Your Scope (pages 11–12) and Organizing Your Ideas (page 13). In Chapter 2, Planning a Document, further evaluate the logic of your organization by reviewing the material on outlining (pages 32–37). For guidance on ensuring that you address the right audience in the right voice, see pages 72–79 in Chapter 3, Drafting a Document. Once you complete this review, you are ready to tackle the smaller, more detailed steps of the process described in the remainder of this chapter.

Coherence

Writing is coherent when the relationship between ideas is clear to your audience. Each idea should relate clearly to the others, with one idea flowing smoothly to the next. Coherence must be tested after writing. As you revise, ask "Can my reader move from this sentence or from this paragraph to the next without feeling a break in meaning?" If there is a break, add a transitional phrase or sentence to explain it.

The basic building blocks of a coherent draft are paragraphs. Effective paragraphs must be unified around a central idea so that every sentence is related to that idea. Paragraphs must also be coherent, with all ideas arranged in a logical order and with transitional devices linking sentences and paragraphs throughout the draft so that the audience can follow your reasoning from sentence to sentence and from paragraph to paragraph.

Paragraph Unity

When every sentence in a paragraph contributes to developing one central idea, the paragraph has unity. If a paragraph contains sentences that do not develop the central idea, it lacks unity.

The most effective way to unify paragraphs is to provide a topic sentence that clearly states the central idea of the paragraph and that directly relates to every other sentence in it. Consider the following example, from a report evaluating possible locations for a company's new distribution center:

> *Probably the greatest advantage of Chicago as the location for our new distribution center is its excellent transportation facilities.* The city is served by several major railroads. In fact, Chicago was at one time the hub of cross-country rail transportation. Chicago is also a major center of the trucking industry, and most of the nation's large freight carriers have terminals there. We are concerned, however, about the delivery problems that we've had with several truck carriers. We've had far fewer problems with air freight. Both domestic and international air-cargo services are available at O'Hare International Airport. Finally, except in the winter months when the Great Lakes are frozen, Chicago is a seaport, accessible through the St. Lawrence Seaway.

Although the paragraph opens with a clearly stated topic sentence (in *italics*) about the advantages of Chicago's transportation facilities, three sentences do not develop that central idea. The sentence about Chicago as the former hub of railroad transportation, although historically accurate, is not relevant to the company's assessment; the two sentences about the relative merits of truck and air-carrier delivery are not relevant here either. Stripped of these digressions, the paragraph becomes unified:

> *Probably the greatest advantage of Chicago as the location for our new distribution center is its excellent transportation facilities.* The city is served by several major railroads. Chicago is also a major center of the trucking industry, and most of the nation's large freight carriers have terminals there. Both domestic and international air-cargo services are available at O'Hare International Airport. Finally, except in the winter months when the Great Lakes are frozen, Chicago is a seaport, accessible through the St. Lawrence Seaway.

For workplace writing, it's best to place a topic sentence at the beginning of a paragraph. In this position, the reader knows immediately what the paragraph is about. This placement also allows the writer to more easily construct a unified paragraph because every subsequent sentence supports the topic sentence and the central idea it expresses.

A paragraph should be just long enough to deal adequately with the central idea stated in its topic sentence. Begin a new paragraph whenever you change the subject significantly. Keep in mind that long paragraphs can intimidate your reader by failing to provide manageable subdivisions of thought. Overly short paragraphs have a disadvantage, too: They may make it difficult to adequately develop the point stated in the topic sentence. A series of short paragraphs can also sacrifice unity by breaking a single idea into several pieces.

Transitions

Effective paragraphs take the reader logically from one idea to the next. Providing transitions will help you achieve a smooth flow of ideas from sentence to sentence, paragraph to paragraph, and subject to subject. Transition is a two-way indicator of what you have said and what you are about to say; it provides readers with guideposts for linking ideas and clarifying the relationship between them.

Transitions Between Sentences

Within a paragraph, transitional expressions clarify and smooth the movement from idea to idea. The representative sample of words and phrases in Table 4–1 commonly functions as transitional devices. Some words and phrases in this table are nearly synonymous but imply somewhat different logical connections. Be sure that the transitional words and phrases you choose convey the precise meaning you intend.

You can achieve effective transitions between sentences by repeating key words or key ideas from preceding sentences and by using pronouns that refer to antecedents in previous sentences. Consider the following short paragraph, which uses both of those means:

> Over the past several months, I have heard complaints about the Merit Award *Program*. Specifically, many employees feel that this *program* should be linked to annual *salary*

TABLE 4–1 A Sampling of Common Transitional Terms

To add information	also	in addition	finally	first, second, etc.
To give an example or to illustrate a point	for example	to illustrate	specifically	in this case
To compare or contrast	on the other hand	on the contrary	likewise	however
To prove	because	therefore	thus	hence
To show time	initially	eventually	during	previously
To show sequence	next	now	concurrently	simultaneously
To conclude	in conclusion	to summarize	finally	as a result
To make connections	and	or	so	but

increases. They believe that *salary increases* would provide a much better incentive than the current $2,000 and $2,500 *cash awards* for exceptional service. In addition, these *employees* believe that their supervisors consider the *cash awards* a satisfactory alternative to *salary increases*. Although I don't think this practice is widespread, the fact that the *employees* believe that it is justifies a reevaluation of the Merit Award *Program*.

Transitions Between Paragraphs

Transitional language between paragraphs serves the same function as it does between sentences: It signals the relationship between one paragraph and the next. For paragraphs, however, longer transitional elements are often necessary. One technique is to begin a new paragraph with a sentence that summarizes the preceding paragraph, as in the following excerpt from an environmental report:

> Each year, forest fires in our region cause significant environmental and economic damage. For example, wood ashes washed into streams after a fire often kill large numbers of fish. In addition, the destruction of the vegetation along stream banks causes water temperatures to rise, making the streams unfit for several varieties of cold-water fish. Forest fires, moreover, hurt the tourist and recreation business because vacationers are not likely to visit flame-blackened areas.
>
> *These losses—and many other indirect losses caused by forest fires—damage not only the quality of life but also the economy of our region.* They also represent a huge drain on the resources and personnel of the Department of Natural Resources. For example, our financial investment last year in fighting forest fires . . . .

If used sparingly, another effective transitional device between paragraphs is to ask a question at the end of one paragraph and answer it at the beginning of the next.

> New workplace technology has always been feared because it has at times displaced some jobs. Historically, however, it has created many more jobs than it has eliminated. Almost always, the jobs eliminated by technological advances have been menial, unskilled jobs, and workers who have been displaced have been forced to increase their skills, which resulted in better and higher-paying jobs for them. *In view of these facts, is new workplace technology a threat to unskilled workers?*
>
> Certainly technology has given us unparalleled access to information and created many new roles for employees. . . .

When you use this transitional device, make sure that the second paragraph does, in fact, answer the question posed in the first.

WRITER'S CHECKLIST
Creating Effective Paragraphs

- ✔ Unify the paragraph around a central idea in a topic sentence.
- ✔ Ensure that every sentence relates to the topic sentence.
- ✔ Arrange ideas in a logical order around the central idea.
- ✔ Use transitions to help readers follow the sequence of ideas.

Emphasis

Effective writing is emphatic writing — it highlights the facts and ideas that the writer considers most important and subordinates those of less importance. By focusing the reader's attention on key elements, emphatic writing enables the reader to determine how one fact or idea in a sentence is related to another. You can achieve emphasis by using any number of the techniques described in this section.

Active and Passive Voice

A sentence is in the active voice if the subject of the sentence acts; it is in the passive voice if the subject is acted on.

ACTIVE	Rajesh Patel prepared the design for the new pump. [The subject — *Rajesh Patel* — acts on *the design* — the direct object.]
PASSIVE	The design for the new pump was prepared by Rajesh Patel. [The subject — *the design* — receives the action.]

In workplace writing, it is often important to emphasize who or what performs an action. Because the active voice is generally more direct, more concise, and easier for readers to understand, use the active voice unless the passive voice is more appropriate. Doing so allows your audience to move quickly and easily from the actor (the subject) to the action performed (the verb) to the receiver of the action (the direct object).

The passive voice, however, can be useful, too. For example, when the doer of the action is less important than the receiver of the action, the writer can emphasize the receiver by making it the subject of the sentence.

EFFECTIVE PASSIVE	Sharon Gleason was appointed chief pathologist of Pine Cone County Hospital by the hospital's board of directors.

The important person in this sentence is Sharon Gleason, not the board of directors who made the appointment. To give her — the receiver of the action — the needed emphasis, the sentence makes sense in the passive voice. The same principle holds true in the sciences for situations where the data are more important than the scientist collecting those data. Laboratory or test reports are good examples of the proper use of the passive voice.

EFFECTIVE PASSIVE	The test was conducted to identify the soil pH levels at the site.

The passive voice is also useful when the performer of the action either is not known or is not important. Finally, although different languages place different values on the use of active and passive voice, active voice is highly valued in English.

EFFECTIVE PASSIVE	The wheel was invented thousands of years ago. [Who invented it is not known.]

As you revise, select the voice, active (usually) or passive (occasionally), appropriate to your purpose and topic.

ETHICS NOTE: Do Not Use Passive Voice to Evade Responsibility Do not use the passive voice to avoid responsibility for an action or to obscure an issue, as in the following examples: "Several mistakes were made in the processing of your claim" (Who made the mistakes?) and "It has been decided that annual bonuses will be discontinued this year" (Who has decided?). Although writers sometimes need to use the passive voice or they use it unintentionally, their attempts to evade responsibility for a problem or future commitment clearly involve an ethical choice.

Subordination

First drafts are often plagued by an overabundance of short, staccato-like sentences, as in the following passage:

> The landscape design firm submitted its proposal. The design recommends the use of native species. The proposal is extensively illustrated.

The passage is monotonous because every sentence has the same subject-verb structure; it also lacks focus because each idea is given equal weight. The key to transforming a series of repetitive, unemphatic sentences is *subordination*, a technique in which a fact or an idea is shown to be secondary to another fact or idea in the same sentence. You can subordinate an element in a sentence by making it a dependent clause, a phrase, or a single modifier.

DEPENDENT CLAUSE	The landscape design firm's proposal, *which recommends that we use native species*, was extensively illustrated.
PHRASE	The landscape design firm's proposal, *recommending our use of native species*, was extensively illustrated.
SINGLE MODIFIER	The landscape design firm's *illustrated* proposal recommends that we use native species.

You can also shift the focus from one idea to another by its placement in a sentence. If you wish to highlight an item, place it either at the beginning or at the end of the sentence; if you wish to subordinate an item, place it in the middle of the sentence.

WITHOUT SUBORDINATION	Poison ivy grows throughout the United States except in Alaska, Hawaii, and parts of the West Coast. It can grow as a vine or a shrub.
EMPHASIZES GEOGRAPHICAL RANGE	Poison ivy, which can grow as a vine or shrub, can be found throughout the United States except in Alaska, Hawaii, and parts of the West Coast.

EMPHASIZES PLANT TYPE Poison ivy, found throughout the United States except in Alaska, Hawaii, and parts of the West Coast, can grow as a vine or a shrub.

Although subordination can help you to write clear and readable sentences, it can be overdone. Be careful not to pile one subordinating clause on top of another — doing so will force your reader to work harder than necessary to understand what you are saying. The following sentence is hard to read because the bottleneck of subordinate clauses prevents the reader from moving easily from one idea to the next.

TOO MUCH SUBORDINATION When the two technicians, who had been trained to repair Maurita printers, explained to the administrative assistant that the Maurita 5090 printer, which she had told them was not working properly, needed a new fuser unit, she decided that until the part arrived, the department would have its sales letters reproduced by an independent printing supplier.

EFFECTIVE SUBORDINATION The administrative assistant told the two Maurita technicians that the Maurita 5090 printer was not working properly. The technicians examined the printer and explained to her that it needed a new fuser unit. She decided that until the part arrived, the department would have its sales letters reproduced by an independent printing supplier.

ETHICS NOTE: Highlight Advantages but Acknowledge Disadvantages
Highlighting the advantages of a product or service in a document is appropriate, but subordinating or failing to mention related disadvantages could easily mislead the audience. Even making a bulleted list of advantages, where they stand out, and then burying a disadvantage in the middle of a paragraph could unfairly mislead the target audience. You might also be tempted to dramatically highlight a feature or service that your audience would find attractive but that may be available only with some models of a product or at extra cost. In that case, the audience could justifiably object that you have given them a false impression in order to sell a product or service, especially if any extra cost was also deemphasized.

Parallel Structure

Parallelism can produce an economy of language, clarify meaning, and indicate the equality of related ideas. It can also promote emphatic writing by linking ideas in a recognizable pattern. A reader who has sensed the pattern of a sentence can go from one idea to another more quickly and confidently.

Parallel structure requires that sentence elements — words, phrases, and clauses — that are alike in function be alike in structure as well. The wording you choose to make a sentence parallel depends on the degree of emphasis you wish to create: Words produce some emphasis, phrases produce more emphasis, and clauses produce the most emphasis.

WORDS Customer-service representatives must be *punctual, courteous,* and *conscientious.*

PHRASES Customer-service representatives must recognize the importance *of punctuality, of courtesy,* and *of conscientiousness.*

CLAUSES Customer-service representatives *must arrive punctually*, they *must behave courteously*, and they *must work conscientiously*.

To make the relationship among parallel units clear, repeat the word (or words) that introduces the first unit.

▶ The advantage is not in the pay but ^in the greater opportunity.

▶ The study of electronics is a necessity and ^a challenge to the trainees.

At the paragraph level, parallel words and phrases clarify the relationships between more complex ideas. Using parallel structure, the following paragraph concisely balances two contrasting functions of the human immune system.

▶ Sometimes the immune system overreacts to things it should simply ignore, like cat dander, eggs, peanuts or pollen. Those are allergies. And sometimes the immune system turns on the body itself, attacking the cells we need to produce insulin (Type 1 diabetes) or hair follicles (alopecia) or even targeting the central nervous system (multiple sclerosis). Those are autoimmune disorders.[2]

Lists

Lists are vertically arranged words, phrases, or sentences that can save readers time by allowing them to see at a glance specific items, questions, or directions. Items in the list are highlighted by bullets, numbers, or letters to set them apart from the surrounding text. Lists also help readers by breaking up complex statements and by focusing on steps in a sequence, materials or parts needed, findings and recommendations, and the like. When you use a list of phrases or short sentences, be sure to keep all elements grammatically parallel, as in the following example:

▶ Please note the following policy changes for corporate correspondence:

- Ensure that all claims made about product safety are qualified by the phrase "provided that normal safety precautions are taken."
- Consider the content of your message, especially e-mails, in the light of the fact that they may be viewed by someone other than the intended recipient.
- Discuss information about the recipient's age, gender, occupation, or other privacy information only if it is relevant to the correspondence.
- Finally, be mindful of tone. Avoid sarcasm, irony, or any other hostile tone that would offend the recipient.

To make sure a list fits with the surrounding sentences, provide adequate transition before and after it. Introduce each list with a sentence or phrase that puts it in context. Otherwise, readers may have to guess why it's there. And although lists help focus reader attention, their overuse can confuse readers. When a document consists almost entirely of lists, the audience lacks the context to be able to distinguish their relative importance or understand how they are related to one another.

---

[2]"The Secret Life of Dirt," *Smithsonian Magazine,* April 2013, p. 43.

WRITER'S CHECKLIST

Using Lists

Follow the practices of your organization or use these guidelines for consistency and formatting.

Consistency

- ✔ Do not overuse lists or create extended lists in documents or in presentation slides.
- ✔ List only comparable items, such as tasks or equipment, that are balanced in importance.
- ✔ Begin each listed item in the same way — whether with nouns, verbs, or other parts of speech — and maintain parallel structure throughout.
- ✔ List bulleted items in a logical order, keeping your audience and purpose in mind.

Formatting

- ✔ Capitalize the first word in each listed item, unless doing so is visually awkward.
- ✔ Use periods or other ending punctuation when the listed items are complete sentences.
- ✔ Avoid commas or semicolons following items and do not use the conjunction *and* before the last item in a list.
- ✔ Use numbers to indicate sequence or rank.
- ✔ Follow each number with a period and start the item with a capital letter.
- ✔ Use bullets (round, square, arrow) when you do not wish to indicate rank or sequence.
- ✔ When lists need subdivisions, use letters with numbers.

Other Ways to Achieve Emphasis

You can create a feeling of anticipation in your audience by arranging a series of facts or ideas in ascending order of importance. Begin such a series with the least important or lowest impact idea and end it with the most important or highest impact one.

▶ The hostile takeover of the company will result in some employees being relocated to different cities, some being downgraded, and some being laid off.

The writer leads the audience step by step from the lowest potential impact on employees to the highest: (1) employee relocation, (2) downgraded jobs, and (3) loss of jobs. Note how the sentence presents these three potential outcomes in parallel structure.

An abrupt change in sentence length can also highlight an important point.

▶ We have already reviewed the problems that the accounting department identified during the past year. We could continue to examine the causes of our problems and point an accusing finger at all the elements beyond our control, but in the end it all leads to one simple conclusion: *We must cut costs.*

Sometimes, simply labeling ideas as important creates emphasis.

▶ *But most important*, we can do everything in our power to make sure that we are producing the best telecommunication equipment on the market.

If you don't overuse them, direct statements such as *most important* should make your audience notice what follows.

Important information may also be brought to the audience's attention by a special format — the material may be boxed, for instance — or by attention-getting devices such as dashes, ALL-CAPITAL letters, underlined words, or a distinctive typeface, such as **boldface**, color, or *italics*. These features can be used to emphasize important words and phrases in warnings. Overuse of such typographical devices may cancel their effectiveness, however. Readers quickly learn to gloss over these devices if they are used for subordinate as well as truly important material.

◆ *For additional highlighting devices, see pages 215–217 in Chapter 7, Designing Documents and Visuals.*

> **WARNING**
>
> **DO NOT** proceed to the next instruction until you have unplugged the equipment. **The electrical power generated by this equipment can kill!**

WRITER'S CHECKLIST

Achieving Emphasis

- ✔ Use the active voice, as appropriate.
- ✔ Subordinate secondary ideas.
- ✔ Use parallel structure to focus attention on how ideas are related.
- ✔ Use lists to highlight ideas by setting them apart from surrounding text.
- ✔ Arrange ideas in least important to most important order.
- ✔ Label key ideas as important.
- ✔ Selectively use typographical devices such as ALL-CAPITAL LETTERS, underlined text, *italics*, color, or **boldface** type.

Point of View

Point of view shows the writer's relation to the information presented. First-person point of view indicates that the writer is a participant or an observer. Second- and third-person points of view indicate that the writer is giving directions, instructions, or advice, or is writing about other people or something impersonal.

FIRST PERSON *I* scrolled down to find the Settings option.

SECOND PERSON Scroll down to find the Settings option and double-click. [*You* is understood.]

THIRD PERSON *He/she/they* scrolled down to find the Settings option.

Many people think they should avoid the pronoun *I* in their workplace writing. Doing so, however, often leads to inappropriate passive constructions or to awkward sentences in which writers refer to themselves as *one* or as *the writer* instead of as *I*.

- ~~It is regrettable~~ *I regret* that *we cannot accept* the equipment shipped on the 12th ~~is unacceptable~~.
- ~~One~~ *I* can only conclude that the bond rate is too low.

Do not use the personal point of view, however, when you need to emphasize the subject matter over the writer or the reader. In the following example, the use of *I* communicates no useful information and is less tactful than the impersonal version.

PERSONAL	I received objections to my proposal from several of your managers.
IMPERSONAL	Several managers have raised objections to the proposal.

Whether you adopt a personal or an impersonal point of view depends on your purpose and readers. In an informal e-mail to an associate, for example, you would most likely adopt a first-person voice because you know the recipient. However, in a report to a large group, you would probably emphasize the subject by using the impersonal third-person point of view.

In some cultures, stating an opinion in writing is considered impolite or unnecessary, but in primarily English-speaking countries, readers expect to see a writer's opinion stated clearly and explicitly.

ETHICS NOTE: Use Pronouns in Organizational Correspondence Carefully

In correspondence on company stationery, statements made using the pronoun *we* may be interpreted as reflecting company policy, whereas using *I* clearly reflects the writer's personal opinion. Use the appropriate pronoun according to whether the matter discussed in the letter is a corporate or an individual concern.

- *I* understand your frustration with the price increase, but we must now include the cost of the recent import tax in our pricing.

This example discusses neither corporate nor individual concerns and could just as easily be written in third person because the writer merely enunciates company policy, not his or her personal decision on the matter.

Language

The words you use matter. Focus on them carefully as you revise. Ensure that you use the right word in the right context throughout and that your writing is economical by eliminating redundant or otherwise needless language. Now is also the time to evaluate your draft for any stated or implied bias toward people or groups. Finally, consider whether you have used technical, legal, or other specialized vocabulary that may be inappropriate for some members of your audience. In digital documents, specialized terms can be defined using a mouse-over feature or can be hyperlinked to a glossary or other document with explanatory content. The plainer your language, or the easier it is for readers to find definitions, the more time, effort, and potential confusion you will save your readers.

Context and Word Choice

As Mark Twain once said, "The difference between the right word and almost the right word is the difference between 'lightning' and 'lightning bug.' " Precision requires that you choose the right word.

Be alert to the effect that a word may have on your audience — and try to avoid words that might, by the implications they carry, confuse, distract, or offend your audience. For example, in describing a piece of machinery that your company recently bought, you might refer to the item as cheap — meaning inexpensive. However, because "cheap" often suggests "of poor quality" or "shoddily made," your audience may picture the new equipment as unreliable or on the verge of falling apart.

In selecting the appropriate word, keep in mind the *context* — the setting in which the word appears. Suppose instead of "cheap" you call the new machine "inexpensive." But the use of the word will depend on the context. While a $1,000 desktop laser printer might be overpriced, an audience unfamiliar with the cost of printing equipment might be surprised to learn that an on-demand printing system at $8,000 is a good buy. It is up to you, the writer, to provide your readers with the context — to let them know, in this case, the relative costs of on-demand printing equipment.

The context will also determine whether a word you choose is specific enough. When you use the word *machine*, for instance, you might be thinking of an automobile, a lathe, a robot, or a laboratory centrifuge. *Machine* is an imprecise word that must be qualified or explained. Conversely, to include printer model numbers in a company's annual report, a detailed parts list in a sales brochure, or specialized technical language in a memo to the accounting department would also be inappropriate. In Figure 4–1, for example, the specific automobile models (in italics) listed in an annual report on an organization's environmental protection practices are an inappropriate level of detail for an overview aimed at the report's general readers.

In all workplace writing, use the words and ideas best suited to your audience and to the context in which the information will be used.

REDUCING MOBILE EMISSIONS

Automobiles, trucks, and buses have been identified as significant sources of both ozone and particulate matter in the region, with their emissions accounting for more than 30 percent of the smog precursors emitted countywide. In response, Gillette County has adopted a "technology neutral" plan to use all available technologies that provide the least amount of emissions, while conserving natural resources until a completely sustainable transportation source is discovered. Although both compressed natural gas and diesel technologies were already a part of the county fleet, hybrid and all-electric sedans and buses have been added, including two hybrid and one all-electric vehicle used by the Department of Environmental Services. . . . *These vehicles include a Ford Fusion Hybrid (4 cyl. gas/electric) Sedan, GMC Sierra Hybrid (8 cyl. gas/electric), and a Chevrolet Spark EV (all-electric, hatchback).*

Inappropriate level of detail

Figure 4–1 Information Too Detailed for Audience and Context

ETHICS NOTE: Use Language Carefully to Avoid Deception Use words correctly and appropriately. Consider the company document that stated, "A nominal charge will be assessed for using our conference facilities." When clients objected that the charge was actually quite high, the writer pointed out that the word *nominal* means "the named amount" as well as "very small." In this situation, the audience had a strong case in charging that the company was attempting to deceive. In other circumstances, various abstract words, technical or legal jargon, and euphemisms — when used to mislead an audience or to hide a serious or dangerous situation — are unethical, even though their meanings (like *nominal*) may be ambiguous.

Conciseness

As you revise, focus on removing unnecessary words, phrases, clauses, and sentences from your writing. Wordiness, as well as stilted or pretentious language, can place a barrier between you and your audience by obscuring your essential meaning. Be particularly alert for two types of wordiness: redundancy and padded phrases.

Redundancy

Modifiers — whether adjectives, adverbs, prepositional phrases, or subordinate clauses — make the words they describe accurate and specific. However, avoid modifiers used to emphasize a point but that merely repeat the idea contained in the word they modify, such as the expressions in the following list:

blue in color	plan ahead
resume again	basic essentials
square in shape	attach together
brief in duration	visible to the eye
completely finished	present status
final outcome	round circle

Padded Phrases

A padded phrase expresses in several words an idea that could easily be expressed in one. *Due to the fact that* is a wordy way of saying *because.* Examine your work for language often padded with the following words: *case, fact, field, factor, manner,* and *nature.*

Sometimes, however, longer wording or phrasing clarifies meaning.

▶ *In terms of* gross sales, the year has been successful; *in terms of* net income, however, it has been discouraging.

Instead of being redundant, the phrase *in terms of* balances the sentence and highlights the contrast in meaning. Expressions such as these must be evaluated individually. If the expression does not contribute to the meaning of the sentence, use a simpler substitute.

Bias

Biased words and expressions offend because they make inappropriate assumptions or stereotypes about gender, ethnicity, physical or mental disability, age, or sexual orientation.

Sexist Language

Sexist language can be an outgrowth of sexism, the arbitrary stereotyping of men and women. Its use can breed and reinforce inequality. To avoid sexism in your writing, treat men and women equally, and do not make assumptions about traditional or occupational roles. Accordingly, use nonsexist occupational descriptions.

Instead of	Consider
chairman	chair *or* chairperson
foreman	supervisor
manpower	staff, personnel, *or* workers
policeman *or* policewoman	police officer
salesman *or* saleswoman	salesperson
male nurse	nurse
female chemist	chemist

Use comparable terms to describe men and women.

Instead of	Consider
man and wife	husband and wife
Ms. Jones and Bernard Weiss	Ms. Jones and Mr. Weiss *or* Mary Jones and Bernard Weiss
ladies and men	ladies and gentlemen *or* women and men

Unintended sexism can creep into your writing by the unthinking use of male pronouns where a reference could apply equally to a man and a woman. One way to avoid such usage is to rewrite the sentence in the plural.

All employees *their managers* *their travel vouchers.*
▶ ~~Every employee~~ will have ~~his manager~~ sign ~~his travel voucher.~~

Other possible solutions are to use *his or her* instead of *his* alone or to omit the pronoun completely if it is not essential to the meaning of the sentence.

an
▶ Everyone must submit ~~his~~ expense report by Monday.

He or she can become monotonous when repeated frequently, and a pronoun cannot always be omitted without changing the meaning of a sentence. Another solution is to omit troublesome pronouns by using the imperative mood whenever possible.

Submit all
▶ ~~Everyone must submit his or her~~ expense reports by Monday.

Other Types of Biased Language

Identifying people by racial, ethnic, or religious categories is simply not relevant in most workplace writing. Telling readers that an engineer is Native American or that a professor is African American almost never conveys useful information. Similarly, linking a profession or a characteristic to race or ethnicity reinforces stereotypes, implying that it is rare or expected for a person of a particular background to have achieved a certain position.

When the context requires it, such as when discussing software tools available to assist individuals with disabilities, consider how you refer to people with disabilities. If you refer to "a disabled employee," you imply that the part (*disabled*) is as significant as the whole (*employee*). Use "an employee with a disability" instead. Similarly, the preferred usage is "a person who uses a wheelchair" rather than "a wheelchair-bound person"; the latter expression inappropriately equates the wheelchair with the person. Likewise, references to a person's age can also be inappropriate, as in expressions like "middle-aged manager" or "young cyber security analyst."

In most workplace writing, such issues are simply not relevant. Of course, in some contexts, race, ethnicity, religion, disability, or age should be identified. For example, if you are writing an Equal Employment Opportunity Commission report about your firm's hiring practices, the racial and gender composition of the workforce is relevant. In such cases, you need to present the information in ways that are accurate and that respect the individuals or groups to which you refer.

PROFESSIONALISM NOTE: Avoid Biased Words and Ideas The simplest way to avoid bias is to not mention differences among people unless the differences are relevant to the topic. Keep current with accepted usage and, if you are unsure of the appropriateness of an expression or the tone of a passage, have several colleagues review the material and give you their opinions.

Plain Language

Plain language is writing that is logically organized and understandable on the first reading. A key to this type of writing is to use language that is both uncomplicated and accurate. Such writing avoids unnecessary jargon, affectation, and technical terminology. Even with the best of intentions, however, you cannot always avoid using specialized terms and concepts. This section will help you sort out the difference between writing that is plain and accurate and writing that is either too complicated or too simplistic.

Assess your audience carefully to ensure that your language connects with their level of knowledge. Replace jargon and complex legal wording with familiar words or terms when possible.

COMPLEX	The systems integration specialist must be able to visually perceive the entire directional response module.
PLAIN LANGUAGE	The operator must be able to see the entire control panel.

If you are a health-care provider, for example, use the appropriate plain-language equivalent for medical terminology with patients in conversations and written guidelines: *bleeding* instead of *hemorrhaging*; *heart attack* instead of *myocardial infarction*; *cast* instead of *splint*; *stitches* instead of *sutures*. If a plain-language alternative does not exist, define or explain a technical term on its first use and include visuals where necessary.

WRITER'S CHECKLIST
Using Plain Language

✔ Identify your average reader's level of technical knowledge.

✔ Avoid unnecessary jargon and legal language.

✔ Avoid confusing terms and constructions.
- Define necessary abbreviations and acronyms.
- Use the same words consistently for the same things.
- Do not give an obscure meaning to a word.

✔ Use the active voice for directness and for identifying the doer of an action.

✔ Use the second person (*you/yours*) or imperative mood to write directly to the reader.

✔ Write sentences understandable on a first reading.
- Aim for one message in each sentence.
- Break up complex information into smaller, easier-to-understand units.
- Use positive writing and the present tense as much as possible.

✔ Select word placement carefully.
- Keep subjects and objects close to their verbs.
- Put *only, always,* and other conditional words next to the words they modify.

Affectation

Do not use language that is more formal, technical, or showy than it needs to be to communicate with your reader. Such inflated language creates a smoke screen that the audience must penetrate to discover your meaning. Consider the following example, in which a company needs to tell employees about its policy for personal phone calls.

INFLATED It is the policy of the company to provide the proper telephonic apparatus to enable each employee to conduct the interoffice and intra-business communication necessary to discharge his or her responsibilities; however, it is contrary to company policy to permit telephones to be utilized for any but select personal employee communications.

PLAIN Your cell phone is provided for company business; use it for personal calls only if they are essential.

Most people would have to read the first version of the policy several times before deciphering its message. The meaning of the revised version, which uses direct, simple, and precise language, is evident at a glance.

Another common type of affectation is adding prefixes and suffixes to simple words. For example, *analyzation*, *summarization*, and *notation* are simply fancy-sounding versions of *analysis*, *summary*, and *note*. The extra syllables tacked onto such words do not make them mean anything more precise; they make them incorrect and longer.

Understanding the possible reasons for affectation is the first step toward avoiding it. Review and revise your writing if you recognize any of the following tendencies:

- *Impression.* Pretentious language used in an attempt to impress others. Evidence and logic will be more convincing and create a more positive impression than a smoke screen of obscure terms.
- *Insecurity.* Language used to cover gaps in a lack of facts, conclusions, or arguments. Continue to research the topic until you are certain of what to say.
- *Imitation.* The tendency to imitate the poor writing of supervisors or colleagues. This practice (such as writers in a company referring to themselves as *one* rather than *I*) is frequently the result of bad habits thoughtlessly repeated rather than because of formal company policies. At least find out if they are policies before falling into the habit with everyone else.
- *Initiation.* Overuse of technical terminology and jargon by those who have just completed their education or training for an occupation. Be especially careful to minimize this habit when writing for senior officials or customers. These readers are much less likely to be as knowledgeable or technically current as you and will struggle to understand your content.

WRITER'S CHECKLIST
Avoiding Affectation

- ✔ Do not refer to yourself as *the writer* or *one*; use the first person (*I*).
- ✔ Choose simple words that say exactly what you mean — do not substitute big, imprecise, or unusual words for well-thought-out, precise language.
- ✔ Avoid trying to impress your reader with pretentious language — such as *aforesaid, hereto* — or with vague or trendy language — such as *calendarize, monetize, locavore, nutraceutical.*
- ✔ Be certain of your facts, conclusions, and arguments. Insecurity in these areas can lead to inflated language.

ETHICS NOTE: Avoid Ambiguous Language Avoid opaque and ambiguous language in descriptions that appear to finesse troublesome situations. Precise language is especially important in health and safety communications, but it is also crucial to investment- and financial-planning guidance because the information involves financial risk.

Technical Terminology

Technical terms are standard, universally recognized words used in a particular field to refer to specific principles, processes, or devices. Unlike inflated language, technical terms are essential for communicating information accurately. The term *divestiture*, for example, has a specific meaning for audiences familiar with management strategies. Similarly, the term *logic gate* would be understood by an audience who studied computer science or electrical engineering.

If you are certain that your audience (and potential audience) will understand a technical term, use it to ensure precision. If you are at all uncertain, however, define the term in plain language when you first use it. If your audience is likely to be confused by a concept, explain it, perhaps including an easy-to-understand example. A brief explanation, though less efficient than using a technical term, is sometimes required to make your writing understandable for the widest possible audience—which is your ultimate goal.

Jargon

Jargon is highly specialized technical slang that is unique to an occupational group. If you are addressing a particular occupational group, jargon (like technical terminology) is a time-saving and an efficient way of communicating with the members of that group. For example, human resources professionals adopted the term *headhunters* to describe the specialists who recruit professional and executive personnel. Such terms should be used only in the appropriate context. Jargon is not a satisfactory substitute for everyday language outside the field in which it is standard.

When jargon becomes so specialized that it applies only to one company or subgroup of an occupation, it is referred to as "shop talk." For example, an automobile manufacturer might produce a "pollution-control valve—Model LV-20." In the department where the device is built, it may be referred to as an "LV-20." Obviously, shop talk is appropriate only for those familiar with its special vocabulary and should be reserved for speech, informal notes, e-mail messages, and, in some cases, formal memos to other departments within a company.

◆ ***For guidance on how to define terms accurately and incorporate them smoothly into your writing, see pages 83–85 in Chapter 3, Drafting a Document.***

WRITER'S CHECKLIST

Revising for Clarity

- ✔ Check the soundness of your organization by outlining your draft and reorganize your content as necessary.
- ✔ Use effective transitions between sentences, paragraphs, and sections.
- ✔ Be consistent in your point of view toward your topic.
- ✔ Emphasize key ideas and subordinate ancillary ideas.
- ✔ Choose precise language to ensure accuracy and to eliminate vagueness and ambiguity.
- ✔ Strive for conciseness by eliminating words, phrases, and sentences that are not necessary to your subject, purpose, and audience.

Proofreading

Proofreading is your final opportunity to review your content for accuracy and for sentence-level corrections in grammar, punctuation, mechanics, and spelling. Even though you are familiar with your content at this point, inadvertent errors can remain unless you methodically examine the draft for them.

Above all, your information must be accurate. Although accuracy is important in all types of writing, it takes on special significance when you write on the job. One misplaced decimal point, for example, can create a staggering financial error. Incorrect or imprecise instructions can cause injury to a worker. At the very least, inaccuracies will cause readers to question your trustworthiness. Put yourself in their place. If a figure or fact in your text differs from one in a chart or graph, which one are they to believe is accurate? These kinds of inaccuracies are easily overlooked as you write a first draft, so you must correct them during revision.

◆ *For an easy-access reference to grammar, punctuation, mechanics, and spelling while revising, see Appendix B, Revision Guide.*

Whether you examine your own or someone else's writing, consider reviewing and proofreading in several stages. Although you need to tailor the stages to the specific document and to your own problem areas, the following Writer's Checklist (Proofreading in Stages) provides a useful starting point for this process. For using Comment and Track Changes in word-processing programs, see the Digital Tip: Incorporating Tracked Changes on page 133 of Chapter 5.

DIGITAL TIP: Grammar Checkers and Spell Checkers

Do not rely uncritically on computer grammar and spell checkers. They may help with proofreading, but they can make writers overconfident. If a typographical error results in a legitimate English word (for example, *coarse* instead of *course*), the spell checker will not flag the misspelling. Moreover, spell checkers will not be familiar with proper names, technical terminology, and non-English expressions. Because grammar checkers cannot anticipate the meaning of your sentences, they may occasionally flag proper usage as incorrect and suggest inappropriate revisions. Therefore, even while using grammar and spell checkers as aids, you still must proofread your work carefully — both on your monitor and on paper.

WRITER'S CHECKLIST
Proofreading in Stages

First-Stage Review

- ✔ Appropriate format, as for reports or correspondence
- ✔ Typographical consistency (headings, spacing, fonts)

Second-Stage Review

- ✔ Specific grammar and usage problems
- ✔ Appropriate punctuation
- ✔ Correct abbreviations and capitalization
- ✔ Correct spelling (especially names and places)
- ✔ Accurate web, e-mail, and other addresses
- ✔ Accurate figures and consistent units of measurement in tables and lists
- ✔ Cut-and-paste errors resulting from moved or deleted text and numbers

Final-Stage Review

- ✔ Final check of your goals: readers' needs and purpose
- ✔ Appearance of the document (see pages 212–220 in Chapter 7, Designing Documents and Visuals)
- ✔ Review by colleague for crucial documents

Use the standard proofreaders' marks shown on page 612, especially for proofreading someone else's document.

PROFESSIONALISM NOTE: Proofread with Care Proofreading not only demonstrates respect for your readers — who can be distracted, irritated, or misled by errors in your text — but also reflects your commitment to accuracy in the way you approach all your work.

Physical Appearance

The most thoughtfully prepared, carefully written, and conscientiously revised writing will quickly lose its effect if it has a poor physical appearance. In the classroom or on the job, a sloppy document will invariably lead your reader to assume that the work that went into preparing it was also sloppy. In the classroom, that carelessness will reflect on you; on the job, it can reflect on both you and your employer. Unless your instructor provides other specific instructions, use the following guidelines for preparing your paper documents:

◆ *For format guidelines for letters and memos, see Chapter 8, Writing E-mails, Memos, and Letters*

◆ *For guidance for formal reports, see Chapter 11, Writing Formal Reports.*

◆ *For guidance on page design, see Chapter 7, Designing Documents and Visuals.*

- Use good-quality, white paper.
- Check that your printer produces a clear, dark image.
- Use at least one-inch margins on all sides of the page.
- Number all appropriate pages.
- Leave ample white space around visuals and to indicate divisions between separate sections.

@ **DIGITAL TIP: Proofreading for Format Consistency**

To check your documents for consistency and accuracy, use both an overview and up-close analysis of your content. Visualizing a whole page in your word processor will show you the general appearance of your document and help you spot any problems with your document's layout, format, or structure. Printing your document and examining it slowly and carefully will help you notice inconsistencies in the details, such as typography, line spacing, and indentation.

Case Study: Revising the Lifemaker Brochure

A variety of the revision techniques discussed in this chapter apply to the Lifemaker sales brochure that was outlined and drafted in Chapters 2 and 3. In Figure 4–2, the writer has taken her second draft and, after allowing for a cooling-off period, critiqued

The Lifemaker System 40—DRAFT

The Compact, Affordable Home Gym Designed for Maximum Fitness Conditioning

Home gyms were designed to eliminate the hassle and expense of going to a health club to work out, but most of them are too bulky and awkward to fit either your budget or your wallet. The Lifemaker System 40 is designed for limped living space, a modest budget, and maximum fitness needs.

Compact Design

The Lifemaker's multiple stations provide a technologically sophisticated strength training program, and is architecturally configured for minimal space and maximal efficiency. At 4 fete wide and 7 feet long, your living room can easily accommodate the Lifemaker with more ease than other home systems. At the same time, the Lifemaker offers more stations and more exercises.

One need not compromise your exercise needs with an overside or ineffective system. Our home gym lets you integrate a complete home exercise system into your available space and your budget.

Cast-Iron Weight Stack

The dual cast-iron weight stacks totals 200 pounds. Which can be arranged to offer a resistance range of 10 to 150 pounds. In addition, Lifemaker offers the only weight system on the market that can be adjusted in multiplied increments.

Adjustable Cables

The Lifemaker's unique cable system allows quick reconfiguring of the weight stacks without taking apart the entire system. Just pulling the center rod and one can add or remove as many plates as you need.

Figure 4–2 Draft Sales-Brochure Copy (Marked for Revision) *(continued)*

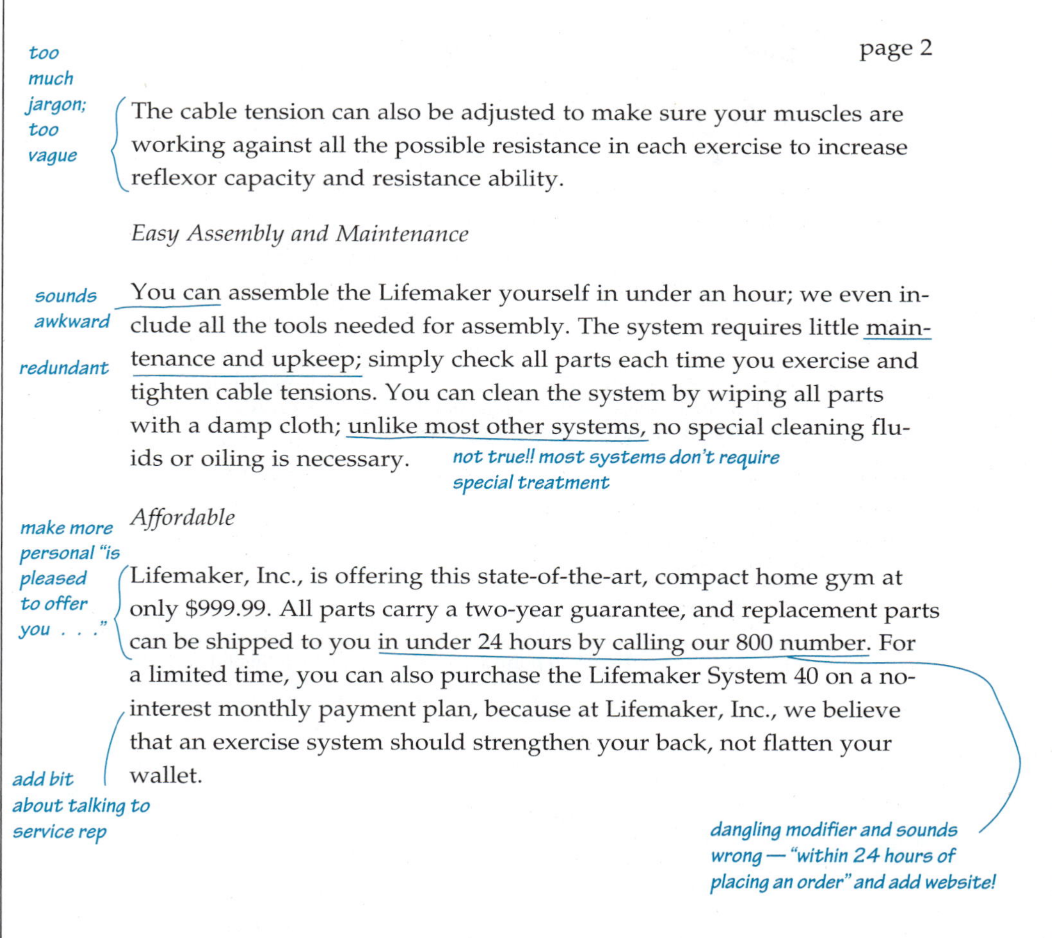

page 2

The cable tension can also be adjusted to make sure your muscles are working against all the possible resistance in each exercise to increase reflexor capacity and resistance ability.

Easy Assembly and Maintenance

You can assemble the Lifemaker yourself in under an hour; we even include all the tools needed for assembly. The system requires little maintenance and upkeep; simply check all parts each time you exercise and tighten cable tensions. You can clean the system by wiping all parts with a damp cloth; unlike most other systems, no special cleaning fluids or oiling is necessary.

Affordable

Lifemaker, Inc., is offering this state-of-the-art, compact home gym at only $999.99. All parts carry a two-year guarantee, and replacement parts can be shipped to you in under 24 hours by calling our 800 number. For a limited time, you can also purchase the Lifemaker System 40 on a no-interest monthly payment plan, because at Lifemaker, Inc., we believe that an exercise system should strengthen your back, not flatten your wallet.

Figure 4–2 Draft Sales-Brochure Copy (Marked for Revision) *(continued)*

her work, using the main points covered in this chapter as her guide. Figure 4–3 on page 120 shows a revised version of the draft. Notice that the writer has not simply made mechanical, sentence-level corrections to her work; she used her marginal comments to revise the structure and organization as well as its sentences. Figure 4–4 on page 121 shows a copy of the published sales brochure.

The Lifemaker System 40

The Compact, Affordable Home Gym
Designed for Maximum Fitness Conditioning

Introduces major benefits from Figure 2–2

Home gym systems are designed to eliminate the hassle and expense of working out at a health club, but most systems take up too much space and can injure both your budget and your back. The Lifemaker System 40 offers a solution to the problem of oversized, overpriced, and ineffective home gyms, because Lifemaker is designed to fit a limited living space, a modest budget, and maximum fitness requirements. Purchasing a Lifemaker System 40 will let you integrate a complete weight-and-cable exercise system into your living space and your budget.

Headings make brochure inviting to readers

Compact Design

The Lifemaker's comprehensive strength-training program is designed to occupy minimal space. The system offers more than 40 exercise combinations, but because it measures only 4 feet wide and 7 feet long, Lifemaker will fit easily into almost any room.

Expands equipment, fitness, maintenance, and affordability benefits from introductory paragraph

Multiple Stations

Three workout stations let you move through your conditioning program as efficiently as if you owned a roomful of weight-and-cable machines. In addition, the multiple stations are designed so that two people can work out at the same time.

Cast-Iron Weights

The Lifemaker features dual weight stacks, totaling more than 200 pounds of cast-iron plates. The dual stacks offer a resistance range of 10 to 150 pounds; resistance can be adjusted in 5-, 10-, or 15-pound increments.

Adjustable Cables

A unique cable system allows you to reconfigure the dual weight stacks without taking apart the entire system. Simply pull the rod located between the stacks and you can add or remove as many plates as you need for a particular exercise. The cable tension can also be adjusted to increase or decrease the amount of resistance within exercise sets.

Easy Assembly, Easy Maintenance

The Lifemaker System 40 can be assembled in less than an hour; no special tools are needed for assembly. You can maintain the Lifemaker in good condition simply by wiping down the system with a damp cloth; no oiling or scrubbing of parts is ever necessary. All parts carry a two-year guarantee and can be shipped to you within 24 hours of your placing an order.

Affordable

Lifemaker, Inc., is pleased to offer you this state-of-the-art, compact home gym for only $999.99. You can also purchase the Lifemaker on a low-interest monthly payment plan. Contact us at www.lifemaker.com or call (800) 554-1234 and we will be happy to arrange a plan that works with your financial needs. At Lifemaker, Inc., we believe that owning a home-gym system should strengthen your back, not flatten your wallet.

Figure 4–3 Final Sales-Brochure Copy

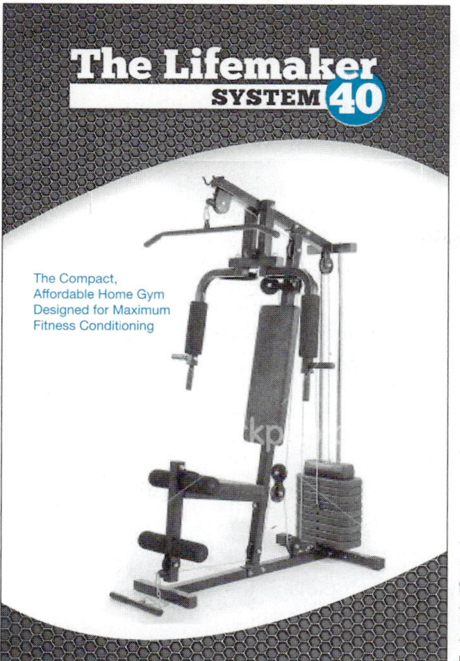

Erdosain/Getty Images

The Lifemaker
SYSTEM 40

The Compact, Affordable Home Gym Designed for Maximum Fitness Conditioning

Home gym systems are designed to eliminate the hassle and expense of working out at a health club, but most systems take up too much space and can injure both your budget and your back. The Lifemaker System 40 offers a solution to the problem of oversized, overpriced, and ineffective home gyms, because Lifemaker is designed to fit a limited living space, a modest budget, and maximum fitness requirements. Purchasing a Lifemaker System 40 will let you integrate a complete weight-and-cable exercise system into your living space and your budget.

Compact Design

The Lifemaker's comprehensive strength-training program is designed to occupy minimal space. The system offers more than 40 exercise combinations, but because it measures only 4 feet wide and 7 feet long, Lifemaker will fit easily into almost any room.

Multiple Stations

Three workout stations let you move through your conditioning program as efficiently as if you owned a roomful of weight-and-cable machines. In addition, the multiple stations are designed so that two people can work out at the same time.

Cast-Iron Weights

The Lifemaker features dual weight stacks, totaling more than 200 pounds of cast-iron plates. The dual stacks offer a resistance range of 10 to 150 pounds; resistance can be adjusted in 5-, 10-, or 15-pound increments.

Erdosain/Getty Images

Adjustable Cables

A unique cable system allows you to reconfigure the dual weight stacks without taking apart the entire system. Simply pull the rod located between the stacks and you can add or remove as many plates as you need for a particular exercise. The cable tension can also be adjusted to increase or decrease the amount of resistance within exercise sets.

Easy Assembly, Easy Maintenance

The Lifemaker System 40 can be assembled in less than an hour; no special tools are needed for assembly. You can maintain the Lifemaker in good condition simply by wiping down the system with a damp cloth; no oiling or scrubbing of parts is ever necessary. All parts carry a two-year guarantee and can be shipped to you within 24 hours of your placing an order.

Affordable

Lifemaker, Inc., is pleased to offer you this state-of-the-art, compact home gym for only $999.99. You can also purchase the Lifemaker on a low-interest monthly payment plan. Contact us at www.lifemaker.com or call (800) 554-1234 and we will be happy to arrange a plan that works with your financial needs. At Lifemaker, Inc., we believe that owning a home-gym system should strengthen your back, not flatten your wallet.

Juice/Getty Images

Figure 4–4 Published Lifemaker Sales Brochure

CHAPTER 4 SUMMARY: REVISING A DOCUMENT

Use the following checklist to help you remember the various aspects of revision covered in this chapter. Refer to this list both before and after you write the final draft of any document; fix any problems before your reader sees them.

- Have I allowed a cooling period?
- Have I included all the information my readers need?
- Is the writing organized logically?
- Do any potential ethical problems need to be resolved?
- Does each paragraph have a topic sentence?
- Are the sentences in each paragraph related to the paragraph's central idea?
- Have I included transitional words and phrases so that readers can follow the relationships among ideas?
- Are active and passive voices used appropriately?
- Are secondary ideas subordinated to primary ideas?
- Are ideas of equal importance written in grammatically parallel structure?
- Are other highlighting devices used appropriately?
- Is the point of view appropriate and consistent?
- Does the language accurately and precisely suit the topic and the audience?
- Is the writing concise?
- Is the writing free of actual or implied bias?
- Does the vocabulary avoid unnecessary technical terminology and jargon?
- Have all errors — grammatical and factual — been corrected during proofreading?
- Is the document appropriately formatted?
- Is the document's appearance crisp and clean?

Exercises

1. Well-constructed paragraphs enable readers to quickly understand their content and writers to achieve their purpose. Read the following paragraph and then (a) underline its topic sentence and (b) cross out any sentences that do not contribute to paragraph unity.

   ▶ Frequently, department managers and supervisors recruit applicants without working through our corporate human resources office. Our human resources departments at all of our locations across the country have experienced this problem. Recently, the manager of our tool-design department met with a recent industrial-design graduate to discuss an opening for a tool designer. The graduate was sent to the human resources department, where she was told that no such position existed. When the tool-design manager asked the director of human resources about the matter, the manager learned that the company president had ordered a hiring freeze for two months. I'm sure that our general employment situation will get better. As a result of the manager's failure to work through proper channels, the applicant was not only disappointed but also bitter.

2. The sentences in the following paragraph have been purposely placed in the wrong order. Examine key terms and transitional devices, and then rearrange the sentences so that the paragraph moves smoothly and logically from one sentence to the next.

Indicate the correct order of the sentences by placing the sentence numbers in the order in which the sentences should appear.

- (1) If such improvements could be achieved, the consequences would be significant for many different applications. (2) However, the most challenging technical problem is to achieve substantial increases in the quantities of electrical energy that can be stored per unit weight of the battery. (3) The overall process yields about 70 percent of the electricity originally put into the battery. (4) A storage battery is a relatively efficient way of storing energy.

3. Each of the following pairs of sentences lacks a transition from the first sentence to the second. Beginning with the partial list of transitional devices in Table 4–1, select the most appropriate one — or a similar choice — for each sentence pair. Then rewrite the sentences as necessary.
   a. The Doctors Clinic was able to attain its fund-raising goal on time this year. Mercer Street Hospital was forced to extend its fund-raising deadline for three months.
   b. When instructing the new tellers, the branch manager explained how to deal with impatient customers. The personal-banking assistant told the new employees that they should consult her if they had difficulty handling those customers.
   c. A car may skid on ice for several reasons. The driver may be going faster than road conditions warrant.
   d. Unit sales dropped 12 percent between the first and second quarters. Revenue increased by 6 percent.
4. Bring to class or submit online a document that you have written either in this (or another) class or at your job. Under the direction of your instructor, take the following steps:
   a. Create a rough outline of your document by writing a one-sentence summary of each paragraph in the order that the paragraphs appear.
   b. Determine whether your sequence of points is logical and effective.
   c. Make a note of any information that you could have added or deleted to make the document more effective.
   d. If you find a problem with the logic of the sequence or with the amount or type of information included or omitted in your paper, revise the outline and then your draft.
5. Bring to class or submit online a document that you have written either in this (or another) class or at your job. (You may use the same document you examined for Exercise 4 if you wish.) Under the direction of your instructor, take the following steps:
   a. Circle all the words or phrases that provide transition between sentences.
   b. If you find two sentences that do not have adequate transition, place an X in the space between them.
   c. For sentences that seem not to have adequate transition, insert a word, phrase, or clause that will improve the transition.
6. To persuade readers to take a specific course of action, successful workplace writers support their suggestions with evidence. When such details are missing in a first draft, they must be added at the revision stage. Referring to the opening and closing paragraphs you wrote for Exercises 1 and 2 in Chapter 3, outline and draft a letter that takes into account the following questions:
   a. What concrete details can you include in your letter to persuade your audience?
   b. What specific examples, facts, and statistics will you include as evidence?
   c. What point of view (first person, second person, or third person) would be most effective for your purpose?

7. Rewrite the following sentences to eliminate excessive subordination:
   a. The duty officer who was on duty at 3:30 a.m. was the one who took the call that there was a malfunction in the Number 3 generator that had been repaired at approximately 9:00 a.m. the previous morning.
   b. I have referred your letter that you wrote to us on June 20 to our staff attorney who reviewed it in the light of corporate policy that is pertinent to the issue that you raise.
8. Each of the following sentences contains a redundant word, phrase, or clause. Rewrite the sentences to eliminate the redundant elements.
   a. The field of engineering is a profession that offers great opportunities.
   b. The human resources manager spoke to the printing-plant supervisor with regard to the scheduling of employee vacations.
   c. Our experienced salespeople, who have many years of work behind them, will plan an aggressive advertising campaign to sell your upgraded widget.
9. The following passages contain unnecessary jargon, padded phrases, and affectation. Revise the passages to eliminate this language.
   a. I hereby designate Mr. Samson, who has been holding the position and serving in the capacity of assistant technical supervisor, to be named and appointed to the position and function of deputy director of customer relations. In his newly elevated position Mr. Samson will report, in the first instance, directly to the department director — that is, to me.
   b. Purchasers of the enclosed substance should carefully and thoroughly follow the instructions provided herein for the use of the substance, and should in no case whatsoever consume, or otherwise partake of, said substance without proceeding in the manner set forth on the accompanying circular of instructions.
10. Some of the following sentences violate the principles of parallel structure. Identify the incorrect sentences and revise to make them parallel. The sentences may be correctly changed in more than one way.
   a. We expected to be disappointed and that we would reject the proposal.
   b. Etiquette is important in social life, and you need it in business too.
   c. Do you prefer organizing conferences, data entry, or balancing the budget?
   d. The mailing notation should not only appear on the original but also on the copies.
   e. The office has not only been cleaned but also newly decorated.
   f. Ms. Jory either wants Anna or me to proofread the galleys for our annual report.
   g. The desk was neither the correct size nor the right model.
   h. You may either send a check or a money order or use a debit card.

Collaborative Classroom Projects

1. Affected language can confuse both native and nonnative speakers. During the next 15 minutes, in groups try to figure out common proverbs buried in these overwritten substitutes. Then, translate these proverbs and put them into regular sentences that might appear in a business-oriented document. When finished, exchange papers with members of your group to evaluate the results.

   EXAMPLE Everything that coruscates with effulgence is not ipso facto aureous.

   TRANSLATION Everything that glitters is not gold.

REWRITE Sometimes things that appear valuable are not as valuable as they seem: "Despite the large amount of advertising and public relations that went into the shoe company's new product line, the design of its new athletic shoes is really not appealing to consumers."

a. Never calculate the possible number of juvenile poultry until the usual period of incubation has been accomplished.
b. People who reside in transparent domiciles should not cast geological specimens.
c. The warm-blooded, feathered, egg-laying vertebrate animal that is among the first invariably comes in the possession of a small, legless crawling invertebrate animal.
d. Where there is gaseous evidence of flammable matter, there is an indicated insinuation of incendiary pyrotechnic.
e. Ornithological specimens of identical plumage tend to congregate in close proximity.
f. Do not utter loud or passionate vocal expressions because of the accidental overturning of a receptacle containing a whitish nutritive liquid.
g. Do not traverse a structure erected to afford passage over a waterway prior to the time of drawing nigh to the same.
h. Hemoglobin is incapable of being extracted from the edible root of brassica rapa.

2. Rewrite each of the following sentences so that the verb is in the active voice. Whenever a potential subject is not given in a sentence, supply one as you write. With these examples fresh in your thinking, seek out other inappropriate examples in cookbooks, product instructions, e-mails, and even in your own writing. After you have each found five examples, divide into groups to share and discuss them. Is there much variation in the wording of your sentences? Is the meaning of the sentence affected by the differences in wording? Is a different tone implied?
   a. The entire building was spray painted by Charles and his brother.
   b. It was assumed by the superintendent that the trip was postponed until next Tuesday.
   c. The completed form should be submitted to Tim Hagen by the 15th of every month.
   d. The fluid should be applied sparingly and should be allowed to dry for eight to ten seconds.
   e. The metropolitan area was defined as groups of counties related by commuting patterns by the researchers.

Research Projects

1. As discussed in this chapter, affected language is very hard to read. To strike a blow for readability, go in small groups to at least two federal or state government agency websites and review their plain-language guidelines. You can find them by typing "Plain Language Initiative" into a search engine. What are these government agencies, and what is the purpose of their communications with U.S. citizens? What guidelines are these agencies implementing? What are the agencies' goals in implementing these guidelines as they relate to U.S. citizens reading their material? Divide the work so that each person in the group performs one of the following tasks: (1) researches the history of plain language at that site, (2) describes what it is, (3) examines samples of government documents in technical and then in plain-language style, or (4) makes a list of ways to use plain language. Write a draft of your findings and be ready to submit it to the class. (Your instructor can determine if your work should be peer reviewed in

stages by different groups.) Distribute your final document or present your findings to the class, as your instructor directs. (You may want to review Chapter 14, Giving Presentations.)

2. Find a document (instructions, advertisements, or other sample) or website that you believe demonstrates one or more of the ethical problems discussed in this chapter: using language that attempts to evade responsibility, to mislead the audience, to deemphasize or suppress important information, or to emphasize misleading or incorrect information. As your instructor directs, (a) report what ethical problems you see and describe how the document might be revised to eliminate those problems, and (b) rewrite the samples to eliminate the ethical problems.

3. Consider that you work for the Office of Human Resources at a large metropolitan hospital. The hospital needs to hire a variety of different types of nurses (prenatal, triage, and so on) in the coming months, and you are part of a committee that is working to find the best candidates. This is a competitive market, and your hospital's online and social-media ads have not been attracting the most qualified candidates. For example, one of the ads reads: "Desperately need hospital nurses for multiple locations and shifts. We offer lots of benefits like daily pay, 401(k), and uniform programs!"

   a. You have been asked to review the ads of local hospitals in your metropolitan area to see why their recruitment efforts are more successful. Go to the Web and social-media sites of several local hospitals and make notes about their nursing ads (be careful to note what kind of nurse each ad refers to) and compare them to one another.
   b. In a memo to the head of Human Resources, discuss how your ad could be more appealing. Based on your research, revise this ad for a particular type of nurse so that it attracts the right candidates and persuades them to contact your office. In preparing your recommendation, refer to the section titled Content and Organization on pages 97–98.

PART 2

Methods and Design

Part 1 discussed the general principles that apply to all on-the-job writing; Part 2 focuses on skills that you will need to approach more complex projects requiring collaboration, research, and design. The following chapters will help you prepare for the specific writing and communicating presented in Part 3 — such as writing correspondence, reports, and proposals, and developing presentations.

- **Collaboration.** Chapter 5 discusses the importance of writing strategies learned in Chapters 1 through 4 to collaborative writing projects on the job, whether you are a member of a collaborative writing team or the team leader. This chapter also describes the rich variety of digital programs available to facilitate the work of collaborative writing teams.
- **Research.** Chapter 6 provides extensive treatment of gathering and evaluating the appropriateness of information for your subject, including using the Internet and library, interviewing, using questionnaires, and making first-hand observations. You will also find advice for using the APA (American Psychological Association) and MLA (Modern Language Association) styles of documenting your research.
- **Design.** Chapter 7 gives detailed advice on designing effective documents — printed and electronic; developing informative and uncluttered illustrations, charts, and graphs for domestic and international audiences; and successfully integrating them into your text. Attention to format and design is crucial to your success in creating instructions, reports, proposals, presentations, and other communications that are clear and appealing to your audience.

5 Collaborating on a Document

Contents

Workplace writing is often collaborative writing — working with other people on a team to produce a proposal, report, website, blog, or other workplace communication. Like any team project, it requires the cooperation of people with different personalities and backgrounds working toward a common goal. Achieving the goal can be stressful but rewarding. This chapter describes the following classroom- and workplace-tested processes for successful collaboration:

On the job or in the classroom, no one works in a vacuum. To some degree, everyone must rely on the help of others to do his or her job. Collaborative writing typically occurs when two or more people work together, as a team, on a single writing project, with each team member contributing to the planning, designing, and writing. The teams that collaborate best are composed of people who are professionally competent, who have mutual respect for the abilities of the other members, and who are compatible enough to work together harmoniously toward a common goal. They also share equal responsibility for the end product.

Collaborative writing is generally done for one of three reasons:

1. The project requires expertise or specialization in more than one subject area.
2. The project will benefit from merging different perspectives into a unified perspective.
3. The size of the project, time constraints, or importance of the project to your organization requires a team effort.

The larger and more important the document, the more likely it is to be produced collaboratively. Sales and grant proposals, for example, often require contributions from many different types of experts (financial specialists, sales managers, systems analysts, engineers, lawyers, and so on). Formal reports, technical specifications, white papers, and journal articles in engineering and medicine are among other documents that are commonly written by teams. For collaborative writing projects, the writing process described throughout this text varies only by the addition of a team-review step; otherwise, the process itself is no different, consisting of planning, researching, writing, reviewing, and revising. In collaborative writing projects, typically one person edits the final draft for clarity and consistency and manages the reproduction and distribution, both online and in print, of the finished document.

Advantages and Disadvantages of Collaborative Writing

Collaborative writing offers many benefits.

- *Many minds are better than one.* Collaborative teams usually produce work that is considerably better than the work produced by any one member. Team members stimulate each other to consider ideas and perspectives different from those they would have explored individually.
- *Team members provide immediate feedback.* Collaborating is like having your own set of critics who have a personal stake in helping you do a good job. Even if it is sometimes contested and debated, feedback is one of the great advantages of collaborative writing. Fellow team members may detect problems with organization, clarity, logic, and substance — and point them out during review. Receiving multiple responses also makes criticism easier to accept; if all team members make the same point, you can more readily accept its validity.
- *Team members play devil's advocate for each other.* That is, they take contrary points of view in an attempt to make certain that all important points are covered and that all potential problems have been exposed and resolved.
- *Team members help each other past the frustrations and stress of writing.* When one team member needs to make a decision, someone is always available to talk it through.
- *Team members write more confidently.* Knowing that peers are depending on your contribution and will offer constructive criticism — not to find fault but to make the end product better — boosts confidence in what you produce.
- *Team members develop a greater tolerance of and respect for the opinions of others.* Team members become more aware of and involved in the planning of a document than if they were working alone. The same is true of reviews and revisions.

The primary disadvantages of collaborative writing include the demand it can place on your time, energy, and ego as a writer. Conflicts can also arise when not all team members participate or share equally in the team's work. Other difficulties can occur when team members are not in the same physical location (or even the same time zone). And unless the final document is edited for clarity and consistency, it will be difficult to read and possibly incorrect. These stresses and how to overcome them are discussed on pages 138–139.

Functions of a Collaborative Writing Team

Writing teams collaborate on every facet of the writing process:

- Planning the document
- Researching the subject
- Writing the draft
- Reviewing the drafts of other team members
- Revising the draft on the basis of comments from all team members

Planning

The team collectively identifies the readers, purpose, and scope of the project, whether it is a major proposal, investigative report, business plan, or environmental impact assessment. It then creates a broad outline of the document, divides the work into sections, and assigns each section to individual team members, usually on the basis of their subject expertise. Ideally, all team members gather around a conference table to plan the project. However, some team members will be separated from the others by miles or even continents. These members can participate in team meetings by speakerphone, videoconference, or online collaborative writing programs. Collaborative writing efforts should still follow these same general guidelines, but team participation may alter depending on the software you use and how you choose to caucus with others in the team.

In preliminary planning discussions, the team also produces a schedule for each stage of the project. The agreed-on schedule should include due dates for drafts, for team reviews of drafts, and for revisions. (Individual team members must plan how they will meet their assigned responsibilities.) The other team members will have the opportunity to comment on drafts and suggest improvements.

Selecting the Publication Medium

At this point, the team selects the media most appropriate for the finished document. Will the document be publicly available? If so, meet with the publications, Web, and social-media staffs to plan printing and web-coding time frames and public-release dates. In some cases, the document will also warrant a press release. If the document is for internal use only, arrange for it to be distributed to the appropriate officials and, if necessary, for its availability on the company's intranet.

Agreeing on Style Standards

As part of the planning process, the team should also agree on a standard reference guide for style and format, such as the *Publication Manual of the American*

Psychological Association or the *MLA Style Manual*. Because different members of the team are producing separate sections of the same document, the guidelines should provide for uniformity and consistency of style. Lacking a standard guide, the team should establish project style guidelines that address the following issues:

- Levels of headings and their style: all-capital letters, all underlined, first letter capitalized, boldfaced, italicized, or some combination of these
- Spacing and margin guidelines
- Research sources that must be cited and those that need not be cited
- Use of the active voice, the present tense, and the imperative mood
- Format for References or Works Cited (if they are used)
- Capitalization of words and abbreviations in the text (*A.M.* versus *a.m.*)
- Abbreviations, acronyms, and symbols
- Standards for terms that could be written as one word, two words, or hyphenated (*on site/onsite, e-mail/email, on-line/online*)
- Number standards (whether to spell out or use numerals)
- Units of measurement — to use the International System of Units (SI) or non-SI units
- Format for and placement of visuals, including organization-specific materials, like logos and seals
- Format and wording of disclaimers (to satisfy legal or policy requirements)

◆ ***Read pages 498–507 in Chapter 14, Giving Presentations and Conducting Meetings before calling your first meeting.***

To achieve document layout and format consistency, consider using style templates featured by your word-processing software (for example, for automated placement of headers, footers, table of contents listings, and more). (For additional information, see Digital Tip: Creating Styles and Templates for Informal Reports, page 339 of Chapter 10.)

◆ ***The revision strategies outlined in Chapter 4, Revising a Document, work well for most collaborative work.***

Collaborating Electronically

E-mail encourages members of a writing team to communicate with each other often, share information, ask questions, and solve problems. A draft sent as an attachment enables team members to solicit feedback electronically and revise the original draft based on comments received, until all sections are in final form and ready for consolidation into the master copy maintained by the team leader.

The team leader should require that each draft be identified with a revision number (for example, "merger proposal — rev 3") so that team members know they are commenting on the latest version. Although e-mail can reduce the frequency of face-to-face communication, it does not eliminate the need for a group to meet in person when possible, especially during project planning periods. If this isn't physically possible, consider making conference calls or using videoconferencing so that everyone can take part.

Collaborative writing software (CWS), like wikis, Google Drive, or company intranets, helps teams of students, employees, researchers, and others work together on a common writing task — whether in the same office or separated by great distances.

Collaborative writing software systems also make it easy to conduct live chat sessions for brainstorming ideas, to share documents with new collaborators, to track changes from one version of a document to the next, to alert collaborators when a document is altered, and to export documents for offline editing. Both CWS and word-processing systems also permit team members to draft, review, edit, and comment on one another's collective work as well as to add track changes in the text, a feature that permits readers to evaluate and accept or reject each change. Some systems allow reviewers to add voice annotations to the text to explain their comments in more detail.

DIGITAL TIP: Incorporating Tracked Changes

When colleagues review your document, they can "track" changes and insert comments within the document itself. Tracking and commenting vary with types and versions of word-processing programs, but in most programs you can view the document with all reviewers' edits and comments highlighted, or see the document as it would look if you accepted any changes made.

WRITER'S CHECKLIST

Planning a Collaborative Writing Project

- ✔ Establish guidelines to ensure that all team members are working toward the same goal.
- ✔ Agree on a standard reference guide for matters of style and format.
- ✔ Make sure that work assignments are appropriate to each person's subject-matter knowledge. Establish a schedule that includes due dates for drafts, for team reviews of drafts, and for revisions.
- ✔ Agree on how to exchange digital project files and whether to use collaborative writing software.

Research and Writing

The planning stage is followed by the research and writing stages. These are periods of intense independent activity by the individual team members. At this point, you gather and research information for your assigned segment of the document, create a master outline of the segment, flesh out the outline by providing the necessary details, and produce a first draft.

Collaboration requires flexibility. The team should not insist that individual members rigidly follow an agreed-on outline if it proves to be inadequate or faulty in one or more areas. For instance, a writer may find that the general outline for his or her segment was based on insufficient knowledge and is not appropriate, or even accurate, as written. During the research process, in particular, a writer may discover highly relevant

◆ *For guidelines on planning and writing a rough draft, see Chapter 2, Planning a Document, and Chapter 3, Drafting a Document.*

◆ *For a detailed explanation of the research process, see Chapter 6, Conducting Research for a Document.*

information that is not covered in the team's working outline. In such cases, the writer must have the freedom to alter the outline. If the deviation is great enough, or will change other parts of the document, the writer should consult the team leader before proceeding.

Revise your draft until it is as good as you can make it. Then, by the deadline established, send copies of the draft to all other team members for their review. You may circulate the draft by distributing hard copy, by sending an attachment through e-mail, or by sharing files in a collaborative writing system. Be sure to uniquely identify each draft before circulating it for comment. Collaborative writing systems automatically identify the author, revision number, and date and time a draft was completed. For other types of drafts, however, you must add unique file names.

PROFESSIONALISM NOTE: Meet Deadlines Deadlines must be met because team members rely on each other; one missed deadline can delay the entire project. A missed project deadline can also result in a lost opportunity or, in the case of a proposal, disqualify a submission. Team members must adjust their schedules and focus on their own part of the task to finish drafts, to consider other team member reviews, and to meet the overall project schedule.

When setting your document's file name and location, follow the recommendations and practices of your organization, but if none exist, construct file names beginning with the most general detail to the most specific detail. If your document is part of a larger category, consider beginning with the category and follow that with the specific section and date (c:\AnnualReport-Introduction-2016_Mar16.pdf). At the same time, work to achieve balance between providing enough detail to make finding the file as easy as possible, while avoiding providing so much detail that the file name becomes excessively and unworkably long. End with the version of the document, such as V2 to indicate a second revision or FinalDraft to indicate the final contribution.

WRITER'S CHECKLIST

Naming Files

- ✔ *Alphabetize documents.* Most collaborative-writing document-management systems default to alphabetical order, while easily allowing for other sorting or searching methods.
- ✔ *Order by using names and year.* Names should begin with the surname followed by the first initial or name (JohnsonS) and use the year, month, day order (2016_Oct23).
- ✔ *Construct file names beginning with the most general to specific detail.* However, keep in mind any naming conventions enforced by a document-management program.
- ✔ *Use capital letters, hyphens, underscore, and periods to divide sections within a file name.* Avoid spaces or other punctuation that could make your document inaccessible.
- ✔ *Strive for consistency.* Be aware of how existing files are saved and mimic the existing structure.

Review and Revision

During the review stage, each team member reviews the work of the other team members carefully and critically (but also with sensitivity to the person whose work is being reviewed), checking for problems in content, organization, and style. A good reviewer evaluates a document in terms of audience, purpose, coherence, emphasis, and accuracy. Team members also try to anticipate questions that might arise for a given reader — a customer, a senior official in the organization, or the board of directors, for example. For a document intended for an international audience, this is the stage to have it reviewed by someone familiar with the country or culture of that audience. (For a discussion of interacting productively with other members, see pages 138–139.)

The review stage may lead to additional planning. If, for example, a review of the first draft reveals that the original organization for a section was not adequate or correct or if new information becomes available, the team must return to the planning stage for that segment of the document to incorporate the newer knowledge and understanding.

Figures 5–1 on page 136 and 5–2 on page 137 represent one section of a proposal that was written by Brady Associates to persuade a prospective client to merge a company's profit-sharing plans. Two people collaborated to prepare the document; Figure 5–1 shows one team member's initial draft with the other's review comments and Figure 5–2 shows the revised section, addressing those draft comments. The proposal describes the merger process and shows its associated costs. Because the final report will be submitted to a company president whose time is limited and who has only a general knowledge of profit-sharing plans and mergers, the reviewer carefully noted any parts of the proposal that were not appropriate for a nonexpert reader.

◆ *For a discussion of writing for international audiences, see pages 74 of Chapter 3, Drafting a Document, and pages 320–323 of Chapter 9, Writing Routine and Sensitive Messages.*

Revising collaborative writing is much like revising any other type of writing: The writer considers suggested changes, checks questionable facts, and reworks the draft as appropriate. At this point, you, as a writer, must be careful not to let your ego get in the way of good judgment. Consider each suggestion objectively on the basis of its merit, rather than reacting negatively to criticism of your writing. Writers who are able to openly discuss and accept criticism and use it to craft a better draft contribute to the most productive kind of collaboration.

WRITER'S CHECKLIST
Reviewing Drafts by Other Writers

- ✔ Does it meet the established purpose of the document?
- ✔ Does it meet the needs of the target audience?
- ✔ Does the content fall within the planned scope of coverage?
- ✔ Does it generally follow the agreed-on outline?
- ✔ Is the content complete?
- ✔ Does it contain technical errors? Does anything seem technically questionable?
- ✔ Do details and examples support the main points?

Team members comment on need to clarify title, eliminate redundancy, and sharpen focus on topic.

****DRAFT****

Part II. Merger of Plans/Amending and Restating Plans/Applications for Determination Letters

Comment [EMK1]: Title is too technical —"Costs/Benefits of Merging"?

We can no longer test the Oakite product services 401(k) Profit Sharing Plan separately for coverage and nondiscrimination because combined, Oakite products and Oakley services have fewer than 50 employees. The merger of the 401(k) Profit Sharing Plans takes care of this problem while reducing the implementation and audit costs. We wil need to amend and restate the new plan to bring itinto compliance with tax law 409921-65.

Comment [WO2]: This is covered in Part I (make this into transition).

Comment [WO3]: sp

Comment [WO4]: #

The cost of merging, amending, restating, and redesigning the surviving 401(k) Profit Sharing Plan and for filing of notices 54-90 and 36-98 and applications 56-98 and 45-98 would be between $18,000 and $25,000.

Comment [EMK5]: Too technical and you need to emphasize benefits.

Comment [WO6]: Cost reduction over 2 years

Additional Comments: Team Member #2 (B. Reisner, Sales Development)

Information sounds correct, but the prospective client will need definitions and explanations for many terms and names (notices 54-90 and 36-98). Also I suggest noting in your opening that Part I explains the problems associated with maintaining separate plans. Doing so will give you a better lead into your section than you've got at this point.

Further, break down specific financial costs and benefits that will result from the merger. Don't go into detail here; remember, Part III describes the details of the merger process. Simply note specific costs for specific services in a table, and give an estimate of the client's projected financial gain. NOTE: The range for costs is $19,000 to $26,000, not $18,000 to $25,000. CHECK: Can client deduct merger costs from gross profit?

Finally, I think it would be good to promote our services with more vigor. You're not simply reporting information so that Mr. B. can phone up another company to do the merger — you're talking him into working with Brady Associates.

Figure 5–1 Draft Section of a Proposal, with Comments of a Team Member

PART II. BENEFITS AND COSTS OF MERGING CURRENT PROFIT-SHARING PLANS

Note new title

As Part I of this report explains, the separate profit-sharing plans for your two companies, Oakite Products and Oakley Services, can no longer ensure that each employee is assigned the correct number of shares and the correct employer contribution. In addition, administrative costs for maintaining separate plans are high. If you commissioned Brady Associates to merge the plans, however, adequate tests could be performed to ensure accuracy, and administrative costs would be greatly reduced. Further, although a merger would require you to make certain changes to your current profit-sharing procedures, Brady Associates would help you amend and restate the new plan so that it complies with the most recent tax legislation.

Introduction sharpens focus on problem and proposed solution

Brady Associates will also prepare and file necessary merger documents with the Departments of Taxation and Labor. The estimated cost for merging, amending, and refiling the profit-sharing plans would be between $19,000 and $26,000. Please see Table 1 for a breakdown of specific costs.

Second paragraph revised to clarify additional advantages of merging plans

Because of reduced administrative costs, you would in reality incur no cost if Brady Associates merged your profit-sharing plans. According to our estimates, the merger would give you a yearly net reduction of $36,000 in administrative costs. Thus, you would save approximately $11,000 during the first year of administering the plan and at least $36,000 annually after the first year. See Table 2 for a breakdown of net reductions in administrative costs.

Strengthens case for Brady's services by including specific expenses and savings

Figure 5–2 Revised Section of Draft Proposal in Figure 5–1

DIGITAL TIP: Using Word Processing to Review Collaborative Documents

Adobe Acrobat and many word-processing packages have options for adding comments on draft documents. You can add text or voice annotations to the text, allowing your readers to read or hear your comments; you can also add track changes in your text and allow readers to accept or reject each change. In Acrobat, you can use a drawing tool to input traditional proofreaders' marks.

WRITER'S CHECKLIST
Writing Collaboratively

- ✔ Designate one person as the team coordinator.
- ✔ Identify the audience, purpose, context, and scope of the project.
- ✔ Create a project plan, including a schedule and style or format standards.
- ✔ Create a working outline of the document.
- ✔ Assign sections or tasks to each team member.
- ✔ Research and write drafts of each document section.
- ✔ Use the agreed-upon standards for style and format.
- ✔ Exchange sections for team member reviews.
- ✔ Revise sections as needed.
- ✔ Meet the established deadlines for drafts, revisions, and final versions.

The Role of Conflict in Collaborative Writing

It is critically important to the quality of any team-written document that all contributors' viewpoints be considered. However, when writers collaborate, conflicts can occur. These may range from a relatively minor difference over a grammatical point (such as whether to split an infinitive) to a major argument over the basic approach to a document (such as how much detail is necessary). Regardless of the severity of a conflict, it must be worked through to a conclusion or compromise that all team members can accept, even though all might not entirely agree. When a group can tolerate some disharmony and work through conflicting opinions to reach a consensus, the final document benefits.

Although mutual respect among team members is necessary, too much deference can inhibit challenges — which reduces the team's creativity. You have to be willing to challenge another team member's work while still being sensitive to that person's ego. The same rule applies to collaborative writing whenever critical give-and-take occurs: Focus on the problem and how to solve it rather than on the person.

Conflicts over valid issues almost always generate more innovative and creative work than does passive acceptance. However, even though the result of conflict in a peer-writing team is usually positive, it can sometimes produce doubt about you or your team members. Remember that conflict is a natural part of group work. Learn to harness it and turn it into a positive force.

To maximize the benefits and minimize the negative effects of conflict, team members should emphasize areas of agreement. They then should identify differences of opinion and ask why they exist. If differences occur over facts, simply determine which are or are not correct. If there is a problem of differing goals, review the project's purpose statement to ensure common understanding. When conflict arises for other reasons, define the problem, describe or brainstorm possible solutions, and select the one solution — or compromise — that best satisfies the views of each team member and of the overall team.

PROFESSIONALISM NOTE: Manage Conflict with Proven Strategies The following suggestions can help you manage conflict:

- Avoid taking a win-or-lose stand, which gains one person's victory at another person's expense. This approach is not constructive because, by definition, there must be a loser. Most conflicts don't start out this way, but when a team member faces personal defeat, reaching a productive compromise is almost impossible. It might also discourage that team member from contributing as freely in the future.
- Avoid accusations, threats, or disparaging comments. Instead, emphasize common interests and mutual goals, bearing in mind that conciliation fosters cooperation. Expressing a desire for harmonious relations can have a very disarming effect on an aggressive personality in the group.
- Support your position with facts. Show how your position is consistent with precedent, prevailing norms, or accepted standards (if true, of course). Point out the ways that your position could benefit the team's ultimate goal and tactfully point out any disadvantages or logic errors in the other person's point of view. Again, focus on the problem and its solution, not on the person.

- Use bargaining strategies to exchange concessions until a compromise is reached. Both parties win through a compromise. Even if you settle for less than you initially wanted, you don't risk losing out altogether as in a win-or-lose struggle. A successful compromise satisfies each participant's minimum needs.

Used well, collaboration resolves conflicts. Each team member must accept the group's goals, and all must work to achieve the best outcome for the team. A flexible, exploratory attitude is a prerequisite for collaboration; always strive to understand each other's points of view and meet the group's goals.

WRITER'S CHECKLIST
Working in a Collaborative Group

- ✔ Know the people on your team and establish a good working rapport with them.
- ✔ Put the interests of your team ahead of your own.
- ✔ Think collectively, as a group, but respect the views of members with subject-area expertise.
- ✔ Participate constructively in group meetings.
- ✔ Be an effective listener (see pages 495–497 in Chapter 14, Giving Presentations).
- ✔ Be receptive to constructive criticism.
- ✔ Provide constructive feedback to your team members.
- ✔ Meet your established deadlines.

Leading a Collaborative Writing Team

Although the team may designate one person as its leader, that person shares decision-making authority with the others while assuming the responsibility for coordinating the team's activities, organizing the project, and producing the final product. Leadership can be granted by mutual agreement to one team member or it can be rotated if the team produces many documents over time.

On a practical level, the team leader's responsibilities include scheduling and leading meetings, writing and distributing minutes of meetings, selecting the tools the team will use (from Web meeting or CWS, to e-mail and word-processing options), and maintaining the master copy of the document during all stages of its development. To make these activities as efficient as possible, the leader should prepare and distribute forms to track the project's status. These forms should include style guidelines mutually agreed to in the project planning meeting (covering the issues listed on page 132), a project schedule, and transmittal sheets to record the status of reviews. Collaborative writing software systems usually include a variety of features for tracking the status of writing projects: a calendar for posting due dates, identifiers for each team member, and time and date stamps and unique revision numbers for all drafts.

Schedule

◆ *For guidance on creating project-tracking graphs, called Gantt charts, see page 233 in Chapter 7, Designing Documents and Visuals.*

All team members must know not only what is expected of them but also when it is expected. The schedule provides this information. Schedules come in different formats. Figure 5-3, for example, shows a schedule used for a class project for a business-writing class. Figure 5-4 shows a bar-chart schedule for the production of a software user's manual that required coordination among the writing, review, and production staffs over a five-month period. Regardless of the format, the schedule must state explicitly who is responsible for what and when the draft of each section is due.

Review Transmittal Sheet

If drafts will be circulated on paper, as is common in small companies and consulting firms, the team leader should provide review transmittal sheets. Writers attach the sheets to their drafts or to a file folder or an envelope that holds the draft. Each reviewer signs off after reviewing the draft and then distributes it to the next reviewer on the list. The review transmittal sheet shows at a glance where the project is in its progression through the review cycle. It also lists in order those who must review the draft, as shown in Figure 5-5 on page 142.

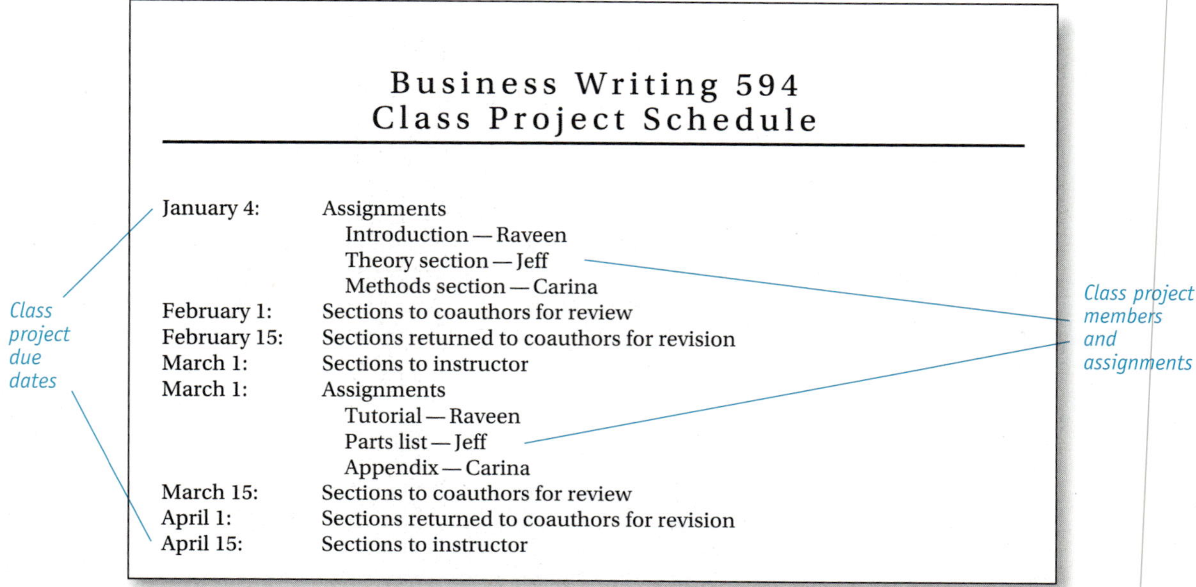
Business Writing 594
Class Project Schedule

January 4:	Assignments Introduction — Raveen Theory section — Jeff Methods section — Carina
February 1:	Sections to coauthors for review
February 15:	Sections returned to coauthors for revision
March 1:	Sections to instructor
March 1:	Assignments Tutorial — Raveen Parts list — Jeff Appendix — Carina
March 15:	Sections to coauthors for review
April 1:	Sections returned to coauthors for revision
April 15:	Sections to instructor

Figure 5–3 Class Project Schedule

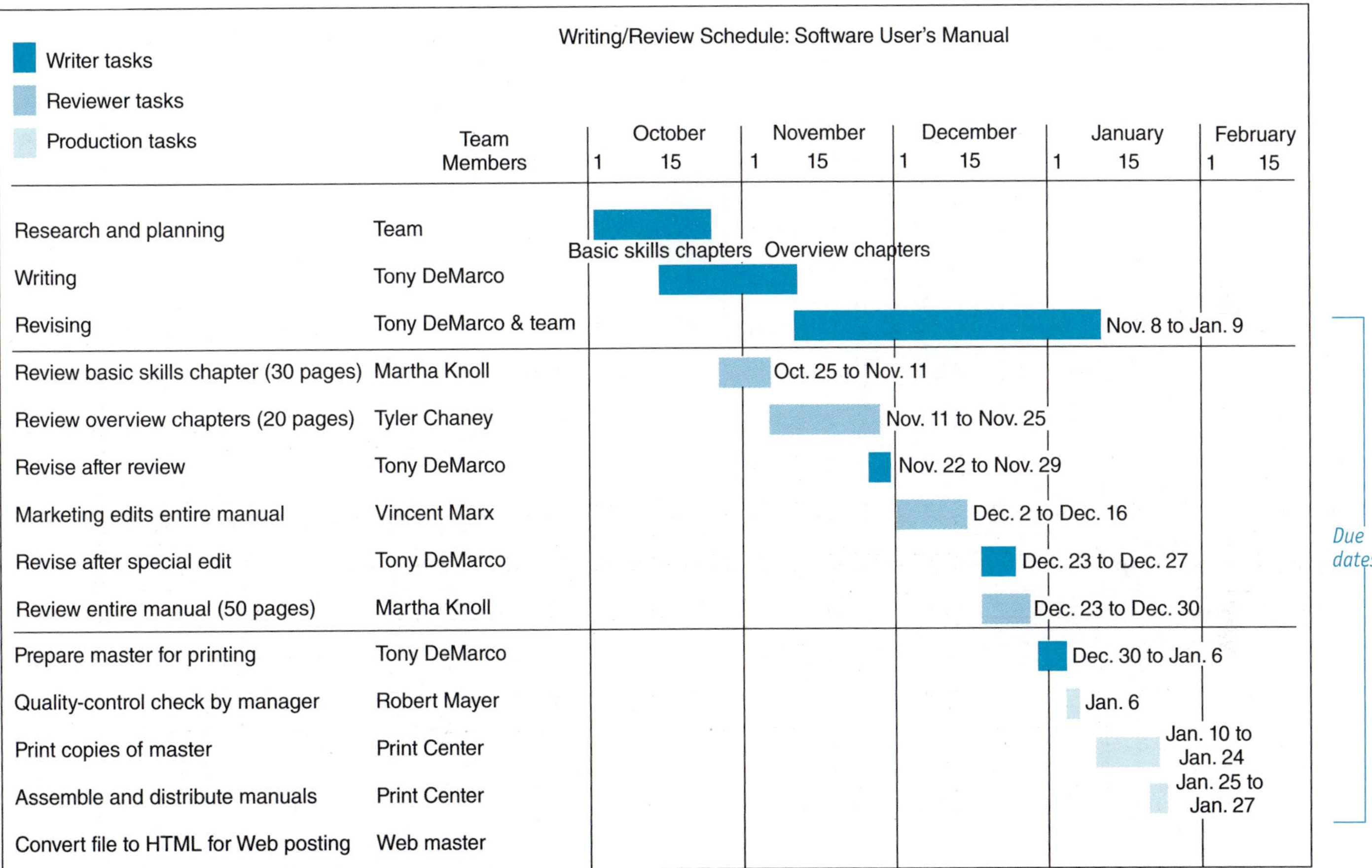

Figure 5–4 Class Project Schedule Presented as a Gantt Chart (Workplace Project)

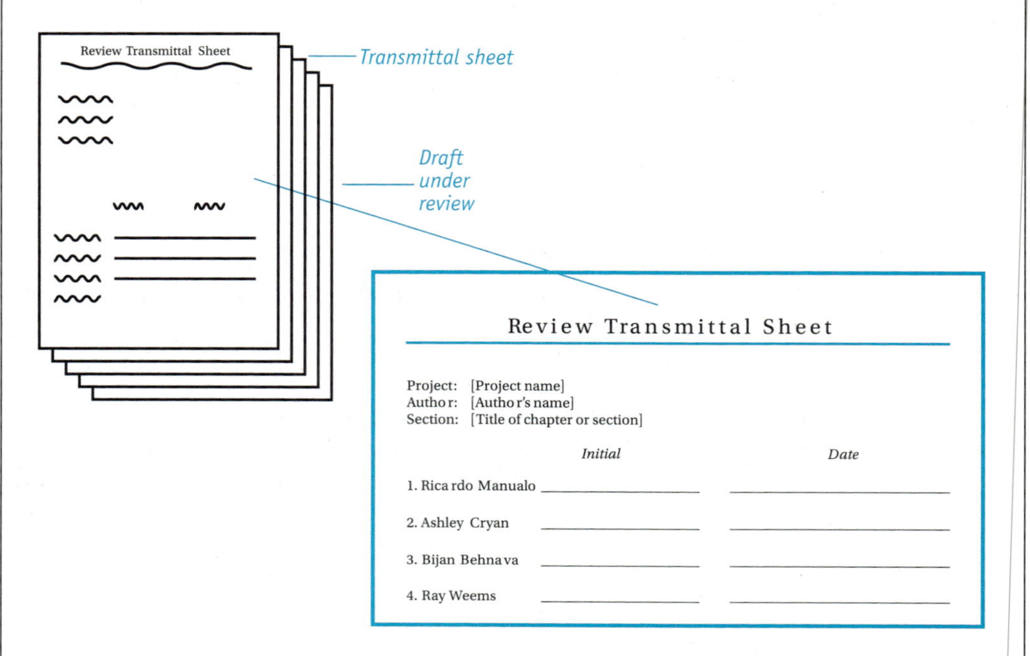

Figure 5–5 Review Transmittal Sheet Attached to a Draft

DIGITAL TIP: Online Transmittal Sheets

Online transmittal sheets provide easy access for the whole team. They can range from simple to-do lists, like those found at www.rememberthemilk.com, to shared reminders on Microsoft Outlook, to more complicated project software like Basecamp (http://basecamphq.com).

Collaborating with Other Departments

In some work settings, writing-team leaders also arrange for the cooperation of different departments within the organization in the creation and publication of their final documents. For example, the team leader may need to meet with art, social media, or media production staff to do the following:

- Plan for the creation of graphs, charts, drawings, maps, or other visuals.
- Plan for design of the document's cover.

- Arrange for photographs to be taken or scanned.
- Determine the date and file format for posting the document to the organization's website and for highlighting its content on the organization's social-media platforms.

The team leader may also meet with print production staff or an off-site printer to do the following:

- Inform the staff or the printer when to expect the manuscript.
- Discuss any special printing requirements, such as color, special binding, document size, foldout pages, and so on.
- Ensure that the publication date meets the project deadline.

In addition, the team leader may need to obtain reviews and approval from other departments, such as the sales, legal, and public-affairs departments. (In the classroom, your instructor or group team leader may take these roles.)

◆ ***For guidance on posting documents to websites, see Appendix A, Writing in an Online Environment.***

CHAPTER 5 SUMMARY: COLLABORATING ON A DOCUMENT

Form a collaborative writing team when:

- Your project requires specialists in more than one subject area.
- Your project would benefit from the merging of different perspectives.
- Your project's size, importance, or deadline requires a team effort.

As a member of a collaborative writing team, you are expected to:

- Work with others as a team of peers to plan, research, and write a single document.
- Research the topics of your assigned section.
- Write your draft.
- Revise your draft based on comments from other team members.
- Review the work of other team members.
- Adhere to the project schedule.
- Share equal responsibility for the end product.
- Respect the opinions of others.

As a team leader, you are expected to:

- Share decision-making authority with other team members.
- Coordinate the activity of team members.
- Maintain the project schedule.
- Solicit legal, policy, or similar reviews before publication.
- Coordinate production (web, print, other) of the final product.

Exercises

1. Schedule a telephone, an e-mail, an online (such as through a social-networking site), or a personal interview with a health-care, a business, a technology, or an industry representative who is part of a collaborative writing team. Before the interview, review this chapter to help you prepare a list of questions to ask about details of the collaborative writing style used by his or her group or company. Keep your telephone or face-to-face interview to no more than 20 to 30 minutes or to two or three e-mails, depending on the type of interview. Consider asking about planning meetings and how they are conducted, collaboration with other specialists or peer reviewers, preparing drafts of documents and how they are circulated and commented on for revision, and any positive or negative experiences your interviewee found most helpful during the collaborative writing process. After the interview, prepare an outline, a draft, and a final report on your findings. Be ready to share your interview report with your classmates, and send the person you interviewed a thank-you letter.
2. Form a collaborative writing team with your classmates based on common occupational interests, such as agriculture, nursing, early childhood education, or engineering. Assume that you have been asked by your university's recruiting staff to create a document based on your experience as a student, explaining why your campus is a great place to prepare for the occupational interest you and your team have chosen. In your group, appoint a team leader and a team record keeper, and decide how to organize and write this assignment so that recruiters can use your material to persuade students to attend your university.
3. Collaborate with a classmate to develop a process that your class can follow to review and comment on each other's written work. Before you begin, review this chapter. Then create an outline and a rough draft for a plan that facilitates peer feedback. Highlight the specific benefits of your plan and be ready to share your plan with the rest of the class.
4. Form a collaborative group of no more than six members in which (if possible) both genders are represented equally. Appoint a group leader and a group recorder. Based on your personal experiences, brainstorm as a group to create a list of gender-related issues that you have encountered as college students, such as the stereotyping of women and men with regard to verbal or mathematical abilities or technological skills. Use your collaborative lists to generate a brief report about these campus gender issues for your college's Office of Diversity (or comparable unit) that includes the ideas of each group member. Be ready to share your report with the rest of the class or write an individual report, summarizing the personal interactions of your group during your meetings.

Collaborative Classroom Projects

1. An important stage of the collaborative writing process is the planning stage, during which time all members of the team need to work toward the same goal, select a reference guide, set up a schedule, and agree on how to enforce the standards that have been established. Assume that your manager has given you a collaborative writing assignment on a topic specific to the company's main product. In groups of five or fewer, take the next 30 minutes to do the following:

a. Become acquainted with one another's expertise by asking each person to talk about his or her background for two minutes or less.
b. Select a team leader.
c. Decide the schedule for making initial assignments and for submitting drafts, coauthor reviews, and revisions.
d. Decide what method you will use to enforce the time line.
e. Decide what other guidelines are necessary to ensure the group's success. Keep in mind that unstated policies can lead to confusion about responsibilities; therefore, when your group has agreed on project guidelines, the team leader will summarize these policies in a list.

2. Imagine that several of you have been hired as a collaborative writing team for a national home decor and architecture magazine. This magazine has won awards for its high-end presentation of celebrity homes and parties, but its senior editor and upper management have recently been lured away by a competing publication. The last two issues have suffered as new hires and interns struggle to come up with successful story ideas, coordinate celebrity interviews and photo shoots, get error-free copy from advertisers and freelance writers on time, coordinate with the graphics department so that the issues are laid out properly, and meet the printer's deadlines. The magazine publisher is very worried about the upcoming holiday issue, which is usually popular with readers and advertisers.

   Magazines typically have a six-month lead time. For example, December magazine articles are assigned to writers in July. Choose someone to be team leader, then, using Figures 5–3, 5–4, and 5–5, create a schedule and transmittal sheets for the holiday issue. Decide on the final production deadline (when everything is ready to go to the printer) and then individual production deadlines for the following:

   a. Help the editorial staff determine all of the copy (written material) that will be included in the issue, the dates freelance and staff writers need to start writing the copy, and the copy deadlines (make the copy due at least six weeks before the production due date). Don't forget to include the time the editorial staff will need to edit the copy and fact check it. Create a Review Transmittal Sheet (see Figure 5–5) to ensure that all the editors, proofreaders, and fact checkers have reviewed the drafts. Check with your instructor about online tools that would be suitable for this assignment.
   b. Help advertising staff determine the number of ads for this issue and make the ads due at least seven weeks before the production due date. Then help the graphics staff determine when they need to have the artwork for the ads (display artwork) completed (no more than a week or two after the ads come in). Remember to have the artwork and ads proofread by members of the editorial staff.
   c. Help the graphics staff schedule the time needed to lay out the entire magazine and then have it proofread by members of the editorial staff to make sure that everything was included in the issue and that copy or ads weren't accidentally forgotten.

Research Projects

1. Form a collaborative writing team to research and write a major report for a department manager, recommending the purchase of tablet computers for traveling staff. In your proposal, identify the type and brand of computer you will be evaluating, as well

as how and where you will gather information on the product (in person at a retail location, on the Internet, and so on).

a. Decide on a team leader and an evaluation board, then do the following:
   - Write a memo requesting your instructor's approval for your team to undertake the project and to evaluate specific tablet brands and models.
   - Create biweekly progress reports, to start as soon as your team has received project approval and to continue for the duration of the project.

b. Have the team leader delegate research responsibilities so that members are able to collect information that answers why the computers are needed and how many are needed; describe the specific features the tablet computers should have (such as memory size, operating speed, and compatibility with desktop computers already installed at the company); describe the types of software that should be installed; define what the total cost will be and whether an educational discount or a quantity discount is available; and explain how the computers should be kept secure and how borrowing them would be controlled.

c. Decide collaboratively on dates for submission of the proposal, progress reports (every two weeks from project approval), the final report, and the final presentation.

d. Present an oral description of your research to the other team members, as well as a report on the results of your preliminary evaluation. Each team member should do the same.

e. Have the team leader present the final results of the project and the recommendations to an evaluation board.

f. Prepare and submit a joint (single) copy of the proposal, progress reports, and formal report, and make group oral presentations. Provide handouts of any printed information you have obtained or of any important text from your proposal (see page 487 in Chapter 14, Giving Presentations). As a team, consider how much the visual appearance of your report will influence whether your recommendations receive approval. If the department manager likes what he or she reads, your report may be attached to his or her budget request to demonstrate why the computers are needed (this is commonly known as "the justification"). Consequently, the quality of your report, both in appearance and in content, can help convince those readers who will approve the expenditure for your request. Your instructor will award a group mark for each assignment, which all team members will receive.[1]

2. Teamwork is used in corporations around the globe. On your own or with a collaborative writing team, research at least two countries' perspectives on the need for teamwork in the workplace. Compare those perspectives with the American perspective on teamwork in the workplace. Present your findings to the class. As your instructor directs, use some of the strategies from earlier collaborative writing assignments.

3. One of the major experts in teamwork and corporate success is W. E. Deming, who created total quality management (TQM). Form a collaborative group. Then research and write a report about Deming and TQM. The presentation should consist of an introduction and a conclusion and the following three parts that form the middle of the report:

---

[1]This project is adapted, with permission, from "An Integrated Collaborative Writing Project" by Ron S. Blicq, in *Collaborative Technical Writing: Theory and Practice,* ed. Richard Louth and Martin Scott (Hammond, LA: Association of Teachers of Technical Writing, n.d.), pp. 57–60.

a. A definition and an explanation of TQM, with background on the history of TQM and its creator.
b. An explanation of TQM's 14 principles and how TQM supports teamwork. Give examples of why companies like General Motors have used or continue to use TQM.
c. An explanation of both the positive and the negative issues that need to be addressed regarding TQM or other teamwork programs. One might be that people from different cultures may have different problems adapting to teamwork. For example, many Americans value individualism, which may at times conflict with teamwork principles.

4. Many successful companies encourage collaborative writing on the job. Search the Web to learn how such companies advertise their team approach when hiring. You might explore the job listings on websites for companies such as Google and the Kimberly-Clark Corporation, as well as the job descriptions on career sites such as Monster.com and Indeed.com. Outline the kinds of collaborative writing assignments that a writer at a particular company might encounter. Your outline should cover areas such as product information, warranty information, employment training, management styles, and so on.

6 Conducting Research for a Document

Contents

This chapter discusses tools, strategies, and resources for researchers of various levels of expertise.

Tom Cabines, production manager of Nebel Desktop Publishers, received an e-mail from Alice Enklend, purchasing director, asking him how many copies of an employee manual a corporate customer had commissioned the firm to print. Tom probably had the answer at his fingertips or was able to find it after a quick look at his intranet invoicing program. Tom's *research* — or tracking down of information on the topic — would be minimal.

Suppose, instead, that Tom were asked to write a market-research report for the president of Nebel about moving the company's working and archived files off-site to a cloud computing account. Would doing so save money? compromise security and confidentiality? free computer technology staff for other tasks? provide emergency backup? How would Tom go about obtaining the necessary information? For this task, he would have to do some extensive work, which could involve primary research — conducting interviews or even collecting questionnaire responses on the topic — or secondary research — gathering published information from the Internet, attending a webinar, reviewing blogs, and the like.

Conducting Primary Research: Experience, Interviews, Observations, and Questionnaires

Primary research is the gathering of raw data from such sources as firsthand experience, interviews with experts, direct observations of activities, and questionnaires to specific populations. In fact, direct observation and interaction are the only ways to obtain certain kinds of information, such as human and animal behavior, natural phenomena, and the operation of systems and equipment. For example, you might use primary research to test the usability of instructions you have created to submit quarterly financial data to an updated spreadsheet system. You can also conduct primary research on the Internet by participating in discussion groups and online forums, by attending Webinars, and by using e-mail to request information from people knowledgeable in your area of interest.

In college, you may talk about resources with other students, your instructors, and especially a research librarian. On the job, you may rely on your own knowledge and experience and that of your colleagues, in addition to the Internet. Other primary sources of workplace information include marketing data, questionnaire and survey results, focus-group opinions, shareholder meetings, and the like. In this setting, begin by brainstorming with colleagues about what sources will be most useful for your project and how you can find them.

Beginning with Your Experience

If your research topic deals with something familiar (a hobby or a voluntary activity, for example) or relates to an occupation you are in or hope to be in, you may already know enough to get started. You can also check your home or office files for any materials you have acquired on the subject and, importantly, how much you need to find out. Based on this background, make a rough outline — it will reveal how much you already know about the topic. Use the outline as a starting point from which to expand your knowledge by locating and using other sources discussed in this chapter.

◆ *For additional guidance on brainstorming, see pages 8–9 in Chapter 1, Understanding the Workplace Writing Context: A Case Study.*

◆ *For detailed advice on using outlines, see pages 32–36 in Chapter 2, Planning a Document.*

Interviewing for Information

To learn from the knowledge and experience of others, interview an expert on the subject where you work or elsewhere. Frequently, the interview involves asking a few questions of a colleague in person or by e-mail. For scheduled, sit-down interviews, first determine the proper person to interview, then prepare for the interview, determine the best medium to use, conduct the interview, and expand your notes immediately after the interview.

Determining Whom to Interview

Many times, your subject or purpose logically points to the proper person to interview for information. If, for instance, you were writing a feasibility report about marketing consumer products in India, you would seek out business people with such experience. Without an obvious source of information, use the following sources to identify an appropriate expert: (1) workplace colleagues or faculty in relevant academic departments, (2) a local firm or organization whose staff includes experts on your subject, (3) information from Internet research, and (4) local chapters or websites of professional societies.

PROFESSIONALISM NOTE: Explain the Purpose of Your Interview When you contact the prospective interviewee, explain who you are, why you would like the interview, the subject and purpose of the interview, and generally how much time it will take. Ask permission if you plan to record the interview and let the interviewee know that you will allow him or her to review your draft.

Even if geography or scheduling prevents you from interviewing an expert in person, you may be able to conduct a telephone or an e-mail interview. To locate an expert's telephone number or e-mail address, check company, organization, or university websites, which often include staff directories with contact information. Many scholarly publications, particularly in engineering and the sciences, include the author's e-mail address; these addresses are often available in specialized library databases as well. To locate these sources, contact a reference librarian.

PROFESSIONALISM NOTE: Save Time by Conducting an E-mail Interview When you are sending questions by e-mail, be as concise and informative as possible in the subject line. Send the request from your school or work e-mail account to avoid the impression that your request is spam, and do not include any attachments. In the body of your message, briefly describe your purpose, write out a few questions, and ask your expert for a referral if he or she is unable to respond. Above all, remember that the person you're writing to is not obligated to answer your e-mail. To improve your chances of a reply, be brief, clear, and respectful.

Preparing for the Interview

After you have made the appointment for the interview, prepare a list of questions for your interviewee and send it before the meeting. Avoid vague, general questions such as "Does the Internet help your business?" Instead, ask specific but open-ended questions such as "Has your company's blog improved communications with your customers?" or "Do your website's usage statistics help focus your organization's marketing strategies?" Such questions prompt interviewees to provide specific information.

Organize your questions so that you begin with the least complex aspects of the topic, then move to the more complex aspects.

ETHICS NOTE: Do Not Misquote or Misrepresent Your Interviewees Aim for accuracy as you take notes to avoid misrepresenting or misquoting your source. Do not surprise the interviewee by setting up a recorder. Obtain the interviewee's permission to do so beforehand. Also let your interviewee know that you will allow him or her to review your draft if possible given your deadline.

Conducting the Interview

Arrive for your interview on time and be prepared to guide the discussion. Once you've introduced yourself, take a few minutes to chat informally—this will help both you and your interviewee to relax. During the interview, follow the guidelines listed in the Writer's Checklist: Interviewing Successfully.

See also pages 495–497 about effective listening in Chapter 14, Giving Presentations.

WRITER'S CHECKLIST
Interviewing Successfully

- ✔ Be pleasant but purposeful. You are there to get information, so don't be timid about asking focused questions on the subject.
- ✔ Start with the list of questions you have prepared, beginning with the less complex or controversial topics to get the conversation started and then moving on to the more complex or controversial topics.
- ✔ Let your interviewee do most of the talking. Remember that he or she is the expert.
- ✔ Be objective. Don't offer your opinions on the subject unless you think a follow-up question would elicit more helpful information from the interviewee. Some answers will prompt additional questions, so ask them as they arise.
- ✔ Stay on track. If the interviewee strays too far from the subject, ask a specific question to redirect the conversation.
- ✔ Be flexible. If a prepared question is no longer suitable, or has already been answered, move to the next question.
- ✔ When recording the interview, do not let it lull you into relaxing so that you neglect to ask crucial questions. Take brief, memory-jogging notes even as you record the interview. Doing so will promote active listening and draw your attention to questions that still need to be addressed.
- ✔ As the interview comes to a close, take a few minutes to skim your notes. If time allows, ask the interviewee to clarify anything that is ambiguous. After thanking the interviewee, ask if you can telephone or e-mail with a follow-up query to clarify a point or two as you complete your interview notes.

Expanding Your Notes After the Interview

Immediately after leaving the interview, use your memory-jogging comments to help you mentally go over the interview and record your detailed notes. Review your comments, fill in any material that is obviously missing, and summarize the speaker's remarks. Do not postpone this step. No matter how good your memory is, you will forget some important points if you do not do this at once. As soon as possible, convert the notes to complete sentences. Select the important information you need and transfer it to your outline or working draft.

A day or two after the interview, thank the interviewee in a brief e-mail message.

Observing Firsthand

◆ *For more on usability testing, see pages 417–418 in Chapter 12, Writing Instructions.*

Visiting a location and conducting firsthand observations may provide valuable information about how a process or procedure works or how a group interacts. If you are planning research that involves observation, choose your sites and times carefully, and be sure to obtain permission in advance. During your observations, remain as unobtrusive as possible and keep accurate, complete records that indicate date, time of day, duration of the observation, and so on. Save interpretations of your observations for future analysis.

ETHICS NOTE: Obtain Institutional Review Board Approval When Appropriate
If you are conducting an observation or distributing a questionnaire at your university or college, ask your instructor whether you need to file an application with your school's institutional review board (IRB). An IRB reviews all research studies that involve humans and animals. A review may be necessary if you plan to present or publish the results of your research, but it may not be required for an in-class project.

Using a Questionnaire

Consider expanding the number of people you gather information from beyond those you've interviewed by using a questionnaire — a series of questions on a particular topic, sent to a number of people you believe will best represent your target audience. It has several advantages over the personal interview, as well as several disadvantages.

Advantages

- You can gather information from more people more quickly than you could through personal interviews.
- You can obtain responses from people in scattered geographical locations.
- Respondents have more time to think through their answers than they would under the pressure of composing thoughtful and complete answers in an interview.
- Questionnaires may yield more objective data because it reduces the possibility that the interviewer's tone of voice or facial expressions might influence an answer.
- The cost of distributing and tabulating a questionnaire — online or on paper — is lower than the cost of conducting numerous personal interviews.
- Online questionnaire results can be tabulated quickly, offering near-immediate results.

Disadvantages

- The results of a questionnaire may be slanted in favor of those people who have strong opinions on a subject because they are more likely to respond than those with only moderate views.
- Even if a questionnaire is designed to let one question lead logically to another, the questionnaire may not allow follow-up to specific answers. However, some online questionnaires can be customized to ask follow-up questions when, for example, responders give a product or service a low rating. The follow-up question may appear: "Please choose one or more of the following reasons listed for your rating."

- Recipients may not respond to your questionnaire in time to meet your deadline.
- Some survey populations may have limited Internet access or English fluency.

Selecting Questionnaire Recipients

Selecting the proper recipients for your questionnaire is crucial if you are to gather representative and usable data. If you wanted to survey the opinions of large groups in the general population — for example, all medical technologists working in private laboratories or all independent garage owners — your task would not be easy. Because you cannot include everybody in your survey, you need to choose a representative cross section — for example, include enough people from around the country, of both genders, and with varied educational training. Only then could you make a generalized statement based on your findings from the sample. (The best sources of information on sampling techniques are market-research and statistics texts.)

PROFESSIONALISM NOTE: Protecting Respondent Confidentiality Follow your company's policy or applicable laws in requesting information about the respondent's age, gender, occupation, or other privacy information. Include such information only if it will be of value in interpreting the answers. Also be clear about whether the respondent's identity and any information the respondent provides will be kept confidential.

Preparing and Designing Your Questionnaire

Keep the questionnaire as brief as possible. The longer it is, the less likely the recipient will complete and return it. Next, create questions that are easy to understand. Recipients should be able to answer most questions with a "yes" or "no" or by checking or circling a choice among several options. Such answers are simple to tabulate and require minimum effort to complete, thus increasing your chances of obtaining a response.

> Do you recommend that the flextime program be made permanent?
>
> ❑ Strongly agree ❑ Agree ❑ No opinion ❑ Disagree ❑ Strongly disagree

If you need more information than such questions produce, provide an appropriate range of answers:

> How many hours of overtime would you be willing to work each week?
>
> ❑ 4 hours ❑ 8 hours ❑ More than 10 hours
>
> ❑ 6 hours ❑ 10 hours ❑ No overtime

ETHICS NOTE: Do Not Skew Questions Questions should be neutral; their wording should not lead respondents to give a particular answer, which can result in inaccurate or skewed data.

SLANTED	Would you prefer the freedom of a four-day workweek?
NEUTRAL	Would you choose to work a four-day workweek, ten hours a day, with every Friday off?

You can access a variety of online questionnaire-generating programs, such as Survey Monkey, Survey Gizmo, and more. To locate them, type "survey-generating programs" into your search engine.

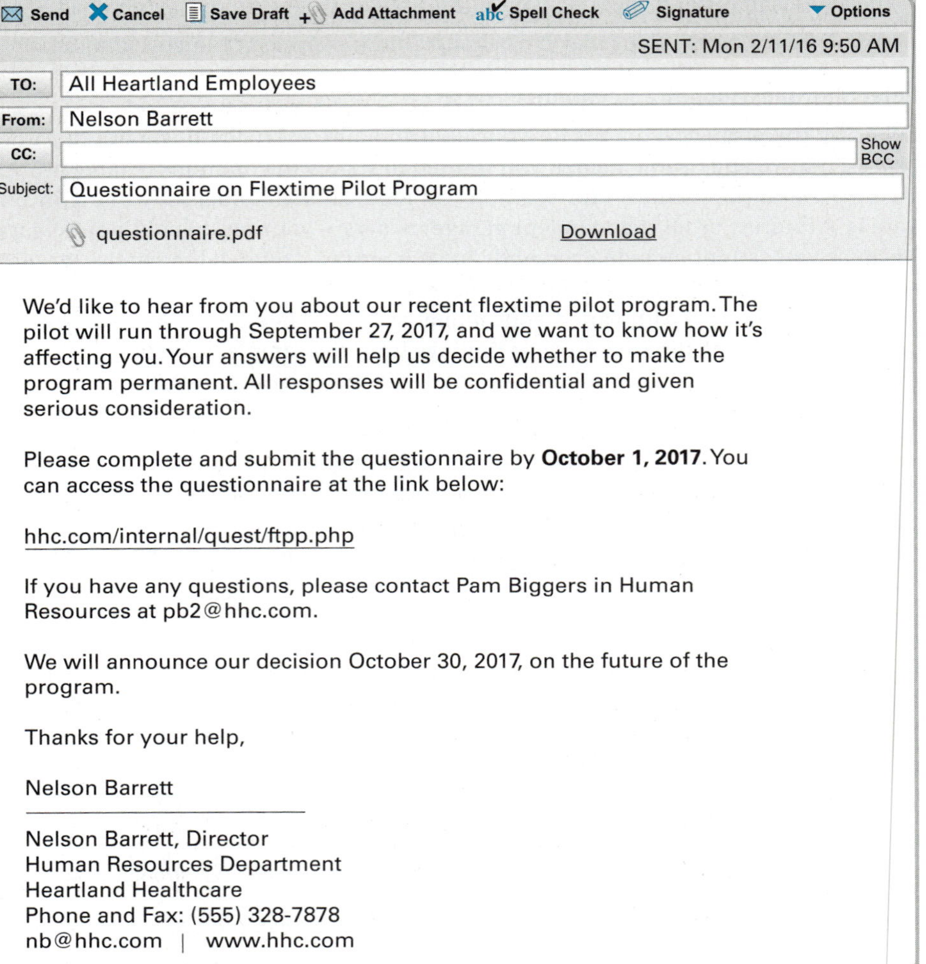

Send | Cancel | Save Draft | Add Attachment | Spell Check | Signature | Options

SENT: Mon 2/11/16 9:50 AM

TO: All Heartland Employees
From: Nelson Barrett
CC:
Subject: Questionnaire on Flextime Pilot Program

questionnaire.pdf Download

We'd like to hear from you about our recent flextime pilot program. The pilot will run through September 27, 2017, and we want to know how it's affecting you. Your answers will help us decide whether to make the program permanent. All responses will be confidential and given serious consideration.

Please complete and submit the questionnaire by **October 1, 2017**. You can access the questionnaire at the link below:

hhc.com/internal/quest/ftpp.php

If you have any questions, please contact Pam Biggers in Human Resources at pb2@hhc.com.

We will announce our decision October 30, 2017, on the future of the program.

Thanks for your help,

Nelson Barrett

Nelson Barrett, Director
Human Resources Department
Heartland Healthcare
Phone and Fax: (555) 328-7878
nb@hhc.com | www.hhc.com

Figure 6–1 Questionnaire Cover E-mail Message

The sample cover e-memo and link to a questionnaire in Figures 6–1 and 6–2 were sent to employees who had participated in a large organization's six-month pilot program of flexible working hours.

Questionnaire

Heartland Healthcare **Flexible Working Hours Program**

Questionnaire

1. **What kind of position do you occupy?**
   - ☐ Supervisory
   - ☐ Nonsupervisory

2. **Indicate to the nearest quarter of an hour when you begin work under flextime.**
   - ☐ 7:00 a.m.
   - ☐ 7:15 a.m.
   - ☐ 7:30 a.m.
   - ☐ 7:45 a.m.
   - ☐ 8:00 a.m.
   - ☐ 8:15 a.m.
   - ☐ 8:30 a.m.
   - ☐ 8:45 a.m.
   - ☐ 9:00 a.m.
   - ☐ Other (specify) ______

3. **Where do you live?**
   - ☐ Talbot County
   - ☐ Montgomery County
   - ☐ Greene County
   - ☐ Other (specify) ______

4. **How do you usually travel to work?**
   - ☐ Drive alone
   - ☐ Bus
   - ☐ Train
   - ☐ Bicycle
   - ☐ Walk
   - ☐ Carpool
   - ☐ Motorcycle
   - ☐ Other (specify) ______

5. **How has flextime affected your commuting time?**
   - ☐ Increase: Approximate number of minutes ______
   - ☐ Decrease: Approximate number of minutes ______
   - ☐ No change

6. **If you drive alone or in a carpool, has flextime increased or decreased the amount of time it takes you to find a parking space?**
   - ☐ Increased ☐ Decreased ☐ No change

7. **How has flextime affected your productivity?**
   a. Quality of work
      ☐ Increased ☐ Decreased ☐ No change

   b. Accuracy of work
      ☐ Increased ☐ Decreased ☐ No change

   c. Quiet time for uninterrupted work
      ☐ Increased ☐ Decreased ☐ No change

8. **Have you had difficulty contacting coworkers who are on different schedules from yours?**
   - ☐ Yes ☐ No

Figure 6–2 Questionnaire

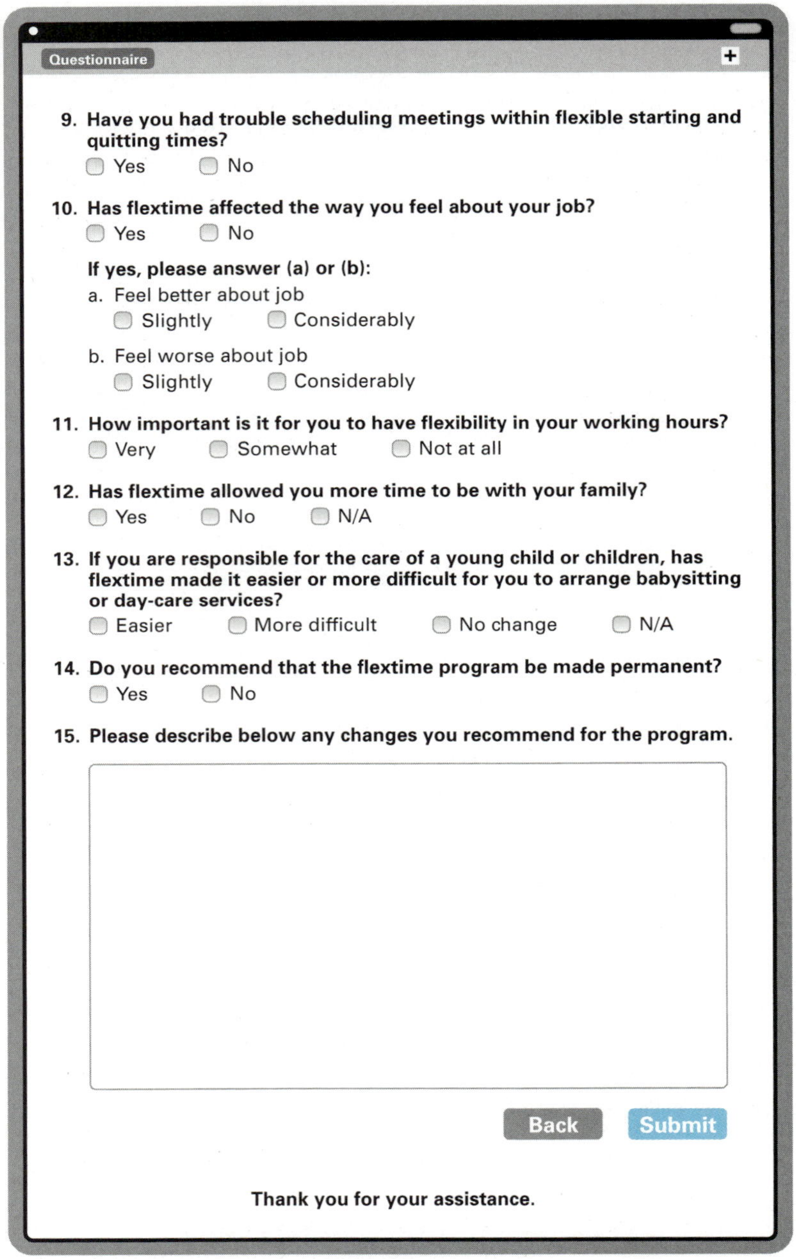

Questionnaire

9. **Have you had trouble scheduling meetings within flexible starting and quitting times?**
   - ▢ Yes ▢ No

10. **Has flextime affected the way you feel about your job?**
    - ▢ Yes ▢ No

    If yes, please answer (a) or (b):

    a. Feel better about job
       - ▢ Slightly ▢ Considerably

    b. Feel worse about job
       - ▢ Slightly ▢ Considerably

11. **How important is it for you to have flexibility in your working hours?**
    - ▢ Very ▢ Somewhat ▢ Not at all

12. **Has flextime allowed you more time to be with your family?**
    - ▢ Yes ▢ No ▢ N/A

13. **If you are responsible for the care of a young child or children, has flextime made it easier or more difficult for you to arrange babysitting or day-care services?**
    - ▢ Easier ▢ More difficult ▢ No change ▢ N/A

14. **Do you recommend that the flextime program be made permanent?**
    - ▢ Yes ▢ No

15. **Please describe below any changes you recommend for the program.**

Back Submit

Thank you for your assistance.

Figure 6–2 Questionnaire *(continued)*

WRITER'S CHECKLIST
Creating a Questionnaire

- ✔ Prepare a cover letter, a memo, an e-mail, or introductory text for an online survey, explaining who you are, the questionnaire's purpose, the date by which you need a response, and how and where to send the completed questionnaire. Include your contact information (mailing address, phone number, and e-mail address).
- ✔ For paper questionnaires, include a stamped, self-addressed envelope if you are using regular mail.
- ✔ Construct as many questions as possible that can be quickly answered with "yes," "no," or a checkmark.
- ✔ Include a section for additional comments, where respondents may clarify their overall attitude toward the subject.
- ✔ Consider offering some tangible appreciation to those who answer the questionnaire by a specific date, such as a copy of the results or, for a marketing questionnaire, a gift certificate.

Conducting Secondary Research: The Workplace, the Library, and the Internet

Secondary research involves gathering information that has been previously analyzed, assessed, evaluated, compiled, or otherwise organized into accessible form. Secondary sources include books and articles, as well as reports, Web documents, online discussion forums, audio and video recordings, podcasts, business letters, minutes of meetings, operating manuals, brochures, and so forth. When used to frame your ideas in context, these sources provide your reader with useful information that enhances your credibility. To find these materials, you will need to conduct research using workplace sources relevant to your needs, your library, and the Internet.

Developing a Search Strategy

Developing an effective search strategy entails considering what you already know and ferreting out further questions about the topic. Early stages may have dead ends and enticing side trips as you begin to focus your topic. Start your research with a question or purpose statement. If your topic is unfamiliar, try to find background information about it through general Internet sources, such as online encyclopedias, reference sites, or other sources that summarize the history of the topic. Keep certain questions in mind to guide your search: What have other people asked about my topic? What aspects of my topic are generating the most interest? What terms and phrases are repeatedly used to describe my topic? Familiarizing yourself with the issues surrounding your topic will help you clarify a preliminary question or purpose statement.

When you have a general understanding of the topic, focus on sources of information specific to your needs. Knowing what *types* of information will be most useful will help you to pinpoint where to look. For example, if you need the latest data on obesity-prevention programs, you might start by reviewing the data available on the U.S. Department of Agriculture website or by checking your library's subject directory for current medical and statistical sources. For additional information, you could then search a database — such as Academic Search Premier or Google Scholar — for recent journal articles on the subject. Do you want to include opinions about the impact of the number of vehicular accidents for the past five years associated with distracted driving by professional drivers? Search a newspaper or business database for periodicals, surveys, or influential blogs. For an overview of a subject, check your library's reference materials or its catalog for recently published books or videos. For in-depth or historical discussions, the best resources are often books and periodicals.

Finally, limit the scope of your search. Do you need to describe why the topic is important? Will the chronology of changes in the topic strengthen your argument? Once you have clearly defined the focus of your search, sum up your research question or thesis statement in two or three key terms. What words might you use to conduct keyword or key subject searches?

WRITER'S CHECKLIST

Developing a Search Strategy

Your answers to the following questions will help to narrow your focus and determine where you should look.

- ✔ What is the scope of your project? Is it a five-minute oral presentation? a 20-page research paper? a group presentation?
- ✔ Is only the most current information relevant to your topic?
- ✔ What kinds of sources best support your topic — existing workplace information? websites? blogs? journal and encyclopedia articles? books? something else?
- ✔ What formats (visual images, audio, print, or electronic) are needed?
- ✔ Do you need a range of opinions or points of view? fact-based research findings? some combination of both?
- ✔ What are your deadlines?

As you look for sources, keep in mind that in many cases the more recent the information, the better. Articles in periodicals and newspapers provide current sources. Academic (.edu), organizational (.org or .com), and government (.gov) websites may include recent research, works in progress, interviews, articles, papers, and conference proceedings. When a resource seems useful, consider its authorship and other aspects of a text or document, as outlined in Evaluating Sources (page 172). Then read the material carefully and take notes that include any additional questions about your topic. Some of your questions may eventually be clarified in other sources; questions that remain unanswered may point to future research projects.

Workplace Sources of Information

The workplace is a rich source of primary information gathered from interviews, firsthand observations, and surveys. But the workplace is an equally valuable source of secondary information — existing content suitable for your research. Such content may be found in a company's existing online and printed technical and promotional works—in white papers, manuals, blogs, and other Web postings; in technical specifications; and in a variety of reports (annual, laboratory, feasibility, investigative, and more). In large organizations, this content is maintained in document-management systems. These systems house collections of documents and related items, most created by employees but from outside sources as well. For example, product photographs, competitor sales sheets, topical e-mails, and scanned magazine or journal articles can be housed under a single directory or document group. Copying or converting such content, when it is suitable to your purposes, is called *repurposing*.[1] If you are preparing a promotional brochure, for example, you may be able to reuse material from a product or service description currently published on your organization's website.

Repurposing saves time because content that often requires substantial effort to develop need not be re-created for each new application. Reusing it may be as simple as copying and pasting content from one document into another. But do so only if it fits the scope, audience, and purpose of the new setting (document, blog, website). If necessary, adapt it to fit the new context. Revise the tense, voice, tone, grammar, and point of view to make the repurposed content fit seamlessly.

You may need to revise the boilerplate for a new medium, as well. A printed brochure or fact sheet may not work as effectively at a website. Blocks of text separated by white space on the printed page may be easy to read in a brochure but not on the Web. Readers scan text differently when they are reading on the Web; they find text divided into bulleted lists or very short paragraphs easier to read. Adapt content accordingly.

ETHICS NOTE: Acknowledge Repurposed Content When Necessary In the workplace, repurposing content within an organization does not violate copyright because the organization owns the information it creates and can share it across the company. Likewise, a writer in an organization may use and repurpose material in the public domain and, with some limitations, content that is licensed under Creative Commons (see http://creativecommons.org/about).

In the classroom, of course, the use of content or someone else's unique ideas without acknowledgment or the use of someone else's exact words without enclosing them in quotation marks and giving appropriate credit is plagiarism.

Library Research

Libraries provide organized paths into scholarship, information, and the ever-expanding Internet. Library resources include (1) online catalogs useful for locating books, videos, and government documents; (2) licensed online databases and indexes of scholarly articles; (3) specialized tools; and (4) subject directories for using the Web. Start with your college or university library. As a student or an affiliate of the school, you will have access to resources not otherwise available to you, such as subscription-only databases of recently published journal articles. Although you may be able to find listings or abstracts of such articles on your personal computer, you can access the full article text only through your school's library, which has already purchased a subscription to the database.

One of the most valuable resources in the library isn't a book or reference tool but the librarians who work there. They can tell you where to begin, how to refine your

[1]Workplace information used for more than one purpose is also called "boilerplate."

search strategy, and how to find research materials related to your topic. They can also interpret your questions and guide your search toward the best print or online resources for your topic, often saving you time. A brief conversation may help to focus your research and alert you to the most productive information sources. In addition to providing help in person and on the phone, an increasing number of libraries now offer e-mail or live chat access for answering reference questions and giving research support. Use your school library's home page, like the one shown in Figure 6–3, to access this feature, as well as the library catalog, article databases, Web directories, and more.

Using Library Catalogs to Locate Books

A library's catalog — Figure 6–4 shows a typical catalog dialogue box — allows you to search a library's books, journals, and videos; tells you an item's location and availability; and may even permit you to search the holdings of other libraries in the region or around the world. (Check with the library staff or the library home page for interlibrary-loan policies and requirements.)

Methods for searching library catalogs vary. Typically, you can search by author, title, subject, or keyword. Become familiar with the way your library's catalog works. If you are at the library, ask a reference librarian to give you a brief tour of the catalog; otherwise, check for guidelines or FAQs (Frequently Asked Questions). Help screens, like the author search screen in Figure 6–4, can be particularly useful in learning the best strategies for locating appropriate materials. Knowing how to use a few basic tools will prepare you to start your research and will often help you streamline the search process.

Follow these basic steps to search a library catalog:

- *Consider multiple search terms.* Unlike a search engine for websites, library catalogs don't search the full text of books; instead, they categorize the main subject of the book as a whole. If your initial search doesn't find anything about your specific topic, broaden your search terms.
- *Skim subject headings.* Librarians use consistent terminology when they describe the subject of a book. If you find a listing for one book that looks useful, the subject headings on the screen may lead you to other relevant sources. You'll have the best results if you search using the same terms catalogers do.
- *Browse the shelves.* In addition to categorizing books by subject, librarians shelve related books together. Combine searching the catalog with browsing the shelves.
- *Consider e-books.* Many academic libraries have e-book collections. These tend to be more academic in nature than those you can buy online. In some cases, the books are large pdf files that you can simply save one chapter at a time. Others are Web-based versions of reference books, offering brief background articles on a wealth of topics. Still others require that you install special software to view them. Be sure to ask a reference librarian for help if you run into difficulties using library e-books.
- *Don't overlook reference books.* Reference books offer valuable nuggets of information and authoritative overviews of topics. However, it can be hard to know which reference book will cover your specific topic; ask a librarian for suggestions. Note that reference books in a library's collection cannot be checked out but are useful for consultation in the library.

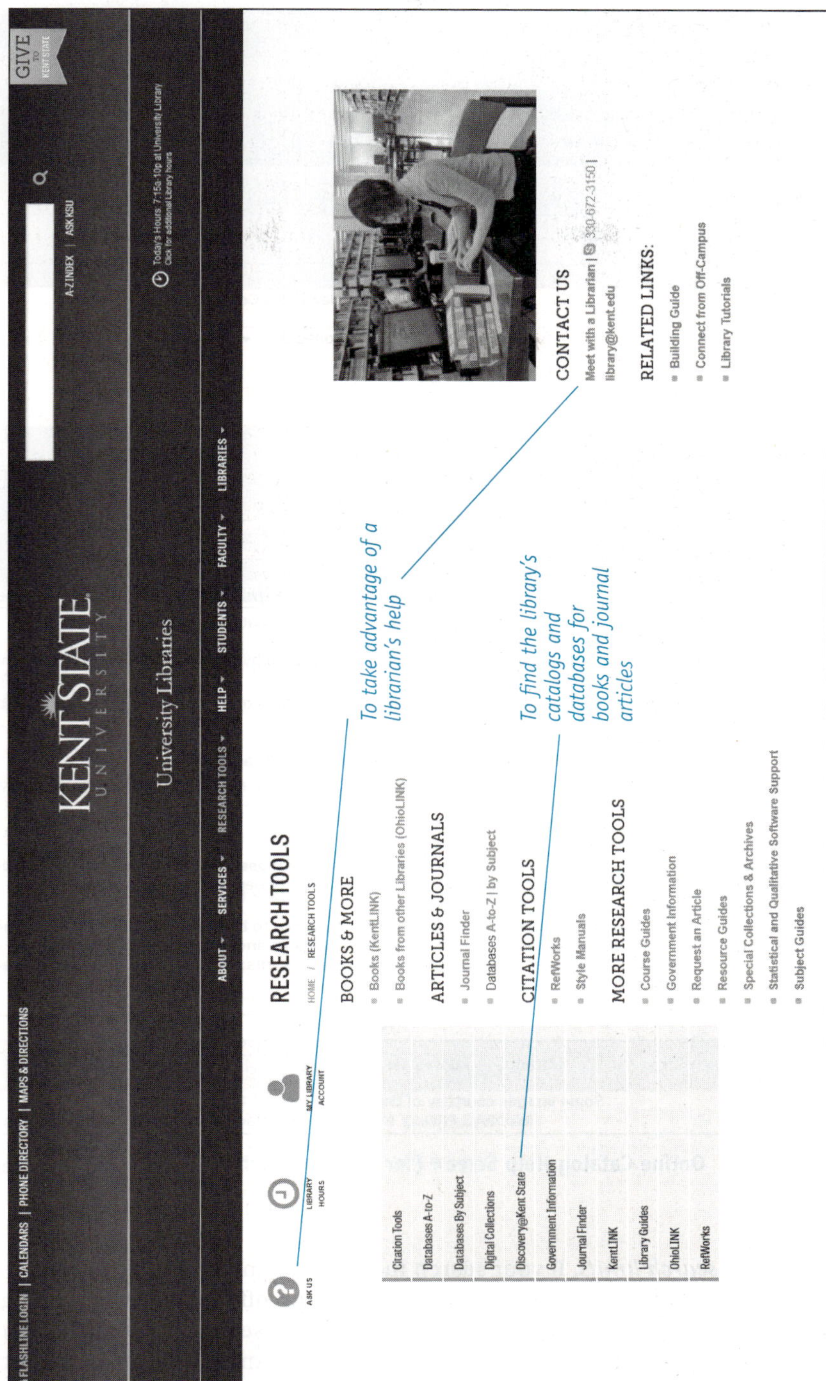

Figure 6–3 College Library Home Page *Source:* http://www.library.kent.edu/research-tools.

Using Databases to Locate Articles

Libraries subscribe to databases that provide citations for print resources and electronic collections of full-text articles; they can be searched within the library or through remote access available to registered students, faculty, and staff. If you are no longer a student, you can access your college library online or in person on alumni status or use a public library. Figure 6–6 is an example of a library database page that provides access to articles in journals organized by subject area. A library's database and index subscriptions might include any or all of the following:

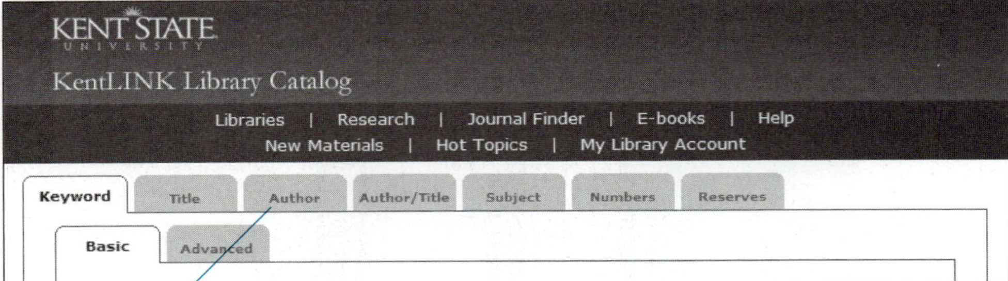

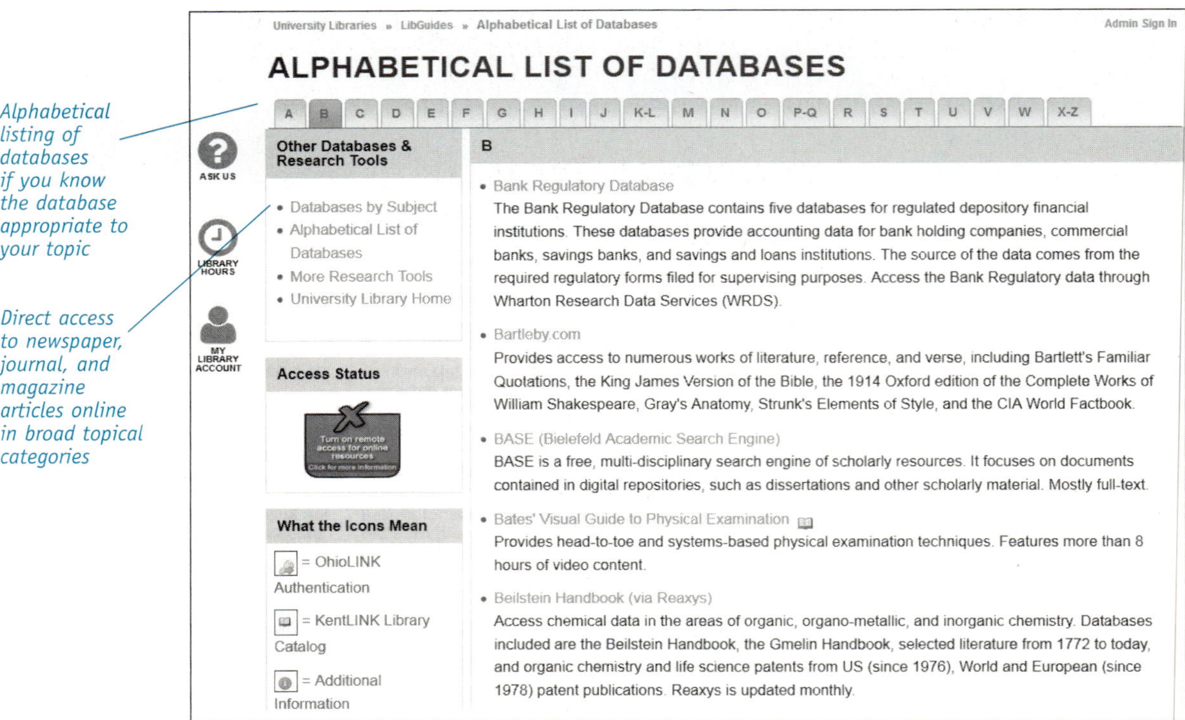

Figure 6–6 College Library Database Page *Source:* http://libguides.library.kent.edu/content.php?pid=347090&sid=2839466.

- *EBSCOhost's Academic Search Premier:* a large multidisciplinary database providing full text for nearly 4,500 periodicals, including more than 7,400 abstracted and indexed peer-reviewed journals
- *Gale's Expanded Academic ASAP:* a large database covering general-interest and scholarly journals plus business, law, and health-care publications (many in full text)
- *ERIC (Educational Resources Information Center):* a U.S. Department of Education database providing access to journals and reports in education
- *JSTOR:* a full-text, archival collection of journals in humanities, social sciences, and sciences
- *LexisNexis Academic:* a collection of databases that is particularly strong for news, business, legal, and corporate and financial information (most articles in full text) as well as congressional, statistical, and government resources

These databases, sometimes called periodical indexes, are excellent resources for articles published within the past 10 to 20 years. Some include descriptive abstracts and full texts of articles. To find older articles, you may need to consult a print or an online index, such as the *Readers' Guide to Periodical Literature* and the *New York Times Index.*

To locate articles within a particular database, conduct a keyword search. If your search turns up too many results, narrow your search by connecting two search terms with AND—"business writing AND employment"—or use other options offered by the database, such as a limited, a modified, or an advanced search, as shown in Figure 6–7.

DIGITAL TIP: Storing Search Results

Databases offer various ways to save your results. You may be able to save your searches and results within the database itself by creating a personal account, sending selected references and full-text articles to an e-mail account, or exporting them to citation-management software such as RefWorks, Endnote, or Zotero. These programs allow you to build your own database of references from multiple sources, sort them into folders, and generate bibliographies in the format of your choice. Database search tools and citation-management software will vary from library to library, so contact a reference librarian for usage guidance at your library.

Using Reference Works to Locate Facts and Topic Overviews

In addition to articles, books, and online sources, you may want to consult reference works such as specialized encyclopedias, dictionaries, and manuals for a brief overview of your subject. Ask your reference librarian to recommend reference works and bibliographies that are most relevant to your topic. Many are located online and can be accessed through your library's home page. Those in a library's collection cannot be checked out.

Encyclopedias. Encyclopedias are comprehensive, multivolume collections of articles arranged alphabetically. Some, such as the *Encyclopaedia Britannica,* cover a wide range of subjects, while others, such as *The Encyclopedia of Careers and Vocational Guidance* and the *McGraw-Hill Encyclopedia of Science and Technology,* are dedicated to specific subjects. For almost every academic discipline, there is at least one specialized encyclopedia with its entries written by noted scholars in the field. The free online encyclopedia *Wikipedia* (www.wikipedia.org) can be used as a starting point for a topic overview because site users continually update entries, but with only varying degrees of editorial reviews for accuracy. Even so, many *Wikipedia* entries include references to additional information on the topic.

Dictionaries. General and specialized dictionaries are available in print and online. General dictionaries can be compact or comprehensive in scope. Specialized

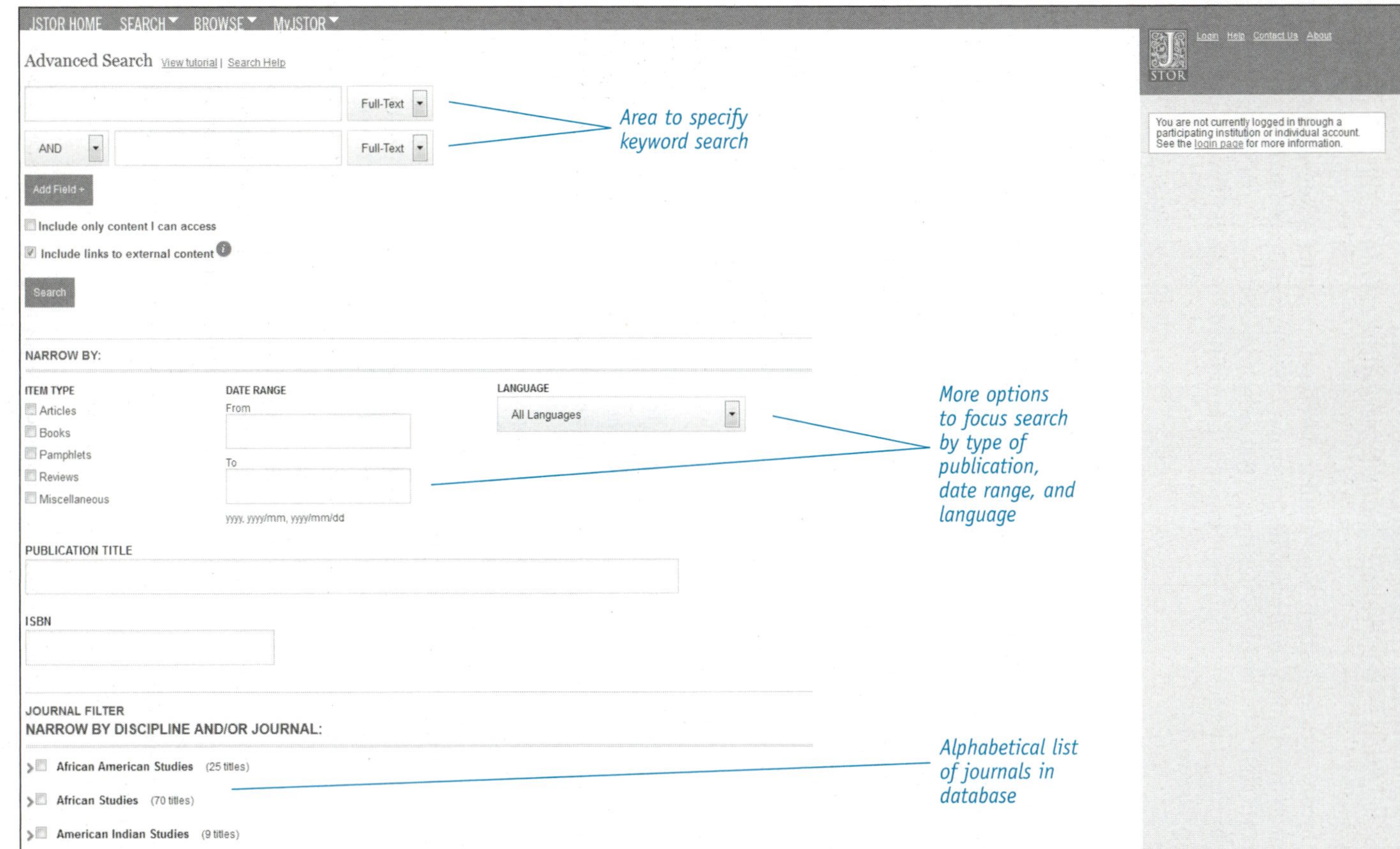

Figure 6–7 Keyword Search for Advanced Database Search *Source:* http://www.jstor.org/action/showAdvancedSearch.

dictionaries narrow their focus to terms used in a particular field, such as engineering, computer science, nursing, architecture, or consumer affairs.

Handbooks and Manuals. Handbooks and manuals are typically one-volume compilations of frequently used information in a variety of fields: the construction and maintenance trades (millwrights, HVAC technicians, pipefitters, crane and rigging specialists, etc.), medical and dental support professions (laboratory, cytology, and respiratory-care technicians; dental hygienists; etc.), and criminal investigative sciences (criminalist, forensic-science technician, DNA analyst, etc.) to name only a few. They offer brief definitions of terms or concepts, standards for presenting information, procedures for documenting sources, and visuals such as graphs and tables.

Bibliographies. Bibliographies list books, periodicals, and other research materials published in areas such as business, medicine, the humanities, and the social sciences.

General Guides. The Guide to Reference at www.guidetoreference.org can help you locate reference books, indexes, and other research materials.

Other Library Resources

Many libraries offer special kinds of research information. For example, a library may provide access to data that can be downloaded into statistical packages, such as SPSS (statistical package for the social sciences), for manipulation. Others offer GIS (geographic information systems) software that links data to spatial information, allowing the researcher to create detailed maps that show factors such as income, ethnicity, or purchasing habits. Many of the features available in these tools are also available online, through free or low-cost alternatives. If a work site doesn't provide access to a specific tool, a quick Internet search might provide a useful alternative.

WRITER'S GLOSSARY

Using Common Library Terms

- ✔ *Abstract:* a brief version of a long document that gives the reader the document's main points.
- ✔ *Bibliographic information:* the author, title, and publication information needed to locate an item in a journal article or book.
- ✔ *Bibliography:* a listing of sources used in the writing of a document; in MLA format, it is called "Works Cited" and in APA format, it is called "References."
- ✔ *Bound periodical:* several issues of a journal or magazine that are secured together in book form.
- ✔ *Call number:* the number assigned to every item in the library to help locate the item.
- ✔ *Circulation desk:* the desk where a patron can check out, return, and renew library materials.
- ✔ *Database:* a searchable electronic catalog of articles from journals, newspapers, and magazines accessible by subscription only but free to library patrons.

- ✔ *Interlibrary loan:* material requested from another library and sent to the patron's library for use.
- ✔ *Journal:* a periodical containing peer-reviewed scholarly articles written by experts in a particular subject area.
- ✔ *Magazine:* a popular periodical meant for the general public; articles are written by paid journalists and are edited but not peer reviewed.
- ✔ *Microform:* older books, journal articles, government documents, and more in film or fiche (i.e., greatly reduced) format that must be viewed in the library on a magnifying device. Many microform texts have also been converted to Web-accessible and searchable documents.
- ✔ *Peer review:* the journal-publishing practice in which experts review articles for accuracy, completeness, and adherence to the highest research standards prior to publication.
- ✔ *Periodical:* a publication issued at regular intervals (daily, weekly, monthly), such as a newspaper, magazine, or journal.

Searching the Web

Although the Internet contains a wealth of information, it has no one indexing scheme, that is, no single catalog that brings the information together for browsing or easy access, unlike the information in a library. However, search engines and Web directories can streamline your Internet search. A *search engine* locates information based on words or combinations of words that you specify. It finds documents or files that contain one or more of these words in their titles, descriptions, or text. Most search engines provide "advanced search" options that can help you narrow your results.

Your best strategy is to investigate how your favorite search engines work; nearly all provide detailed instructions on their help pages. Although search engines vary in what and how they search, you can use some of the basic strategies in Digital Tip: Using Search Engines and Keywords (page 171).

A *subject directory* organizes information by broad subject categories (business, entertainment, health, sports) and related subtopics (marketing, finance, investing). Figure 6–8 shows the home and the business and economics pages of a Web directory organized and maintained by ipl2 (http://ipl.org), a consortium of university library and information-science specialists with volunteer assistance. A subject-directory search eventually produces a list of specific sites that contain information about the topics you request. Once you locate a site of interest that you want to revisit, you can bookmark it.

Most major search engines, such as Bing and Yahoo!, also offer directories. The following search engines and subject directories are among the most widely used on the Web.

Search Engines

Google (www.google.com). The largest and most popular search engine, Google features several specialized search tools, including the following:

Books (http://books.google.com)

Finance (www.google.com/finance)

Geography (http://earth.google.com)

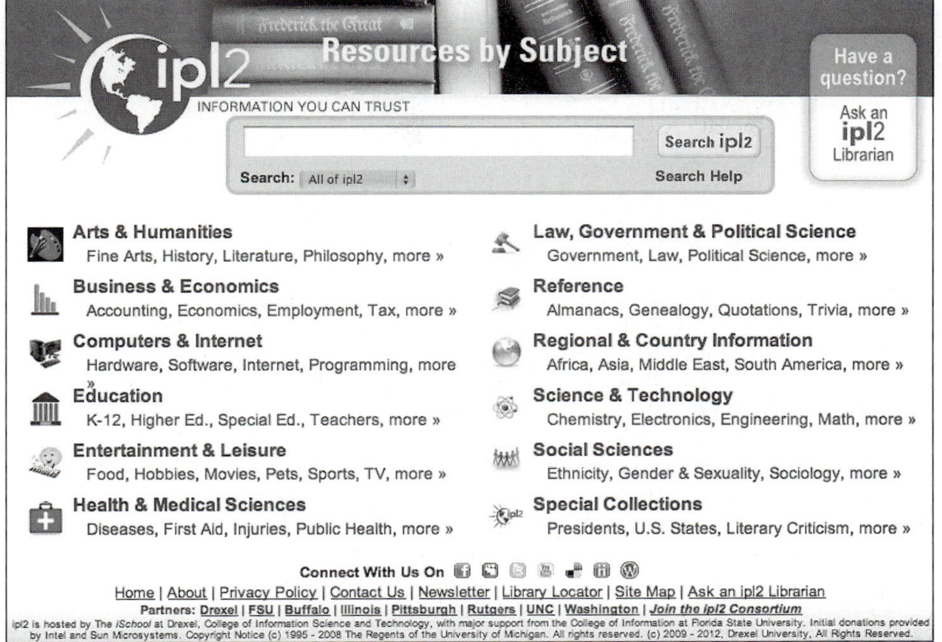

Each site provides detailed sources of information about the broad topic it covers

Figure 6–8 Web Directory Organized by Broad Topic Categories *Source:* http://www.ipl.org/div/subject/.

Images (http://images.google.com)

Maps (http://maps.google.com)

News (http://news.google.com)

Scholarly publications (http://scholar.google.com)

Yahoo! (yahoo.com). Yahoo! and Bing (bing.com) are also popular search engines, directories, and portals.

Subject Directories

The following Web directories offer access to sites selected for their quality. They are a good way to find useful sites when a search engine produces too many results.

Directory Journal (http://www.dirjournal.com) A combined local and Web directory for accessing news, research, and entertainment websites.

globalEDGE (http://globaledge.msu.edu). A directory of sites of particular interest to international business professionals.

Internet Scout Project (http://scout.wisc.edu). Published continually since 1994, Internet Scout presents the efforts of librarians and educators at the University of Wisconsin–Madison, who have selected and annotated more than 10,000 academically useful websites.

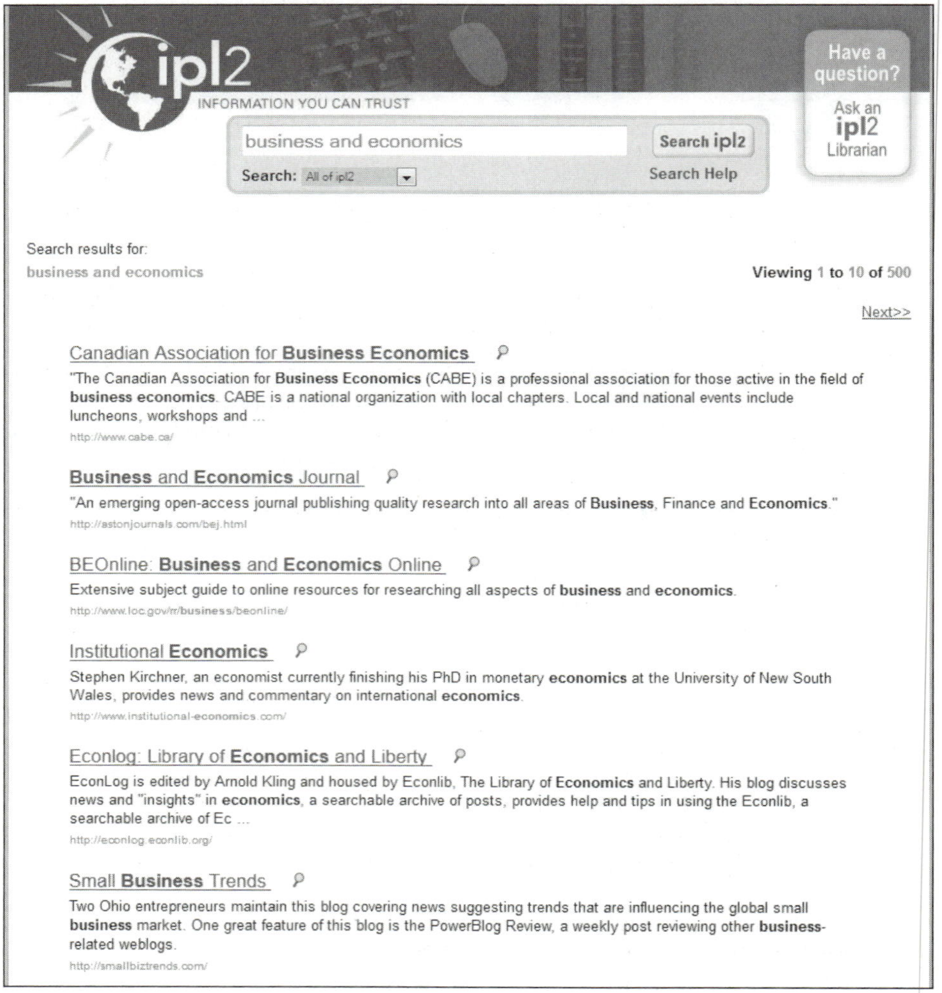

ipl2
INFORMATION YOU CAN TRUST

business and economics | Search ipl2
Search: All of ipl2 | Search Help

Have a question? Ask an ipl2 Librarian

Search results for:
business and economics

Viewing 1 to 10 of 500

Next>>

Canadian Association for **Business Economics**
"The Canadian Association for **Business Economics** (CABE) is a professional association for those active in the field of **business economics**. CABE is a national organization with local chapters. Local and national events include luncheons, workshops and ...
http://www.cabe.ca/

Business and **Economics** Journal
"An emerging open-access journal publishing quality research into all areas of **Business**, Finance and **Economics**."
http://astonjournals.com/bej.html

BEOnline: **Business** and **Economics** Online
Extensive subject guide to online resources for researching all aspects of **business** and **economics**.
http://www.loc.gov/rr/**business**/beonline/

Institutional **Economics**
Stephen Kirchner, an economist currently finishing his PhD in monetary **economics** at the University of New South Wales, provides news and commentary on international **economics**.
http://www.institutional-**economics**.com/

Econlog: Library of **Economics** and Liberty
EconLog is edited by Arnold Kling and housed by Econlib, The Library of **Economics** and Liberty. His blog discusses news and "insights" in **economics**, a searchable archive of posts, provides help and tips in using the Econlib, a searchable archive of Ec ...
http://econlog.econlib.org/

Small **Business** Trends
Two Ohio entrepreneurs maintain this blog covering news suggesting trends that are influencing the global small **business** market. One great feature of this blog is the PowerBlog Review, a weekly post reviewing other **business**-related weblogs.
http://smallbiztrends.com/

Figure 6–8 Web Directory Business and Economics Screen (*continued*) *Source:* http://www.ipl.org/IPL/Finding?Key=business+and+economics&collection=gen.

Jayde (http://www.jayde.com) A business to business (B2B) search engine.

Librarians' Internet Index (www.ip2.org). A searchable, annotated directory of continually updated Internet resources that are evaluated and annotated by research librarians.

ScienceDirect (www.sciencedirect.com). A search engine that focuses on scientific information.

WWW Virtual Library (www.vlib.org). This collection of subject directories was started when the Web was new and continues to be updated.

Metasearch Engines

These programs search other search engines for information about your query and sift through the findings to list relevant results. One such engine is Dogpile (www.dogpile.com).

Web-Based Tools

A growing number of Web-based applications are available to enhance your research, such as the following examples.

- **Create your own maps.** Find maps or create your own customized maps using Google Maps (http://maps.google.com) or the National Atlas (http://nationalatlas.gov).
- **Get the latest blog postings automatically.** Keep up to date with changes on news sites and blogs by using RSS (really simple syndication). To do so, you can either add feeds to your browser toolbar or use a feed aggregator such as Feedly (http://feedly.com) or Inoreader (https://www.inoreader.com).
- **Create graphic representations** of ideas or visualize data using tools such as Mindomo (www.mindomo.com).

◆ *For a discussion about creating blogs, see pages 596–599 in Appendix A, Writing in an Online Environment.*

WRITER'S CHECKLIST

Using Search Engines and Keywords

- ✔ Check any search tips available in the engine you use and consider any additional search phrases the search engine may suggest.
- ✔ Enter precise keywords and phrases that are specific to your topic, such as *nuclear power* rather than only the term *nuclear*, which would also yield listings for *nuclear family*, *nuclear medicine*, and hundreds of other unrelated topics.
- ✔ Try several search engines to get more varied results. Remember that search engines may sell high rankings to advertisers and therefore may not rank as highly the pages most relevant to your search.
- ✔ Consider using a metasearch engine, such as Dogpile (www.dogpile.com), which displays results from multiple search engines.
- ✔ Refine and narrow your terms as you evaluate the results of each search.

Locating Business and Government Sites

The Web includes numerous sites devoted to specific subject areas. Following are some suggested resources for researching business topics.

Business Resources

Business Internet Resources (http://www.loc.gov/rr/business/beonline/subjectlist.php)

Business Reference Services: Science, Technology, and Business Division (www.loc.gov/rr/business). This site is developed and maintained by the Library of Congress. See the Subject Guide to Internet Resources.

Yahoo! Directory: Business and Economy (https://business.yahoo.com/category/Business_and_Economy/Directories)

Government Resources

Government Documents and Reports

- Bureau of Economic Analysis (www.bea.gov)
- Congressional Budget Office (www.cbo.gov)
- Congressional Research Service Reports (https://www.fas.org/sgp/cr)
- Government Accountability Office (www.gao.gov)
- U.S. Government Publishing Office (http://www.gpo.gov)

Sites for Statistics

- Government Sources
  - American FactFinder (http://factfinder.census.gov/faces/nav/jsf/pages/index.xhtml)
  - Bureau of Economic Analysis (www.bea.gov)
  - Bureau of Justice Statistics (http://bjs.ojp.usdoj.gov)
  - Bureau of Labor Statistics (www.bls.gov)
  - Fedstats (http://fedstats.sites.usa.gov/)
  - National Center for Education Statistics (http://nces.ed.gov)
  - National Center for Health Statistics (www.cdc.gov/nchs)
  - United Nations Statistics Division (http://unstats.un.org/unsd)
  - U.S. Census Bureau (www.census.gov)
- Opinion Polls
  - Harris Vault (www.harrisinteractive.com/Insights/HarrisVault.aspx)
  - Pew Global Attitudes Project (http://pewglobal.org)
  - World Public Opinion (www.worldpublicopinion.org)

Evaluating, Recording, and Acknowledging Research Sources

As you research your topic, weigh the merits of your sources carefully. Once you've decided which materials to use, you will need to record information from each source so that you can accurately quote, paraphrase, and summarize it in your paper or report. Recording your sources is especially important so that you can acknowledge where your information came from, thereby avoiding plagiarism.

Evaluating Sources

As you interview for information or work with print or online material, evaluate each source by asking yourself the following questions:

- Is the information accurate and up to date?
- Is the speaker or author reputable and qualified?
- Is the publisher or sponsoring organization well established and respected in the field?

Evaluate the usefulness of information on the Internet with the same standards that you use to evaluate printed material, people you interview, or any other source.

The easiest way to ensure that information is valid is to obtain it from a reputable source. For example, data from the Bureau of Labor Statistics, the Securities and Exchange Commission, and the Bureau of the Census are widely used by U.S. businesses. Likewise, online versions of established, reputable journals in medicine, engineering, computer software, and other fields merit the same level of trust as the printed versions. However, as you move away from established, reputable sites, exercise more caution. Be especially wary of blogs, unmoderated online discussion groups, and public wikis. Remember that anyone with access can place information on the Internet, so for many sources there are no checks and balances on content in place. Collectively generated websites, such as *Wikipedia*, often make no guarantee of the validity of information at their sites (see http://en.wikipedia.org/wiki/Wikipedia:General_disclaimer). Treat information obtained from these sources cautiously.

Use the following domain abbreviations to help you determine an Internet site sponsor, and note that many domain abbreviations, such as *.org*, *.int*, and *.pro*, are not independently evaluated to determine the site sponsor's appropriateness for the site designation.

.aero	aerospace industry	.pro	professionals
.biz	business	.mil	U.S. military
.com	company or individual	.name	individual
.coop	business cooperative	.net	company or individual
.edu	educational institution	.org	general organization
.gov	U.S. government	.info	general use

Keep in mind the following four criteria when evaluating any source, whether print or online: authority, accuracy, bias, and currency.[2]

Authority

Consider the author's reputation: Is the writer an authority in the field? Has he or she written other, highly regarded books or articles? If you don't know, ask a librarian, an instructor, or an expert who is familiar with the subject area whether the author of a book or an article has an established reputation.

Because anyone can publish on the Web, it is sometimes difficult to determine authorship of a document, and frequently a person's qualifications for speaking on a topic are absent or questionable. If you do not recognize the author or the organization sponsoring the site as well known and respected in the field, check the site's "About Us" page or mission statement if available. This information should give you a sense of

[2]Adapted from Leigh Ryan and Lisa Zimmerelli, *The Bedford Guide for Writing Tutors*, 6th ed. (Boston: Bedford/St. Martin's, 2016).

the site's purpose and perspective. Ask the following questions to help you determine the authority of a site or document:

- Is the author's document listed in or linked from a reliable source or document?
- Is the author referenced or mentioned positively by another author or organization whose authority you trust?
- Does the document give ample biographical information about the author so that you can evaluate his or her credentials, or can you get this information by linking to another document?

If the publisher or sponsor is an organization, you can usually assume that the document meets the standards and aims of the group. Consider also the following:

- The suitability of the organization to address this topic.
- Whether this organization or agency is recognized and respected in the field.
- The relationship of the author to the publisher or sponsor. (Does the document tell you something about the author's expertise or qualifications?)

Accuracy

Criteria for evaluating accuracy include the following:

- Other sources that the document relies on are reputable and cited or linked.
- Background information can be verified.
- Methodology is appropriate for the topic.
- With a research project, data that were gathered include explanations of research methods and interpretations.
- The graphs and visuals are free of distortion.
- The site is modified or updated regularly.

Bias

To determine bias, consider how the context reveals the author's knowledge of the subject and his or her stance on the topic. Check for the following:

- The publication or site identifies its audience.
- The book, article, or site was published or developed by a recognized academic institution; government agency; or national, international, or commercial organization with an established reputation in the subject area.
- The author shows knowledge of theories, techniques, or schools of thought usually related to the topic.
- The author shows knowledge of related sources and attributes them properly.

- The author discusses the value and limitations of the approach if it is new.
- The author acknowledges that the subject itself or his or her treatment of it is controversial.

Currency

If your topic involves data or ideas that change frequently or that depend on up-to-date information, look for whether the document has a publication or "last updated" date, includes the date of copyright, gives dates showing when information was gathered, or indicates when new material was updated, when appropriate.

WRITER'S CHECKLIST

Criteria for Evaluating Research Sources

Keep in mind the following criteria when evaluating research sources.[3]

For All Sources

- ✔ Is the resource recent enough and relevant to your topic? Is it readily available?
- ✔ Who is the intended audience? Is it the mainstream public? a small group of professionals?
- ✔ Is the author an authority on the subject?
- ✔ Does the author provide enough supporting evidence and document sources so that you can verify the information's accuracy?
- ✔ Is the information presented in an objective, unbiased way? Are any biases made clear? Are opinions clearly labeled? Are viewpoints balanced, or are opposing opinions acknowledged?
- ✔ Are the language, tone, and style appropriate and cogent?

For a Website

- ✔ Does a reputable group or organization sponsor or maintain the site?
- ✔ Are the purpose and scope of the site clearly stated? Check the "Mission Statement" or "About Us" pages. Are there any disclaimers about the sources or accuracy of content?
- ✔ Is the site updated, thus current? Are the links functional and up to date?
- ✔ Is the documentation authoritative and credible? Check the links to other sources and cross-check facts at other reputable websites, such as academic ones.
- ✔ Is the site well designed? Is the material well written and error free?

For an Article

- ✔ Is the publisher of the magazine or other periodical well known?
- ✔ What is the article's purpose? For a journal article, read the abstract; for a newspaper article, read the headline and first paragraph.
- ✔ Does the article contain informative diagrams or other visuals?

---

[3]For more details, see Leigh Ryan and Lisa Zimmerelli, *The Bedford Guide for Writing Tutors*, 6th ed. (Boston: Bedford/St. Martin's, 2016).

For a Book

✔ Does the preface or introduction indicate the author's or book's purpose?

✔ Does the table of contents relate to your topic? Does the index contain terms related to your topic?

✔ Are the chapters useful? Skim through one chapter that seems related to your topic — notice especially the introduction, headings, and closing.

Taking Notes

Taking notes enables you to condense and record information from books, articles, websites, and other sources. The notes you take will furnish much of the material for your outline and final written work.

Document the following information about any book that you decide to include in your research:

Library call number

Author (if the author is an organization, indicate that fact)

Title

City of publication

Publisher's name

Year of publication

For an article in print, record the following information:

Author

Title of the article

Name of the journal in which the article appears

Journal volume and issue numbers

Date of publication

Page numbers of the article

Database (if you found the article's full text in a library database)

Digital object identifier (DOI; for full-text articles found online)

For online sources, you can print out the search screen containing the full bibliographic citation, download the citation from an online database to your hard drive, or e-mail the citation to yourself. See Digital Tip: Storing Search Results (page 165) for more information on recording online search results.

If you are using Internet sources, you can highlight passages and cut and paste them into a word-processing file, in addition to taking notes. When you cut and paste information from the Internet, be very careful: Consider changing the font or color of the text so that you can easily distinguish borrowed material from your own notes; at the very least, put quotation marks around the material. Always include the source to provide proper credit in your final work. Otherwise, you will be plagiarizing from the source. If the source is copyrighted, you may also be guilty of copyright infringement. (A full discussion of avoiding plagiarism and other intellectual property violations begins on page 181.) When working with paper sources (books and journals), you can photocopy material and highlight important passages with a highlighter, type them into your laptop or desktop computer, or jot notes on index cards.

Whichever method you use, identify the source of the information and include the author's last name (also include first name or initials if you have two authors with the same last name) and the page number or numbers on which the material appears in the original source. If you have consulted more than one book or article by an author, include the title as well; for long titles, you may use a shortened form.

As you take notes, make a list of the topics you will cover in your research. Identify your notes as appropriate with these topics (sometimes called tags). In a word-processing document, for instance, you can create different-colored tags to distinguish topics so that when you need to arrange your notes in preparation for creating an outline, you can use the tags as a guide in organizing your material.

For the sake of accuracy and correctness, be careful to distinguish whether you are quoting directly from your source, paraphrasing (restating the text you're using in your own words), or summarizing (writing down a condensed version of the text). If you are a beginning researcher, you should probably stick to writing down direct quotations. Then, when you turn to actually writing your research paper, you can decide whether you want to quote directly, paraphrase, or summarize.

Quoting from Your Sources

When you quote directly from another source, use only the information you need to make your point. The following section describes long-standing techniques to help you do so and to credit your information sources.

Direct Quotations

A direct quotation is a word-for-word copy of the text of an original source. Choose direct quotations (which can be of a word, a phrase, a sentence, or, occasionally, a paragraph) carefully and use them sparingly. Enclose direct quotations in quotation marks and separate them from the rest of the sentence by a comma or colon. The initial capital letter of a quotation is retained if the quoted material originally began with a capital letter.

- The economist stated, "Regulation cannot supply the dynamic stimulus that in other industries is supplied by competition."

When a quotation is divided, the material that interrupts the quotation is set off, before and after, by commas, and quotation marks are used around each part of the quotation.

- "Regulation," he said in a recent interview, "cannot supply the dynamic stimulus that in other industries is supplied by competition."

Indirect Quotations

An indirect quotation is a paraphrased version of an original text. It is usually introduced by the word *that* and is not set off from the rest of the sentence by punctuation marks.

▶ In a recent interview he said that regulation does not stimulate the industry as well as competition does.

Deletions or Omissions

Deletions or omissions from quoted material are indicated by three ellipsis points (. . .) within a sentence and a period plus three ellipsis points (. . . .) at the end of a sentence.

▶ "If monopolies could be made to respond . . . we would be able to enjoy the benefits of . . . large-scale efficiency. . . ."

When a quoted passage begins in the middle of a sentence rather than at the beginning, ellipsis points are not necessary; the fact that the first letter of the quoted material is not capitalized tells the reader that the quotation begins in midsentence.

▶ Rivero goes on to conclude that "coordination may lessen competition within a region."

Regardless of where the ellipsis points appear, be careful to retain the accuracy and grammatical consistency of the original passage.

Inserting Material into Quotations

When it is necessary to insert a clarifying comment within quoted material, use brackets.

▶ "The industry is an integrated system that serves an extensive [geographic] area, with divisions existing as islands within the larger system's sphere of influence."

When quoted material contains an obvious error or might be questioned in some other way, the expression *sic* (Latin for "thus"), in italic type and enclosed in brackets, follows the questionable material to indicate that the writer has quoted the material exactly as it appeared in the original.

▶ The company considers Baker Industrials to be a "guilt-edged [*sic*] investment."

◀ **ETHICS NOTE: Indicate Any Changes to Quoted Source Material** When you are quoting, do not make any changes or omissions in the quoted material unless you clearly indicate what you have done. For further information on incorporating quoted material and inserting comments, see Avoiding Plagiarism and Other Intellectual Property Violations on page 181 and Incorporating Quotations into Text below. ▶

Incorporating Quotations into Text

Quote word for word only when your source concisely sums up a great deal of information or reinforces a point you are making. Quotations must also relate logically, grammatically, and syntactically to the rest of the sentence and the surrounding text.

◆ *For detailed information about documenting sources of information, see pages 184–206.*

Depending on the length, there are two methods of handling quotations in your text. For APA style, a quotation of fewer than 40 words is incorporated into the text and enclosed in quotation marks. For MLA style, a quotation of no more than four lines is incorporated into the text and enclosed in quotation marks.

Material that runs longer than at least 40 words (APA style) or four lines (MLA style) is usually set off from the body of the text by being indented from the left margin one-half inch (APA style) or one inch (MLA style). The quoted passage is spaced the same as the surrounding text and is not enclosed in quotation marks, as shown in the following example, which uses APA style. If you are not following a specific style manual, you may block indent one inch from both the left and right margins for reports and other documents.

▸ After reviewing a large number of works in business and technical communication, Alred sees an inevitable connection between theory, practice, and pedagogy:

> Therefore, theory is necessary to prevent us from being overwhelmed by what is local, particular, and temporal. In turn, pedagogy both mediates practice and transforms our theory. Indeed, one reason I find this work rewarding is that I sense it puts me at the intersection of theory, practice, and pedagogy as they are involved with writing in the workplace. (585)

The use of the Web today has reinforced this connection because it calls on the Web-page designer to engage in a teaching function as well as reflect on the practice of Web design. For example, the widespread use of . . .

Notice that the quotation blends with the content of the surrounding text, which uses transitions to introduce and comment on the quotation. At the end of the document, the following entry appears in the list of references as the source of the quotation in the example.

Alred, G. J. (2003). Essential works on technical communication. *Technical Communication, 50,* 585–616.

Do not rely too heavily on the use of quotations in the final version of your document. Generally, avoid quoting anything that is more than one paragraph.

Paraphrasing

Paraphrasing is restating or rewriting in your own words the essential ideas of another writer. Because the paraphrase does not quote the source word for word, quotation marks are not necessary. However, paraphrased material should be credited because the ideas are taken from someone else. The following example is an original passage explaining the optical concept of object blur. The paraphrased version restates the essential information of the passage in a form appropriate for a report.

ORIGINAL One of the major visual cues used by pilots in maintaining precision ground reference during low-level flight is that of object blur. We are acquainted with the object-blur phenomenon experienced when driving an automobile. Objects in the foreground appear to be rushing toward us, while objects in the background appear to recede slightly.

—Wesley E. Woodson and Donald W. Conover, *Human Engineering Guide for Equipment Designers*

PARAPHRASED

Object blur is an optical illusion that affects people in fast-moving vehicles: Nearby objects seem to rush toward the observer, while distant objects seem to move away slightly (Woodson and Conover).

Strive to put the original ideas into your words without changing them or taking them out of context in a way that distorts the author's intended meaning.

Summarizing

A summary is a condensed version, in the researcher's own words, of an original passage. Summaries present only the essential ideas or conclusions of the original and are considerably shorter than paraphrases of the same passage. As with directly quoted and paraphrased material, the source of summarized information must be credited in a footnote.

Following this passage is a brief summary of its content.

ORIGINAL

Now that we have learned something about the nature of elements and molecules, what are fuels? Fuels are those substances that will burn when heat is applied to them. Some elements, in themselves, are fuels. Carbon, hydrogen, sulfur, magnesium, titanium, and some other metals are examples of elements that can burn. Coal, charcoal, and coke, for example, are almost pure carbon; hydrogen, another element, is a highly flammable gas. But the most familiar combustible materials are not pure elements; they are compounds and mixtures. Wood, paper, and grass are principally composed of molecules of cellulose, a flammable substance. If we examine the chemical makeup of this compound, we will discover what elements form the basic fuels in most solid materials. The cellulose molecule contains twenty-one atoms: six carbon, ten hydrogen, and five oxygen atoms: $C_6H_{10}O_5$. Since oxygen is not flammable . . . , it follows that the carbon and hydrogen found in most common combustible solids are the elements that burn. This conclusion becomes even stronger when we look at common flammable liquids. Gasoline, kerosene, fuel oils, and other petroleum compounds are composed of only carbon and hydrogen atoms, in varying amounts. These compounds, called hydrocarbons (hydrogen + carbon), will all burn.

—James H. Meidl, *Flammable Hazardous Materials*

SUMMARIZED

The chemical makeup of a substance determines whether it is flammable. Carbon and hydrogen are highly flammable elements, so materials made up largely of these elements, called hydrocarbons, are good fuels (Meidl 8–9).

Summarize a source to remind yourself of the substance of a research source. Summarized information can also be useful to your reader because it condenses passages that give more details than the reader needs.

Avoiding Plagiarism and Other Intellectual Property Violations

Plagiarism is the use of someone else's ideas without acknowledgment or the use of someone else's exact words without quotation marks and appropriate credit. Plagiarism is the theft of someone else's creative and intellectual property and is unacceptable in business, science, journalism, academia, or any other field. If you intend to publish, reproduce, or distribute material that includes quotations from published works, like websites, blogs, podcasts, Facebook, YouTube, Twitter, or other digital sources, you may need to obtain written permission from the copyright holders of those works.

Acknowledging Your Sources

The gold standard for avoiding ethical and legal problems is to carefully document your sources of information. This standard applies both in the classroom and on the job, regardless of whether your primary audience is your instructor, your company management, or the readers of a publication or website. (Details regarding commonly used systems for documenting sources begin on page 185.)

Quoting a passage — including cutting and pasting a passage from an Internet source into your work — is permissible only if you enclose the passage in quotation marks and properly cite the source. Likewise, you may paraphrase the words and ideas of another *if you document your source*. Although you do not enclose paraphrased ideas or materials in quotation marks, you must document their sources. Paraphrasing a passage without citing the source is permissible only when the information paraphrased is common knowledge.

Even websites that grant permission to copy, distribute, or modify material under the "copyleft" principle, such as *Wikipedia*, nonetheless caution that you must give appropriate credit to the source from which material is taken (see http://en.wikipedia.org/wiki/Wikipedia:Citing_Wikipedia).

Common Knowledge

Common knowledge refers to information that is widely known and readily available in handbooks, manuals, atlases, and other references. For example, the "law of supply and demand" is common knowledge and is found in every economics and business textbook. Likewise, the distances between two cities, the names of routes, and the geographic features of an area found on virtually every travel map qualify as common knowledge. You need not document the source of such information. Common knowledge also refers to information within a specific field that is generally known and understood by most others in that field — even though it may not be widely known by those outside the field. For example, the fact that the 1918 Spanish flu pandemic killed millions of Americans is common knowledge among public health officials, epidemiologists, and historians. The source for this information need not be documented. However, the number of deaths caused by the 1918 flu among members of the U.S. military or among the population of a North American city would not be common knowledge and would require a citation. An indication that something is common knowledge is whether it is repeated in multiple sources without citation. If you are in any doubt about whether information meets this standard, document its source.

Copyrights, Patents, and Trademarks

Most published material—written or visual—is copyrighted. In workplace writing, you must obtain prior approval to reproduce virtually all copyrighted information and cite the source of that information in your final work. However, small amounts of material from a copyrighted source may be used, especially for educational purposes, without permission or payment as long as you indicate that it is someone else's material and your use satisfies the fair-use criteria of the U.S. Copyright Office. U.S. law also protects two other intellectual property rights: patents and trademarks. Though they differ from copyright in their applicability, they both afford important protections in workplace contexts.

Copyrights

Copyright establishes legal protection for original works of authorship, including literary, dramatic, musical, artistic, and other intellectual works in printed or electronic form; it gives the copyright owner exclusive rights to reproduce, distribute, perform, or display a work. Copyright protects all original works from the moment of their creation, regardless of whether they are published or contain a notice of copyright (©).

ETHICS NOTE: Obtain Permission Before Using Copyrighted Information If you plan to reproduce copyrighted material in your own publication or on your website, you must obtain permission from the copyright holder. To do otherwise is a violation of U.S. law.

Permissions

To seek permission to reproduce copyrighted material, you must write to the copyright holder. In some cases, it is the author; in other cases, it is the editor or publisher of the work. For websites, read the site's "terms-of-use" information (if available) and e-mail your request to the appropriate party. State specifically which portion of the work you wish to reproduce and how you plan to use it. The copyright holder has the right to charge a fee and specify conditions and limits of use.

Exceptions

Some print and Web material—including text, visuals, and other digital forms—may be reproduced without permission. The rules governing copyright can be complex, so it is prudent to carefully check the copyright status of anything you plan to reproduce.

- *Fair use.* A small amount of material from a copyrighted source may be used for educational purposes (such as classroom handouts), commentary, criticism, news reporting, and scholarly reports without permission or payment as long as the use satisfies the "fair-use" criteria, as described at the U.S. Copyright Office website, (www.copyright.gov). Whether a particular use qualifies as fair use depends on all the circumstances.

◆ *See the Ethics Note on page 159 of this chapter regarding the repurposing of in-house content.*

- *Company boilerplate.* Employees often borrow material freely from in-house manuals and reports, as well as other company documents in doing work for the company to save time and ensure consistency. Using such "boilerplate," or "repurposed," material is not a copyright violation because the company is considered the author of works prepared by its employees on the job.

- *Public domain material.* Works created by or for the U.S. government and not classified or otherwise protected are in the public domain — that is, they are not copyrighted. The same is true for older written works when their copyright has lapsed or never existed. Be aware that some works in the public domain may include "value-added" features — such as introductions, visuals, and indexes — that may be copyrighted separately from the original work and may require permission even if the main work is in the public domain.
- *Copyleft Web material.* Some public access websites, such as *Wikipedia*, follow the "copyleft" principle and grant permission to freely copy, distribute, or modify material, but the modified material is also required to be made freely available on the same basis.[4]

ETHICS NOTE: Give Credit to All Content Obtained from the Internet The Internet has changed the face of copyright, creating an illusion of universal access to online material, when in fact permission is often required to alter or use it in any way. Alternative forms of permissions — like those offered by Creative Commons — allow users to freely incorporate specific content into their documents and to license their own original content. Still, even when you use material that may be reproduced or published without permission, you must nonetheless give appropriate credit to the source from which the material is taken.

See Acknowledging Your Sources, page 181.

Patents

The United States Patent and Trademark Office (USPTO) defines a patent as an intellectual property right granted by the U.S. government to an inventor for a limited time in exchange for public disclosure of the invention when the patent is granted. U.S. patents differ from copyright in that they protect inventions rather than written, musical, and artistic works. The USPTO grants three types of patents:

- *Utility patents* cover inventions of machinery, manufacturing processes, or new materials (for example, a personal three-dimensional printer, composite material for a car bumper, a technique to mine the seabed for minerals) and are valid for 20 years.
- *Design patents* cover the invention of new designs for manufactured items (for example, a design for a mobile phone, desk chair, or car hood) and are valid for 14 years.
- *Plant patents* cover inventions for new plant varieties (for example, an ornamental shrub or a disease-resistant orange tree) and are valid for 20 years.

[4]"Copyleft" is a play on the word *copyright* and is the effort to free materials from many of the restrictions of copyright. See http://en.wikipedia.org/wiki/Copyleft.

To obtain information about international patents, links to patent offices around the world, and tutorials on patent laws in different countries and regions, visit the global online patent resource The Lens at www.lens.org.

Trademarks

A trademark is a word, phrase, graphic symbol, logo, or another device that identifies and distinguishes the source of the goods of one merchant or manufacturer from those of others. The two primary marks are trademarks and service marks.

- *Trademarks* identify physical commodities (for example, automobiles, computers, shoes) distributed through interstate commerce.
- *Service marks* identify services (for example, the preparation and sale of food, the provision of transportation or lodging, the sale of life or health insurance). The term *trademark* is often used to refer to both trademarks and service marks.[5]

Trademarks for goods and services registered with the USPTO include the ® symbol or the phrase "Reg. U.S. Pat. & TM Off." The phrase "Patent Pending" on a manufactured item means that the inventor has applied for a patent on the item. Before trademarks are registered with the USPTO, service providers commonly use the superscript symbol SM. Trademark names are proper nouns and must be capitalized. When citing a trademark, include the superscript trademark symbol ® if it's used in the trademark name. To obtain additional information about patents and trademarks, go to the FAQ page of the U.S. Patent and Trademark Office website at www.uspto.gov/faq/index.jsp.

Documenting Sources

By documenting your sources, you identify where you obtained the facts, ideas, quotations, and paraphrases you used in preparing your content. This information can come from Web sources; books; newspaper, magazine, or trade-journal articles; manuals; proposals; investigative reports; interviews; e-mail; and other sources. Documenting sources achieves three important purposes:

- It allows readers to locate and consult the sources used and to find further information on the subject.
- It enables writers to support and lend credibility to their assertions and arguments.
- It helps writers to give proper credit to others and thus avoid plagiarism by identifying the sources of facts, ideas, quotations, and paraphrases.

This section shows citation models and sample pages for two principal documentation systems: APA and MLA.

---

[5]The USPTO registers other less frequently used types of marks that have different registration requirements than trademarks and service marks: certification marks, collective marks, collective trademarks, and collective service marks. They are described at www.uspto.gov.

American Psychological Association. *Publication Manual of the American Psychological Association*. 6th ed. Washington, DC: American Psychological Association, 2010. See also www.apastyle.org.

The APA system of citation is often used in the social sciences. It is referred to as an author-date method of documentation because parenthetical in-text citations and a references list (at the end of the paper) emphasize the author(s) and date of publication so that the currency of the research is clear.

MLA Handbook for Writers of Research Papers. 7th ed. New York: Modern Language Association of America, 2009. See also www.mla.org.

The MLA system is used in the humanities. This style uses parenthetical citations and a list of works cited (at the end of the paper), and it places greater importance on the pages on which cited information can be found than on the publication date.

APA Style

APA In-Text Citations

To document direct quotations in text, give the author's last name, the year of publication, and the page number in parentheses. APA style requires that you use only the past or present perfect tenses for introducing cited material; *Hanley claimed* or *Hanley has claimed*, not *Hanley claims*.

▶ Environmental groups battling global warming need to convince the public that "a low-impact lifestyle" is both worthwhile and doable (Sylvan, 2011, p. 42).

The page number is optional, although its use is encouraged, for paraphrased information and ideas.

▶ Despite its gains, the environmental movement has struggled to keep pace with the problems of globalization (Sylvan, 2011).

If the author's name is mentioned in the text, give only the year of publication and the page number in parentheses.

▶ According to Sylvan (2011), environmental groups are working hard to sell the "low-impact lifestyle" to the public (p. 42).

Include no more information than is necessary to enable readers to find the corresponding entry in the references list. If the author's name and the year of publication are mentioned in the text, give only the page number for direct quotations.

▶ As Sylvan pointed out in his 2011 volume, "Sadly, natural disasters may be the best way to draw attention to the problem of global warming" (p. 184).

Omit parenthetical information for paraphrased material.

▶ In his 2011 volume, Sylvan pointed out the attention-getting impact of natural disasters.

If the citation follows a block quotation, place the citation after the final punctuation mark, as shown in Figure 6–9 on page 193. Use the spacing shown in the examples. Within the citation itself, separate the name, date, and page number with commas. Allow one space after each comma. Use the abbreviation *p.* or *pp.* (not italicized) before page numbers.

If your references list includes more than one work by the same author published in the same year, list the works alphabetically by title and add the lowercase letters *a, b, c,* and so forth, to the year in both the references-list entries and the text citations: (Ostro, 2011b, p. 347). When a work has two authors, cite both names joined by an ampersand: (Maddie & Khoshaba, 2012). For the first citation of a work with three, four, or five authors, include all names.

▶ As Burns, Brooks, and MacNeil (2011) argued . . .

For subsequent citations, include only the name of the first author followed by *et al.* (not italicized).

▶ Burns et al. (2011) put forth the alternate theory . . .

For a work with six or more authors, use the name of the first author followed by *et al.* in all citations.

▶ Their findings led to a burgeoning interest in the new theories of child development (Hargrove et al., 2012, p. 21).

When two or more works by different authors are cited in the same parentheses, list the citations alphabetically and use semicolons to separate the citations: (Loftus, 2010; Testerman, Kuegler, & Dowling, 2009; Van Gremergen, 2011).

If you are citing a source created by a corporation or an organization, use its name as the author.

▶ However, high employment rates in the Midwest affected this trend considerably (U.S. Department of Labor, 2010).

If you are quoting a source by an unknown author, use a brief version of the title in your citation.

▶ Textile manufacture had replaced the local maritime trade well before the mid-nineteenth century ("A Short History," 2010).

If two or more sources have authors with the same last name, use first initials in your citation: (J. Kellogg, 2011). When citing e-mail, phone calls, or personal interviews, use the words *personal communication* in your parenthetical citation.

▶ Linda Waters (personal communication, November 28, 2011), an executive at CorTex, stated the case succinctly. . . .

To refer to an entire website (not just to a particular article or document at that site), include the URL in your parenthetical citation.

▶ The U.S. Department of Commerce provides current statistics on international trade at the Bureau of Economic Analysis website (http://www.bea.gov).

However, do not cite the entire website in your references list. To cite a specific document from a website, follow the format that you would for a print document (citing the author, year, and page or paragraph number).

▶ Sokol (2012) argued that funding for technical assistance must keep pace with the needs of local communities (para. 8).

If there are no stable page or paragraph numbers in the online document, include information to help the reader find the passage you are citing, such as a heading.

▶ In his previous address to the group, he expressed his belief in the value of using technology in the classroom (Maxwell, 2011, Technology section).

APA Citation Format for a References List

Begin the references list on the first new page following the end of the text and title it "References." Begin each new entry at the left margin and indent the second and subsequent lines one-half inch from the left margin. (Your instructor may require you to use a paragraph indent instead. If so, begin at a paragraph indent, with subsequent lines continuing at the left margin.) Double-space within and between entries.

Include full page numbers when citing a range of pages for articles (119–124, not 119–24) and indicate with a comma if the page flow of an article is interrupted (119–124, 128–132). Use the abbreviation *p.* or *pp.* only with articles in newspapers (not in magazines or other sources), chapters in edited books, or proceedings.

Include only sources that were essential to the preparation of your document; do not include background reading. Do not include forms of personal communication, such as letters, e-mail, personal interviews, and telephone conversations. Cite these sources only in the text.

The following listing specifies the APA format and order of elements in a references list.

Author

- Alphabetize the list by author's last name and initials.
- List multiple works by the same author in publication date order, from earliest to latest. Give each a separate entry.
- For works by corporations or government agencies, alphabetize by organizational name.
- When no author is given, alphabetize by the first significant word in the title.

- For works by multiple authors, list the authors in the order in which they appear on the title page of the work, last name first. Separate author names with commas and insert an ampersand (&) before the last author's name. If there are eight or more authors, as there may be on some research articles, provide the first six names followed by three ellipsis dots and the last author's name.

Publication Date

- Enclose in parentheses.
- For journals and books, give only the year.
- For periodicals other than journals, give the year, comma, and month and day.

Title

- Capitalize the first word of the title and subtitle of books, articles, or chapters.
- Lowercase all other words except proper nouns.
- Italicize the titles of books.
- Do not use quotation marks or italics for titles of articles or chapters from books.
- End titles with a period.

Multiple Volume or Series Publications

- List the series number following the title, enclosed in parentheses.
- List the volume number following the title, enclosed in parentheses.
- List the edition number following the title, if it is not the first, enclosed in parentheses.

Publishing Information

- List the publishing information last for citations to books, pamphlets, and conference proceedings.
- Show a shortened form of the publisher's name.
- Include the publisher's city and state, even if the publisher's city is well known (*New York, NY*). Exception: Omit the state if the name of the publisher includes the state, as in the case of a university press.
- Abbreviate the state name using the two-letter postal code.
- Omit terms like *Publisher, Co.*, and *Inc.*
- Do not abbreviate the words *Books* and *Press.*

Periodicals

- Show the title of a journal, magazine, or newspaper in uppercase and lowercase letters.
- List the volume and page numbers after the title.
- List the issue number (in parentheses) for journals that do not have continuous page numbering throughout a volume.
- Italicize the title and volume numbers.

- Separate elements with commas and end with a period.
- If a journal article has been assigned a digital object identifier (DOI), insert it after the page numbers.

Online Sources

- Review the specific models for citing electronic sources on pages 190–191. Figure 6–10 on page 194 shows a sample APA-style references page.

APA Documentation Models

Books

Single Author

Black, A. (2015). *How business works: A graphic guide to business success.* London, UK: Dorling Kindersley.

Multiple Authors

Jain, P., & Sharma, P. (2014). *Behind every good decision: How anyone can use business analytics to turn data into profitable insight*. New York, NY: AMACOM.

Corporate Author

DK Publishing. (2014). *The business book (big ideas simply explained)*. London, UK: Dorling Kindersley.

Edition Other Than First

FitzGerald, J., Dennis, A., & Durcikova, A. (2014). *Business data communications and networking* (12th ed.). Hoboken, NJ: Wiley.

Multivolume Work

Standard and Poor's. (2013). *Standard and Poor's 500 guide, 2013 edition*. New York, NY: McGraw-Hill.

Work in an Edited Collection

Judah, B. (2014). London's laundry business. In D. Starkman, M. M. Hamilton, & R. Chittum (Eds.), *The best business writing, 2014 edition* (pp. 78–99). New York, NY: Columbia University Press.

Encyclopedia or Dictionary Entry

Brewer, D.J., & Picus, L.O. (Eds.). (2014). Access to education. In *Encyclopedia of education economics and finance*. Thousands Oaks, CA: Sage.

Articles in Periodicals

Magazine Article

Kuttner, R. (2015, Spring). The wealth problem. *The American Prospect, 26*(2), 33–37.

Journal Article

Wales, W., Wiklund, J., & McKelvie, A. (2015). What about new entry? Examining the theorized role of new entry in the entrepreneurial orientation-performance relationship. *International Small Business Journal, 33*(4), 351–373.

Newspaper Article

Hiltzik, M. (2015, June 12). Emissions cap-and-trade program is working well in California. *Los Angeles Times*, p. 17.

Article with Unknown Author

Put up the firewalls. (2015, June 11). *The Economist*, 23–24.

Electronic Sources

Document on a Website with an Author

Harvey, C. (2015, March). *We are killing the environment one hamburger at a time*. Retrieved from http://www.businessinsider.com/one-hamburger-environment-resources-2015-2

Document on a Website with a Corporate or an Organizational Author

Centers for Disease Control and Prevention. (2015). Healthy food service guidelines. Retrieved from http://www.cdc.gov/obesity/strategies/food-serv-guide.html

Document on a Website with an Unknown Author

Facebook news feed algorithm now considers time spent looking at a post. (2015). Retrieved from http://www.forbes.com/sites/amitchowdhry/2015/06/13/facebook-news-feed-algorithm-now-considers-time-spent-looking-at-a-post

Article with a Digital Object Identifier (DOI)

Lukason, O., & Hoffman, R. C. (2014). Firm bankruptcy probability and causes: An integrated study. *International Journal of Business and Management, 9*(11), 72–79. doi:10.5539/ijbm.v9n11p80

Article or Other Work from a Database

Velinov, A., & Chen, W. (2015). Do stock prices reflect their fundamentals? New evidence in the aftermath of the financial crisis. *Journal of Economics and Business, 80*, 1–20. Retrieved from http://www.sciencedirect.com/science/article/pii/S0148619515000119

Article in an Online Periodical

Goldman, D., & Pagliery, J. (2015, June 13). Net neutrality is here. What it means for you. *CNNMoney*. Retrieved from http://money.cnn.com/2015/06/12/technology/net-neutrality

Online Book

World Bank, Development Research Center of the State Council, & the People's Republic of China. (2014). *Urban China: Toward efficient, inclusive, and sustainable urbanization*. Retrieved from https://openknowledge.worldbank.org/handle/10986/18865

E-mail

Personal communications (including e-mail and messages from discussion groups and electronic bulletin boards) are not cited in an APA references list. They can be cited in the text as follows: "According to J. D. Kahl (personal communication, October 2, 2014), web pages need to reflect. . . ."

Entry in a Wiki

Pedagogical scenarios. (n.d.). Retrieved December 9, 2014, from http://edutechwiki.unige.ch/en/Category:Pedagogical_scenarios

Message Posted to a Newsgroup, an Online Forum, or a Discussion Board

myrc60. (2014, May 5). Re: Independent Contractors [Online forum]. Retrieved from **https://www.smallbusinessforums.org/showthread.php?850-Independent-Contractors**

Blog Post

Zumbrun, J. (2015, May 29). Today's graduates may have the strongest first decade in the job market of all millennials. [Web log post]. Retrieved from http://blogs.wsj.com/economics/2015/05/29/todays-graduates-may-have-the-strongest-first-decade-in-the-job-market-of-all-millennials/

Publication on CD-ROM

Malkin, M. (2015). *Who built that: awe-inspiring stories of American tinkerpreneurs* [CD-ROM]. New York, NY: Mercury Ink.

Multimedia Sources

Map or Chart

Bhutan Transportation. (2012). [Map]. Retrieved from https://www.cia.gov/library/publications/resources/cia-maps-publications/map-downloads/bhutan_transportation.jpg/image.jpg

Colorado. (2016). [Map]. Chicago, IL: Rand.

Film or Video

McNeal, D. [Host]. (2014). *Entrepreneurial thinking* [DVD]. Waterford, MI: Seminars on DVD.

McDonald, M. [Host]. (2015, June 9). Blue satellite in Decatur. [Video files]. *Illinois stories*. Retrieved from https://www.networkknowledge.tv/service/illinois-stories

Radio or Television Program

Siegel, R. (Host). (2015). Often employees, rarely CEOs: Challenges Asian Americans face in tech. *All things considered* [Radio broadcast]. Philadelphia, PA: WHYY.

Alfonsi, S. (Host). (2015, June 7). The storm after the storm [Television series episode]. In J. Fager (Executive producer), *60 minutes*. Boston, MA: WBZ.

Podcast or Webcast

Tyson, N. D. (2013, January 23). House science & national labs caucus: Neil deGrasse Tyson [Video webcast]. *The Library of Congress literature webcasts*. Retrieved from http://www.loc.gov/today/cyberlc/feature_wdesc.php?rec=5790

Glass, I. (Host). (2014, November 7). The leap [Audio podcast]. *This American life*. Retrieved from http://www.thisamericanlife.org/radio-archives/episode/539/the-leap

Other Sources

Published Interview

Dadich, S. (2014, August 22). The most wanted man in the world: Behind the scenes with Edward Snowden [Interview]. *Wired, 22*(9), 29–35.

Personal Interview and Letters

Personal communications (including telephone conversations) are not cited in a references list. They can be cited in the text as follows: "According to J. D. Kahl (personal communication, October 2, 2014), web pages need to reflect. . . ."

Brochure or Pamphlet

American Cancer Society. (2015). Colorectal cancer screening [Brochure]. Atlanta, GA: Author.

Government Document

U.S. Department of Labor, Bureau of Labor Statistics. (2014, October). *Female self-employment in the United States: An update to 2012*. Washington, DC: Government Printing Office.

Report Published in a Collection

Cady, L. E., & Fessenden, T. (2013). Gendering the divide: Religion, the secular, and the politics of sexual difference. In L. E. Cady & T. Fessenden (Eds.), *Religion, the secular, and the politics of sexual difference* (pp. 3–24). New York, NY: Columbia University Press.

Report Published Separately

Mitchell, A. (2015). *State of the news media 2015*. Washington, DC: Pew Research Center.

Unpublished Data

Kavsan, G., & Hersom, P. (2014). [Oregon small-business statistics, by county]. Unpublished raw data.

APA Sample Pages

ETHICS CASES 14

This report examines the nature and disposition of the 3,458 ethics cases handled companywide by CGF's ethics officers and managers during 2014. The purpose of such reports is to provide the Ethics and Business Conduct Committee with the information necessary for assessing the effectiveness of the first year of CGF's Ethics Program (Davis, Marks, & Tegge, 2004). According to Matthias Jonas (2004), recommendations are given for consideration "in planning for the second year of the Ethics Program" (p. 152).

The Office of Ethics and Business Conduct was created to administer the Ethics Program. The director of the Office of Ethics and Business Conduct, along with seven ethics officers throughout CGF, was given the responsibility for the following objectives, as described by Rossouw (2000):

> Communicate the values, standards, and goals of CGF's Program to employees. Provide companywide channels for employee education and guidance in resolving ethics concerns. Implement companywide programs in ethics awareness and recognition. Employee accessibility to ethics information and guidance is the immediate goal of the Office of Business Conduct in its first year. (p. 1543)

The purpose of the Ethics Program, established by the Committee, is to "promote ethical business conduct through open communication and compliance with company ethics standards" (Jonas, 2006, p. 89). To accomplish this purpose, any ethics policy must ensure confidentiality and anonymity for employees who raise genuine ethics concerns. The procedure developed at CGF guarantees that employees can . . .

Shortened title and page number

One-inch margins. Text double-spaced

Long quote indented one-half inch, double-spaced, without quotation marks

In-text citation gives name, date, and page number

Figure 6–9 APA Sample Page (from a Report)

APA

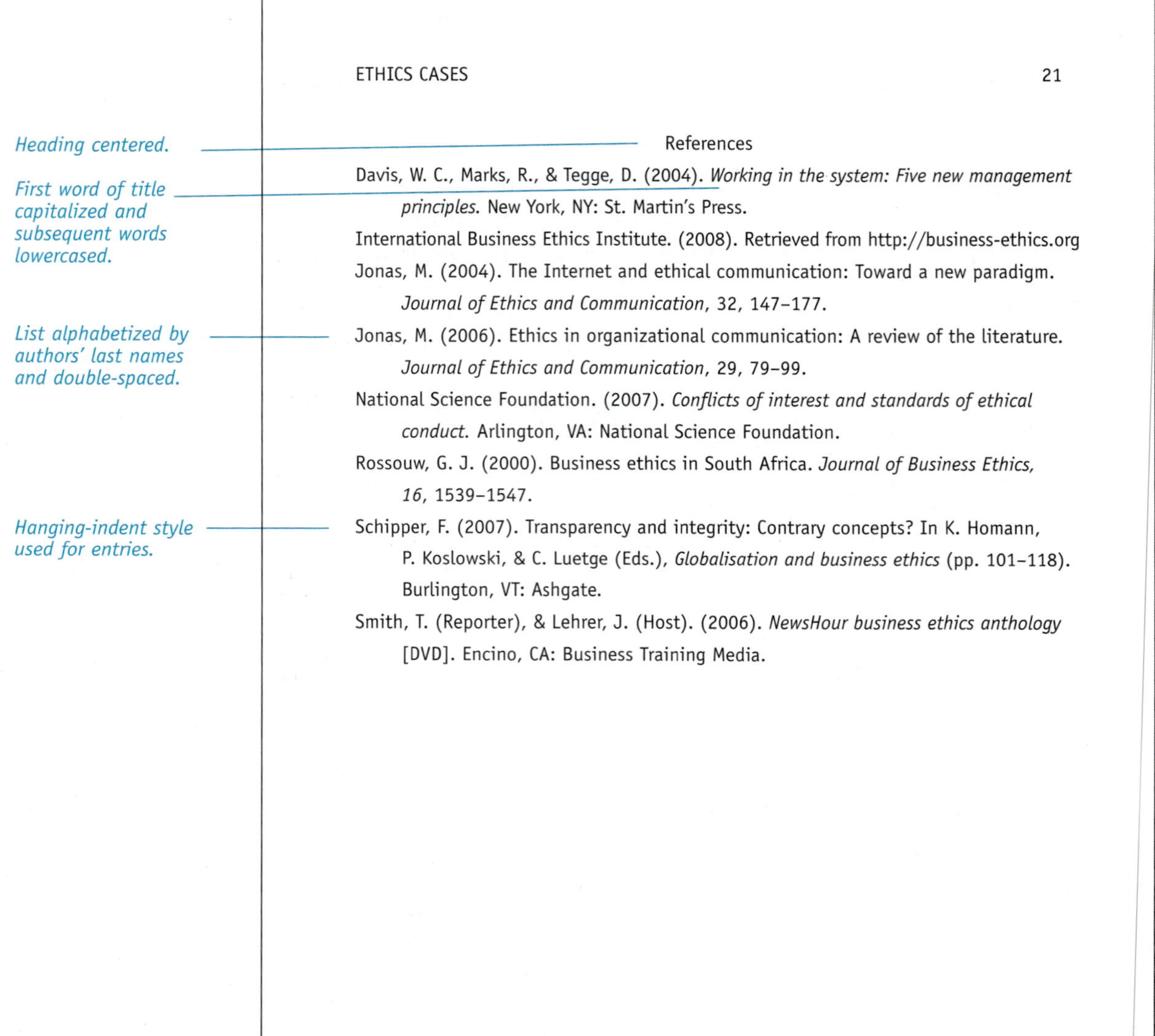

Heading centered.
First word of title capitalized and subsequent words lowercased.
List alphabetized by authors' last names and double-spaced.
Hanging-indent style used for entries.

ETHICS CASES 21

References

Davis, W. C., Marks, R., & Tegge, D. (2004). *Working in the system: Five new management principles.* New York, NY: St. Martin's Press.

International Business Ethics Institute. (2008). Retrieved from http://business-ethics.org

Jonas, M. (2004). The Internet and ethical communication: Toward a new paradigm. *Journal of Ethics and Communication*, 32, 147–177.

Jonas, M. (2006). Ethics in organizational communication: A review of the literature. *Journal of Ethics and Communication*, 29, 79–99.

National Science Foundation. (2007). *Conflicts of interest and standards of ethical conduct.* Arlington, VA: National Science Foundation.

Rossouw, G. J. (2000). Business ethics in South Africa. *Journal of Business Ethics, 16*, 1539–1547.

Schipper, F. (2007). Transparency and integrity: Contrary concepts? In K. Homann, P. Koslowski, & C. Luetge (Eds.), *Globalisation and business ethics* (pp. 101–118). Burlington, VT: Ashgate.

Smith, T. (Reporter), & Lehrer, J. (Host). (2006). *NewsHour business ethics anthology* [DVD]. Encino, CA: Business Training Media.

Figure 6–10 APA Sample List of References

MLA Style

MLA In-Text Citations

When you cite a source in text, give only the author's last name and the page number or numbers in parentheses.

> Preparing a videotape of measurement methods is cost-effective and can expedite training (Peterson 151).

If the author's name is mentioned in the text, give only the page number of the source in parentheses.

> Peterson summarized the results of these measurements in a series of tables (183–91).

If two or more sources have authors with the same last name, include their initials (or first names if their names begin with the same letter) to avoid confusion.

> These results were summarized 40 years ago (R. Peterson 183–91). S. Peterson has recently suggested the reevaluation of these findings (29).

Include no more information than is necessary to enable readers to find the corresponding entry in the list of works cited. To cite an entire work rather than a particular page in a work, mention the author's name in the text and omit the parenthetical citation.

Place a parenthetical citation in the text between the closing quotation mark or the last word of the sentence (or clause) and the end punctuation mark (usually a period). Use the spacing shown in the examples.

> The results of these studies have led even the most conservative managers to adopt technologies that will "catapult the industry forward" (Peterson 183–84).

If the parenthetical citation refers to an indented quotation, however, place it outside the last sentence of the quotation, as shown in Figure 6–11 on page 203.

If you are citing a page or pages of a multivolume work, give the volume number, followed by a colon, a space, and the page number(s): (Jones 2: 53–56). If the entire volume is being cited, identify the author and the volume: (Smith, vol. 3).

For more than one work by the same author, give the title of the work (or a shortened version if the title is long) in the parenthetical citation, unless you mention it in the text. If, for example, your list of works cited includes more than one work by Thomas J. Peters, the citation for his book *The Pursuit of Wow: Every Person's Guide to Topsy-Turvy Times* would appear as (Peters, *Pursuit* 93). Use only one space between the title and the page number.

To cite a source written by two or three authors, include all of the names in your parenthetical citation: (Rotherson and Peters 467–75); to cite a source written by four or more authors, include the first author's name followed by the phrase *et al.* ("and others," not italicized) or give all the authors' last names (depending on the style used in the works-cited list). To cite a source in which a separate work is quoted, provide the name of the person being quoted.

> According to Billings, there is "a greater potential for a small business to succeed in an urban area" (qtd. in Kooper et al. 421).

To quote a source written by a corporation or an organization, use that name as the author.

> However, many declining industries that fueled the economy of the 1950s are now being faced with a government mandate to clean up and preserve the environment (Environmental Protection Agency 16–17).

To quote a source by an unknown author, use a brief version of the title in your citation. (Put titles of articles in quotation marks and titles of books in italics.)

> The benefits of this treatment have been known since the early 1980s ("Audio Therapy" 56).

For a sentence that refers to two separate sources, include both in your parenthetical citation, separating them with a semicolon.

> Some analysts believe that the impact of electronic commerce caused the extreme market fluctuations of the late 1990s (Jones 174; Dragonetti 267).

To cite electronic sources, follow the same rules that you would for print sources, including as much identifying information as available (e.g., names and page numbers).

> As pointed out in a recent *Slate.com* article, America's poor are more numerous but less visible than ever (Connors).

If no names are indicated in the electronic source, use the title (full or shortened) in your citation; if no page numbers are indicated, do not cite any numbers, unless there are paragraph or section numbers. In this case, use the abbreviation *par.* or *sec.* (not in italics). Do not include URLs in your parenthetical citations or in your works-cited list.

> According to one online article, the organization's stated mission is to connect North American exporters with appropriate markets in Eastern Europe ("Business to Go," par. 18).

MLA Citation Format for a List of Works Cited

Begin the list of works cited on the first new page following the end of the text. Each new entry should begin at the left margin, with the second and subsequent lines within an entry indented one-half inch from the left margin. Double-space within and between entries. The correct format for dates is as follows: day, month, year, with no commas (18 Jan. 2013). Abbreviate all months except May, June, and July.

The following listing specifies the format of the elements in a list of works cited.

Author

- Alphabetize the list by the author's last name for a single author and by the last name of the first author for works with more than one author.

- List multiple works by the same author in alphabetical order by first significant word in the title. Put three hyphens and a period in place of the author's name for the second and subsequent titles.
- When a corporation or government agency is the author, alphabetize by organizational name, followed by a period.
- When no author is given, alphabetize by the first significant word in the title.
- For edited works, follow the editor's name with a comma and *ed.* or *eds.* (for more than one editor, not italicized).

Title

- Capitalize the first word in the title and subtitle and all significant words thereafter.
- Italicize the title of a book or pamphlet.
- Put quotation marks around the titles of articles in periodicals, essays in collections, or papers in proceedings.
- End titles with a period.

Multiple Volume or Series Publications

- Specify the edition, if not the first, after the title.
- Give the name of the series and series number after the publication information.
- When you cite one volume, include the volume number after the title and the total number of volumes at the end of the entry; otherwise, include the total number of volumes before the publication information.

Publication Information

- List the city of publication, publisher's name, and date of publication.
- Use a shortened form of the publisher's name.
- When publication information cannot be found, use *n.p.* (no publication place), *n.p.* (no publisher), and *n.d.* (no date).
- For familiar reference works, list only the edition and year of publication.

Medium Consulted

- Include the medium of the work you consulted: *Print, Web, MP3 file, DVD, Lecture, MS* (for a handwritten manuscript or letter), *TS* (for a typescript or typed letter).
- In most cases, the medium is listed at the end of the entry.
- For online entries, the medium is listed before the date of access.

See the documentation models for placement of the medium.

Periodicals

- For journal articles, list the volume number and issue number, date, and page numbers after the title of the periodical.
- For an article in a magazine or newspaper, omit the volume and issue numbers.

- For a newspaper, give the edition and page number(s).
- For a magazine article, give the page number(s).

Online Sources

Standards continue to evolve for citations of online and electronic sources. When citing online information, the two primary goals are to give credit to the author and to enable readers to retrieve the source. The MLA no longer requires the use of URLs but instead assumes readers will be able to find a source by entering the author, title, and other relevant information in a search engine or database.

Review the following guidelines for citing online sources:

- Begin with the author, the title of the work, and, if the work also appears in a printed version, the print publication information.
- Italicize the name of the website and follow it with the sponsor or publisher of the website. (The sponsor can usually be found in the site's copyright notice.) Then list the date of publication or most recent update, the medium (*Web*), and the date of access.
- For works accessed through a library database, insert the name of the database (in italics) after any print publication information. After the database name, list the medium (*Web*) and the date of access.
- For specific works found online, such as podcasts, wikis, and postings to a discussion group, consult the models in the following section.

See Figure 6–12 (page 204) for a sample list of works cited in MLA style.

MLA Documentation Models

Books

Single Author

Black, Alexandra. *How Business Works: A Graphic Guide to Business Success*. London: Dorling Kindersley, 2015. Print.

Multiple Authors

Jain, Piyanka, and Puneet Sharma. *Behind Every Good Decision: How Anyone Can Use Business Analytics to Turn Data into Profitable Insight*. New York: AMACOM, 2014. Print.

Corporate Author

DK Publishing. *The Business Book (Big Ideas Simply Explained)*. London: Dorling Kindersley, 2014. Print.

Edition Other Than First

FitzGerald, Jerry, Alan Dennis, & Alexandra Durcikova. *Business Data Communications and Networking*. 12th ed. Hoboken: Wiley, 2014. Print.

Multivolume Work

Dubofsky, Melvyn, and Paul S. Boyer, eds. *The Oxford Encyclopedia of American Business, Labor, and Economic History*. 2 vols. Oxford: Oxford UP, 2013. Print.

Work in an Edited Collection

Judah, Ben. "London's Laundry Business." *The Best Business Writing, 2014 edition.* Ed. Dean Starkman, Martha M. Hamilton, and Ryan Chittum. New York: Columbia University Press, 2014. 78–99. Print.

Encyclopedia or Dictionary Entry

"Access to Education." *Encyclopedia of Education Economics and Finance*. Ed. Dominic J. Brewer and Lawrence O. Picus. 2014. Print.

Articles in Periodicals

Magazine Article

Kuttner, Robert. "The Wealth Problem." *The American Prospect* 15 Mar. 2015: 33–37. Print.

Journal Article

Wales, William, Johan Wiklund, and Alexander McKelvie. "What About New Entry? Examining the Theorized Role of New Entry in the Entrepreneurial Orientation-Performance Relationship." *International Small Business Journal* 33.4 (2015): 351–373. Print.

Newspaper Article

Hiltzik, Michael. (2015, June 12). "Emissions Cap-and-Trade Program Is Working Well in California." *Los Angeles Times* 12 June 2015: B2. Print.

Article with Unknown Author

"Put Up the Firewalls." *Economist* (US) 11 June 2015: 23–24.

Electronic Sources

Entire Website

GreenpeaceBlogs.org. Greenpeace, n.d. Web. 20 Sept. 2014.

Short Work from a Website, with an Author

Harvey, Chelsea. (2015, March). "We Are Killing the Environment One Hamburger at a Time." *Business Insider*. *Business Insider*, Inc., 5 Mar., 2015. Web. 18 Apr. 2015.

Short Work from a Website, with a Corporate Author

Centers for Disease Control and Prevention. "Healthy Food Service Guidelines." CDC.gov. USA.gov, 20 Jan. 2015. Web. 22 Feb. 2015.

Short Work from a Website, with an Unknown Author

"Facebook News Feed Algorithm Now Considers Time Spent Looking at a Post." *Forbes.com*. Forbes, 2015. Web. 13 June 2015.

Article from a Database (Subscription)

"From Rock to Crock: The Economics of the Music Industry." *The Economist* [US] 4 June 2015: 14. Expanded Academic ASAP. Web. 7 July, 2015.

Article in an Online Journal

McGowan, Pauric, Sarah Cooper, Mark Durkin, and Caroline O'Kane. "The Influence of Social and Human Capital in Developing Young Women as Entrepreneurial Business Leaders." *Journal of Small Business Management* 53.3 (2015): 645–661. Web. 11 July 2015.

Article in an Online Magazine

Thomsen, Jacqueline. "'Less Soda Means More Adderall': What Happens When a College Campus Bans Sugary Drinks?" *Slate*. The Slate Group, 19 June 2015. Web. 5 Oct. 2015.

Article in an Online Newspaper

Vanderkam, Laura. "Working Mothers Who Make It All Work." *Wall Street Journal*. Dow Jones, 19 June 2015. Web. 5 Nov. 2015.

Online Book

World Bank, Development Research Center of the State Council, & the People's Republic of China. *Urban China: Toward Efficient, Inclusive, and Sustainable Urbanization*. Washington, DC: World Bank, 2014. *Open Knowledge Repository*. Web. 12 Dec. 2014.

Publication on CD-ROM

Malkin, Michelle. *Who Built That: Awe-Inspiring Stories of American Tinkerpreneurs.* New York: Mercury Ink, 2015. CD-ROM.

E-mail Message

Kahl, Jonathan D. "Re: Web page." Message to the author. 2 Oct. 2014. E-mail.

Blog

You're the boss. New York Times Co., n.d. Web. 31 Oct. 2014.

Entry or Comment on a Blog

Zumbrun, Josh. "Today's Graduates May Have the Strongest First Decade in the Job Market of all Millennials." *Real Time Economics*. Dow Jones, 29 May 2015. Web. 7 Sept. 2015.

Posting to an Online Discussion Group

Kelly, Will. "Online Meeting Tools and Technical Communication Teams." Techwr-l. TechWhirl.com, 1 Jan. 2013. Web. 15 Oct. 2015.

Multimedia Sources

Entry in a Wiki

"Come Unto Him (Johnson, Edward F.)." *MSLP: Petrucci Music Library*. International Music Score Project, 30 Aug. 2031. Web. 25 Oct. 2015.

Map or Chart

Colorado. Map. Chicago: Rand, 2016. Print.

"San Francisco." Map. *Google Maps*. Google, 2015. Web. 7 Sept. 2015.

Film or Video

Entrepreneurial Thinking. Narr. Delatorro McNeal. Seminars on DVD, 2014. DVD.

McDonald, Mark. (2015, June 9). "Blue Satellite in Decatur." *Illinois Stories*. Network Knowledge, 11 Dec. 2013. Web. 5 Jan. 2015.

Radio or Television Program

"Massive Cyberattack on Federal Government." The Situation Room. Host Wolf Blitzer. CNN. 4 June 2015. Television.

Glinton, Sonari. "How a Tax on Chicken Changed the Playing Field for U.S. Automakers." Morning Edition. Hosts Steve Inskeep and David Greene. Natl. Public Radio. WBEZ, Chicago, 19 June 2015. Radio.

Television Interview

Brokaw, Tom. Interview by Charlie Rose. *The Charlie Rose Show*. PBS. WGBH, Boston, 11 May 2015. Television.

Podcast

Green, Sarah. "Why Leadership Feels Awkward." *HBR IdeaCast*. Harvard Business Review, 12 Feb. 2015. MP3 file. 22 Oct. 2015.

Other Sources

Published Interview

Snowden, Edward. "The Most Wanted Man in the World." Interview by Scott Dadich. *Wired*. Conde Nast, 22 Aug. 2014. Web. 18 Oct. 2015.

Personal Interview

Sariolgholam, Mahmood. Personal interview. 29 Nov. 2014.

Personal Letter

Pascatore, Monica. Letter to the author. 10 Apr. 2015. TS.

Brochure or Pamphlet

American Cancer Society. *Colorectal Cancer Screening*. Atlanta: American Cancer Society, Inc., 2015. Print.

Government Document

United States. Dept. of Labor. Bureau of Labor Statistics. *Female Self-Employment in the United States: An Update to 2012*. Washington: GPO, 2014. Print.

Lecture or Speech

Morehead, Shellee. "Sex, DNA, and Family History." Local and Family History Lecture Ser. Boston Public Lib. 29 May 2015. Lecture.

MLA Sample Pages

Litzinger 14

Author's last name and page number.

This report examines the nature and disposition of the 3,458 ethics cases handled companywide by CGF's ethics officers and managers during 2014. The purpose of such reports is to provide the Ethics and Business Conduct Committee with the information necessary for assessing the effectiveness of the first year of CGF's Ethics Program (Davis, Marks, and Tegge 142). According to Matthias Jonas, recommendations are given for consideration "in planning for the second year of the Ethics Program" ("Internet" 152).

One-inch margins. Text double-spaced.

The Office of Ethics and Business Conduct was created to administer the Ethics Program. The director of the Office of Ethics and Business Conduct, along with seven ethics officers throughout CGF, was given the responsibility for the following objectives, as described by Rossouw:

> Communicate the values, standards, and goals of CGF's Program to employees. Provide companywide channels for employee education and guidance in resolving ethics concerns. Implement companywide programs in ethics awareness and recognition. Employee accessibility to ethics information and guidance is the immediate goal of the Office of Business Conduct in its first year. (1543)

Long quote indented one inch, double-spaced, without quotation marks.

The purpose of the Ethics Program, according to Jonas, is to "promote ethical business conduct through open communication and compliance with company ethics standards" ("Ethics" 89). To accomplish this purpose, any ethics policy must ensure confidentiality for anyone . . .

In-text citations give author name and page number. Title used when multiple works by same author cited.

Figure 6–11 MLA Sample Page (from a Report)

MLA

Heading centered.

List alphabetized by authors' last names or title and double-spaced.

Hanging-indent style used for entries.

Litzinger 14

Works Cited

Davis, W. C., Roland Marks, and Diane Tegge. *Working in the System: Five New Management Principles*. New York: St. Martin's, 2004. Print.

International Business Ethics Institute. Inter. Business Ethics Inst., 14 Jan. 2008. Web. 19 June 2014.

Jonas, Matthias. "Ethics in Organizational Communication: A Review of the Literature." *Journal of Ethics and Communication* 29.2 (2006): 79–99. Print.

---. "The Internet and Ethical Communication: Toward a New Paradigm." *Journal of Ethics and Communication* 32.1 (2004): 147–77. Print.

Rossouw, George J. "Business Ethics in South Africa." *Journal of Business Ethics* 16.14 (2000): 1539–47. Print.

Sariolghalam, Mahmood. Personal interview. 29 Jan. 2008.

Schipper, Fritz. "Transparency and Integrity: Contrary Concepts?" *Globalisation and Business Ethics*. Ed. Karl Homann, Peter Koslowski, and Christoph Luetge. Burlington: Ashgate, 2007. 101–18. Print.

Smith, Terrence. "Legislating Ethics." *NewsHour Business Ethics Anthology*. Host Jim Lehrer. Encino: Business Training Media, 2006. DVD.

United States. Natl. Science Foundation. *Conflicts of Interest and Standards of Ethical Conduct*. NSF Manual No. 15. Arlington: Natl. Science Foundation, 2007. Print.

Figure 6–12 MLA Sample List of Works Cited

Other Style Manuals

Many professional societies, publishing companies, and other organizations publish manuals that prescribe bibliographic reference formats for their publications or for publications in their fields. In addition, several general style manuals are well known and widely used.

Biology

Council of Science Editors. *Scientific Style and Format: The CSE Manual for Authors, Editors, and Publishers.* 7th ed. Reston: Council of Science Editors, 2006. Print.

See also councilscienceeditors.org.

Chemistry

Dodd, Janet S., ed. *ACS Style Guide: A Manual for Authors and Editors.* 2nd ed. Washington: Amer. Chemical Soc., 1997. Print.

See also www.acs.org.

Government Documents

United States. Government Printing Office. *Style Manual.* 30th ed. Washington: GPO, 2008. Print.

Journalism

Christian, Darrell, Sally Jacobson, and David Minthorn, eds. *Associated Press Stylebook and Briefing on Media Law.* 46th ed. New York: Basic Books, 2011. Print.

See also www.apstylebook.com.

Law

Harvard Law Review et al. *The Bluebook: A Uniform System of Citation.* 18th ed. Cambridge: Harvard Law Rev. Assn., 2005. Print.

See also www.legalbluebook.com.

Medicine

Iverson, Cheryl, et al. *American Medical Association Manual of Style: A Guide for Authors and Editors.* 10th ed. Oxford: Oxford UP, 2007. Print.

See also www.ama-assn.org.

Political Science

American Political Science Association. *APSA Style Manual for Political Science.* Rev. ed. Washington: APSA, 2006. Print.

See also www.apsanet.org.

Social Work

National Association of Social Workers. *Writing for the NASW Press: Information for Authors.* National Association of Social Workers. Web. http://www.naswpress.org/authors/guidelines/00-contents.html.

CHAPTER 6 SUMMARY: CONDUCTING RESEARCH FOR A DOCUMENT

Information sources available to you as you research job-related topics include firsthand observations that you gather directly and the results of research published by others that is available in print or online.

- Interview yourself. Your own knowledge, training, and experience may provide essential information.
- Personal interviews with subject-matter experts can provide up-to-date information not readily available elsewhere, but interviews require thoughtful preparation.
    - Select the subject-matter expert most likely to be helpful.
    - Prepare specific questions before the interview.
    - Take careful notes during the interview.
    - Review and summarize your notes immediately after the interview.
- Firsthand observations and experiments are essential to gather information about behavior, natural phenomena, and the functions of processes or equipment. To gather observational information:
    - Choose sites and times carefully and, as necessary, request permission in advance.
    - Keep complete, accurate records and note dates, times, durations, and other details.
    - Remain as unobtrusive as possible to not interfere with the process under observation.
- Questionnaires permit you to obtain the views of groups of people without the time and expense necessary for conducting numerous personal interviews.
    - Design the questionnaire to gather as much information as you need with as little effort as possible on behalf of those answering the questions.
    - Formulate questions so that the answers can be readily tabulated.
    - Carefully select respondents to ensure that their responses represent a cross section of the population about which you wish to generalize your results.
- Use workplace content already available when it's suitable for your purpose.
    - Adapt the content to fit the new context.
    - Revise as necessary when the material is repurposed for a different medium.
- Libraries provide organized access to a wealth of information in their print, audiovisual, and digitized collections. Researchers can access the information through
    - Library catalogs
    - Databases
    - Reference works
- The Internet provides online access to immense amounts of information, although its lack of a coherent organization makes locating salient information a challenge. To increase the odds of locating what you need, use search engines, subject directories, and metasearch engines.
    - Evaluate print and online sources of information for their relevance, timeliness, and accuracy.
    - Review the information source for its depth and breadth of coverage of your topic.
    - Ensure that the source is reputable.
    - Evaluate the information for any evidence of bias.
    - Keep detailed records of these sources for your bibliography.

- Take notes that accurately summarize the information relevant to your topic.
- Avoid plagiarism and other intellectual property violations by giving complete and accurate credit to all your information sources, which will do the following:
  - Allow readers to locate the source of the information given.
  - Establish your credibility by supporting your work with information from existing sources.
  - Give proper credit to your sources.
- Document the information that you quote, paraphrase, or summarize in your text in brief parenthetical in-text citations, with full information in an alphabetical list of references or works cited at the end of the text.
- Follow the guidelines of a documentation system like APA or MLA, or another system for a specific field.

Exercises

1. Review the online catalog search in this chapter (illustrated in Figures 6–4 through 6–6 on pages 162–164). Choose a topic related to your area of study and conduct a step-by-step online catalog search by keyword. What three to five books would you consider using, and why? Using the same topic, conduct the same step-by-step search using an Internet search engine. What three to five books would you consider using based on this second search, and why?
2. For each sentence in the following passage, decide whether it is necessary to add quotation marks or cite a source. Explain your reasoning.

   ▶ Many people have made money investing in real estate in the past couple of years. However, what goes up, comes back down (1). EZHomeBuilders, a corporation that builds luxury homes, announced that falling real estate values are causing them to scale back some projects and cancel others (2). After they announced this, shares of EZHomeBuilders fell 50 percent on the New York Stock Exchange, closing at $27.14 per share (3). Shares of other major builders fell as well (4).

   My aunt, Shelly Maughn, who is a residential real estate broker, says she thinks the market will return to the way it was about a decade ago, with prices increasing more slowly (5). She also used to work in retail sales and sold furnishings and appliances for homes where she watched sales go up and down with the housing market (6). When business for home builders slowed, business slowed for us, she says (7).

   I worked as an intern in Aunt Shelly's real estate office last summer and I really enjoyed it (8). One day, I hope to become a residential real estate broker and investor even though real estate can be a challenging career (9).
3. Prepare an APA-style references list or an MLA-style works-cited list, as directed by your instructor, using your course written assignments' references lists.
4. Use one of your library's online periodical databases (such as CQ Researcher) to find articles related to a recent discovery or an important trend in your field. Write a three-page report of your findings, using the APA or MLA style of documentation. Cite your sources within your text and include an APA-style references list or an MLA-style list of works cited.
5. For Research Project 2 in Chapter 1, you interviewed instructors about how they prepare their class lectures for their different groups of students. Go back to your

interview transcripts and incorporate at least two direct quotes and two paraphrases of your interviewees' comments into your written findings.

6. The use of cell phones, laptop computers, and digital cameras has created a growing need for the recycling of portable rechargeable batteries. Many retail stores are promoting goodwill with their customers and helping to preserve the environment by shipping spent battery packs to recycling centers. Create an online questionnaire using one of the free online tools for doing so to determine if people are aware of the need to recycle portable rechargeable batteries and how people feel about companies that provide recycling programs. Invite at least 20 people to participate, collate your results, and present your findings to the class. Use a table or graph to illustrate your findings.

Collaborative Classroom Projects

1. Bring to class information related to your area of study from three websites. Print out relevant pages from each site and draft a brief synopsis of the resources provided there. Form groups with three to five students who share your major. Review the guidelines in this chapter for evaluating a website and draft a list of questions to consider when evaluating a website as a research resource specific to your field. Evaluate and compare each of the sites that your group members have found and decide which sites would be the most valuable for your research. Write a brief group summary of your findings to share with the class.
2. Using the online sources that you brought to class for Collaborative Classroom Project 1, work in a group of three to five students to create an APA-style list of references and an MLA-style works-cited list from your collective online sources. (Refer to the Documenting Sources section on pages 184–206 of this chapter as needed.)

Research Projects

1. Prepare to interview someone who is now in the career you seek. You can find someone in your field through the campus career-development office, through local professional organizations related to your field, or even through relatives and friends. Submit the name and position of the individual as well as a list of questions you plan to ask to your instructor for approval. Write a short report in which you incorporate the information you gathered at your interview and document the interview in APA or MLA style. Submit to your instructor your organized notes of the interview and the letter or e-mail that you sent to request the interview.
2. Assume you are a manager at a small manufacturing firm (you may choose the product that your company produces). Because of a rising national concern about the environment and land use, the board of directors has asked your department to develop a policy statement outlining your corporation's views on the conservation of natural resources. Use your library's Web subject directory to locate information about how government environmental policy affects your business. Submit your list of at least five sites with your notes, describing the information contained at each site and giving reasons why you chose these sites. Include with your notes an APA-style references list or an MLA-style list of works cited.

3. Imagine that you work in public relations at an engineering college and your department is hosting a "brain teaser" competition for local high school students as a strategy to get more of them interested in the sciences and engineering, especially at your university. Many engineering professors and consultants will be in the audience. You decide to create a list of questions about the possibility of human travel to Mars. You research several websites to gather information about current knowledge of the planet (based on spacecraft fly-bys and surface explorations with the Mars Rover program) and how and why human travel would expand that knowledge. You also want to include questions about the technical and habitat problems needing solutions before such missions become feasible. It is very important not only that you have accurate answers for your questions but also that you have credible sources in case someone doubts your answers.

7 Designing Documents and Visuals

Contents

Workplace — and classroom — communications require more than words. They often require tables, drawings, photos, maps, graphs, and charts — elements that must be integrated with text on a page or a screen into a unified whole. The integration of text and images is best accomplished by understanding several key principles of document and visual design. These principles establish the foundation for the practical guidelines provided throughout the rest of the chapter.

This chapter is divided into two main parts. The first, Designing Documents, offers detailed information for document layout and design; the second, Creating Visuals, provides guidelines and models for designing illustrations, for integrating illustrations into the text, and for using graphics to communicate with an international audience.

Clarity and consistency are important not only for good writing but also for the design and layout of any document — especially one that includes visuals — and for the creation and use of the visuals themselves. Effectively designed documents help readers locate the information they need and grasp how the parts of the document fit together. The Designing Documents section describes how to achieve these goals by providing your readers with carefully selected visual cues. Whether you are creating a memo, a report, or a newsletter, everything from your choice of type size and style to the arrangement of text and visuals on each page contributes to your reader's comprehension.

The Creating Visuals section of this chapter focuses on how to use visual aids to increase your reader's understanding of your topic. Tables, graphs, drawings, charts, maps, and photographs — often collectively called *visuals* — can express ideas or convey information that words alone cannot. Presented with clarity and consistency, visuals can help readers focus on the key concepts in your document, presentation, or website.

Understanding Design Principles

To be able to create effective documents and visuals, it helps to understand basic principles of design. In fact, the same set of principles applies to both documents and visuals. These principles are grounded in the observation that visual perception is an active thinking process that depends on context. Essentially, when you look at a document or at a visual within a document, you are looking at it with a particular goal or purpose that, along with your past experience and expectations, helps to determine what you notice.

For example, assume that your university has published a planning document that includes a bar graph of expected tuition increases for the next ten years. If you're currently a sophomore, you are primarily interested in tuition costs for the next couple of years. When you look at the graph, your goal (figuring out what *you* will have to pay in tuition) determines where you focus your attention, and your past experience reading bar graphs helps you interpret the information you find.

Even though an object is made up of multiple parts — lines, shapes, colors, and so on — we typically perceive the object as a whole, not as a collection of individual parts. In other words, when you look at that bar graph of expected tuition increases, you don't necessarily take note of the fact that the bars are blue rectangles with a black border; you tend instead to see the overall patterns, such as the fact that the bars quickly get taller, meaning that you'll be paying more for tuition by the time you graduate.

Psychologists have identified a number of perceptual principles based on these underlying concepts that form the foundation of effective design. Three of the most important include:

- Grouping
- Contrast
- Repetition

Grouping

Grouping helps readers see relationships among items on a page or screen, which in turn helps them grasp how information is organized and what is most important. Grouping can occur in several different ways.

- *Proximity:* Items that are close together seem like part of a group, while items that are far apart seem dissimilar. Related items (for example, a heading and the paragraph that follows it) should be closer together than less closely related items (a heading and the paragraph above the heading).
- *Similarity:* Items that share qualities (such as size, shape, color) are viewed as similar and tend to be associated as part of a group.
- *Alignment:* Items that are aligned tend to be grouped. If the items in a bulleted list are aligned with one another and indented from the rest of the text, for example, readers immediately recognize them as related.

Contrast

Contrast sets items apart and helps readers quickly grasp which items are different from one another. For example, to emphasize one data bar in a graph, you might give it a different color or pattern from the other bars. Likewise, to highlight one sector of a pie chart, show it slightly ajar from the other sectors. To give readers an easy way to navigate a long document, you might contrast the headings from the body text by making them larger or a different color from the surrounding text.

Repetition

Repetition communicates consistency and predictability through repeated patterns of design elements whether on a page, screen, table, or visual. Inconsistencies in these patterns are confusing and distracting. If like items on a page (headings, footers, bulleted lists) vary slightly from one another in their design, readers do not know whether the items are supposed to be a related group. Consistency ensures that the patterns in a document or visual are clear and unambiguous. Repetition thus allows the users of a document to focus on the things they should pay attention to (the things that you, as the author, want them to pay attention to) instead of spending time trying to interpret the design.

Adhering to these foundational design and rhetorical principles will help you create documents and visuals that convey your content clearly and unambiguously for ease of understanding. In the sections that follow, we discuss how these principles apply to elements of document layout, such as typography, headings, and columns, and to different types of visuals, such as tables and line graphs.

Designing Documents

Most memos, letters, meeting minutes, progress reports, internal and external Web pages, and other routine communications are formatted according to standards in an organization's style book or other organizational guidance document. In this text, business-correspondence formats are discussed in Chapter 8, Writing E-mails, Memos, and Letters; formal-report formats are discussed in Chapter 11, Writing Formal Reports. However, certain high-visibility, complex, or special-purpose documents, such as those aimed at customers, stockholders, or clients, require special layout-and-design consideration.

This section introduces you to the document layout-and-design principles for such nonroutine materials. Thoughtfully applied, these principles will make even the most complex information look accessible and give readers a favorable impression of the organization that produced it. To accomplish these goals, any document's design should do the following:

- Offer a simple, uncluttered presentation of the topic.
- Highlight the content's structure, hierarchy, and order.
- Help readers find information easily.
- Reinforce an organization's image.

The same content can read differently with and without a well-designed page layout. Figure 7–1, for example, is a sample page from a software instruction manual without any conscious design devices. Note the effort necessary to follow the logic of the instructions — the words and sentences run together without any breaks or pointers to the content's organization and logic. Figure 7–2 shows the same information with a layout that both highlights the content's sequence and cues the reader to the location of this material within the manual.

Effective design is based on visual simplicity, consistency, and harmony, such as using compatible fonts, colors, and the same highlighting device for similar items. Design should reveal hierarchy by signaling the difference between topics and subtopics, between primary and secondary information, and between general points and examples that support those points. Writers can achieve these goals by intentionally selecting fonts, choosing devices to highlight information, and arranging text and visual components on a page. In addition to making information easy to find, the design should project the appropriate image of an organization. For example, clients paying a high fee for consulting services may expect a report of study findings with a sophisticated design, high-quality paper, color images, and imaginative typography. Employees inside an organization or taxpayers in a community may expect management or community officials to be frugal, so they may accept — even expect — publications printed in black and white with simple designs.

Reference numbers have three parts: the basic reference number, a transposition check digit (TCD) that helps verify correct entry of the number, and a suffix that lets the system link related reference numbers such as an incoming message and the reply to that message. The system adds hyphens to longer reference numbers to make them easier to read. Parts of a reference number: in the sequence 123-456789-B123, 123-456789 is the basic reference number, B is the TCD, and 123 is the suffix.

System messages are informational, advisory, or error messages that appear on screens. Simple messages appear on the last line of any screen. Multiple messages appear on the Message Screen, which is accessed by pressing MESSAGE. The start of the message indicates the message type. Information Message is a confirmation that the system accepts your transaction. ⊵ Important: The most important informational message is TRANSACTION ACCEPTED AND POSTED TO FILES, which indicates the transaction has been successfully completed and is now part of the record for that account, instrument, or instruction. Look for this message as you post each message.

Figure 7–1 Page with Poorly Designed Layout

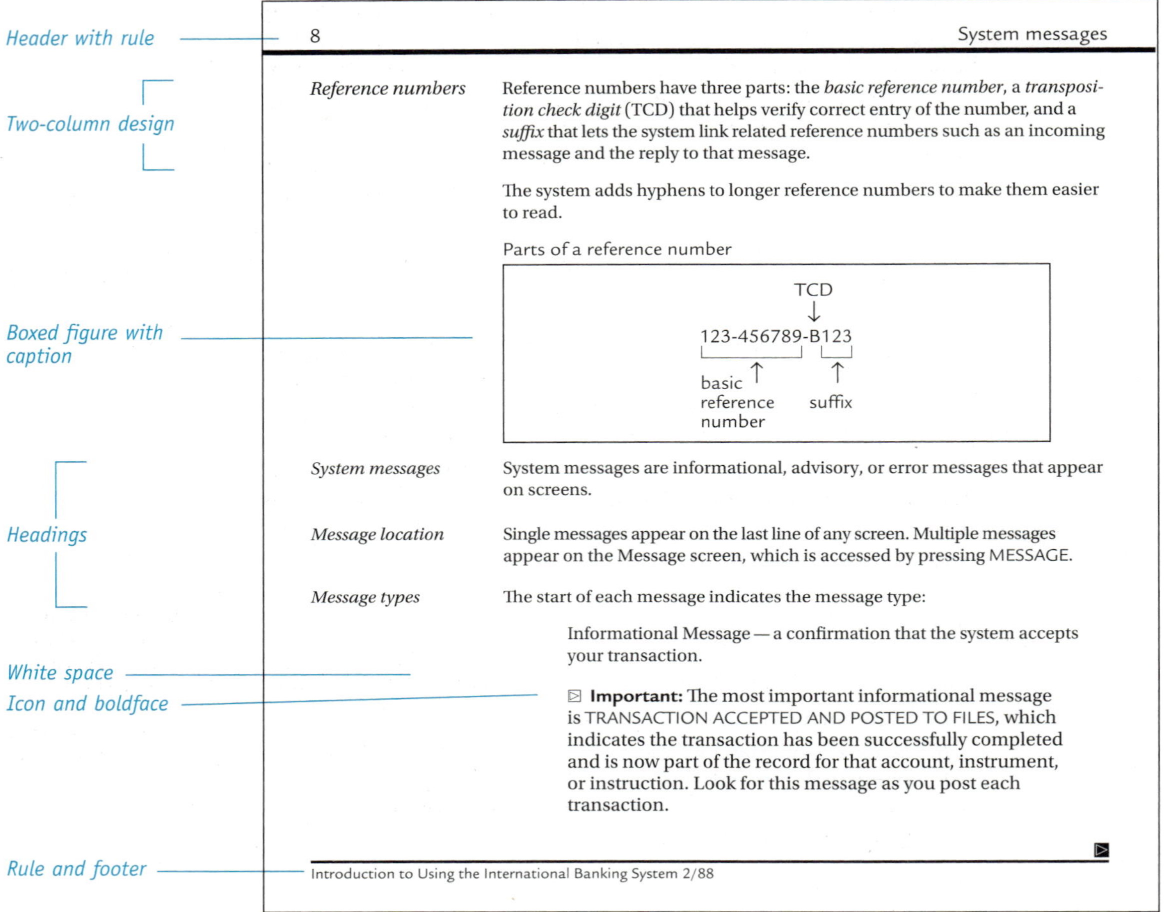
Header with rule
8 System messages
Two-column design
Reference numbers
Reference numbers have three parts: the *basic reference number*, a *transposition check digit* (TCD) that helps verify correct entry of the number, and a *suffix* that lets the system link related reference numbers such as an incoming message and the reply to that message.
The system adds hyphens to longer reference numbers to make them easier to read.
Boxed figure with caption
Parts of a reference number
TCD
123-456789-B123
basic reference number
suffix
Headings
System messages
System messages are informational, advisory, or error messages that appear on screens.
Message location
Single messages appear on the last line of any screen. Multiple messages appear on the Message screen, which is accessed by pressing MESSAGE.
Message types
The start of each message indicates the message type:
Informational Message — a confirmation that the system accepts your transaction.
White space
Icon and boldface
Important: The most important informational message is TRANSACTION ACCEPTED AND POSTED TO FILES, which indicates the transaction has been successfully completed and is now part of the record for that account, instrument, or instruction. Look for this message as you post each transaction.
Rule and footer
Introduction to Using the International Banking System 2/88

Figure 7–2 Page Illustrating Well-Thought-Out Design and Layout Choices

Typography

Typography refers to the style and arrangement of type on a printed page. A complete set of all the letters, numbers, and symbols available in one typeface (or style) is called a *font*.

Typeface

For most on-the-job writing, select a typeface primarily for its simplicity and legibility. Avoid typefaces that may distract readers, such as *script* and *cursive* typefaces that mimic calligraphy or handwriting. Let your audience, purpose, and the context guide your choice. You would expect cursive typeface in a wedding invitation but not in an annual or a technical report. One major distinction among typefaces is the presence or absence of serifs. Serifs are the small projections at the end of each stroke in a letter. The text of this book is set in Utopia, a serif typeface, and all headings are in Officina Sans, a sans serif (without serifs) typeface. Serif type is easier to read, especially in the smaller sizes, and it works better for main text than sans serif. Sans serif type, however, works well for headings (like the ones in this book). The simpler design of sans serif letters also makes them ideal for use with text on websites and for use in other documents read on-screen. Choose popular typefaces, such as Times New Roman, or any of the following, especially when preparing text for digital media:

Univers	Century	Gill Sans
Palatino	Garamond	Helvetica

Do not use more than two or three typefaces in a single document—using too many typefaces will confuse readers and create visual disharmony in your document. To create a dramatic contrast between headings and text, as in a newsletter, use a typeface for the heading that is distinctively different from that of the text. You can also use a noticeably different typeface within a graphic element. In any case, experiment before making your final decision. (Keep in mind that not all fonts have the same assortment of symbols and other characters that you may need for your graphics.)

Type Size

Ensure that your text is easily readable. Small print can cause eyestrain and make the text look crammed and intimidating. Six-point type, for example, is too small for almost anything other than classified ads. Likewise, large type makes reading difficult for a general audience, although it may be suitable for readers with visual impairment. Ideal point sizes for text in paper documents range from 10 to 12 points. For documents that will be read from a distance or that are geared toward visually impaired readers, use large type sizes. Figure 7–3 illustrates a range of type sizes.

◆ *Ideal type sizes for presentation slides are discussed in Chapter 14, Giving Presentations, and for websites in Appendix A, Writing in an Online Environment.*

Highlighting Devices

Highlighting devices can give a document a visual logic and clarify its organization. For example, rules and boxes can set off steps in a process and illustrations from surrounding explanations. However, be selective about how you use these devices and

6 pt. This size might be used for dating a source.
8 pt. This size might be used for footnotes.
10 pt. This size might be used for headers and footers.
12 pt. This size might be used for main text and figure captions.
14 pt. This size might be used for section headings.
18 pt. This size might be used for chapter titles.

Figure 7–3 Samples of 6- to 18-Point Type Sizes

◆ *For additional guidance on highlighting facts and ideas, see pages 102–107 in Chapter 4, Revising a Document.*

special graphics; too many design devices clutter a page and interfere with comprehension. And consistency is important: Use the same technique to highlight a particular feature throughout your document. Writers use a number of methods to emphasize important words, passages, and sections within documents:

- Typographical devices
- Headings and captions
- Headers and footers
- Rules, icons, and color

Review Figure 7–2 to see an effective use of these devices.

Typographical Devices

When used sparingly, **boldface**, *italics*, color, and ALL-CAPITAL LETTERS can help you achieve emphasis.

- Use **boldface** type for headings or short passages of text to which you would like to draw attention.
- Use *italics* to highlight a key term or phrase or to slow readers, as in cautions or warnings.
- Use ALL-CAPITAL LETTERS for headings (with or without boldface) or to alert readers to crucial steps in a process, as in instructions, or to indicate danger, such as in a caution or warning message.
- Use color as you would the other devices — sparingly and consistently.

Headings and Captions

Headings — titles and subtitles within the body of a document — divide material into comprehensible segments by highlighting the main topics and signaling topic changes. They indicate the hierarchy within a document and help readers decide which sections they need to read. Captions — titles that highlight or describe illustrations or blocks of text — often appear below figures, above tables, and in the left or right margins next to blocks of text. Note the captions used to describe the figures and tables throughout this book.

Headings appear in many typeface variations (**boldface** being most common) and often use sans serif typefaces. The most common positions for headings and subheadings are centered, flush left, indented, or by themselves in a wide left margin. Insert an additional line of space above a heading to emphasize the division on the page, as shown throughout this text. Major section or chapter headings normally appear at the top of a new page. Never leave a heading as the final line on a page — the heading will be disconnected from its text and thus ineffective. Instead, move the heading to the start of the next page. A heading that appears near the end of a page should be followed by at least two lines of text.

◆ *For detailed advice on using and formatting headings in formal reports, see pages 377 and 382 in Chapter 11, Writing Formal Reports.*

Headers and Footers

A header appears at the top of each page and contains such information as the topic or subtopic of a section, the section number, the date the document was written, the page number, the document name, or the section title; a footer contains similar information at the bottom of each page. These help readers pinpoint their location within a document. (The header at the top of the next page reads "Chapter 7 ◆ Designing Documents and Visuals," and includes the page number.) Document pages may have headers or footers or both, as in Figure 7–2. Although headers and footers are important reference devices, limit the amount of information in them to avoid visual clutter. Headers and footers are usually in a smaller type size than the main text.

Rules, Icons, and Color

Rules are vertical or horizontal lines used to divide one area of the page from another or to create boxes; used in moderation, rules isolate and highlight important information for ease of reading. Figure 7–2 illustrates the effective use of rules to separate the header and footer from the main text.

An icon is a pictorial representation of an idea; it looks like what it represents and can be used to identify specific actions, objects, or sections of a document. It may be literal (an image of a house in a real estate brochure) or metaphorical (the image of a house on a Web browser toolbar that denotes a website home page). Other commonly used icons include the small envelopes on Web pages to symbolize e-mail links and paper clips to denote attachments to an e-mail. Because they convey ideas without words, icons are especially useful in communications with international audiences. To be effective, however, icons must be simple and easily recognizable to your reader. Figures 7–35 and 7–36 on pages 255–256, for example, illustrate internationally recognized icons (also called symbols).

Color and screening (or shading) can distinguish one part of a document from another or unify a series of documents. These techniques can set off sections within a document, highlight examples, or emphasize warnings. These devices are especially useful in graphs, maps, and drawings to differentiate boundaries and to depict the actual colors of geological and biological samples. In tables, you can use screening to highlight column titles or sets of data to which you want to draw the reader's attention. Figure 7–16 on page 235, for example, uses screening to differentiate the nursing education data.

Integrating Other Design Elements

You can choose from a variety of other design elements to enhance the visual logic and coherence of your page. These features can be adjusted within the template options with word-processing and publishing programs, such as MS Word and MS Publisher.

Columns

As you design pages, consider the size and number of columns. A single-column format works well with larger typefaces, double-spacing, and left-justified margins. For smaller typefaces and single-spaced lines, the two-column structure enhances legibility by keeping text columns narrow enough so that readers need not scan back and forth across the width of the entire page for every line. Check and correct your document for single words or parts of words that appear alone as first or last lines of your columns. Figure 7–4 shows a report formatted in two columns.

Columns with left-justified and ragged-right text

Optical and Handwritten Character Recognition Software: Recent Developments

Since the inception of computers, programmers have been teaching them to mimic humans. One such task that humans often take for granted is literacy. The process of reading printed text with a computer is called Optical Character Recognition (OCR). This method is optical because it uses a scanner to measure the reflected light off a piece of paper much like a copy machine does (Srihari and Lam 1–4). Along with OCR technology came handwriting recognition. Handwriting recognition occurs when the computer identifies each character the user writes with an electronic pen. Both OCR and handwriting recognition currently allow the computer almost 100 percent accuracy in understanding the writing of its human counterpart ("Looking Forward" 213).

What Are the Practical Applications?
OCR and handwriting recognition are used daily for such tasks as reading your tax forms and checking your passport at customs. The IRS, for example, receives about 200 million tax forms every year. So OCR is an important technology in processing tax forms because of OCR's speed and accuracy compared with manual interpreta-

to 45,000 pieces of mail an hour (Srihari and Lam 12). . . .

How Does Scanning Work?
When the computer scans a page of text it does so graphically. All the computer sees at first is a grid of many small dots where each dot is either black or white. A typical scanner reads 300 of these dots per square inch.

The letter *R* as printed (*left*) and as scanned into a matrix of dots (*right*).

In the first step of processing a page of text, the computer looks at the whole document and decides which regions contain text, and within regions it searches for individual l

Full-justified text

Uniform right-margin line endings

Optical and Handwritten Character Recognition Software: Recent Developments

Since the inception of computers, programmers have been teaching them to mimic humans. One such task that humans often take for granted is literacy. The process of reading printed text with a computer is called Optical Character Recognition (OCR). This method is optical because it uses a scanner to measure the reflected light off a piece of paper much like a copy machine does (Srihari and Lam 1–4). Along with OCR technology came handwriting recognition. Handwriting recognition occurs when the computer identifies each character the user writes with an electronic pen. Both OCR and handwriting recognition currently allow the computer almost 100 percent accuracy in understanding the writing of its human counterpart ("Looking Forward" 213).

What Are the Practical Applications?
OCR and handwriting recognition are used daily for such tasks as reading your tax forms and checking your passport at customs. The IRS, for example, receives about 200 million tax forms every year. So OCR is an important technology in processing tax forms because of OCR's speed and accuracy compared with manual interpretation to 45,000 pieces of mail an hour (Srihari and Lam 12). . . .

How Does Scanning Work?
When the computer scans a page of text it does so graphically. All the computer sees at first is a grid of many small dots where each dot is either black or white. A typical scanner reads 300 of these dots per square inch.

The letter *R* as printed (*left*) and as scanned into a matrix of dots (*right*).

In the first step of processing a page of text, the computer looks at the whole document and decides which regions contain text, and within those regions it searches for individual letters.

Figure 7–4 Left-Justified (*top*) and Full-Justified (*bottom*) Text Columns

White Space

White space (the area on the page or screen free of text or design elements) visually frames information and breaks it into manageable chunks. For example, white space between paragraphs helps readers see the information in the paragraphs as units. White space between sections is also a visual cue that one section is ending and another is beginning. Use the default-margin setting on your word processor (usually 1 or 1¼ inches), but allow extra space at the left margin if your document will be three-hole punched for binders.

Left- or Full-Justified Text Alignment

Pages with left-justified text are generally easier to read than pages with full-justified text because the uneven contour of the right text margin (called "ragged" right) allows the spacing within and between words to be more uniform. Full justification causes word-processing software to insert irregular-sized spaces between words, producing unwanted gaps or unevenness in blocks of text, often making your document more difficult to read. Full-justified text is more appropriate for publications such as corporate annual reports, consumer booklets, sales brochures, and other documents aimed at a broad readership that expects a more formal, polished appearance. Full justification is often useful with multi-column formats because the spaces between the columns (alleys) need the definition that full justification provides. Figure 7–4 shows the same document with left-justified (*top*) and full-justified (*bottom*) columns.

Lists

Lists are an effective way to highlight words, phrases, and short sentences. They break up complex statements and allow key items to stand out. Further, they are easy to read. Lists are particularly useful for certain types of information:

- Steps in sequence
- Materials or parts needed
- Items to remember
- Criteria for evaluation
- Concluding points
- Recommendations

Avoid both too many lists and too many items in lists. Too many lists without adequate transitional text before and after may leave readers unable to distinguish either their relative importance or how one list is related to another. Too many items will prompt readers to stop paying attention after the fourth or fifth item.

◆ ***For more information about using lists effectively, see pages 105–106 in Chapter 4, Revising a Document.***

Illustrations

Readers notice illustrations, especially large ones, before they notice text. Therefore, choose the size of an illustration according to its relative importance within your document. For newsletter articles and publications aimed at wide audiences, consider especially the proportion of the illustration to the text. In magazine design, for example, page layout is more dramatic and appealing when the major illustration (photograph, drawing, and so on) occupies three-fifths rather than half the available space. The same principle can be used to enhance the visual appeal of a report. Also, place illustrations where they are most useful to your audience. For example, grouping illustrations at the end of a report usually makes the writer's task easier, but placing them in the text closer to their accompanying explanations gives readers more convenient access to them and provides visual breaks from blocks of text. (Creating visuals and integrating them with text is discussed in the next section.)

DESIGNING YOUR DOCUMENT

Laying Out the Page

- Select typefaces for legibility in style and size, not simply for variety.
- Emphasize important information with consistent typographical and design devices, such as the following:
  - Be selective in choosing all-capital, italic, and boldface type styles.
  - Use headings (in boldface or italic type) to denote major sections and topic changes.
  - Create captions to identify figures and tables and to emphasize boxed information.
  - Include headers and footers to orient readers at the page level.
  - Use rules, icons, and color to highlight crucial information.
- Integrate the typographical and page-level design elements into a consistent, coherent whole.
  - Allow adequate white space between paragraphs and around visuals and text boxes.
  - Use lists to highlight comparable types of information by setting them off from the surrounding text.
  - Position visuals in proportion to their importance and set them off with adequate white space.

Creating Visuals

◆ *For more information on incorporating visuals into presentations, see the Writer's Checklist on pages 480–487 in Chapter 14, Giving Presentations.*

◆ *For guidance in preparing graphics for presentations, see the Writer's Checklist on pages 485–486 in Chapter 14, Giving Presentations.*

Visuals can express ideas or convey information in ways that words alone cannot. For example, tables allow readers to easily compare large numbers of statistics that would be difficult to understand in sentence form. Graphs make trends and mathematical relationships immediately evident. Drawings, photographs, charts, and maps render shapes and spatial relationships more concisely and efficiently than text can. By allowing the reader to interpret data at a glance, visuals accelerate understanding and promote efficiency. They can also boost the persuasiveness of your document, presentation, or website by highlighting trends and comparisons important to your content. The guidelines in Table 7–1 can help you select the most appropriate visuals based on their purpose and special features.

Choosing Appropriate Visuals

TO SHOW OBJECTS AND SPATIAL RELATIONSHIPS

Drawings

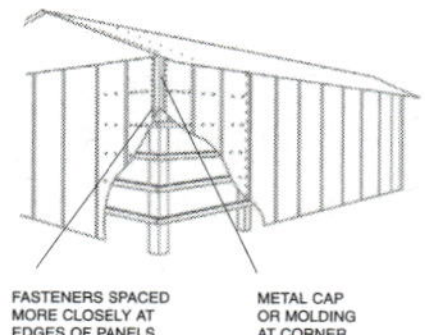

- Depict real objects difficult to photograph
- Depict imaginary objects
- Highlight only parts viewers need to see
- Show internal parts of equipment in cutaway views
- Show how equipment parts fit together in exploded views
- Communicate to international audiences more effectively than text alone

Photographs

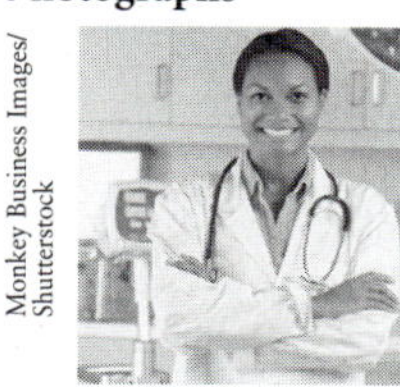
Monkey Business Images/Shutterstock

- Show images of subjects
- Record an event in process
- Record the development of phenomena over time
- Record the as-found condition of a situation for an investigation
- Show the colors essential to the accuracy of information in medical, chemical, forensic, botanical, and other fields

TO DISPLAY GEOGRAPHIC INFORMATION

Maps

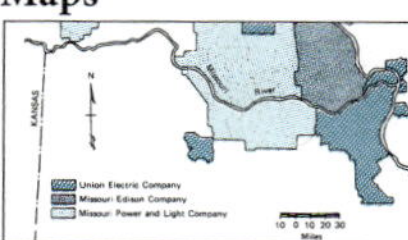

- Show specific geographic features of an area
- Show distance, routes, or locations of sites
- Show the geographic distribution of information (e.g., populations by region)

TO SHOW NUMERICAL AND OTHER RELATIONSHIPS

Tables

Divisions	*Employees*
Research	*1,052*
Marketing	*2,782*
Automotive	*13,251*
Consumer Products	*2,227*

- Organize information systematically in rows and columns
- Present large numerical quantities concisely
- Facilitate item-to-item comparisons
- Clarify trends and other graphical information with precise data

Bar & Column Graphs

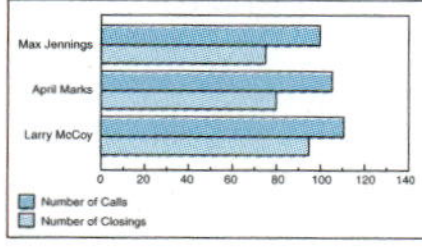

- Depict data in vertical or horizontal bars and columns for comparison
- Show quantities that make up a whole
- Track status of projects from start to finish
- Visually represent data shown in tables

Line Graphs

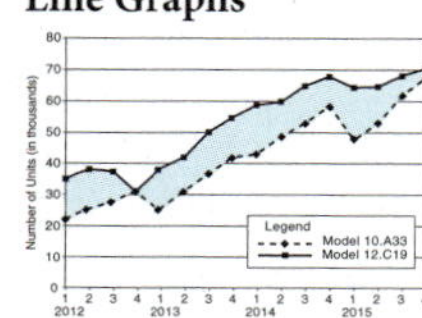

- Show trends over time in amounts, sizes, rates, and other measurements
- Give an at-a-glance impression of trends, forecasts, and extrapolations of data
- Compare more than one kind of data over the same time period
- Visually represent data shown in tables

Table 7–1 Chart for Choosing Appropriate Visuals

Picture Graphs

- Use recognizable images to represent specific quantities
- Help nonexpert readers grasp the information
- Visually represent data shown in tables

Pie Graphs

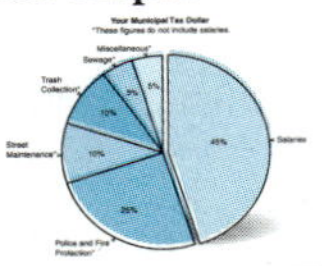

- Show quantities that make up a whole
- Give an immediate visual impression of the parts and their significance
- Visually represent data shown in tables or lists

TO SHOW STEPS IN A PROCESS OR RELATIONSHIPS IN A SYSTEM

Flowcharts

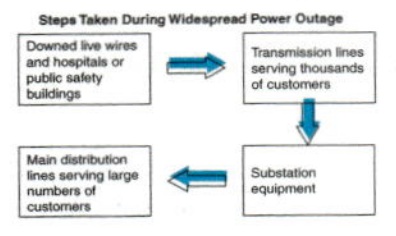

- Show how the parts or steps in a process or system interact
- Show the stages of an actual or a hypothetical process in the correct direction, including recursive steps

Schematic Diagrams

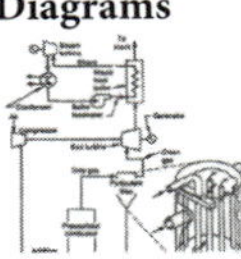

- Show how the components in electronic, chemical, electrical, and mechanical systems interact and are interrelated
- Use standardized symbolic representations rather than realistic depictions of system components

TO GIVE AN OVERVIEW OF A COMPLEX PROCESS OR EVENT

Infographics

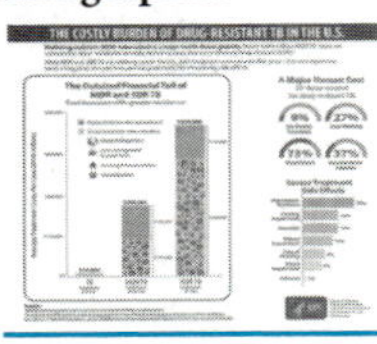

- Integrate text, graphs, images, and numbers to "tell a story"
- Combine the communications advantages of text and graphics to give both an overview and a narrative explanation of a topic
- Organize disparate facts, concepts, images into an understandable whole

TO SHOW RELATIONSHIPS IN A HIERARCHY

Organizational Charts

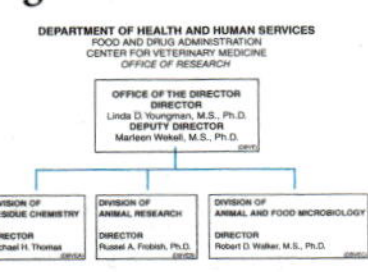

- Give an overview of an organization's depart-mental components
- Show how the components relate to one another
- Depict lines of authority within an organization

TO SUPPLEMENT OR REPLACE WORDS

Symbols & Icons

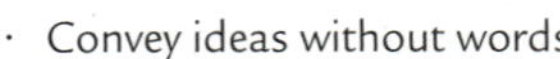

- Convey ideas without words
- Save space and add visual appeal
- Transcend individual languages to communicate ideas effectively for international readers
- Communicate culturally neutral images

Table 7–1 Chart for Choosing Appropriate Visuals *(continued)*

Designing and Integrating Visuals with Text

When using tables, graphs, or illustrations, consider your purpose and your reader carefully. For example, a drawing of the major regions of the brain for a high school science class would be different from an illustration provided for research scientists studying brain abnormalities. Be aware that although visuals can be indispensable to your topic, it is your writing, including headings, captions, and callouts, that must carry the burden of providing their context and pointing out their significance.

To make the most effective use of visuals and to integrate them smoothly with the text of your document, consider your graphics requirements even before you begin to write. Plan your visuals—tables, graphs, drawings, charts, maps, or photographs—when you're planning the scope and organization of your final work, whether it's a report, newsletter, brochure, presentation, or website. Regardless of the setting, purpose, and format of the final product, consider making graphics an integral part of your outline by copying and pasting them into the appropriate places, using your computer's clipboard feature. Like other information in a working outline, these boxes and sketches can be moved, revised, or deleted as required.

◆ *For guidance on graphics and typography for websites and other digital media, see pages 584–586 in Appendix A, Writing in an Online Environment.*

The following guidelines will help you create your visual materials and incorporate them into your documents effectively. (If you have an international audience, be sure to read Using Visuals to Communicate Internationally on pages 251–257.)

◆ *For guidance on preparing presentation graphics, see pages 484–485 in Chapter 14, Giving Presentations.*

- **Why include your visual?** Explain in the text why you've included the illustration and point your readers to it by figure or table number. The description for each visual will vary with its complexity and its importance. Remember your audience: Nonexperts require lengthier explanations than experts do, as a rule.
- **Is the information in your visual accurate?** Gather the information from reliable sources.
- **Is your visual focused and free of clutter?** Include only information necessary to the discussion in the text and eliminate unnecessary parts and components as well as labels, arrows, boxes, and lines.
- **Are terms and symbols in your visual defined and consistent?** Define all acronyms in the text, figure, or table. If any symbols are not self-explanatory, include a listing (known as a *key*) that defines them. Keep terminology consistent. Do not refer to the same data as a "proportion" in the text and as a "percentage" in the illustration.
- **Does your visual specify measurements and distances?** Specify the units of measurement used, when appropriate. Ensure that relative sizes are clear or indicate distance by a scale, as on a map. Avoid mixing English and SI (International System) units or dollars, euros, or other currencies; if both are necessary, include one in parentheses next to the other—"3 miles (5 kilometers)."
- **Is the lettering readable?** Position any explanatory text or labels horizontally for ease of reading, if possible.
- **Is the caption clear?** Give each illustration a concise caption that clearly describes its contents.
- **Is there a figure or table number?** Assign a figure or table number for documents containing five or more illustrations. The figure or table number precedes the title:

▶ Figure 1. Projected research budget for 2012–2017

Note that graphics (photographs, drawings, maps, and so on) are generically labeled "figures"; tables (data organized in rows and columns) are labeled "tables."

- **Are figure or table numbers referred to in your text?** Refer to each visual by its figure or table number in the text of your document.
- **Are visuals appropriately placed?** Place illustrations as close as possible to and following the text where they are discussed. Place lengthy and detailed illustrations that would impede the flow of your text in an appendix and refer to their location in your text.
- **Do visuals stand out from surrounding text?** Allow adequate white space on the page around and within each illustration.
- **Is a list of figures or tables needed?** In documents with more than five illustrations, list the illustrations in a separate section of the front matter by title, together with figure and page numbers, or table and page numbers. Title the list of figures "List of Figures" and the list of tables "List of Tables."

◆ *For more on evaluating sources, see pages 172–176 in Chapter 6, Conducting Research for a Document.*

A discussion of specific types of visuals commonly used in on-the-job writing follows. Your purpose and audience will ordinarily determine the best type of visual to use.

ETHICS NOTE: Create Visuals That Accurately Represent the Source Data Misleading visuals are unethical and can result in a loss of credibility for you and your organization. Sometimes deceptive visuals are based on incorrect statistics; sometimes statistics are manipulated to help a person or an organization improperly achieve goals. In either case, visuals and the statistics that inform them can help or hurt specific groups. (For example, a graph that accurately shows the number of college binge drinkers could help gain support for the creation of a campus substance-abuse counseling center; visuals that inaccurately suggest a lower number of binge drinkers could be used to argue against stricter alcohol regulations on campus.)

Tables

A table organizes data in rows and columns. The data may be numerical, as in Figure 7–5, or verbal, as in Table 7–2 on page 244. Because tables display information in rows and columns, they facilitate item-by-item comparisons more easily than if the data were embedded in the text.

Following are the elements of a typical table, as shown in Figure 7–5, with guidelines:

- *Table number*. Number each table sequentially throughout the text.
- *Table title*. Create a title that describes concisely what the table represents; place it above the table.
- *Boxhead*. In the boxhead (beneath the title) provide column headings that are brief but descriptive. Include units of measurement either as part of the heading or enclosed in parentheses beneath it. Standard abbreviations and symbols are acceptable. When possible, avoid vertical or diagonal lettering.

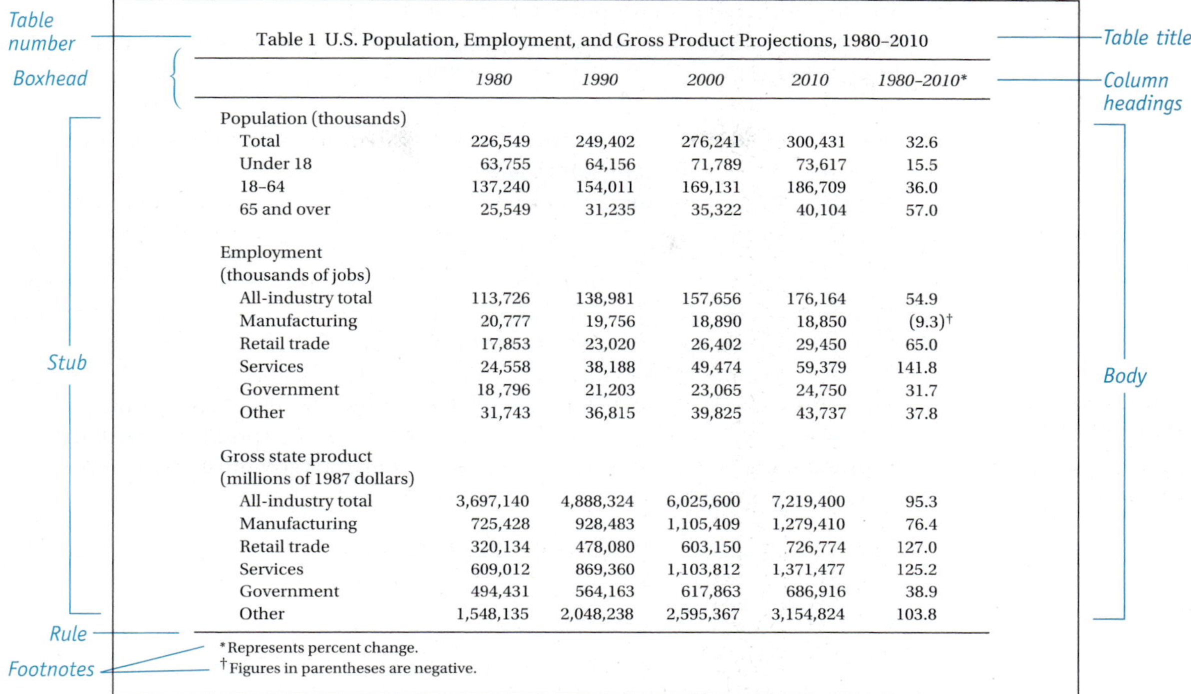

Table 1 U.S. Population, Employment, and Gross Product Projections, 1980–2010

	1980	*1990*	*2000*	*2010*	*1980–2010**
Population (thousands)					
Total	226,549	249,402	276,241	300,431	32.6
Under 18	63,755	64,156	71,789	73,617	15.5
18–64	137,240	154,011	169,131	186,709	36.0
65 and over	25,549	31,235	35,322	40,104	57.0
Employment (thousands of jobs)					
All-industry total	113,726	138,981	157,656	176,164	54.9
Manufacturing	20,777	19,756	18,890	18,850	(9.3)†
Retail trade	17,853	23,020	26,402	29,450	65.0
Services	24,558	38,188	49,474	59,379	141.8
Government	18 ,796	21,203	23,065	24,750	31.7
Other	31,743	36,815	39,825	43,737	37.8
Gross state product (millions of 1987 dollars)					
All-industry total	3,697,140	4,888,324	6,025,600	7,219,400	95.3
Manufacturing	725,428	928,483	1,105,409	1,279,410	76.4
Retail trade	320,134	478,080	603,150	726,774	127.0
Services	609,012	869,360	1,103,812	1,371,477	125.2
Government	494,431	564,163	617,863	686,916	38.9
Other	1,548,135	2,048,238	2,595,367	3,154,824	103.8

*Represents percent change.
†Figures in parentheses are negative.

Figure 7–5 Table *Source:* U.S. Small Business Administration, Office of Advocacy, from data provided by the Bureau of Economic Analysis.

- *Stub.* In the left-hand vertical column of a table, called the stub, list all the items to be shown in the body of the table.
- *Body.* Provide data in the body of your table below the column headings and to the right of the stub. (Each datum element is located in a *cell.*) Within the body, arrange columns so that the terms to be compared appear in adjacent rows and columns. Where no information exists for a specific cell, substitute a row of dots or a dash to acknowledge the gap. If you substitute the abbreviation "N/A" for missing data in a cell, add a footnote to clarify whether it means "not available" or "not applicable."
- *Rules.* Use rules (lines) to separate your table into its various parts. Include horizontal rules below the title, below the body of the table, and between the column headings and the body of the table. You may include vertical rules to separate the columns, but do not use rules to enclose the sides of the table. Side rules do not add a meaningful boundary and are one less element users must decipher.
- *Source line.* Below the table, include a source line to identify where you obtained the data (when appropriate). Many organizations place the source line below the footnotes.

- *Footnotes*. Include a footnote when you need to explain an item in the table. Use symbols (*, †) or lowercase letters (sometimes in parentheses) rather than numbers to make it clear that the notes are not part of the data or the main text.
- *Continuing tables*. When you must divide your table to continue it on another page, repeat the column headings and give the table number at the head of each new page with a "continued" label ("Table 3, continued"), as shown in Figure 7–6.

ETHICS NOTE: Acknowledge the Sources of Borrowed Visuals and Data Whether you reprint a preexisting image or use published information to create your own graph or table, you must acknowledge your borrowings in a source or credit line. Place source information below the caption for a figure and below any footnotes at the bottom of a table. (See Figure 7–5 for an example.) If you wish to use illustrations found on the Web or in printed sources, obtain written permission from the copyright holder. Material that is not copyrighted (generally limited to publications of the U.S. government) can be reproduced without permission, but you must still acknowledge the source in a credit line.

Table 4

Assessment of Electronic Media and Format Standards in Federal Agencies: Number, Percentage, and Basis for Use by Agency

Format	Standard for each format used							
	Agency mandated		Common agency practice		Other		None	
	Number	Percent	Number	Percent	Number	Percent	Number	Percent
Database								
Oracle	7	38.9	8	44.4	1	5.6	1	5.6
WAIS	1	4.3	21	91.3	0	0.0	0	0.0
MARC	1	33.3	1	33.3	0	0.0	0	0.0
Sybase	0	0.0	4	80.0	0	0.0	0	0.0
dBase	0	0.0	8	80.0	0	0.0	0	0.0
Other	2	4.4	21	46.7	12	26.7	9	20.0

Table 4, continued

Assessment of Electronic Media and Format Standards in Federal Agencies: Number, Percentage, and Basis for Use by Agency

Format	Standard for each format used							
	Agency mandated		Common agency practice		Other		None	
	Number	Percent	Number	Percent	Number	Percent	Number	Percent

Figure 7–6 Divided Table (Continued on a Second Page)

To list relatively few items that would be easier for the reader to grasp in tabular form, use an informal table within the text of your document.

▶ The sound-intensity levels (decibels) for the three frequency bands (in hertz) were determined to be the following:

Frequency Band (Hz)	*Decibels*
600–1,200	68
1,200–2,400	62
2,400–4,800	53

Although you need not include titles or table numbers to identify informal tables, do include headings that describe the information provided and properly align columns and rows. You may also need to acknowledge the source of the information, as discussed in the Ethics Note on previous page.

DESIGNING YOUR DOCUMENT

Presenting Information in Tables

- Use tables to present data that you want readers to quickly evaluate and compare but that would be difficult or tedious to present in your main text.
- Identify each table with a concise, descriptive title and a unique table number.
- Use horizontal lettering, if possible.
- Do not enclose the left and right sides with vertical rules.
- Include a source line when necessary to identify where you obtained the data.
- For tables continued on another page, repeat the table number (followed by "continued"), title, and column headings.
- Use informal tables — those without a title or number — when there are only a few items to categorize.

DIGITAL TIP: Creating Simple Tables for a Document

Word-processing programs can automate the creation of tables, as do the many software programs designed to format Web pages. They allow you to specify the number of rows and columns needed for your data, to define the style of the table elements, and to select vertical and horizontal rules.

Graphs

Graphs, also called charts, present numerical data in visual form, showing trends, movements, distributions, and cycles more readily than tables or text do. Although graphs present statistics in a format that is easy to grasp quickly, they cannot show the detailed cell-by-cell data of a table. For this reason, they are often accompanied by tables that give exact numbers. (Note the difference between the graphs and the table showing the same data in Figure 7–7.) To solve the problem of showing only approximate data in graphs, you can include the exact data for each column or fraction of a column — if this will not clutter your graph — giving the reader both a quick overview of the data and precise numbers. (See Figure 7–16 on page 235.) The most commonly used graphs are line graphs, bar graphs, pie graphs, and picture graphs (also called pictographs), all of which can be created once you have entered your data into a spreadsheet or database application.

Line Graphs

The line graph shows the relationship between two or more sets of figures. The graph is composed of a vertical axis and a horizontal axis that intersect at right angles, each representing one set of data. The relationship between the two sets is indicated by points plotted along appropriate intersections of the two axes that are then connected to form a continuous line. The line graph's vertical axis usually represents amounts, and its horizontal axis usually represents increments of time (Figure 7–8). Line graphs with more than one plotted line allow for comparisons between two sets of data. In creating such graphs, label each plotted line, as shown in Figure 7–9. You can emphasize the difference between the two lines by shading the space that separates them. The following guidelines apply to most line graphs:

- Give your graph a title that describes the data clearly and concisely.
- Indicate the zero point (where the two axes meet). If the range of data is too large to begin at zero, insert a break in the scale (Figure 7–10); otherwise, the graph would show a large area with no data.
- Divide the vertical axis into equal portions, from the least amount at the bottom to the greatest amount at the top. The caption for this scale may be placed at the upper left (as in Figure 7–9) or, as is more often the case, along the vertical axis (as in Figure 7–10).
- Divide the horizontal axis into equal units from left to right, and label them to show what values each represents.
- Include enough points to plot the data accurately; too few data points will distort a depiction of the trends (Figure 7–11).
- Keep grid lines to a minimum so that the curved lines stand out. Detailed grid lines are unnecessary because precise values are usually shown either on the graph or in an accompanying table.
- Include a label or a key when necessary to define symbols or visual cues to the data, such as in Figure 7–12.
- Include a source line under the graph, indicating where you obtained the data (see Figures 7–8, 7–9, and 7–12).
- Present all type horizontally if possible. The type for the vertical axis caption, however, is usually presented vertically (see Figures 7–10 and 7–11).

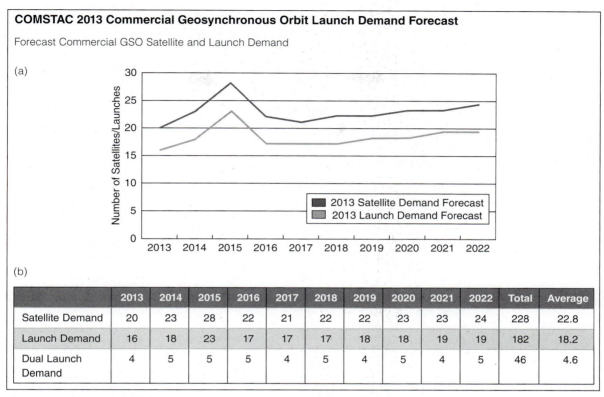

COMSTAC 2013 Commercial Geosynchronous Orbit Launch Demand Forecast

Forecast Commercial GSO Satellite and Launch Demand

(a)

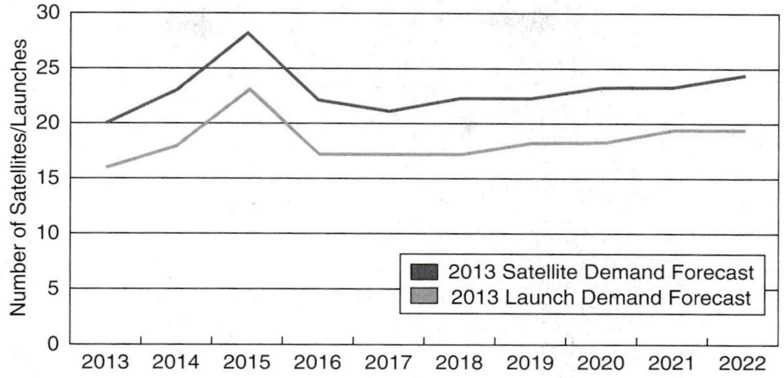

Number of Satellites/Launches

0 5 10 15 20 25 30

2013 2014 2015 2016 2017 2018 2019 2020 2021 2022

2013 Satellite Demand Forecast

2013 Launch Demand Forecast

(b)

	2013	2014	2015	2016	2017	2018	2019	2020	2021	2022	Total	Average
Satellite Demand	20	23	28	22	21	22	22	23	23	24	228	22.8
Launch Demand	16	18	23	17	17	17	18	18	19	19	182	18.2
Dual Launch Demand	4	5	5	5	4	5	4	5	4	5	46	4.6

Figure 7–7 Graph and Table Showing the Same Data *Source:* http://www.faa.gov/about/office_org/headquarters_offices/apl/aviation_forecasts/aerospace_forecasts/2014-2034/media/Commercial_Space_Transportation.pdf.

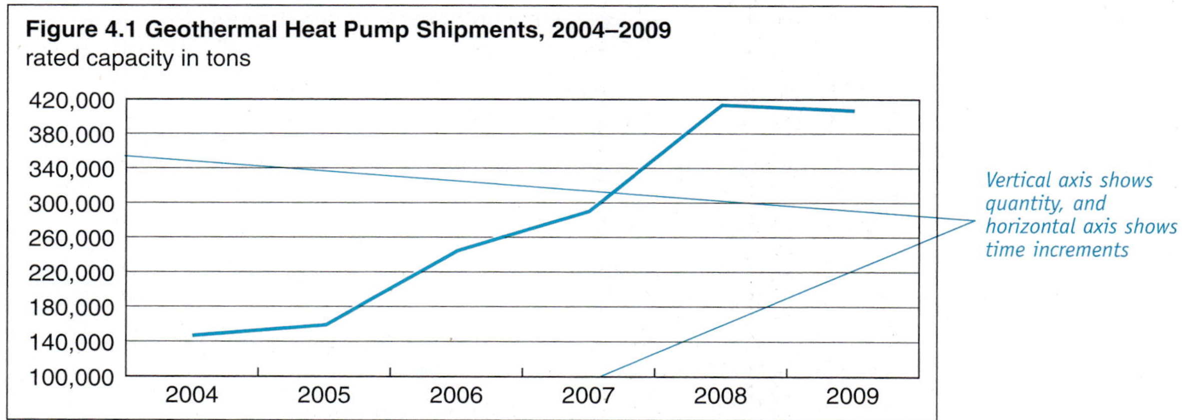

Figure 7–8 Single-Line Graph U.S. Energy Information Administration (EIA).

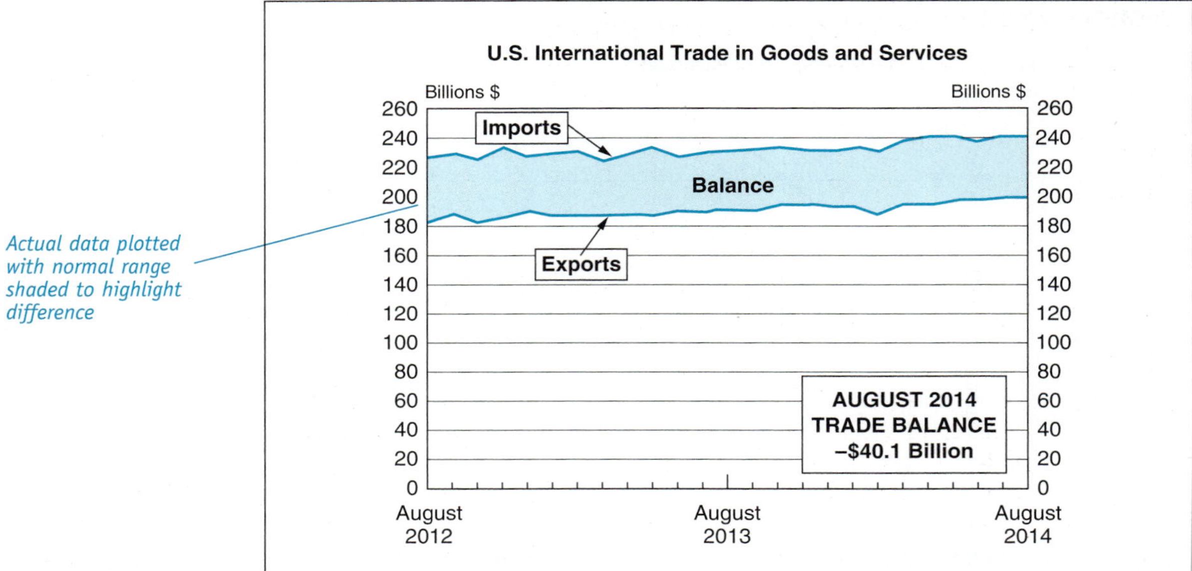

Figure 7–9 Double-Line Graph with Shading *Source:* http://www.census.gov/foreign-trade/Press-Release/2014pr/08/ftdpress.pdf.

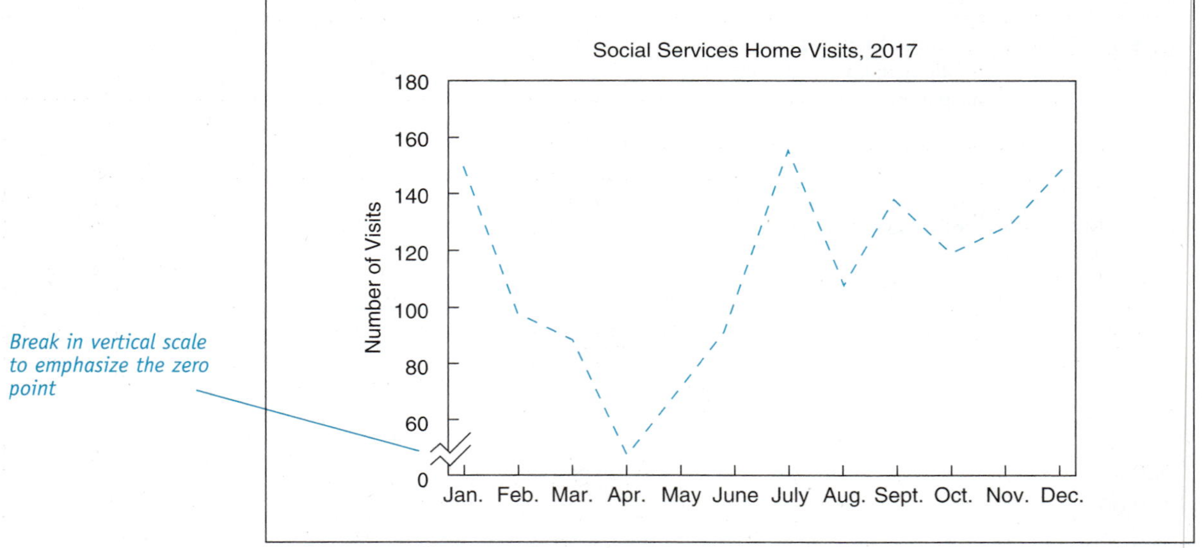

Figure 7–10 Line Graph with Vertical Axis Broken

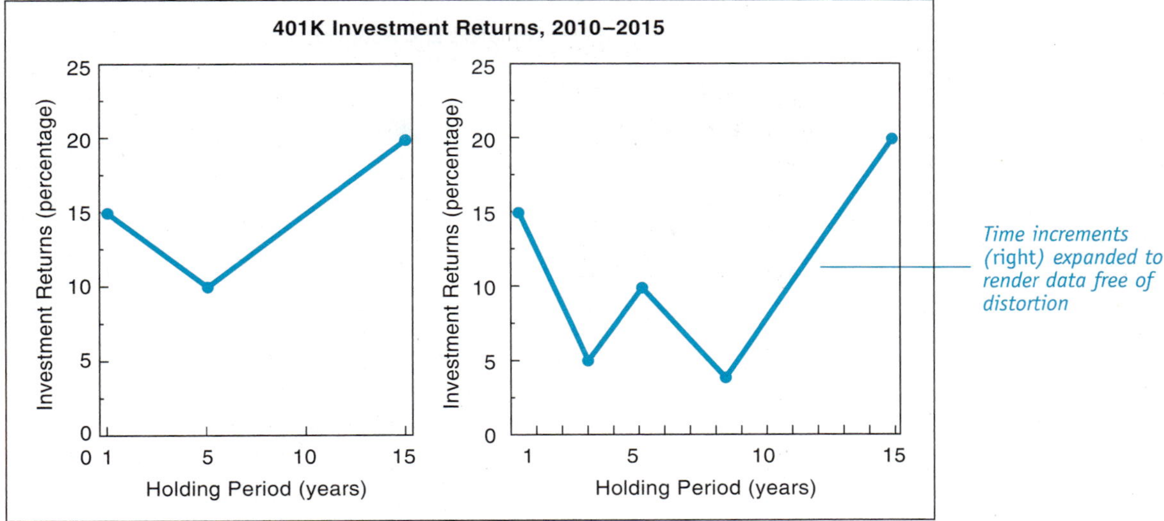

Figure 7–11 Distorted (*left*) and Distortion-Free (*right*) Expressions of Data

ETHICS NOTE: Create Graphs that Accurately Represent Data Be sure to proportion the vertical and horizontal scales so that they present data precisely and without visual distortion—to do otherwise is inaccurate and potentially misleading. In Figure 7-11, the graph on the left gives the appearance of a slight decline followed by a steady increase in investment returns because the scale is compressed, with some of the years selectively omitted. The graph on the right represents the trend more accurately because the years are evenly distributed without omissions.

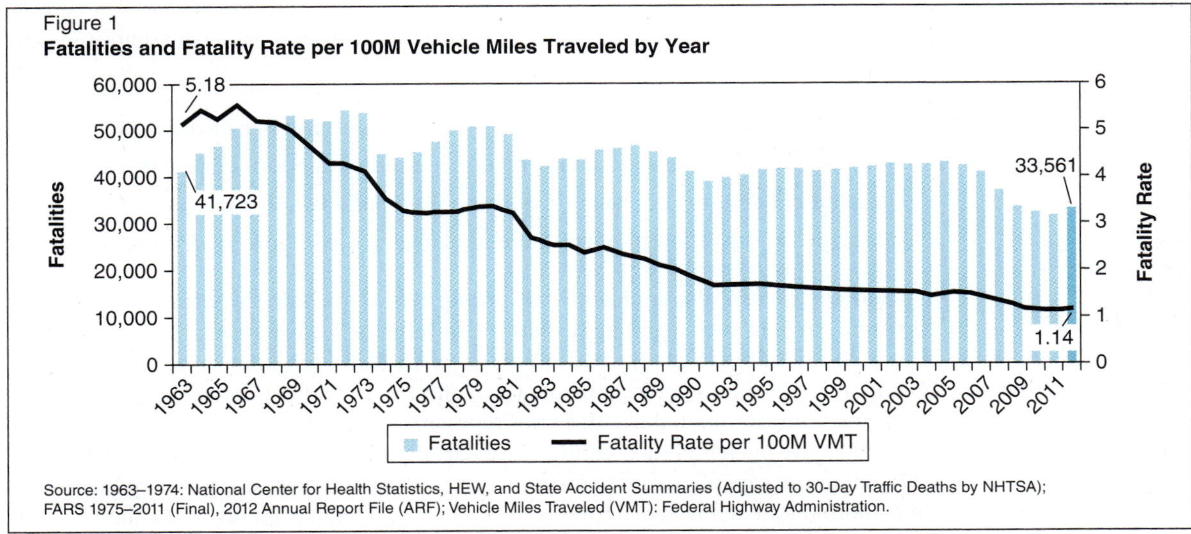

Figure 7–12 Bar Graph of Different Types of Information for Different Periods of Time
Source: U.S. Department of Transportation, http://www-nrd.nhtsa.dot.gov/Pubs/811856.pdf.

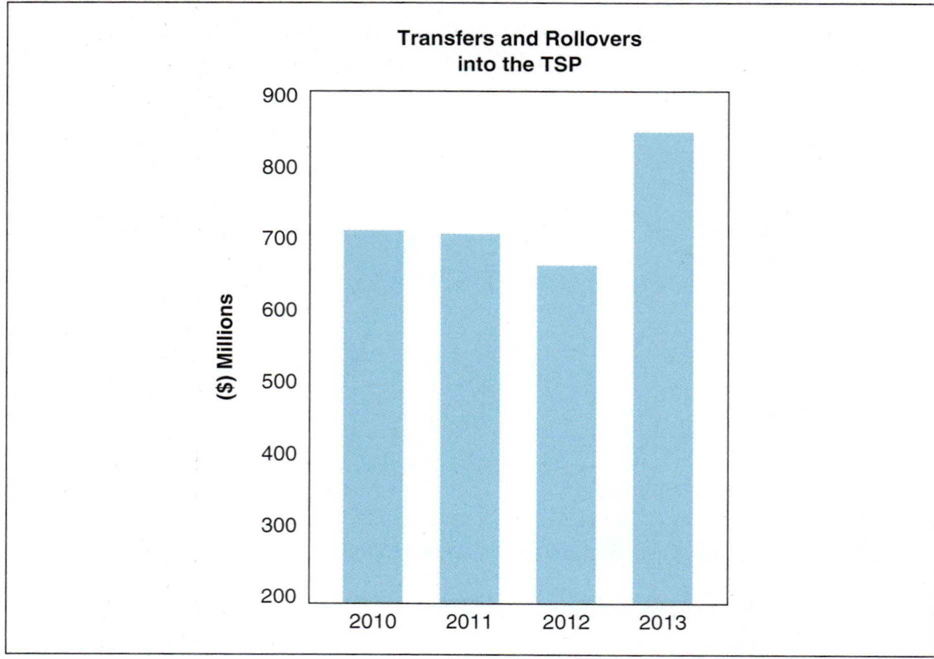

Figure 7–13 Bar Graph Showing Quantities of the Same Kind of Information at Different Periods of Time *Source:* https://www.tsp.gov/PDF/formspubs/tspbk08.pdf.

Bar Graphs

Bar graphs consist of horizontal or vertical bars of equal width but scaled in length or height to represent some quantity. They are commonly used to show the following proportional relations:

- Different types of information during different periods of time (see Figure 7–12)
- Quantities of the same kind of information at different periods of time (Figure 7–13)
- Quantities of different information during a fixed period of time (Figure 7–14)
- Quantities of the different parts that make up a whole (Figure 7–15 on page 234)

Bar graphs can also indicate what proportion of a whole the various component parts represent. In such a graph, the bar, which is theoretically equivalent to 100 percent, is divided according to the proportion of the whole that each item sampled represents. (Compare the displays of the same data in Figures 7–15 and 7–17 on page 236.) In some bar graphs, the completed bar does not represent 100 percent because not all parts of the whole have been included or not all are pertinent in the sample (Figure 7–16 on page 235). Bar graphs are also used to track project schedules, where each bar represents the time allotted for each task of a project. A project-tracking bar graph, also called a *Gantt chart,* is shown in Figure 5–4 on page 141.

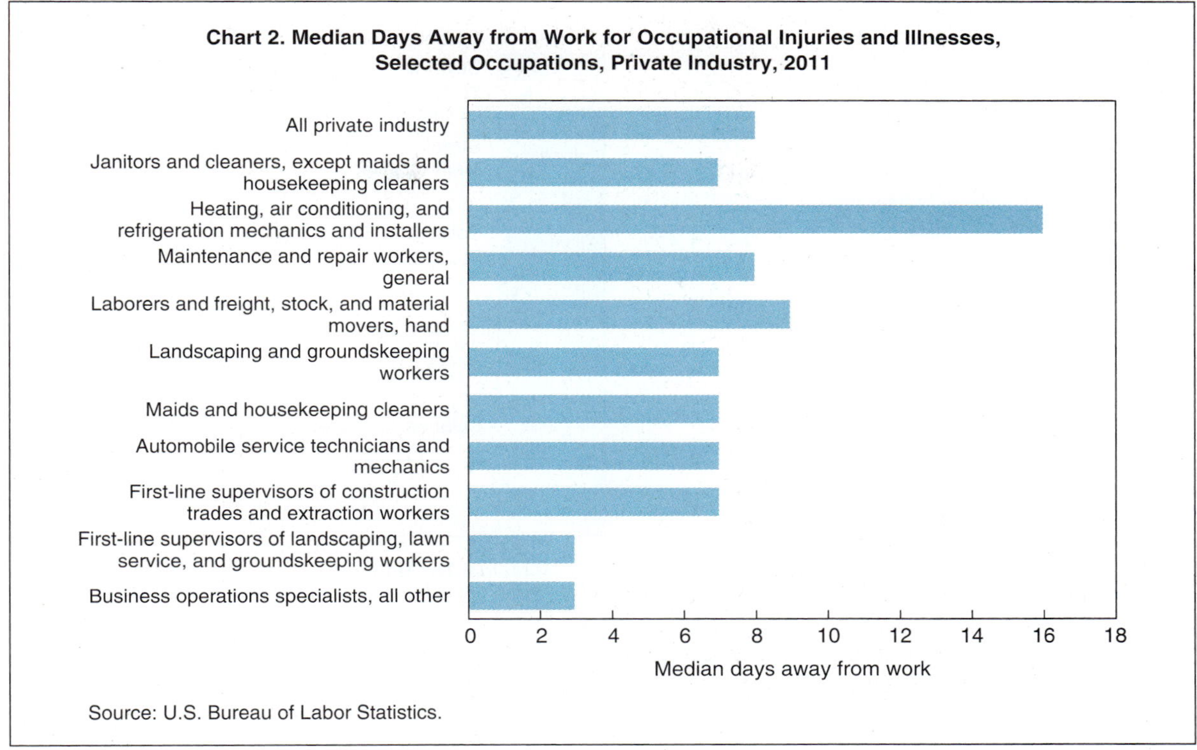

Figure 7–14 Bar Graph Showing Quantities of Different Information During a Fixed Period of Time *Source:* Bureau of Labor Statistics, U.S. Department of Labor, http://www.bls.gov/news.release/pdf/osh2.pdf.

Note that in Figure 7–18 on page 236, a type of bar graph showing travel frequency, the exact quantities appear at the end of each picture column, eliminating the need to have an accompanying table giving the percentages. If the bars are not labeled, the different portions must be clearly indicated by shading, crosshatching, or other devices. Include a key that represents the various subdivisions.

A Gantt chart is a type of horizontal bar graph designed to plan and track the status of projects from beginning to end. As shown in Figure 5–4 on page 141, the horizontal axis represents the length of a class project divided into time increments — days, weeks, or months.

The time line usually runs across the top of the chart. The vertical axis represents the individual tasks that make up the project and can include a second column listing the staff or organization responsible for each task. The horizontal bars in the body of the chart identify each task and show its beginning and end date. Gantt charts are often prepared with spreadsheet or project-management software. For examples, demonstrations, and free Gantt-chart software, see GanttProject at www.ganttproject.biz.

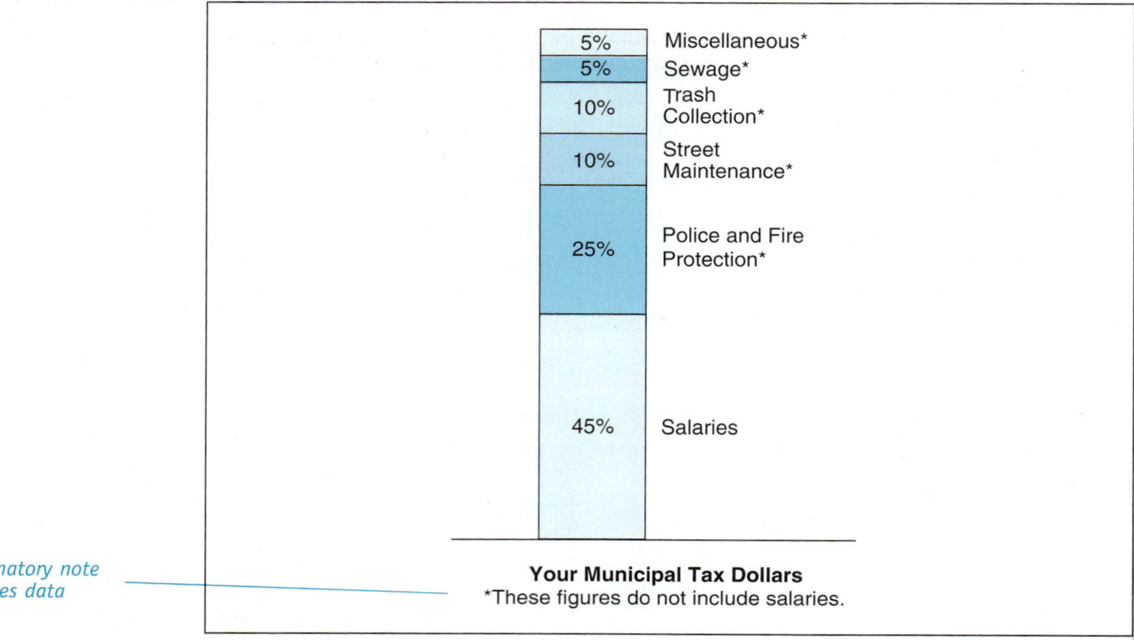

Figure 7–15 Bar (Column) Graph Showing Different Quantities of Different Parts of a Whole

Pie Graphs

A pie graph presents data as wedge-shaped sections of a circle. The circle equals 100 percent, or the whole, of some quantity (a municipal tax dollar, tuition fees for a semester, the hours of a working day), with the wedges representing the various parts into which the whole is divided. In Figure 7–17, for example, the circle stands for a city tax dollar and is divided into units equivalent to the percentages of the tax dollar spent on various city services. Note that the slice representing salaries is slightly offset (exploded) from the others to emphasize that data. This feature is commonly available in spreadsheet and database software.

The relationships among the various statistics presented in a pie graph are easy to grasp, but the information is often general. For this reason, a pie graph is often accompanied by a table that presents the actual figures on which the percentages in the graph are based.

Following are guidelines for constructing pie graphs:

- Keep in mind that the complete 360° circle is equivalent to 100 percent.
- When possible, begin at the 12 o'clock position and sequence the wedges clockwise, from largest to smallest. (This is not always possible because the default setting for some charting software sequences the data counterclockwise.)
- Apply a distinctive pattern, various shades of gray, or different colors for each wedge.

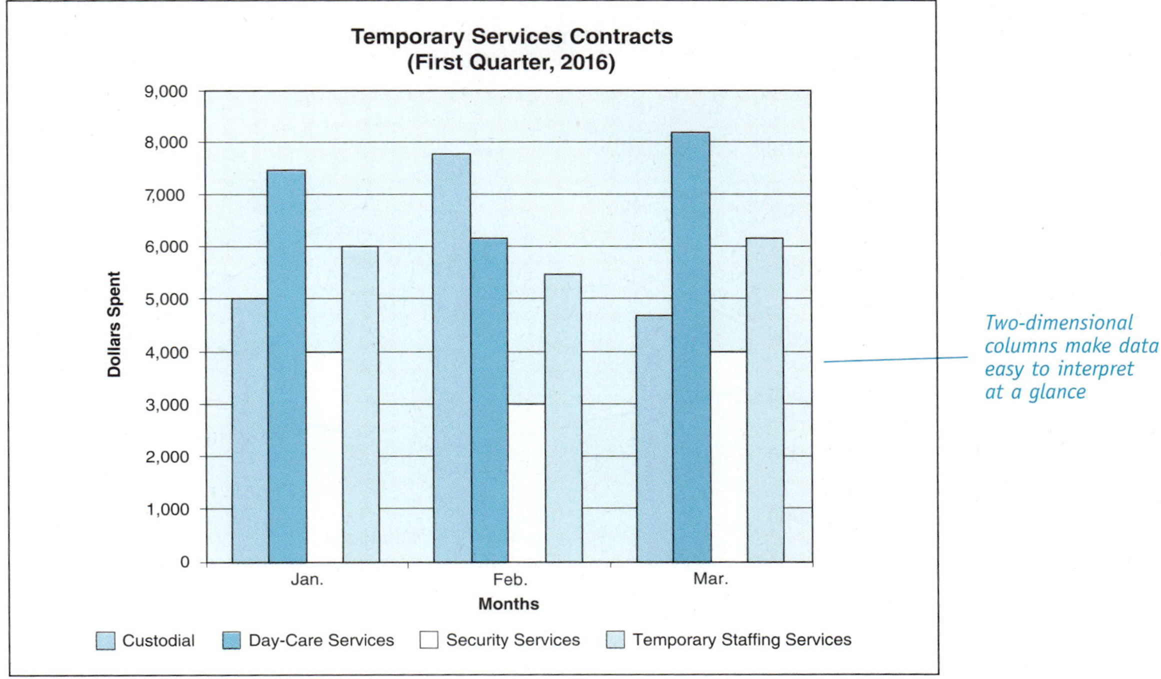

Two-dimensional columns make data easy to interpret at a glance

Figure 7–21 Two-Dimensional Column Graph (Same Data as in Figures 7–19 and 7–20)

entire three-month period in contract expenditures at a glance, the graph in Figure 7–22 is preferable.

When precise dollar amounts for each service are equally important, you can provide a table showing that information. As Figures 7–19 through 7–22 show, the more complicated a graph looks, the harder it is to interpret. On balance, simpler is better for the reader. Use this principle when you review your computer graphics on-screen in several styles and consider your reader's needs before deciding which style to use.

Drawings

Drawings (or *illustrations*) are useful when your reader needs an impression of an object's general appearance or an overview of a series of steps or directions. Note, for example, the sequence of drawings in Figure 12–10 on page 414 that show the steps used to install a waste disposer. Drawings are the best choice when you need to focus on details or relationships that a photograph cannot capture. A drawing can emphasize the significant piece of a mechanism, or its function, and omit what is not significant—for example, a *cutaway drawing* can show the internal parts of a piece of equipment in such a way that their relationship to the overall equipment is clear (Figure 7–23). An *exploded-view drawing* can show the proper sequence in which parts fit together or the details of each individual part (Figure 7–24). For a smaller-scale exploded-view diagram, see Figure 12–3 on page 400.

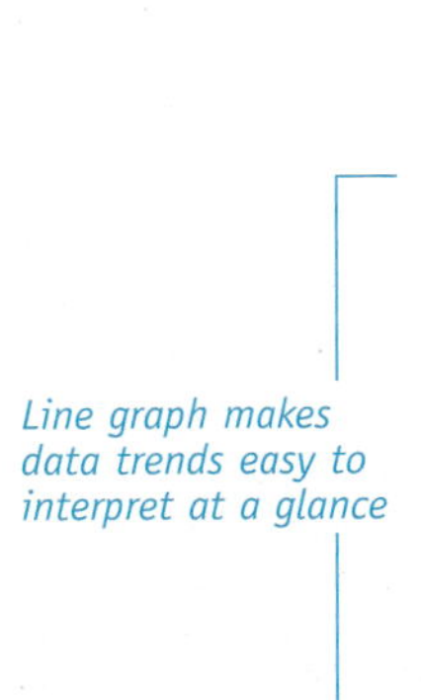

Line graph makes data trends easy to interpret at a glance

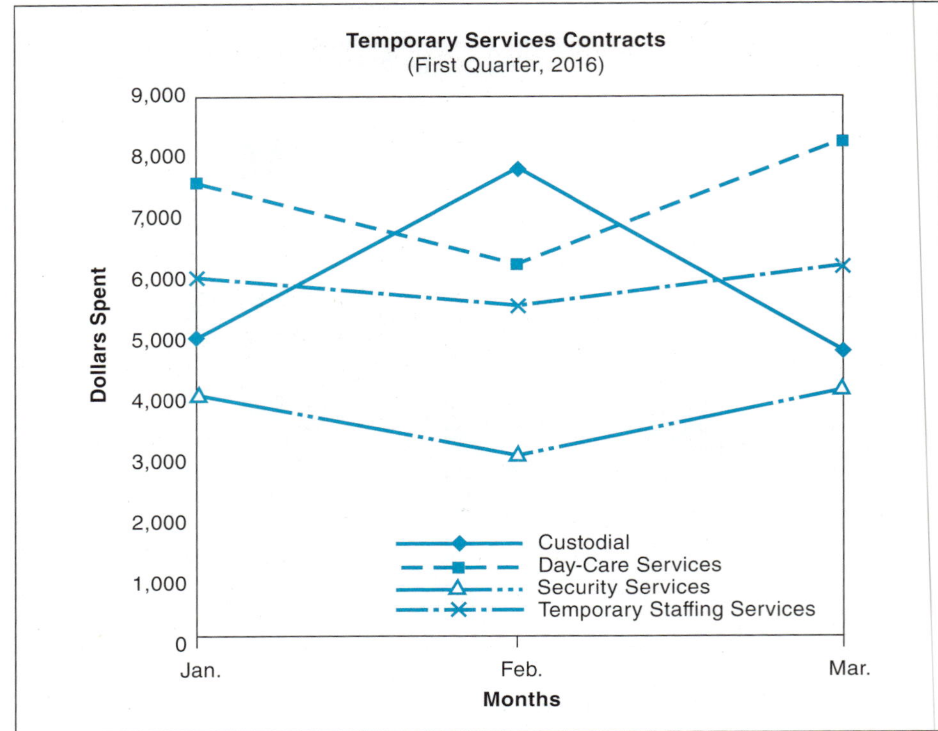

Figure 7–22 Line Graph (Same Data as in Figures 7–19 Through 7–21)

Drawings are also the best option for illustrating simple objects or tasks that do not require photography (Figure 7-25 on page 243). However, if the actual appearance of an object (a dented fender) or a phenomenon (an aircraft wind-tunnel experiment) is necessary to your document, a photograph is essential. When static two-dimensional drawings must show the illusion of motion, graphics designers use a variety of techniques, depending on the motion being represented. These techniques can be used singly or in combination. Table 7-2 defines the most commonly used of these techniques in workplace graphics and shows an example of each. For drawings that require a high degree of accuracy and precision, seek the help of a graphics specialist. Many organizations have their own specifications for drawings and their own teams responsible for putting together or composing drawings. Other organizations rely on images or drawings purchased from online marketers for their purposes. If a project requires that you prepare illustrations yourself, use the following guidelines:

- Show the equipment or other object from the point of view of the person who will use it.
- When illustrating part of a system, show its relationship to the larger system of which it is a part.

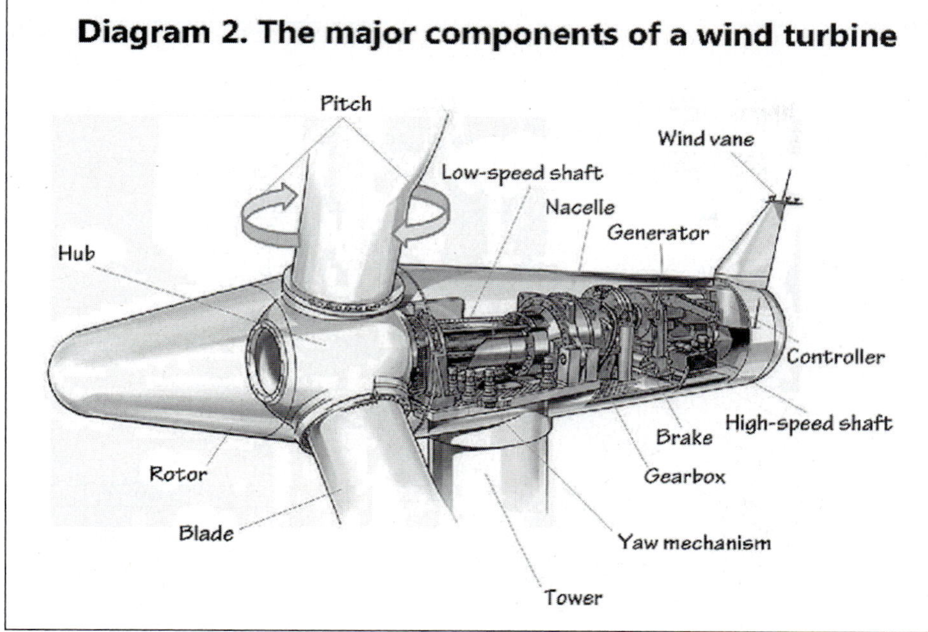

Cutaway shows internal structure of a device (wind turbine)

Figure 7–23 Cutaway Drawing Reprinted by permission of Center on Globalization, Governance and Competitiveness, Duke University (CGGC).

- Draw the different parts of an object in proportion to one another, unless you indicate that certain parts are enlarged.
- For drawings used to illustrate a process, arrange them from left to right and from top to bottom.
- Label important parts of each drawing so that text references to them are clear and consistent.
- Depending on the complexity of what is shown, label the parts themselves — see Figure 7–24 — or use a letter or number key.

Flowcharts

A flowchart is a diagram that shows the stages of a process from beginning to end; it presents an overview that allows readers to grasp essential steps quickly and easily. Flowcharts can illustrate a variety of processes, ranging from the steps required to process an invoice to the stages in the life cycle of the honeybee.

Flowcharts can take several forms to represent the steps in a process: labeled blocks (Figure 7–26), pictorial representations (Figure 7–27), or standardized symbols (Figure 7–28). The items in any flowchart are always connected according to the sequence in which the steps occur. They are typically depicted left to right or top to

Exploded view shows components and their names

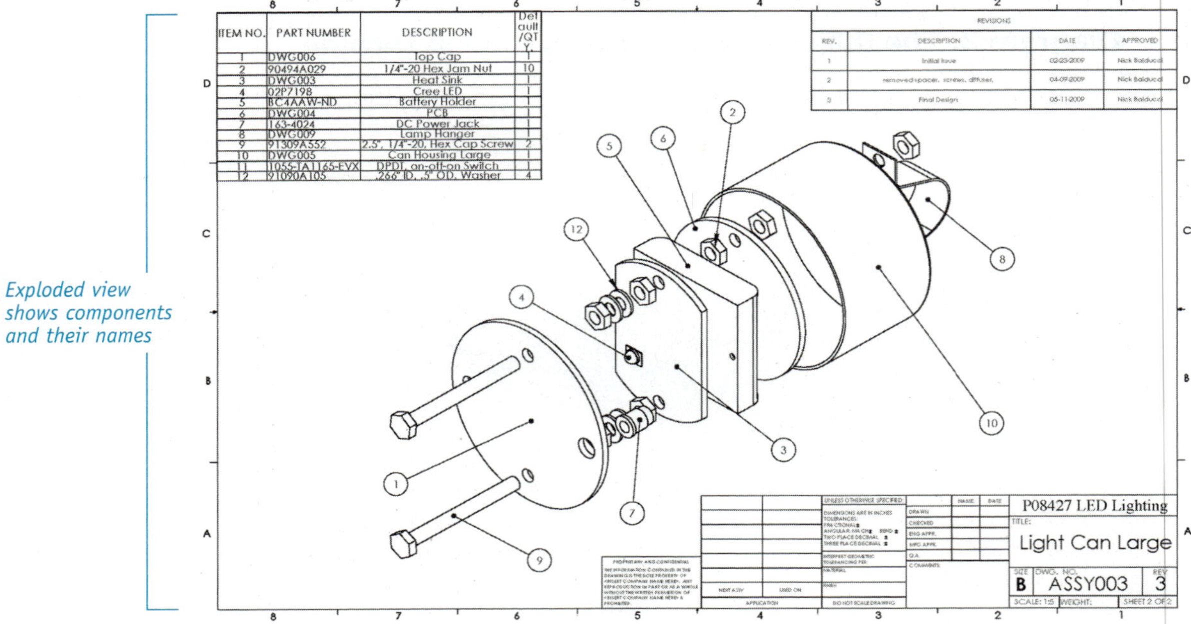

Figure 7–24 Exploded-View Drawing Reprinted by permissions of Nicholas Balducci.

bottom. When the flow is otherwise, indicate it with arrows. Flowcharts that document computer programs and other information-processing procedures use standardized symbols set forth in *Information Processing: Documentation Symbols and Conventions for Data, Program, and System Flow-charts, Program Network Charts, and System Resources Charts* (ISO publication 1985E). (Publication available at www.iso.org.) Many word-processing programs provide flowcharting utilities that can be used to construct flowcharts for documents and presentation slides.

Follow these guidelines when creating a flowchart:

- Label each step in the process or identify it with a conventional symbol. Steps can also be represented pictorially or by captioned blocks.
- With labeled blocks and standardized symbols, use arrows to show the direction of flow, especially if the flow is opposite of left to right or top to bottom. With pictorial representations, number each step and use arrows to show the direction of all flow.
- Include a key if the flowchart contains symbols that your audience may not understand.
- Leave adequate white space on the page. Do not crowd the steps and directional arrows too close together.

Prevent Repetitive-Motion Injuries

Before beginning to type and during breaks throughout the day, take time to do the stretches as shown.

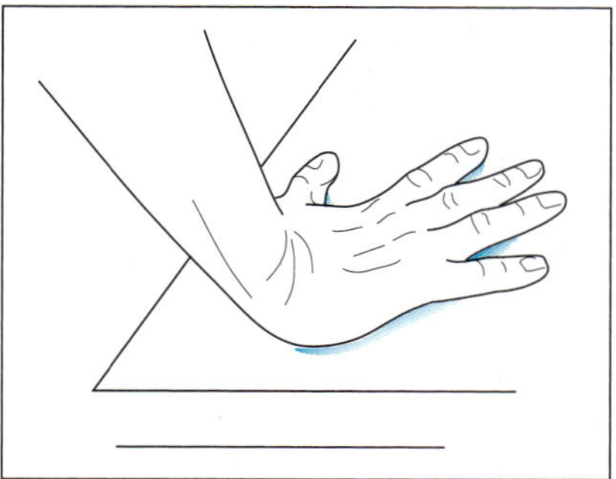

Gently press the hand against a firm flat surface, stretching the fingers and wrist. Hold for five seconds.

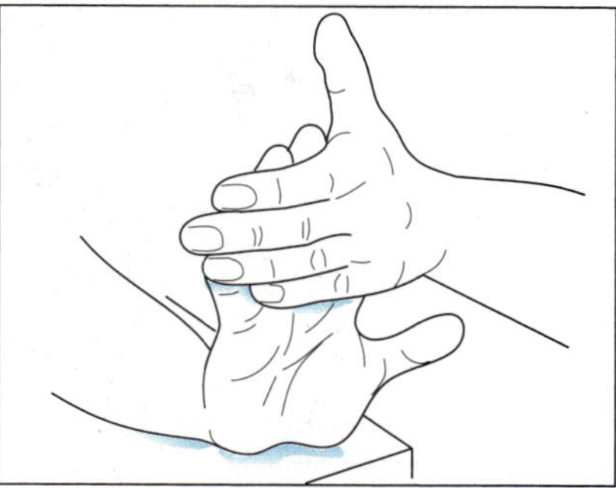

Rest the forearm on the edge of a table. Grasp the fingers of one hand and gently bend back the wrist, stretching the hands and wrist. Hold for five seconds.

Figure 7–25 Drawing

Organizational Charts

An organizational chart shows how the various parts of an organization are related to one another. Such illustrations give readers an overview of an organization or indicate the lines of authority within it (Figure 7–29).

The title of each organizational part (office, section, division) is placed in a separate box. These boxes are then linked to a central authority. If useful to your readers, include the name of the person occupying the position identified in each box. As with all illustrations, place the organizational chart as close as possible following the text that refers to it.

Maps

Maps can be used to show the specific geographic or human-made features of an area (mountains, rivers, roads, dams) or to show information according to geographic distribution (population, housing, manufacturing centers, and so forth) (Figure 7–30). In most cases, maps must be purchased or licensed for use in a document. Online maps, such as those available on GoogleMaps or Mapquest, cannot be used freely in documents and, because they are Web-based, will not print clearly if used in such mediums. However, online interactive sites, like iMapBuilder, Google Earth, and NovaMind, can generate maps for incorporation into publications, websites, and presentations. For additional maps and cartographic resources, see www.lib.utexas.edu/maps.

Table 7–2 Common Graphic Techniques to Represent Motion in Static Images

	Technique	Definition	Purpose	Example
Arrows	Arrowhead at one end		To show the direction or destination of the motion	KevinAlexander-George/Getty Images
	Arrowhead at both ends		To show motion in both directions	Courtesy NASA
Motion Lines	Speed lines	Horizontal lines drawn behind an object	To show an object speeding away in the opposite direction	KreativKolors/Shutterstock
	Guide lines	Straight, dashed, or dotted lines	To show the location of parts/components in exploded-view how-to-assemble drawings	My Product Engineer! © 2013
	Contour lines	Straight or curved lines that follow an object's shape (contour) as after-shadows	To show an oscillating object (vibrating, swinging, shivering)	
	Motion blur	A photographic effect in which an object appears to trace its path through space in blurred lines	To show an object in motion through a trajectory	Mike Powell/Betty Images

Information from Jose M. Bezerra de Souza and Mary Dyson, "An Illustrated Review of How Motion Is Represented in Static Instructional Graphics," http://www.interdisciplinary.net/ci/vl/vl1/Jose%20paper.pdf.

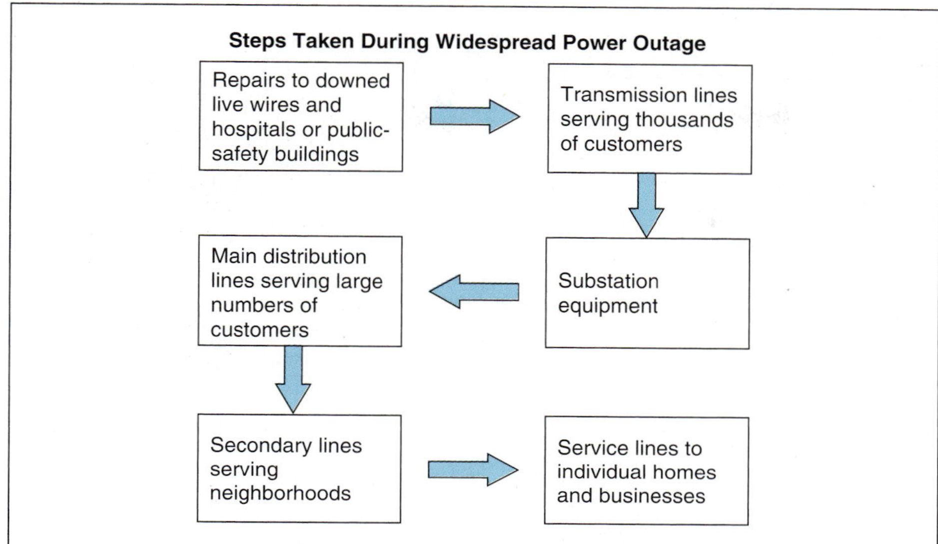

Figure 7–26 Flowchart Using Labeled Blocks (Depicting Electric Utility Power Restoration Process) *Source:* Potomac Electric Power Company.

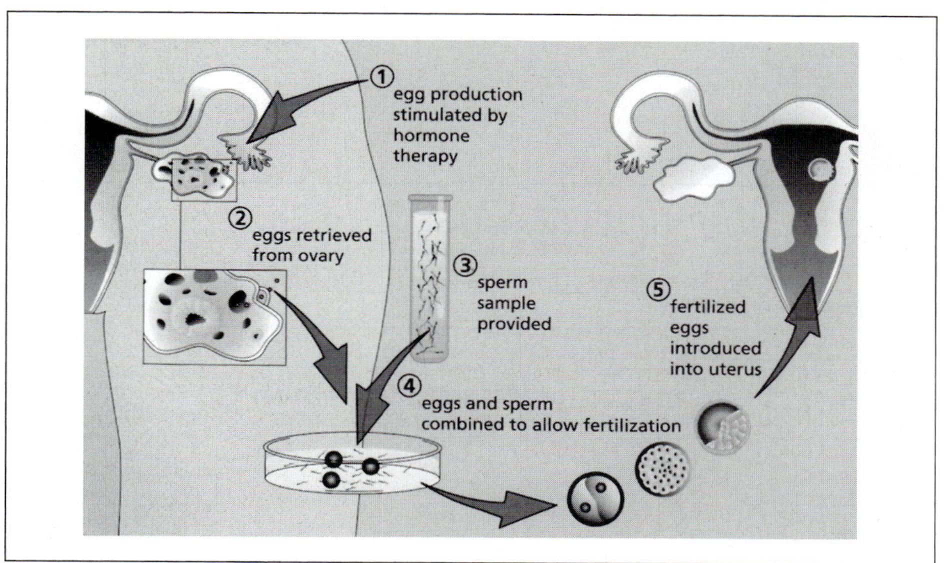

Figure 7–27 Flowchart Using Pictorial Symbols FDA/Renee Gordon.

Pictorial flowchart with numbered steps and directional arrows

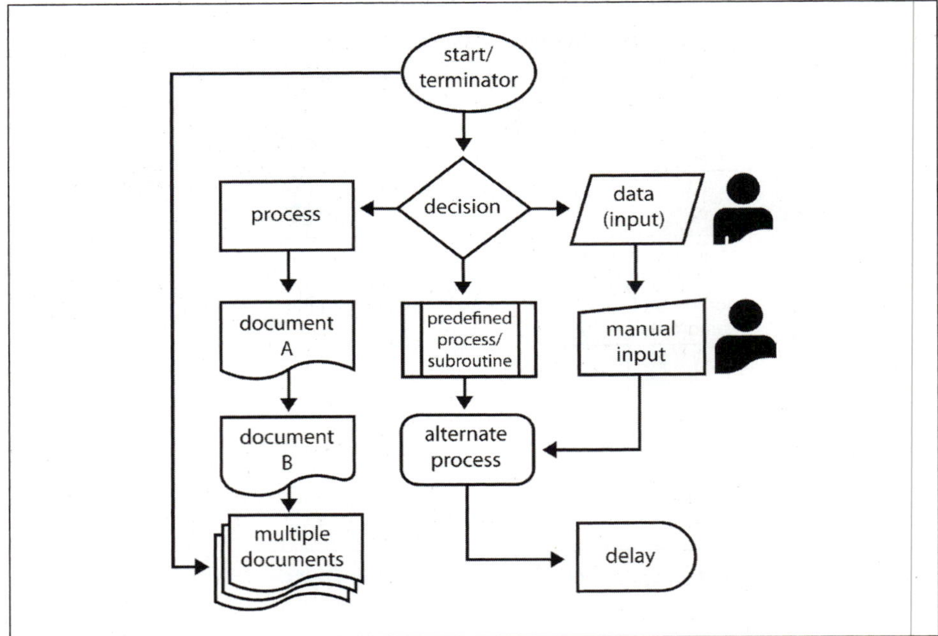

Figure 7–28 Flowchart Using Standardized Information-Processing Symbols
Michael D. Brown/Shutterstock.

Boxes are linked to show hierarchy of and relationships among units in an organization

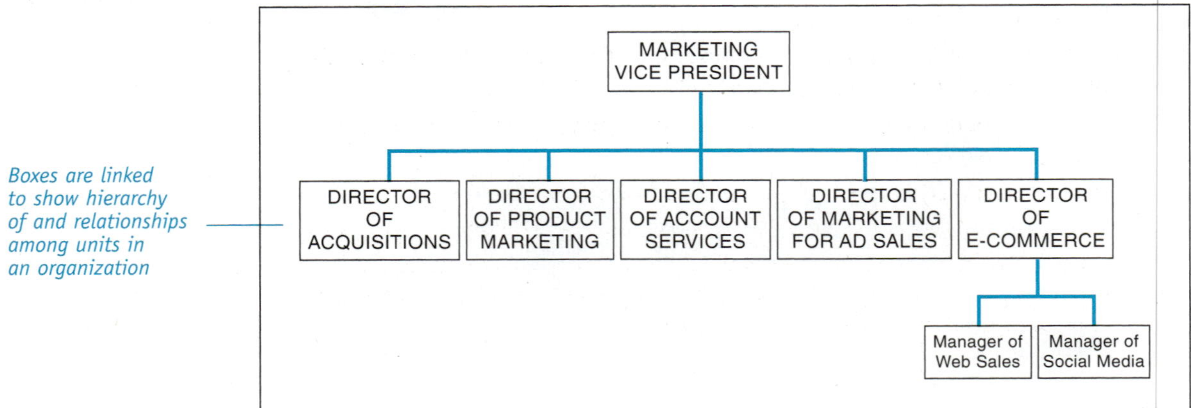

Figure 7–29 Organizational Chart

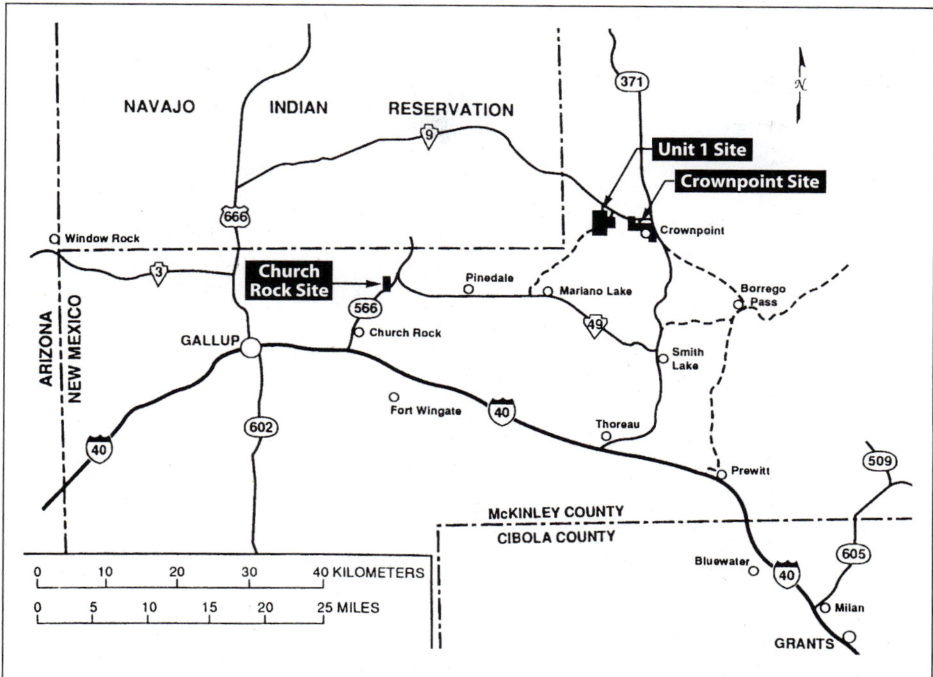

Figure 7–30 Map U.S. Nuclear Regulatory Commission.

Focus of map is location of three sites (highlighted with callouts and arrows)

Note state, reservation, and county boundaries; highways; and scales of distance

Keep in mind the following points as you create maps for use with your text:

- Clearly identify all boundaries within your map. Eliminate those that are unnecessary to the area you want to show.
- Eliminate unnecessary information. For example, if population is the focal point, do not include mountains, roads, rivers, and so on.
- Include a scale of miles or feet, or kilometers or meters, to give your reader an indication of the map's proportions.
- Indicate which direction is north with an arrow or compass symbol.
- Emphasize key features by using color, shading, dots, crosshatching, or appropriate symbols, and include a key telling what the different colors, shadings, or symbols represent (Figure 7–31). Include a key or legend that explains what the colors, shadings, or symbols represent.

◆ ***For more information on researching or creating maps, see Chapter 6, Conducting Research for a Document.***

Photographs

Photographs are vital to show the surface appearance of an object or to record an event or the development of a phenomenon over a period of time. Not all representations, however, call for photographs. They cannot depict the internal workings of

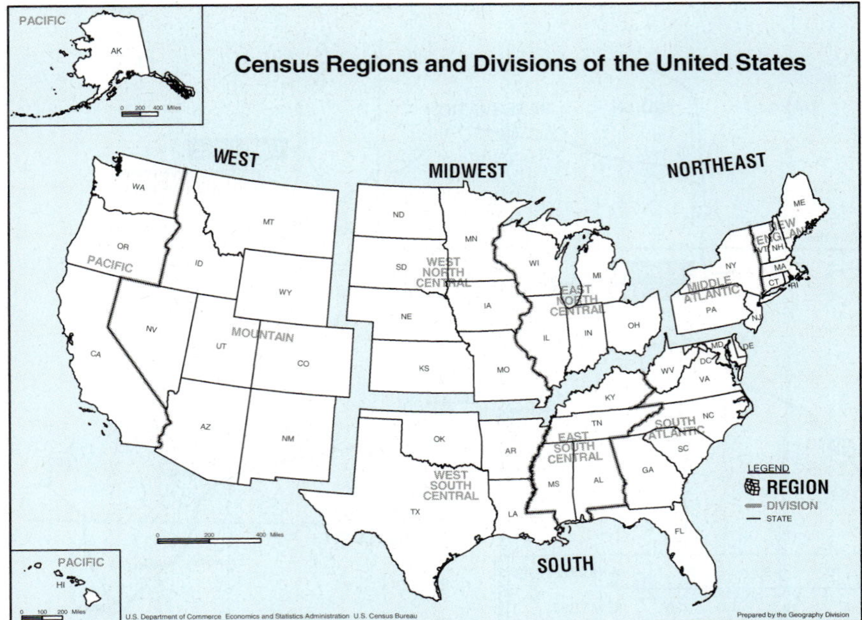

Figure 7–31 Map Showing Legend and Shading to Depict Data U.S. Census Bureau.

a mechanism or below-the-surface details of objects or structures. Such details are better shown in drawings or diagrams.

Highlighting Photographic Objects

Whether you take the photographs yourself or select them from a photo library, ensure that they focus on the details important to your content. To show the relative size of an unfamiliar object, place (or choose a photograph that shows) a familiar object—such as a ruler, a book, a tool, or a person—near the object to be photographed, as shown in Figure 7–32.

Ask the printer reproducing your publication for special handling requirements if you use glossy photographs. If you use digital photos, ask about the preferred resolution of the images before you shoot: the higher the resolution, the better the quality. You can digitize film photos using scanners or create digital photos directly using a digital camera, but ensure that the equipment has the necessary memory for the resolution required by the printer. For Web or other digital sites, ask the Web master or check the site's technical guidelines about the preferred file format (JPEG, GIF, or other) before you submit your photos.

Using Color

Color is, in many cases, the only way to communicate crucial information. In medical, chemical, geological, and botanical publications, for example, readers often need to know exactly what an object or a phenomenon looks like to accurately interpret it.

Figure 7–32 Photograph of Permafrost Soil Sample Courtesy R. Michael Miller, Argonne National Laboratory.

Posting color images online is no more complicated or expensive than posting black-and-white images. For publications, however, preparing and printing color photographs are complex technical tasks performed by graphics and printing professionals. If you are planning to use color photographs in your publication, discuss with these professionals the type, quality, and number of photographs required. Be mindful that color reproduction in printed publications is significantly more expensive than black-and-white reproduction.

Infographics

Infographics are visual forms of communication that make complex information understandable by combining text, numbers, icons, graphs, flowcharts, drawings, and other visuals into a unified whole, as shown in Figure 7–33. They are often used to educate wide audiences and can be especially useful for instructions and presentations. Infographics might be used to show an overview of a process (how to take out a personal loan), a natural phenomenon (the evolution of an animal species), an accident (the anatomy of a train wreck), a project plan (public transportation options in a city and projected passenger usage), instructions (how to assemble modular office furniture), and more. Each of these subjects might prove difficult to concisely illustrate with text or images alone.

Infographics can be static, noninteractive visuals intended for public display, print publication, or high-resolution online download. They can also take digital, interactive forms, including such tools as mouse-over pop-ups that reveal additional details or animated elements that showcase multiple cause-and-effect scenarios.

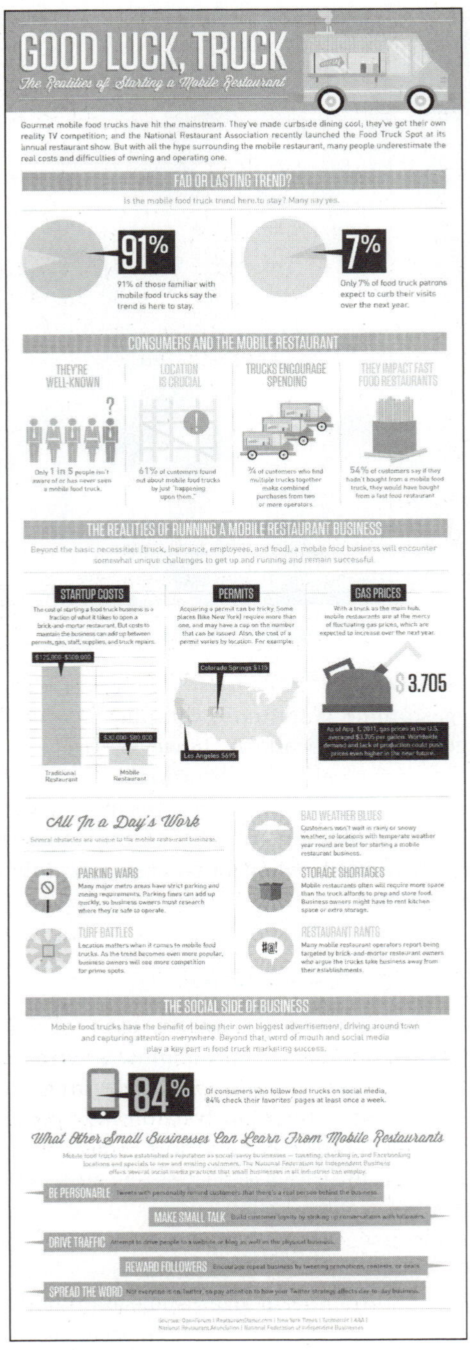

Figure 7–33 Infographic Describing a Process (Partial Image) Reprinted by permission of Intuit.

They are frequently created by graphics designers who collaborate with subject-area experts on the content. However, professionals without a formal design background can also create infographics for the workplace using a range of free online tools. Search for "tools for creating infographics" or visit such sites as piktochart.com, infogr.com, and creately.com.

Note the excerpt from the Good Luck Truck infographic in Figure 7–33. It combines text, typographic devices, data charts, a table and map, icons and images, and boxed content organized into a coherent overview of the costs and difficulties of owning and operating a restaurant in a truck. The text supports and clarifies the data in the graphs and charts and highlights the key features in the illustrations. This process could have been described in a text-heavy booklet, but the infographic's impact and appeal make the content more readily understandable.

WRITER'S CHECKLIST

Creating Infographics

✔ Use images appropriate to the topic and audience.

- Select images (illustrations and icons) where possible that are self-explanatory.
- Arrange text and images in the appropriate sequence to illustrate a process.
- Do not use dated or obsolete images or icons (rotary telephones/modems).
- Use culturally neutral images for international audiences.

✔ Use design elements—logo, typeface, colors—consistent with your company's branding practices.

✔ Ensure that all types of data graphics and illustrations are uniform in color and design.

✔ Use accurate data in text and graphics.

✔ Prepare text that is concise and clear.

✔ Cite your sources of information appropriately.

WEB LINK

Templates for creating infographics for non-professional designers are available for free at http://www.easel.ly/, http://piktochart.com/, http://infogr.am/, http://creately.com/, and http://visual.ly.

Using Visuals to Communicate Internationally

In a global business and technology environment, visuals require the same careful attention given to other features of global communications. The audiences for these communications include clients, business partners, colleagues, and current and potential employees and customers. Even though English is rapidly becoming the global language of business and science, many people speak it as a second or third language. For this reason, graphics offer distinct advantages for communicating in a global business climate.

- They can communicate a message more effectively than text, particularly in the context of safety warnings or cautions.
- They can sometimes replace technical terms that are difficult to translate.

Despite their unquestionable value in communicating with international readers, symbols, images, and even colors are not free from cultural associations: How they are perceived depends on many factors — including the values and norms of a given culture. International graphics standards exist in some fields — computer technology, airport signage, mathematics, and most scientific and engineering disciplines — but generally do not for the vast majority of other images. Writers who create documents

DIGITAL TIP: Using Graphics Software*

- *Vector graphics packages* allow you to manipulate predefined shapes (boxes, circles, arcs, lines, letters) that you then combine to produce images. Vector packages render crisp, high-resolution images that are ideal for producing complex technical graphics (isometric drawings, exploded views, and detailed line drawings), as well as basic images (flowcharts and organizational charts). These images — lines, shapes, letters — retain high-quality resolution regardless of the size at which they are produced.
- *Bitmap (or raster) programs* allow you to manipulate individual pixels (picture elements, or dots) to produce lines, shapes, and patterns. These programs — also called *paint programs* — work best with images that have broad variations in colors, shapes, or hues, such as photos and detailed drawings. Use these programs to edit photos, create Web graphics, or modify screen shots for use in print and online publications. You can alter these images by manipulating the color and intensity of the dots. The resolution quality of the images is affected by the number of dots they contain — more dots equal higher quality. At lower resolution, the images have a fuzzy or jagged appearance.

Which program should you use? Typical vector programs include Visio and Adobe Illustrator. Among the numerous bitmap programs, many students use the freeware program GIMP or the commercial Adobe Photoshop program. Select the program based on the type of image you will produce.

Use a vector program for the following:

- Line drawings
- Blueprints
- Flow and organizational charts
- Isometric drawings
- Network and process diagrams
- Illustrations, graphs, or graphics that will be resized and that require fidelity regardless of size

Use a bitmap program for the following:

- Photographs
- Computer screen shots
- Web graphics

Note that most vector programs can convert vector images to dots to create bitmap images for editing with a bitmap image editor. However, bitmap programs cannot convert bitmap images to vector images.

Information from "An Introduction to Illustration Software" by Bryan J. Follas, *Intercom*, September/October 2001: 6–8.

DIGITAL TIP: Computer Graphics

Creating computer graphics allows you to do the following:

- Save images for future use and update them as necessary.
- Use the same images in reports, other documents, and websites, where appropriate.
- Send images to presentation software programs such as Microsoft PowerPoint or Apple Keynote to create printed transparencies or digital presentations for meetings.
- Communicate image files to others electronically through e-mail.
- Automate sharing and updating data in images created and maintained in different applications — spreadsheet, database, graphics, word-processing, and presentation programs.

for an international audience can avoid confusing and possibly offending their readers by understanding the cultural connotations of visuals, described in the following sections.

Colors

Colors have culture-dependent meanings. A particular color can distort or even change the meaning of a graphic symbol. To cite one example, white in Western culture symbolizes purity. In many Asian cultures, white is associated with death and mourning. Conversely, black is associated with, among other things, death and mourning in Western cultures. Likewise, strong primary colors like red, blue, and yellow vary in their associations, depending on the setting. Red commonly indicates warning or danger in North America, Europe, and Japan. In China, however, red symbolizes joy. In Europe and North America, blue generally has a positive connotation; in Japan, the color represents villainy. In Europe and North America, yellow represents caution or cowardice; in Arab countries, yellow generally means fertility or strength. Although some of these connotations seem clear-cut, be aware that it is difficult to determine how people across the globe will interpret a given color because no universal symbolic standard for color interpretations exists. Seek out natives of the culture for their assistance or review the source cited in the Web Link on this page.

WEB LINK

Intercultural Resources
Intercultural Press publishes "books and training materials that help professionals, businesspeople, travelers, and scholars understand the meaning and diversity of culture." (See www.interculturalpress.com.)

People, Parts of the Body, and Gestures

Depicting people and parts of the body in graphics can be problematic (Table 7–3). If your graphics will reach an international audience, it is better to avoid depictions of people eating or representations of bare arms and feet. Nudity in advertising, for example, generally is acceptable in Europe but not in North America or in predominantly Muslim countries. Even showing isolated body parts could lead to communication difficulties. For example, some Middle Eastern cultures regard the display of the soles of one's shoes to be disrespectful and offensive. Therefore, a technical manual that attempts to demonstrate the ease of running a software program by

TABLE 7–3 International Implications of Gestures and Body Language

Body Part	Gesture	Country	Interpretation
Head	Nodding up and down	Bulgaria	No
Left hand	Showing palm	Muslim countries	Dirty, unclean
Index finger	Pointing to others	Venezuela, Sri Lanka	Rude
Fingers and thumb	Circular OK	Germany, Netherlands	Rude
Ankle and leg	Crossing over knee	Indonesia, Syria	Rude
Eye	Touching finger below eye	Honduras	Caution

showing a user with his or her feet on a desk could be considered offensive to that audience.

Consider the graphic in Figure 7–34, warning weightlifters against the use of steroids. The image is appropriate for North American audiences (and others) but would

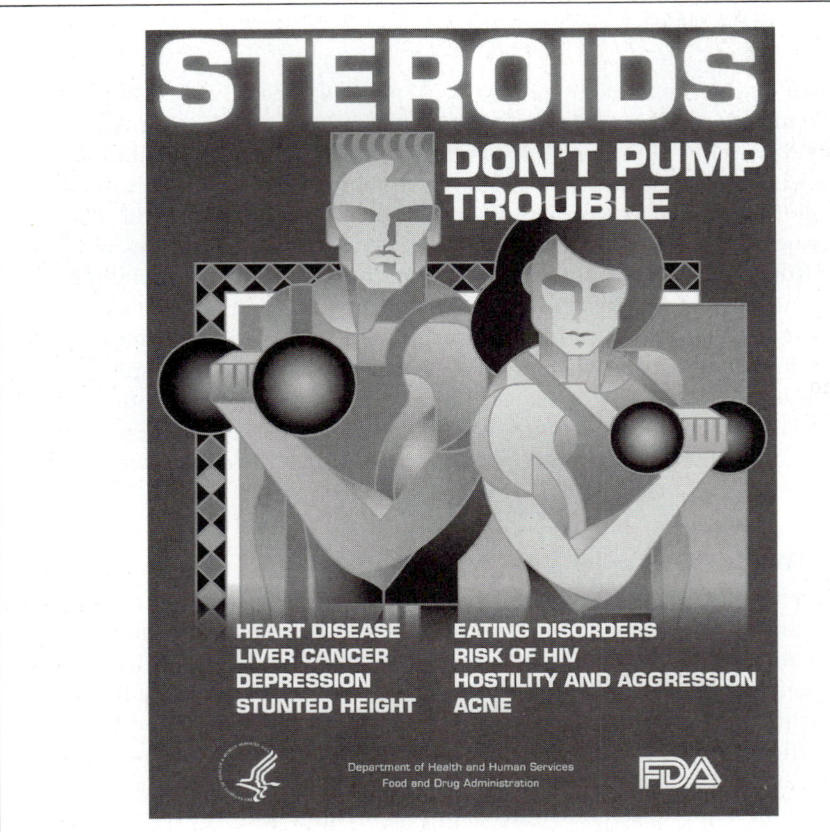

Figure 7–34 Graphic for a U.S. Audience

Figure 7–35 Graphic for a Global Audience

be highly inappropriate in cultures where the image of a partially clothed man and woman in close proximity would be contrary to deeply held cultural beliefs and even laws about the public depiction of men and women. A better choice to illustrate the anti-steroid message for those cultures would be the weightlifter image shown in Figure 7–35. It identifies the target audience (weightlifters) and avoids the connotations associated with more realistic images of people.

Communicators producing instructions often use hand gestures such as the victory sign ( ) or the "OK" sign ( ) as positive motivators. However, the meaning of each of these gestures varies by culture. In Australia, for example, the victory sign conveys the same meaning as holding up the middle finger in North America. Similarly, the gesture that means "OK" in North America can mean "worthless" in France, can mean "money" in Japan, and is a sexual insult in many other parts of the world. Even a smile may have different connotations. In Japan, smiling can be a sign of joy or can be used to hide displeasure; in some Asian cultures, smiling may be considered a sign of weakness.

Further, a manual that contains a pointed finger to indicate "turn the page" might offend someone in Venezuela. A writer preparing a manual for export to Honduras could indicate "caution" by using a picture of a person touching a finger below the eye.

Cultural Symbols

Signs and symbols are so culturally rooted that we often lose sight of the fact that the meaning we intend may be understood only in our culture.

A Michigan manufacturer of window fans, for example, wanted to use easily understood symbols to represent the two speeds of its product: fast and slow. The technical communicators selected a rabbit and a turtle. However, recognition of these animals as symbols of speed and slowness requires familiarity with Aesop's fables — a Western tradition.

Symbols that carry simultaneous religious and nonreligious meanings have long been used in North America, where it is common to use the cross as a symbol for first

Figure 7–36 International Organization for Standardization (ISO) Symbols © ISO. This material is reproduced from the ISO Bulletin, March 2003 with permission of the American National Standards Institute (ANSI) on behalf of ISO. All rights reserved.

aid or a hospital. In Muslim countries, however, a cross solely represents Christianity; a crescent (usually green) is a symbol for first aid.

The symbols or icons we create to represent technology are also laden with cultural assumptions. If users do not have regular contact with computers or mobile communications devices, technical and business communicators cannot predict how those users will interpret representations of such devices. Even punctuation marks are affected by cultural expectations. For example, in English-speaking countries, the question mark generally represents the need for information or the Help function in a computer manual or program. In many countries, this symbol is not a punctuation mark and therefore cannot be understood at all. To avoid confusion, when possible include a key that associates the English-language question mark with the local language's equivalent mark.

These and similar examples suggest why international groups, such as the International Organization for Standardization (ISO), have established agreed-on symbols, such as those shown in Figure 7–36, designed for public signs, guidebooks, and manuals.[1]

Reading Practices

Whether text is read right to left or left to right influences how graphics are sequenced. In the Middle East and in many parts of Asia, for example, text is read from right to left. For these audiences, you will need to alter the design and sequencing of text and graphics. Seek examples of graphics placement in documents and online communications that meet the expectations of such audiences.

Directional Signs

The signs we use to represent direction or time are open to misinterpretation. For example, the arrow sign on shipping cartons can be interpreted to mean either that the carton should be placed with the arrow pointing up to the top of the carton, or pointing down to the carton's most stable position. Western cultures tend to indicate the future (or something positive) by pointing to the right (→) and the past (or something negative) by pointing to the left (←); in the Chinese culture, left represents honor and right self-destruction.

[1]Learn more from the useful illustrations in "The International Language of ISO Graphical Symbols" at www.iso.org/graphical-symbols_booklet.pdf.

PROFESSIONALISM NOTE: Adapt Visuals for International Audiences Careful attention to the different connotations that visual elements may have for an international audience makes translations easier, saves a company from potential embarrassment, and over time earns respect for the company and its products and services.

CONSIDERING AUDIENCE AND PURPOSE

Using International Graphics

- Consult with someone from your intended audience's country or culture who will be able to recognize and explain the effects of subtle visual elements on your intended readers.
- Organize visual information for your intended audiences. North American readers read visuals from left to right in clockwise rotation. Middle Eastern readers read visuals from right to left in counterclockwise rotation.
- Learn about the use of gestures in other cultures as a first step to learning about cultural context because the interpretation of gestures differs widely.
- Be sure that the graphics you use have no unintended religious or symbolic implications.
- As a rule, use few colors in your graphics unless your target audience expects otherwise or the topic requires it. Generally, black-and-white or gray-and-white illustrations are less problematic than color graphics. If you must use color, respect your audience's preferences and taboos.
- Create simple visuals. Simple shapes with few elements are easier to read in most cultures.
- Use outlines or neutral abstractions to represent human beings, such as stick figures for bodies or a circle for a head.
- Be consistent in labeling for all visuals.
- Explain the meaning of icons or symbols. Include a glossary to explain symbols that cannot be changed (for example, company logos).
- Test icons, symbols, and punctuation marks (many languages, for example, do not use a question mark) in context with members of your target audience. Usability testing with cultural experts is critical.

CHAPTER 7 SUMMARY: DESIGNING DOCUMENTS AND VISUALS

Understanding Design Principles

- Do the layout and design of your finished document highlight the organization and hierarchy of your information?
- Does your content use consistent and predictable typographical and design devices?
- Are items similar in content grouped to emphasize their relationship?
- Are items that you wish to emphasize set apart from or shown in contrast to the items around them?

Integrating Visuals and Text

- Have you noted in your document planning outline the approximate location of your visuals?
- Does the text preceding a table or figure make clear why the visual is there and what it shows?
- Do all visuals have clear, concise captions?
- Is the graphic located as close as possible to — but following — the text describing it? Is the language in the text consistent with the language in the visual?
- Have you allowed adequate white space around and within the text and graphics in your documents?
- Have you obtained permission to reproduce copyrighted graphics?

Creating Visuals

- Do your tables organize numerical or verbal information for ease of understanding?
- Are the trends depicted in your graphs free of distortions?
- Are graphs supported by precise data in tables or by exact figures on the graph?
- Are color, shading, or crosshatching patterns on graphs easy to interpret?
- Are graphs free of unnecessary details that obscure at-a-glance interpretations?
- Are drawings shown from the correct perspective and focused on the significant piece of a device or mechanism?
- Do flowcharts indicate the direction of flow?
- Are the steps in a pictorial flowchart labeled?
- Are unfamiliar symbols in a flowchart explained?
- Are the components in an organizational chart linked to show clearly the lines of authority within the organization?
- Are maps free of details that obscure the features you wish to highlight?
- Do photographs show key objects and details from the best perspective and degree of visual clarity?

Using Visuals to Communicate Internationally

- Has someone from your audience's culture or country reviewed your visuals for appropriateness?
- Do visuals feature culturally neutral shapes and designs?
- Are important features, including icons and symbols, labeled on the visual or explained in a glossary or key?

Exercises

1. Assume that you work for PLANET (the Professional Landcare Network), a professional association for landscape designers and contractors. You have been asked to create a table for the organization's website, www.landcarenetwork.org, that shows the seasonal lawn-maintenance tasks landscape services or homeowners might perform over the period of one year. Use the following information to create your table:

   Mow: April to June (every two weeks), July and August (weekly), and September to October (every two weeks)

   De-thatch: April or September

   Aerate: April or September

Fertilize: March, May, July, September, November
Water: Twice a week June through September, or as needed
Apply weed killer: February, April, June, August, October

If PLANET organizers were also considering using your table in their new brochure, what design or formatting differences would you suggest between the Web and print tables?

2. Assume that a survey of 100 companies resulted in the following distribution percentages by type of industry: computer-related, 32 percent; industrial equipment, 7 percent; business services, 8 percent; telecommunications, 10 percent; media and publications, 10 percent; consumer goods, 10 percent; medical and pharmaceutical, 14 percent; other, 9 percent. Prepare a pie graph showing the distribution.

3. Create a line or bar graph that compares sales in thousands of dollars among the various truck-parts divisions of the ABC Corporation for 2014, 2015, and 2016. Sales for each division are as follows:

   - Axles: 2014 ($225K), 2015 ($200K), 2016 ($75K)
   - Universal joints: 2014 ($125K), 2015 ($100K), 2016 ($35K)
   - Frames: 2014 ($125K), 2015 ($100K), 2016 ($50K)
   - Transmissions: 2014 ($75K), 2015 ($65K), 2016 ($50K)
   - Clutches: 2014 ($35K), 2015 ($30K), 2016 ($15K)
   - Gaskets and seals: 2014 ($28K), 2015 ($25K), 2016 ($20K)

4. Briefly explain whether a photograph or a line drawing would better illustrate features of the following subjects: a dry-cell battery (for an article in a general encyclopedia), a flower arrangement (in a florist's brochure), an electrical-outlet box (in a wiring instructions booklet), or the procedure for wrapping a sprained ankle (for a first-aid handbook).

5. Create a flowchart showing a work-related process (administrative, medical, industrial, or other) from start to finish. Label each step showing the directional flow, and, where possible, use symbols or images at the appropriate steps in the process.

6. Create an organizational chart for a campus group to which you belong or for the department in your area of study.

7. Misleading visuals are unethical and can result in a loss of credibility for you and your organization. For each of five subjects from the following list, suggest a potential visual based on statistics and list ways in which that visual might be used to help or hurt the people involved:

   - Immigrants seeking political asylum in the United States
   - Children who are abused or teens who are homeless
   - Elderly people who need financial assistance
   - Children with learning disabilities
   - Women who give birth in prison
   - Homeless people with mental disabilities
   - Former convicts seeking the right to vote
   - Veterans with disabilities
   - Men or women who are subjected to domestic abuse
   - Infants affected by illegal drugs
   - Underpaid health-care workers
   - Adults on Social Security

8. Following up on Exercise 7, imagine that you are planning to create a report for local government leaders on the use and ethics of visuals and statistics as they relate to promoting social programs and public policy. Using the Designing Your Document checklist on pages 220, think strategically about the layout of your pages as a means of persuading this audience. For example, how many columns will you use? What kind of font type and size would promote quick and efficient reading? How will you highlight statistics and other crucial information? (You may want to revisit Chapter 1, Understanding the Workplace Writing Context: A Case Study, for information on audiences and their needs.) Use your answers to create a thumbnail sketch of your report.
9. Create a pie chart that breaks down the expense percentages in your monthly budget, including housing, food, utilities, transportation (car, bus, subway), insurance (car, life, property, medical), school, clothing, entertainment, and the like. Support your pie chart with a detailed table that specifies the exact amount you budgeted for each item.

Collaborative Classroom Projects

1. Divide the class into teams of two to three students and have each team locate websites that use both text and visuals to explain how things work. One source is www.howstuffworks.com. After reviewing the guidelines in this chapter for creating documents and integrating visuals:
   a. Choose an object from one of the sites, print the explanation (including graphics), and have each team evaluate it according to the criteria listed under Designing and Integrating Visuals with Text, pages 223–224.
   b. Mark the pages of the explanation, indicating any changes you would make to improve the explanation. Feel free to sketch out the team's ideas.
   c. Have each team draft a memo to your instructor that explains what does and does not work in the original explanation, supporting your ideas with information from this chapter. Specify how your changes would improve the explanation and associated graphics. Attach to your memo the marked-up printout of the explanation and any sketches the team created.
2. Bring to class a set of illustrated instructions (such as assembly instructions for a bookcase or a quick-start guide for a tablet computer) that you believe could be designed more effectively. Then do the following, as your instructor directs:
   a. Critique the design and create a list of what could be improved.
   b. Recommend specific steps for improving the instruction's clarity.
   c. Create a new set of instructions either yourself or in a group.

Research Projects

1. Imagine that you just got hired as a graphic artist for a marketing company. Your job is to design visuals for a new promotional campaign your company is creating for a famous sneaker company. You come up with the idea for a graphic, featuring a mound of sneakers piled high to the sky. You decide to copyright your idea. You then create the sneaker graphic and register it in your name instead of the marketing company's. You later run into a friend who shows you an interesting graphic, featuring people running.

The artist gave him permission to use that graphic for a project. You ask to use it, too, and your friend gives you permission. Your new boss gets wind of your activities and threatens to fire you unless you learn about copyright laws. Research the basic copyright and fair-use laws regarding graphics to find out what you did wrong. Present your findings to the class in an oral presentation.

2. Create a bar graph showing the median sales price of new single-family homes in the United States for 1990 and at five-year intervals through the most current data available at the website of the U.S. Census Bureau, www.census.gov.

PART 3

Messages and Models

Parts 1 and 2 discuss the principles of effective writing that apply to all on-the-job writing tasks; Part 3 focuses on the practical applications of these principles. Chapters 8 through 15 provide explicit guidelines for writing the most common types of work-related communications and offer plenty of examples: e-mail messages, memos, business letters, instructions, proposals, and a variety of formal and informal reports. Part 3 ends with a chapter that puts everything you have learned in this text to its first practical test: finding a job appropriate to your education and abilities.

8 Writing E-mails, Memos, and Letters

Contents

Business messages among people within an organization, or between those people and their clients or customers, are essential to the success of individuals and businesses. You can communicate your goals and convey a professional image by using the following guidelines essential to successful business messages:

Business messages — whether written on a desktop, laptop, tablet computer, or on paper — must (1) establish or maintain a positive working relationship with readers and (2) convey a professional image of you and your organization. Achieving those goals and fulfilling the specific purpose of your message requires many of the steps that are described in Chapters 1 through 4. Even as you quickly compose an e-mail on a mobile device, for example, you need to consider your readers (audience), study previous messages (research), and then arrange the points you wish to cover (organization). Finally, given the ability in a digital environment to write on the move, transmit messages instantly, and have some messages simultaneously available to large groups, you must not skip revision *and you must think carefully before you send your message.*

Allow a cooling period, especially when the message is sensitive or responds to a problem (see Chapter 4, Revising a Document). Even a lunch-hour break can give you a chance to reconsider any potentially inappropriate statements made in the heat of the situation. *Because it is possible to send and distribute a message instantly, you must consider carefully the impact of your*

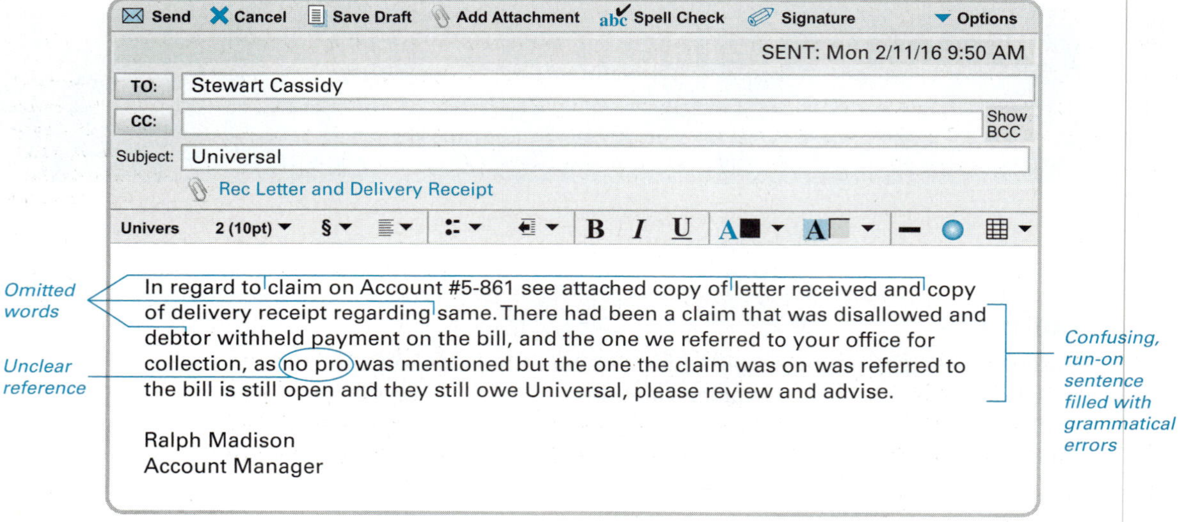

Figure 8–1 Poorly Written Message

message on your recipients, yourself, and your employer. The high cost of writing that is produced quickly and without care is illustrated in Figure 8–1, an actual message sent to a law firm (the names have been changed). What does that client want? What impression do you get of that sender? This case was highly sensitive, so Stewart Cassidy did not want to reply until he was sure how to respond to the message. But the staff at the law firm could not understand it, even though a number of attorneys, paralegals, and assistants who read it were generally familiar with the case. Staff members exchanged messages and even phone calls with Ralph Madison and others at his company to try to clarify the request but without success. This message wasted the time of a highly paid staff — and caused a delay in legal services to Ralph Madison's company. Such carelessly written messages also project a poor image of the writer and can result in other kinds of losses. A reader's negative reaction to an unclear or unprofessional message, for example, can cost a firm its reputation and future business — and can even cost an employee his or her job.

PROFESSIONALISM NOTE: Choose a Medium to Protect Content Privacy Especially in a digital and print-based environment, the writer must consider the method of transmission used to deliver a document. Memos and letters can be mailed, sent as attachments to e-mail messages, or faxed. Instant messages can be composed on a mobile device, through a public website, or through a social-media portal. Each method brings with it privacy and confidentiality considerations that the writer must keep in mind. For example, because fax machines in offices can be located in shared areas, inform the intended recipient before you send confidential or sensitive documents. And, because conversations transmitted through social-media sites often expose your text to professional colleagues, to friends, and potentially to the general public, ensure that such conversations are appropriate for disclosure. For a thorough discussion of selecting the appropriate medium, see Chapter 1, pages 14–19.

For an overview of the writing process at work, see Chapter 1, Understanding the Workplace Writing Context: A Case Study.

Using Professional Style and Tone

Corresponding with others in the workplace enables you to establish or maintain a positive working relationship with your readers and to convey a professional image of yourself and your organization. Your attitude toward the reader (tone) and the way you express yourself (style) determine how readers react to you and your organization.

Audience and Writing Style

Effective messages use an appropriate conversational style. To achieve that style, imagine your reader sitting across from you and write to the reader as if you were talking face to face. Anticipate your reader's needs and feelings. Ask yourself, "How might I feel if I received this message?" and then tailor it accordingly. Remember, an impersonal and unfriendly message to a customer or client can tarnish the image of you and your business, but a thoughtful and sincere one can enhance it.

Whether you use a formal or an informal writing style depends on your reader, your purpose, and the context. You might use an informal (or a casual) style, for example, with a colleague you know well and a formal (or restrained) style with a client you do not know.

CASUAL It worked! The new process is better than we had dreamed.

RESTRAINED You will be pleased to know that the new process is more effective than we had expected.

You will probably find yourself using a slightly more restrained style more frequently than the casual style. Remember that an overdone attempt to sound casual or friendly can sound insincere. However, do not adopt a style so formal that your writing reads like a legal contract. Affectation not only will irritate and baffle readers but also can waste time and produce costly errors.

AFFECTED Per yesterday's e-mail, we no longer possess an original copy of the brochure requested. Please be advised that a PDF copy is attached herewith to this e-mail.

◆ *For detailed advice about adopting an appropriate style in your writing, see pages 102–115 in Chapter 4, Revising a Document.*

IMPROVED — We are out of printed copies of the brochure we discussed yesterday, so I'm attaching a PDF copy to this e-mail.

The improved version is not only clearer and less stuffy but also more concise.

Goodwill and the "You" Viewpoint

Write concisely, but do not be so blunt that you risk losing the reader's goodwill. Responding to a vague written request with "Your request was unclear" or "I don't understand" could offend your reader. Instead, establish goodwill to encourage your reader to provide the information you need.

> I'll be glad to help, but I need more information to find the report you requested. Specifically, can you give me the report's title, release date, or number?

Although this version is a bit longer, it is more tactful and will elicit a faster response.

You can also build goodwill by emphasizing the reader's needs or benefits. Suppose you received a refund request from a customer who forgot to enclose the receipt. In a response to that customer, you might write the following:

WEAK — We must receive the sales receipt before we can process a refund. [The writer's needs are emphasized: "*We* must."]

If you consider how you might keep the customer's goodwill, you could word the request this way:

IMPROVED — Please mail or fax the sales receipt so that we can process your refund. [This is polite, but the writer's needs are still emphasized: "so that *we* can process."]

You can put the reader's needs and interests foremost by writing from the reader's perspective. Often, doing so means using the words *you* and *your* rather than *we*, *our*, *I*, and *mine*—a technique called the "you" viewpoint. Consider the following revision:

EFFECTIVE — So that you can receive your refund promptly, please mail or fax the sales receipt. [The reader's needs are emphasized with *you* and *your*.]

This revision stresses the reader's benefit and interest and is more likely to accomplish its purpose: to get the reader to act.

If overdone, however, goodwill and the "you" viewpoint can produce writing that is fawning and insincere. Messages that are full of excessive praise and inflated language may be ignored—or even resented—by the reader.

EXCESSIVE PRAISE — You are just the kind of astute client that deserves the finest service we can offer—and you deserve our best deal. Knowing how carefully you make decisions, I know you'll think about the advantages of using our consulting service.

REASONABLE — From our earlier messages, I understand your need for reliable service. We work to give all our priority clients our full attention, and after you have reviewed our proposal, I'm confident you will appreciate our "five-star" consulting option.

WRITER'S CHECKLIST

Using Tone to Build Goodwill

Use the following guidelines to achieve a tone that builds goodwill with your recipients.

✔ Be respectful, not demanding.

DEMANDING	Submit your answer in one week.
RESPECTFUL	We would appreciate your answer by the November 15 deadline.

✔ Be modest, not arrogant.

ARROGANT	My attached report is thorough, and I'm sure that it will be essential.
MODEST	The attached report contains details of the refinancing options that I hope you will find useful.

✔ Be polite, not sarcastic.

SARCASTIC	I just now received the shipment we ordered six months ago. I'm sending it back — we can't use it now. Thanks a lot!
POLITE	I am returning the shipment we ordered on March 12. Unfortunately, it arrived too late for us to be able to use it.

✔ Be positive and tactful, not negative and condescending.

NEGATIVE	Your complaint about our prices is way off target. Our prices are definitely not any higher than those of our competitors.
TACTFUL	Thank you for your suggestion concerning our prices. We believe, however, that our prices are comparable to or lower than those of our competitors.

Structuring Effective Messages

Messages need to be structured to meet the readers' needs. This section covers organizational patterns and elements that will help you accomplish your purposes in writing.

Direct and Indirect Patterns

Direct Pattern

The direct pattern is effective in the workplace because readers appreciate messages that get to the main point early — at the outset, if at all possible. This approach begins with the main point, follows with an explanation of details, and provides a goodwill closing that builds a positive relationship with the recipient.

1. Main point of message
2. Explanation of details or facts
3. Goodwill closing

Figure 8–2 shows an example of a reader-focused letter using the direct pattern. By presenting the main point first, you save the reader time, increase the likelihood that the reader will pay careful attention to the supporting details, and generally achieve goodwill from the start.

The direct pattern is especially appropriate for presenting good news, as shown in Figure 8–3 on page 272. This message presents the good news in the opening (the main point), follows with an explanation of facts, and closes by looking toward the future (goodwill). The direct pattern may also be appropriate for negative messages in situations where little is at stake for the writer or reader and the reasons for the negative message are relatively unimportant.

▶ Dear Mr. Coleman:

We do not have the part you requested currently in stock, but we hope to have it within the next month. Our supplier, who has been reliable in the past, assures us that the manufacturer that produces those parts will be able . . . [Continues with details and goodwill closing]

Indirect Pattern

The indirect pattern may be effective when you need to present negative or sensitive messages in correspondence. Research has shown that people form their impressions and attitudes very early when reading correspondence. For this reason, presenting bad news, refusals, or sensitive messages indirectly is often more effective than presenting them directly, especially if the stakes are high.[1]

As with any type of writing, imagine how your audience will react to your message. Consider the thoughtlessness in the job rejection that follows:

▶ Dear Ms. Mauer:

Your application for the position of Records Administrator at Southtown Dental Center has been rejected. We have found someone more qualified than you.

Sincerely,

◆ ***For more guidance on organizing information, see Chapter 2, Planning a Document.***

Although the letter is concise and uses the pronouns *you* and *your*, the writer has not considered how the recipient will feel as she reads the letter. The letter is, in short, rude. The pattern of this letter is (1) bad news, (2) curt explanation, (3) close.

---

[1]Gerald J. Alred, "'We Regret to Inform You': Toward a New Theory of Negative Messages," in *Studies in Technical Communication*, ed. Brenda R. Sims (Denton: University of North Texas and NCTE, 1993), 17–36.

July 28, 2017

Mr. James Longo
Longo's Café and Deli
157 Adams Drive
Trumbull, TN 37802

Dear Mr. Longo:

Would you be willing to share your personal history with the Trumbull Historical Society? Mary Tran recommended you as somebody we should talk to because of your long commitment to neighborhood improvement. — *Main point*

As you may have heard, Historical Society volunteers are interviewing people whose experiences illustrate Trumbull's rich and varied cultural fabric. The oral history project aims both to document local traditions and to demonstrate that Trumbull is a vibrant town with strong community ties. At the same time, by sharing oral histories at public forums, the Historical Society hopes to replace negative stereotypes with a truer picture of what the community means to its residents. — *Explanation*

We would like to add your voice to the official history of Trumbull. If you choose to participate, you will be asked to recall events, experiences, personal or family memories, and cultural traditions that are important to you. You won't be pressed to discuss anything you're not comfortable with, and you will determine the focus of the conversation. Interviews take about an hour and are scheduled at your convenience.

I hope I've piqued your interest. I'll call you in the next couple of weeks to discuss the project, but do feel free to contact me earlier if I can answer any questions. — *Closing*

Thank you,

Margaret Schweinhurt

Margaret Schweinhurt
Project Coordinator
Trumbull Oral History Project
611.999.9999
oralhistory@mas.org

Figure 8–2 Reader-Focused Request Letter

Records offer

Dear Ms. Mauer:

We are pleased to offer you the position of Records Administrator at Southtown Dental Center at the salary of $54,300. Your qualifications fit our needs precisely, and we hope you will accept our offer.

If the terms we discussed in the interview are acceptable to you, please come to the main office at 9:30 a.m. on November 18. At that time, we will ask you to complete our benefits form, in addition to . . .

Our entire office looks forward to working with you. Everyone was favorably impressed with you during your interview.

Sincerely,

Figure 8–3 A Good-News Message

The indirect pattern for such bad-news correspondence allows the explanation or details to lead logically and tactfully to the negative message, as in the following pattern:

1. Context (or "buffer")
2. Explanation or details
3. Bad news or negative message
4. Goodwill closing

◆ *For more examples, see pages 300–319 in Chapter 9, Writing Routine and Sensitive Messages.*

The opening (traditionally called a "buffer") should provide a context for the subject and establish a professional tone. However, it must not mislead the reader to believe that good news may follow and it must not contain irrelevant information.[2]

The body should provide an explanation by reviewing the details or facts that led to a negative decision or refusal. Give the negative message simply, based on the facts; do not belabor the bad news or provide an inappropriate apology. Neither the details nor an overdone apology can turn bad news into something positive. Your goal should be to establish for the reader that the writer or organization has been *reasonable* given the circumstances. To accomplish this goal, you need to organize the explanation carefully and logically.

[2]Kitty O. Locker, "Factors in Reader Responses to Negative Letters: Experimental Evidence for Changing What We Teach," in *Journal of Business and Technical Communication* 13, no. 1 (January 1999): 29.

The closing should establish or reestablish a positive relationship through goodwill or helpful information. Consider, for example, the revised bad-news letter, shown in Figure 8–4. This letter carries the same disappointing news as the letter on page 270, but the writer of this letter begins by not only introducing the subject but also thanking the reader for her time and effort. Then the writer explains why Ms. Mauer was not accepted for the job and offers her encouragement by looking toward a potential future opportunity. Bad news is never pleasant; however, information that either puts the bad news in perspective or makes the bad news reasonable maintains respect between the writer and the reader. The goodwill closing is intended to reestablish an amicable professional relationship.

The indirect pattern can also be used in relatively short e-mail messages and memos. Consider the unintended secondary message a manager conveys in the following notice:

WEAK It has been decided that the office will be open the day after Thanksgiving.

"It has been decided" not only sounds impersonal but also communicates an authoritarian, management-versus-employee tone. The passive voice also suggests that the

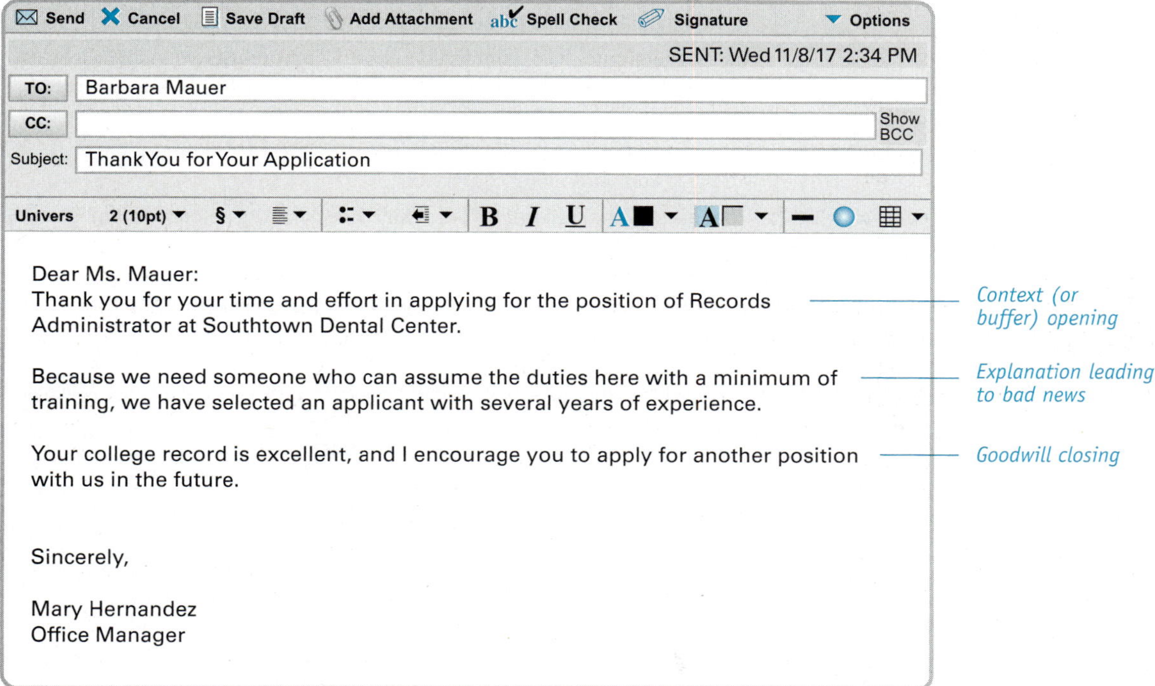

Figure 8–4 Courteous Bad-News Letter

decision maker does not want to say "I have decided" and thus accept responsibility for the decision. One solution is to remove the first part of the sentence.

IMPROVED The office will be open the day after Thanksgiving.

The best solution, however, would be to suggest both that there is a good reason for the decision and that employees are privy to (if not a part of) the decision-making process.

EFFECTIVE Because we must meet the December 15 deadline for submitting the Bradley Foundation proposal, the office will be open the day after Thanksgiving.

By describing the context of the bad news first (the need to meet the deadline), the writer focuses on the reasoning behind the decision to work. Employees may not necessarily like the message, but they will at least understand that the decision is not arbitrary and is tied to an important deadline.

Openings

Openings are crucial because readers in the workplace are busy meeting deadlines and coping with dozens of messages every day. Openings should identify the subject, its relevance to your readers, and often the main point of the message.

E-MAIL Attached is the final installation report, which I hope you can review by Monday, December 11. You will notice that the report includes . . .

MEMO ACM Electronics has asked us to prepare a comprehensive set of brochures for its Milwaukee office by August 9. We have worked with similar firms in the past. . . .

TEXT MESSAGE Reached client location and problem is defective circuit board. Will replace and send report to Dextron.

LETTER Enclosed with this letter is your refund check for the defective compressor, number AJ50172. Also enclosed is our latest . . .

Even if your opening gives the essential background of a problem, state the main point early in the first paragraph.

BACKGROUND Last year we did not hire new staff because of the freeze on hiring. As a result of the increased workload described in this memo, we need to hire two additional application support specialists this year.

When the reader is not familiar with the subject or with the background of a problem, provide an introductory paragraph before stating the main point (shown in italics in the following example) of the memo. Doing so is especially important in correspondence that serves as a record for crucial information months or years later.

MAIN IDEA OBA Electronics has asked us to prepare a comprehensive print and digital brochure for its Milwaukee office by August 11, 2017. We have worked with electronics firms in the past, so this job should not cause significant

> problems. I estimate that it will take two months to complete. Ted Harris has requested time and cost estimates for the project, Fred Moore in production will prepare the cost estimates, and *I would like you to prepare a tentative schedule for the project.*

Generally, longer or complex subjects benefit most from more thorough introductions. However, even when you are writing a short message about a familiar subject, remind readers of the context. In the following examples, words that provide context are shown in italics.

- *As we discussed after yesterday's meeting,* we need to set new guidelines for . . .
- *As Maria recommended,* I reviewed the office reorganization plan. I like most of the features; however, the location of the receptionist and administrative assistant . . .

Do not state the main point first when (1) readers are likely to be highly skeptical or (2) key readers, such as managers or clients, may disagree with your position. In those cases, a more persuasive tactic is to state the problem or issue first, then present the specific points supporting your final recommendation, as discussed in the earlier section on negative messages.

◆ *For more information on openings and closings, see pages 87–90 in Chapter 3, Drafting a Document.*

Because business messages are often more personal than reports and other formal documents, an opening must also establish an appropriate tone that achieves your purpose.

- I'm seeking advice about organizational communication, and several people have suggested that you are an authority on the subject.

The tone of respect in this opening is not only appropriate but also persuasive because it appeals to the reader's pride. Other openings might appeal to the reader's curiosity or personal interests, as in the following:

- I have a problem you may be interested in helping me solve.
- Mr. Walter Jenkens has given us your name as a reference for his company's services. I hope you'll be willing to help us by answering some specific questions about his company.

Closings

An effective closing can accomplish many important tasks, such as building positive relationships with readers, encouraging colleagues and employees, soliciting feedback or the continuation of a discussion, and letting recipients know what you will do or what you expect of them and, if necessary, when an assignment is due.

- I will discuss the problem with the marketing consultant and let you know by Wednesday (August 9) what we are able to change.

Closings can also provide an incentive for the reader to act, as in the following:

- Please consider the highlighted changes on the contract and return it to me with the additional material in the preaddressed envelope. If I receive your approval by

Tuesday, May 5, I can have the amended contract ready for your signature by the end of the week.

Although routine statements are sometimes unavoidable ("If you have further questions, please let me know"), make your closing work for you by providing specific prompts to which the reader can respond.

◆ For more examples of openings and closings in various types of correspondence, review the figures in Chapter 9, Writing Routine and Sensitive Messages.

▸ Thanks again for the report, and let me know if you want me to send you a copy of the test results.

▸ If you would like further information, such as a copy of the questionnaire we used, please reply to this e-mail.

Developing Clarity and Emphasis

Your messages need to be clear and emphasize your main points. To produce a clear message, you need to adequately develop your main points and be as specific as possible, as shown in the following example.

VAGUE Be more careful on the loading dock.

DEVELOPED To prevent accidents on the loading dock, follow this procedure:
1. Check to make sure . . .
2. Load only items that are rated . . .
3. Replace any defective parts . . .

◆ To review the outlining process, see Chapter 2, Planning a Document.

Although the first version is concise, it is not as clear and specific as the "developed" revision. Do not assume your readers will know what you mean: Vague messages are easily misinterpreted. Readers may be pressed for time and misinterpret your message if it is vague.

Lists

◆ For additional guidance on using lists, see the Using Lists checklist on page 106 in Chapter 4, Revising a Document.

Vertically stacked words, phrases, and other items with numbers or bullets can effectively emphasize such information as steps in a sequence, materials or parts needed, key or concluding points, and recommendations. A particularly useful type of list is one that helps define goals.

▸ I recommend we aim to accomplish the following tasks in our meeting:
- Identify and analyze the audiences for our business plan.
- Refine our goals for convincing potential investors to provide financing.
- Assess the profitability and goals for our new business venture.

As described in Chapter 4, Revising a Document, make sure you provide context so that the reader can understand the purpose of the list. Be careful not to overuse lists — a message that consists almost entirely of lists is difficult to understand because it forces readers to connect separate and disjointed items. Further, lists lose their impact when they are overused.

Headings

Another attention-getting device, particularly in long messages, is the use of headings. Headings have a number of advantages:

◆ *For additional guidance on headings, see pages 377 and 382 in Chapter 11, Writing Formal Reports.*

- They divide material into manageable segments.
- They call attention to main topics.
- They signal a shift in topic.

They are especially helpful for messages aimed at different types of audiences because the headings allow each reader to scan them and read only the section or sections appropriate to his or her needs. Notice the effective use of both a list and headings in Figure 8–8 on page 286.

Subject Lines

Although they may seem simple, subject lines for e-mails, memos, and some letters require careful preparation for important reasons:

- They announce the topic and focus of the correspondence.
- They enable recipients to decide at a glance how the message is related to their needs.
- They are important aids to filing and later retrieval.

As these functions suggest, each e-mail or memo should address one subject (as illustrated in Figure 8–6 on page 281 and Figure 8–8 on page 286). A subject area, of course, may contain multiple points or questions. But if you need to cover two subject areas, write two messages. Multisubject e-mails and memos are often confusing to or overlooked by a hurried reader.

Subject lines should be concise yet complete, specific, and accurate to achieve their goals.

VAGUE	Subject: Tuition Reimbursement
VAGUE	Subject: Time-Management Seminar
SPECIFIC	Subject: Tuition Reimbursement for Time-Management Seminar

Capitalize all major words in a subject line except articles, prepositions, and conjunctions with fewer than five letters (unless they are the first or last words). Remember that the subject line should not substitute for an opening that provides context for the message.

Managing Your E-mail and Protocol

E-mail (or *email*) functions in the workplace as the primary medium to exchange information and share electronic files with colleagues, clients, and customers. E-mail messages range from short, informal notes to longer, more formal communications with clients and professionals. You may also attach memos, letters, and other files to e-mails.

Dilbert

Scott Adams, Dilbert cartoon, "My derogatory and condescending e-mail will set things right." Copyright © 1999 by United Features Syndicate. Reprinted with the permission of United Media.

Review and Confidentiality

Avoid the temptation to send the first draft of a message without rereading it for clarity and appropriateness. Your message should include all crucial details and be free of grammatical and factual errors, ambiguities, and unintended implications.

Keep in mind that e-mails are easily forwarded and are never truly deleted. Most companies back up and save all their e-mail messages and are legally entitled to monitor e-mail use. Companies can be compelled, depending on circumstances, to provide e-mail and digital messaging logs in response to legal requests. Consider the content of all your messages in light of these possibilities, and carefully review your message before you click "Send."

◖ **PROFESSIONALISM NOTE: Double-Check Messages for Accuracy and Tact Before Sending Them** Be especially careful when sending messages to superiors in your organization or to people outside the organization. Spending extra time reviewing your e-mail can save you the embarrassment caused by a carelessly written message. One helpful strategy is to write the draft and revise your e-mail before filling in the "To" line with the address of your recipient. ◗

WRITER'S CHECKLIST

Maintaining Professionalism

- ✔ Review your organization's policy regarding the appropriate use of e-mail.
- ✔ Do not forward jokes or *spam*, discuss office gossip, or use biased language.
- ✔ Do not send *flames* (e-mails that contain abusive, obscene, or derogatory language) to attack someone.
- ✔ Avoid abbreviations (BTW for *by the way*, for example) and emoticons used in personal e-mail, discussion forums, text messaging, and instant messaging.

- ✔ Do not write in all lowercase letters or in ALL UPPERCASE LETTERS.
- ✔ Base your e-mail username on your personal name (msmith@domain.com), if possible, and avoid clever or hobby-related names (sushilover@domain.com).
- ✔ Write a cover message when including attachments ("Attached is a copy of . . ."), and double-check that it is indeed attached. See "cover letters" in Chapter 9, page 300.
- ✔ Always sign the e-mail or use a signature block (see Figure 8–6 on page 281) or both; doing so is not only polite but also avoids possible confusion.
- ✔ Send a "courtesy response" informing the sender when you need additional time to reply or when you need to confirm that you have received a message or an attachment.

DIGITAL TIP: Sharing Electronic Files

When you need to send large attachments or a collection of several attachments, consider an alternative: Use one of the many free online services designed for archiving and sharing files. After uploading a file to a specialized website, you will be given a URL that you can share via e-mail, allowing your recipients to download the file at their convenience. Although these tools shouldn't be used for sensitive documents, they work well in most situations.

Writing and Design

Make the main point early, as suggested in this chapter, and use short paragraphs to avoid dense blocks of text. For longer and more detailed messages, provide a brief paragraph overview at the beginning. Adapt forwarded messages by revising the subject line to reflect the current content and cut irrelevant previous text or highlight key text, based on your purpose and context.

Provide a specific subject line, as described on pages 289–290, after composing the message so that your topic is precise and clear to the reader. An empty subject line is unprofessional and may be interpreted as spam, thus routed to junk mail.

Most e-mail programs allow you to provide emphasis with typographical features, such as various fonts and bullets. For systems that do not, consider using a "plain text" setting with alternative highlighting devices, such as asterisks for emphasis, or attaching a highly formatted document to an e-mail. Place your response to someone else's message at the beginning (or top) of the e-mail window so that recipients can see your response immediately.

Adapt your salutation and complimentary closing to your audience and the context.

- When e-mail functions as a traditional business letter, consider the standard salutation (*Dear Ms. Tucker:* or *Dear Docuform Customer:*) and closing (*Sincerely,* or *Best wishes,*).
- When you send e-mail to individuals or small groups inside an organization, you may wish to adopt a more personal greeting (*Dear Andy,* or *Dear Project Colleagues,*) and closing (*Regards,* or *Good luck,*).

- When e-mail functions as a personal note to a friend or close colleague, you can use an informal greeting or only a first name (*Hi Mike,* or *Hello Jenny,* or *Bill,*) and a closing (*Take care,* or *Best,*).

Be aware that in some cultures, professionals do not refer to recipients or colleagues by their first names. See examples of inappropriate and appropriate e-mail messages in Figures 8-5 and 8-6. See also the Writing International Correspondence section in Chapter 9 on page 320.

Many companies and professionals include signature blocks (also called *signatures*) at the bottom of their messages. Signatures, which are set to appear at the end of every e-mail, supply information traditionally provided on company letterhead. Many organizations provide graphic signature forms or formatting standards. If yours does not, consider the following guidelines for formatting text-based signatures:

- Keep line length to 60 characters or fewer to avoid unpredictable line wraps.
- Test your signature block in plain-text e-mail systems to verify your format.
- Avoid using quotations, aphorisms, proverbs, or other sayings from popular culture, religion, or poetry in professional signatures.

The pattern shown in Figure 8–6 is typical.

WRITER'S CHECKLIST

Managing Your E-mail and Reducing Overload*

- ✔ Avoid becoming involved in an e-mail exchange if a phone call or meeting would be more efficient.
- ✔ Consider whether an e-mail message could prompt an unnecessary response from the recipient, and make clear to the recipient whether you expect a response.
- ✔ Send a copy ("cc:") of an e-mail only when the person copied needs or wants the information.
- ✔ Review all messages on a subject before responding to avoid dealing with issues that are no longer relevant.
- ✔ Set priorities for reading e-mail by skimming sender names and subject lines as well as where you appear in a "cc:" address line.
- ✔ Check the e-mail address before sending an e-mail to make sure it is correct.
- ✔ Create e-mail folders using key topics and personal names to file messages.
- ✔ Check your in-box regularly and try to clear it or categorize it and file new messages by the end of each day.
- ✔ Use the search command to find particular subjects and personal names.

---

*For understanding the causes of e-mail overload, see Gail Fann Thomas and Cynthia L. King, "Reconceptualizing E-mail Overload," *Journal of Business and Technical Communication* 20, no. 3 (July 2006): 252–87.

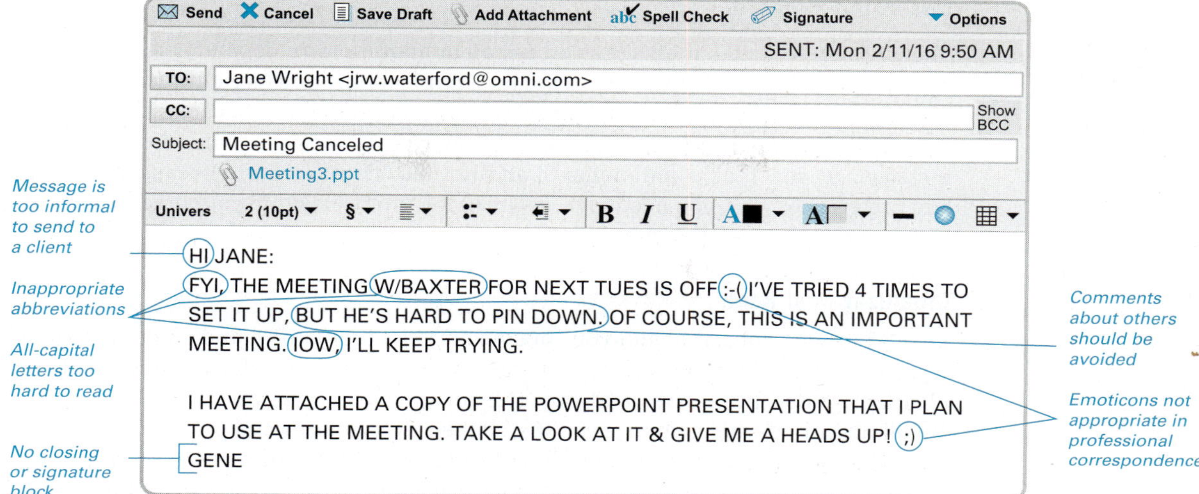
Send Cancel Save Draft Add Attachment Spell Check Signature Options

SENT: Mon 2/11/16 9:50 AM

TO: Jane Wright <jrw.waterford@omni.com>

CC:

Subject: Meeting Canceled

Meeting3.ppt

HI JANE:

FYI, THE MEETING W/BAXTER FOR NEXT TUES IS OFF :-(I'VE TRIED 4 TIMES TO SET IT UP, BUT HE'S HARD TO PIN DOWN. OF COURSE, THIS IS AN IMPORTANT MEETING. IOW, I'LL KEEP TRYING.

I HAVE ATTACHED A COPY OF THE POWERPOINT PRESENTATION THAT I PLAN TO USE AT THE MEETING. TAKE A LOOK AT IT & GIVE ME A HEADS UP! ;)

GENE

Figure 8–5 Inappropriate E-mail Message (with Attachment)

Send Cancel Save Draft Add Attachment Spell Check Signature Options

SENT: Mon 2/11/16 11:16 AM

TO: Jane Wright <jrw.waterford@omni.com>

CC:

Subject: Baxter Meeting Canceled

Meeting3.ppt

Jane:

I need to cancel the meeting with Thomas Baxter for next Friday (Feb. 15). I will work to schedule another meeting because we need to meet with him.

I have attached a copy of the PowerPoint presentation that I'd like to use at the meeting. Let me know if you see possible improvements.

Thanks,
Gene

Gene Marting, Manager
Sales Division, Building Systems, Inc.
3555 South 47th Street, Boise, ID 83703
Off: (208) 719-6620 Fax: (208) 719-5500
http://www.building/sys/com
e-mail: gmarting@buildingsystems.com

Signature block separated from message

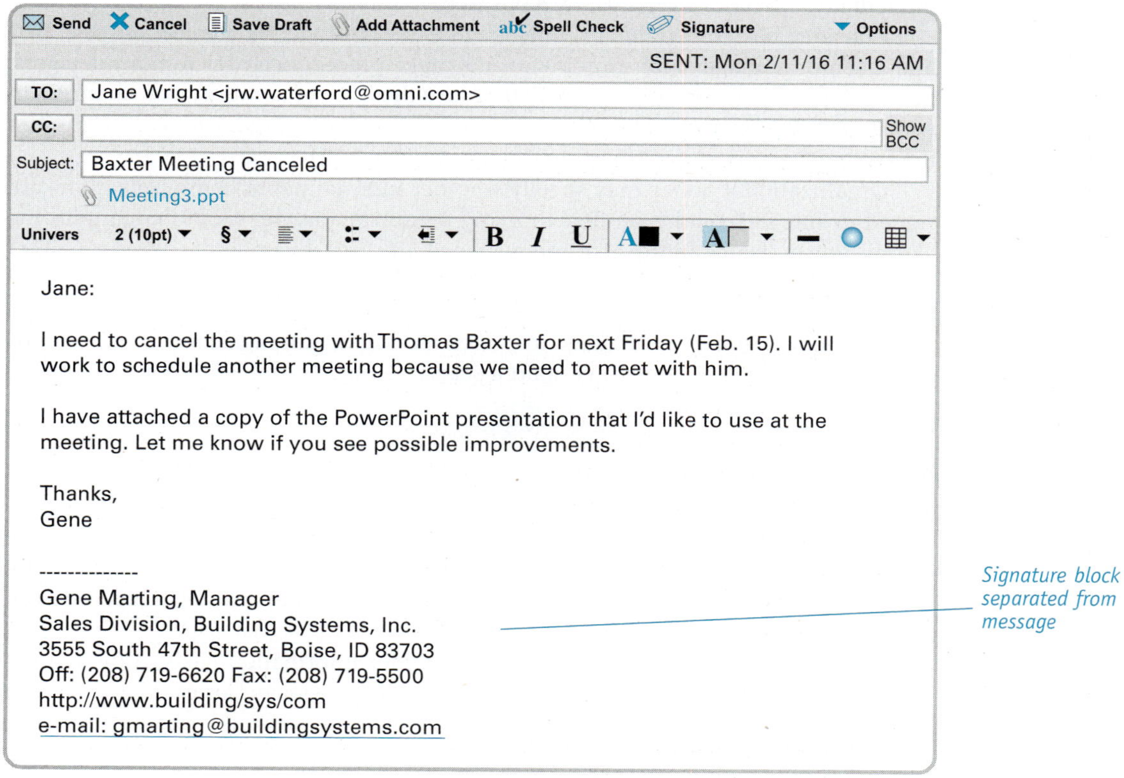

Figure 8–6 Revised, Appropriate E-mail Message (with Attachment)

Observing Protocol

The decision to send a message as an e-mail or another form depends on the organizational practice and the purpose of the communication. Some organizations may use e-mail almost exclusively, not only because of its speed but also because it fosters the easy exchange of information. Other organizations may use printed memos for official messages or attach a formal memo to an informal "cover" e-mail. Because practices and preferences vary, you need to be aware of the protocol within your organization or profession. See pages 266–267.

Organizational Rank

Be alert to the expectations in your organization for who writes and receives certain types of communications. Learn your organization's practices for internal communications. Small businesses and organizations, for example, may not need formal guidelines for internal communications, so their expectations and practices will differ from those of large organizations. In corporations and government agencies, however, protocol for internal communications is usually based on lines of authority. For example, staff members at large companies seldom send recommendations directly to senior executives beyond their immediate manager. Doing so could put the sender's immediate supervisor in an awkward position.

Consider also the order in which addressees should be named on the "To" line — senior managers, for example, usually take precedence over junior managers. An employer's organizational chart determines the lines of authority and channels in which internal communications travel. (For a discussion of organizational charts, see the section Organizational Charts in Chapter 7, page 243.)

Organizational policy may specify whether internal paper communications are signed or initialed by the sender. In many organizations, the sender's name in the "From" line indicates approval of and responsibility for a document's content; in other organizations, the sender's signature or initials on a printed or scanned memo next to the typed name verifies the writer's approval. Signatures or initials are often unnecessary for memos sent as or attached to e-mail messages, although some organizations prefer that a digital document contain a scanned image of the author's signature or initials.

Copy Protocol

The person listed on the e-mail or memo's "To" line is the primary recipient. To share the same message with others, the sender provides each of them a separate or courtesy copy (*cc:*) of the message. This notation (*cc: Jane Doe*) appears in the e-mail or memo heading and informs all the recipients of who else has received the message.

Courtesy copies are usually sent on a for-your-information basis. Although the primary recipient may have to act on a request in the message (for example, approve hiring a new employee), the courtesy-copy recipients are included because they need to know that the request was made.

ETHICS NOTE: Use Blind Copy (BCC) Messages Ethically The blind-copy ("bcc:") function allows writers to send copies of a message to someone without the primary receiver's knowledge.* Use the "bcc:" notation with great care. Sending sensitive or confidential information to a third party as a blind copy without the original recipient's knowledge is unethical when used to play office politics. The blind-copy function is both ethical and useful, however, when used to protect the privacy of the e-mail addresses of a large group of recipients.

Send courtesy copies only to those who need the information, especially when the message contains confidential personnel, medical, or financial information. Unnecessary copies also clog up in-boxes with unwanted information.

Also be aware of lines of authority when you copy recipients. If you send an e-mail or memo to your immediate supervisor about a pet project, for example, do not copy your supervisor's manager unless you are instructed to do so.

Sending Text and Instant Messages

Text messaging, or *texting*, refers to the delivery or exchange of brief written messages between mobile phones over cellular networks. Text messaging is effective for simple messages communicated between people on the move or in nontraditional workplaces (e.g., "Client backup servers down"). Some text messages can include photographs, video, and other digital files. As with your workplace e-mail, consider carefully the content of your messages before sending them. For the real-time exchange of brief messages, the phone or instant messaging may be a better choice. See Table 1-1 in Chapter 1.

PROFESSIONALISM NOTE: Keep Text Messages Short Avoid using text messages to communicate complicated or sensitive information. The abbreviated format does not allow for the transmittal of complex or detailed information, and as the sender you cannot always be certain the text message has been viewed or even received.

Instant messaging (IM) is a communications medium that allows both real-time text communications and the transfer of text or other files, such as an image or a document. Instant messaging is especially useful to those who are working in an environment that demands near-instant, brief written exchanges between two or more participants.

The abbreviation "bcc:" originally referred to the term "blind carbon copy" when copies of letters could be produced only on a typewriter using carbon paper. The "bcc:" notation ("bcc:" Dr. Brenda Shelton*) was separately typed on only the copied pages. Even though technology changed, the abbreviation "bcc:" was retained but is often defined as "blind courtesy copy."

To set up routine IM exchanges, work with those with whom you regularly exchange messages to find the appropriate software or tool to use. Consider available tools, such as computer programs or interfaces built into other electronics, as well as text-message capabilities on a mobile phone. Then add to your contact list the user names of those with whom you regularly exchange messages. Choose a screen name that your colleagues will recognize. If you use IM routinely as part of your job, set an "away" status (or message) that signals when you are not available for IM sessions.

When writing instant messages, keep them simple and to the point, covering only one subject in each message to prevent confusion and inappropriate responses. Because screen space is often limited and speed is essential, many who send instant messages use abbreviations and shortened spellings ("u" for "you"). Be sure that your reader will understand such abbreviations; when in doubt, avoid them.

In Figure 8–7, the manager of a software-development company in Maine ("Diane") is exchanging instant messages with a business partner in the Netherlands ("Andre"). Notice that the correspondents use an informal style that includes personal and professional abbreviations with which both are familiar ("NP" for *no problem* and "QSG" for *Quick Start Guide*). These messages demonstrate how IM cannot only help people exchange information quickly but also build rapport among distant colleagues and team members.

ETHICS NOTE: Adhere to Organizational Policies on the Personal Use of Computers Be sure to follow your employer's IM policies, such as any limitations on sending personal messages during work hours or requirements concerning confidentiality. If no specific policy exists, check with your management before using this medium.

messages from Andre — Last message received at 09:04 AM

8:58 AM	Andre: Hi Diane! me: good morning
9:00 AM	Andre: Time for a quick question? me: NP! Andre: How is it going with the QSG?
9:01 AM	Andre: Will you be finished soon? me: I am working on it. me: I am targeting Friday
9:02 AM	Andre: If you are not quite finished, send me what you have. me: I would recommend finishing the QSG before we focus on user guide.
9:03 AM	Andre: good idea Andre: ok, I won't keep you any longer Andre: bye
9:04 AM	me: Talk to you later.

Figure 8–7 Instant-Message Exchange

WRITER'S CHECKLIST
Instant-Messaging Privacy and Security

- ✔ Set up distinct business and professional contact lists (or accounts) to avoid inadvertently sending a personal message to a business associate.
- ✔ Learn the options, capabilities, and security limitations of your IM system and set the preferences that best suit your use of the system.
- ✔ Save significant IM exchanges (or logs) for your future reference.
- ✔ Be aware that instant messages can be saved by your recipients and may be archived by your employer. (See the Professionalism Note below.)
- ✔ Do not use professional IM for office gossip or inappropriate exchanges.

PROFESSIONALISM NOTE: Send Text Messages Only to Those Who Want Them Don't assume that a contact wants or is able to receive text or instant messages. Just because an individual called you from his or her mobile phone doesn't mean that you should use text messages to communicate a response.

Designing Memos

Memos are documents that use a standard form (*To: From: Date: Subject:*) whether sent on paper or as attachments to e-mail messages. They may be used within organizations for routine correspondence, short reports, proposals, and other internal documents.

Even in organizations where e-mail messages have largely taken the function of memos, a printed or an attached memo with organizational letterhead can communicate with formality and authority in addition to offering the full range of digital features. Paper memos are also useful in manufacturing and service industries, as well as in other businesses where employees do not have easy access to e-mail.

Memo Format

The memo shown in Figure 8–8 illustrates a typical memo format. As this example illustrates, the use of headings and lists often fosters clarity and provides emphasis in memos. For a discussion of subject lines, see page 289–290.

PROFESSIONALISM NOTE: Adhere to Organizational Ranking Protocol When Sending Memos As with e-mail, be alert to the practices of addressing and distributing memos in your organization. Consider who should receive or needs to be copied on a memo and in what order — senior managers, for example, take precedence over junior managers. If rank does not apply, alphabetizing recipients by last name is safe.

Some organizations ask writers to initial or sign formal memos that are printed (*hard copy*) to verify that the writer accepts responsibility for a memo's content.

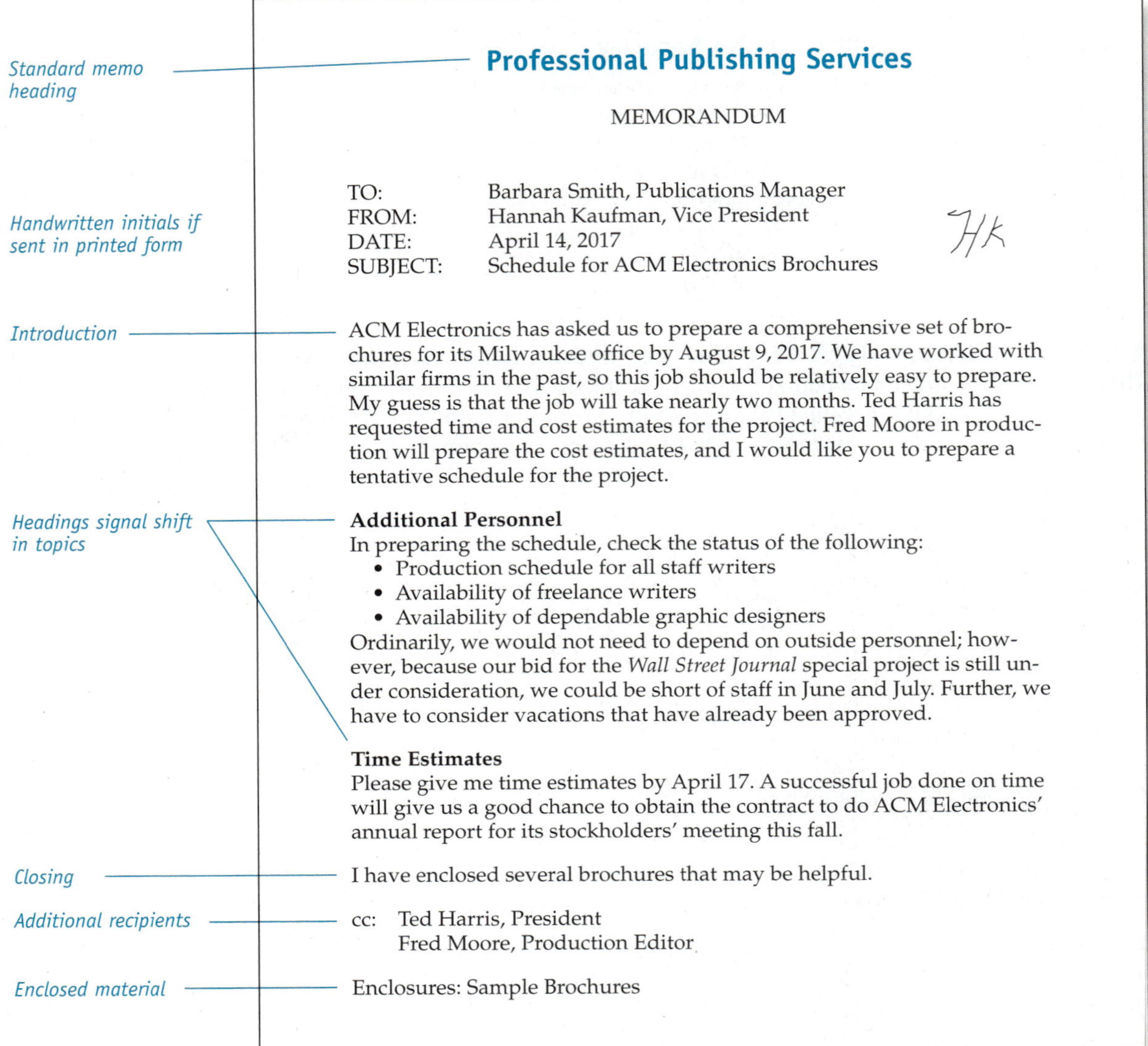

Standard memo heading
Handwritten initials if sent in printed form
Introduction
Headings signal shift in topics
Closing
Additional recipients
Enclosed material
Professional Publishing Services
MEMORANDUM
TO: Barbara Smith, Publications Manager
FROM: Hannah Kaufman, Vice President
DATE: April 14, 2017
SUBJECT: Schedule for ACM Electronics Brochures
HK
ACM Electronics has asked us to prepare a comprehensive set of brochures for its Milwaukee office by August 9, 2017. We have worked with similar firms in the past, so this job should be relatively easy to prepare. My guess is that the job will take nearly two months. Ted Harris has requested time and cost estimates for the project. Fred Moore in production will prepare the cost estimates, and I would like you to prepare a tentative schedule for the project.
Additional Personnel
In preparing the schedule, check the status of the following:
• Production schedule for all staff writers
• Availability of freelance writers
• Availability of dependable graphic designers
Ordinarily, we would not need to depend on outside personnel; however, because our bid for the Wall Street Journal special project is still under consideration, we could be short of staff in June and July. Further, we have to consider vacations that have already been approved.
Time Estimates
Please give me time estimates by April 17. A successful job done on time will give us a good chance to obtain the contract to do ACM Electronics' annual report for its stockholders' meeting this fall.
I have enclosed several brochures that may be helpful.
cc: Ted Harris, President
Fred Moore, Production Editor
Enclosures: Sample Brochures

Figure 8–8 Typical Memo Format (Printed with Sender's Handwritten Initials)

When memos require more than one page, use a second-page header and always carry at least two lines of the body text over to that page. The header should include the recipient's name or, if there are too many names to fit, an abbreviated subject line; the page number; and the date. Place the header in the upper left-hand corner or across the page, as shown in Figure 8–9.

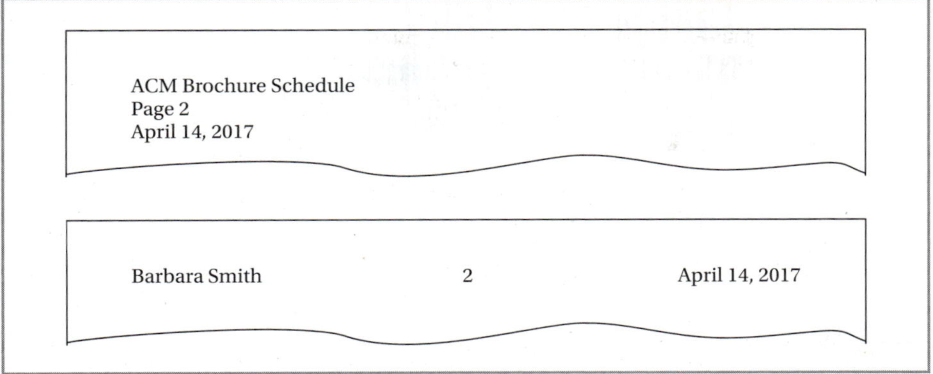

Figure 8–9 Headers for the Second Page of Memos

Designing Letters

Business letters — correspondence written for those outside an organization — are often the most appropriate choice for formal communications with professional associates, clients, or customers. Letters may be especially effective for those people who receive a high volume of e-mail and other electronic messages. Letters printed on organizational letterhead communicate formality, respect, and authority.

Although word-processing software provides templates for correspondence, the templates may not provide the appropriate dimensions and elements you need. The following sections offer specific advice on formatting and related etiquette for business letters.

Letter Format

If your employer requires a particular letter format, use it. Otherwise, follow the design guidelines shown in Figure 8–10. Figure 8–10 illustrates the popular *full-block style* in which the entire letter is aligned at the left margin. To achieve a professional appearance, center the letter on the page vertically and horizontally. Regardless of the default margin provided in a word-processing program, it is more important to establish a picture frame of blank space surrounding the text of the letter. When you use organizational stationery with letterhead at the top of the page, consider the bottom of the letterhead as the top edge of the paper. The right margin should be approximately as wide as the left margin. To give a fuller appearance to very short letters, increase both margins to about an inch and a half. Use your full-page or print-preview feature to check for proportion.

Heading

Unless you are using letterhead stationery, place your full return address and the date in the heading. Because your name appears at the end of the letter, it need not be

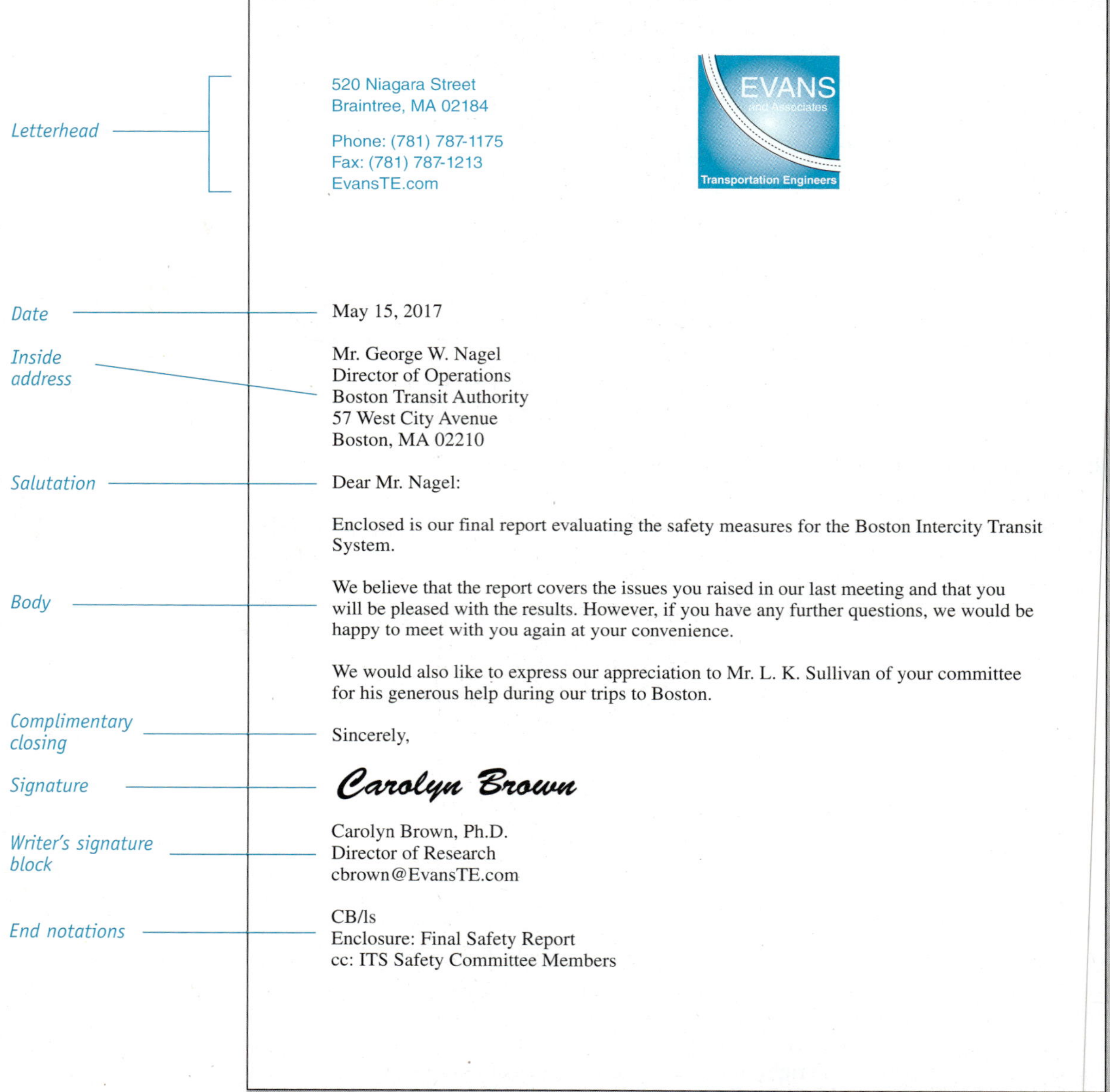

520 Niagara Street
Braintree, MA 02184

Phone: (781) 787-1175
Fax: (781) 787-1213
EvansTE.com

May 15, 2017

Mr. George W. Nagel
Director of Operations
Boston Transit Authority
57 West City Avenue
Boston, MA 02210

Dear Mr. Nagel:

Enclosed is our final report evaluating the safety measures for the Boston Intercity Transit System.

We believe that the report covers the issues you raised in our last meeting and that you will be pleased with the results. However, if you have any further questions, we would be happy to meet with you again at your convenience.

We would also like to express our appreciation to Mr. L. K. Sullivan of your committee for his generous help during our trips to Boston.

Sincerely,

Carolyn Brown

Carolyn Brown, Ph.D.
Director of Research
cbrown@EvansTE.com

CB/ls
Enclosure: Final Safety Report
cc: ITS Safety Committee Members

Figure 8–10 Full-Block-Style Letter (with Letterhead)

included in the heading. Spell out words such as *street*, *avenue*, *first*, and *west* rather than abbreviating them. You may either spell out the name of the state in full or use the standard postal service abbreviation available at usps.com. The date usually goes directly beneath the last line of the return address. Do not abbreviate the name of the month. Begin the heading about two inches from the top of the page. If you are using letterhead that gives the company address, enter only the date, three lines below the last line of the letterhead.

Inside Address

Include the recipient's full name, title, and address in the inside address, two to six lines below the date, depending on the length of the letter. The inside address should be aligned with the left margin, and the left margin should be at least one inch wide.

Salutation

Place the salutation, or *greeting*, two lines below the inside address and align it with the left margin. In most business letters, the salutation contains the recipient's personal title (such as *Mr.*, *Ms.*, *Dr.*) and last name, followed by a colon. If you are on a first-name basis with the recipient, use only the first name in the salutation.

Address women as *Ms.* unless they have expressed a preference for *Miss* or *Mrs.* However, professional titles (such as *Professor*, *Senator*, *Major*) take precedence over *Ms.* and similar courtesy titles.

When a person's first name could refer to either a woman or a man, one solution is to use both the first and last names in the salutation (*Dear Pat Smith:*).

For multiple recipients, the following salutations are appropriate:

- Dear Professor Allen and Dr. Rivera: [two recipients]
- Dear Ms. Becham, Ms. Moore, and Mr. Stein: [three recipients]
- Dear Colleagues: [*Members*, or other suitable collective term]

Subject Line

An optional element in a letter is a subject line, which should follow the salutation. Insert one blank line above and one blank line below the subject line. The subject line in a letter functions as it does for e-mail and other correspondence as an aid in focusing the topic and filing the letter. (For information on creating subject lines, see pages 289–290.)

Subject lines are especially useful if you are writing to a large company and do not know the name or title of the recipient. In such cases, you may address a letter to an appropriate department or identify the subject in a subject line and use no salutation.

▶ National Medical Supply Group
501 West National Avenue
Minneapolis, MN 55407

Attention: Customer Service Department

Subject: Defective Cardio-100 Stethoscopes

I am returning six stethoscopes with damaged diaphragms that . . .

In other circumstances in which you do not know the recipient's name, use a title appropriate to the context of the letter, such as *Dear Customer* or *Dear IT Professional.*

Body

The body of the letter should begin two lines below the salutation (or any element that precedes the body, such as a subject or an attention line). Single-space within and double-space between paragraphs, as shown in Figure 8–10. To provide a fuller appearance to a very short letter, you can increase the side margins or increase the font size. You can also insert extra space above the inside address, the writer's signature block, and the initials of the person typing the letter—but do not exceed twice the recommended space for each of these elements.

Complimentary Closing

Type the complimentary closing two spaces below the body. Use a standard expression such as *Sincerely, Sincerely yours,* or *Yours truly.* (If the recipient is a friend as well as a business associate, you can use a less formal closing, such as *Best wishes* or *Best regards* or, simply, *Best.*) Capitalize only the initial letter of the first word, and follow the expression with a comma.

Writer's Signature Block

Type your full name four lines below and aligned with the complimentary closing. On the next line include your business title, if appropriate. The following lines may contain your individual contact information, such as a telephone number or an e-mail address, if not included in the letterhead or the body of your letter. Sign the letter in the space between the complimentary closing and your name.

End Notations

Business letters sometimes require additional information that is placed at the left margin, two spaces below the typed name and title of the writer in a long letter, four spaces below in a short letter.

Reference initials show the letter writer's initials in capital letters, followed by a slash mark (or colon), and then the initials of the person typing the letter in lowercase letters, as shown in Figure 8–10. When the writer is also the person typing the letter, no initials are needed.

Enclosure notations indicate that the writer is sending material (such as an invoice or an article) along with the letter. Note that you should mention the enclosure in the body of the letter. Enclosure notations may take several forms:

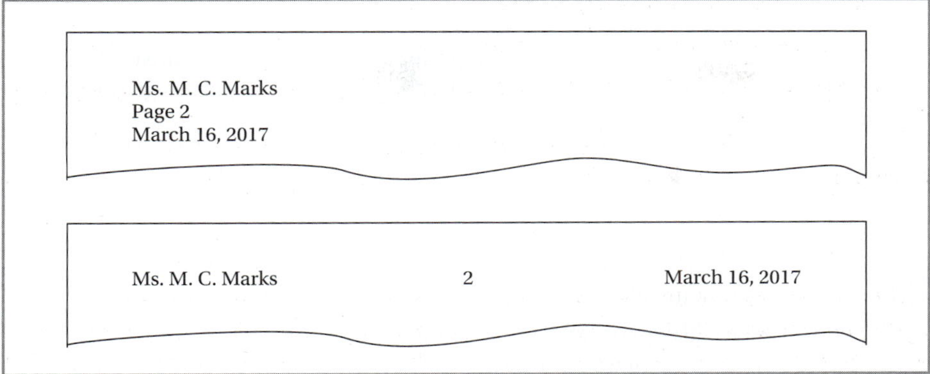
Ms. M. C. Marks
Page 2
March 16, 2017

Ms. M. C. Marks 2 March 16, 2017

Figure 8–11 Alternative Headers for the Second Page of a Letter

- Enclosure: Final Safety Report
- Enclosures (2)
- Enc. *or* Encs.

Copy notation ("cc:") tells the reader that a copy of the letter is being sent to the named recipient(s) (see Figure 8–10). Use a blind-copy notation ("bcc:") when you do not want the addressee to know that a copy is being sent to someone else. A blind-copy notation appears only on the copy, not on the original ("bcc: Dr. Brenda Shelton"). See the Ethics Note on page 283.

Continuing Pages

If a letter requires a second page (or, in rare cases, more), always carry at least two lines of the body text over to that page. Use plain (nonletterhead) paper of quality equivalent to that of the letterhead stationery for the second page. It should have a header with the recipient's name, the page number, and the date. Place the header in the upper left-hand corner or across the page, as shown in Figure 8–11.

MEETING THE DEADLINE: The Time-Sensitive Message

More than once in your career you will be asked to do a seemingly impossible task—write a crucial e-mail, an important memo, or a relatively high-profile letter that requires some research—all in less than an hour! These messages are often written for the signature of someone else who is higher up in the organization. When you get such an assignment, do not panic. Instead, use the following straightforward principles drawn from this book to focus your energies on the task at hand.

Understand the Assignment

Nothing could be worse than to waste time under a short deadline by misunderstanding the purpose or intended reader of such a writing task. Ask the person giving you the assignment to be as explicit as possible about the following:

- The topic
- The reader(s) and the reader's background
- The purpose and intended outcome
- The key points that must be covered
- The person who will sign or send the document

Gather Information

The essential background information for your research can almost always be located within your company or organization. Sources include previous e-mails, letters, memos, press releases, websites (internal or external), contracts, budget data, handbooks, speeches by senior officials, legal opinions, and the like. Be careful to gather *only* the information pertinent to the correspondence. The person assigning the job will usually provide essential background information or tell you where to find it. If the information is not readily available, be sure to ask for it.

As long as the information originated in your organization, fits your context, and is accurate and well written, use as much of it as you need without citation unless references to the source would help your readers. If necessary, revise such material for consistency of content, style, and format as you prepare the draft. When using information from other sources, make sure you avoid plagiarism and any violation of copyright (see pages 181–183 in Chapter 6, Conducting Research for a Document).

On the job, you will have another source of information that you may not always have in the classroom — your experience. In fact, one reason you may receive such an assignment is because of your knowledge of the subject, reader, organization, or professional area. Brainstorming using your own knowledge, as discussed on pages 8–9, will prepare you to draw the most benefit from your experience when you are under pressure.

Organize Your Thoughts

◆ *For typical organizing strategies, see Table 2-1 in Chapter 2, Planning a Document.*

Do not overlook this important step. Your message should have an opening, a middle (body), and a closing. Organizing the information into this structure does not have to be a formal process — you won't have time to create a full-blown outline, nor should one be necessary. Jot down the points you need to make in a sequence that makes sense. Keep it simple. In some cases, you will organize by classifying and dividing your subject matter, presenting the information on one subject before going on to another subject. Sometimes a problem-and-solution order makes sense. At other times, a chronological, sequential, or general-to-specific order will be appropriate.

Write the Draft

With the right information and a structure for organizing it, the writing will not be difficult. Stick to your plan—your rough outline—and begin. Make the structure easy for you and your reader to follow. Cover only one subject in each paragraph. After a topic sentence, provide essential supporting information—facts, examples, policy, procedures, guidelines.

Write a quick draft first; you can polish it after it is on the screen or paper. Write without worrying about grammar, sentence structure, or spelling. Given the limited time available, your main focus should be on getting your ideas down.

Polish the Draft

You will not have much time left, but discipline yourself to read the draft several times, concentrating on different elements each time.

First, concentrate on larger issues. Is the information accurate? Is it complete? Have you made all your points? Are your points organized in the right sequence? Have you provided too much information? Revise accordingly.

Next, focus on polishing at the sentence and word level. Aim for simple sentences in the active voice. Include some longer sentences to avoid the monotony of too many simple sentences strung together. Structure longer sentences so that subjects and verbs agree and primary ideas are distinct from subordinate ideas. Use parallel structure to convey matching ideas. Use lists where possible. Don't forget to review punctuation. A misplaced comma or semicolon can change the meaning of a sentence. In this situation, you do not have time for a cooling period, so watch for and tone down any emotionally charged language.

As a final review, use spelling and grammar checkers, but don't rely on them to catch all of your errors or to respond accurately—you must make the final decisions. Make sure you read through a paper version of the final draft at least once to catch any remaining errors. If you have time, ask a second reader to help.

Take a Well-Deserved Break

After your draft is written, you may e-mail it to a superior for review before you prepare the final form for signature and distribution. Now sit back and enjoy the sense of professional pride you have earned from a job well done under pressure!

CHAPTER 8 SUMMARY: WRITING E-MAILS, MEMOS, AND LETTERS

Selecting the Appropriate Media

- Consider your audience, purpose, and context to select the appropriate media for messages.
- Use e-mail as a primary correspondence medium.
- Choose texting and instant messaging for simple messages and brief exchanges.

- Use printed and attached formal memos for workplaces without easy access to e-mail.
- Choose business letters for formal correspondence outside an organization.

Using Professional Style and Tone

- Focus on a positive relationship and professional image.
- Choose a writing style appropriate to the topic and audience.
- Use goodwill and the "you" viewpoint.

Structuring Effective Messages

- Use the direct pattern for goodwill and positive messages:
  1. Main point or good news
  2. Explanation of details or facts
  3. Goodwill closing
- Use the indirect pattern for some negative messages:
  1. Context (or buffer)
  2. Explanation or details
  3. Bad news or negative message
  4. Goodwill closing
- Organize your ideas into an opening, a body, and a closing.

Developing Clarity and Emphasis

- Develop thoughts adequately to be clear for the reader.
- Use lists for emphasizing main points without overusing them.
- Consider headings for long messages to segment subtopics.
- Write a subject line that is complete and helpful, yet concise.

Managing Your E-mail and Protocol

- Follow your organization's confidentiality policies and maintain professionalism.
- Use an appropriate and clear writing style that conveys a professional image.
- Maintain professionalism in your messages.
- Consider the format and design needs of e-mail messages.
- Create an appropriate salutation, closing, and signature block.
- Manage your e-mail by prioritizing, using folders, and reviewing messages.
- Observe business protocol for ranking recipients and copying messages.

Sending Text and Instant Messages

- Use text messaging for simple messages for those coworkers in nontraditional workplaces.
- Keep text messages brief and include only appropriate attachments.
- Use instant messaging for real-time exchanges between two or more participants.
- Use only IM abbreviations your recipients understand.
- Maintain accurate and current contact lists.

Designing Print and Attached Memos

- Use an appropriate organizational format.
- Determine if the memo should be printed or attached to a cover e-mail.
- Include a continuing page header, if needed.

Designing Business Letters

- Determine if a letter printed on organizational letterhead is appropriate.
- Follow the letter format appropriate to the context or required by your employer.
- Prepare a heading or use printed letterhead.
- Provide an inside address, appropriate salutation, body, and complimentary close.
- Add your signature block and end notations below the complimentary close.
- Include a continuing page header, if needed.

Meeting the Deadline: The Time-Sensitive Message

- Make sure that you understand the assignment.
- Gather pertinent background information.
- Organize your major points into a sequence that makes sense.
- Write the draft quickly, covering only one subject in each paragraph.
- Polish the draft — focus on content and organization before revising at the sentence and word level.

Exercises

1. You are the manager of accounting for a company that sells computer-software packages. You have just received word from the comptroller that there has been a change in the expense allowances for employees using their own cars on business. Previously, one rate was applied to all employees, but now there will be different allowance rates for regular and nonregular drivers. Effective immediately, regular drivers will receive $1.00 per mile for the first 650 miles driven per month, and 25¢ for each additional mile; nonregular drivers will receive 80¢ per mile for the first 150 miles per month, and 25¢ for each additional mile. Regular drivers are those who use their own cars frequently on the job to drive to their sales territories. Nonregular drivers are those employees — such as home-office personnel — who only occasionally use their cars on business. To ensure that these categories are used properly, you have requested that the manager of each department notify Accounts Payable, in writing, which employees in his or her department should be classified as regular drivers. Accounts Payable will reimburse those employees not identified by the letter according to the nonregular-driver formula. Prepare a memo or an e-mail message to communicate this information to all employees.
2. Complete this assignment either on your own or as part of a collaborative team.
   a. You are director of corporate communications for a nationwide insurance company called The Provider Group. Management has asked you to design a letterhead that reflects a "modern, yet responsible image." For this project, collect as many samples of letterhead stationery as you can. Then, using word-processing software with graphics capability, design a letterhead for The Provider Group (using a local address, phone number, and any other appropriate details). As you design, consider the image and personality your design will project, as well as the amount of information you should provide.
   b. Survey three or four organizations in your area (including your college) to determine the standard letter formats they use (full block, modified block, and so on). Evaluate the formats using the guidelines provided in this chapter and in Chapter 7, Designing Documents and Visuals.

c. Using the results in parts *a* and *b*, determine the best format for letters sent to clients by The Provider Group.

3. Briefly describe a work- or school-related e-mail message that you have received that was inappropriate, using specific points from the e-mail professionalism guidelines in this chapter.

4. Rewrite the following statements, improving them as indicated.

   a. Make the following statement more positive and less blunt:

      ▶ I will not pay you because you have not sent the final software upgrade. If you do not send the right one immediately, I will not pay you at all.

   b. Make the following passage friendlier:

      ▶ I bought the Music Collection you advertised on TV, and, not only did it take six weeks to become available, but the downloads were in the wrong format and unusable. Can't you get anything right? I'm contesting the charge on my credit card and am deleting the worthless files!

   c. Make the following passage clear and unpretentious:

      ▶ With reference to your recent automobile accident, I have been unable to contact you due to the fact that I have been in Chicago working day and night on a proposal—a biggie. I should be back in the office in the neighborhood of the 15th or so. In the unforeseen and unlikely event that I should be delayed, you can utilize Mr. Strawman, of my office, who will also endeavor in your behalf.

5. Imagine that you work for a company where many of the new hires have been using instant messaging to pass on confidential material to each other or relay emergency information. This greatly concerns the chief executive officer (CEO), who especially has a problem with employees using business IM names like "Sexyguy2012" and "Squirrelgirl42." Draft a company memo, to be sent by the CEO, detailing proper IM etiquette.

6. Based on your own experience as a student, write a memo to your instructor on one of the following topics in less than one hour.

   a. Should student tickets to athletic events on campus be included with the price of tuition?
   b. Should the library add a coffee kiosk in the reserve room?
   c. Should the college offer more (or fewer) online courses?

   Be sure to cover the points you feel must be included to support your conclusion.

7. You work for Smith Consultants, and your manager has asked you to draft a complaint letter to the software-supply company that developed your new customer-service database—the level of service and technical support to date has not met your manager's expectations. Include the following points:

   a. Telephone calls from your employees to the company's technical support department are often not returned in a timely fashion. Sometimes they are not returned at all.
   b. Software-assistance personnel often blame your hardware for the problem; however, when consulted, the hardware representative reports that the problem is with the software.
   c. Promised monthly four-hour in-service training sessions have not been scheduled for the past three months.

   You must also mention that your company is considering not paying the software provider the remaining 30 percent of the purchase amount. However, this is a very delicate matter because Smith Consultants has already invested thousands of dollars in the software system and would like to resolve the problem without losing the investment.

Following the principles of business correspondence offered in this chapter, submit your draft in correct business-letter format to your instructor.

8. Explore the templates offered by your word-processing software. Most word-processing packages offer several styles of business-document templates, both contemporary and traditional. (Check your software's "help" menu for "templates.") Use a template for letters offered by your software to format a letter you have composed. Print out the letter and submit it to your instructor with a memo that addresses the following questions:
   a. Why did you choose this particular template?
   b. Did the template make writing your letter easier? Why or why not?
   c. Why might businesses request that their employees use a template when formatting business letters?
   d. What are the drawbacks, if any, of using templates?

Collaborative Classroom Projects

1. Divide into small groups (three or four students) and elect a group leader. As a writing team, draft a letter explaining the changes in shipping charges to customers of your wholesale office-supply company.

   For more than five years, your company has been able to offer online customers a flat shipping rate of $5.95 for any order under $300. This has been a strong advertising point for the company. However, profits have fallen steadily in the past two years, so the president of your company has announced that shipping charges will increase in two months. Shipping will be $12.95 for orders over $300 and will increase by $3 for each additional $100 worth of product.

   Your writing team must inform your existing customers of the change—a difficult task because the customers have been conditioned by your marketing representatives to expect "the industry's most reasonable" shipping charges. The letter should provide the context and an explanation of the charges, the bad news, and a goodwill close. Follow the guidelines in this chapter for reference.

2. Imagine that members of your group work as interns for a new local nonprofit organization that works with parents to teach expressive skills to autistic toddlers. The organization has received several financial and automobile donations in response to a recent fund-raising drive, and it needs to send a form letter to donors that thanks them for their generosity and subtly encourages them to give again in the future. Because some donors have asked how they can write off their car donations, the organization has decided to supplement the letter with an information sheet that explains how to deduct noncash contributions from their income taxes. Create a thank-you letter and an information sheet as follows:
   a. For the letter:
      - Create a name and letterhead for the charity.
      - Begin with the donor's inside address and a salutation with the donor's name.
      - Write the letter using a "we" or "I" viewpoint.
      - Thank the donor for the contribution to your charity and detail the amount donated.
      - Describe the good works of the charity (who is helped by the charity and how).
      - Let donors know that because no goods or services were exchanged, the donation is tax-deductible and they should keep this letter for their tax records.
      - Provide a contact name and number.
      - Use your name to sign the letter as the director of the charity.

b. For the information sheet, use the following information paraphrased from the IRS website. Be sure to organize it logically and attractively (see Chapter 7, Designing Documents and Visuals) and use the "you" viewpoint.

   - If a donor claims a deduction on his or her return of over $500 for all contributed property, the donor must attach a Form 8283 (PDF), *Noncash Charitable Contributions*, to the return.
   - If a donor claims a total deduction of $5,000 or less for all contributed property, the donor need complete only Section A of Form 8283.
   - If a donor claims a deduction of more than $5,000 for an item or a group of similar items, the donor generally needs to complete Section B of Form 8283, which usually requires a qualified appraiser to appraise the vehicle and its value.
   - The donor will need to keep records of the donation and substantiate the car's current fair market value. The charity will need to provide written acknowledgment (a description of the car and whether the charity provided any goods or services in exchange, including their value) if the donor is claiming a deduction of $250 or more for the car.

3. Divide into two groups of equal numbers. One group represents the local electric company's consumers, and the other group represents the company's marketing representatives. If you are in the consumer group, write a letter as a team to the utility commissioner asking that the rate increase requested by the electric company not be granted. If you are in the marketing group, write a letter as a team asking the utility commissioner to grant your rate-increase request. Each group has 30 minutes to write the letter, which should address the following issues:

   a. Dependability of service of the utility
   b. Need for a rate increase or reason to deny the increase
   c. Ability of customers to pay for the increase

   Trade letters and, during the next 30 minutes, work as a group to write bad-news response letters from the utility commissioner's office. If you are writing to the consumers, break the bad news that the rate increase will be necessary. If you are writing to the electric company's marketing representatives, break the bad news that a rate increase will not be granted. Remember to provide a context, an explanation, the bad news, and a goodwill close when drafting your replies.

Research Projects

1. Imagine that several administrative assistants in your company have been sending sales letters to female customers randomly using *Ms.* and *Mrs.* as titles. Research the history of the title *Ms.* and write a memo to the assistants detailing when the term was coined and for what reasons and explaining the conventions they should use when addressing women in their written correspondence.
2. Search newspaper websites available only through your campus library for three recent articles about e-mail etiquette. Write a brief analysis in which you compare and contrast the content of the articles. E-mail your analysis to your instructor and include links to the articles analyzed.

9 Writing Routine and Sensitive Messages

Contents

There are almost as many types of workplace messages as there are reasons for writing. This chapter discusses some of the most frequently written and challenging types, including international correspondence, focusing in particular on the style and tone suitable to each type.

For each of these types of messages, you must also determine what form — such as e-mail, memo, or letter — and what transmittal method — such as e-mail attachment, fax, or mailed correspondence — is best. Keep in mind any company or organizational practices regarding the form and transmittal methods for specific types of messages.

This chapter builds on and applies the strategies described in Chapter 8 to widely used and often challenging types of workplace messages. Much of this correspondence involves routine information exchanges, but even straightforward communications provide opportunities to benefit you and your recipient. Equally important is correspondence that promotes a positive image of your organization's product or service. Finally, and most challenging, is correspondence that communicates sensitive or negative information.

◆ *For information on formatting memos and letters, see pages 285–293 in Chapter 8, Writing E-mails, Memos, and Letters.*

Routine and Positive Messages

The types of correspondence discussed in this section provide the opportunity to build goodwill with readers and to create a positive image of your organization.

Cover Messages (or Transmittals)

◆ *For advice on proposal cover letters and a sample, see pages 442 and 444 in Chapter 13, Writing Proposals.*

◆ *For advice on writing cover messages to résumés, see Writing an Effective Letter of Application on pages 551–557.*

When you send a formal report, proposal, brochure, or similar material, you should include a cover message to identify what you are sending. This message might be an e-mail with material attached or a printed memo or letter with the material enclosed. Because of the amount of e-mail exchanged on the job, a cover message is especially important when sending an attached file. The cover message also provides you with a record of when and to whom you sent the material.

Open by explaining what is being sent and why. A cover letter that accompanies a report, for example, may identify the report's title, briefly describe its contents, state its purpose, and note who requested it. In an optional second paragraph, you might summarize the information or point out any sections of particular interest to the reader. This paragraph could mention the conditions under which the material was prepared, such as limitations of time or budget. Your closing paragraph should contain acknowledgments of help received, offer more assistance, or express the hope that the material will fulfill its purpose. If your letter accompanies a proposal, you could mention a key point or two as to why your firm is the best one to do the job.

Figure 9–1 is an example of a cover message that is brief and to the point. Figure 9–2 on page 302 shows a cover letter that is a bit more detailed, touching on the manner in which the information was gathered.

Acknowledgments

When a colleague or client sends you something or makes a request, you should acknowledge what was sent, respond to the request, or explain that you cannot respond to the request immediately in a short, polite note. The example shown in Figure 9–3 on page 302 is typical.

Inquiries

◆ *For job applications and another type of inquiry letter, see Chapter 15, Writing Résumés and Cover Letters.*

An inquiry letter or e-mail message can be as simple as a request for a free brochure or as complex as asking a consultant to define specific requirements for a usability testing lab.

The two broad categories of inquiries include those that benefit the recipient and those that benefit the writer. Inquiries of obvious benefit to the recipient include requests

Ecology Systems and Services
39 Beacon Street, Boston, MA 02106
telephone: (617) 351-1223 fax: (617) 351-2121
ecologysystems.com

May 24, 2017

Mario Espinoza, Chief Engineer
Louisiana Chemical Products
3452 River View Road
Baton Rouge, LA 70893

Dear Mr. Espinoza:

Enclosed is the final report on our installation of pollution-control equipment at Eastern Chemical Company, which we send with Eastern's permission. Please call me (ext. 1206) or e-mail me at the address below if you have any questions.

Identification of enclosure

Offer of assistance

Sincerely,

Susan Wong

Susan Wong, Ph.D.
Technical Services Manager
swong@ecologysystems.com

SW/ls
Enclosure

Figure 9–1 Brief Cover Letter (for a Report)

for information about a recently advertised product. Inquiries that primarily benefit the writer include, for example, a request to a professional association for demographic information about its members. If your inquiry is of the second kind, be particularly considerate of your reader's needs. Your objective will probably be to obtain, within a reasonable time, answers to specific questions. You will be more likely to receive a prompt, helpful reply if you follow the guidelines listed in Considering Audience and Purpose: Writing Inquiries on page 303 and illustrated in Figure 9–4 on page 303.

Send | Cancel | Save Draft | Add Attachment | Spell Check | Signature | Options

SENT: Mon Fri 9/9/16 2:32 PM

TO: AHammersmith@IDC.com

CC:

Show BCC

Subject: Annual Energy Estimate Report

AnnualEnergyEstimate.sc.pdf Download

Dear Mr. Hammersmith:

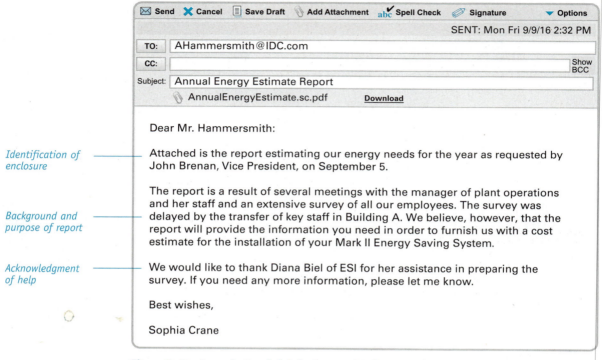

Identification of enclosure — Attached is the report estimating our energy needs for the year as requested by John Brenan, Vice President, on September 5.

Background and purpose of report — The report is a result of several meetings with the manager of plant operations and her staff and an extensive survey of all our employees. The survey was delayed by the transfer of key staff in Building A. We believe, however, that the report will provide the information you need in order to furnish us with a cost estimate for the installation of your Mark II Energy Saving System.

Acknowledgment of help — We would like to thank Diana Biel of ESI for her assistance in preparing the survey. If you need any more information, please let me know.

Best wishes,

Sophia Crane

Figure 9–2 Cover Letter (with Background Information)

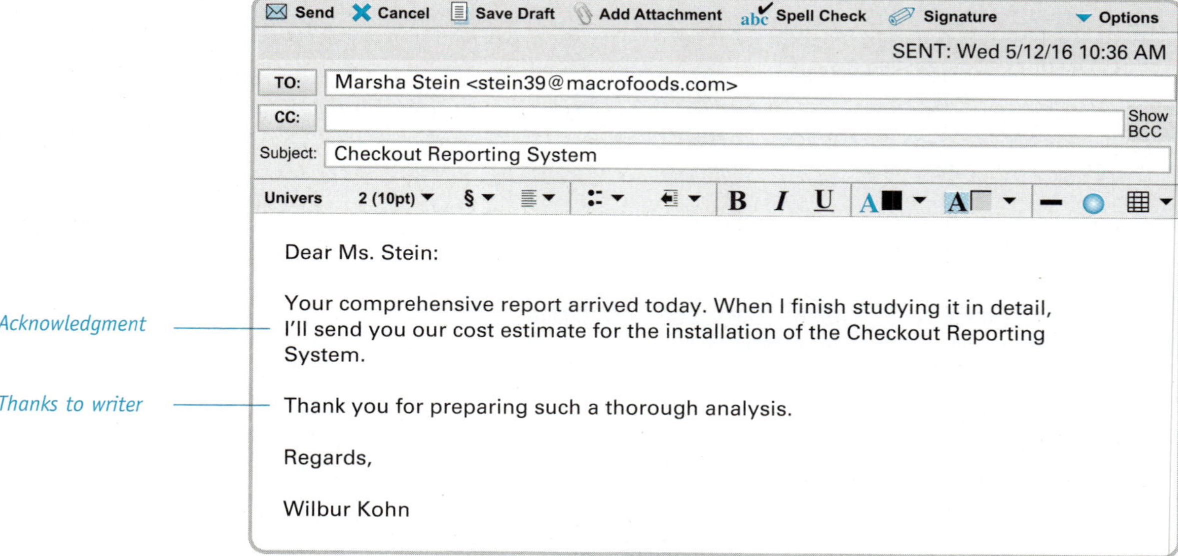

Send | Cancel | Save Draft | Add Attachment | Spell Check | Signature | Options

SENT: Wed 5/12/16 10:36 AM

TO: Marsha Stein <stein39@macrofoods.com>

CC:

Show BCC

Subject: Checkout Reporting System

Univers 2 (10pt)

Dear Ms. Stein:

Acknowledgment — Your comprehensive report arrived today. When I finish studying it in detail, I'll send you our cost estimate for the installation of the Checkout Reporting System.

Thanks to writer — Thank you for preparing such a thorough analysis.

Regards,

Wilbur Kohn

Figure 9–3 Acknowledgment (Sent as an E-mail Message)

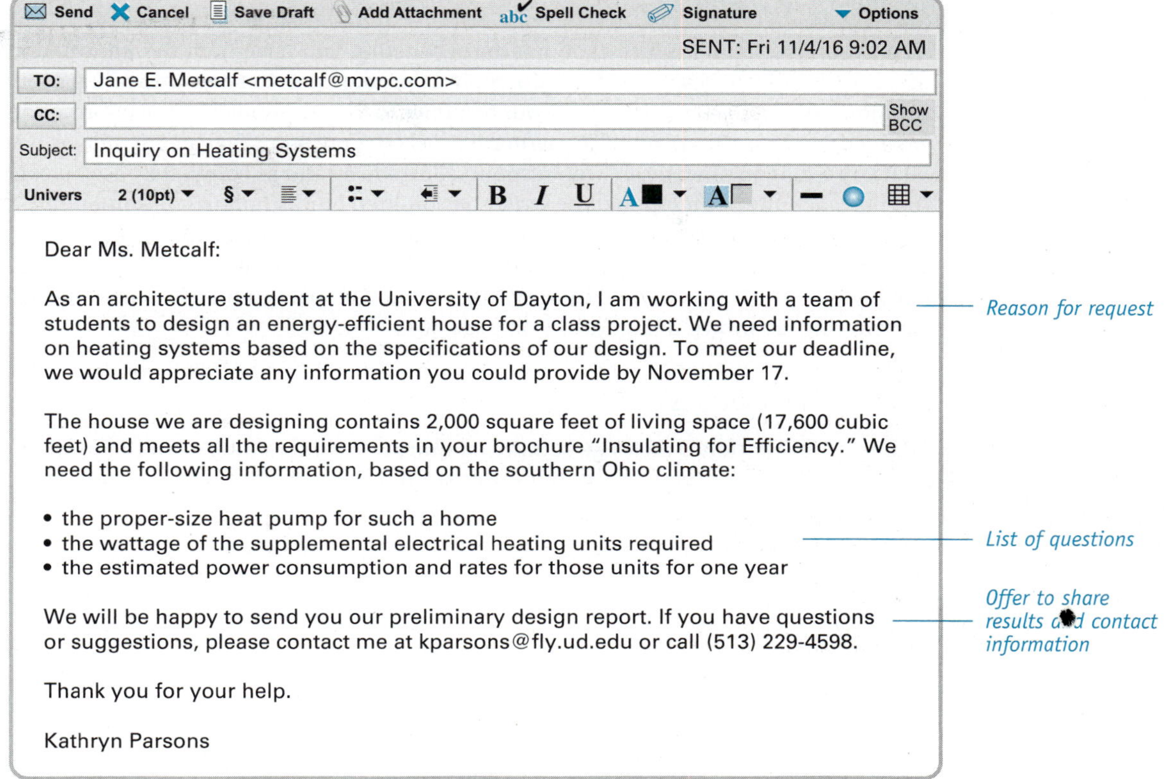
Send Cancel Save Draft Add Attachment Spell Check Signature Options

SENT: Fri 11/4/16 9:02 AM

TO: Jane E. Metcalf <metcalf@mvpc.com>

CC:

Subject: Inquiry on Heating Systems

Dear Ms. Metcalf:

As an architecture student at the University of Dayton, I am working with a team of students to design an energy-efficient house for a class project. We need information on heating systems based on the specifications of our design. To meet our deadline, we would appreciate any information you could provide by November 17.

The house we are designing contains 2,000 square feet of living space (17,600 cubic feet) and meets all the requirements in your brochure "Insulating for Efficiency." We need the following information, based on the southern Ohio climate:

- the proper-size heat pump for such a home
- the wattage of the supplemental electrical heating units required
- the estimated power consumption and rates for those units for one year

We will be happy to send you our preliminary design report. If you have questions or suggestions, please contact me at kparsons@fly.ud.edu or call (513) 229-4598.

Thank you for your help.

Kathryn Parsons

Figure 9–4 Inquiry (Sent as an E-mail Message)

CONSIDERING AUDIENCE AND PURPOSE

Writing Inquiries

- Make your questions specific, clear, and concise. Phrase your questions so that the reader will know immediately the type of information you are seeking, why you need it, and how you will use it.
- If appropriate, present your questions in a numbered or bulleted list to make it easy for your reader to respond.
- Keep the number of questions to a minimum to improve your chances of receiving a prompt response.
- If possible, offer some inducement for the reader to respond, such as promising to share the results of what you are doing.
- Promise to keep responses confidential, if appropriate, and provide a date by which you need a response.
- Close by thanking the reader for taking the time to respond. Provide contact information, such as a phone number or an e-mail address, to simplify a reply.

Responses to Inquiries

When you receive an inquiry, first determine whether you have both the information and the authority to respond. If you do, reply as promptly as you can, answering every question asked. Adjust the length of your response to the questions and the information provided by the writer. Even if the writer has asked a question that seems silly or has what you feel is an obvious answer, respond courteously and as completely as you can. You may tactfully point out that the writer has omitted or misunderstood something.

If you feel you cannot answer an inquiry, find out who can and forward the inquiry to that person. Notify the writer that you have forwarded the inquiry, as shown in Figure 9–5. If you reply to a forwarded inquiry, state in the first paragraph why someone else is answering, as shown in Figure 9–6 on page 306.

Sales and Promotions

A sales or promotional message requires a thorough understanding of the product, service, or business and the potential customer's needs. For this reason, many

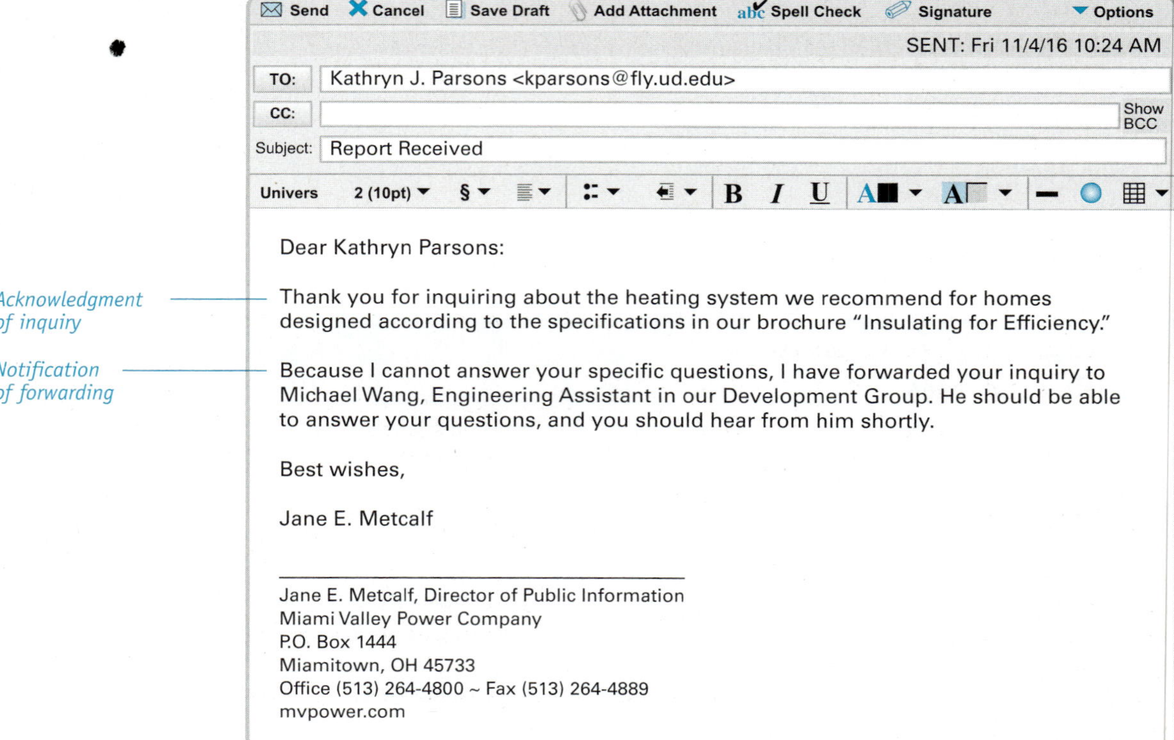
Send Cancel Save Draft Add Attachment Spell Check Signature Options

SENT: Fri 11/4/16 10:24 AM

TO: Kathryn J. Parsons <kparsons@fly.ud.edu>

CC:

Subject: Report Received

Dear Kathryn Parsons:

Thank you for inquiring about the heating system we recommend for homes designed according to the specifications in our brochure "Insulating for Efficiency."

Because I cannot answer your specific questions, I have forwarded your inquiry to Michael Wang, Engineering Assistant in our Development Group. He should be able to answer your questions, and you should hear from him shortly.

Best wishes,

Jane E. Metcalf

Jane E. Metcalf, Director of Public Information
Miami Valley Power Company
P.O. Box 1444
Miamitown, OH 45733
Office (513) 264-4800 ~ Fax (513) 264-4889
mvpower.com

Figure 9–5 Acknowledgment of an Inquiry (Indicating That the Request Has Been Forwarded)

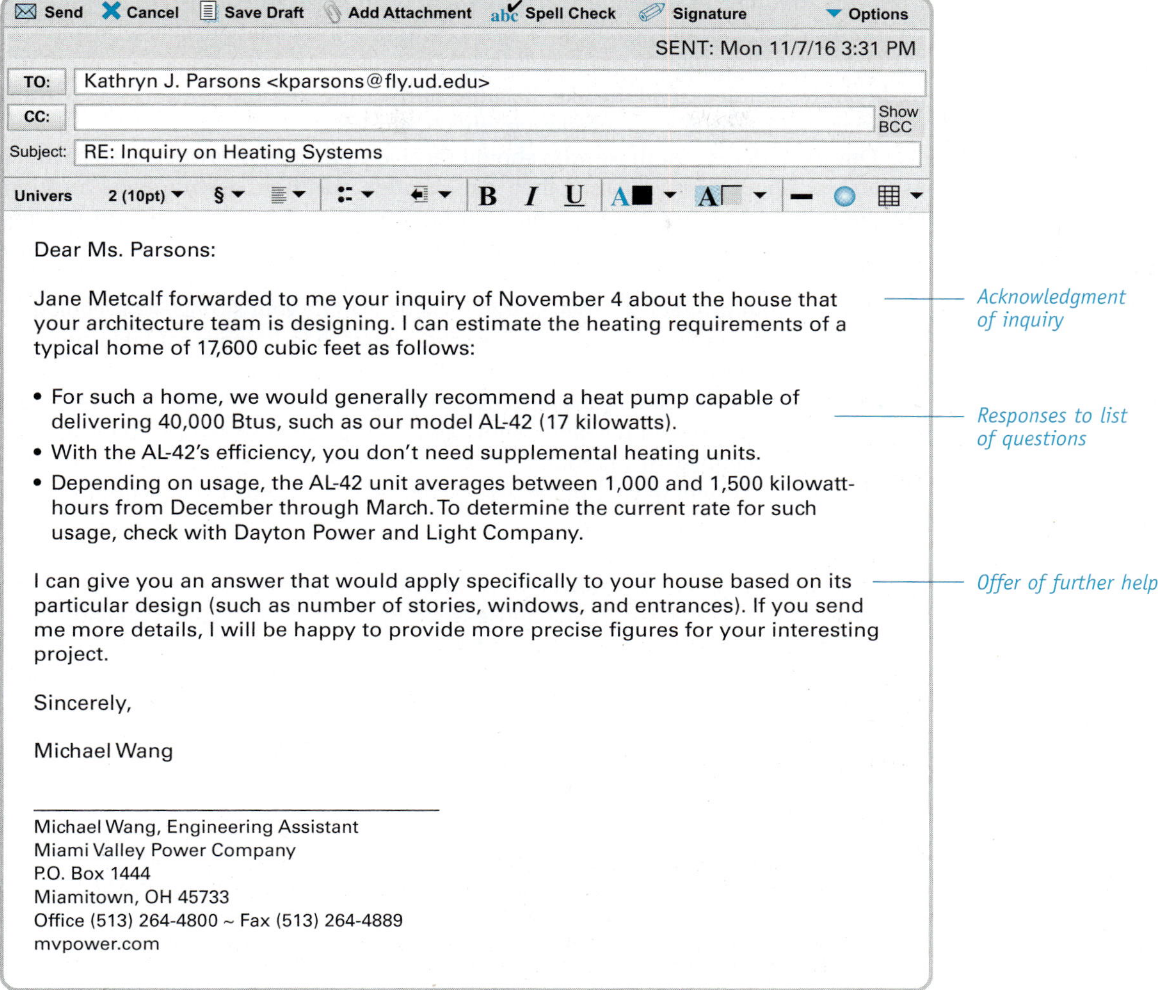

Send Cancel Save Draft Add Attachment Spell Check Signature Options

SENT: Mon 11/7/16 3:31 PM

TO: Kathryn J. Parsons <kparsons@fly.ud.edu>

CC:

Subject: RE: Inquiry on Heating Systems

Dear Ms. Parsons:

Jane Metcalf forwarded to me your inquiry of November 4 about the house that your architecture team is designing. I can estimate the heating requirements of a typical home of 17,600 cubic feet as follows:

- For such a home, we would generally recommend a heat pump capable of delivering 40,000 Btus, such as our model AL-42 (17 kilowatts).
- With the AL-42's efficiency, you don't need supplemental heating units.
- Depending on usage, the AL-42 unit averages between 1,000 and 1,500 kilowatt-hours from December through March. To determine the current rate for such usage, check with Dayton Power and Light Company.

I can give you an answer that would apply specifically to your house based on its particular design (such as number of stories, windows, and entrances). If you send me more details, I will be happy to provide more precise figures for your interesting project.

Sincerely,

Michael Wang

Michael Wang, Engineering Assistant
Miami Valley Power Company
P.O. Box 1444
Miamitown, OH 45733
Office (513) 264-4800 ~ Fax (513) 264-4889
mvpower.com

Figure 9–6 Response to an Inquiry (Sent as an E-mail Message)

businesses (such as major retailers) employ specialists to compose their sales and other promotional material. However, if you work in a small business or are self-employed, you may need to write and design sales messages yourself. An effective sales message accomplishes the goals described in the Writing Sales Letters checklist on page 309.

Your first task is to identify your audience: those who should receive your letter, postcard, e-mail, or other material. If you do not select your recipients carefully, your message will likely be dismissed as junk mail or e-mail spam. Appropriate recipients may include existing customers or people who have purchased a product or service from you and may do so again. You also might want to seek new customers who may be interested in certain products or services. Companies that specialize in marketing techniques compile and sell such lists of members of professional organizations, trade-show attendees, and the like. Because purchasing lists and printing and mailing materials can be expensive, select recipients with care.

Once you decide on those who should receive your sales message, learn as much as you can about them, such as their age, gender, vocation, geographical location, educational level, financial status, and interests. You must be aware of your readers' needs so that you can effectively tell them how your product or service will satisfy those needs.

Analyze your product or service carefully to determine your strongest psychological sales points — the product's intangible benefits rather than its physical features — and build your sales letter around those points. Begin by identifying how your product or service will make your reader's job easier, status higher, personal life more pleasant, and so on. Then in the body of the letter, show how your product or service can satisfy the need or desire identified in your opening. Describe the physical features of your product in terms of their benefit to your reader. Help your reader imagine using your product or service — and enjoying its benefits.

If the price of your product or service is especially competitive, you may decide to emphasize the cost. However, if your product or service is relatively costly (even if priced competitively), you may choose to emphasize its high quality, reliability, or special benefits instead. If you feel a need to minimize the negative effect of price, you might state the cost in terms of a unit rather than a set ($20 per item instead of $600 per set); identify the daily, the monthly, or even the yearly cost based on the estimated life of the product; suggest a series of payments rather than the total; or compare the cost with that of something the reader accepts readily ("costs the same as a movie and a dinner out").

ETHICS NOTE: Ensure That Sales Message Claims Are Valid Be certain that any claim you make in a sales message is valid. To claim that a product is safe guarantees its absolute safety; therefore, say the product is safe "provided that normal safety precautions are taken." Further, do not exaggerate or speak negatively about a competitor. Because of the ethical and sometimes legal concerns inherent in a sales letter, always have someone else — a coworker, manager, or member of your company's legal staff — review the letter for accuracy. For further ethical and legal guidelines, visit the Direct Marketing Association at www.dmaresponsibility.org. See also the ethics note on page 110 in Chapter 4, Revising a Document.

Notice the informal, friendly tone of the typical sales letter, as shown in Figure 9-7 — an approach frequently used by small, local businesses to make the reader feel comfortable about coming to them. The signature line of sales letters often shows the name of the company rather than the name of an individual, as is the case in this example. Sales letters sent by e-mail are often more economical than print options, especially for large groups of potential and existing customers, as shown in

Janice's Ski & Cycle
775 First Avenue, Ottumwa, IA 52501
(515) 273-5111 • fax (515) 273-5511

April 5, 2017

Mr. Raymond Sommers
350 College Place
Sharpsville, IA 52156

Dear Mr. Sommers:

Are you ready to go bike riding this spring—but your bike isn't? — *Needs of reader*

Janice's Ski & Cycle will get your bike in shape for the beautiful days ahead. We will lubricate all moving parts; check the tires, brakes, chain, lights, horn, and other accessories; and make any minor repairs—all for only $45.95 with the coupon enclosed with this letter. — *Benefits of service*

Just stop in any day, Monday through Saturday, between 8:00 a.m. and 9:00 p.m. We are conveniently located at the corner of First and Walker. If you bring your bike in before 10:00 a.m., you can enjoy a spring bike ride that evening. — *Convenience of service*

Happy riding!

Janice's Ski & Cycle

  Find us on Facebook or follow us on Twitter @janiceskicycle!

Figure 9–7 Sales Letter

Figure 9–8. If you choose e-mail as a medium, consider laws related to e-mail marketing, such as the CAN-SPAM Act (www.business.ftc.gov/documents/bus61-can-spam-act-compliance-guide-business). Consider as well how e-mail offers the ability to include multimedia (such as video and purchase links) and the need to keep content targeted and short.

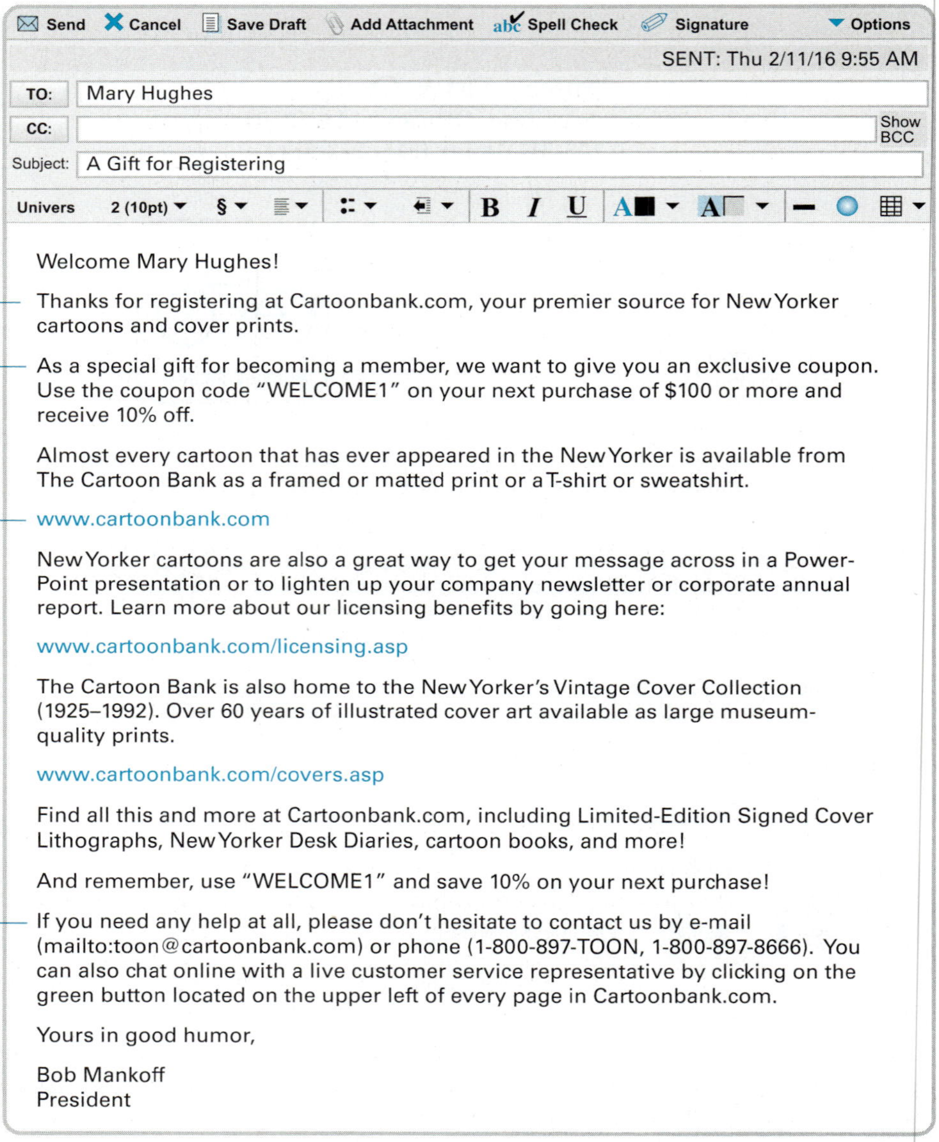

Send | Cancel | Save Draft | Add Attachment | Spell Check | Signature | Options

SENT: Thu 2/11/16 9:55 AM

TO: Mary Hughes

CC:

Show BCC

Subject: A Gift for Registering

Univers 2 (10pt)

Welcome Mary Hughes!

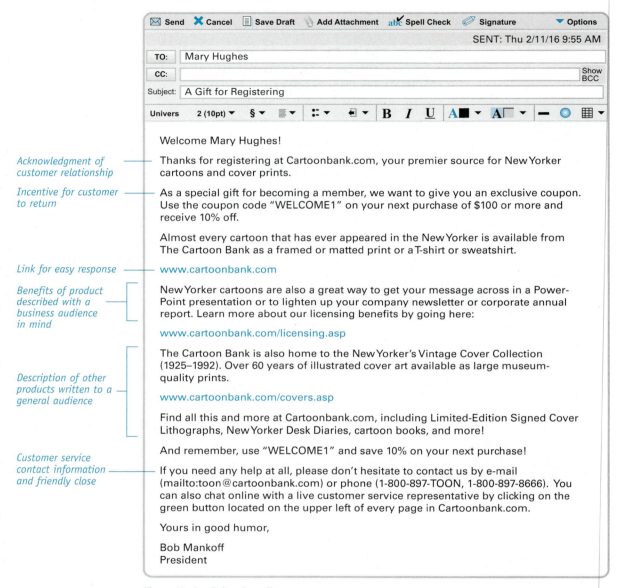

Acknowledgment of customer relationship

Thanks for registering at Cartoonbank.com, your premier source for New Yorker cartoons and cover prints.

Incentive for customer to return

As a special gift for becoming a member, we want to give you an exclusive coupon. Use the coupon code "WELCOME1" on your next purchase of $100 or more and receive 10% off.

Almost every cartoon that has ever appeared in the New Yorker is available from The Cartoon Bank as a framed or matted print or a T-shirt or sweatshirt.

Link for easy response

www.cartoonbank.com

Benefits of product described with a business audience in mind

New Yorker cartoons are also a great way to get your message across in a Power-Point presentation or to lighten up your company newsletter or corporate annual report. Learn more about our licensing benefits by going here:

www.cartoonbank.com/licensing.asp

Description of other products written to a general audience

The Cartoon Bank is also home to the New Yorker's Vintage Cover Collection (1925–1992). Over 60 years of illustrated cover art available as large museum-quality prints.

www.cartoonbank.com/covers.asp

Find all this and more at Cartoonbank.com, including Limited-Edition Signed Cover Lithographs, New Yorker Desk Diaries, cartoon books, and more!

And remember, use "WELCOME1" and save 10% on your next purchase!

Customer service contact information and friendly close

If you need any help at all, please don't hesitate to contact us by e-mail (mailto:toon@cartoonbank.com) or phone (1-800-897-TOON, 1-800-897-8666). You can also chat online with a live customer service representative by clicking on the green button located on the upper left of every page in Cartoonbank.com.

Yours in good humor,

Bob Mankoff
President

Figure 9–8 Sales E-mail

WRITER'S CHECKLIST
Writing Sales Letters

- ✔ Attract your readers' attention and pique their interest in the opening, for example, by describing a product's feature that would appeal strongly to their needs.
- ✔ Convince readers that your product or service is everything you say it is through case histories, free-trial use, money-back guarantee, or testimonials and endorsements.*
- ✔ Suggest ways readers can make immediate use of the product or service. Include a brochure or a Web link with photos or videos.
- ✔ Minimize the negative effect price can have on readers.
    - Mention the price along with a reminder of the benefits of the product.
    - State the price in terms of units rather than sets ($20 per item, not $600 per set).
    - Identify the daily, monthly, or even yearly cost based on the estimated life of the product.
    - Suggest a series of payments rather than one total payment, if possible.
    - Compare the cost of your product with that of something readers accept readily. ("This entire package costs no more than a dinner and a concert.")
- ✔ Make it easy and worthwhile for customers to respond: Include instructions for ordering online or by phone, information about free delivery, or special discount codes.
- ✔ Include links to social media and invite readers to become part of the conversation and community surrounding the product, service, or brand. Doing so also fosters the organization's Web presence.

Sensitive and Negative Messages

Writing sensitive or negative messages requires careful thought. You must decide the goal of your message and the approach you need to take. Then write in a way that maintains a professional relationship with a correspondent despite any difficult circumstances.

Routine and High-Stakes Refusals

When you receive a request to which you must give a negative reply, you may need to write a refusal message containing bad news. The difficulty of writing refusals depends on the stakes for the writer or the reader. As the stakes build, you need to increase your effort to analyze the situation and carefully develop your strategy as shown in Figures 9–9 through 9–12.

The refusal in Figure 9–9 declines an invitation to speak at a meeting, and the stakes for the writer are relatively low; however, the writer wishes to acknowledge the honor of being asked. Figure 9–10 on page 311 shows a letter rejecting a job applicant in which the stakes are somewhat higher.

*For detailed advice, search "advertising disclosure guidelines" on the official site of the Federal Trade Commission, www.ftc.gov.

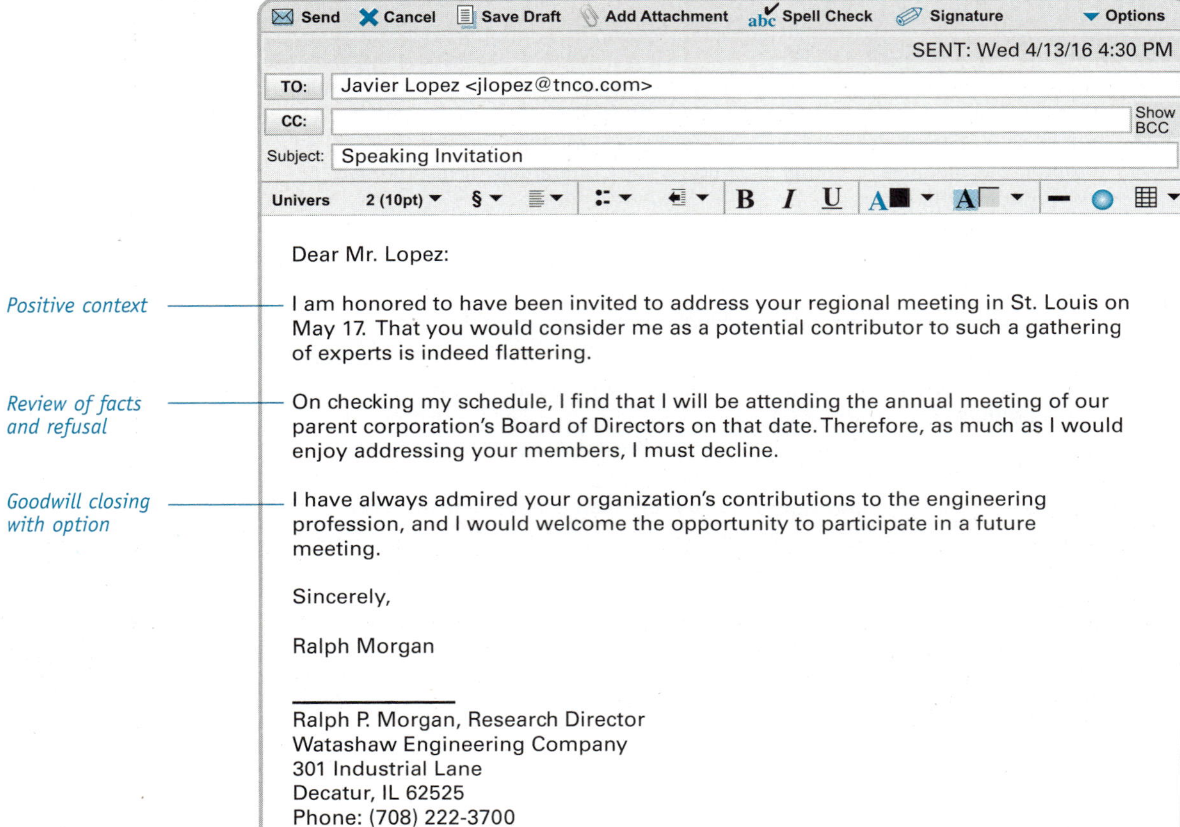

SENT: Wed 4/13/16 4:30 PM

TO: Javier Lopez <jlopez@tnco.com>

CC:

Subject: Speaking Invitation

Dear Mr. Lopez:

I am honored to have been invited to address your regional meeting in St. Louis on May 17. That you would consider me as a potential contributor to such a gathering of experts is indeed flattering.

On checking my schedule, I find that I will be attending the annual meeting of our parent corporation's Board of Directors on that date. Therefore, as much as I would enjoy addressing your members, I must decline.

I have always admired your organization's contributions to the engineering profession, and I would welcome the opportunity to participate in a future meeting.

Sincerely,

Ralph Morgan

Ralph P. Morgan, Research Director
Watashaw Engineering Company
301 Industrial Lane
Decatur, IL 62525
Phone: (708) 222-3700
wec.com

Figure 9–9 E-mail Refusing a Speaking Invitation

Figure 9–11 on page 312 shows a refusal sent to a supplier whose product was not selected, yet the writer wishes to maintain a harmonious relationship. Opening with the bad news and following it with reasons may give readers the impression that the reasons merely prop up the bad news in a high-stakes negative message. The ideal in such cases says *no* in such a way that you not only avoid antagonizing your reader but also maintain goodwill. To do so, you must convince your reader that the bad news is *based on reasons that are logical or at least understandable.* The following pattern, introduced on page 272 in Chapter 8, Writing E-mails, Memos, and Letters, is often a useful approach to this problem:

1. *Context.* In the opening, introduce the subject, but do not provide irrelevant information or mislead the reader that good news may follow.
2. *Explanation.* Review the facts or details that lead logically to the bad news, trying to see things from your reader's point of view.

Liberty Associates
3553 West Marshall Road
San Diego, CA 92101

Phone (619) 555-1001
Fax (619) 555-0110

January 18, 2017

Ms. Sonja Yadgar
2289 South 63rd Street
Hartford, CT 06101

Dear Ms. Yadgar:

Thank you for your interest in financial counseling at Liberty Associates. I respect your investment experience and professionalism, and I enjoyed our conversation. — *Positive context*

Shortly after our meeting, an especially appropriate, well-qualified internal candidate applied for the position, and we have decided to offer the job to that individual. The decision was very difficult. Both Nancy Linh and I were impressed with your qualifications and believe that you have a great deal to offer our profession. — *Review of facts and refusal*

Best wishes for the future. — *Goodwill closing*

Sincerely,

Meike Künkel
Vice President
Director of Development

www.libertyassociates.com

Figure 9–10 Letter Rejecting a Job Applicant

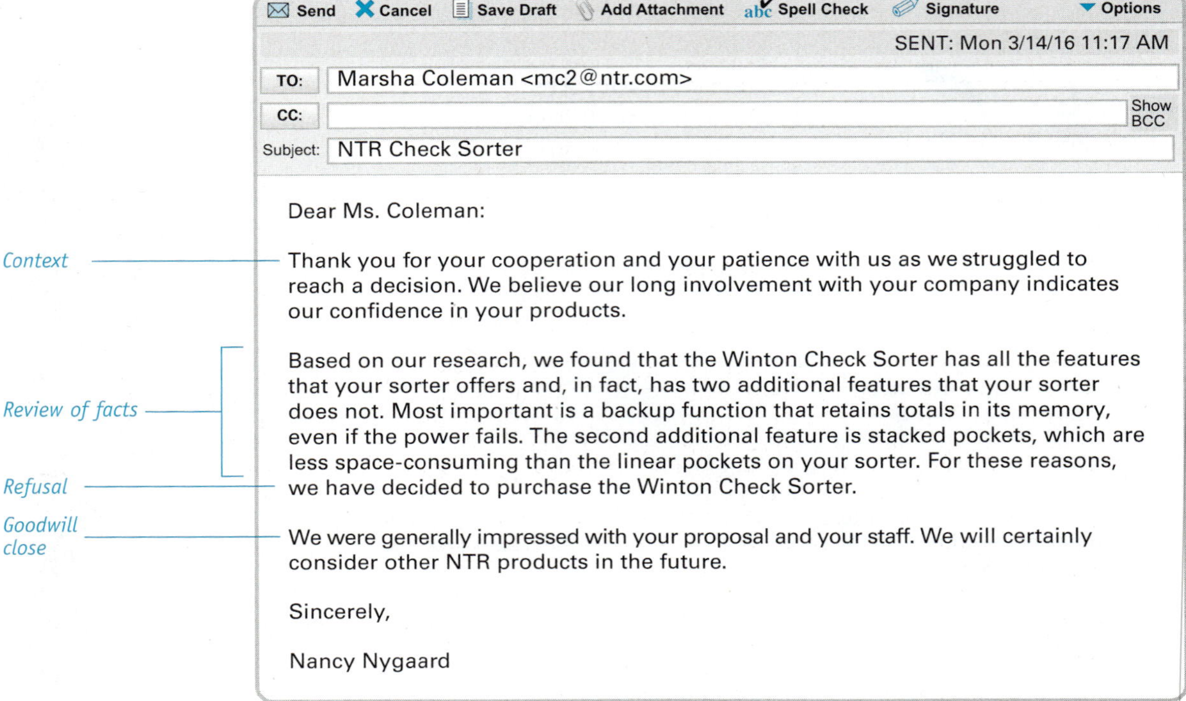

Send | Cancel | Save Draft | Add Attachment | Spell Check | Signature | Options

SENT: Mon 3/14/16 11:17 AM

TO: Marsha Coleman <mc2@ntr.com>

CC:

Show BCC

Subject: NTR Check Sorter

Dear Ms. Coleman:

Thank you for your cooperation and your patience with us as we struggled to reach a decision. We believe our long involvement with your company indicates our confidence in your products.

Based on our research, we found that the Winton Check Sorter has all the features that your sorter offers and, in fact, has two additional features that your sorter does not. Most important is a backup function that retains totals in its memory, even if the power fails. The second additional feature is stacked pockets, which are less space-consuming than the linear pockets on your sorter. For these reasons, we have decided to purchase the Winton Check Sorter.

We were generally impressed with your proposal and your staff. We will certainly consider other NTR products in the future.

Sincerely,

Nancy Nygaard

Figure 9–11 E-mail Rejecting a Sales Proposal

3. *Bad news.* State your refusal or negative message, based on the facts, concisely and without apology.
4. *Goodwill.* In the closing, establish or reestablish a positive relationship by providing an alternative if possible, assure the reader of your high opinion of his or her product or service, offer a friendly remark, or simply wish the reader success.

In the case of the rejected proposal shown in Figure 9–12, the writer expresses appropriate and genuine appreciation for the reader's time, effort, and interest. Then the writer thoroughly details the reasons for the refusal in order to convince the reader that the conclusion is reasonable. It states the negative message concisely, clearly, and as positively as possible. It then closes by working to reestablish goodwill and avoids rehashing the bad news. (Do not write, "Again, we're sorry we can't use your idea.")

◆ *See also Goodwill and the "You" Viewpoint on pages 268–269, Direct and Indirect Patterns on pages 269–274, and Sending a Resignation Letter or Memo on pages 568–570.*

Complaints

When you experience a problem in the workplace, you first use and exhaust all the standard approaches to solving the problem—calls to customer-service personnel and messages to those you have dealt with in an organization. By the time you need to write a formal complaint message or letter (sometimes called a *claim letter*), you

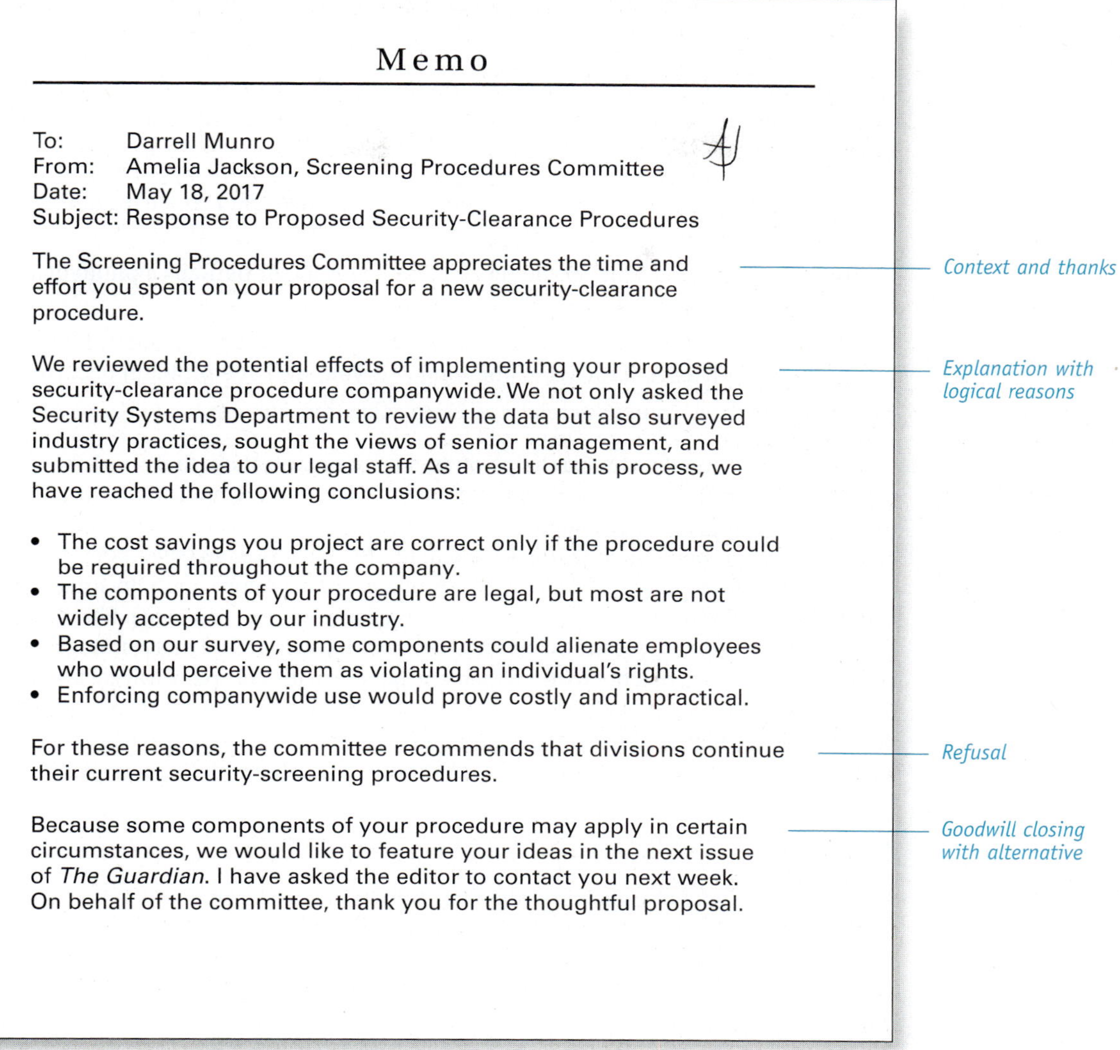

Memo

To: Darrell Munro
From: Amelia Jackson, Screening Procedures Committee
Date: May 18, 2017
Subject: Response to Proposed Security-Clearance Procedures

The Screening Procedures Committee appreciates the time and effort you spent on your proposal for a new security-clearance procedure.

We reviewed the potential effects of implementing your proposed security-clearance procedure companywide. We not only asked the Security Systems Department to review the data but also surveyed industry practices, sought the views of senior management, and submitted the idea to our legal staff. As a result of this process, we have reached the following conclusions:

- The cost savings you project are correct only if the procedure could be required throughout the company.
- The components of your procedure are legal, but most are not widely accepted by our industry.
- Based on our survey, some components could alienate employees who would perceive them as violating an individual's rights.
- Enforcing companywide use would prove costly and impractical.

For these reasons, the committee recommends that divisions continue their current security-screening procedures.

Because some components of your procedure may apply in certain circumstances, we would like to feature your ideas in the next issue of *The Guardian*. I have asked the editor to contact you next week. On behalf of the committee, thank you for the thoughtful proposal.

Figure 9–12 Memo Rejecting an Internal Proposal

may be irritated and angry. If you write a complaint that reflects only your annoyance and anger, you may simply seem petty and irrational. Likewise, immediately posting a complaint to a company's social-media site or to a public forum might be seen as an attack and not as an honest attempt to work out a problem and reach a resolution. The best complaints—the ones taken most seriously—do not sound complaining. Remember, too, that the person who receives your complaint may not be the one who was directly responsible for the situation. An effective message or letter should assume that the recipient will conscientiously correct the problem. However, anticipate reader reactions or rebuttals.

◆ *For advice about writing resignation and job-refusal letters, see Chapter 15, Writing Résumés and Cover Letters.*

- I reviewed my user manual's "safe operating guidelines" carefully before I installed the device. [Assures readers you followed instructions.]

Without such explanations, readers may be tempted to dismiss your complaint. Although the circumstances and severity of the problem may vary, effective complaint letters (or e-mails) should generally follow this pattern:

1. Identify the problem or faulty item(s) and include relevant invoice numbers, part names, and dates.
2. Include or attach a copy of the receipt, bill, contract, or perhaps a photo of a damaged part and keep the original for your records.
3. Explain logically, clearly, and specifically what went wrong, especially for a problem with a service. (Avoid guessing why you think the problem occurred.)
4. State what you expect the reader to do to solve the problem.

To reach someone who can help you in a large organization, first check its website or call its main office so that you can address your letter to the appropriate department (often Customer Service, Consumer Affairs, or Adjustments). Some websites not associated with the company, such as that for the Better Business Bureau (www.bbb.org) or that of a state consumer affairs office, may also provide contact information. In smaller organizations, you might write to a vice president in charge of sales or service. For very small businesses, write directly to the owner. As a last resort, you may find that sending copies of a complaint message or letter to more than one person in the company will get fast results. Each employee who receives the complaint will know (because of the copy notations) that others, possibly higher in the organization, have received the letter and will take note of whether the problem is solved. Figure 9–13 shows a typical complaint message.

Adjustments

An adjustment letter or e-mail is written in response to a complaint and tells a customer or client what your organization intends to do about the complaint. Although sent in response to a problem, an adjustment letter actually provides an excellent opportunity to build goodwill for your organization. An effective adjustment letter, such as the examples shown in Figures 9–14 and 9–15 on pages 316 and 317, respectively, can not only repair any damage done but also restore the customer's confidence in your company.

No matter how unreasonable the complaint, the tone of your response should be positive and respectful. Avoid emphasizing the problem, but take responsibility for it when appropriate. Focus your response on what you are doing to correct the problem. Settle such matters quickly and courteously, and lean toward giving the customer or client the benefit of the doubt at a reasonable cost to your organization. See also "Routine and High-Stakes Refusals" in Chapter 9 and "Goodwill and the 'You' Viewpoint" in Chapter 8.

Full Adjustments

Before granting an adjustment to a claim for which your company is at fault, first determine what happened and what you can do to satisfy the customer. Be certain

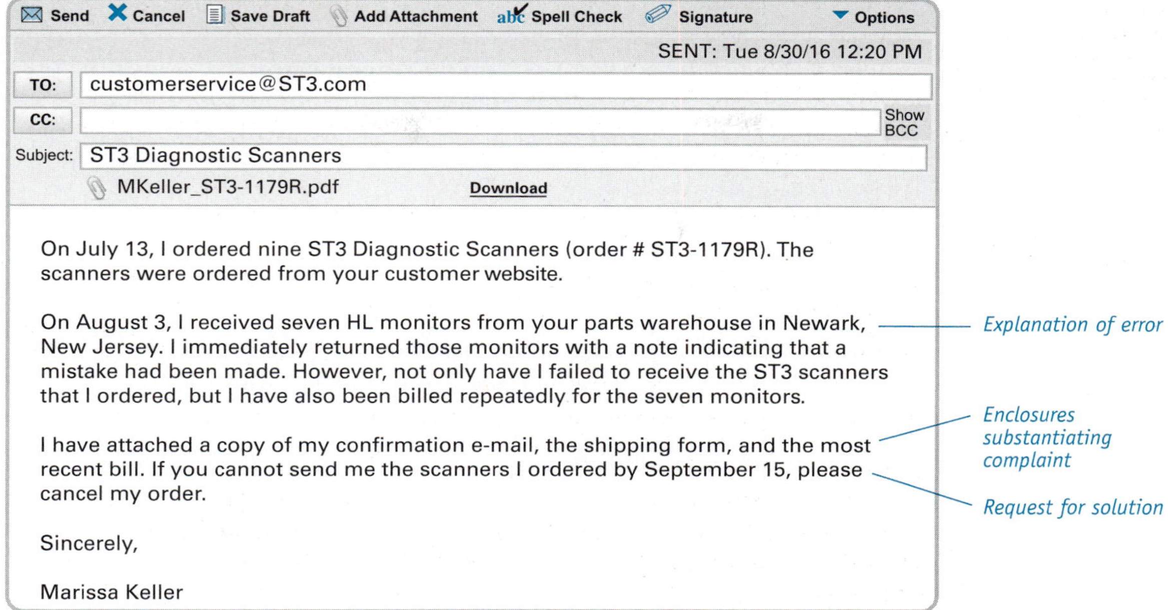
Send | Cancel | Save Draft | Add Attachment | Spell Check | Signature | Options

SENT: Tue 8/30/16 12:20 PM

TO: customerservice@ST3.com

CC:

Subject: ST3 Diagnostic Scanners

MKeller_ST3-1179R.pdf Download

On July 13, I ordered nine ST3 Diagnostic Scanners (order # ST3-1179R). The scanners were ordered from your customer website.

On August 3, I received seven HL monitors from your parts warehouse in Newark, New Jersey. I immediately returned those monitors with a note indicating that a mistake had been made. However, not only have I failed to receive the ST3 scanners that I ordered, but I have also been billed repeatedly for the seven monitors.

I have attached a copy of my confirmation e-mail, the shipping form, and the most recent bill. If you cannot send me the scanners I ordered by September 15, please cancel my order.

Sincerely,

Marissa Keller

Figure 9–13 Complaint Message Detailing a Billing Problem

that you are familiar with your company's adjustment policy — and be careful with word choice.

- We have just received your letter of May 7 about our defective gas grill.

Saying something is "defective" could be ruled in a court of law as an admission that the product is in fact defective. When you are in doubt, seek legal advice.

Grant adjustments graciously: A settlement made grudgingly will do more harm than good. Not only must you be gracious, but you must also acknowledge the error in such a way that the customer will not lose confidence in your company. Emphasize early what the reader will consider good news.

- Enclosed is a replacement for the damaged part.
- Yes, you were incorrectly billed for the delivery.
- Please accept our apologies for the error in your account.

Professionalism Note: Be Forthright and Respectful When Responding to Adjustment Correspondence If an explanation will help restore your reader's confidence, explain what caused the problem. You might point out any steps you are taking to prevent a recurrence of the problem. Explain that customer feedback helps your firm keep the quality of its product or service high. Close pleasantly, looking toward the future, and avoid recalling the problem in your closing (do not write, "Again, we apologize . . .").

INTERNET SERVICES CORPORATION
10876 Crispen Way
Chicago, IL 60601

May 5, 2017

Mr. Jason Brandon
4319 Anglewood Street
Tacoma, WA 98402

Dear Mr. Brandon:

Gracious tone

Adjustment

We are sorry that your experience with our customer support help line did not go smoothly. We are eager to restore your confidence in our ability to provide dependable, high-quality service. Your next three months of Internet access will be complimentary as our sincere apology.

Providing dependable service is what is expected of us, and when our staff doesn't provide quality service, it is easy to understand our customers' disappointment. I truly wish we had performed better in our guidance for setup and log-in procedures and that your experience had been a positive one. To prevent similar problems in the future, we plan to use your letter, anonymized, in training sessions with customer support personnel.

Positive closing

We appreciate your taking the time to write us. It helps to receive comments such as yours, and we conscientiously follow through to be sure that proper procedures are being met.

Yours truly,

Inez Carlson

Inez Carlson, Vice President
Customer Support Services

www.isc.com

Figure 9–14 Adjustment Letter (Company Takes Responsibility)

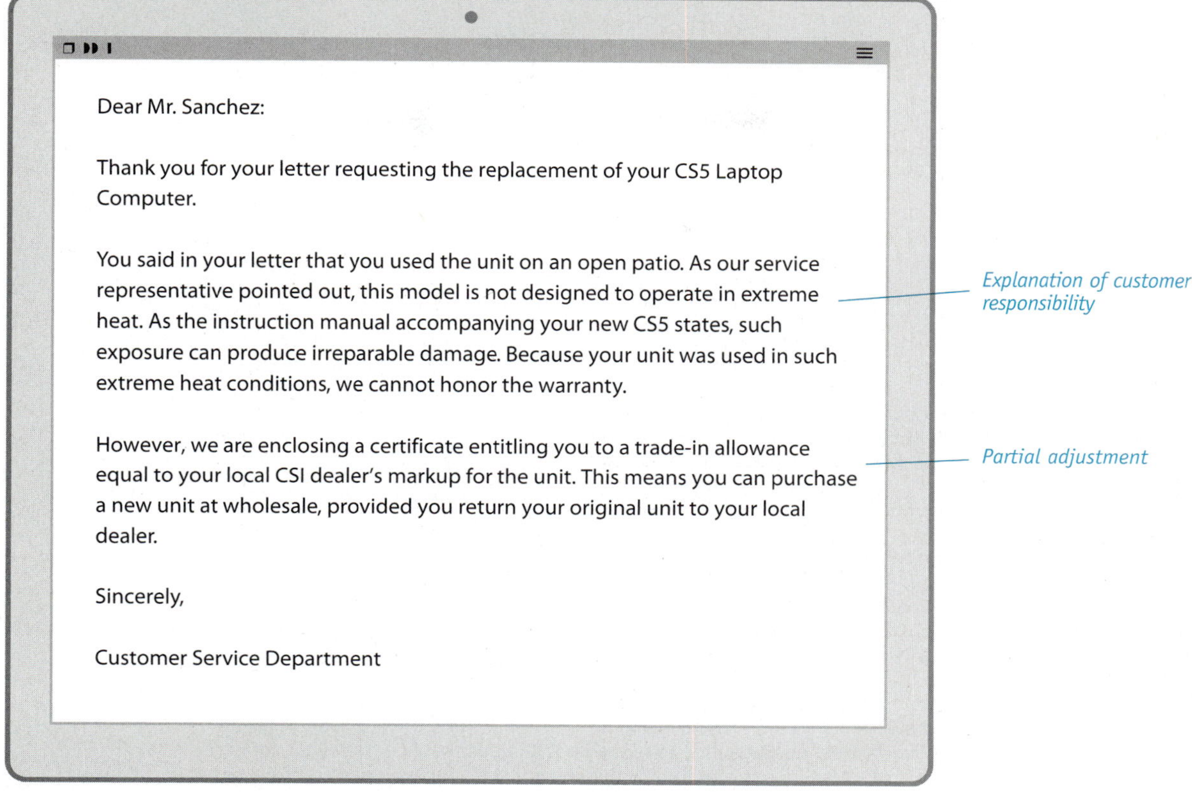
Dear Mr. Sanchez:

Thank you for your letter requesting the replacement of your CS5 Laptop Computer.

You said in your letter that you used the unit on an open patio. As our service representative pointed out, this model is not designed to operate in extreme heat. As the instruction manual accompanying your new CS5 states, such exposure can produce irreparable damage. Because your unit was used in such extreme heat conditions, we cannot honor the warranty.

However, we are enclosing a certificate entitling you to a trade-in allowance equal to your local CSI dealer's markup for the unit. This means you can purchase a new unit at wholesale, provided you return your original unit to your local dealer.

Sincerely,

Customer Service Department

Figure 9–15 Partial Adjustment (Accompanying a Product)

The adjustment letter in Figure 9–14, for example, begins by accepting responsibility and offers an apology for the customer's inconvenience, as well as complimentary Internet service (note the use of the pronouns *we* and *our*). The second paragraph expresses a desire to restore goodwill and describes specifically how the writer intends to make the adjustment. The third paragraph expresses appreciation to the customer for calling attention to the problem and assures him that his complaint has been taken seriously.

Partial Adjustments

You may sometimes need to grant a partial adjustment—even if a claim is not really justified—to regain the lost goodwill of a customer or client. If, for example, a customer incorrectly uses a product or service, you may need to help that person better understand the correct use of that product or service. In such a circumstance, remember that your customer or client believes that his or her claim is justified. Therefore, you should give the explanation before granting the claim—otherwise, your reader may never get to the explanation. If your explanation establishes customer responsibility, do so tactfully. Figures 9–15 and 9–16 are examples of partial adjustment letters.

Swelco Coffeemaker, Inc.

9025 North Main Street
Butte, MT 59702

Phone: (800) 233-5656
Fax: (800) 233-3010

August 21, 2017

Mr. Carlos Ortiz
638 McSwaney Drive
Butte, MT 59702

Dear Mr. Ortiz:

Enclosed is your SWELCO Coffeemaker, which you sent to us on August 16.

Education of customer

In various parts of the country, tap water may have a high mineral content. If you fill your SWELCO Coffeemaker with water for breakfast coffee before going to bed, a mineral scale will build up on the inner wall of the water tube — as explained on page 2 of your SWELCO Instruction Booklet.

Adjustment and instruction

We have removed the mineral scale from the water tube of your coffeemaker and thoroughly cleaned the entire unit. To ensure the best service from your coffeemaker in the future, clean it once a month by operating it with four ounces of white vinegar and eight cups of water. To rinse out the vinegar taste, operate the unit twice with clear water.

Positive closing

With proper care, your SWELCO Coffeemaker will serve you faithfully and well for many years to come.

Sincerely,

Helen Upham

Helen Upham
Customer Services

HU/mo
Enclosure

swelco.com

Figure 9–16 Educational Adjustment Letter

Collections

Collection letters serve two purposes: (1) to collect an overdue bill and (2) to preserve the customer relationship. In some states, collection letters need to be prepared by attorneys because certain language and requirements must be followed to demand payment. However, even if you never need to write a collection letter, understanding the principles behind such letters offers important insights into the strategies of sensitive correspondence.

Most companies use a series of collection letters in which the letters become increasingly demanding and urgent. The series usually proceeds in three stages, each of which may include several e-mails and letters as well as follow-up phone calls. All letters should be courteous and show a genuine interest in the customer and whatever problems may be preventing prompt payment.

The first stage consists of reminders stamped on the invoice ("overdue"), form letters, or brief personal notes. These early reminders should maintain a friendly tone that emphasizes the customer's good credit record until now. They should remind the customer of the debt and may even solicit more business by including or attaching promotional material for new items. As in the example in Figure 9–17, you might suggest that nonpayment may be a result of a simple error or oversight.

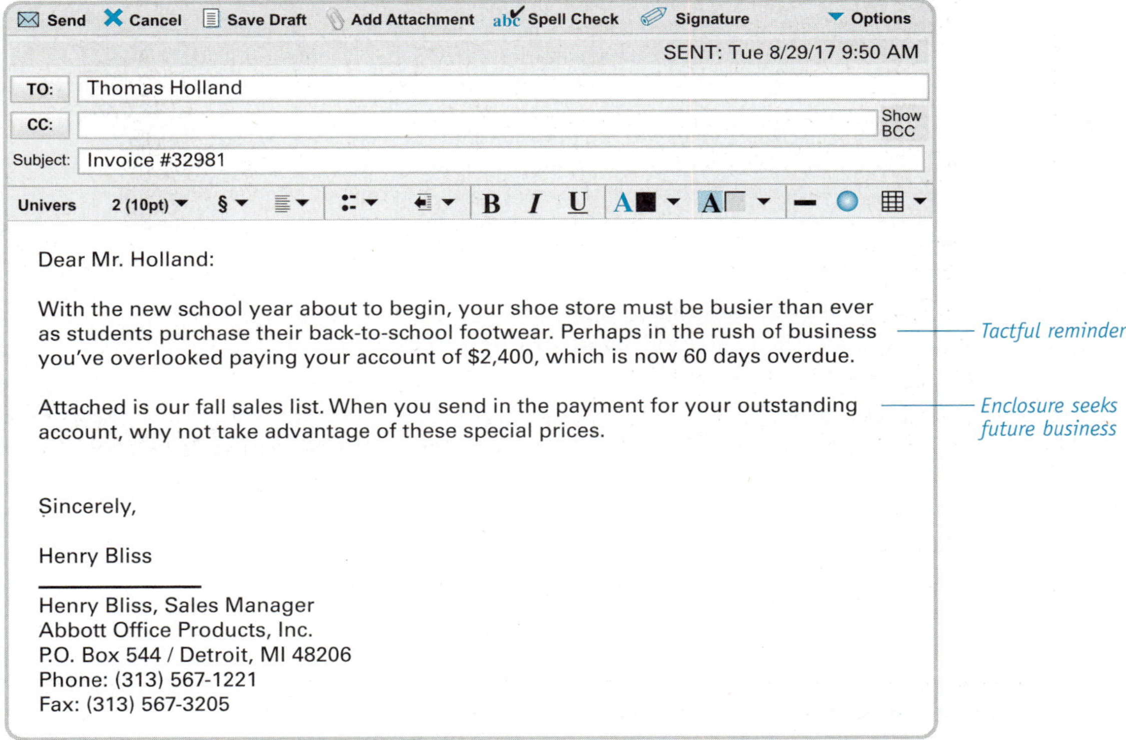

Figure 9–17 First-Stage Collection Message

ABBOTT OFFICE PRODUCTS, INC.

P.O. Box 544
Detroit, MI 48206
Phone (313) 567-1221
Fax (313) 567-2112
abbott.com

November 8, 2017

Mr. Thomas Holland
Walk Softly Shoes
1661 East Madison Boulevard
Garfield, AL 36613

Dear Mr. Holland:

Inquiry about problems

We are concerned that we have not heard from you about your overdue account of $2,400 even though we have written three times in the past 90 days. Because you have always been one of our best customers, we have to wonder if some special circumstances have caused the delay. If so, please feel free to discuss the matter with us.

Direct request

By sending us a check today, you can preserve your excellent credit record. Because you have always paid your account promptly, we are sure that you will want to settle this balance now. If your balance is more than you can pay at present, we will be happy to work out mutually satisfactory payment arrangements.

Options for response

Please use the enclosed envelope to send in your payment, or call 800-526-1945 to discuss your account.

Sincerely,

Henry Bliss
Sales Manager
hb@abbott.com

Figure 9–18 Second-Stage Collection Letter

ABBOTT OFFICE PRODUCTS, INC.

P.O. Box 544
Detroit, MI 48206
Phone (313) 567-1221
Fax (313) 567-2112
abbott.com

December 29, 2017

Mr. Thomas Holland
Walk Softly Shoes
1661 East Madison Boulevard
Garfield, AL 36613

Dear Mr. Holland:

Your account in the amount of $2,400 is now 180 days overdue. You have already received a generous extension of time and, in fairness to our other customers, we cannot permit a further delay in payment.

Urgent request

Because you have not responded to any of our letters, we must turn your account over to our attorney for collection if we do not receive payment immediately. Such action, of course, will damage your previously fine credit rating.

Explicit demand

Why not avoid this unpleasant situation by making a fund transfer or sending your check in the enclosed return envelope within 10 days or by calling 800-526-1945 to discuss payment.

Options for response

Sincerely,

Henry Bliss

Henry Bliss
Sales Manager
hb@abbott.com

Figure 9–19 Third-Stage Collection Letter

In the second stage, the messages are more than just reminders. You now assume that some circumstances are preventing payment. Ask directly for payment, and inquire about possible problems, perhaps inviting the customer to discuss the matter with you. You might suggest an optional installment payment plan if you are able to offer one. Mention the importance of good credit, appealing to the customer's pride, self-esteem, and sense of fairness. Remind the customer that he or she has always received good value from you. Make it easy to respond with a return envelope, a telephone or fax number, or an e-mail or Web address where the payment can be made. At this stage, your tone should be firmer and more direct than in the early stage, but it should never be rude, sarcastic, or threatening. Notice how the second-stage letter shown in Figure 9–18 is more direct than the first-stage letter but no less polite. Consider in this stage and certainly in the final stage using a transmittal method that provides proof of receipt.

Third-stage collection letters reflect a sense of urgency, since the customer has not responded to your previous letters. Although your tone should remain courteous, make your demand for payment explicit. Point out how reasonable you have been, and urge the customer to pay at once to avoid a collection service or legal action or damage to the recipient's credit rating, as shown in Figure 9–19 on page 322. Again, make it easy to respond by providing a return envelope, a telephone or fax number, or an e-mail or Web address.

Writing International Correspondence

With so many companies operating globally, you may need to write letters, memos, or e-mail messages to readers from other cultures. Because English is widely taught and used in international business, you will be able to send most international correspondence in English. If you must use a translator, however, be sure that the translator understands the purpose of your correspondence. It is also prudent to let your reader know (in the letter itself or in a postscript) that a translator helped write the letter. For first-time contacts, consider sending both the English version and a translation in the reader's native language. If at all possible, have someone from your intended reader's culture or with appropriate expertise review your draft before you complete your final proofreading.

Culture and Business-Writing Style

When you read correspondence from businesspeople in other cultures or countries, be alert to differences in such features as customary expressions, openings, and closings. Business writers in some cultures, for example, traditionally use indirect openings that may express good wishes about the recipient's family or compliment the reader's success or prosperity. Consider deeper issues as well, such as how writers from other cultures express bad news. Some cultures traditionally express negative messages, such as refusals, indirectly to avoid embarrassing the recipient. Such cultural differences are often based on perceptions of time, face-saving, and other traditions.

Cross-Cultural Examples

Figures 9–20 and 9–21 show a draft and a final version of a letter written by an American businessperson to a Japanese businessperson. The opening and closing of the draft in Figure 9–20 do not include enough of the politeness strategies that are important in Japanese culture, and the informal salutation inappropriately uses the recipient's first name (*Dear Ichiro:*). This draft also contains idioms (*looking forward, company family*), jargon (*transport will be holding*), contractions (*I'm, don't*), informal language (*just e-mail or fax, Cheers*), and humor and allusion (*"ptomaine palace" across from our main offices*).

Compare that letter to the one in Figure 9–21, which is written in language that is courteous, literal, and specific. This revised letter begins with concern about the recipient's family and prosperity because that opening honors traditional Japanese patterns in business correspondence. The letter is free of slang, idioms, and jargon. The sentences are shorter than in the draft; in addition, bulleted lists break up the paragraphs, contractions are avoided, months are spelled out, and 24-hour-clock time is used.

When writing for international readers, rethink the ingrained habits that define how you express yourself, learn as much as you can about the cultural expectations of others, and focus on politeness strategies that demonstrate your respect for readers. Doing so will help you achieve clarity and mutual understanding with international readers.

WRITER'S CHECKLIST

Writing International Correspondence

- ✔ Observe the guidelines for courtesy, such as those in the *Writer's Checklist: Using Tone to Build Goodwill* in Chapter 8 on page 269.
- ✔ Write clear and complete sentences: Unusual word order or rambling sentences will frustrate and confuse readers.
- ✔ Avoid an overly simplified style that may offend or any affectation that may confuse the reader.
- ✔ Avoid humor, irony, and sarcasm; they are easily misunderstood outside their cultural context.
- ✔ Do not use idioms, jargon, slang expressions, unusual figures of speech, or allusions to events or attitudes particular to American life.
- ✔ Consider whether necessary technical terminology can be found in abbreviated English-language dictionaries; if it cannot, carefully define such terminology.
- ✔ Do not use contractions or abbreviations that may not be clear to international readers.
- ✔ Avoid inappropriate informality, such as using first names too quickly.
- ✔ Write out dates, whether in the month-day-year style (*June 11, 2017* not *6/11/17*) used in the United States or the day-month-year style (*11 June 2017* not *11/6/17*) used in many other parts of the world.
- ✔ Specify time zones or refer to international standards, such as Greenwich Mean Time (GMT) or Universal Time Coordinated (UTC).
- ✔ Use international measurement standards, such as the metric system (*18°C, 14 cm, 45 kg*), where possible.
- ✔ Ask someone from your intended audience's culture or with appropriate expertise to review your draft before you complete your final proofreading.

DRAFT FOR REVIEW

Dear Ichiro:

I'm writing to confirm travel arrangements for your visit to Tucson next month. We at Sun West are looking forward to meeting you and cultivating a successful business relationship between our two companies.

I understand that you will arrive on 3/20/17 on Delta flight #186 at 1:30 p.m. (itinerary enclosed). When you pick up your baggage at Tucson, go directly toward the "taxi-limo" area where our transport will be holding a card with your name and can take you directly to Loewes Ventana Canyon Resort. The resort has an excellent restaurant—we promise not to take you to the "ptomaine palace" across from our main offices!

We are excited to meet you. We want you to meet our company family. After you meet everyone, you will enjoy a catered breakfast in our conference room. Events include presentations from the president of the company and from departmental directors on several topics.

I have enclosed a guidebook and map of Tucson and material on our company. If you see anything that interests you, let me know, and we will be happy to show you our city and all it has to offer. And if you have any questions about the company before we see you, just e-mail or fax (I don't think regular mail will get to us in time).

Cheers,

Ty Smith
Vice President

U.S. writer moves too quickly to use of first name

Contraction (I'm) is too informal and may not appear in an English dictionary

Jargon ("transport") is inappropriate

The use of "family" is a figure of speech that could be confusing

Abrupt and informal: add more goodwill to closing

"Looking forward" is an idiom that may not be clear

First paragraph gets to business abruptly: add more personal greeting

Abbreviated with U.S. date format: use March 20, 2017

Inappropriate humor and allusion

First three sentences use overly simplified style

Figure 9–20 Inappropriate International Correspondence (Draft Marked for Revision)

Sun West Corporation, Inc.

2565 North Armadillo
Tucson, AZ 85719
Phone: (602) 555-6677
Fax: (602) 555-6678
sunwest.com

March 6, 2017

Ichiro Katsumi
Investment Director
Toshiba Investment Company
1-29-10 Ichiban-cho
Tokyo 105, Japan

Dear Mr. Katsumi:

I hope that you and your family are well and prospering in the new year. We at Sun West Corporation are very pleased that you will be coming to visit us in Tucson this month. It will be a pleasure to meet you, and we are very gratified and honored that you are interested in investing in our company.

So that we can ensure that your stay will be pleasurable, we have taken care of all of your travel arrangements. You will

- Depart Narita–New Tokyo International Airport on Delta Airlines flight #75 at 1700 on March 20, 2017.
- Arrive at Los Angeles International Airport at 1050 local time and depart for Tucson on Delta flight #186 at 1205.
- Arrive at Tucson International Airport at 1330 local time on March 20.
- Depart Tucson International Airport on Delta flight #123 at 1845 on March 27.
- Arrive in Salt Lake City, Utah, at 1040 and depart on Delta flight #34 at 1115.
- Arrive in Portland, Oregon, at 1210 local time and depart on Delta flight #254 at 1305.
- Arrive in Tokyo at 1505 local time on March 28.

If you need additional information about your travel plans or information on Sun West Corporation, please call, fax, or e-mail me directly at tsmith@sunwest.com. That way, we will receive your message in time to make the appropriate changes or additions.

Figure 9–21 Appropriate International Correspondence

Mr. Ichiro Katsumi 2 March 6, 2017

After you arrive in Tucson, a chauffeur from Skyline Limousines will be waiting for you at Gate 12. He or she will be carrying a card with your name, will help you collect your luggage from the baggage claim area, and will then drive you to the Loewes Ventana Canyon Resort. This resort is one of the most prestigious in Tucson, with spectacular desert views, high-quality amenities, and one of the best golf courses in the city. The next day, the chauffeur will be back at the Ventana at 0900 to drive you to Sun West Corporation.

We at Sun West Corporation are very excited to meet you and introduce you to all the staff members of our hardworking and growing company. After you meet everyone, you will enjoy a catered breakfast in our conference room. At that time, you will receive a schedule of events planned for the remainder of your trip. Events include presentations from the president of the company and from departmental directors on

- The history of Sun West Corporation
- The uniqueness of our products and current success in the marketplace
- Demographic information and the benefits of being located in Tucson
- The potential for considerable profits for both our companies with your company's investment

We encourage you to read through the enclosed guidebook and map of Tucson. In addition to events planned at Sun West Corporation, you will find many natural wonders and historical sites to see in Tucson and in Arizona in general. If you see any particular event or place that you would like to visit, please let us know. We will be happy to show you our city and all it has to offer.

Again, we are very honored that you will be visiting us, and we look forward to a successful business relationship between our two companies.

Sincerely,

Ty Smith

Ty Smith
Vice President

Enclosures (2)

Figure 9–21 Appropriate International Correspondence *(continued)*

MEETING THE DEADLINE: Writing a Sensitive Message

Emma Davis is the human resources manager for Apex Medical Systems.* Emma needs to inform all employees that the tuition reimbursement program will be discontinued immediately. Apex recently lost 30 percent of its sales of diagnostic equipment to Mega Medical Products, a newly merged, larger company that recently began an aggressive marketing campaign to many of Apex's clients. Apex's business model will now need to be modified to successfully compete with Mega Medical Products.

One program that will need to be eliminated is the very popular but costly tuition reimbursement program for employees. The program has allowed employees who have been working at the company for at least three years to be fully reimbursed for their tuition up to two classes per semester if they received grades of a "B" or higher. Apex has been generous with this benefit because the program has been proven to increase employees' productivity and commitment to the company. Obviously, many employees will be disappointed and, possibly, angered by this change. Because management has taken pride in the tuition reimbursement program, it has decided to support employees currently enrolled in courses or who have fewer than four courses left to receive a graduate degree. Emma knows this will be a tough writing assignment.

The Emma Davis "early draft" (Figure 9-22 on page 328) and "final draft" (Figure 9-23 on page 329) follow.

*Samples based on student submissions for the Business Writing Awards at the University of Wisconsin-Milwaukee.

CHAPTER 9 SUMMARY: WRITING ROUTINE AND SENSITIVE MESSAGES

Routine and Positive Messages

- *Cover (or transmittal)* messages accompany material sent to a recipient, identify what is being sent, and explain why it is being sent.
- *Acknowledgments* build goodwill with colleagues and clients by confirming the arrival of something they sent and expressing thanks.
- *Inquiries and responses* state clearly the information wanted, who wants it, and why. Answer inquiries by responding to all the questions or forwarding the inquiry to someone who can.
- *Sales and promotions* attract the reader's attention to a product, service, or business by arousing interest, emphasizing benefits, and inviting a response.

Sensitive and Negative Messages

- *Refusals* deny requests or give negative replies while working to maintain goodwill.
- *Complaints* use a professional tone to describe a problem and how you expect it to be corrected.
- *Adjustments* tell customers how your company intends to redress a complaint and apologize if the company is at fault.
- *Collections* work to preserve the customer relationship while collecting payment on an overdue account.

Subject line announces negative message prior to the context

Paragraph contains excessive praise and overstatement that obscures negative message

Using "anger and disappointment" suggests reactions that may not be the case—it may even prompt them

Good points, but repeats negative message ("Employees . . . will not receive tuition reimbursement. . . .")

Stating that the changes "may be temporary" (although conceivable) offers false hope to readers

Suggesting that the sacrifice will "not go unrewarded" is unjustified

APEX MEDICAL SYSTEMS
Memorandum

TO: Apex Medical Employees
FROM: Emma Davis, Human Resources Manager
DATE: October 20, 2017
SUBJECT: Cancellation of Tuition Reimbursement Program

You are all invaluable members of the Apex Medical Systems team. The beauty of being part of a team is that major problems can be solved on the large scale by working together and making small-scale changes. Recently a substantial portion of our business was lost to Mega Medical Products. Consequently, our relatively small company is struggling to remain financially viable with our current business model. To keep our company, some employee benefits must be altered. One of these benefits is the tuition reimbursement program. This program is a life-changing opportunity for our ambitious employees working to further their educations. The decision to end the program was a difficult one and will rightfully cause anger and disappointment. To relieve some of this disappointment, I will explain the changes to the program more thoroughly.

Tuition Reimbursement Changes
Conditions of the tuition reimbursement program changes include:

- Full tuition reimbursement for employees currently enrolled in courses
- Full tuition reimbursement for employees with fewer than four courses left to receive a graduate degree
- No tuition reimbursement until further notice for employees planning to enroll in courses in the future
- Resources about outside funding and scholarships for employees interested in furthering their education

If you have any questions about the changes, don't hesitate to ask.

Moving Forward
Keep in mind, these changes may be temporary. The more we can work together as a team to get our company back on track, the sooner programs like tuition reimbursement will return. Together, we can keep our small business fighting against larger businesses like Mega Medical Products. Your sacrifice during this difficult time warrants many thanks and will not go unrewarded.

Figure 9–22 Early Draft of Message

APEX MEDICAL SYSTEMS
Memorandum

TO: Apex Medical Employees
FROM: Emma Davis, Human Resources Manager *ED*
DATE: October 20, 2017
SUBJECT: Tuition Reimbursement Program

Subject line announces the topic and the focus of the message

As a member of the Apex Medical Systems team, you may know that recently a substantial portion of our business was lost to Mega Medical Products. Consequently, Apex is struggling to remain financially viable. In addition to adjusting our business model for at least the short term, some employee benefits must be altered.

Paragraph provides context and explanation for message

One of these benefits is the tuition reimbursement program, which has provided important opportunities for employees to further their education and has been a source of pride for management. Given our current budget, we made the difficult decision to discontinue the tuition reimbursement program.

Provides details that make the "difficult decision" reasonable

Currently Enrolled Employees
We hope to minimize the impact of this change on those employees currently enrolled in courses and advanced programs by providing the following:

- Full tuition reimbursement for employees currently enrolled in courses
- Full tuition reimbursement for employees with fewer than four courses left to complete a graduate program
- Resources and advice for alternatives or outside funding for employees who wish to further their education

Makes good points in fostering a positive relationship with employees

Human Resources Assistance
I would like to invite you to meet with me or one of our staff members to explore several options if you wish to continue your education. We have contacts in the student financial assistance and career development offices at several local colleges. Further, Larry Sanders in our office has experience in identifying local nontraditional programs that are particularly related to our industry.

Provides alternatives that build on last point in previous section

Contact information: Emma Davis (edavis@apex.com)
Larry Sanders (lsanders@apex.com)

Thank you for your patience as we move forward with this change. We appreciate all your hard work and dedication as a part of our team.

Offers helpful information to build goodwill and teamwork

Figure 9–23 Final Draft of Message

Writing International Correspondence

- Determine whether to use English only or to include a translated version.
- Adjust for cultural preferences in pacing and organizing ideas.
- Avoid using humor and slang.
- Proofread carefully for ambiguity and confusing sentence structure.
- Check for appropriate forms of dates, times, and measurements.

Exercises

1. Find an article in a print or an online business magazine on the importance of workplace communication and either photocopy it or attach it to an e-mail to your instructor. Write a cover letter or an e-mail message to your instructor that describes why the article is interesting or helpful to you. Review both cover letters, in this chapter, and e-mail, in Chapter 8, Writing E-mails, Memos, and Letters, before you send the message.
2. The following situations require different types of correspondence. Read *a* through *e*, and then write the letters, memos, or e-mail messages assigned by your instructor, using the proper format for each.
   a. You are writing a letter requesting a free booklet that explains how college students can apply for scholarships to study abroad. Address the letter to Nancy Reibold, the executive director of the Global Initiative Center at 1012 Third Avenue, New York, NY 10021. You learned about this booklet when you were surfing the Web and came upon the Global Initiative Center website.
   b. Assume that you are Nancy Reibold and you received the request for the booklet. You are out of copies at the moment, however, because you have received more requests than anticipated. You expect to receive more copies within two weeks. Write a response to the inquiry, explaining these circumstances. Tell the reader that you will send the booklet, titled "Study Abroad," as soon as you can—and offer the alternative of downloading a document that you will make available at your website.
   c. You are Nancy Reibold's assistant at the Global Initiative Center, and you are both angry. You have just received 10,000 copies of the booklet from the Jones Printing Company, 105 East Summit Street, New Brunswick, NJ 08910. When you opened the carton, you discovered each booklet is missing several pages. This is the second printing mistake made by Jones Printing, and the shipment is late as well, even though Robert Mason, the sales representative, had promised that you would have no problems this time. Nancy Reibold wants to "get this problem corrected immediately." Write a complaint letter to Robert Mason for Ms. Reibold to sign.
   d. Assume that you are Robert Mason. You have received the complaint letter about the printing mistake. After checking, you discover that the booklets sent to the Global Initiative Center had been subcontracted to another printing firm (ILM Printing Company) because of the backlog at Jones. You know that Jones Printing will not be billed for the booklets if you return them to ILM Printing within five working days. You decide that you must write an adjustment letter to Ms. Reibold quickly, asking her to return the booklets.
   e. Assume that you are Robert Mason. Send a convincing, detailed memo to J. R. Jones, your boss and president of Jones Printing, recommending that ILM Printing Company not be used for future subcontracting work.

3. You manage Sunny River Resort. Charles James, director of the Sunny River Business League, has requested the free use of your lodge for a two-day staff meeting. You'd like the business league to use your meeting room, but you have a problem: You charge any group $1,500 per day to use the room. You can't afford to give it away. The room has a number of fixed and variable costs required to clean, pay for lighting and air-conditioning, and supply and repair equipment. Also, what might happen if others knew you had provided the room at no cost? Write an e-mail to Mr. James selling him on the idea of using your lodge while holding to the $1,500 fee. Use tact, a positive tone, and persuasive details.
4. You are the manager of Hamon's Fine Clothing. Dr. Klaus Müller, a busy cardiac surgeon, has purchased two suits (total $1,578) from you and is six months overdue in paying for them despite several standard form notices. You'll now need to start a series of collection letters, but you want to make the pace slow. Dr. Müller is highly respected in the community. Write a series of collection letters, spacing them appropriately (date the first letter January 4).
5. You are the membership director of a fitness center that caters to professional women. You decide to bring in additional revenue by offering personal training sessions at $90 per hour and hire three fitness instructors who have been certified as personal trainers by the Aerobics and Fitness Association of America. Unfortunately, clients have been slow to sign up. Write a sales letter to existing members, announcing your fitness center's personal training program. In addition to convincing your readers of the benefits of personal training, the letter should introduce the trainers, describe their backgrounds and interests, and emphasize the extensive training they received in their certification workshops. Their training includes the following:
   - Anatomy and kinesiology
   - Fitness-assessment testing procedures (including skin-fold caliper measuring and sit-up, reach, and abdominal strength tests)
   - Weight management and nutrition for the average person as well as those with special medical needs
   - Motivation
6. Imagine that the sales letter in Exercise 5 worked well and that many people signed up with the three trainers, especially C. J., who really knows how to motivate people. However, a rumor spreads through the fitness center that she isn't certified, and members begin to complain about paying $90 an hour for an uncertified trainer. You check with a source at the Aerobics and Fitness Association of America who confirms that C. J. never completed the certification workshop. Write an adjustment letter to the members who scheduled personal training sessions with C. J. You'll want to consider that C. J. has a loyal following, but your fitness center's credibility or liability is at risk. What solution can you offer that might appease C. J.'s clients and keep your fitness center's credibility intact?
7. You have recently purchased a local high-end camera store and wish to build your business. You have a mailing list of former customers, but many of them were unhappy with the previous owner's products and service. You would like to win them back. You specialize in the highest-quality digital and single-lens reflex (SLR) cameras as well as accessories. The shop is also an authorized repair service for Nikon and Sony cameras and lenses. Your partner is highly qualified as a photographer and is an expert in digital imaging for commercial and Web applications. The community you serve is relatively affluent, but the former owner's reputation included overcharging customers and refusing to service what he sold. Your store is located on East Capitol Drive near a variety of appliance stores and restaurants, and a chain electronics store that sells cameras but is not known for quality service. You believe that satisfied customers will improve your

business. Write a sales letter, addressed to former customers, effectively promoting your services. Plan to use this letter as the basis for other promotional materials.

8. Eight years ago, you opened Tiny Tots Day Care with six children, and it has grown to a capacity of 65 children. Its reputation is so high that there is a waiting list of 78 children. As the director and owner of the center, you now face a problem that you have never before encountered. You must expel a child from the center. You need to write a letter to Mr. and Mrs. Brady, telling them that their four-year-old son, Brett, is being expelled from Tiny Tots. Since Brett entered your center, things haven't been the same. This child is not able to get along with other children. In his two months at Tiny Tots, he has bitten six children (causing one child to require stitches); kicked a teacher; and regularly scratched, hit, and pulled hair. Several parents have threatened to pull their children out of your center if Brett does not leave. Despite several conferences with Brett's parents, who seem reasonable and concerned about their son, you have observed no changes in his behavior. Write the letter to the Bradys, following the pointers for a refusal letter. Remember that this is the Brady's only child, so choose your words carefully.

9. Prepare an e-mail to inform a group of international customers of the following: Your company's newsletter will now be delivered electronically, by e-mail, and will be updated monthly instead of bimonthly. Customers who wish to receive the print version of the newsletter will be charged an annual handling fee of $30. New items listed in the newsletter can be ordered at your company's website at a 10 percent discount. Customers need to inform the company if they wish to cancel their subscriptions to the newsletter. Be sure to present these changes positively—with your customers' point of view in mind. Refer to page 277, Managing Your E-mail and Protocol, in Chapter 8, Writing E-mails, Memos, and Letters, and page 320, Writing International Correspondence, in this chapter.

10. Draft an inquiry letter to Mr. José Espinosa of the Spanish Tourist Bureau in Madrid, Spain, asking for information about work opportunities in Spain. Explain that you are interested in relocating to Spain after you graduate. To draft the letter, first gather information about both the proper protocol and the format of the letter. With the approval of your instructor, ask an instructor at your college who teaches Spanish (and would understand the form and protocol of such a letter) to comment on the appropriateness of the letter you have drafted.

Collaborative Classroom Projects

1. Form groups of five or fewer members. Your company, an office-supply business, has just mistakenly sent a promotion to all your customers offering a 20 percent discount off the total of their next order. The promotion was supposed to have offered a 20 percent discount off *the most expensive item* in their next order. After receiving input from all appropriate departments, the company president has decided the business cannot afford to grant the overall 20 percent discount. You have been instructed to draft a correction e-mail to your customers explaining the mistake and clarifying that they will be allowed to take 20 percent off only the most expensive item, not the entire order. Your company president asks that you appeal to your customers' vested interest in your company's ability to keep prices competitive and advises you to ask for their understanding of the error. Appoint a team leader and, as a group, take no more than 20 minutes to brainstorm the points you want to include in the e-mail. Then, during the next 20 minutes, draft your letters individually. As a group, select one letter that best represents your group's ideas.

2. Your class has been asked to organize a three-hour workshop on business writing for your university's continuing-education department. As a class, you have discussed this workshop with your instructor and decided that because of your course loads, your jobs, and other outside responsibilities, you are unable to volunteer to conduct a successful workshop at this time. Appoint a class leader or facilitator and a class recorder. As a group, draft a letter to the Department of Continuing Education explaining why your class cannot help. Brainstorm to develop a list of points to include in your letter. Open the letter with an explanation of the context, introducing the subject and establishing the tone. Then explain the facts, lead logically to your refusal, and conclude with goodwill to retain a positive relationship with the department. (Keep in mind that your class's refusal creates a sensitive situation for your instructor, who will be working again with the Department of Continuing Education.) After you have completed your letter, your instructor may want to give the class feedback.

Research Projects

1. Choose one of the following topics:
   - How to write effective sales letters (or, generally, how to write persuasively)
   - How to write effective refusal letters ("bad news" or "negative messages")
   - How to write effective complaint letters
   - How to respond to complaint letters

   Find at least three recent articles on your topic in an academic journal or periodical, such as the *Journal of Business Communication* or *Business Communication Quarterly.* (Your reference librarian can suggest indexes or abstracting services that will help you find articles.) Write a brief critical analysis of what you find. Compare and contrast the articles and, in conclusion, give your opinion on the article with the most helpful advice. Support your analysis with examples from the articles.

2. Assume you work for a company that is expanding to include several international branches. Research and write an informal investigative report on cultural differences in workplace communication: slang expressions and technical jargon, methods of addressing people, punctuation marks, colors, references to body parts, physical gestures, technology symbols, cultural symbols, or other aspects of written communication. You may choose one culture to compare to the United States in great detail or more than one culture to compare on different points. Before beginning your research and writing, determine your audience, your purpose, and the scope of your report.

3. Imagine that your company is eager to sell its new nonlinear video editing system internationally, starting in Canada and then moving on to Switzerland. Your marketing director, who is very industrious, has already created business cards, brochures, and other marketing materials and planned a public relations campaign that will launch in six weeks. Unfortunately, she did not do enough research into Canadian business practices to know that the country is officially bilingual and the province of Quebec requires that there be a French translation for all promotional materials. You suspect there may be similar issues with the Swiss campaign. Address the situation by doing the following:
   a. Research official language requirements and business etiquette in Canada and Switzerland. A good starting point is Executive Planet at www.executiveplanet.com.
   b. Search the Web for professional translation services and find a rough estimate for the cost of translating an eight-page brochure into French on a rush basis. Find out also what additional translations for the Swiss campaign might cost.

c. Write a memo that commends the marketing director for working hard on the project but also describes the current translation issue. Being aware of your tone, advise the director of the need to thoroughly research any countries the system will be marketed in before creating final material, and give two or three examples of other issues she may find with regard to doing business in Canada and Switzerland. Advise the director to quickly have the materials translated into French by a professional translating service and describe how much money will be allocated from the marketing department's budget for this service and why (again, be aware of your tone). Conclude your memo with a form of goodwill that encourages the director to be as industrious as she has been but to also be aware of cultural differences and the impact they can have on companies trying to do business internationally.

4. You work for a small, budget-conscious company of fewer than 50 employees. Your supervisor has asked you to investigate one of the items listed below for possible purchase by your company. Your supervisor's primary consideration is cost. Using the Web, review information provided by at least three online vendors about the product or service you are interested in. With your instructor's approval, e-mail the vendors to obtain any further information you may need. Which vendor offers the best value? Write a persuasive memo to your supervisor that explains your recommendation for the product or service. Include key points from your research, and support your recommendation with specific details. Possible products and services to investigate include the following:

   - A wireless communication system
   - A company vehicle (for purchase or lease)
   - A computer software package
   - A security system
   - An accounting or other business-related service

10 Writing Informal Reports

Contents

The successful operation of many companies and organizations depends on reports that are either circulated internally or submitted to customers, clients, and others. This chapter discusses report-writing strategies (see pages 335–338) and the most common types of informal reports:

What is a report? Although the term is used to refer to hundreds of different types of written communications, a *report* can be defined as an organized presentation of factual information prepared for a specific audience.

Reports fall into two broad categories: formal and informal. Formal reports, described in detail in Chapter 11, Writing Formal Reports, generally grow out of projects that are large in scope and require the collaboration of many people. They may range from several dozen to hundreds of pages and usually include a table of contents and other devices to aid the reader because of their length and scope of coverage. Informal reports, however, generally run from a few paragraphs to a few pages, though some are longer. They include only the essential elements of a report: an introduction, a body, conclusions, and, when appropriate, recommendations. Because of their brevity and limited scope, informal reports may be written as letters, e-mails, or memos attached to e-mails (for recipients outside a company) or as e-memos, e-mails, or intranet postings (for recipients within an organization).

Planning and Writing Informal Reports

Informal reports often describe specific incidents, note the progress of ongoing activities or projects, or summarize the results of a completed project or investigation. They may also recommend follow-up work that should be performed based on the conditions described.

Considering Your Audience

◆ *For additional guidance on audience analysis, see pages 6–7 in Chapter 1, Understanding the Workplace Writing Context: A Case Study.*

As with all workplace writing, first consider the makeup of your audience. An informal report is almost always written for a specific small group of readers (or a single reader)—usually at their request. As a result, readers will likely be familiar with the subject of the report, making it easier for you to determine how much background information to provide and how much specialized or technical language to use. Note, for example, that the writer of the periodic report in Figure 10–3 on pages 343–344 assumes it's unnecessary to spell out the acronyms used throughout the report (SVR, LAR, ERCAR, AREDOT, etc.) because its readers are familiar with them. Without such knowledge, readers would be slowed significantly as they hunted for the meanings of these abbreviations.

Collecting Information

◆ *For more on note-taking, see pages 176–177 in Chapter 6, Conducting Research for a Document.*

◆ *For more on organizing information, see Chapter 2, Planning a Document.*

For a report to be effective, you need to include all the information that will help you meet your objective (such as describing the status of an office remodeling project or explaining the need to upgrade a staff training program) and address your reader's needs (such as keeping a project on schedule or having enough data to make a decision). To achieve these goals, keep notes through every stage of the activity on which you will be reporting. Otherwise, you may have trouble obtaining or trying to remember information when the time comes to write the report. Because many companies use Web-based report templates to collect and compile information, especially about incidents, keep in mind the required fields that you may need to complete as you collect information.

CONSIDERING AUDIENCE AND PURPOSE

Planning and Evaluating Informal Reports

- Who is the audience for your report? Are the audience members knowledgeable about the topic?
- What specifically have your readers requested? Are there legal or rule-based requirements at your company or organization that determine the information needed in your report?
- Have you selected the right medium—e-mail, memo, company report templates, website, or letter—for your readers?
- Does your introduction frame the topic for your audience and provide necessary background information?
- Do your graphics depict the findings accurately and clearly for your intended audience?
- Is the report well organized and sufficient in scope so that your audience can understand and interpret your findings, conclusions, and recommendations?

Your notes should record, in abbreviated form, the background information that will go into your report. Do not make your notes so brief, however, that you forget what you intended when you wrote them. When you are ready to draft your report, organize your notes into a sequence that makes sense from the perspective of your objective and audience. If you are working with an outline, add your notes to the appropriate places to flesh it out.

Parts of the Informal Report

Most informal reports have three or four main parts: the introduction, the body, conclusions, and recommendations. For routine reports, the introduction may be replaced by an opening that simply announces the subject — "Monthly Customer Services, June 2016." Likewise, the conclusion may consist of a closing statement or sentence signaling the end of the report — "If you wish to discuss the summary of sales prospects for June, please contact me directly."

Introduction

The introduction announces the subject of the report, explains its purpose, and, when appropriate, names anybody who assisted with or provided information for the report. It may describe the scope of information covered, any limitations of the topic, or the reason for the amount of detail presented. A trip report, for example, could note the facilities or customers visited, the reason for the visits, and an explanation for any delays or problems encountered. It may also provide any essential background information about the subject of the report. The introduction may also concisely summarize any conclusions, findings, or recommendations made in the report. An overview is useful because it saves your readers time by providing essential information at a glance and helps focus their thinking for the discussion that follows.

◆ *For a discussion of openings and closings, see pages 87–90 in Chapter 3, Drafting a Document.*

Body

The body presents a clearly organized account of the report's subject — the results of a market survey, the findings of a test carried out, the status of a construction project, and so on. The amount of detail you include in the body depends on your objective, the complexity of your subject, and your readers' familiarity with the subject. This information is frequently supported by tables, graphs, drawings, and other visuals to clarify ideas and concepts in ways that words alone cannot, as well as to save space.

◆ *For detailed advice on creating and using visuals, see Chapter 7, Designing Documents and Visuals.*

Conclusions and Recommendations

The conclusion summarizes your findings and tells readers what you think the significance of those findings may be. The conclusion may make a judgment or prediction, issue a call for action, or suggest ideas for further action. It should not go outside the scope of topics discussed in the report.

Recommendations, when included, are sometimes combined with conclusions in one section at the end of the report. In this section, you recommend a course of action that you believe is warranted by your findings. Recommendations can cover a broad range of options, from suggesting new safety procedures based on findings about an accident, to developing new products or marketing campaigns based on consumer surveys, to hiring new employees as a result of growing business.

Reaching logical conclusions in workplace writing requires using trustworthy evidence, especially when making recommendations based on your conclusions. However, illogical, biased, or emotional thinking about evidence can adversely influence the conclusions and recommendations you reach. To avoid these pitfalls, review the following guidance:

- Explaining Cause and Effect (Chapter 3, pages 85–86)
- Evaluating Sources (Chapter 6, pages 172–184)

Types of Informal Reports

Because there are so many different types of informal reports and because the categories sometimes overlap (a trip report, for example, might also be a progress report), it would be unrealistic to attempt to study or try to itemize every type. However, it is possible to become familiar with report writing in general and to examine some of the most frequently written kinds of informal reports in the workplace:

- Progress reports
- Periodic reports
- Investigative reports
- Incident reports
- Trip reports
- Test reports

Progress and Periodic Reports

Both progress reports and periodic reports are written to inform decision makers about the status of work performed over the course of an ongoing project. The chief difference between them is when they are written. The progress report is issued at certain milestones during a project. Construction and manufacturing projects, for example, must be done in stages: Whether the project involves adding a sunroom to a private residence or building a deep-sea oil-drilling rig, it follows a coordinated sequence. *Progress reports* describe in detail the status of activities at each stage in the sequence: work in progress, work completed, special problems or delays, costs, worker availability, and anything else that may affect the schedule for completing the project. *Periodic reports*, sometimes called status reports, detail the status of an ongoing project at regular intervals — weekly, monthly, quarterly. Both types of reports may be required for work being performed within an organization or by an outside contractor or consultant. In some of these organizations, progress and periodic reports may be completed electronically. The information for the report is collected through a website or on a company-provided template and is compiled electronically. Its availability is then announced to the appropriate audience.

Progress Reports

The purpose of a progress report is to keep others — usually management or a client — informed of the status of significant milestones during a project. For a companywide computer-network upgrade, for example, the significant stages or milestones could include completion of electrical power enhancements; delivery, installation, and testing of hardware and software; and completion of employee training.

The projects most likely to generate progress reports are long-term and fairly complex. The construction of a building, the development of a new product, the opening of a branch office in another part of town, and a major redesign of a company's website are examples of such projects. Progress reports are usually specified in the contract for a project that will take weeks, months, or longer to complete.

Progress reports allow managers and clients to keep track of the project and to make any necessary adjustments in assignments, schedules, and budget allocations while the project is under way. Such reports can, on occasion, avert crises. If a hospital had planned to open a new wing in February, for instance, but a shortage of wallboard caused a two-month lag in construction, a progress report would alert hospital managers to the delay in time for them to make alternative plans.

All reports issued during the life of a project should be submitted in the same format to make it easier for readers to recognize at a glance where they need to focus their attention. Reports sent outside the company are normally prepared as letters; those circulated within the company can be written as memos attached to e-mails. The first report in the series should identify the project in detail and specify what materials will be used and what procedures will be followed throughout the project. Later reports in the series contain only a transitional introduction that briefly reviews the work discussed in the previous report. The body of the reports should describe in detail the current status of the project. Every report should end with any conclusions or recommendations — for instance, alterations in schedule, materials, or procedures. Collectively, the reports provide a complete picture of the development of a given project. This "timeline" often proves useful for planning future projects, making the progress report even more valuable.

In the example shown in Figure 10–1, a contractor reports to the county administrator on the progress in renovating the county courthouse. Notice that the emphasis is on meeting specified costs and schedules. In Figure 10–2 on page 341, a real-world progress report created by a second-grade teacher spells out her expectations for a student and how they are being met and sometimes even surpassed. She also describes current classroom work, which allows the parent to consider the report in the context of the class curriculum.

DIGITAL TIP: Creating Styles and Templates for Informal Reports

Most word-processing programs enable you to create templates that automate the visual appearance of text elements such as headings, paragraphs, and lists throughout a document. Once you specify your styles, save the template and use it each time you create a report. Keep in mind that many organizations may already provide such templates for informal and formal reports, so check before you create your own.

Hobard Construction Company
9032 Salem Avenue
Lubbock, TX 79409

www.hobardcc.com
(808) 769-0832
Fax: (808) 769-5327

August 14, 2016

Walter M. Wazuski
County Administrator
109 Grand Avenue
Manchester, NH 03103

Dear Mr. Wazuski:

Subject line identifies topic

Subject: Courthouse Progress Report 8 for July 31, 2016

Project status summary

The renovation of the County Courthouse is progressing on schedule and within budget. Although the cost of certain materials is higher than our original bid indicated, we expect to complete the project without exceeding the estimated costs because the speed with which the project is being completed will reduce overall labor expenses.

Detailed status of project

Costs

Materials used to date have cost $178,600, and labor costs have been $293,000 (including some subcontracted plumbing). Our estimate for the remainder of the materials is $159,000; remaining labor costs should not exceed $400,000.

Work Completed

As of July 31, we finished the installation of the circuit-breaker panels and meters, the level-one service outlets, and all the subfloor wiring. The upgrading of the courtroom, the upgrading of the records-storage room, and the replacement of the air-conditioning units are in the preliminary stages.

Work Scheduled

We have scheduled the upgrading of the courtroom to take place from August 28 to October 9, the upgrading of the records-storage room from October 13 to November 17, and the replacement of the air-conditioning units from November 24 to December 17. We see no difficulty in having the job finished by the scheduled date of December 22.

Sincerely yours,

Tran Nuguélen

Tran Nuguélen
ntran@hobardcc.com

Figure 10–1 Progress Report (Letter to a Client)

PROGRESS REPORT

Student: Jared Greene
Teacher: Melissa Holman
Report: December 2016

Melissa Holman

It has been a pleasure to welcome Jared to second grade. He is a responsible member of our classroom community, his behavior at school is respectful and appropriate, and he is a student who can be counted on to do the right thing. At all times, he works hard, takes pride in his work, and is eager to share what he has accomplished with teachers, family members, and classmates.

Introduction summarizes student's evaluation

Reading: The reading curriculum is taught through the structure of Reading Workshop. This includes reading independently, reading with a teacher, reading with other students in a weekly reading group, and taking lessons on reading strategies and phonics. . . . Jared is an enthusiastic participant during group meetings. He likes to discuss literature, and he frequently makes text connections and predictions during group mini-lessons.

Writing and Spelling: During Writers' Workshop, instruction has focused on generating story ideas; developing one idea into a story with a beginning, a middle, and an end; "reading like a writer" to notice choices authors make in the structure and language of their published works; and expanding "small moments" into detailed stories. Jared is working on a research piece about the Wampanoag (Native American) language. Jared has a strong sense of story structure (beginning, middle, end) as well as many of the conventions of nonfiction (table of contents, index, glossary).

Mathematics: We have completed three units in our Everyday Math curriculum, incorporating lessons in money, telling time, addition and subtraction, place value, and "number stories" (word problems). Mathematical thinking is an area of true strength for Jared. He understands concepts of operation (addition, subtraction, etc.) and demonstrates comfort with basic and more complex math facts. He is growing increasingly limber with his use of numbers and is able to see that there are many strategies for solving any given problem.

Social Studies and Science: We are wrapping up the work of our first three Charles River research units, which focused on river geology and erosion, mapping, and the water cycle. Jared has been an active participant in our Charles River research. He is naturally inquisitive, enthusiastic about the material, and careful in his hypotheses and observations. He is able to record detailed notes and enjoys predicting the outcome of experiments and projects.

Body assesses student's progress in each area of the curriculum

It has been wonderful to have Jared in my classroom this year. I look forward to fostering his intellectual and social development throughout the year.

Conclusion ends with positive assessment and looks ahead to the remaining school year

Figure 10–2 Progress Report (Elementary Education Teacher)

Periodic Reports

Periodic reports (also called *activity reports*) are written by employees and managers to their supervisors at regular intervals — daily, weekly, monthly, quarterly, annually — to record or describe the status of ongoing workplace tasks. Many kinds of routine status information do not require a narrative explanation and can be recorded on forms, entered into networked computer databases or spreadsheets, or printed as graphs or tables in the body of a written report. Examples include human resources, accounting, and inventory records; production and distribution figures; sales numbers; and travel and task logs.

Other types of tasks, like ongoing projects or initiatives, may require a brief narrative description to document changes over time. Employees routinely submit status reports (also called *activity reports*) to their supervisors about their ongoing projects. In some organizations, periodic reports are fully automated: For assembly-line positions in which each day ends with a review of work done, periodic reports are computer-generated to summarize the day's work.

Most other kinds of periodic reports seldom run longer than a page or two. Like progress reports, they are most often written as memos or e-mail messages within an organization and as letters when sent to clients and customers outside an organization. Quarterly and annual status reports, because of their scope, are usually longer and may even be submitted to senior management as formal reports, with a cover page, table of contents, and separate sections describing the activities of each subdivision of a company or an organization.

◆ *For a discussion of the scope and format of formal reports, see Chapter 11, Writing Formal Reports.*

One- and two-page periodic reports can be organized in a variety of ways, depending on your reader's reporting requirements. Once you have established a format and an organization, create a template and use it consistently for each subsequent report.

The sample periodic report in Figure 10–3 is sent monthly from a company's district sales manager to the regional sales manager as an attachment to a brief e-mail message. Notice that there is no traditional opening and closing, both of which are superfluous because the report is routine; that is, the report goes to the same person every month and covers the same topics. It also goes to a high-level manager who receives many such reports each month, so he or she does not have time to read

DESIGNING YOUR DOCUMENT
Formatting Progress and Periodic Reports

- For internal distribution, send the report as a memo. If an organization requires the use of an existing template or provides a website through which to submit the report, then opt for the method provided.
- If the report will be sent to clients or others outside your organization, format it as a letter, unless they prefer receiving an e-mail attachment.
- Keep narrative information brief and use headings to organize the content.
- Present routine and numerical data in tables or graphs.
- Create a template and use the same format — headings, tables, organization, and so on — for each consecutive report in a series.

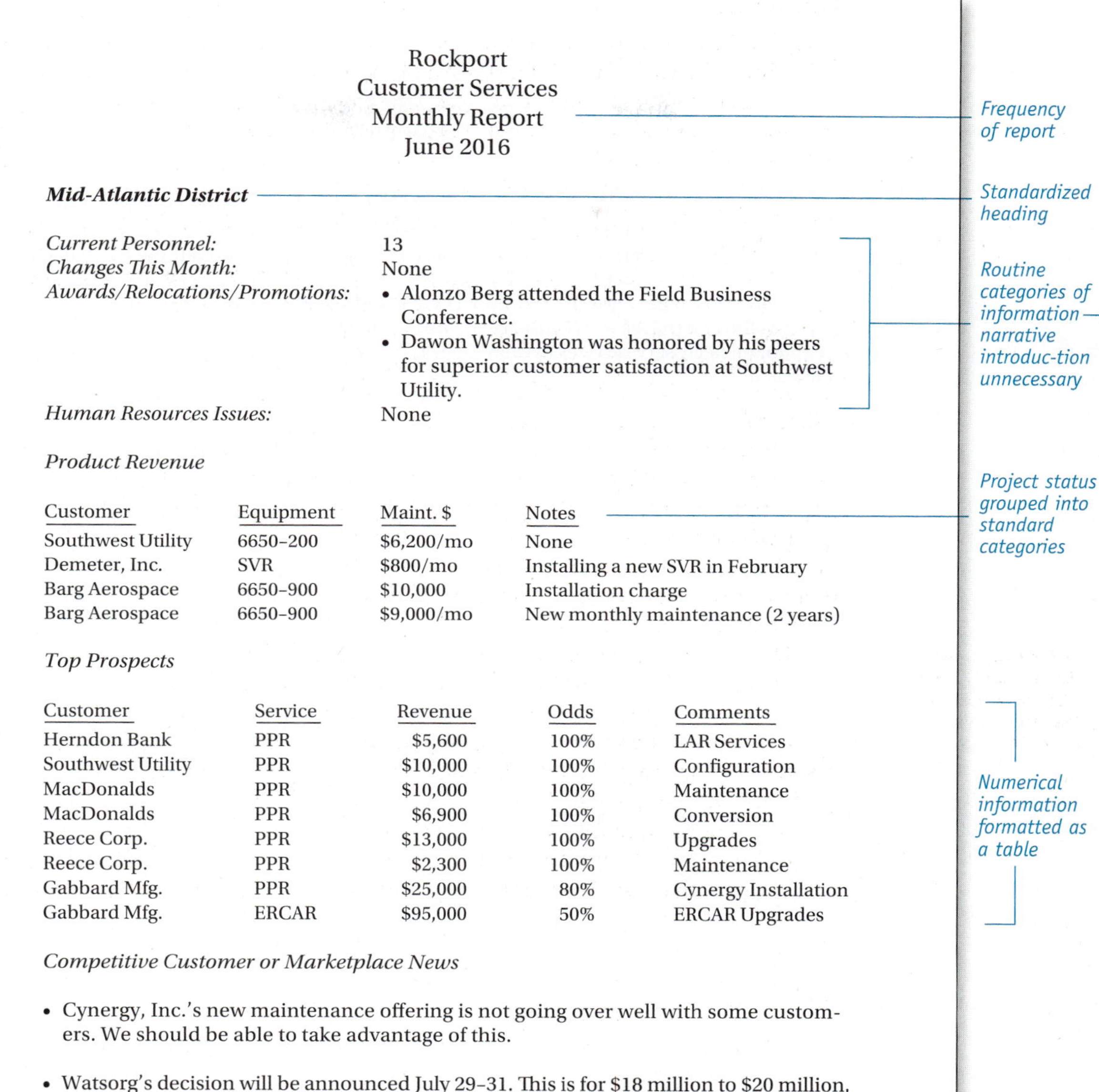

Rockport
Customer Services
Monthly Report
June 2016

Mid-Atlantic District

Current Personnel:	13
Changes This Month:	None
Awards/Relocations/Promotions:	• Alonzo Berg attended the Field Business Conference. • Dawon Washington was honored by his peers for superior customer satisfaction at Southwest Utility.
Human Resources Issues:	None

Product Revenue

Customer	Equipment	Maint. $	Notes
Southwest Utility	6650-200	$6,200/mo	None
Demeter, Inc.	SVR	$800/mo	Installing a new SVR in February
Barg Aerospace	6650-900	$10,000	Installation charge
Barg Aerospace	6650-900	$9,000/mo	New monthly maintenance (2 years)

Top Prospects

Customer	Service	Revenue	Odds	Comments
Herndon Bank	PPR	$5,600	100%	LAR Services
Southwest Utility	PPR	$10,000	100%	Configuration
MacDonalds	PPR	$10,000	100%	Maintenance
MacDonalds	PPR	$6,900	100%	Conversion
Reece Corp.	PPR	$13,000	100%	Upgrades
Reece Corp.	PPR	$2,300	100%	Maintenance
Gabbard Mfg.	PPR	$25,000	80%	Cynergy Installation
Gabbard Mfg.	ERCAR	$95,000	50%	ERCAR Upgrades

Competitive Customer or Marketplace News

- Cynergy, Inc.'s new maintenance offering is not going over well with some customers. We should be able to take advantage of this.
- Watsorg's decision will be announced July 29–31. This is for $18 million to $20 million, going either to us or to Cynergy. The problem is that we finished our "best and final" presentation in the first week of February, and Watsorg gave Cynergy an extension to the end

Figure 10–3 Periodic Report

Monthly Report, Mid-Atlantic District June 2016

of the month. Dragging this out increases Cynergy's odds of winning. However, the last word is that the negotiations are not going well with Cynergy, so we are keeping our fingers crossed.

- AREDOT is installing the largest Saki tape library system in the world. The sales rep said that Saki had been working with a company to develop a "virtual tape system" when Embry was sold to Jordan. This resulted in Jordan not getting the contract.

- Charlestown Customer Services met with a CARL team director from Columbus, Ohio, to discuss future services with CARL. He is considering Rockport as the prime contractor for all necessary services in Charlestown. He will base his decision on the cost analysis.

Headings announce topic change

Significant Wins and Accomplishments

- Hector Martinez convinced Barg Aerospace to acquire two additional 6650A–900s from us on a rental basis with a two-year maintenance contract worth $9,000 per month per machine. The installation team has installed the second 900 and will install the third in the coming weeks.

- Charlestown Customer Services completed installation of a Cynergy 2063 and a Rockport 1006 at Ft. Lee, Virginia. We partnered with Rathbone Corporation to win the business.

Product Issues

Secard performance issues have continued from last month. We applied new code with high hopes, but no improvement was noted by the customer. Currently, ERT traces are running to gather more information. The customer is getting very concerned with this issue, and they are our only Secard customer in Charlestown.

2

Figure 10–3 Periodic Report *(continued)*

unnecessary narrative. Because this report is written to someone completely familiar with the background details of the projects discussed, the district sales manager can write a spare narrative with many shorthand references to equipment, customers, and project status. For example, the writer mentions a "best and final" presentation to Watsorg rather than writing that Rockport, his company, has presented its final sales proposal to Watsorg, Inc., for equipment and services. The writer need not describe the details of the project because the regional sales manager is already familiar with them. Such an abbreviated narrative is appropriate for the intended reader.

Investigative Reports

Investigative reports are systematic studies or research assessments of something or someone. In law enforcement, industrial, and medical settings, they are used to examine how and why crimes, accidents, disease outbreaks, and the like occurred, and they may include recommendations about how to prevent their recurrence. In business settings, investigative reports are written to examine business trends, product and investment opportunities, alternative procedures for performing a task, employee incentives to spur productivity, tax strategies, fleet vehicle purchases, and the like. Investigative reports are usually prepared as *e-memos* if written within an organization and as *letters* if written by an outside consultant. They may also be written in the narrative section of routine forms. The results of long, complex investigations are usually written as formal reports. For memo and letter reports, open with a brief introductory summary of the topic of the investigation, any relevant background as to why the investigation was necessary, and the name of the person who requested it (someone inside your organization or an outside client). Then, in the body of the memo or letter, describe the extent of or method used for your investigation. Finally, state your findings and any recommendations based on the findings.

◆ *For guidance on writing and formatting letters and memos, see Chapter 8, Writing E-mails, Memos, and Letters.*

In the example shown in Figure 10–4 on pages 346–347, a store manager has investigated three alternative ways of reducing shoplifting in his store and recommended the one most suitable for the store's size and budget.

◆ *For guidance on writing and organizing formal reports, see Chapter 11, Writing Formal Reports.*

Incident Reports

Incidents involving personal injuries, accidents, and work stoppages (those caused by equipment failures, worker illnesses, and so on) occur in many industrial and construction settings. Problematic episodes may also occur in health-care, social-work, and criminal-justice settings. Every such incident must be reported so that management can determine its cause and take any necessary steps to prevent or reduce the impact of a recurrence. An incident report — also called an accident report, depending on the situation — is the record of a mechanical breakdown, a medical emergency, or a personnel confrontation in an institution. The report may be used by the police or by a court of law in establishing guilt or liability.

The report is usually written by the person in charge of the site where the incident occurred and addressed to his or her superior. (Some organizations have printed forms for specific types of reports, which include a section for the writer to

Green Department Stores Memo

To: William Bernardi, Regional Manager
From: Julius Chernoff, Department Manager JC
Date: September 24, 2016
Subject: Shoplifting at Store E-5150

Introduction and background

As we have discussed over the last several months, shoplifting at Store E-5150 has increased since the store opened one year ago this month. Although we have budgeted $30,000 a year for shoplifting losses, our monthly inventory check shows that we have lost $47,800 in merchandise this year. The loss was especially evident during the summer months. It is time to take action to reverse this trend.

Section heading and overview of options

Proposed Solutions

My staff and I have researched several options for minimizing shoplifting in our store. They include hiring security guards, using strategically placed security cameras in the store, and using undercover employees. In investigating options available to us, we considered effectiveness, convenience, and cost.

First option investigated, with findings

Security Guards

We first considered hiring security guards. I met with the president of Hall Security on July 26. Hall Security is a local company that has been in business ten years. I also talked to other store managers in the area who have contracts with Hall Security — all are very pleased with the service and its effectiveness. They believe that the presence of uniformed security guards in their stores discourages theft. The managers surveyed report shoplifting reduction rates of from 50 to 70 percent. I can provide you with detailed data from these interviews at your request.

If we decide to have one security guard on duty during all store hours, we would pay a flat monthly rate of $4,300. One guard on duty from 4 p.m. until 10 p.m. daily, our busiest hours, would cost $2,100 a month. We are not considering the option of a night guard because we have not had any problems with break-in burglaries after hours.

Second option investigated, with findings

Security Cameras

We next considered the use of security cameras. The cameras provide a record of thefts in progress and make prosecuting shoplifters much easier once they're caught. The technicians from TSC, Inc., a camera service company, visited our store on August 6. They studied the floor plan to determine the most effective placement of cameras throughout the store. They recommend six cameras placed so that we have a view of the whole store at all times. We would need to purchase a single monitor that would display each camera's view

Figure 10–4 Investigative Report (Memo with Recommendations)

William Bernardi 2 September 24, 2016

on a rotational basis every ten seconds. The monitor would be located in the store manager's office where I or, in my absence, someone I designate, can observe activity throughout the store's retail space. The videotapes can be kept for a week and then recorded over.

TSC, Inc., would install the system and train our employees to operate it. TSC, Inc., also provides a five-year on-site service warranty for the cameras and monitor. They make service calls to the store during business hours within four hours of being called. Total cost, including installation, will be $7,500. We were impressed with the knowledge, experience, and professionalism of the TSC representatives. They provided data for stores comparable to ours that showed an average 60 to 75 percent drop in the incidence of shoplifting after cameras were installed. I called several store managers where the cameras are in use, and they verified these results.

Impressions of second option

Undercover Employees

The third option examined is the use of undercover employees. This option involves having store employees who pose as customers as they stroll through the store monitoring customers for shoplifting. We estimate that this option would require two employees each shift. They would alternate between their regular duties, such as stocking shelves and performing inventory-control tasks. If we also employ security guards, these two units could work in conjunction to help discourage theft.

Third option investigated, with findings

However, the option has some risks associated with it. It would require that our employees receive training in the legal rights of customers and could potentially put our employees at risk in encounters with criminals. Hall Security can provide training over a one-week period at a cost of $1,500 per employee.

Risks associated with option

Recommendations

Section heading and recommendations based on findings

After completing our research on these possibilities for theft prevention, my staff and I believe that the best option is the installation of security cameras. After comparing the cost of the system with the amount of merchandise we are losing, we believe that the expense is worth the investment. Once the system is installed, there will be negligible expense in its use and maintenance. Our research shows that theft has declined in more than 90 percent of the stores that have had security cameras installed. Pending our approval, TSC, Inc., can install the system in four days. Once it is installed, we would evaluate the effectiveness of the system on a monthly basis, and I would provide you with a monthly status report. I look forward to your assessment of this recommendation.

Figure 10–4 Investigative Report (Memo with Recommendations) *(continued)* describe in detail what happened.) Make certain that all circumstances about the incident are known before writing the report. Figure 10–5 shows an incident report written by a safety officer after interviewing all the people involved in a work-site accident.

ETHICS NOTE: Be Thorough, Accurate, and Objective When Writing Incident Reports Because insurance claims, workers' compensation awards, and even lawsuits may hinge on the information contained in an incident report, be sure to include precise times, dates, locations, treatment of injuries, names of any witnesses, and any other crucial information. Be thorough and accurate in your analysis of the problem and support any judgments or conclusions with facts. Be objective: Always use a neutral tone and avoid assigning blame. If you speculate about the cause of the problem, make clear to your reader that you are speculating. (Note the factual detail and objective tone in Figure 10–5.)

WRITER'S CHECKLIST

Writing an Incident Report

✔ On the subject line of your memo, state what you are reporting:

SUBJECT: Personal-Injury Accident in Section A-40.

✔ Write a brief introductory summary of the incident.

✔ In the body of your memo:

- State exactly when and where the accident, breakdown, emergency, or conflict took place.
- Describe any physical injury or any property damage that occurred.
- Itemize any expenses that resulted from the incident (for example, an injured employee may have missed a number of workdays or an equipment failure may have caused a disruption in service to the company's customers).
- Include precise data on times, dates, location, treatment of injuries, names of any witnesses, and any other crucial information.

✔ In your conclusion, provide a detailed analysis of what you believe caused the trouble.

- Avoid condemnation or blame; be thorough, exact, and objective, and support any opinion you offer with facts.
- Avoid correcting the conditions that may have led to the incident until you have heard from the workers' compensation group or from those responsible for reviewing details of the incident.

✔ Include your recommendations for preventing further incidents (such as increased training in safety precautions, improved equipment, and protective clothing). If you are speculating on the cause of the accident, make sure that this is clear to the reader.

Evaluating and Revising an Incident Report

✔ Who is the audience for the report?

✔ Do you need to interview workers or others about the accident or incident?

Consolidated Energy, Inc.

To: Marvin Lundquist, Vice President
Administrative Services
From: Kalo Katarlan, Safety Officer KK
Field Service Operations
Date: August 20, 2016
Subject: Field Service Employee Accident on August 4, 2016

The following is an initial report of an accident that occurred on Monday, August 4, 2016, involving John Markley, and that resulted in two days of lost time.

How accident was evaluated

Accident Summary

John Markley stopped by a rewiring job on German Road. Chico Ruiz was working there, stringing new wire, and John was checking with Chico about the materials he wanted for framing a pole. Some tree trimming had been done in the area, and John offered to help remove some of the debris by loading it into the pickup truck he was driving. While John was loading branches into the bed of the truck, a piece broke off in his right hand and struck his right eye.

What happened, who was involved, what injury resulted

Accident Details

1. John's right eye was struck by a piece of tree branch. John had just undergone laser surgery on his right eye on Friday, July 31, to reattach his retina.
2. John immediately covered his right eye with his hand, and Chico Ruiz gave him a paper towel with ice to cover his eye and help ease the pain.

Events listed in order of occurrence

7. On Thursday, August 6, John returned to his eye surgeon. Although bruised, his eye was not damaged, and the surgically reattached retina was still in place.

Recommendations

To prevent a recurrence of such an accident, the Safety Department will require the following actions in the future:

- When working around and moving debris such as tree limbs or branches, all service crew employees must wear safety eyewear with side shields.
- All service crew employees must always consider the possibility of shock for an injured employee. If crew members cannot leave the job site to care for the injured employee, someone on the crew must call for assistance from the Service Center. The Service Center phone number is printed in each service crew member's handbook.

List of corrective actions

FIGURE 10–5 Incident Report (Memo with Recommendations)

- ✔ Are your notes thorough enough to accurately summarize the accident or incident?
- ✔ Have you organized your thoughts into a concise outline to guide your writing?
- ✔ Does the introduction state the subject and purpose of the report?
- ✔ Does the body include sufficient detail to lead the reader to the same findings and conclusions that you present?
- ✔ Do the findings and conclusions logically follow from the details described in the body?
- ✔ Do the recommendations make sense based on your conclusions?

Trip Reports

A trip report (also called a *site-visit report*) provides a permanent record of a business trip and its activities or accomplishments: sites visited, customers and clients met, tasks completed, problems encountered and solved. The report provides managers with essential information and can enable other employees to benefit from the information, such as the need for revised procedures, equipment or design upgrades, customer preferences, and more.

A trip report is normally written as an e-mail message and addressed to an immediate supervisor, as shown in Figure 10–6. On the subject line, give the destination (or purpose) and dates of the trip. Explain the purpose of the trip in a brief introductory summary and note whom or where you visited and what you accomplished. The report should be organized in chronological order and devote a brief section to each major event. Include a heading for each section, although you needn't give equal space to each event; instead, elaborate on the more important events. End the report with any appropriate conclusions and recommendations. Finally, if required, attach a record of expenses to the trip report.

Test Reports

Test reports, also called laboratory reports for tests performed in laboratories, record the results of tests and experiments. Tests that form the basis of these reports are not limited to any particular occupation; they are common in many fields, from chemistry to fire science, from metallurgy to medical technology, and include studies on vehicles, blood, mercury thermometers, pudding mixes, smoke detectors — the list goes on. They are conducted in many settings, from laboratories and test kitchens to vehicle test tracks and field engineering sites. Information collected in testing may be used to upgrade or discontinue products or to streamline testing or manufacturing procedures.

Because accuracy is the essential goal of a test report, take careful notes while you are performing the test. Then state your findings in specific, precise, and unambiguous language. Test procedures and findings are usually written in passive voice: "arsenic values *are based* on wet-weight determination," "airborne asbestos *was collected*. . . ." Use tables, graphs, or illustrations if they will help interpret the findings. As with other reports, the format in which test reports are prepared depends on the intended

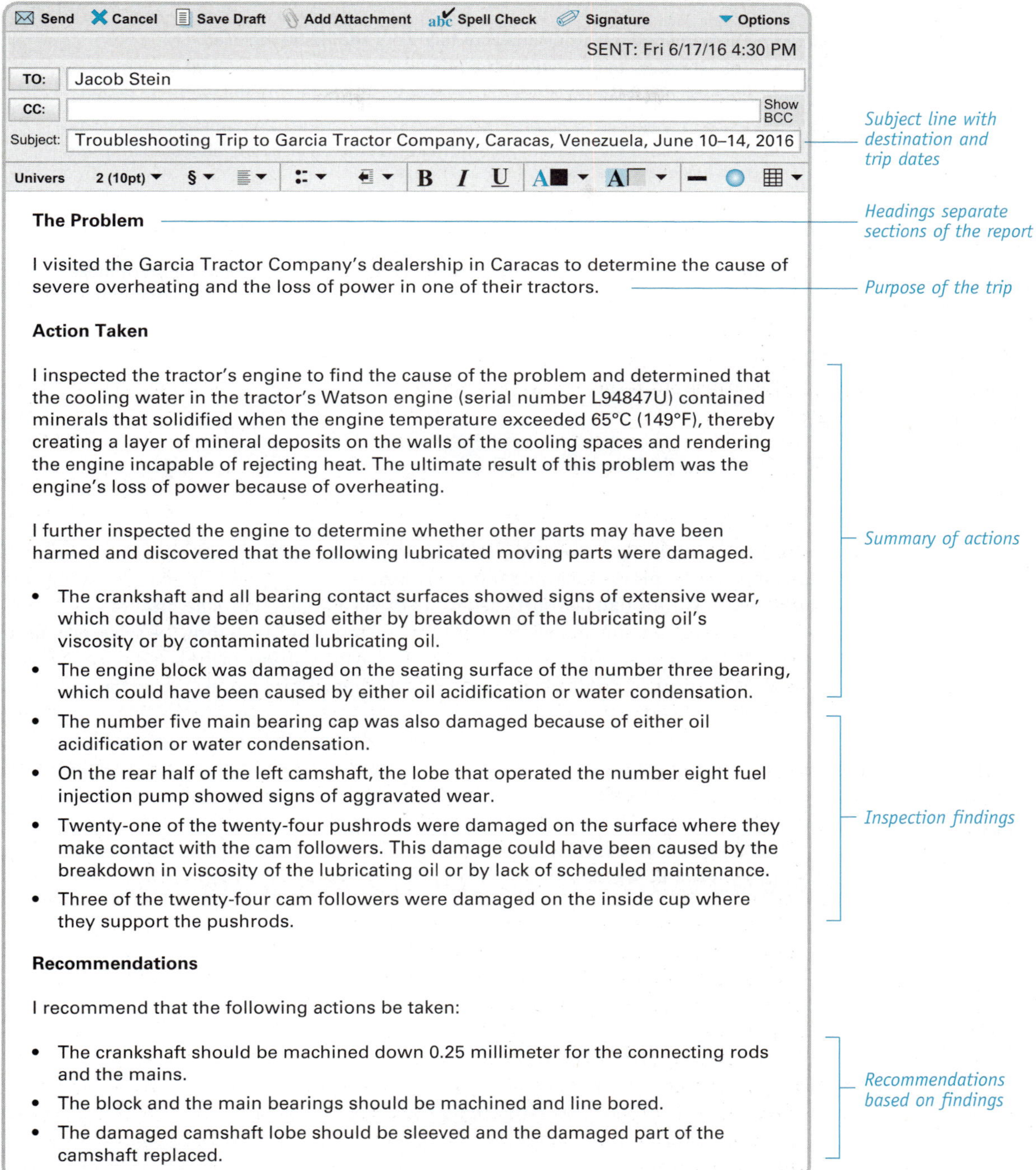

Send
Cancel
Save Draft
Add Attachment
Spell Check
Signature
Options
SENT: Fri 6/17/16 4:30 PM
TO: Jacob Stein
CC:
Show BCC
Subject: Troubleshooting Trip to Garcia Tractor Company, Caracas, Venezuela, June 10–14, 2016
Univers
2 (10pt)

The Problem

I visited the Garcia Tractor Company's dealership in Caracas to determine the cause of severe overheating and the loss of power in one of their tractors.

Action Taken

I inspected the tractor's engine to find the cause of the problem and determined that the cooling water in the tractor's Watson engine (serial number L94847U) contained minerals that solidified when the engine temperature exceeded 65°C (149°F), thereby creating a layer of mineral deposits on the walls of the cooling spaces and rendering the engine incapable of rejecting heat. The ultimate result of this problem was the engine's loss of power because of overheating.

I further inspected the engine to determine whether other parts may have been harmed and discovered that the following lubricated moving parts were damaged.

• The crankshaft and all bearing contact surfaces showed signs of extensive wear, which could have been caused either by breakdown of the lubricating oil's viscosity or by contaminated lubricating oil.
• The engine block was damaged on the seating surface of the number three bearing, which could have been caused by either oil acidification or water condensation.
• The number five main bearing cap was also damaged because of either oil acidification or water condensation.
• On the rear half of the left camshaft, the lobe that operated the number eight fuel injection pump showed signs of aggravated wear.
• Twenty-one of the twenty-four pushrods were damaged on the surface where they make contact with the cam followers. This damage could have been caused by the breakdown in viscosity of the lubricating oil or by lack of scheduled maintenance.
• Three of the twenty-four cam followers were damaged on the inside cup where they support the pushrods.

Recommendations

I recommend that the following actions be taken:

• The crankshaft should be machined down 0.25 millimeter for the connecting rods and the mains.
• The block and the main bearings should be machined and line bored.
• The damaged camshaft lobe should be sleeved and the damaged part of the camshaft replaced.

Subject line with destination and trip dates
Headings separate sections of the report
Purpose of the trip
Summary of actions
Inspection findings
Recommendations based on findings

Figure 10–6 Trip Report Information adapted from a report prepared by Johan DeBeer of Mitsubishi Engines, N.A.

- The damaged pushrods and cam followers should be replaced.
- The vibration damper should be remanufactured to prevent heat developed by the engine from solidifying the viscous oil and nullifying the damping action.

I requested a sample of used oil from the engine, but the oil had been drained and discarded before my arrival. I recommend that the oil viscosity be tested after the engine has been operated for several hours.

Suggested Follow-Up

Additional recommendation

Because Garcia Motors uses many additional Watson engines that potentially could also be damaged, I strongly recommend sending a detailed report of these problems to the client and commissioning a set of Spanish-language maintenance guides for current and future customers in Venezuela.

Sincerely,

Wilhelm Kurtz
Engine Specialist

Figure 10–6 Trip Report (*continued*)

audience: letters for customers outside your organization and e-mails or intranet postings for employees within your organization. Test reports can also be submitted electronically, through a Web-based form, or via a digital template file.

◆ *For guidance in preparing visuals, see Chapter 7, Designing Documents and Visuals.*

On the subject line, identify the test you are reporting, including the reference number, if any, assigned to the project or specific test. If the purpose of the test is not obvious to your reader, explain it in the body of the report. Then, if it is helpful to your reader, specify the testing procedures or methodology. You need not give a detailed explanation of how the test was performed, but a summary is usually expected to give a general idea of the testing methods. Next, present the data — the results of the test. If an interpretation of the results is expected, furnish such an analysis in your conclusion. Close the report with any recommendations based on test results.

◆ *For a discussion of the use of active versus passive voice, see pages 102–103, Chapter 4, Revising a Document.*

Figure 10–7 on page 353 shows a test report that notes briefly how the test was conducted. Figure 10–8 on page 354 shows a test report that explains in detail how the tests were performed and describes the federal standards on which the testing was based.

4928 Wyaconda Road
Rockville, MD 20852
Phone (301) 492-3331
Fax (301) 492-1832
biosphericsinc.com

March 15, 2016

Mr. Luigi Sebastiani, General Manager
Midtown Development Corporation
114 West Jefferson Street
Milwaukee, WI 53201

Report in letter format for a customer

SUBJECT: Results of Analysis of Soil Samples for Arsenic

Test identified in subject line

Dear Mr. Sebastiani:

The results of our analysis of your soil samples for arsenic showed considerable variation; a high iron content in some of the samples may account for these differences.

Following are the results of the analysis of eight soil samples. The arsenic values listed are based on a wet-weight determination. The moisture content of the soil is also given to allow conversion of the results to a dry-weight basis if desired.

Testing methodology

Hole	Depth	Moisture (%)	Arsenic Total (ppm)
1	12"	19.0	312.0
2	Surface	11.2	737.0
3	12"	12.7	9.5
4	12"	10.8	865.0
5	12"	17.1	4.1
6	12"	14.2	6.1
7	12"	24.2	2,540.0
8	Surface	13.6	460.0

Table of areas tested and findings

I noticed that some of the samples contained large amounts of metallic iron coated with rust. Arsenic tends to be absorbed into soils high in iron, aluminum, and calcium oxides. The large amount of iron present in some of these soil samples is probably responsible for retaining high levels of arsenic. The soils highest in iron, aluminum, and calcium oxides should also show the highest levels of arsenic, provided the soils have had approximately equal levels of arsenic exposure.

Interpretation of test findings

If I can be of further assistance, please do not hesitate to contact me.

Yours truly,

Gunther Gottfried

Gunther Gottfried, Chemist
ggottfried@biosphericsinc.com

Figure 10–7 Test Report (Letter to Customer)

BIOSPHERICS Inc.

4928 Wyaconda Road
Rockville, MD 20852
Phone (301) 492-3331
Fax (301) 492-1832
biosphericsinc.com

April 5, 2016

Report in letter format for a customer

Mr. Leon Hite, Administrator
The Angle Company, Inc.
1869 Slauson Boulevard
Waynesville, VA 23927

Dear Mr. Hite:

Purpose and scope of test

On March 22, Biospherics Inc. performed asbestos-in-air monitoring at your Route 66 construction site, near Front Royal, Virginia. Six persons and three construction areas were monitored.

Testing methodology

All monitoring and analyses were performed in accordance with "Occupational Exposure to Asbestos," U.S. Department of Health and Human Services, Public Health Service, National Institute for Occupational Safety and Health, 1995. Each worker or area was fitted with a battery-powered personal sampler pump, operating at a flow rate of approximately two liters per minute. The airborne asbestos was collected on a 37-mm Millipore-type AA filter mounted in an open-face filter holder. Samples were collected over an eight-hour period.

Test findings

In all cases, the workers and areas monitored were exposed to levels of asbestos fibers well below the standard set by the Occupational Safety and Health Administration. The highest exposure found was that of a driller exposed to 0.21 fiber per cubic centimeter. The driller's samples were analyzed by scanning electron microscopy followed by energy-dispersive X-ray techniques that identify the chemical nature of each fiber, to identify the fibers as asbestos or other fiber types. Results from these analyses show that the fibers present are tremolite asbestos. No nonasbestos fibers were found.

Yours truly,

Allison Jones

Allison Jones, Chemist
AJ/jrm
ajones@biospherics. com

Figure 10–8 Test Report with Methodology Explained (Letter to Customer)

CHAPTER 10 SUMMARY: WRITING INFORMAL REPORTS

Check informal reports to make sure the following is done:

- The introduction states the subject and purpose and summarizes conclusions and recommendations.
- The body presents a detailed account of the work reported on.
- The conclusion summarizes findings and indicates their significance.
- The recommendations describe actions that should be taken based on the findings and conclusions.

The following types of informal reports are typical:

- Progress and periodic reports
  - Inform the reader of the status of an ongoing project either at certain stages (progress) or at regular intervals (periodic).
  - Alert readers to any necessary adjustments in scheduling, budgeting, and work assignments.
- Investigative reports
  - Open with a statement of the topic being examined.
  - Define the extent of the investigation.
  - Present the findings, interpretations, conclusions, and, when appropriate, recommendations.
- Incident reports
  - Identify the precise details, such as time and place of an accident or other incident.
  - Indicate any injuries or property damage.
  - State a likely cause of the accident or incident.
  - Specify what should be done to prevent a recurrence, if doing so is part of the reporting requirement.
- Trip reports
  - Include the destination and dates of the trip.
  - Explain why the trip was made, who was visited, and what was accomplished.
  - State any findings or recommendations based on the purpose of the trip.
- Test reports
  - State the purpose of the test and indicate the procedures used to conduct the test.
  - Indicate the results of the test or experiment and any interpretations helpful to the reader.

Exercises

1. Assume that you are the traffic manager of a trucking company that has had four highway accidents within a one-week period. Using the following facts, write an incident report to your company president, Michael Spangler.
   - Your company operates in your state.
   - The four accidents occurred in different parts of the state and on different dates (specify the date and location of each).

- Each accident resulted in damage not only to the truck (specify the dollar amount of the damage) but to the cargo (specify the type of cargo and the dollar amount of the damage).
- Only one of the accidents involved another vehicle (a company truck swerved into a parked car when a tire blew out). Give the make and year of the damaged car and its owner's name.
- Only one of the accidents involved injury to a company driver (give the driver's name and specify the injury and his current condition).
- Your maintenance division traced all four of the accidents to faulty tires, all the same brand (identify the brand) and all purchased at the same time and place (identify the place and date).
- The tires have now been replaced, and your insurance company, Acme Underwriters, has brought suit against the tire manufacturer to recover damages, including lost business while the four trucks were being repaired (specify the dollar amount of the lost business).

2. Workers' compensation allows employees who are injured on the job to receive benefits like medical expenses and lost wages, depending on when the injury happened, how the injury happened, and the severity of the injury. Imagine that you work for a human resources manager of a large online retailer. Most of your company's workers spend their days packing books, DVDs, and other products into mailing boxes, then lifting the boxes and putting them onto carts and pulling the carts to the mailing rooms. Your manager asks you to draft an investigative end-of-the-year report in the form of a memo that details the most common type of employee injury and other yearly information. Your research uncovers the following:

   - Back injuries are the most common, occurring mostly in the warehouse.
   - In 2013–2016, 956 injuries occurred.
   - The total cost of the injuries was $3.5 million.
   - There is still a cost of $8.2 million for all open claims.
   - This information reflects a significant loss in productivity.

   Be sure to open your memo with a brief introductory summary that details the information you were seeking, the reason the investigation was necessary, and the person who requested it. In the body of the memo or letter, describe the extent of or method used for your investigation. Then state your findings and any recommendations based on the findings.

3. As the medical staff administrative assistant at a hospital, write a progress report to the director of the hospital outlining the current status of the annual reappointment of committees. Use the following facts to write the report:

   - A total of ten committees must be staffed.
   - The chief of staff has telephoned each person selected to chair a committee, and you have sent each of them a follow-up e-mail of thanks from the chief.
   - You have written e-mails to all physicians who are currently on committees but are not being reappointed, informing them of the fact.
   - You have written e-mails to all physicians being asked to serve on committees.
   - You expect to receive e-mail replies from those physicians declining the appointment by the 15th of the following month.
   - Once committee assignments have been completed, you will create the membership lists of all committees and e-mail them to the complete medical staff.

4. You are a field-service engineer for a company that markets diesel-powered emergency generators. Based on the following information, write a trip report.

You have just visited five cities to inspect the installation of your company's auxiliary power units in hospitals and you need to report to your manager about your findings. You visited the following hospitals and cities:

- May 20: Our Lady of Mercy Hospital in San Antonio
- May 21: Dallas Presbyterian Hospital in Dallas
- May 22: St. Elizabeth Hospital in Oklahoma City
- May 23: New Orleans General Hospital in New Orleans
- May 24: Emory University Hospital in Atlanta

You found that each installation was properly done. With the cooperation of the administrators, you switched each hospital to auxiliary power for a one-hour trial run. All generators functioned as designed. You held a brief training session for the maintenance staff at each hospital about how to manually switch to generator power and how to regulate its speed to produce 220 volts of electricity at 60 hertz. You want to commend your company's sales staff and field personnel for creating a positive image of your company in the minds of all five customers you visited.

5. Locate a laboratory report prepared by a private or government agency on the Web, as directed by your instructor. Compare elements of the report to the guidelines in this chapter. To what extent does the actual laboratory report match the chapter guidelines, and how could they help to improve the report? Comment on any differences you see based on the context of the report and the organization that produced it. Submit your report in memo form to your instructor.

6. Each of the following topics presents a situation in which a company plans a significant change that could threaten its existing customer base. Select one of the following topics (or create your own topic based on your area of study and professional interest) and write a memo in which you offer your recommendations for ensuring that the change that your company proposes will not jeopardize its existing customer base. With your customers in mind, make specific suggestions for facilitating as smooth and positive a transition as possible.

   a. Assume that you are part of the management team of a fast-food restaurant with a "burgers only" identity — and a loyal customer base — that wants to add distinctive and healthful menu items.
   b. Assume that you are part of the management team for an apparel manufacturing firm (men's or women's clothing) known for its conservative fashions. Your firm is about to introduce a new line of clothing with a distinctly contemporary appeal.
   c. Assume that you work for a small medical insurance company concerned with the rising number of medical claims being submitted by your customers. To combat this, your company has initiated a campaign designed to entice your customers to adopt healthier lifestyles and has begun sending brochures and personalized letters to customers. Some customers have expressed concern that this is an indication that the company will become more reluctant to pay their claims.

Collaborative Classroom Projects

1. In Collaborative Classroom Project 3 in Chapter 8, Writing E-mails, Memos, and Letters, your class broke into two groups, the local electric company's consumers and the company's marketing representatives. Both sides wrote letters asking that a rate increase be rejected or accepted, respectively. Now assume that before the marketing

representatives wrote their letter, they had investigated the company's need for a rate increase to build a fourth natural-gas–fired generating unit. The investigation uncovered the following information:

- The electric company supplies electricity to three cities and more than 1.65 million customers.
- Population growth is beginning to add strain to an already overloaded system (the company currently generates power using nuclear, coal, natural gas, and oil plants at 12 different sites).
- Customers set two peak records for summer usage in 2016: They used approximately 8,992 megawatt-hours (MWh) of electricity on July 16 between 4:00 and 5:00 p.m., and approximately 9,027 MWh on July 19 in the same time period.
- Despite the summer heat, peak energy use occurs during the winter: The highest demand (10,142 MWh) was recorded on January 15, 2016.
- Company engineers report that a new natural-gas–fired generating unit would add approximately 500 megawatts of capacity, which could generate electricity for about 320,000 additional consumers.

Rewrite your group's marketing representatives' letter to include the research. When you are finished, exchange letters for peer reviews. Comment on the level of persuasion that these letters now contain with the added details and facts.

2. As a class, plan to visit a lab or learning center on campus, preferably one outside your department. Determine as a group which lab you would like to visit and the specific purposes of your visit. The lab may be a science lab, a computer lab, an engineering lab, or a writing center. After an explanation of the lab's procedures and a tour of the lab or center, your class will reconvene in your own classroom and write a trip report about the visit. Include the date of the visit, your destination, the purpose of your trip, and an explanation of what you learned during the visit.

Research Projects

1. The use of cell phones, laptop and tablet computers, digital cameras, and other devices has created a growing need for the recycling of portable rechargeable batteries. Many retail stores are helping to preserve the environment by shipping spent battery packs to recycling centers. In Chapter 6, Conducting Research for a Document, Exercise 6, you created a questionnaire designed to determine if people are aware of the need to recycle portable rechargeable batteries and how people feel about companies that provide recycling programs. Expand your investigation and write an investigative report on the recycling of portable rechargeable batteries. In this report, be sure you do the following:

   a. Describe the many different types of rechargeable batteries being used today (like nickel cadmium and lithium ion).
   b. Explain how the recycling is accomplished.
   c. List the local businesses in your city or area that participate in recycling programs.
   d. Include the findings from your questionnaire.

2. You have been asked to determine for your campus organization where members can volunteer 10 to 12 hours a week for local community service.

   a. Begin by investigating at least three organizations that accept volunteers, such as nursing homes, hospitals, political and civic groups, or schools. Detail the type of volunteer help needed, the hours and days when the help is needed, whether any training is required, and to whom the volunteer will report. Also be sure to find out if volunteers do hands-on work with people — such as playing games with children or adults or bathing, lifting, or turning those who aren't mobile — or if volunteers work behind the scenes, making solicitation calls, addressing envelopes, stocking supplies, and so on.

b. Then write a three- to five-page investigative report in which you evaluate each of the three organizations given the criteria above, as well as from the point of view of your own background, experience, and future vocational goals that are similar to those members of your organization.

c. Finish by selecting the one that is most suitable for members of your organization and explain the reasons for your selection.

3. Assume that you work for a small business and the company president has asked you to gather information from the Small Business Administration (SBA) that will benefit your company, such as opportunities for government contracts or special programs or training available through the SBA. Visit the SBA website at www.sba.gov and prepare an investigative report of 300 to 500 words to be submitted to your instructor.

4. Many large international companies target sections of their websites to the different world markets where their products are sold. For example, McDonald's (www.McDonalds.com) includes customized pages for each of the 50-plus countries where its restaurants are established. Assume that you work for a company that is considering expanding its website for international markets. You have been assigned to investigate and report your findings on the differences and similarities between the regional sections of other companies' sites. To research your report, examine the websites of at least three international corporations. You might visit, for example, McDonald's American and European sites, or Sony's Asian and Eastern European sites. Note the translations of the company's slogan, the colors and graphics used on the sites, the presentation of products, and so on. (You may want to revisit the sections on international correspondence [pages 320–327] in Chapter 9, Writing Routine and Sensitive Messages; on using graphics to communicate to global audiences [pages 251–257] in Chapter 7, Designing Documents and Visuals; and on considering international Web users [page 595] in Appendix A: Writing in an Online Environment.)

11 Writing Formal Reports

Contents

This chapter discusses the parts of formal reports, the information they typically include, and how best to organize them into an effective final product. Depending on the subject, objective, and scope, a formal report is typically divided into three major parts — front matter, body, and back matter — and contains the following elements:

Formal reports are written accounts of major projects that require substantial research and often involve more than one writer. Such projects include research into new developments in a field, explorations of the feasibility of a new product or a new service, or an organization's end-of-year review. Because of the variety of purposes they serve, formal reports can be called by many different names: feasibility study, annual report, investigative report, research report, analytical report, and the like. The purpose, scope, and complexity of the project will determine which components will be included and how those components are organized. Most formal reports require signposts, whether within the printed document or as links in the online version, that point to the material in the report. A table of contents, for example, gives readers an overview of the content and how it is organized. Creating a formal topic outline, which lists the report's major facts and ideas and indicates their relationship to one another, should help you to write a well-organized report.

Formal reports are organized to address the needs of more than one audience. These audiences will occupy a variety of positions, have different levels of knowledge about your topic, and be responsible for reading and responding to different parts of the report. Few in the audience will read the entire report, so the executive summary and abstract must make sense independently of the rest of the report. Although everybody will skim the table of contents, managers and other decision makers will focus on the executive summary because it concisely summarizes the report in full. These readers need to know the "bottom line" quickly for its potential impact on their staffing, organizational, and budget decisions. They may also need to refer to the report's glossary for definitions of special terms. Technical experts, however, will be responsible for implementing the report's recommendations, so they need to understand in detail how the conclusions and recommendations were reached. General readers whose needs are less immediate may read only the abstract to decide whether to read the whole report. Therefore, overlapping content is appropriate in the introduction, executive summary, and abstract, as well as in the conclusions and recommendations.

As you read this chapter, keep in mind all that you've learned about the process of drafting and revising on-the-job writing tasks because careful planning, drafting, and revising, as much as using the organizational frameworks covered in this chapter, form the basis for a successful formal report.

In the workplace, formal reports are often written by a team of specialists assembled for that purpose. Each member of the team is selected to contribute material based on his or her specialty or background and collaborates on every facet of the writing process:

◆ *For guidance on working collaboratively on team projects, review Chapter 5, Collaborating on a Document.*

- Planning the report
- Researching the subject and writing a chapter or section of the report
- Reviewing the drafts of other team members
- Revising their drafts on the basis of comments from the team members
- Publishing the final report

◆ *For guidance on conducting research, see Chapter 6, Conducting Research for a Document.*

A team leader usually coordinates the team's work by setting a schedule for the work, leading the effort to plan the report, assigning responsibilities, coordinating all

◆ *For brainstorming strategies, see Chapter 1, Understanding the Workplace Writing Context: A Case Study.*

◆ *For outlining, see Chapter 2, Planning a Document.*

◆ *For advice on planning, creating, and integrating visuals, see Chapter 7, Designing Documents and Visuals.*

◆ *For a review of revising strategies, see Chapter 4, Revising a Document.*

content reviews, editing the final draft to ensure a consistent voice, and overseeing production and distribution of the final report. The team leader also performs the essential task of controlling the master draft to ensure that it is current and accurate and that no parts are confused with earlier drafts that have been revised and superseded.

DIGITAL TIP: Creating Styles and Templates for Formal Reports

You can use a word-processing program to create time-saving templates that automate the visual appearance of text elements such as headings, paragraphs, and lists throughout a document. Once you specify your styles, save the template and use it each time you create a formal report. Many organizations provide such templates for their formal and informal reports, so check before you create your own.

Transmittal Letter or Memo

◆ *Examples of transmittal letters are also shown in Figures 9–1 and 9–2 (on pages 301–302).*

Formal reports are usually requested by a client or senior executive in an organization. When you submit the formal report, include with it a brief transmittal (or cover) message that identifies the report topic and explains why the report was prepared. The transmittal often opens with a brief paragraph (one or two sentences) explaining what is being sent and why. The next paragraph concisely summarizes the report's contents or stresses a finding or conclusion important to the audience. This section may also mention any special conditions under which the material was prepared (limitations of time or money, for instance). The closing paragraph may acknowledge any help received in preparing the report or express the hope that the information fulfills its purpose.

Typically, transmittal letters and memos are brief—usually one page. Figure 11–1 shows a sample transmittal memo.

Front Matter

The front matter, which includes all the elements that precede the body of the report, serves several purposes: (1) it explains the topic, organization, and purpose of the report; (2) it indicates whether the report contains the kind of information that the audience is looking for; and (3) it lists where in the report the audience can find specific chapters, headings, illustrations, and tables. Not all formal reports require every one of these elements. A title page and table of contents are usually mandatory, but whether the remaining items are included will depend on the scope of the report and its intended audience. Scientific and technical reports, for example, often include a separate listing of abbreviations and symbols; in most business reports, such lists are unnecessary. The front-matter pages are numbered with lowercase Roman numerals, as shown in Figures 11–3, 11–4, and 11–5 (on pages 366, 367, and 369, respectively). Throughout the report, page numbers are often centered either near the bottom or near the top of each page.

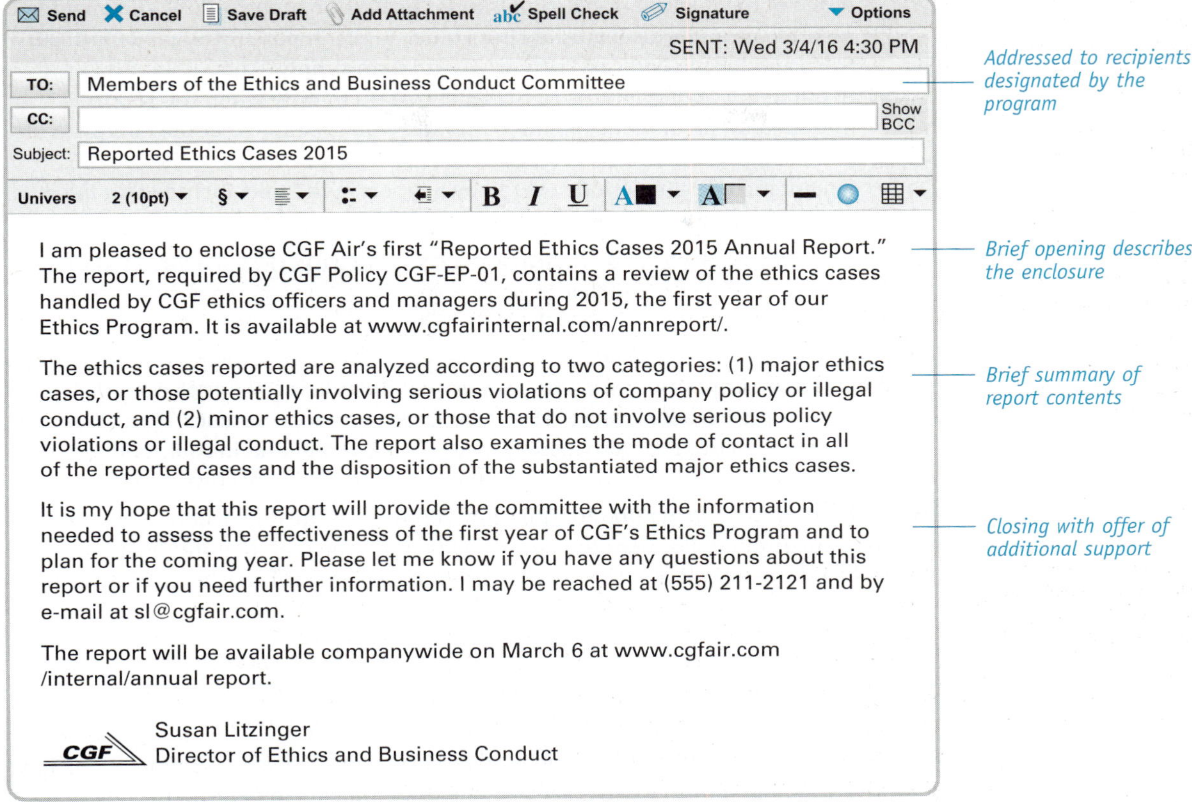
Send | Cancel | Save Draft | Add Attachment | Spell Check | Signature | Options

SENT: Wed 3/4/16 4:30 PM

TO: Members of the Ethics and Business Conduct Committee

CC:

Subject: Reported Ethics Cases 2015

I am pleased to enclose CGF Air's first "Reported Ethics Cases 2015 Annual Report." The report, required by CGF Policy CGF-EP-01, contains a review of the ethics cases handled by CGF ethics officers and managers during 2015, the first year of our Ethics Program. It is available at www.cgfairinternal.com/annreport/.

The ethics cases reported are analyzed according to two categories: (1) major ethics cases, or those potentially involving serious violations of company policy or illegal conduct, and (2) minor ethics cases, or those that do not involve serious policy violations or illegal conduct. The report also examines the mode of contact in all of the reported cases and the disposition of the substantiated major ethics cases.

It is my hope that this report will provide the committee with the information needed to assess the effectiveness of the first year of CGF's Ethics Program and to plan for the coming year. Please let me know if you have any questions about this report or if you need further information. I may be reached at (555) 211-2121 and by e-mail at sl@cgfair.com.

The report will be available companywide on March 6 at www.cgfair.com /internal/annual report.

CGF
Susan Litzinger
Director of Ethics and Business Conduct

Figure 11–1 Transmittal Memo for a Formal Report Reprinted and adapted by permission of Susan Litzinger, a student at Pennsylvania State University, Altoona.

Title Page

Although the formats of title pages vary, the page could include the following information: (1) the full title of the report; (2) the name(s) of the writers, principal investigators, or compilers who prepared it; (3) the date the report was issued; (4) the name of the organization for which the writer(s) works; and (5) the name of the organization or person to whom the report is submitted.

1. *Full title of the report.* The title should reflect the topic as well as the scope and objective of the report. Titles often provide the only basis on which audiences can decide whether to read a report. Aim for accuracy and conciseness: Titles too vague or too long can confuse the audience and prevent efficient filing by topic for later retrieval. Follow these guidelines when creating the title:
   - Focus on the subject matter. Avoid titles that begin "Notes on," "Studies on," "A Report on," or "Observations on." These phrases are often redundant and state the obvious. However, phrases such as "Annual Report" or "Feasibility Study" should be used in a title or subtitle because they help define the purpose and

scope of the document. The title should be unique to the report, allowing the report to be easily distinguished from other similar reports. "Annual Report: 2017 Sales and Profits Forecast" is more useful than simply "Annual Report."

- Avoid using abbreviations in the title. Use them only when the report is intended for an audience familiar enough with the topic that the abbreviation will be understood.
- Do not include the period covered by a report in the title; include that information in a subtitle:

▶ **EFFECTS OF PROPOSED HIGHWAY CONSTRUCTION ON PROPERTY VALUES**
Tri-State Regional District
Annual Report, 2016

2. *Names of the writers, principal investigators, or compilers, as appropriate.* Frequently, contributors simply list their names. Sometimes they identify themselves by their job titles in the organization (Jane R. Lihn, Cost Analyst; Rodrigo Sánchez, Head, Research and Development). They also identify themselves by their tasks in contributing to the report (Antoine Baume, Compiler; Wanda Landowska, Principal Investigator).
3. *Date or dates of the report.* For one-time reports, list the date when the report is to be distributed. For periodic reports, which may be issued monthly or quarterly, list the period that the present report covers in a subtitle, as well as the date when the report is to be distributed.
4. *Name of the organization for which the writer works.*
5. *Name of the organization or individual to whom the report is being submitted,* if the work is being done for an organization other than your own.

These categories are standard on most title pages, although some organizations may require additional information. A sample title page appears in Figure 11–2.

The title page, although unnumbered, is considered page i (small Roman numeral one). The back of the title page, which is blank and unnumbered, is considered page ii, and the abstract then falls on page iii so that it appears on a right-hand (that is, an odd-numbered) page. For reports with printing on both sides of each sheet of paper, it is a long-standing printer's convention that right-hand pages are always odd-numbered and left-hand pages are always even-numbered. (Note the pagination in this book.) New sections and chapters of reports typically begin on a new right-hand page. Reports with printing on only one side of each sheet can be numbered consecutively regardless of where new sections begin.

Abstract

An abstract is a condensed version of a report or journal article that summarizes and highlights its major points. Abstracts enable prospective readers to decide quickly whether the topic is relevant to them. Usually 200 to 250 words long, abstracts must make sense independently of the work they summarize because they often appear without the report in databases or in online citations. Depending on the kind of information they contain, abstracts are usually classified as either *descriptive* or *informative.*

A *descriptive* abstract includes information about the purpose, scope, and methods used to arrive at the findings contained in the report. It is thus a slightly expanded

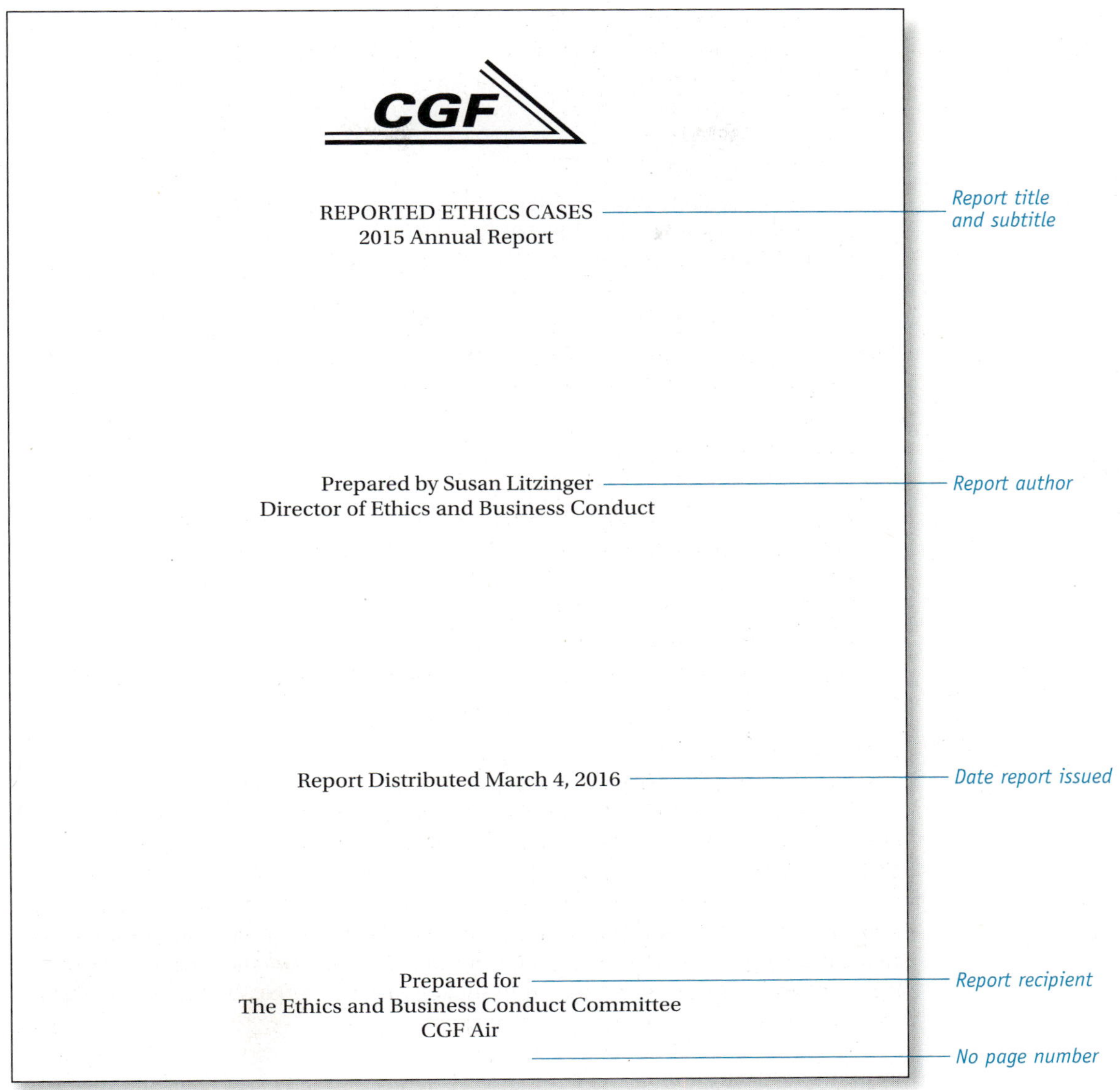

Figure 11–2 Title Page of a Formal Report Susan Litzinger.

table of contents in paragraph form. Provided that it adequately summarizes the information, a descriptive abstract need not be longer than several sentences (Figure 11–3 on page 366).

An *informative* abstract is an expanded version of the descriptive abstract. In addition to information about the purpose, scope, and research methods of the original report, the informative abstract summarizes the results, conclusions, and, if any, recommendations. The informative abstract thus retains the tone and essential scope of the report while omitting its details (Figure 11–4).

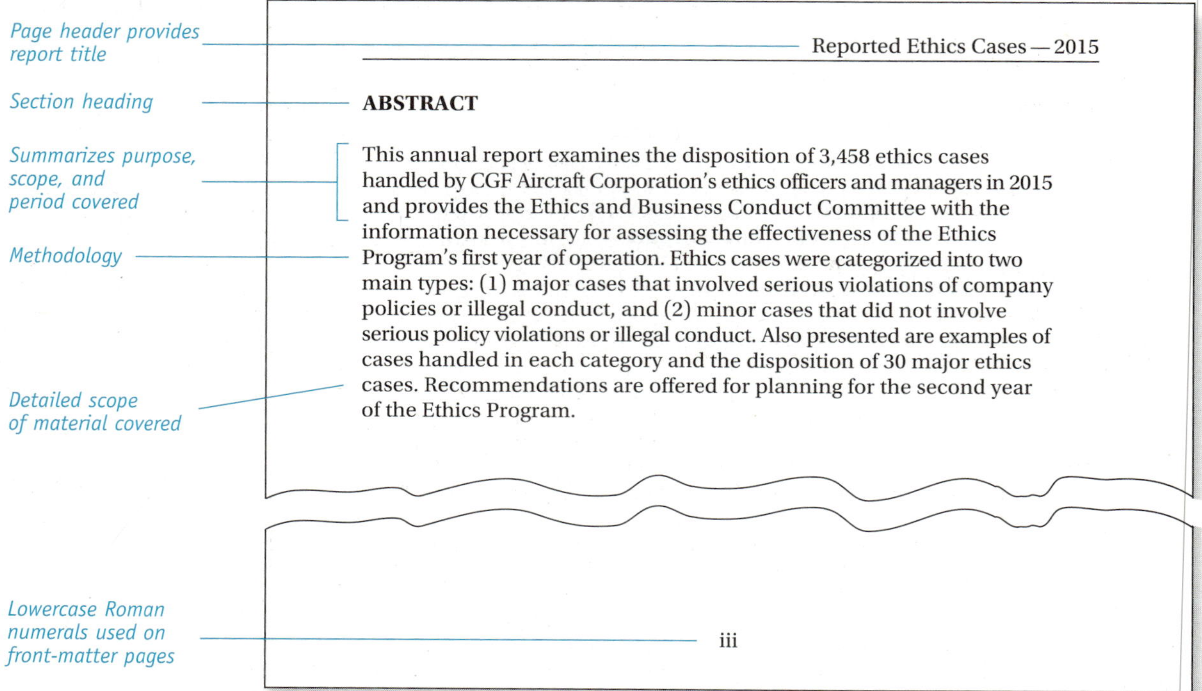
Page header provides report title
Reported Ethics Cases — 2015
Section heading
ABSTRACT
Summarizes purpose, scope, and period covered
This annual report examines the disposition of 3,458 ethics cases handled by CGF Aircraft Corporation's ethics officers and managers in 2015 and provides the Ethics and Business Conduct Committee with the information necessary for assessing the effectiveness of the Ethics Program's first year of operation. Ethics cases were categorized into two main types: (1) major cases that involved serious violations of company policies or illegal conduct, and (2) minor cases that did not involve serious policy violations or illegal conduct. Also presented are examples of cases handled in each category and the disposition of 30 major ethics cases. Recommendations are offered for planning for the second year of the Ethics Program.
Methodology
Detailed scope of material covered
Lowercase Roman numerals used on front-matter pages
iii

Figure 11–3 Descriptive Abstract of a Formal Report Susan Litzinger.

Which type of abstract should you write? If your employer or client has a preference, use it. Otherwise, the answer depends on your topic. Informative abstracts satisfy the needs of the widest possible audience because of their scope. Descriptive abstracts, however, are appropriate for information surveys, progress reports that combine information from more than one project, and any report that compiles a variety of information. For these types of reports, conclusions and recommendations either do not exist in the original or are too numerous to include in an abstract. Typically, an abstract follows the title page and is numbered page iii.

Write the abstract after finishing your report. Otherwise, your abstract may not accurately reflect the final version. Begin with a topic sentence that announces the subject and scope of the report. Then, using the major and minor heads of your table of contents to distinguish primary from secondary ideas, decide what material is relevant to your abstract. Write clearly and concisely, eliminating unnecessary words and ideas, but do not omit articles (*a, an, the*) and important transitional words and phrases (*however, therefore, but, in summary*). Write complete sentences, but avoid stringing a group of short sentences end to end; instead, combine ideas by using subordination and parallel structure. As a rule, spell out most acronyms and all but the most common abbreviations (°C, °F, mph). Finally, as you summarize, keep the tone and emphasis consistent with the original report.

◆ ***For additional guidance on summarizing content, review pages 179–180 in Chapter 6, Conducting Research for a Document.***

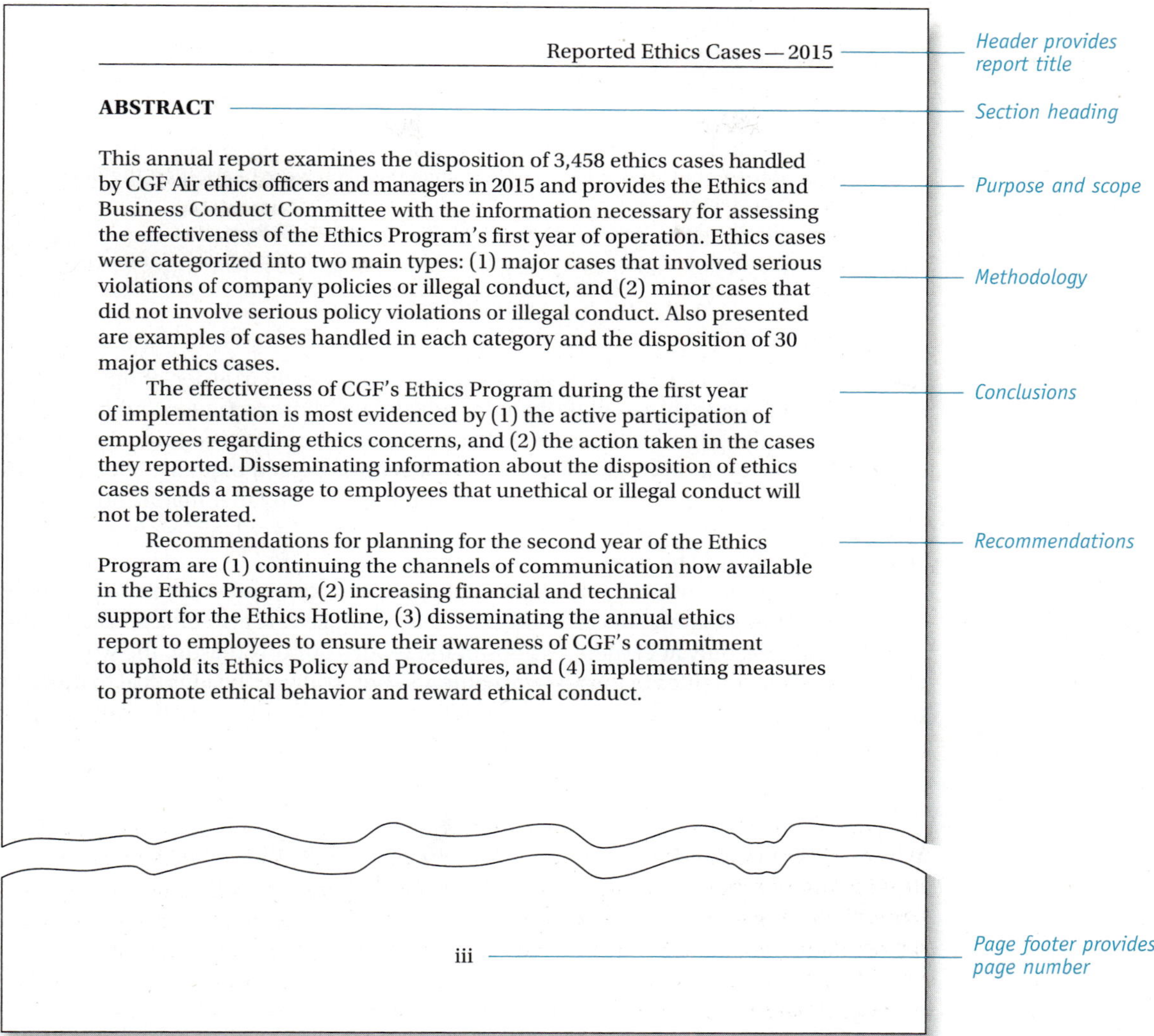

Reported Ethics Cases — 2015

ABSTRACT

This annual report examines the disposition of 3,458 ethics cases handled by CGF Air ethics officers and managers in 2015 and provides the Ethics and Business Conduct Committee with the information necessary for assessing the effectiveness of the Ethics Program's first year of operation. Ethics cases were categorized into two main types: (1) major cases that involved serious violations of company policies or illegal conduct, and (2) minor cases that did not involve serious policy violations or illegal conduct. Also presented are examples of cases handled in each category and the disposition of 30 major ethics cases.

The effectiveness of CGF's Ethics Program during the first year of implementation is most evidenced by (1) the active participation of employees regarding ethics concerns, and (2) the action taken in the cases they reported. Disseminating information about the disposition of ethics cases sends a message to employees that unethical or illegal conduct will not be tolerated.

Recommendations for planning for the second year of the Ethics Program are (1) continuing the channels of communication now available in the Ethics Program, (2) increasing financial and technical support for the Ethics Hotline, (3) disseminating the annual ethics report to employees to ensure their awareness of CGF's commitment to uphold its Ethics Policy and Procedures, and (4) implementing measures to promote ethical behavior and reward ethical conduct.

iii

Figure 11–4 Informative Abstract of a Formal Report Susan Litzinger.

WRITER'S CHECKLIST

Writing Abstracts

Include the following information:

- ✔ Subject
- ✔ Scope
- ✔ Purpose
- ✔ Methods used

- ✔ Results obtained (informative abstract only)
- ✔ Recommendations made, if any (informative abstract only)

Do not include the following kinds of information:

- ✔ Detailed discussion or explanation of the methods used
- ✔ Administrative details about how the research was undertaken, who funded it, who worked on it, and the like, unless such details have a bearing on the document's purpose
- ✔ Illustrations, tables, charts, maps, and bibliographic references
- ✔ Any information that does not appear in the original document

Table of Contents

A table of contents lists all the headings of the report in their order of appearance, along with their page numbers. It includes a listing of all front matter and back matter except the title page and the table of contents itself. In printed reports, the table of contents begins on a new right-hand page. For reports posted digitally, left align and single-space the text and use Arabic or Roman numerals to label major topics. Note that in Figure 11–5 the table of contents is numbered page v because it follows the abstract (page iii) and because page iv is blank.

Along with the abstract, a table of contents gives your audience an overview of the scope of information covered and how it is organized. It also aids a reader who may want to look only at certain sections of the report. For this reason, the wording of chapter and section titles in the table of contents should always be identical to those in the text. For digital versions of the report, link the table of contents to the appropriate sections or chapters in the body of the report.

List of Figures

When a report contains more than five figures, list them by title, along with their page numbers, in a separate section beginning on a new page and immediately following the table of contents. Number figures consecutively throughout the report with Arabic numbers.

List of Tables

When a report contains more than five tables, list them, along with their titles and page numbers, in a separate section immediately following the list of figures (if there is one). Number tables consecutively throughout the report with Arabic numbers.

Foreword

A foreword is an optional introductory statement written by someone other than the author. It generally provides background information about the publication's significance and places it in the context of other works in the field. The author of the foreword is usually an authority in the field or an executive of the company. The author's name and affiliation and the date the foreword was written appear on a separate line below the foreword.

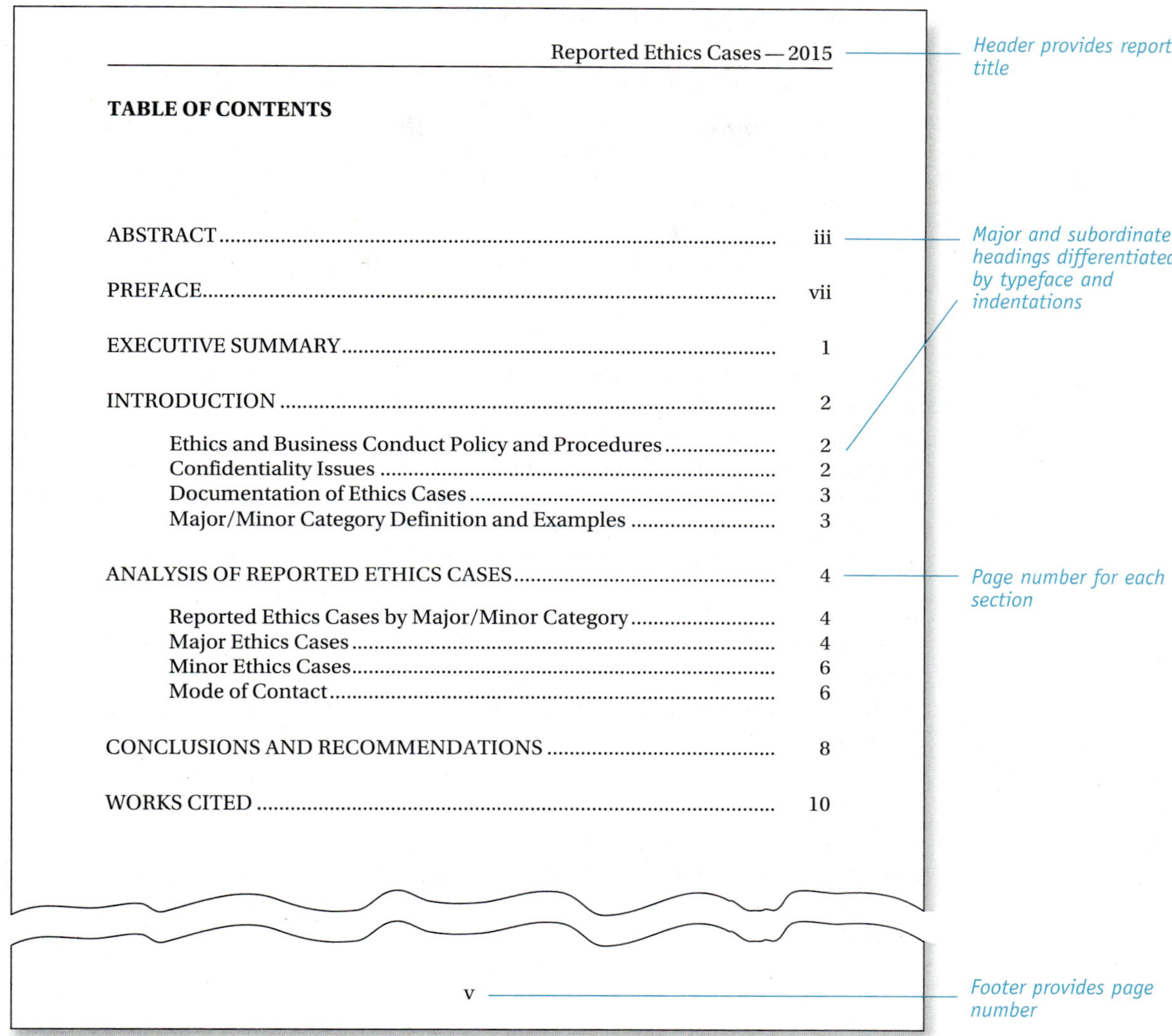
Reported Ethics Cases — 2015

TABLE OF CONTENTS

v

Figure 11–5 Table of Contents of a Formal Report Susan Litzinger.

Preface

A preface is an optional introductory statement written by the author to announce the purpose, background, or scope of the report. Sometimes a preface specifies the audience for whom the report is intended; it may also highlight the relationship of the report to a given project or program. A preface may contain acknowledgments of help received in the preparation of the report. It may also cite permission obtained for the use of copyrighted works. If a preface is not included, place this type of information, if essential, in the introduction (discussed later in this chapter). Figure 11–6 shows a sample preface.

The preface follows the table of contents (and the lists of figures and tables and the foreword, if these are present). It begins on a separate page, is numbered with Roman numerals, and is titled "Preface."

List of Abbreviations and Symbols

When the abbreviations and symbols used in a report are numerous, and when there is a chance that the audience will not be able to interpret them, include a list of all abbreviations and symbols and what they stand for in the front matter of the report. Such a list, which follows the preface, is particularly appropriate for technical reports whose audience is not restricted to technical specialists. For digital versions of the report, add hyperlinks to their definitions or cursor-over pop-up definitions.

Figure 11–7 on page 372 shows an example of a list of symbols that appear in a report as part of equations that calculate the transfer of heat and water vapor from the surface of cooling ponds at industrial sites. The author assumes that the report readers have a technical education, however, because BTU (British thermal unit), Hg (chemical symbol for mercury), and similar terms are not defined.

■ Body

◆ *For guidance about page-level layout and design elements — typography, margins, columns, headers and footers, and the like — see Chapter 7, Designing Documents and Visuals.*

The body is the section of the report that describes in detail the methods and procedures used to generate the report, demonstrates how results were obtained, describes the results, draws conclusions, and, if appropriate, makes recommendations. It usually includes the following components:

- Executive summary
- Introduction
- Text (including headings, tables, and illustrations)
- Conclusions and recommendations
- Works cited or references

Number the first page of the body page 1, using Arabic rather than Roman numerals.

Executive Summary

The body begins with an executive summary that provides a more complete overview of the report than the abstract does. The summary states the purpose of the investigation and gives major findings; provides background; states the scope; includes conclusions; and, if any are made, gives recommendations. It also describes the procedures or methodology used to conduct the study. Executive summaries are optional, but they are strongly recommended for reports with multiple readers with different levels of knowledge about the topic of a report.

Reported Ethics Cases — 2015

PREFACE

The CGF Aircraft Corporation takes its commitment to an ethical work environment seriously. Throughout its 64-year history, CGF has fostered high ethical standards in its relations with its customers, suppliers, and employees. The size, diversity, and decentralized locations of our workforce make it imperative that CGF's ethical commitment — both in principle and in practice — be formalized. To this end, the CGF Aircraft Corporation established a corporationwide Ethics Program in August 2014. The goal of the program is to "promote a positive work environment that encourages open communication regarding ethics and compliance issues and concerns."

The Office of Ethics and Business Conduct (OEBC) was created to implement and administer the program. The director of the OEBC and seven ethics officers from throughout the corporation are responsible for the following program objectives:

- Communicate the values and standards for CGF's Ethics Program to employees.
- Inform employees about company policies regarding ethical business conduct.
- Establish companywide channels for employees to obtain information and guidance in resolving ethics concerns.
- Implement companywide ethics awareness and education programs.

This report examines the nature and disposition of the ethics cases handled by the OEBC in 2015, the first year of operation. The report was compiled to provide the corporation's Ethics and Business Committee of the OEBC with the information necessary to assess the effectiveness of the first year of CGF's Ethics Program.

This report represents the efforts of the dedicated staff of the OEBC, the ethics officers, and the many managers and employees throughout CGF. We wish to acknowledge their active support and contributions to this report and to the program.

vii

Header provides report title

Section heading

Background and purpose of program

Program background

Bulleted list makes objectives easy to read

Purpose and scope of report

Audience for report

Acknowledgment of help in preparation of report

Footer provides page number

Figure 11–6 Preface of a Formal Report Susan Litzinger.

SYMBOLS

A	Pond surface area, ft^2 or acres
A_0	One-half the daily insulation, BTU/ft^2
A_n	Surface area of *n*th segment of the plugflow model, ft^2
C	Cloud cover in tenths of the total sky obscured
C_1	Bowen's ratio, 0.26 mmHg/°F
C_P	Heat capacity of water, BTU/lb/°F
E_1, E_2	Estimation of equilibrium temperatures using data from off-site and on-site records, respectively, °F
E(x)	Estimation of equilibrium temperature using monthly average meteorologic data, °F
e_a	Saturation pressure of air above pond surface, mmHg
e_s	Saturation pressure of air at surface temperature, T_s, mmHg
g	Skew coefficient
H	Heat content, BTU

Symbols arranged in alphabetical order

Figure 11–7 List of Symbols for a Technical Report

Although more complete than an abstract, the executive summary should not contain a detailed description of the work on which the findings, conclusions, and recommendations were based. Note that this section *summarizes* rather than repeats verbatim this information. The length of the summary is proportional to the length of the report; typically, the summary should be approximately 10 percent of the length of the report. Like the abstract, the executive summary should be written after the report is finished.

Some executive summaries follow the organization of the report. Others highlight the findings, conclusions, and recommendations by summarizing them first, before going on to discuss procedures or methodology.

Like the abstract, the executive summary should be written so that it can be read independently of the report. It must not refer by number to figures, tables, or references contained elsewhere in the report. Because executive summaries are frequently read in place of the full report, all uncommon symbols, abbreviations, and acronyms must be spelled out.

Figure 11–8 shows an executive summary of the report on the Ethics Program at CGF Air.

WRITER'S CHECKLIST

Writing Executive Summaries

- ✔ Write the executive summary after you have completed the original report.
- ✔ Avoid using terminology that may not be familiar to your readers.
- ✔ Spell out all uncommon symbols, abbreviations, and acronyms.

Reported Ethics Cases — 2015

Header provides report title

EXECUTIVE SUMMARY

This report examines the nature and disposition of the 3,458 ethics cases handled by the CGF Air ethics officers and managers during 2015. The purpose of this report is to provide CGF's Ethics and Business Conduct Committee with the information necessary for assessing the effectiveness of the first year of the company's Ethics Program.

Purpose

Ethics information and guidance were available to employees through managers, ethics officers, and an ethics hotline.

Major ethics cases — defined as those situations potentially involving serious violations of company policies or illegal conduct — included cover-up of defective workmanship or use of defective parts in products; discrimination in hiring and promotion; involvement in monetary or other kickbacks; sexual harassment; disclosure of proprietary or company information; theft; and use of corporate Internet resources for inappropriate purposes, such as for conducting personal business, gambling, or access to pornography.

Scope

Minor ethics cases — all reported concerns not classified as major ethics cases — included informational queries from employees, situations involving coworkers, and situations involving management.

Scope

The effectiveness of CGF's Ethics Program during the first year of implementation is most evidenced by (1) the active participation of employees in the program and the 3,458 contacts employees made regarding ethics concerns through the various channels available to them, and (2) the action taken in the cases reported by employees, particularly the disposition of the 30 substantiated major ethics cases.

Conclusions

Based on these conclusions, recommendations for planning the second year of the Ethics Program are (1) continuing the channels of communication now available in the Ethics Program, (2) increasing financial and technical support for the Ethics Hotline, the most used mode of contact in the ethics cases reported in 2015, (3) disseminating this report in some form to employees to ensure their awareness of CGF's commitment to uphold its Ethics Policy and Procedures, and (4) implementing some measure of recognition for ethical behavior, such as an "Ethics Employee of the Month" award to promote and reward ethical conduct.

Recommendations

1

Footer provides page number

Figure 11–8 Executive Summary of a Formal Report Susan Litzinger.

- ✔ Do not refer by number to figures, tables, or references contained elsewhere in the report.
- ✔ Make the summary concise, but do not omit transitional words and phrases (such as *however, moreover, therefore, for example,* and *in summary*).
- ✔ Include only information discussed in the original document.

Introduction

The introduction provides your audience with any general information — such as why the report has been written — needed to understand the details of the rest of the report. State the subject, the purpose, the scope, and the way you plan to develop the topic. You may also describe how the report will be organized, but, as with the descriptive abstract, exclude specific findings, conclusions, and recommendations. Figure 11–9 shows the introduction to the report on the CGF Ethics Program. Note that the contents of the introduction and the contents of the preface and executive summary may overlap in some cases.

Introducing the Subject

The introduction should state the subject of the report. To provide context for the audience, it should also include a summary of background information on the definition, history, or theory of the report's subject.

Stating the Purpose

The statement of the purpose in your introduction should function as a topic sentence does in a paragraph. It should make your audience aware of your goal as they read the supporting statements and examples and it should tell them whether your material provides a new perspective or clarifies an existing perspective.

Stating the Scope

The statement of scope tells the audience how much or how little detail to expect. Does your report present a broad survey of the topic, or does it concentrate on one part of the topic? What period does it cover? Is it confined to a specific work site or geographic area? Once you state your scope broadly, stop. Save the details for the main body of the report.

Previewing How the Topic Will Be Developed

In a long report, state how you plan to develop or organize your topic. Is the report an analysis of the component parts of some whole? Is it an analysis of selected parts (or samples) of a whole? Is the material presented in chronological order? Does it move from details to general conclusions or from a general statement to the details that verify the statement? Does it set out to show whether a hypothesis is correct or incorrect? Stating your topic allows your audience to anticipate how the subject will be presented and gives them a basis for evaluating how you arrived at your conclusions or recommendations.

Reported Ethics Cases — 2015

Header provides report title

INTRODUCTION

This annual report examines the disposition of the 3,458 reported ethics cases in 2015 and provides the Ethics and Business Conduct Committee with the information necessary for assessing the effectiveness of the first year of CGF's Ethics Program. Recommendations are given for planning the second year of the Ethics Program.

Purpose

Ethics and Business Conduct Policy and Procedures

Subheading signals shift in topic

Effective January 1, 2015, the Ethics and Business Conduct Committee implemented Policy CGF-EP-01 and Procedure CGF-EP-02 for the administration of CGF's new Ethics Program. The purpose of the Ethics Program is to "promote ethical business conduct through open communication and compliance with company ethics standards" (CGF, "Ethical Business Conduct").

Background

The Office of Ethics and Business Conduct (OEBC) administers the Ethics Program. The director of the OEBC, along with seven ethics officers throughout CGF, is responsible for the following objectives:

- Communicate the values, standards, and goals of CGF's Ethics Program to employees.
- Inform employees about company ethics policies.
- Provide channels for employee education and guidance in resolving ethics concerns.
- Implement companywide programs in ethics awareness, education, and recognition.

Bulleted list makes information easy to read

Employee accessibility to ethics information and guidance became the immediate goal of the OEBC in its first year of operation. The following channels were set up in 2015:

- Managers throughout CGF received intensive ethics training, and employees were encouraged to go to their managers as the first point of contact.
- Ethics officers were available to employees and managers through face-to-face or telephone contact, through the Ethics Hotline, and by e-mail.
- The Ethics Hotline was available to all employees, 24 hours a day, 7 days a week, to report ethics concerns anonymously.

Background

Confidentiality Issues

Subheading

CGF's Ethics Policy ensures confidentiality and anonymity for employees who raise genuine ethics concerns. Procedure CGF-EP-02 guarantees appropriate discipline, including dismissal, for retaliation or retribution against any employee who reports any genuine ethics concern.

2

Footer provides page number

Figure 11–9 Introduction to a Formal Report Susan Litzinger.

Reported Ethics Cases — 2015

Subheading

Documentation of Ethics Cases

Methodology

The following requirements were established by the director of the Office of Ethics and Business Conduct as uniform guidelines for the documentation by managers and ethics officers of all reported ethics cases:

Bulleted list highlights guidelines

- Name, position, and department of the individual initiating contact, if available
- Date, time, and mode of contact
- Name, position, and department of the person contacted
- Category and resolution of ethics case

Managers and ethics officers entered the required information in each reported ethics case into an ACCESS database file, enabling efficient retrieval and analysis of the data.

Subheading

Major/Minor Category Definition and Examples

Methodology

Major ethics cases were defined as those situations potentially involving serious violations of company policies or illegal conduct. Procedure CGF-EP-02 requires notification of the Internal Audit and the Law departments in serious ethics cases. The staffs of the Internal Audit and the Law departments assume primary responsibility for managing major ethics cases and for working with the employees, ethics officers, and managers involved in each case.

Examples of situations categorized as major ethics cases:

Bulleted list highlights examples

- Cover-up of defective workmanship or use of defective parts in products
- Discrimination in hiring and promotion
- Involvement in monetary or other kickbacks from customers for preferred orders
- Sexual harassment
- Disclosure of proprietary customer or company information
- Theft
- Use of corporate Internet resources for inappropriate purposes

Minor ethics cases were defined as including all reported concerns not classified as major ethics cases. Minor ethics cases were classified as follows:

- Informational queries from employees
- Situations involving coworkers or management

Footer provides page number

3

Figure 11–9 Introduction to a Formal Report *(continued)*

Text (Body)

Generally the longest section of the report, the text (or body) presents the details of how the topic was investigated, how the problem was solved, how the best choice from among alternatives was selected, or whatever else the report covers. This information is often clarified and further developed by the use of illustrations and tables and may be supported by references to other studies.

Most formal reports have no single best organization — the organization of the report will depend on the topic, on how you have investigated it, and on your audience's needs. The text is ordinarily divided into several major sections, comparable to the chapters in a book. These sections are then subdivided to reflect logical divisions within your main sections. The sample table of contents (see Figure 11-5, page 369) indicates how the text was organized for the report on the Ethics Program at the CGF Aircraft Corporation. Figure 11-10 shows the body of the same report.

Headings

Headings (or *heads*) are the titles or subtitles of sections within the body of the report. They make the report more accessible to the audience by (1) calling attention to the main topics, (2) signaling changes of topic, and (3) dividing the body into manageable segments. Especially for long and complicated reports, you may need several levels of headings to indicate major divisions and subdivisions of the topic. Make headings most effective by following these guidelines:

◆ *For guidance on creating templates that automate heading styles, see the Digital Tip: Creating Styles and Templates for Formal Reports, page 362.*

- Use headings to signal a new topic or subtopic within the larger topic.
- Ensure that headings at the same level are of relatively equal importance and word them in parallel grammatical structure.
- Subdivide sections only as needed; not every section requires its own lower-level headings.
- Subdivide a section with two or more headings (a topic cannot logically be divided into fewer than two parts).
- Do not allow a heading to substitute for discussion; the text should read as if the heading were not there.
- Avoid too many or too few headings or levels of headings; too many clutter a document and too few fail to provide a recognizable structure.
- Use varying type styles and formatting conventions to distinguish among levels of headings (see Figure 11-11 on page 382 and Designing Your Document on page 383).
- Do not leave a heading as the final line of a page. If two lines of text cannot fit below a heading, start the section at the top of the next page.
- Hyperlink headings in digital formal reports to send readers to corresponding segments in the report; this facilitates easier navigation for your readers.

Figure 11-11 illustrates this system.

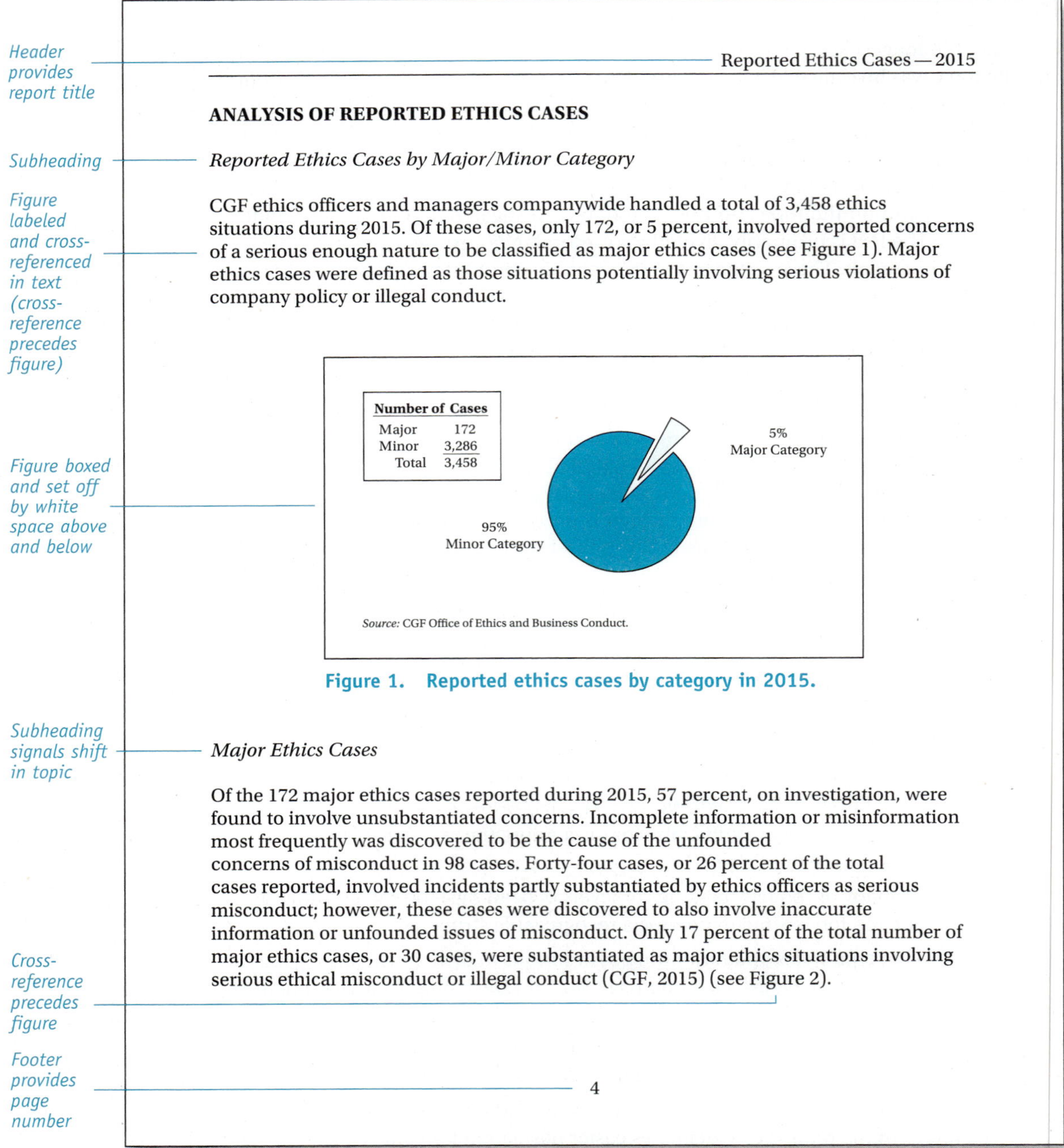

Reported Ethics Cases — 2015

ANALYSIS OF REPORTED ETHICS CASES

Reported Ethics Cases by Major/Minor Category

CGF ethics officers and managers companywide handled a total of 3,458 ethics situations during 2015. Of these cases, only 172, or 5 percent, involved reported concerns of a serious enough nature to be classified as major ethics cases (see Figure 1). Major ethics cases were defined as those situations potentially involving serious violations of company policy or illegal conduct.

Number of Cases	
Major	172
Minor	3,286
Total	3,458

Source: CGF Office of Ethics and Business Conduct.

Figure 1. Reported ethics cases by category in 2015.

Major Ethics Cases

Of the 172 major ethics cases reported during 2015, 57 percent, on investigation, were found to involve unsubstantiated concerns. Incomplete information or misinformation most frequently was discovered to be the cause of the unfounded concerns of misconduct in 98 cases. Forty-four cases, or 26 percent of the total cases reported, involved incidents partly substantiated by ethics officers as serious misconduct; however, these cases were discovered to also involve inaccurate information or unfounded issues of misconduct. Only 17 percent of the total number of major ethics cases, or 30 cases, were substantiated as major ethics situations involving serious ethical misconduct or illegal conduct (CGF, 2015) (see Figure 2).

4

Figure 11–10 Body of a Formal Report Susan Litzinger.

Text (Body)

Generally the longest section of the report, the text (or body) presents the details of how the topic was investigated, how the problem was solved, how the best choice from among alternatives was selected, or whatever else the report covers. This information is often clarified and further developed by the use of illustrations and tables and may be supported by references to other studies.

Most formal reports have no single best organization — the organization of the report will depend on the topic, on how you have investigated it, and on your audience's needs. The text is ordinarily divided into several major sections, comparable to the chapters in a book. These sections are then subdivided to reflect logical divisions within your main sections. The sample table of contents (see Figure 11–5, page 369) indicates how the text was organized for the report on the Ethics Program at the CGF Aircraft Corporation. Figure 11–10 shows the body of the same report.

Headings

Headings (or *heads*) are the titles or subtitles of sections within the body of the report. They make the report more accessible to the audience by (1) calling attention to the main topics, (2) signaling changes of topic, and (3) dividing the body into manageable segments. Especially for long and complicated reports, you may need several levels of headings to indicate major divisions and subdivisions of the topic. Make headings most effective by following these guidelines:

◆ *For guidance on creating templates that automate heading styles, see the Digital Tip: Creating Styles and Templates for Formal Reports, page 362.*

- Use headings to signal a new topic or subtopic within the larger topic.
- Ensure that headings at the same level are of relatively equal importance and word them in parallel grammatical structure.
- Subdivide sections only as needed; not every section requires its own lower-level headings.
- Subdivide a section with two or more headings (a topic cannot logically be divided into fewer than two parts).
- Do not allow a heading to substitute for discussion; the text should read as if the heading were not there.
- Avoid too many or too few headings or levels of headings; too many clutter a document and too few fail to provide a recognizable structure.
- Use varying type styles and formatting conventions to distinguish among levels of headings (see Figure 11–11 on page 382 and Designing Your Document on page 383).
- Do not leave a heading as the final line of a page. If two lines of text cannot fit below a heading, start the section at the top of the next page.
- Hyperlink headings in digital formal reports to send readers to corresponding segments in the report; this facilitates easier navigation for your readers.

Figure 11–11 illustrates this system.

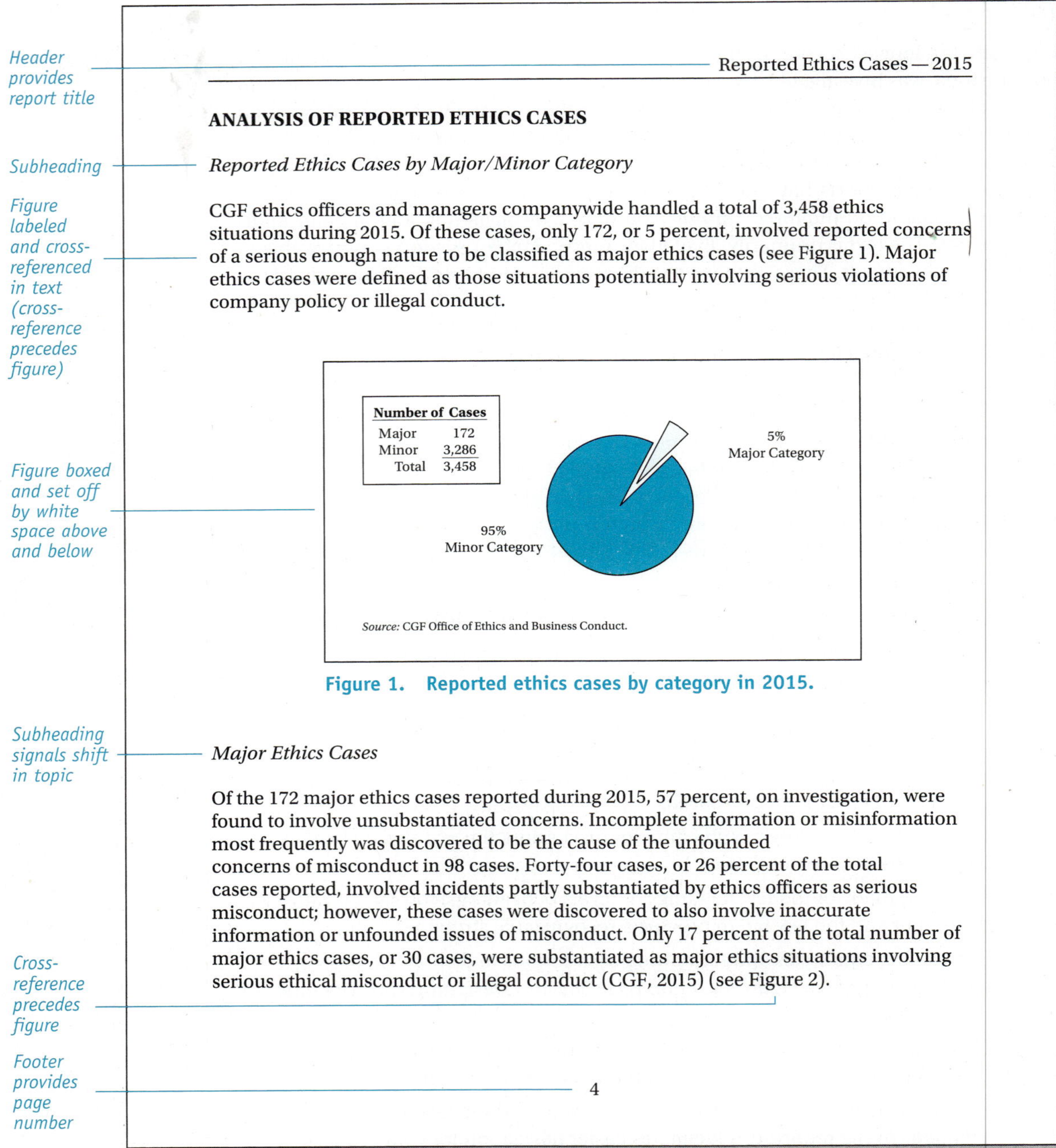

Header provides report title
Reported Ethics Cases — 2015
ANALYSIS OF REPORTED ETHICS CASES
Subheading
Reported Ethics Cases by Major/Minor Category
Figure labeled and cross-referenced in text (cross-reference precedes figure)
CGF ethics officers and managers companywide handled a total of 3,458 ethics situations during 2015. Of these cases, only 172, or 5 percent, involved reported concerns of a serious enough nature to be classified as major ethics cases (see Figure 1). Major ethics cases were defined as those situations potentially involving serious violations of company policy or illegal conduct.
Figure boxed and set off by white space above and below
Number of Cases
Major 172
Minor 3,286
Total 3,458
5% Major Category
95% Minor Category
Source: CGF Office of Ethics and Business Conduct.
Figure 1. Reported ethics cases by category in 2015.
Subheading signals shift in topic
Major Ethics Cases
Of the 172 major ethics cases reported during 2015, 57 percent, on investigation, were found to involve unsubstantiated concerns. Incomplete information or misinformation most frequently was discovered to be the cause of the unfounded concerns of misconduct in 98 cases. Forty-four cases, or 26 percent of the total cases reported, involved incidents partly substantiated by ethics officers as serious misconduct; however, these cases were discovered to also involve inaccurate information or unfounded issues of misconduct. Only 17 percent of the total number of major ethics cases, or 30 cases, were substantiated as major ethics situations involving serious ethical misconduct or illegal conduct (CGF, 2015) (see Figure 2).
Cross-reference precedes figure
Footer provides page number
4

Figure 11–10 Body of a Formal Report Susan Litzinger.

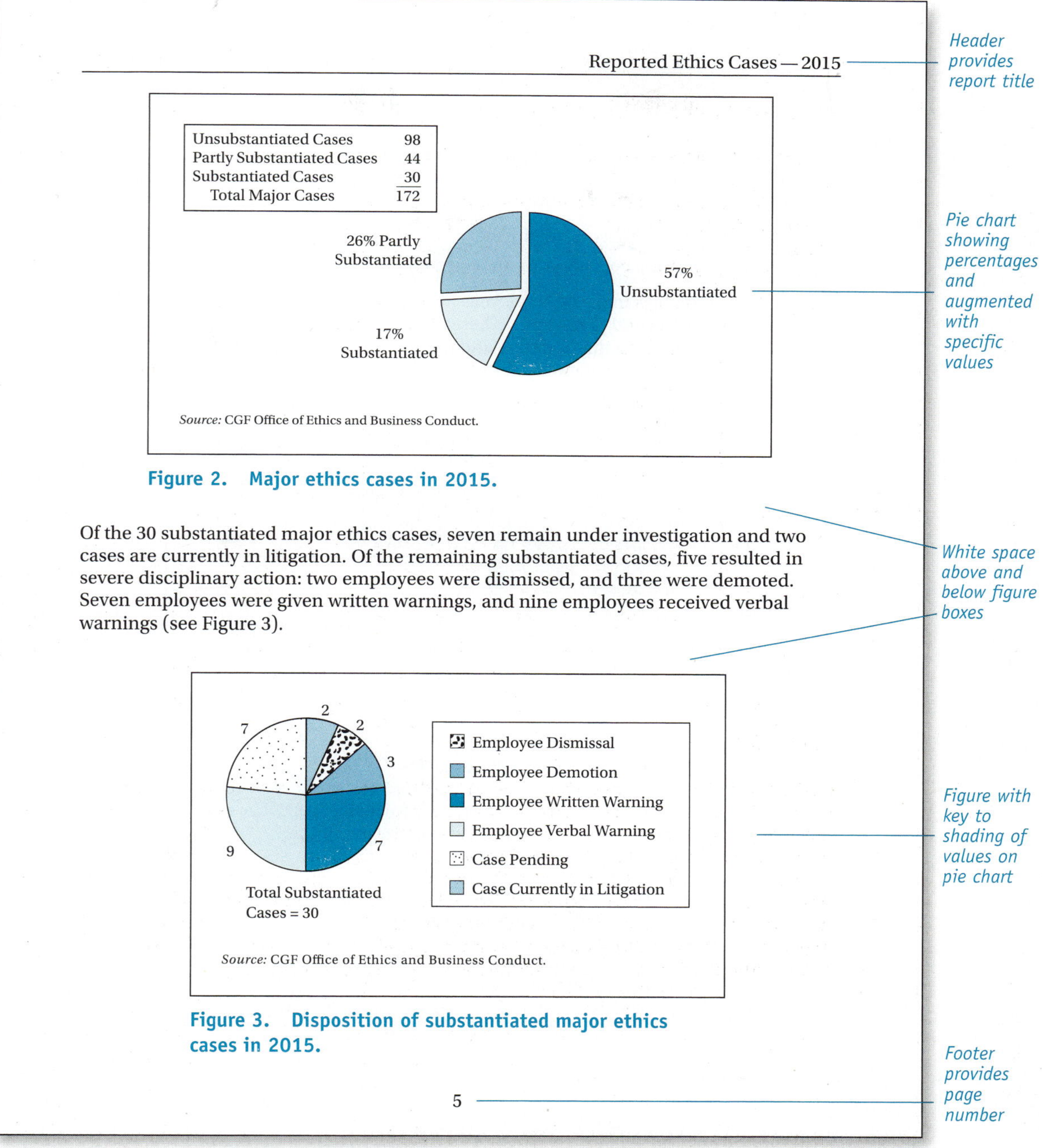

Reported Ethics Cases — 2015
Header provides report title
Unsubstantiated Cases 98
Partly Substantiated Cases 44
Substantiated Cases 30
Total Major Cases 172
26% Partly Substantiated
57% Unsubstantiated
17% Substantiated
Pie chart showing percentages and augmented with specific values
Source: CGF Office of Ethics and Business Conduct.
Figure 2. Major ethics cases in 2015.
Of the 30 substantiated major ethics cases, seven remain under investigation and two cases are currently in litigation. Of the remaining substantiated cases, five resulted in severe disciplinary action: two employees were dismissed, and three were demoted. Seven employees were given written warnings, and nine employees received verbal warnings (see Figure 3).
White space above and below figure boxes
2
2
3
7
7
9
Total Substantiated Cases = 30
Employee Dismissal
Employee Demotion
Employee Written Warning
Employee Verbal Warning
Case Pending
Case Currently in Litigation
Figure with key to shading of values on pie chart
Source: CGF Office of Ethics and Business Conduct.
Figure 3. Disposition of substantiated major ethics cases in 2015.
5
Footer provides page number

Figure 11–10 Body of a Formal Report *(continued)*

Header provides report title

Subheading

Minor Ethics Cases

Minor ethics cases included those that did not involve serious violations of company policy or illegal conduct. During 2015, ethics officers and company managers handled 3,286 such cases, classified as follows:

Bulleted list highlights information

- Informational queries from employees
- Situations involving coworkers or management

The majority of contacts made by employees were informational, involving questions about the new policies and procedures. These informational contacts comprised 65 percent of all contacts of a minor nature and numbered 2,148. Employees made 989 ethics contacts regarding coworkers and 149 contacts regarding management (see Figure 4).

Cross-reference precedes figure

White space above and below figure box

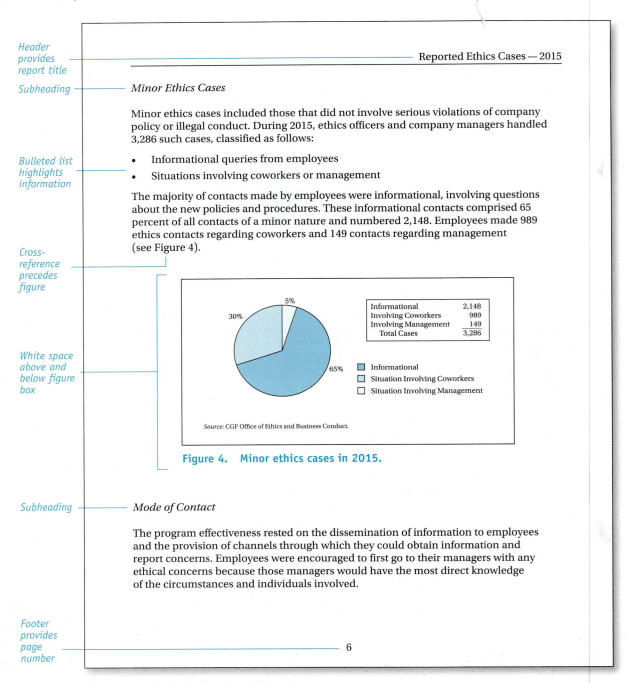

Informational	2,148
Involving Coworkers	989
Involving Management	149
Total Cases	3,286

Source: CGF Office of Ethics and Business Conduct.

Figure 4. Minor ethics cases in 2015.

Subheading

Mode of Contact

The program effectiveness rested on the dissemination of information to employees and the provision of channels through which they could obtain information and report concerns. Employees were encouraged to first go to their managers with any ethical concerns because those managers would have the most direct knowledge of the circumstances and individuals involved.

Footer provides page number

Figure 11–10 Body of a Formal Report *(continued)*

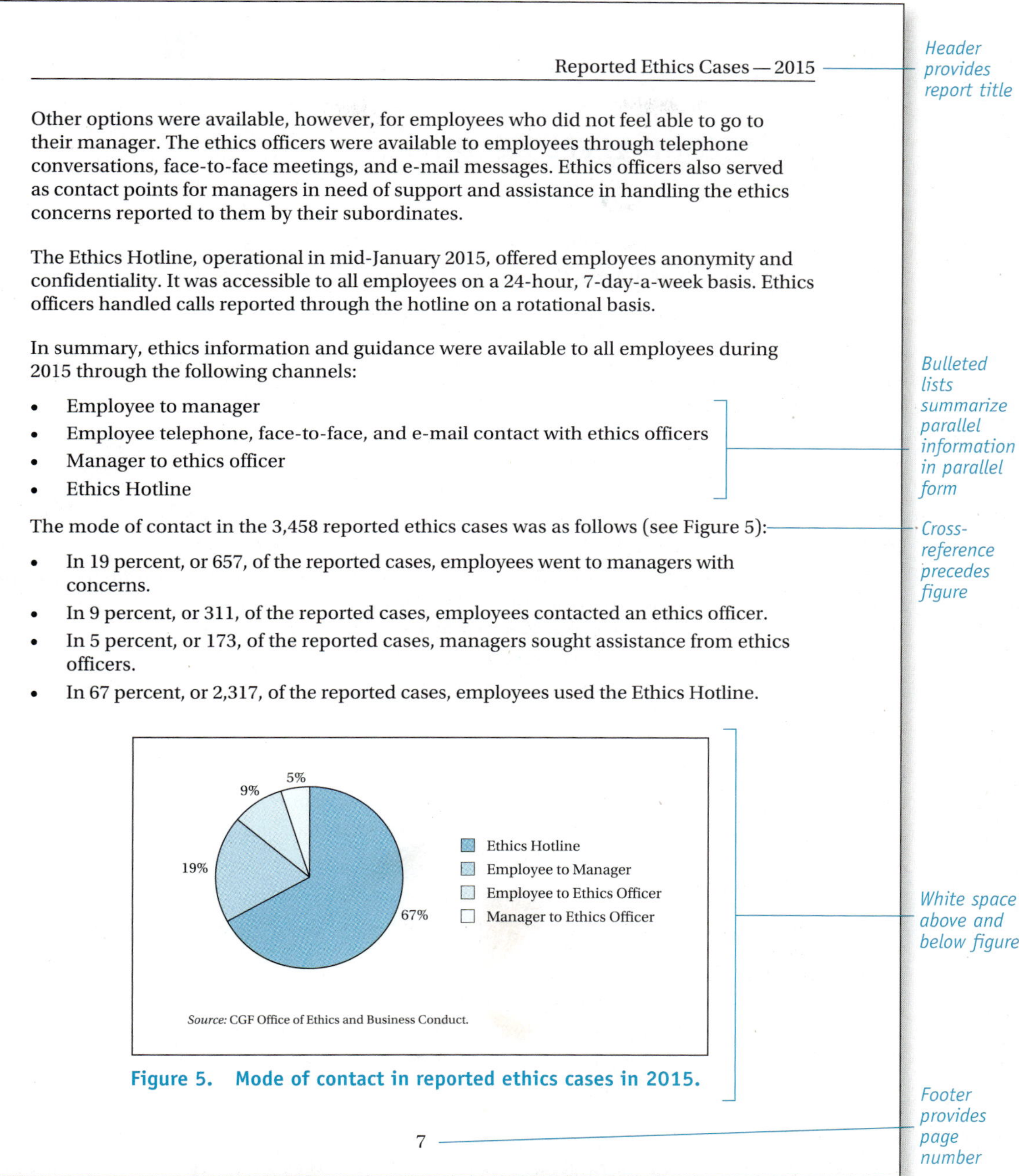

Reported Ethics Cases — 2015

Other options were available, however, for employees who did not feel able to go to their manager. The ethics officers were available to employees through telephone conversations, face-to-face meetings, and e-mail messages. Ethics officers also served as contact points for managers in need of support and assistance in handling the ethics concerns reported to them by their subordinates.

The Ethics Hotline, operational in mid-January 2015, offered employees anonymity and confidentiality. It was accessible to all employees on a 24-hour, 7-day-a-week basis. Ethics officers handled calls reported through the hotline on a rotational basis.

In summary, ethics information and guidance were available to all employees during 2015 through the following channels:

- Employee to manager
- Employee telephone, face-to-face, and e-mail contact with ethics officers
- Manager to ethics officer
- Ethics Hotline

The mode of contact in the 3,458 reported ethics cases was as follows (see Figure 5):

- In 19 percent, or 657, of the reported cases, employees went to managers with concerns.
- In 9 percent, or 311, of the reported cases, employees contacted an ethics officer.
- In 5 percent, or 173, of the reported cases, managers sought assistance from ethics officers.
- In 67 percent, or 2,317, of the reported cases, employees used the Ethics Hotline.

Figure 5. Mode of contact in reported ethics cases in 2015.

7

Figure 11–10 Body of a Formal Report *(continued)*

FIRST-LEVEL HEADING

The text of the document begins here.

SECOND-LEVEL HEADING

The text of the document begins here.

Third-Level Heading

The text of the document begins here.

Fourth-Level Heading

The text of the document begins here.

Fifth-level heading. The text of the document begins here and continues normally to the next line of the page.

Figure 11–11 Common Type Style for Headings

The decimal numbering system uses a combination of numbers and decimal points to subordinate levels of headings in a report. The system is used primarily for scientific and technical reports. The outline in Figure 11–12 shows the correspondence between different levels of headings and the decimal numbers used. (Note that although the second-, third-, and fourth-level headings are indented in an outline or a table of contents as headings, they align with the left margin in the body of the report.)

Explanatory Notes

Occasionally, reports contain notes that clarify content for some readers that would be a distraction for others. This type of explanation is generally placed at the foot of the page on which the idea appears.

1 MAJOR IDEA
1.1 Supporting idea for 1
1.2 Supporting idea for 1
1.2.1 Example or illustration of 1.2
1.2.2 Example or illustration of 1.2
1.2.2.1 Detail for 1.2.2
1.2.2.2 Detail for 1.2.2
1.3 Supporting idea for 1
2 MAJOR IDEA

Figure 11–12 Decimal Numbering System for Headings

A description of the 76 variables identified for inclusion in the regression equations, together with their method of construction, data, source, means, and ranges, is given in Appendix A. The following discussion elaborates on those variables that proved most important in explaining housing-price variations.[1]

[1]The number in parentheses in the following discussion refers to the variable number as used in regression equations.

If such comments are very long, or if offering them as footnotes would crowd the pages of the report body, they may appear in a separate "Notes" page at the end of the section, chapter, or report.

DESIGNING YOUR DOCUMENT

Heading Styles

Although various systems exist like the guidelines for headings and seriation established by the American Psychological Association, the following guidelines for formatting up to five levels of headings are common. Format your document according to the documentation style best suited for the project.

First-Level Head

- All-capital letters underlined or in 18-point boldface type
- Centered or flush left on a line by itself
- Two spaces above and one below

Second-Level Head

- All-capital letters underlined or in 14-point boldface type
- Flush left on a line by itself
- One space above and one space below

Third-Level Head

- Capital and lowercase letters underlined or in boldface type
- Flush left on a line by itself
- One space above and one space below

Fourth-Level Head

- Capital and lowercase letters not underlined or in boldface type
- One space above and one space below

Fifth-Level Head

- Indented as a paragraph on the same line as the first line of material it introduces
- Underlined or in italic type
- First letter capitalized; all others lowercase except proper nouns
- Ends with a period
- One space above the heading

Graphic and Tabular Matter

Formal reports often contain illustrations and tables that clarify and support the text. These materials may be numbered and sequenced in varying ways. If your employer or client has a preferred system, use it. If not, the following guidelines offer a typical system for numbering and smoothly integrating such materials into the text.

Identify each figure with a title and a number, in Arabic numerals, above or below the figure. For fairly short reports, number figures sequentially throughout the report (Figure 1, Figure 2, and so forth). For long reports, number figures by chapter or by section. According to this system, the first figure in Chapter 1 would be Figure 1.1 (or Figure 1–1), and the second figure would be Figure 1.2 (or Figure 1–2). In Chapter 2, the first figure would be Figure 2.1 (or Figure 2–1), and so on.

◆ *For a full discussion of creating and using illustrations, see Chapter 7, Designing Documents and Visuals.*

In the text, refer to figures by number rather than by location ("Figure 2.1" [or "Figure 2–1"] rather than "the figure below"). When the report is laid out and printed, the figures may not fall exactly where you originally expected. The figure or table should always be placed *after* its first mention in the text.

Identify each table with a title and a number, centering both of these lines above the table. For fairly short reports, number the tables sequentially throughout the report (Table 1, Table 2, and so on). For long reports, number tables by chapter or by section, according to the system described for figure numbering. As with figures, refer to tables in the text by number rather than by location ("Table 4.1" [or "Table 4–1"] rather than "the above table").

Conclusions

The conclusions section of a report pulls together the report's results or findings and interprets them in the light of its purpose and methods. Consequently, this section is the focal point of the work, the reason for the report in the first place. The conclusions must grow out of the findings discussed in the body of the report; moreover, they must be consistent with the purpose stated in the introduction and with the report's methodology. For instance, if the introduction states that the report's objective is to assess the market for a new product, then the conclusion should focus on the requirements of the market examined and on how appropriate the new product is for that market.

Recommendations

Recommendations, which are sometimes combined with the conclusions, suggest a course of action that should be taken based on the results of the study. (Decide whether the report should make recommendations when the report is being planned.) What consulting group should the firm hire for a special project? With which Web-page designer should the company sign a contract? What new and emerging markets should the firm target? Which make of delivery van should the company purchase to replace the existing fleet? The recommendations section says, in effect, "I think we should purchase this, or do that, or hire them."

The emphasis here is on the verb *should*. Recommendations advise the audience on the best course of action based on the researcher's findings. In general, a decision maker in the organization, or a customer or client, makes the final decision about whether to accept the recommendations.

Figure 11–13 shows the conclusions and recommendations from the report on the CGF Ethics Program.

ETHICS NOTE: Review Reports Before Distribution for Compliance with Policy, Disclosure, and Prior-Approval Requirements Formal reports frequently appear at the issuing organization's website. Whether a report is printed, posted to a website, published in PDF format, or formatted for a tablet computer, all versions should be identical in content. If the printed version is shortened or revised for online posting, the online version should be marked accordingly, as in the following example, so that readers know how it differs from the original.

> *The data in Appendix A of this report are updated monthly and vary from the data in the printed report, which is published each February.

Regardless of the transmittal method, all versions of the report should be reviewed before posting to ensure the following:

- They comply with the organization's guidelines for release of information to the public.
- Their content is consistent with the organization's current policies.
- They do not contain proprietary, classified, or private information.
- Each has been granted permission by the copyright holder to publish copyrighted text, tables, or images.

Works Cited (or References)

If you refer to material in, or quote directly from, a published work or other research source, you must cite those sources in the body of the text and provide a list of references in a separate section. Citing sources and listing references allows readers to locate and consult your sources to find further information about the subject; the practice also enables you to avoid plagiarism while supporting your assertions and arguments with expert opinion and valid data. If your instructor or employer has a preferred reference style, follow it; otherwise, use the APA or MLA documentation guidelines shown in Chapter 6, Conducting Research for a Document. (*Note:* In APA style, the list is titled "References"; in MLA style, the list is titled "Works Cited.") For a relatively short report, place the references at the end of the body of the report, as shown in Figure 11–14 on page 388. For a report with a number of sections or chapters, place the references at the end of each major section or chapter. In either case, title the reference or works-cited section as such and begin it on a new page. If a particular reference appears in more than one section or chapter, repeat it in full in each appropriate reference section.

For detailed guidance on documenting sources and avoiding plagiarism, see pages 172–184 in Chapter 6, Conducting Research for a Document.

Header provides report title

Reported Ethics Cases — 2015

CONCLUSIONS AND RECOMMENDATIONS

Conclusions

The effectiveness of CGF's Ethics Program during the first year of implementation is most evidenced by (1) the active participation of employees in the program and the 3,458 contacts employees made regarding ethics concerns through the various channels available to them, and (2) the action taken in the cases reported by employees, particularly the disposition of the 30 substantiated major ethics cases.

One of the 12 steps to building a successful Ethics Program identified by Frank Navran in *Workforce* magazine is an ethics communication strategy. Navran explains that such a strategy is crucial in ensuring "that employees have the information they need in a timely and usable fashion and that the organization is encouraging employee communication regarding the values, standards, and the conduct of the organization and its members" (p. 119).

APA-style in-text citation

The 3,458 contacts by employees during 2015 attest to the accessibility and effectiveness of the communication channels that exist in CGF's Ethics Program.

An equally important step in building a successful ethics program is listed by Navran (2010) as "Measurements and Rewards," which he explains as follows:

Indented quotation set off for emphasis

> In most organizations, employees know what's important by virtue of what the organization measures and rewards. If ethical conduct is assessed and rewarded, and if unethical conduct is identified and dissuaded, employees will believe that the organization's principals mean it when they say the values and code of ethics are important. (p. 121)

APA-style in-text citation

Disseminating information about the disposition of ethics cases, particularly information about the severe disciplinary actions taken in major ethics violations, sends a message to employees that unethical or illegal conduct will not be tolerated. Making public the tough-minded actions taken in cases of ethical misconduct provides "a golden opportunity to make other employees aware that the behavior is unacceptable and why" (Ferrell & Gardiner, 2001, p. 129).

APA-style in-text citation

Footer provides page number

8

Figure 11–13 Conclusions and Recommendations of a Formal Report Susan Litzinger.

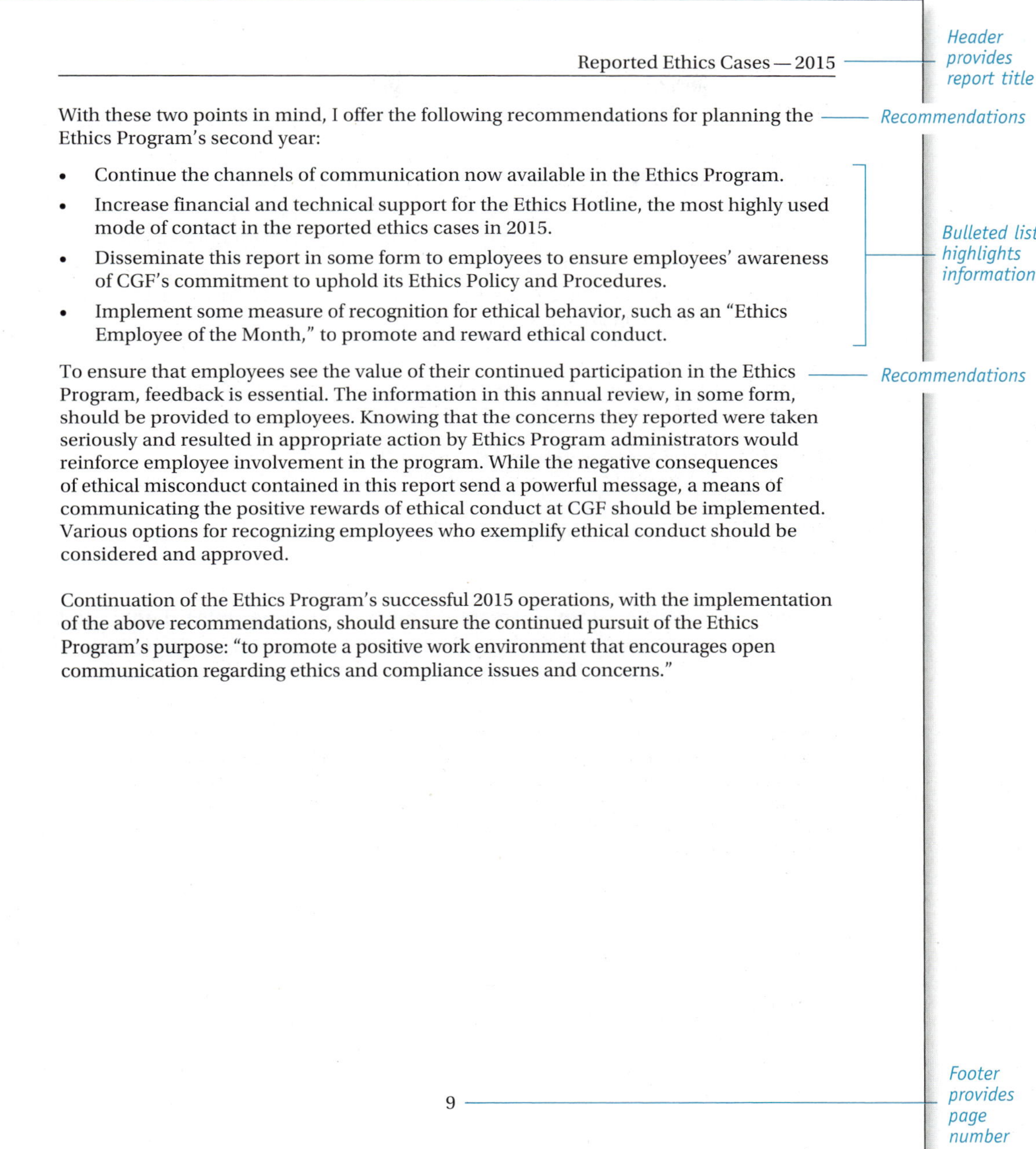
Reported Ethics Cases — 2015

With these two points in mind, I offer the following recommendations for planning the Ethics Program's second year:

- Continue the channels of communication now available in the Ethics Program.
- Increase financial and technical support for the Ethics Hotline, the most highly used mode of contact in the reported ethics cases in 2015.
- Disseminate this report in some form to employees to ensure employees' awareness of CGF's commitment to uphold its Ethics Policy and Procedures.
- Implement some measure of recognition for ethical behavior, such as an "Ethics Employee of the Month," to promote and reward ethical conduct.

To ensure that employees see the value of their continued participation in the Ethics Program, feedback is essential. The information in this annual review, in some form, should be provided to employees. Knowing that the concerns they reported were taken seriously and resulted in appropriate action by Ethics Program administrators would reinforce employee involvement in the program. While the negative consequences of ethical misconduct contained in this report send a powerful message, a means of communicating the positive rewards of ethical conduct at CGF should be implemented. Various options for recognizing employees who exemplify ethical conduct should be considered and approved.

Continuation of the Ethics Program's successful 2015 operations, with the implementation of the above recommendations, should ensure the continued pursuit of the Ethics Program's purpose: "to promote a positive work environment that encourages open communication regarding ethics and compliance issues and concerns."

9

Figure 11–13 Conclusions and Recommendations of a Formal Report *(continued)*

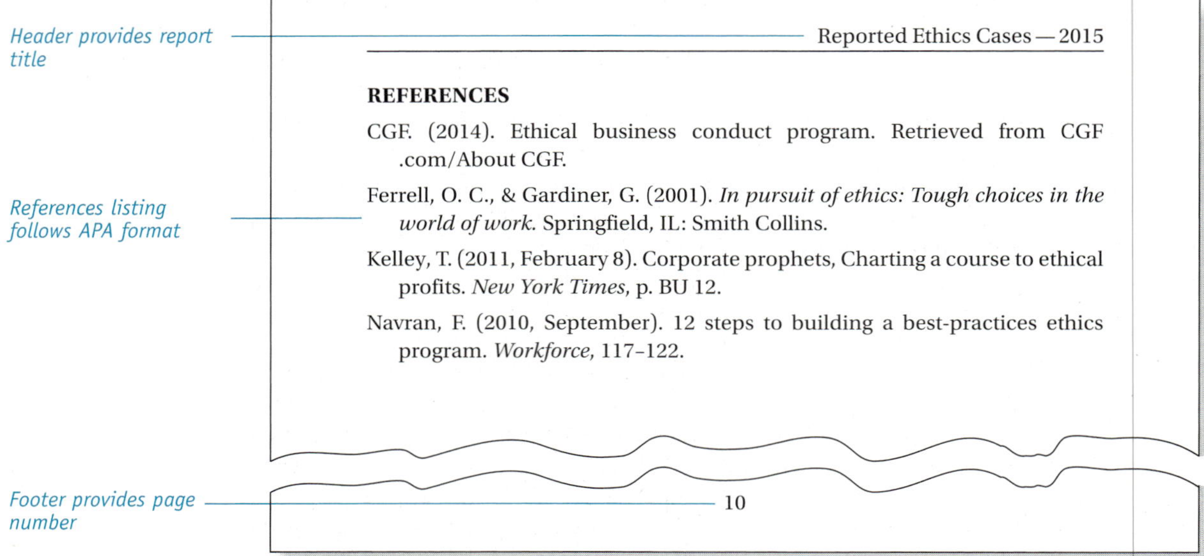

Header provides report title
Reported Ethics Cases — 2015
REFERENCES
CGF. (2014). Ethical business conduct program. Retrieved from CGF .com/About CGF.
Ferrell, O. C., & Gardiner, G. (2001). In pursuit of ethics: Tough choices in the world of work. Springfield, IL: Smith Collins.
Kelley, T. (2011, February 8). Corporate prophets, Charting a course to ethical profits. New York Times, p. BU 12.
Navran, F. (2010, September). 12 steps to building a best-practices ethics program. Workforce, 117–122.
References listing follows APA format
Footer provides page number
10

Figure 11–14 References Section of a Formal Report Susan Litzinger.

ETHICS NOTE: Cite Research Sources in Line with Legal and Ethical Standards Always identify the sources of any facts, ideas, quotations, and paraphrases you include in a report (unless the information was taken from existing company documents, which usually do not require documentation). Plagiarism — even if unintentional — is unethical and in some cases illegal. Plagiarism in a college course may result in formal academic misconduct charges; on the job, it can get you fired. Avoid trouble by giving proper credit to others.

Back Matter

The back matter of a formal report contains supplementary material — such as where to find additional information about the topic (bibliography) — and expands on certain subjects (appendixes). Other back-matter elements define the terms used (glossary) and provide information on how to easily locate information in the report (index). For very long formal reports, back-matter sections may be individually numbered.

Bibliography

The bibliography is an alphabetical listing of all the sources you consulted to prepare the report — not just the ones you cite specifically in the report — and suggests additional resources readers might want to consult. Accordingly, the bibliography may be longer than the works-cited section. A bibliography is not necessary if the Works Cited (or References) page contains a complete list of sources. Like other elements in the front and back matter, the bibliography starts on a new page and is labeled by name.

Entries in a bibliography are listed alphabetically by the author's last name. If an author is unknown, the entry is alphabetized by the first word in the title (other than *A*, *An*, or *The*). Entries also can be grouped by subject and then ordered alphabetically within those categories.

An annotated bibliography includes complete bibliographic information about a work (author, title, place of publication, publisher, and publication date) followed by a brief description or evaluation of what the work contains.

Appendixes

An appendix clarifies or supplements information in the body with content that is too detailed or lengthy for the primary audience but that is relevant to secondary audiences. Appendixes might provide long charts and supplementary graphs or tables, copies of questionnaires and other material used in gathering information, verbatim transcripts of interviews, pertinent correspondence, and explanations too long for explanatory footnotes. Generally, each appendix contains one type of material. For example, a report may have one appendix presenting a questionnaire and a second, separate appendix with a detailed tabulation of questionnaire results.

Place the first appendix on a new page directly after the bibliography; each additional appendix also begins on a new page. Appendixes are ordinarily labeled Appendix A, Appendix B, and so on and identified with a title: Appendix A: Sample Questionnaire. If your report has only one appendix, label it "Appendix," followed by the title. To call it Appendix A implies that an Appendix B will follow.

If a report has only one appendix, the pages are generally numbered 1, 2, 3, and so forth. If it has more than one appendix, the pages are double-numbered according to the letter of each appendix (for example, the first page of Appendix B would be numbered B–1).

Glossary

A glossary is an alphabetical list of definitions of specialized terms used in a formal report. Include a glossary if a report will go to readers unfamiliar with the topic-specific terms you use. If you do include a glossary, keep the entry definitions concise and be sure they are written in plain language to improve reader understanding.

▶ *Capital gain*: The difference between an asset's purchase price and selling price, when the difference is positive.

Arrange the terms alphabetically, with each entry beginning on a new line. The definitions then follow the terms, dictionary style. In a formal report, the glossary appears as a separate section after the bibliography and appendix(es), and it begins on a new page.

Regardless of whether you include a glossary, define any specialized terms when they are first mentioned in the text.

DIGITAL TIP: Digitally Enhancing Formal Reports

Many organizations publish formal reports as PDF files or Web documents. Digital versions of formal reports can offer tables of contents that link directly to the individual sections within a report. You can add hyperlinks or mouseover elements that provide definitions of specialized terms or links to supplemental information.

Index

An index is an alphabetical list of all the major topics and subtopics found in the report. It cites the pages where each topic can be found and allows readers to locate information on particular topics quickly and easily, as shown in Figure 11–15. Indexes are especially useful for reports that will serve as reference documents in a subject area for at least several years. The index always comes at the very end of the report.

Do not attempt to compile an index until the final manuscript is completed because terminology and page numbers will not be accurate before then. The key to a useful index is selectivity. Instead of listing every possible reference to a topic, select references to passages where the topic is discussed fully or where a significant point is made about it. Use the words or phrases that best represent a topic — those that a reader would most likely look for in an index. For example, the key terms in a reference to the development of legislation about environmental impact statements would probably be *legislation* and *environmental impact statement*.

DIGITAL TIP: Creating an Index

Most word-processing programs can save you time by creating an index automatically based on keywords that you mark while composing the report.

An index entry can consist solely of a main entry and its page number; it can also include a main entry, subentries, and even sub-subentries, as shown in Figure 11–15. The first word of an entry should be the principal word because the reader will look for

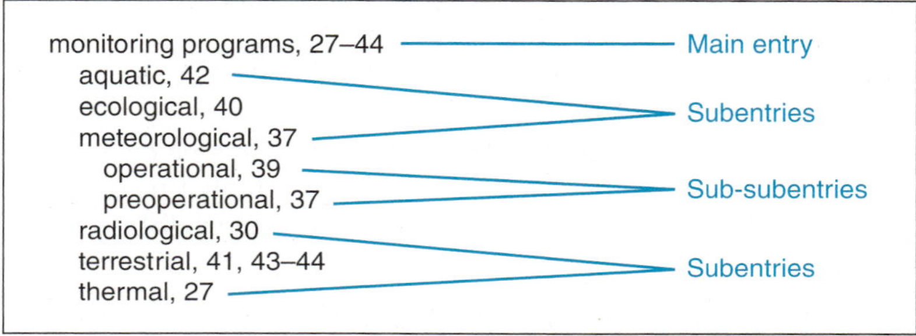

Figure 11–15 Index Entry (with Main Entry, Subentries, and Sub-subentries)

topics alphabetically by their main words. An index entry should be written as a noun or a noun phrase rather than as an adjective alone.

When you have compiled a list of key terms and cross-references for the entire work, sort the main entries alphabetically, and then sort all subentries and sub-subentries alphabetically beneath their main entries.

CHAPTER 11 SUMMARY: WRITING FORMAL REPORTS

Formal reports require thoughtful planning because of their varied audiences, purposes, scope, and complexity. To ensure that they are adequately planned and written, review the following summary checklist.

- Who is the principal audience for the report? Who is the secondary audience?
- Is the transmittal message necessary and addressed to the person or organization requesting the report?
- Are the elements that make up the front matter, body, and back matter of the report organized in the correct sequence?
- Does the title page include the report title, date, preparer, and recipient?
- Does the abstract concisely highlight the report's major points?
- Does the table of contents list section titles exactly as they appear throughout the report?
- Does the executive summary describe the purpose, major findings, conclusions, recommendations, and methodology used to reach the findings? Can it be read independently of the report?
- Does the introduction state the purpose of the report, the scope of material it covers, how you plan to develop the topic, and how the report will be organized?
- Does the body of the report enable the principal audience to interpret your findings, conclusions, and recommendations?
- Is the body of the report organized into logically divided sections that best represent how the topic was developed to reach its findings, conclusions, and recommendations?
- Do the conclusions grow logically from the report's findings?
- Do the recommendations advise the audience on the appropriate course of action to take based on the findings?
- Do the works cited or references provide enough information to permit a reader to locate a source of interest?
- Is the material in the appendixes important enough to be included but not so voluminous or ancillary that its presence in the body of the report would impede the reader?
- Does the report include a large number of technical terms that should be defined for your audience in an alphabetically arranged glossary?
- Are the index terms sufficiently selective that they allow the audience to locate key topics throughout the report quickly and accurately?

Exercises

1. Prepare a statement that defines the scope of a formal report, covering the benefits, risks, and costs of establishing an on-site fitness center at a local business with more than 200 employees.

2. The following is an audience-profile questionnaire for the fitness-center report in Exercise 1 or for a hypothetical research, investigative, or annual report that you have been asked to prepare. Briefly explain the topic of your formal report before answering the questions:
   a. Who is your audience? (Write a 75- to 100-word description.)
   b. What does your audience already know about the subject?
   c. What do you want your audience to know?
   d. What might be your readers' attitude toward the topic? (Explore several alternatives.)
   e. Why will your audience be reading the report?
   f. How will your readers' perception of the report affect the project?
3. Keeping in mind that design is an important part of a formal report, prepare a title page for the fitness-center report in Exercises 1 and 2, or for a hypothetical research, investigative, or annual report that you have been asked to prepare, and bring it to class. Explain the reasons for your design decisions, including the placement of information and the choice of illustrations. Refer to pages 363–364 for guidelines as you design your title page.
4. Considering your audience and purpose, determine what elements you would need to include in the fitness-center or hypothetical report from Exercises 1, 2, and 3. Then prepare a table of contents that details the materials the final report would include.
5. Assume you are starting a business of your own. First, determine what type of business you would start, depending on your knowledge or experience. Based on what you know about such a business, write an introduction for a formal report, explaining what your business will be and identifying what city would be the best location for your business and why. Assume that you are preparing this report to attach to a request for funding from the Small Business Administration. Submit an outline to your instructor before you begin your draft.
6. Assume that you work in the corporate office of a high-end automotive manufacturer and that you are coordinating a report that analyzes the effectiveness of new management initiatives that have gone into effect in the past year. Two of the people on your team, who have been lax in meeting periodic deadlines, submit hastily written drafts on the day before the entire report must be printed. To your dismay, you realize that each of them has peppered his section with abbreviations for trendy managerial phrases, such as "JIT" for "just-in-time" delivery and "CSR" for "corporate social responsibility." There is no time left to revise these sections, but you know that several of the report's readers will not understand the abbreviations. Using the following terms, create a List of Abbreviations for the report to explain what phrases they stand for and what those phrases mean. (You may have to do a little research to learn what the abbreviations stand for and what business concepts they refer to.)

ALF	BID	MOP
ALO	FMCG	SONTTAP
ASK	KAS	
ATNA	KISS	

7. Using the guidelines on pages 390–391, create an index for the sample formal report reprinted in Figures 11–9, 11–10, 11–13, and 11–14 (on pages 375, 378, 386, and 388, respectively). As your instructor directs, exchange your index with that of another student and make a list of terms that differ in the indexes. Discuss with your partner

potential reasons for the discrepancies between your lists, and decide which words would be prudent for you to add.

Collaborative Classroom Projects

1. Bring to class or post online in a discussion forum a sample abstract for a journal article related to your major field of study. Divide into teams with classmates who share a similar major area of study. Appoint a group leader and a recorder. As a group, review the abstracts and answer the following questions about each:
   a. How many words are in the abstract?
   b. Is the abstract descriptive or informative? How do you know?
   c. What is the abstract's purpose? What is its scope?
   d. Is the abstract clear and concise?
   e. Does the abstract encourage you to read the rest of the report?
   f. How would you improve the abstract?
2. As a class, discuss the executive summary shown in Figure 11–8 on page 373. Assume that the audience is, for example, the board of directors of CGF Aircraft Corporation. Consider the following questions:
   a. How does the executive summary introduce the report? Does it include the appropriate information?
   b. Is the background information sufficient?
   c. What is the purpose of the report?
   d. What is the scope of the report?
   e. Are costs an important concern of this report?
   f. Are the conclusions effective?
   g. How long would you expect the report to be?

Research Projects

1. Imagine that you work for a consulting firm that specializes in attractions, such as theme parks, aquariums, and zoos. Your firm has been hired by TRC, Inc., a company that owns several theme parks in the United States and is now interested in opening a new park in your state.
   a. Write an investigative report for TRC, Inc. that includes the following (as directed by your instructor):
      - An introduction
      - A short history of theme parks
      - The current state of the theme-park industry across the country and in your state (number and types of parks, attendee demographic trends, gross and net income, and any other relevant data)
      - An analysis of what makes theme parks successful (like popular themes that appeal to families, cutting-edge rides, quality service and cleanliness, and acceptable admissions prices)
      - The local audience for theme parks (demographics) and what appeals to them
      - A description of the competition in the area and their strong and weak points
      - Developing trends in theme parks (what the theme park of the future will look like and offer to the public)

- Conclusions
- Recommendations
- References (APA style)

b. Include the following visuals in your report (be sure to cite them and label them as described in Chapter 7, Designing Documents and Visuals):

- A line graph of attendance at theme parks across the country during the past five years
- A chart of services and offerings that make theme parks successful and the national theme parks that offer all or some of those services and offerings
- A pie graph of tourism in your state, broken down by the popularity of each kind of tourist activity (for example, theme parks, nature activities, museums, and so on)
- Photographs of local theme parks

2. Using the *Occupational Outlook Handbook* at the Bureau of Labor Statistics website at www.bls.gov/ooh/, write a formal report in which you analyze two different job positions in your major area of study. Include in your report the required background, working conditions, pay scale, geographic expectations, and job outlook. Prepare your report as if you are trying to decide objectively between two occupations, and include a conclusion and recommendations section.

3. The Federal Highway Administration (FHWA) of the U.S. Department of Transportation (DOT) works with states to conduct studies that explore the funding and feasibility of highway projects. According to the FHWA's Procedural Guidelines for Highway Feasibility Studies, six to nine tasks must occur within studies. See www.fhwa.dot.gov/planning/border-planning/corbor/feastudy.cfm. Only the last two steps of each case involve drafting the report; the first steps involve gathering and analyzing data.

   a. Write an abstract of the FHWA's Procedural Guidelines. Include a breakdown of the tasks required for (1) "improving an existing facility" or (2) "making major improvements to . . . a multi-State transportation corridor."

   b. Visit your state's DOT website and find a link to current construction projects. You can also research a project that local citizens and government officials are exploring, like light rail, express bus, monorail, or other services.

   c. Imagine that you work for your state's DOT and you've been asked to draft an outline of a feasibility study for one or two current or future construction projects to get funding from the FHWA. Consider how you would address each task leading to the final report. Describe what kind of information you would try to put in each task and from where you would get these data. Sources could include the public-affairs office of the local DOT, local newspapers, and the U.S. DOT's website links to transportation information regarding each state. Create a transmittal memo directed to the secretary of transportation for your state.

12 Writing Instructions

Contents

When you tell someone how to perform a procedure or task, you are giving instructions. Instructions may describe how to carry out a particular task in the workplace (send a file to a digital copier); perform a procedure (process a Medicare form); operate equipment (use a spray-paint gun); or assemble, repair, or maintain equipment (replace a seal on a high-pressure pump).

This chapter provides guidance for the following:

How many times have you heard people complain about instructions being unclear, inaccurate, or poorly illustrated? Poor instructions can cause miscommunication and delays in an important project or, worse, be directly responsible for an injury, which could result in damage claims and lawsuits. If your instructions are based on clear thinking and careful planning, they should enable your audience to carry out the procedure or task successfully. Clear, easy-to-follow instructions can also build goodwill for your company. Keep in mind that the most effective instructions often combine written and visual elements that reinforce each other. Consider too the most effective medium for your instructions. Although many companies continue to produce instructions in print, most can also be found online at company or product websites, often in downloadable versions and, increasingly, posted as videos. Finally, consider testing your instructions with someone unfamiliar with them, recording and evaluating their behavior as they perform a task.

Planning Instructions

To write effective instructions, you must thoroughly understand the process, system, or device you are describing. Often, you can do so by observing someone else perform a task or, better yet, performing it yourself and recording the details for each step from start to finish. Then assess your audience. Are they fellow employees within your firm, North American customers for your company's products, or non-English readers? Adapt your language and the design features of your instructions—their layout and packaging—for your target audience. After writing an introduction, listing or describing any essential tools or materials as necessary, organize the instructions in the sequence and exact number of steps necessary to perform the task.

Learn to Perform the Operation Yourself

Without a thorough understanding of the task you are describing, your instructions could be inaccurate or even dangerous. For example, the container of a brand-name drain cleaner directs the user to do the following:

> Fill sink with 1 to 2 inches of water, then close off drain opening.

Users would find it difficult to raise the water level in the sink *before* closing the drain! The writer of these instructions did not carefully observe the actual sequence of steps required to use the product. In this case, users simply ignored the instructions and performed the task according to common sense. Suppose, however, such confusing instructions were given for administering an intravenous fluid or for assembling high-voltage electrical equipment. The results of such inaccurate instructions could be both dangerous and costly.

The writer of the drain-cleaning instructions undoubtedly knew better and was just careless. Sometimes, though, a writer may be asked to write instructions for a procedure that he or she does not understand adequately. Don't let that happen to you. If you cannot perform a task yourself, request permission to watch someone else do it. As you watch, take careful notes and ask questions about any step that is not clear to you. Direct observation should enable you to write instructions that are exact, complete, and clear. Also make certain that you know the reason for the procedure, the materials and tools required, and the end result of the task.

Once you understand the procedure, you must determine the most effective way to present it to your audience.

Assess Your Audience and Purpose

In the workplace, you may need to prepare instructions for coworkers, domestic and international customers, or other users of your company's products or services. Start by determining who will use your instructions. Remember that you and your readers share a common purpose: the successful completion of a task or procedure after reading your instructions. To best meet reader requirements, learn as much as you can about your audience. You and your coworkers, for example, share a large amount of knowledge already. For customers and others outside the company, begin by learning their level of knowledge and experience, and try to put yourself in their position as they follow your instructions. Is the audience skilled in the kind of task for which you are writing instructions? If they are knowledgeable about the subject, use the specialized vocabulary and abbreviations appropriate to the subject. If they have little or no knowledge of the subject, use plain language or include a glossary that defines specialized terms in plain language. For international readers, learn about their proficiency in English and tailor the language accordingly.

◆ *For guidance on using plain language, see page 113 of Chapter 4, Revising a Document.*

◆ *For advice on creating a glossary, see Chapter 11, Writing Formal Reports.*

Coworkers

Employees write many kinds of informal, nontechnical instructions to coworkers every day. The advantage of communicating with coworkers is that they share your familiarity with the company's organization and hierarchy, job titles, products, customers, and numerous other details that need not be spelled out. In the e-mail instructions in Figure 12–1, for example, a budget analyst requests data about an office's copier use to plan for the upcoming fiscal year's budget. Note that this information is sent annually to the office manager, so both the sender and the recipient are familiar with the process. The scope of the request, its language ("seven-year life cycle"), and the shared access to an online form require no special explanations.

More detailed instructions to coworkers may describe how to perform routine workplace activities. The instructions in Figure 12–2 on page 399 address the crucial corporate responsibility of responding to consumer correspondence in a timely and responsible manner. They lay out the steps from the point when the correspondence is received until the company's response is sent. Note the use of headings, the step-by-step organization of the required tasks, and the uncomplicated language of the memo. These instructions assume that all recipients are familiar with the company's departments and job titles.

Consumers

Some instructions are intended to help customers assemble and maintain products. The instructions can range in scope from directions for operating a kitchen blender to guidance for installing and testing software on the computer network of a multi-branch commercial bank. These instructions tend to be formally written and carefully reviewed for accuracy and for their adherence to policy and legal requirements before they are used. The requirements common to all such instructions are that they be accurate, written in language appropriate to the audience, illustrated in sufficient detail (if necessary), and packaged in the medium most useful to the customer—brochure, digital or printed manual, or website. Keep in mind that each medium brings with it advantages and challenges. For example, using a website might be best for instructions that are subject to frequent changes, but doing so requires an audience familiar with the Internet.

Assess your customers carefully to meet these requirements. Consider their familiarity with your product based on their previous knowledge or experience, how broad your audience is (Is it a narrow group of specialists or a large cross section of the population?), and the medium most useful for your customers' needs. Also consider your audience's motivation for reading your instructions. Although instructions are essential to the successful use of consumer products, many readers ignore them. To increase the likelihood that readers will look at your instructions, see Design for Ease of Use on page 414. Figure 12–3 on page 400 shows a set of online instructions to repair a leaking compression faucet. Intended for home-repair users, the instructions describe how the faucet works, give step-by-step directions for the repair, and show an exploded-view diagram of the faucet's construction. Written in the imperative mood, the instructions also include a link to step-by-step drawings of the repair process.

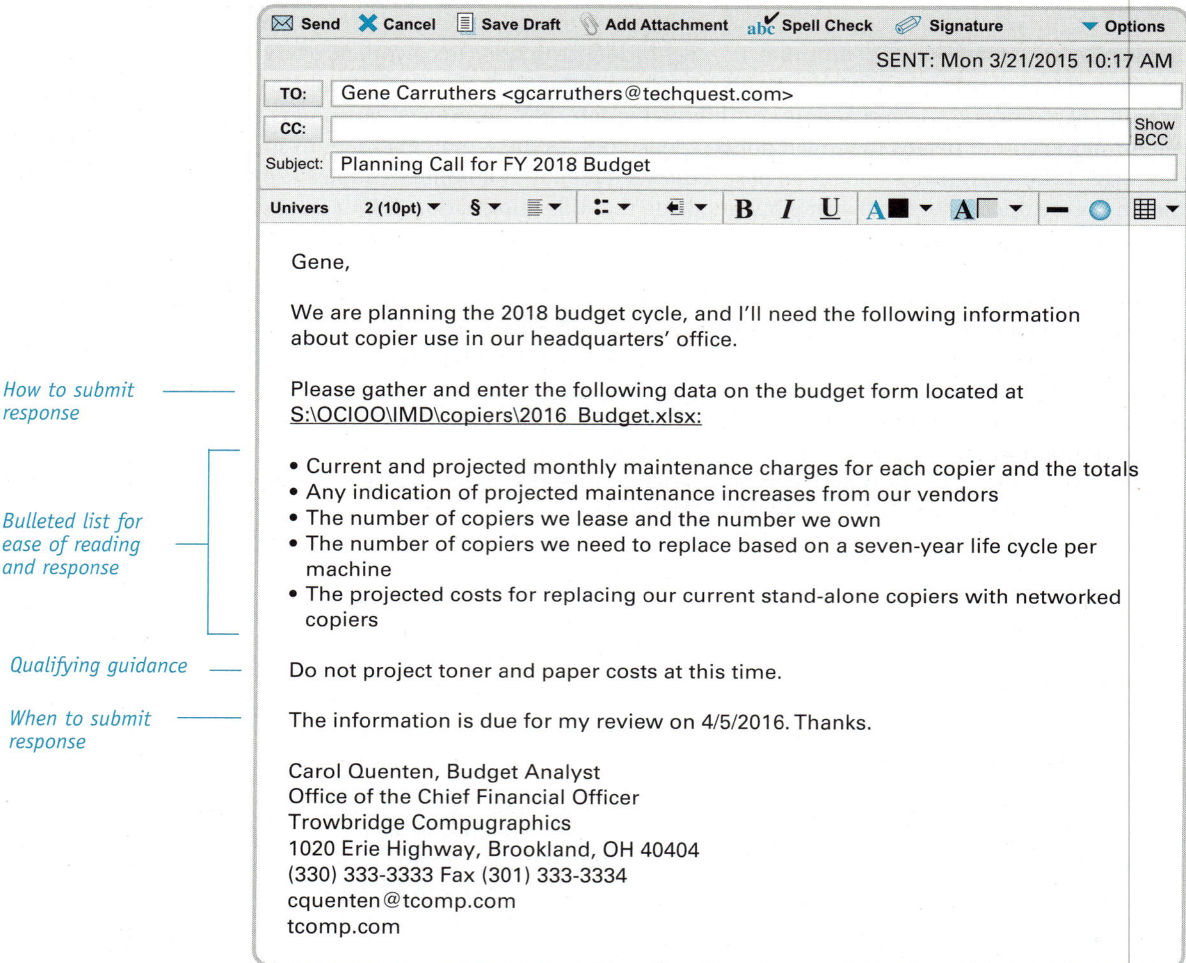
Send | Cancel | Save Draft | Add Attachment | Spell Check | Signature | Options

SENT: Mon 3/21/2015 10:17 AM

TO: Gene Carruthers <gcarruthers@techquest.com>

CC:

Subject: Planning Call for FY 2018 Budget

Gene,

We are planning the 2018 budget cycle, and I'll need the following information about copier use in our headquarters' office.

How to submit response — Please gather and enter the following data on the budget form located at S:\OCIOO\IMD\copiers\2016_Budget.xlsx:

Bulleted list for ease of reading and response

- Current and projected monthly maintenance charges for each copier and the totals
- Any indication of projected maintenance increases from our vendors
- The number of copiers we lease and the number we own
- The number of copiers we need to replace based on a seven-year life cycle per machine
- The projected costs for replacing our current stand-alone copiers with networked copiers

Qualifying guidance — Do not project toner and paper costs at this time.

When to submit response — The information is due for my review on 4/5/2016. Thanks.

Carol Quenten, Budget Analyst
Office of the Chief Financial Officer
Trowbridge Compugraphics
1020 Erie Highway, Brookland, OH 40404
(330) 333-3333 Fax (301) 333-3334
cquenten@tcomp.com
tcomp.com

Figure 12–1 Informal Employee-to-Employee Instructions

International Readers

Language differences create the biggest obstacle to writing instructions for readers whose primary language is not English. For such audiences, find out as much as possible about their English-language proficiency and adjust your writing accordingly. If your text will be translated into another language, write to the extent possible in plain language and define specialized terms or abbreviations in a glossary. If your instructions are going to be transmitted digitally and if your organization relies on software to translate its website automatically, be sure to have an expert review the translations of your instructions before posting them for public access. Help your audience by becoming familiar with their terminology for important concepts or even the

Proctor Electronic Corporation

Consumer Response Department

Procedures for Handling Correspondence

1. **Intake**
   When the Customer Response Department receives an e-mail, Twitter, Facebook, or website consumer query or comment, the department assistant
   - Logs the message into the online tracking system.
   - Forwards the message to the section analyst for review.
   - Retains a copy of the message in the section tracking file folder.
2. **Content Review**
   The department analyst
   - Reviews the content.
   - Meets with the department chief to discuss response strategy, staff assigned to respond, and date due to the department supervisor.

   The due date is two working days before the response is due to the vice president for consumer affairs.
3. **Staff Assignment**
   The department analyst
   - Informs the department assistant of who will respond and the due date.
   - Meets with the assistant and provides any necessary background for the reply.
4. **Staff Response**
   - The respondent e-mails the draft reply to the department assistant on or before the due date.
   - The department assistant logs the draft into the database and forwards it to the department analyst for review.
5. **Response Review**
   The department chief and department analyst jointly
   - Make any necessary revisions to the draft.
   - Forward the draft to the department assistant for incorporation into the final draft.

   The department assistant
   - Enters the final draft into the company electronic document database.
   - Maintains a record of approvals on the final draft.
   - Prepares a version for e-signature.
6. **Approval**
   - The department supervisor approves the draft.
   - The department assistant forwards the final draft to the vice president for consumer affairs for review, e-signature, and response to the consumer.

Instructions arranged in sequential order

Bullets identify tasks within each major step

Boldface headings identify major steps

Figure 12–2 Coworker Instructions for Processing Correspondence

tip # 1

REPAIRING A LEAKY WASHER-TYPE FAUCET

Washer-type faucets work with a rubber or composition washer that closes onto a metal washer seat **(Fig. 1)**. The washer can become hardened, worn or the seat wears, causing the faucet to leak. You can close the faucet tighter to stop the leaking temporarily, but this increases the internal damage to the faucet.

To repair the leak, first turn off the water. If there's a shutoff valve beneath the fixture, turn off the water at that point. Otherwise, turn it off at the main house shutoff valve in the basement, utility room, or crawlspace. Turn off the hot water supply at the water heater.

Fig. 1 Compression faucet

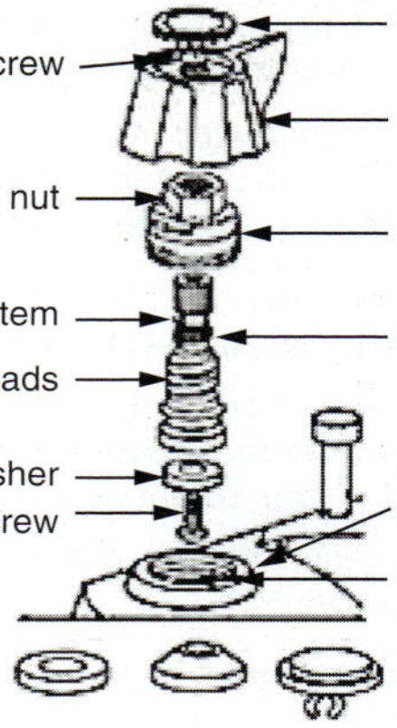

cap
handle screw
handle
stem nut
packing nut
stem
packing
threads
seat washer
washer screw
faucet body
valve seat
washers

Take the faucet apart by removing the handle (this may not be necessary on some older faucets). Loosen the Phillips-head screw, which usually is beneath a decorative cap in the center of the handle. The cap either unscrews or snaps off when you pry it with a knife blade.

Instructions written in the imperative mood

If you must use pliers on decorative faucet parts, pad them with electrical tape or cloth to protect the finish. And take special care with the plastic parts found on many modern faucets. Next, lift or pry the handle off its broached stem. Unscrew the packing nut beneath the handle, exposing the rest of the stem. Remove the stem by rotating it in the "on" direction. It will thread out. Reinstall the handle if you have difficulty turning it (Fig. 1). Clean chips from the faucet cavity, but do not use harsh abrasives or a file.

Exploded-view diagram shows proper sequence of parts and their names.

Examine the stem. If the threads are badly corroded or worn, take it to your retailer and get a new stem to match. Clean the stem if it's dirty.

Now look at the washer, which is located on the lower end of the stem and held in place by a brass screw. If the washer is squeezed flat or has a groove worn in it, replace it—this should stop any dripping. Take the washer with you to your dealer to ensure an exact match in size and style. If the brass screw is damaged, too, replace it with a new brass screw.

Figure 12–3 Product Repair Instructions Reprinted by permission of National Retail Hardware Association.

names of commonly used objects. Consider, for example, the following passage from a computer-printer service manual that was translated from Japanese to English by the manufacturer for American field engineers.

> Remove cover panel with great care, using plus driver to remove screws. Inside control box, wires are held in place with different screws. Take minus driver and loosen screws to remove wire from red and green terminals.

The terms "plus driver" and "minus driver" refer to a Phillips-head screwdriver and a flat-head screwdriver. The Japanese translator apparently did not know the appropriate American terminology for the tools, so he used what seemed to be logical descriptions of them. (The Phillips-head screwdriver can look like a plus sign; the flat-head screwdriver looks like a minus sign.) The result was a lot of confusion by English-speaking readers over what these terms could mean.

Well-illustrated instructions are especially effective in clarifying directions for international readers. In fact, instructions for many kinds of devices that require assembly or steps in a safety procedure are completely visual, such as the laminated cards aboard airplanes that illustrate how to evacuate the plane in an emergency. Visual instructions for international audiences avoid the pitfalls common when information is translated from one language to another. The instructions in Figure 12–4 illustrate how to install a box shelf on drywall. The product, manufactured in China, is sold internationally. The instructions show images of all parts provided and the tools needed to complete installation. They convey important image-only information about the shelving, like the weight, capacity, placement, and positioning. Even so, the instructions assume that consumers are familiar with the tools needed for assembling and mounting the shelving—a level, pencil, screwdriver, and power drill. If visual-only instructions are not possible, consult with someone from your intended audience's country as you plan and draft your instructions.

The need for cross-cultural understanding of commonly used concepts led the International Organization for Standardization (ISO) to develop agreed-on symbols like those shown in Figure 7–36 on page 256 for use in public signs, guidebooks, and manuals.

◆ *For a fuller discussion of writing for international readers, see page 74 in Chapter 3, Revising a Document; pages 251–257 in Chapter 7, Designing Documents and Visuals; and pages 320–326 in Chapter 9, Writing Routine and Sensitive Messages.*

Organize the Instructions

To make your instructions easy to follow, divide them into short, simple steps, and arrange the steps in the correct sequence. The steps can be given in either of two ways. You can label each step with a sequential number, as follows:

1. Connect each black cable wire to a brass terminal.
2. Attach one 4-inch green jumper wire to the back.
3. Connect both jumper wires to the bare cable wires.

Or, you can use words that indicate time or sequence, as follows:

> *First*, assess the problem that the customer reports to you. *Next*, observe and test the system in operation. *At that time*, question the customer until you understand the problem completely. *Then*, test the following. . . .

Think ahead for your reader. If the instructions in step 2 will affect a process in step 9, say so in step 2. Sometimes your instructions have to make clear that two operations must be performed simultaneously. Either state that fact in an introduction to the specific instructions or include both operations in the same step.

CONFUSING	1. Hold down the Control key.
	2. Press the Delete key before releasing the Control key.
CLEAR	1. While holding down the Control key, press the Delete key.

If your instructions involve many steps, break them into stages, each with a separate heading so that each stage begins with step 1. Using headings as dividers is especially important if your reader is likely to be performing the operation as he or she

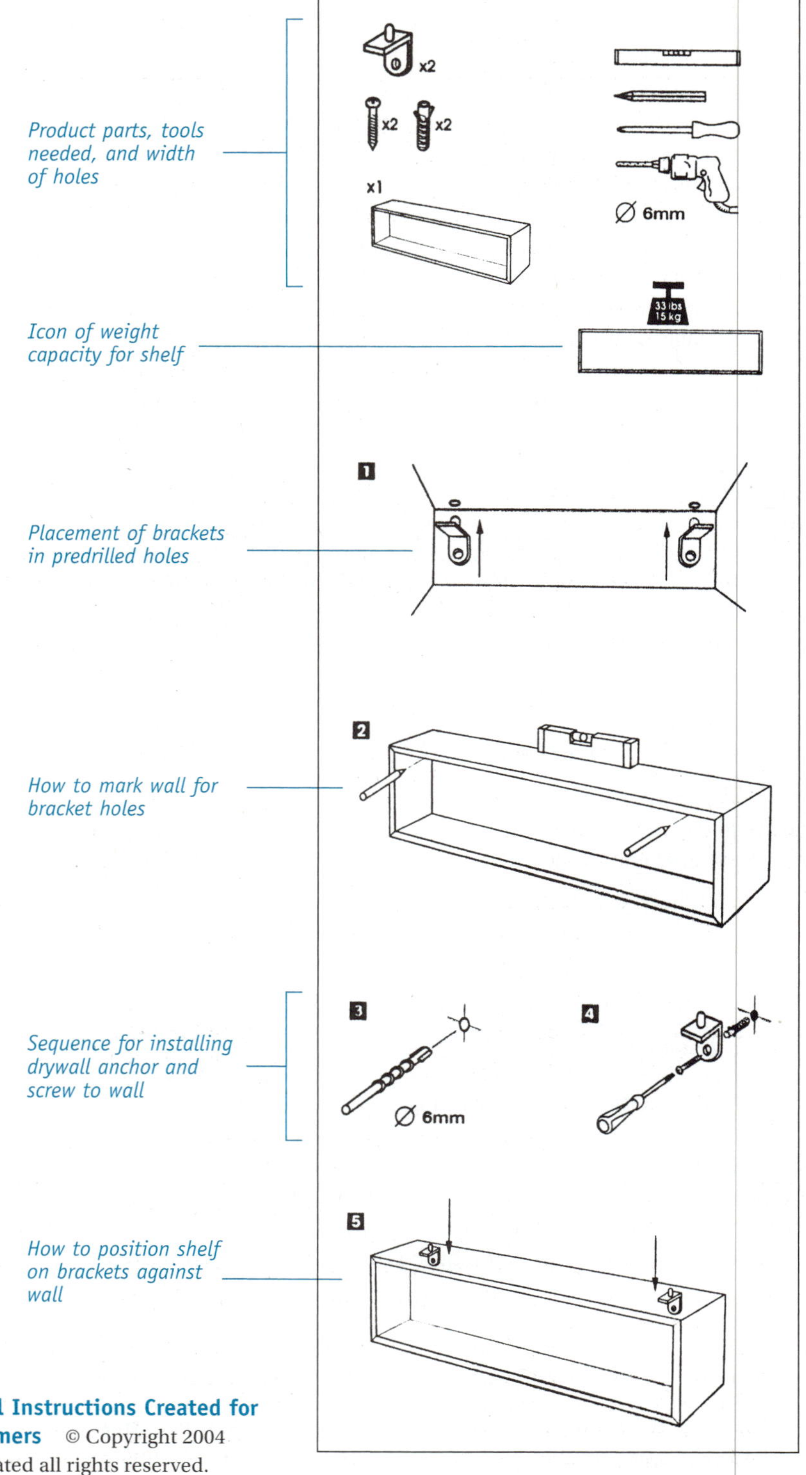

Figure 12–4 Visual Instructions Created for International Customers © Copyright 2004 Rubbermaid Incorporated all rights reserved.

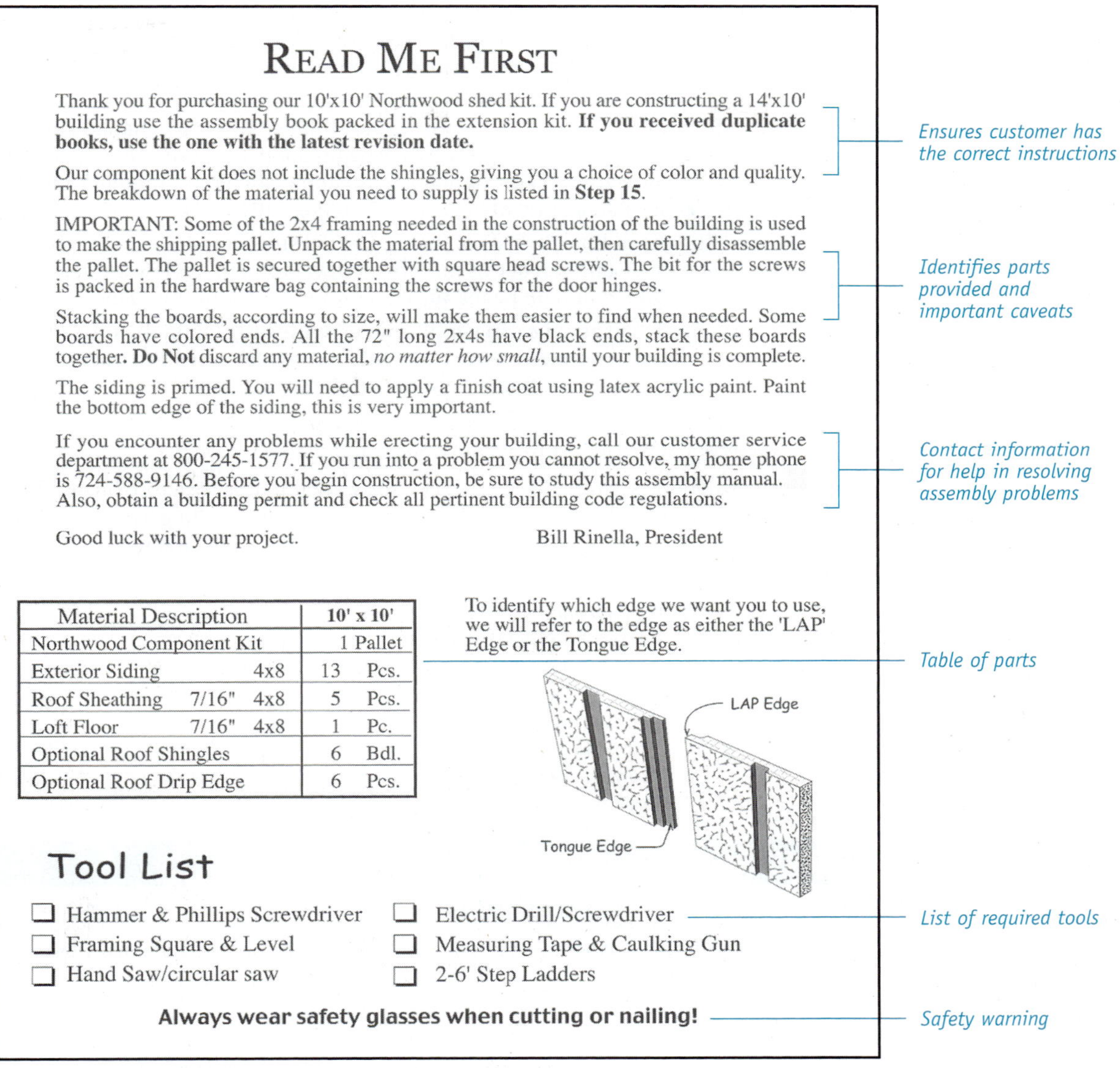

Read Me First

Thank you for purchasing our 10'x10' Northwood shed kit. If you are constructing a 14'x10' building use the assembly book packed in the extension kit. **If you received duplicate books, use the one with the latest revision date.**

Our component kit does not include the shingles, giving you a choice of color and quality. The breakdown of the material you need to supply is listed in **Step 15**.

IMPORTANT: Some of the 2x4 framing needed in the construction of the building is used to make the shipping pallet. Unpack the material from the pallet, then carefully disassemble the pallet. The pallet is secured together with square head screws. The bit for the screws is packed in the hardware bag containing the screws for the door hinges.

Stacking the boards, according to size, will make them easier to find when needed. Some boards have colored ends. All the 72" long 2x4s have black ends, stack these boards together. **Do Not** discard any material, *no matter how small*, until your building is complete.

The siding is primed. You will need to apply a finish coat using latex acrylic paint. Paint the bottom edge of the siding, this is very important.

If you encounter any problems while erecting your building, call our customer service department at 800-245-1577. If you run into a problem you cannot resolve, my home phone is 724-588-9146. Before you begin construction, be sure to study this assembly manual. Also, obtain a building permit and check all pertinent building code regulations.

Good luck with your project. Bill Rinella, President

Material Description		10' x 10'
Northwood Component Kit		1 Pallet
Exterior Siding	4x8	13 Pcs.
Roof Sheathing	7/16" 4x8	5 Pcs.
Loft Floor	7/16" 4x8	1 Pc.
Optional Roof Shingles		6 Bdl.
Optional Roof Drip Edge		6 Pcs.

To identify which edge we want you to use, we will refer to the edge as either the 'LAP' Edge or the Tongue Edge.

Tool List

- ☐ Hammer & Phillips Screwdriver
- ☐ Framing Square & Level
- ☐ Hand Saw/circular saw
- ☐ Electric Drill/Screwdriver
- ☐ Measuring Tape & Caulking Gun
- ☐ 2-6' Step Ladders

Always wear safety glasses when cutting or nailing!

Figure 12–5 Introduction for Instructions Reprinted by permission from Barnkits.com.

reads the instructions. Many instructions for product assembly are organized into four parts: Introduction, Required Equipment and Materials, Procedure, and Conclusion.

1. *Introduction.* Use an introduction to provide any needed background information, to state the purpose of the procedure, or to offer a theory of operation to help your audience understand why the product works the way it does. Figure 12–5 shows the introduction to the instructions for assembling a 10-by-10-foot backyard shed, the Northwood. The text identifies the shed by size, indicates which set of instructions to

use for its assembly, describes the material included in the shed kit (with a table of parts), shows a drawing of the siding, lists the tools needed, provides a customer-service telephone number, and ends with a warning about the need for safety glasses.

2. *Required Equipment and Materials.* If special equipment, tools, or materials are needed to follow your instructions, provide a well-labeled section that tells your audience clearly what they need before they begin the procedure — don't let them get well into the procedure before you tell them about such requirements. (Note the tools and materials section of Figure 12–5 on page 403.)
3. *Procedure.* The procedure consists of the sequential steps required to complete the task. For a full discussion of this method of development, review the section on sequential organization on pages 40–42 in Chapter 2, Planning a Document.
4. *Conclusion.* Brief instructions can simply end with the last step in the procedure. For longer and more complex instructions, add a conclusion section that satisfies your audience's sense of confidence about completing the job successfully.

> Congratulations on successfully assembling your [product name]. With proper care, it will serve you well for many years to come.

Many instructions are organized into sections similar to this structure but are titled to more specifically describe the process. The instructions for installing a ceramic countertop in a kitchen or bathroom, for example, are organized into the following sections:

1. Introduction
2. Tools Needed
3. Surface Preparation
   - Choosing the Edge Trim
   - Selecting the Sink
4. Planning the Layout
5. Setting the Tile
6. Applying Grout
7. Caulking and Sealing the Grout

CONSIDERING AUDIENCE AND PURPOSE

Planning to Write Instructions

- Can you perform or carefully observe others perform the task you are describing?
- Will someone unfamiliar with the task you are describing be able to follow your instructions?
- What vocabulary is appropriate to your audience?
- Are your instructions to coworkers sufficiently specific to ensure that the task can be completed accurately and within the allotted schedule?
- Have you organized the instructions in the proper sequence for the task?
- Did you take into account your customers' level of knowledge about your product before you began writing?
- Are your instructions written and illustrated appropriately for international readers?
- What is the best medium for transmitting the instructions to your audience? In which other mediums might the instructions also be made available? How do these choices provide specific advantages and challenges to you as you compose the instructions?

Writing Instructions

Effective instructional writing follows a precise pattern dictated by the instruction writer's goal: telling someone how to perform a task. The most direct way of doing so is to word the instructions as commands, using the imperative mood: (1) Perform step 1. (2) Wait 5 minutes and perform step 2, and so on.

Assume that the reader will not be familiar with the task or procedure described. For that reason, use the plainest language possible to communicate with the broadest audience.

Finally, you are obligated to warn the audience explicitly of any potential risks or hazards associated with the task being explained. These warnings must be clearly spelled out; must stand out from the surrounding text; and, if possible, must be illustrated. (This topic is discussed in more detail in the section titled Include Warnings and Cautions on page 409.)

Write Directly to Your Reader

The clearest and simplest instructions are written as commands. Address each sentence directly to your audience in the imperative mood and the active voice to make your instructions easier to follow and less wordy than if written in the passive voice.

PASSIVE	The access lid should be closed by the operator.
ACTIVE/IMPERATIVE	Close the access lid.

Although instructions should be concise, do not try to achieve conciseness by leaving out needed words such as *a, an, the,* pronouns (*you, this, these*), and verbs. Doing so will certainly shorten sentences, but sentences shortened this way usually have to be read more than once to be understood — defeating the purpose of brevity. The following instruction for cleaning a power punch press assembly (a machine that punches holes and other patterns into materials), for example, is not easily understood at first reading.

UNCLEAR	Pass brush through punch area for debris.

The meaning of the phrase *for debris* needs to be made clearer. Revised, the instruction is readily understandable.

CLEAR	Pass a brush through the punch area to clear away any debris.

In any operation, certain steps must be performed with more exactness than others. Anyone who has boiled a three-minute egg for four minutes understands this all too well. Alert your audience to the steps that require exact timing or measurement.

VAGUE	Let the liquid cool.
PRECISE	Let the liquid cool for 30 minutes at room temperature.

The example in Figure 12-6 is from an online pamphlet for patients who have had a cast removed from an injured wrist. After opening with general guidance (elevate the hand, apply ice, etc.), the guide continues with specific illustrated instructions for exercises that will promote recovery. Note that the instructions are written in

Bulleted list of routine therapeutic practices for injured wrists

Introduction to specific exercises

Arrows point to direction of motion

Disclaimer statement

Wrist Mobility Exercises (after cast)

Pain, swelling and stiffness in your wrist and hand are common following wrist injury or after wearing a cast. Follow these tips to improve pain, motion and swelling.

To Reduce Swelling and Pain:

- Elevate your hand above your heart as much as possible throughout the day to reduce your swelling. Keep your hand higher than the level of your heart.
- Ice: Use ice 15-20 minutes, 2-4 times per day as long as your wrist is warm, painful or swollen. Place a cold pack on your wrist with a thin towel between your skin and the cold pack to prevent a rash or burn.
- Contrast baths: Fill a large bowl with warm water and another with cold water. Alternate placing your hand and wrist between warm and cold water. 30 seconds in warm, followed by 30 seconds cold. Always finish with the cold. Repeat 4 times. Do this 2-4 times per day.
- Massage: While keeping your hand elevated, begin with gentle massage on the back of your fingers and hand. Stroke from the fingertips towards the wrist and forearm.
- Use your hand for light activities.
- Do the exercises below.

Exercises for Range of Motion:

Do the exercises below 5-10 times each. Do them 3-4 times per day. Hold each stretch for 5-10 seconds.

Palm up (supination)

Keep your elbow by your side with your elbow bent at 90 degrees; turn you palm up toward the ceiling. You may use the other hand to assist.

Palm down (pronation)

Keep your elbow by your side with your elbow bent at 90 degrees turn your palm down toward the floor. You may use the other hand to assist.

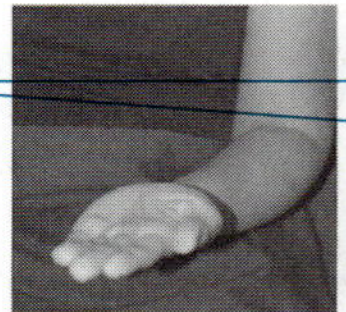

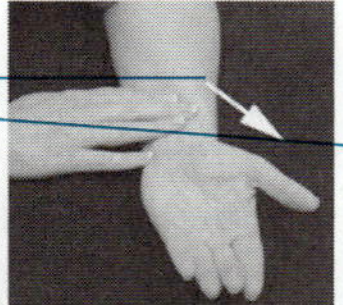

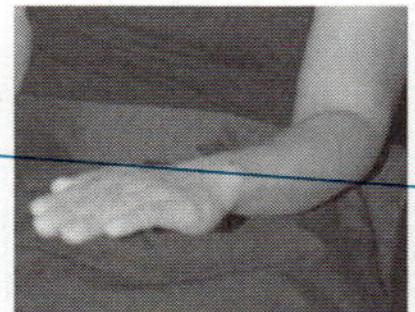

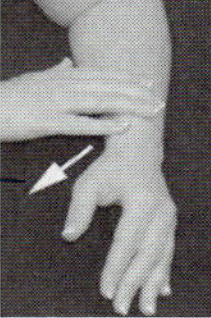

Wrist Bending

Begin by bending your hand up at the wrist as far as you can. Then bend your hand down at the wrist as far as you can.

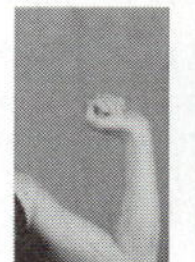

Consult with your physical or occupational therapist or doctor if you experience an increase in your symptoms with recommended exercises, or if you develop new symptoms of numbness, tingling, or a spread of the pain. This information is not intended to diagnose health problems or to take the place of medical advice or care you receive from your physician or other health care professional. If you have persistent health problems, or if you have additional questions, please consult with your doctor. If you have questions or need more information about your medication, please speak to your pharmacist.

Physical Therapy

KAISER PERMANENTE®

012701-025 (5-15)

Figure 12–6 Instructions for Wrist Mobility Therapy Courtesy of Kaiser Permanente Northern California.

Wrist Mobility Exercises (after cast)

Wrist Bending using clasped hands:
You can assist the wrist bending by clasping your hands together and bending back and forth. You can also move your clasped wrists from side to side.

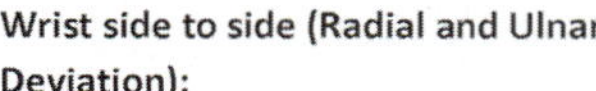

Wrist side to side (Radial and Ulnar Deviation):
Bend you hand toward the thumb side as far as you can and then toward the little finger side as far as you can.

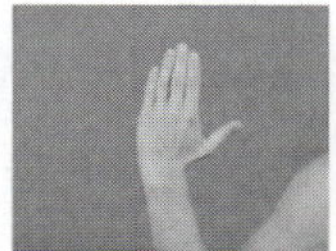

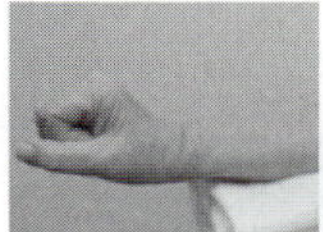
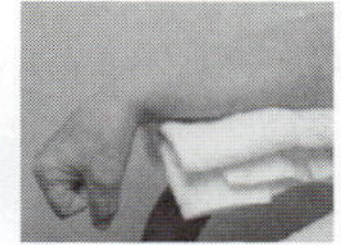

Wrist bending (flexion and extension)
Progress your bending exercises by Doing them over the edge of a table or your arm rest. Make a fist. Bend your wrist to move your hand upward, then bend your wrist down.

Prayer Stretch
Progress stretching by adding the prayer stretch when the exercises above become easier or you are not seeing the progress you expect. Start with your palms together in front of your chin. Slowly lower your hands toward your waistline, keeping your hands close to your stomach and your palms together until you feel a mild to moderate stretch under your forearms. Hold for at least 15-30 seconds. Repeat 2-4 times

Multiple photographs per exercise to show extent of movement

Thumb Exercises:
Make large circles in both directions with your thumb. Reach small finger and slide your thumb down to the base of your small finger.

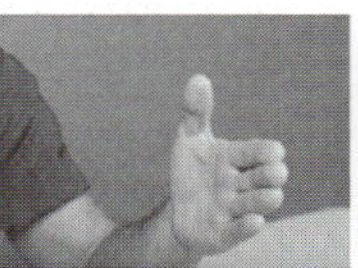
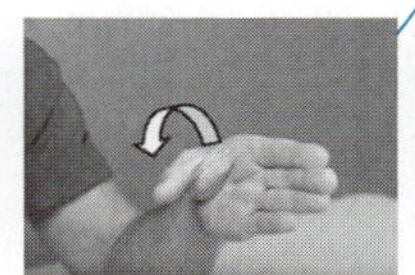
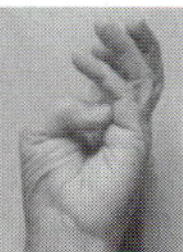

Consult with your physical or occupational therapist or doctor if you experience an increase in your symptoms with recommended exercises, or if you develop new symptoms of numbness, tingling, or a spread of the pain. This information is not intended to diagnose health problems or to take the place of medical advice or care you receive from your physician or other health care professional. If you have persistent health problems, or if you have additional questions, please consult with your doctor. If you have questions or need more information about your medication, please speak to your pharmacist.

Physical Therapy

KAISER PERMANENTE®

012701-025 (5-15) REVERSE

Figure 12–6 Instructions for Wrist Mobility Therapy (*continued*) Courtesy of Kaiser Permanente Northern California.

Photographs keyed to each variation of related set of exercises

Wrist Mobility Exercises (after cast)

Finger Exercises:

A. Straighten all your fingers.

B. Spread fingers apart.

C. Touch the tip of each finger.

D. Make a closed fist.

E. Bend at the tips into a hook fist.

F. Bend at big knuckles, keep fingers straight like you are trying to form a table top.

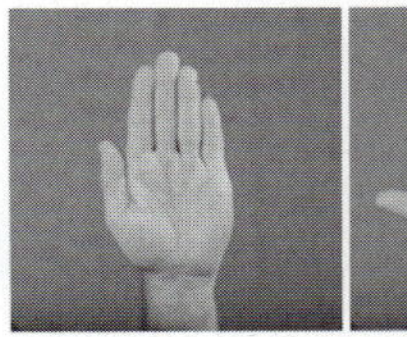
A.

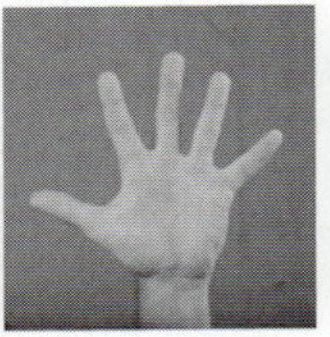
B.

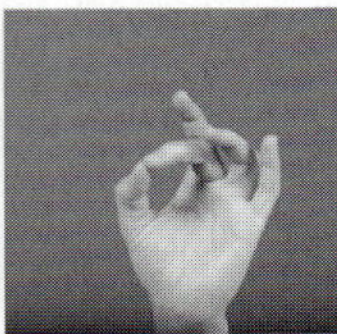
C.

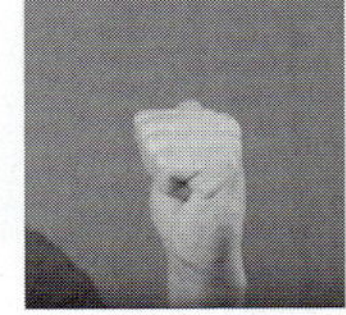
D.

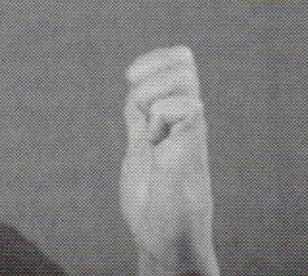
E.

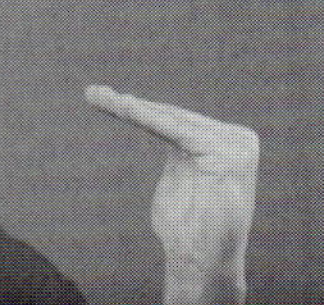
F.

You may assist with the other hand to straighten your fingers and bend your fingers if they are stiff.

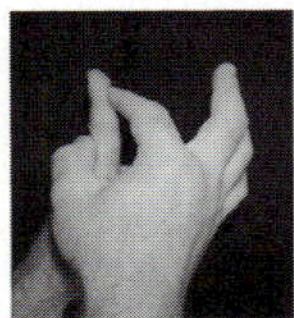

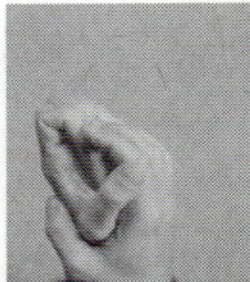

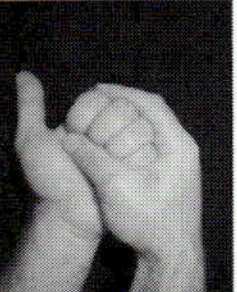

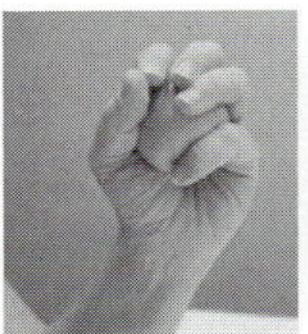

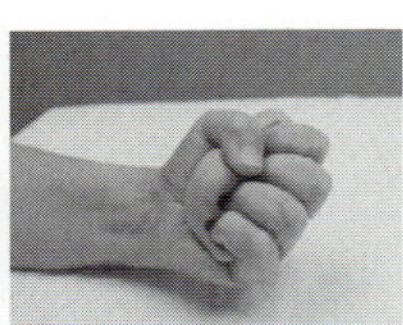

Hand squeeze

Hold a sponge, putty or rolled up sock in your hand. Make a fist around the putty and squeeze. Squeeze the putty and work it around in your hand for up to 5 minutes at a time. Do the putty exercise 3-6 times every day. You may squeeze a sponge in a basin of warm water.

Consult with your physical or occupational therapist or doctor if you experience an increase in your symptoms with recommended exercises, or if you develop new symptoms of numbness, tingling, or a spread of the pain. This information is not intended to diagnose health problems or to take the place of medical advice or care you receive from your physician or other health care professional. If you have persistent health problems, or if you have additional questions, please consult with your doctor. If you have questions or need more information about your medication, please speak to your pharmacist.

Physical Therapy

012701-025 (5-15)

Figure 12–6 Instructions for Wrist Mobility Therapy *(continued)* Courtesy of Kaiser Permanente Northern California.

plain language and in the imperative mood. When used, medical terms are defined (*supination/pronation*). The instructions also specify the number of repetitions for and duration of each exercise — information crucial to any therapy regimen. The photographs are taken from the optimal angle for the patient performing the exercises and enhanced with arrows that show direction and range of motion. When necessary, the photographs are keyed (A., B., C., etc) to a specific sequence of instructions.

◆ *See also pages 112–113 in Chapter 4, Revising a Document.*

WRITER'S CHECKLIST

Writing Instructions in Plain Language

✔ Keep in mind your average reader's level of technical knowledge.

✔ Avoid confusing terms and constructions; for example,
- Do not include undefined abbreviations and acronyms.
- Do not use two different words for the same thing.
- Do not give an obscure meaning to a word.
- Do not use unnecessary jargon.

✔ Write in the imperative mood.

✔ Use the active voice.
- The active voice makes clear who is supposed to do what.
- The active voice uses fewer words.

✔ Use *you* and other pronouns.
- Pronouns allow you to write directly to the reader rather than to a group.
- Pronouns pull the reader into the writing and make the writing relevant to the reader.

✔ Write short sentences.
- Aim for one message in each sentence.
- Break up information into smaller, easier-to-understand units.

✔ Use the present tense as much as possible.

✔ Select word placement carefully.
- Keep subjects and objects close to their verbs.
- Put *only, always,* and other conditional words next to the words they modify.
- Put *if* phrases after the main clauses to which they apply, not before.

Include Warnings and Cautions

Warnings and cautions are essential to instructions involving potentially hazardous equipment or materials. Many processes in industrial, medical, law-enforcement, military, and other settings involve the use of potentially dangerous equipment, chemicals, and explosives. Instruction writers have legal and ethical reasons for ensuring that warnings and cautions are included with such instructions. Even instructions for tasks not overtly hazardous may require cautionary statements, as described in the following Ethics Note. In either case, you may need legal guidance on the appropriate language to use.

ETHICS NOTE: Ensure That Instructions Warn Users of Potential Dangers

Product liability laws require a manufacturer to warn potential users of (1) dangers in the normal use of a product and (2) dangers in the foreseeable misuse of a product. A manufacturer, however, need not warn of open and obvious dangers. Hence, instructions for an electric knife need not warn the user to not use the knife for shaving a beard — an obvious danger that is also neither "normal use" nor "foreseeable" by the manufacturer. Instructions for an electric knife would need to warn users to take care when holding food to be sliced because a slip of the hand could result in injury — a danger in normal use. Even if the danger is open and obvious, the manufacturer may have a duty to warn users who may not be aware of the extent or degree of danger. If the likelihood of injury is serious, the manufacturer is also required to display a warning on the product itself.

Language of Warnings

In general, all instructions for the proper use of a product should be *clear, readable,* and *understandable*. However, readers must also be warned specifically of dangers that they might expect and dangers that they might not. Remember, a danger that is obvious to you as the writer of the instructions may not be obvious to the user. Instructions not only must warn of all risks and hazards but also must warn *adequately*. An adequate warning must do three things:

- Identify the hazard and the potential seriousness of the risk.
- Give the likely results of ignoring the warning.
- Describe how to avoid the hazard and thus the injury.

To ensure that a warning is adequate, the language in it must be clear and explicit.

VAGUE	Failure to disengage the blades may result in bodily harm.
EXPLICIT	If you do not disengage the blades, they can amputate your fingers.

Avoid words that are open to interpretation or need further defining: *proper, excessive, frequently, often, seldom, may, might, could, recommended, occasionally*. Instead, include specific time references (*every 90 days*) and use definitive verbs (*should, must*). If potential users are diverse, consider their familiarity (if any) with the product, their level of literacy, and their nationality.

Visual Symbols and Signal Words

Alert your readers to any potentially hazardous materials or actions before they reach the step for which the material is needed or in which the action will be performed. Caution readers handling hazardous materials about any requirements for special clothing, tools, equipment, and other safety measures. Highlight warnings, cautions, and precautions to make them stand out visually from the surrounding text — use an open, uncrowded format so that they do not blend in with the instructions. A clear border of heavy lines or white space adds visual emphasis to warnings. You can also

READ SAFETY SIGNS CAREFULLY AND FOLLOW THEIR INSTRUCTIONS

Danger signs identify the most serious hazards and are attached to machines near specific hazard areas.

Keep safety signs in good condition. Replace any missing or damaged safety signs.

Icons depict types of hazards

Kathy Konkle/Getty Images

Figure 12–7 Typical Warning Icons with Text

place warning notices in all uppercase letters, in large and distinctive fonts, or in color. When instructions are presented in digital mediums, warnings often rely on color and movement to draw the reader's attention and can even require a reader's acknowledgment before allowing them to proceed to the next steps.

Use symbols and icons in the text to reinforce warnings, as illustrated in Figure 12–7. Use line drawings of products that depict the physical sources of hazards and, if possible, the nature of the hazard. Cartoons can be especially helpful in instructions or warnings for adolescents and children. Another common feature of warnings is a picture of what *not* to do, typically a slash (/) through the image, as shown in Figure 12–8.

Warning words, symbols, icons, and labels are increasingly becoming standardized, although industry practices do vary. Certain signal words in boldface and their corresponding colors are becoming standards in North America and are used in both instructional material and on road signs:

> **DANGER** (red): hazard or unsafe practice that *will* result in severe injury or death
> **WARNING** (orange): *could* result in severe injury or death
> **CAUTION** (yellow): could result in *minor* injury or property damage
> **NOTICE** (blue): information unrelated to safety

The hazard-alert symbol — an international standard — should appear with the signal word:

Use cautions and warnings only when necessary, however. Too many may cause your audience to ignore those that are essential.

Figure 12–8 Icon Depicting a Prohibited Activity

Using Illustrations and Design Principles

Well-thought-out illustrations can make even the most complex instructions easier to understand. In addition to demonstrating the steps of your instructions, line art, photographs, diagrams, and even cartoon-style drawings can help your audience identify parts and the relationships among them. In fact, some instructions, including those for international audiences, use only illustrations (see Figure 12–4 on page 402).

Consider the layout and design of your instructions to most effectively integrate text and visuals. Highlight important visuals, like warnings, by making them stand out from the surrounding text. Consider using boxes and boldface or distinctive headings. Experiment with font style, size, and color to determine which devices are most effective. If you use color, be aware that certain colors (red, green, and yellow, for example) have well-established meanings in North America but may be interpreted differently in other countries. Also keep in mind that your chosen medium and transmittal method allow for or restrict you to additional design elements. For example, instructions on the Web or presented as an e-book might require that the reader agree before moving forward, and can include extensive videos and dynamic how-to illustrations.

◆ *For a discussion of cultural differences in the use of color, see page 253 in Chapter 7, Designing Documents and Visuals.*

Illustrate for Clarity

The value of illustrations will depend on your audience's needs and on the nature of the project. In general, instructions for inexperienced readers should be more thoroughly illustrated than those for experienced readers. Enhance the value of the illustration by referring to it in the instructions to explain what it shows, by labeling relevant parts to further clarify its purpose, and by wording figure captions concisely and accurately.

Ensure that step-by-step instructions are placed next to the steps illustrated or that illustrations are labeled with step numbers so that the audience immediately recognizes the connection between the two. Figure 12–9 shows instructions that guide a medical lab technician through the steps of streaking a saucer-sized disk of material

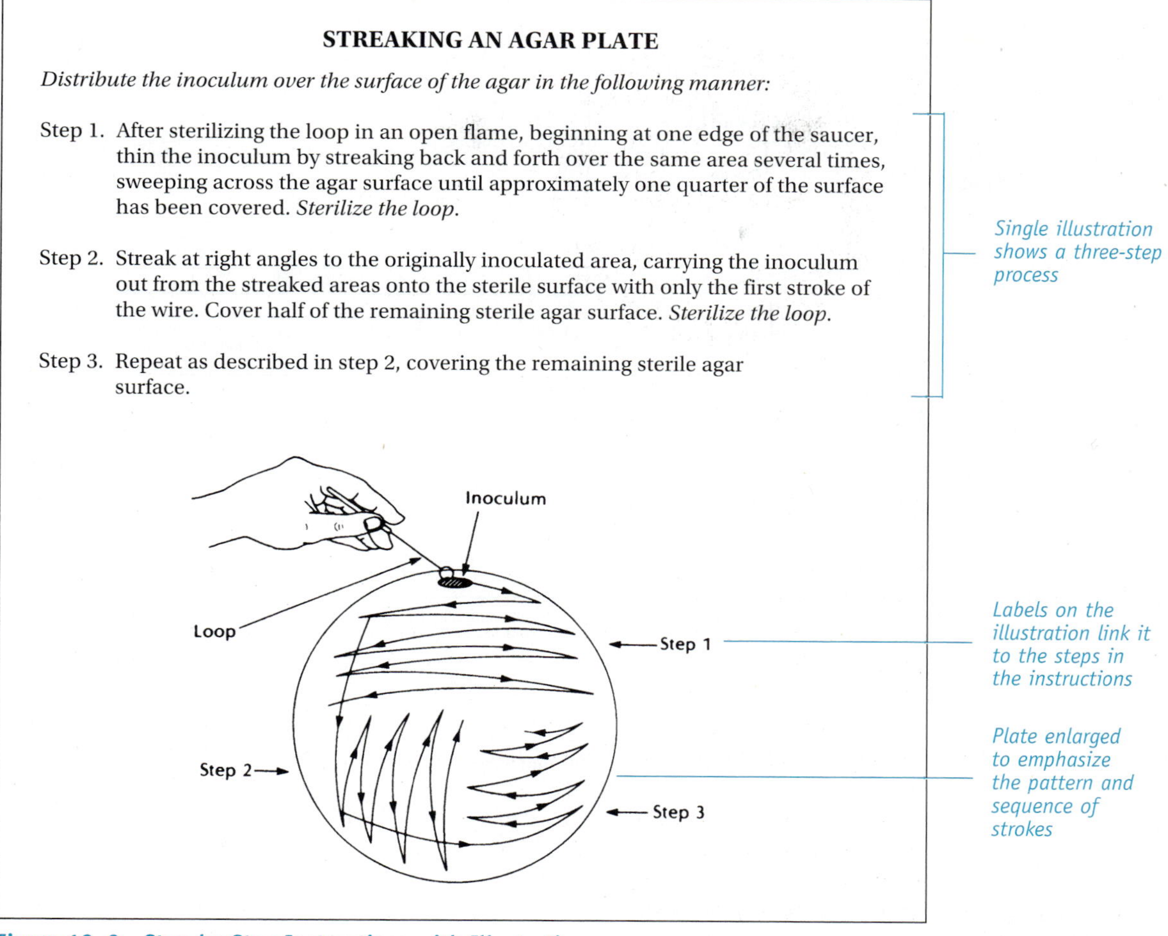
STREAKING AN AGAR PLATE
Distribute the inoculum over the surface of the agar in the following manner:
Step 1. After sterilizing the loop in an open flame, beginning at one edge of the saucer, thin the inoculum by streaking back and forth over the same area several times, sweeping across the agar surface until approximately one quarter of the surface has been covered. Sterilize the loop.
Step 2. Streak at right angles to the originally inoculated area, carrying the inoculum out from the streaked areas onto the sterile surface with only the first stroke of the wire. Cover half of the remaining sterile agar surface. Sterilize the loop.
Step 3. Repeat as described in step 2, covering the remaining sterile agar surface.
Inoculum
Loop
Step 1
Step 2
Step 3
Single illustration shows a three-step process
Labels on the illustration link it to the steps in the instructions
Plate enlarged to emphasize the pattern and sequence of strokes

Figure 12–9 Step-by-Step Instructions with Illustration

(called *agar*) used to grow bacterial colonies for laboratory examination. In this case, the purpose is to thin out the original specimen (the *inoculum*) so that bacteria will grow in small, isolated colonies. When necessary or advisable, illustrate each step in your instructions (Figure 12–10), making certain that the illustration represents the current model of the equipment.

A technique especially useful for inexperienced readers is to show a close-up of a portion of a larger image. Figure 12–11 on page 415, for example, illustrates a coronary bypass procedure required by the decreased blood flow through a partially clogged artery, which is shown in close up. The "magnified" image can show essential details impossible to see in a larger picture. Linking the two images visually puts the close-up in context for the reader.

◆ *For a complete discussion of how to create and use effective illustrations, see Chapter 7, Designing Documents and Visuals.*

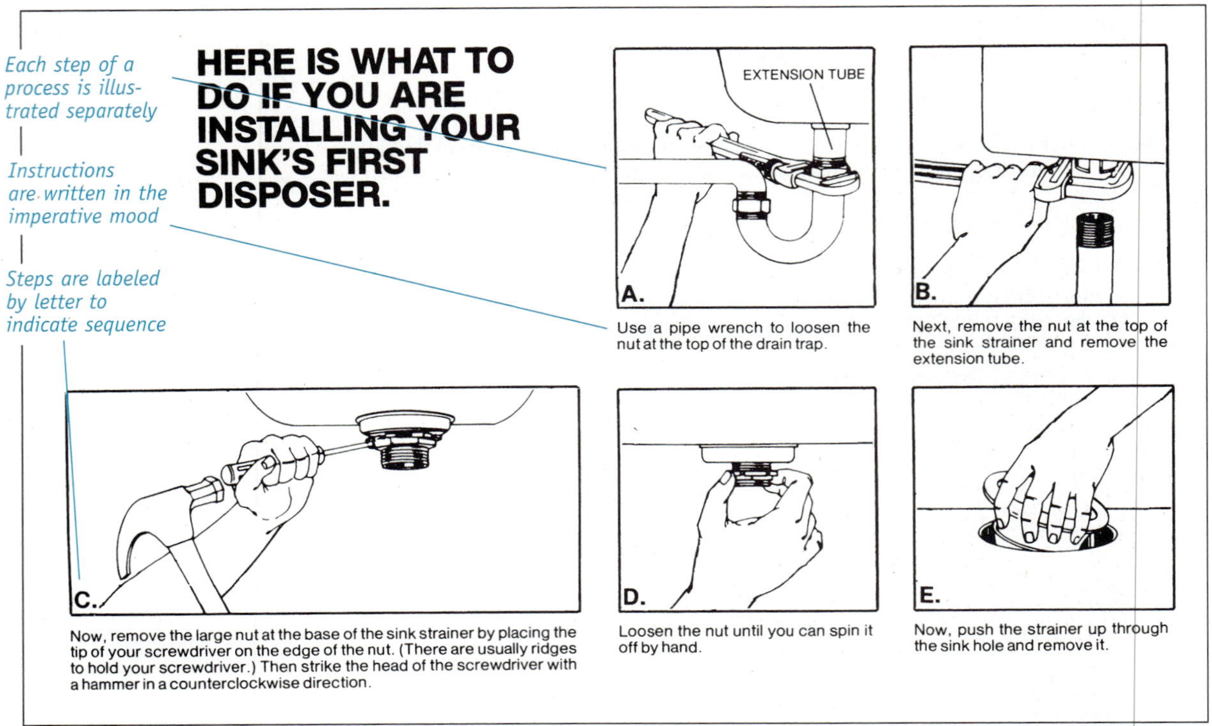

Each step of a process is illustrated separately

Instructions are written in the imperative mood

Steps are labeled by letter to indicate sequence

HERE IS WHAT TO DO IF YOU ARE INSTALLING YOUR SINK'S FIRST DISPOSER.

Use a pipe wrench to loosen the nut at the top of the drain trap.

Next, remove the nut at the top of the sink strainer and remove the extension tube.

Now, remove the large nut at the base of the sink strainer by placing the tip of your screwdriver on the edge of the nut. (There are usually ridges to hold your screwdriver.) Then strike the head of the screwdriver with a hammer in a counterclockwise direction.

Loosen the nut until you can spin it off by hand.

Now, push the strainer up through the sink hole and remove it.

Figure 12–10 Illustrating Each Step in a Set of Instructions *Source:* "Kenmore Food Waste Disposers. Installation, Care, and Use Manual" at http://www.managemylife.com/mmh/lis_pdf/OWNM/L0411040.pdf.

Design for Ease of Use

Even clear, well-illustrated instructions are of no value if no one reads them. Customers want to use a new device as soon as they receive it. However, if the product comes with a thick user's manual of dense, legalistic text, they will avoid it. This attitude can lead to accidents, increased online queries and calls to customer help lines, dissatisfied customers, and lost time and productivity.

To address this problem, many firms use a three-tier approach in their instructions. In addition to a full-scale user's manual — essential for products such as automobiles, cell phones, washers, dryers, and ovens — companies also produce a condensed version of the manual with pictures, easy-to-follow diagrams, and minimal text. They also include instructional text embedded in their digital devices that direct readers to perform a task to access a particular feature — "Slide to unlock" or "Enter the following code to start your link." The full-scale owner's manual usually contains information important to customers, like warranties,

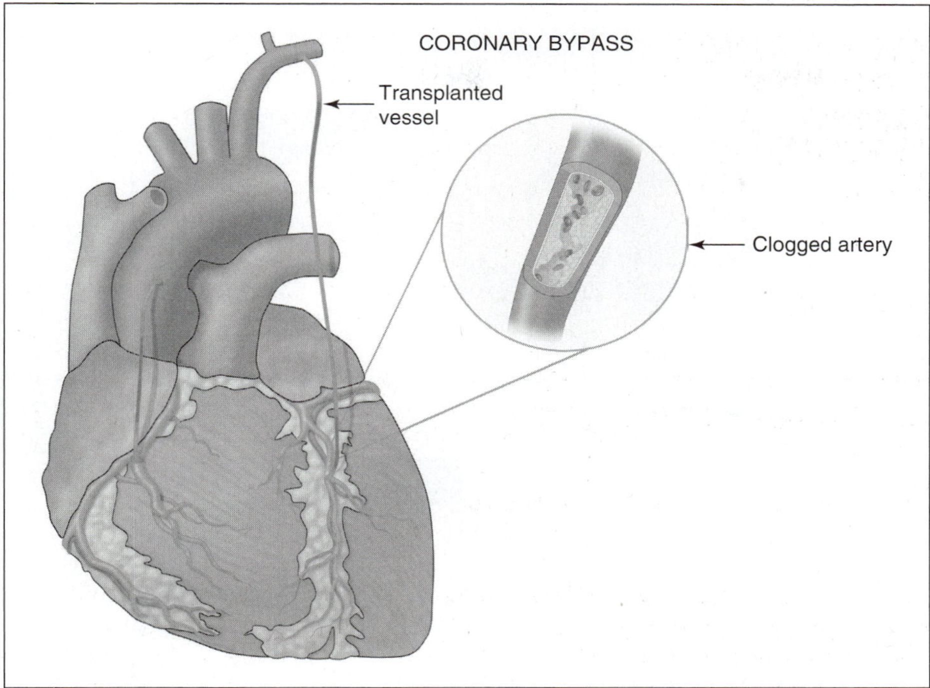

Figure 12–11 Close-up of Equipment to Illustrate Details Monica Schroeder/Science Source.

maintenance recommendations, service locations, and troubleshooting guides. However, when users are given a choice between a 200-page owner's manual and an 8-page glossy color booklet, they opt for the booklet. In another approach, many companies now provide heavily illustrated quick-reference guides with few words and large photographs that are often color coded to parts on the equipment. Figure 12–12 shows a quick-start guide for setting up a wireless monitor that transfers patient cardiac data to a physician. The guide also includes brief introductory text about the optimal location for the device to transmit its cellular signal. The guides may range in size from posters to a single sheet of paper. Other firms produce booklets with indexed tabs and FAQs (frequently asked questions) sections that permit readers to find at a glance what they are looking for — the correct air pressure for tires, how to set an oven timer, and the like, as shown in Figure 12–13 on page 417. Other options include 3-by-5-inch laminated cards (for phone use), stickers (warning of poisons and providing information about emergency treatment), and even magnets. To create instructions for complex procedures, consider using the two-tier approach. (Many other options exist for providing customers with product help, such as websites, customer forums, help lines, instructor-led classes, blogs, Webinars, and FAQs.)

◆ *For more information about blogs, podcasts, and FAQs, see pages 596–603 in Appendix A, Writing in an Online Environment.*

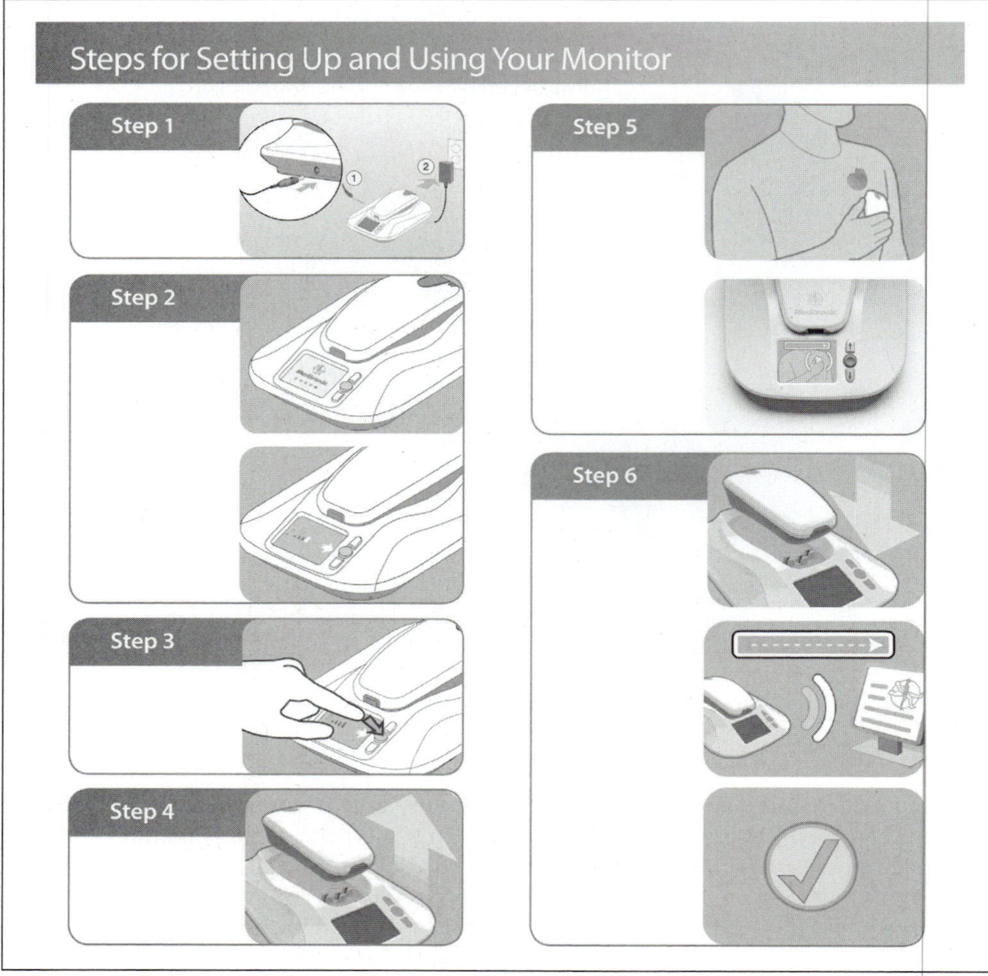

Figure 12–12 Simplified Quick Setup Guide Reproduced with permission of Medtronic, Inc.

WRITER'S CHECKLIST

Advantages of Quick-Reference Guides

- ✔ Help customers who won't read comprehensive guides
- ✔ Give users basic but essential information in a format that gets them started accurately and as soon as possible
- ✔ Especially suited to products or equipment that require a one-time setup
- ✔ Reduce company installation and service support costs
- ✔ Give users the satisfaction of performing a task quickly and effectively

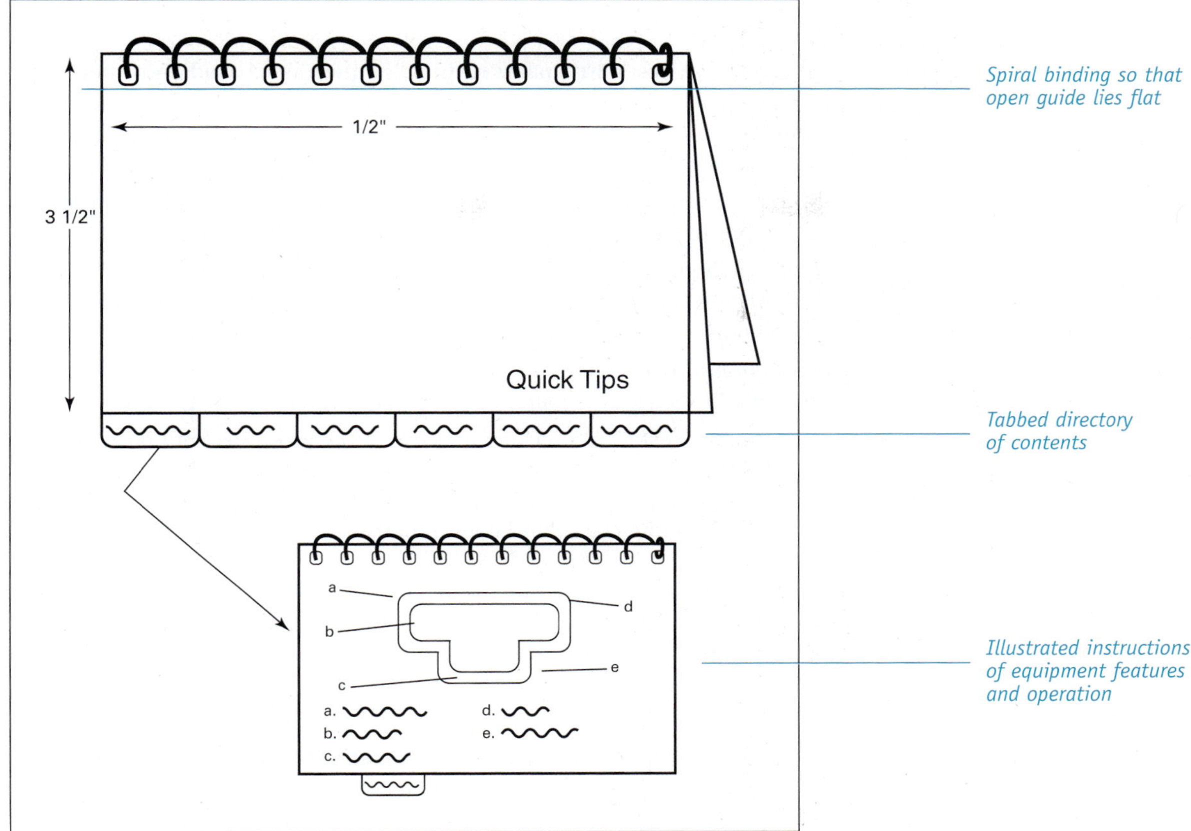

Figure 12–13 Laminated Pocket-Size Owner's Guide

Testing for Usability

To test the accuracy and clarity of your instructions, ask someone who is not familiar with the operation to use the instructions you have written to perform the task or procedure. A first-time user of your instructions can spot missing steps or point out passages that should be worded more clearly. As you watch your tester follow your instructions, note any steps that seem especially puzzling or confusing and revise them for clarity.

Usability test participants typically are members of the target audience for the product or procedure. If the participants encounter problems, it is likely that other users will experience similar problems. For example, if instructions for filling out a section of a tax form are unclear to test participants, they are likely to be confusing to most taxpayers.

Usability tests can rely on one or more of the following methods:

- *Read-and-locate test.* Test participants respond to questions based on content found in the instructions. Testers record whether and how participants find answers and how long it takes them to do so. This test evaluates ease of navigation, document format, and organization for instructions.
- *User edit.* Testers watch participants perform real tasks while using the instructions to predict if other users will be able to understand and follow them.
- *Protocol and method.* Test participants comment aloud as they read and respond to instructional text and graphics. This test can reveal a wide variety of format and wording problems.
- *Comprehension test.* Test participants take a written quiz to measure comprehension and recall of instructional content, including visuals.
- *Survey or interview.* Testers ask participants the same questions both before and after they read the instructions to determine whether their comprehension of the instructions has improved, or they ask questions only after participants read instructions to determine clarity and comprehension of the document.

Some companies use in-house or commercial software to conduct usability testing; these programs can provide feedback almost instantly, capturing and recording a tester's keystroke, screen, and mouse movements, then evaluating these results against the instructions.

ETHICS NOTE: Obtain Written Permission from Usability-Test Participants Prior to Testing Before beginning work with test participants, explain to them the purpose of the activity and describe what you'll ask them to do. Assure them that their participation is voluntary and that they can stop participating at any time. Then, obtain their written permission to talk to them, observe their work, and use the results of these observations in your project. You especially need permission if you plan to record them in audio or video media. Also, avoid asking participants to do anything they find uncomfortable, unethical, or coercive. Check with your instructor for classroom projects or with your legal staff in the workplace about wording these permission releases.[1]

[1]Adapted from Miles A. Kimball and Ann R. Hawkins, *Document Design: A Guide for Technical Communicators* (Boston: Bedford, 2008).

Analyzing the results of those test methods can help instructional specialists detect and resolve problems before the instructions are put to use. If test participants have trouble understanding the instructions, the language and organization, as well as the layout and design, may need to be revised. Although usability testing can be time-consuming, the extra time can pay off in greater safety, improved efficiency, increased productivity, and fewer customer complaints.

CHAPTER 12 SUMMARY: WRITING INSTRUCTIONS

Planning Instructions

- Make sure you understand the task thoroughly. (For technical instructions to accompany products, learn to perform the operation yourself or carefully observe others performing the operation.)
- Learn the needs and experience level of your audience.
- Organize the task into short, simple steps.
- Present each step in the correct sequence.

Writing Instructions

- Write directly to your readers, using the active, imperative voice.
- Write clearly and concisely—short sentences are best.
- In an introduction at the beginning of your instructions:
    - Mention any necessary details, background information, and preparation.
    - List all required equipment and materials.
- Use plain language (avoid technical jargon).
- Include warnings and cautions for potentially hazardous equipment or materials.

Using Illustrations and Design Principles

- Use visuals to illustrate steps and procedures where needed.
- Create visuals at the level of detail appropriate to your audience.
- Create quick-start guides with images, easy-to-follow diagrams, and minimal text for users averse to reading manuals.

Testing for Usability

- Test the readability and effectiveness of your instructions by having someone unfamiliar with the task test them while you observe.
- Analyze the results of your observations to improve the instructions.
- Revise the instructions as necessary.

Exercises

1. Write a set of instructions for either of the following topics. Assume that your audience has no knowledge of the subject. Use illustrations where they would be helpful to your audience.
    a. How to program your DVR to record a television show that will be broadcast in several hours from the time you programmed your machine
    b. How to incorporate a visual into a text document
2. Create a set of interview questions that you could rely on as a means of checking the usability of the instructions you created in Exercise 1. Remember that you would interview users both before and after they read the instructions to determine their comprehension and attitudes and the clarity of what they have read.

3. Collect examples of instructions written in the passive voice and rewrite them using the active voice.
4. As this chapter describes, many firms have developed a two-tier approach for instructions because consumers will gravitate toward illustrated quick-start guides, easy-to-follow diagrams, and booklets instead of 200-plus-page instruction manuals. Locate a large instructional book or manual (for example, for new software or a new automobile), or go to a website that features lengthy instructions for consumer goods, and create a set of 3-by-5-inch laminated cards or a four- to eight-page booklet that will be easy to follow and thus encourage consumers to follow instructions.
5. Review the instructions at your school's website for how to get from the nearest airport to your school student center or other central location. Write a critique of the instructions from the perspective of a nonnative speaker of English. (See Chapter 8, Writing E-mails, Memos, and Letters, for helpful information on international communication strategies.)
6. Collect examples of instructions that are written using ambiguous words like "might" or "may" and revise them using explicit words.
7. Many supermarkets and other large retailers now offer self-checkout systems that encourage customers to scan, pay for, and bag their merchandise themselves. These systems allow the store to place employees in other areas where one-on-one attention is needed, and they reduce the need to hire more cashiers. Imagine that you work for a company that manufactures these checkout systems. Write a set of instructions for store managers that will help them prevent the following problems that could discourage customers from using the equipment. (*Hint:* Many of these problems could be prevented before the customer has to face them.)
   - The customer is unfamiliar or uncomfortable with the self-checkout system.
   - The customer scans the bar code, but the product does not appear in the register's inventory database.
   - The customer has difficulty following the steps needed to work the self-checkout system (for example, he or she can't figure out how to use the scales to weigh produce or how to pay for the purchase).

Collaborative Classroom Projects

1. In groups of four to six, write assembly instructions for a product in the classroom. For example, assume that the instructor's desk needs to be assembled. Write an introduction, a required equipment and materials section, a procedure section, and a conclusion. Share your instructions with the class.
2. For any of the exercises or projects in this chapter that ask you to create instructions, conduct a usability test with protocols as a means of checking the usability of those instructions. Sit next to your usability test participants as they comment aloud while they follow the instructions and perform the tasks. This should reveal their thought processes, attitudes, and reasons for decision-making, which should help you to determine areas of helpfulness or confusion in your instructions. Form groups of three or four, as directed by your instructor.
3. Rewrite the assembly instructions you created in Collaborative Classroom Project 1 for the Web. Conduct the same usability testing procedures you used in Collaborative Classroom

Project 2 to compare the usability across transmittal methods. Were the print or Web instructions easier for your participants to follow? Share your results with the class.

Research Projects

1. Numerous chemicals are used in the cleaning of educational institutions' bathrooms, office carpeting, locker rooms, and so on. For this assignment, research and write a formal report on the cleaning products used by your institution's cleaning or maintenance crews. Include formal-report elements based on your instructor's specific directions.

   a. Begin by interviewing the director of maintenance (or someone in a similar position) at your institution about the kinds of cleansers and chemicals used for specific types of cleaning. Ask about the precautions needed and specific instructions given to those who work with these chemicals. Ask about the amount and cost of these products on a monthly or yearly basis.
   b. Inquire about training given to employees in the use of these chemicals (your Human Resources Department may conduct this training). Ask how much training and instruction are offered and what subjects are covered. Ask if any special sessions are offered to nonnative speakers or readers of English.
   c. Research "green," or environmentally friendly, products that can be used in place of more toxic cleansers. Be sure to address the ability of such cleansers to clean heavily populated environments, the potential cost of such products, and the training or instruction needed for their use.

   Write a formal report to the head of maintenance that summarizes your findings, makes recommendations on product safety and worker training and instruction, and recommends a course of action regarding the use of traditional cleansers, environmentally friendly cleansers, or a combination of both. Include a graph or chart with your report.

2. As explained in this chapter, warning words, symbols, icons, and labels are increasingly standardized, although industry practices do vary. Certain signal words in boldface and their corresponding colors are becoming standards in North America, like **DANGER** in red, **WARNING** in orange, and **CAUTION** in yellow. And certain icons, like the no-smoking symbol depicted in Figure 12–8 on page 412, are universally understood. Research appropriate icons that you could place in the formal report described in Research Project 1. For example, what icons and signal words with corresponding colors would you use, or would you create, that might represent a dangerous bathroom-cleaning product used by your university? How would you differentiate it from a product that might be less toxic but is still dangerous if ingested? Report your findings to your instructor in a memo.

3. Explore the following two websites to discover how they use illustrations to help convey their messages to the consumer: SafetyStore at www.safetystore.com, an online catalog of safety and preparedness products, and the U.S. Coast Guard, Office of Boating Safety at www.uscgboating.org. Make a list of the variety of illustrations used and their individual purposes. Analyze the style of text that accompanies the illustrations. Determine the goals of these sites and whether these sites accomplish their goals. Support your conclusions with examples, as directed by your instructor.

4. Imagine that you give how-to-travel seminars for people in different occupational fields who will be flying on airlines throughout the United States. In your earlier seminars,

some people were confused about what is allowed in carry-on luggage and what has to be checked into the cargo bay. You decide to create lists for your seminar attendees that break down acceptable and prohibited items by the following categories: male and female models traveling to fashion shoots, semiprofessional athletes traveling to their sporting events, construction vendors heading for conventions, and martial artists heading to competitions. Using the list of permitted and prohibited carry-on items from the Transportation Security Administration at www.tsa.gov/travelers/airtravel/prohibited/permitted-prohibited-items.shtm, create two handouts for one or two of the groups listed above, complete with the appropriate symbols or icons, to accommodate members of these groups that include the following:

a. English-speaking American travelers
b. American immigrants and international travelers who are not familiar with symbols and icons used in the United States and for whom English is a second language

13 Writing Proposals

Contents

This chapter discusses the audience for, the management and organization of, and the writing strategies used to develop the following kinds of proposals:

A proposal is a document written to persuade members of a company or other organization that what is proposed will benefit them by solving a problem or fulfilling a need. To succeed, the proposal must, therefore, convince your audience that they need what you are proposing, that it is practical and appropriate, and that you are the right person or organization to provide the proposed product or service. To persuade your organization's management to make a change or an improvement or perhaps to fund a project you would like to launch, you would write an *internal proposal.* To persuade someone outside your company to purchase your product or service, you would write an *external proposal,* such as a sales proposal. A *grant proposal,* another type of external proposal, is written to a nonprofit, educational, or governmental organization to request funding for projects that would benefit their mission.

Planning and Writing Proposals

Regardless of the type of proposal you write — internal, external, sales, or grant — begin by considering whether your company or organization can complete the project being proposed in a request for proposals (RFP). (RFPs are described in detail beginning on page 465.) Do you have the right staff expertise and facilities to address questions about your competence to complete the project effectively, on time, and within the agreed-on budget? If not, can you get the necessary help elsewhere? If you can perform the task required, you are ready to plan and draft the proposal.

Audience and Purpose

Put yourself in the position of those reviewing your proposal — does it convincingly fulfill their needs and goals? Consider what information would convince you to make the decision you are asking them to make. Then, being as specific as possible, provide the following:

1. Sufficient background information to describe how you can solve their problem (if the information is based on research, cite your sources) or provide them the services they request.
2. The methods or optional approaches to be used in achieving the proposed solution
3. Information about equipment, materials, and staff requirements
4. An itemized list of costs
5. A schedule for completing the project broken down into separate tasks

Each of these items is central for a persuasive and complete proposal; you can see detailed examples of each in the figures later in this chapter. As you consider what your readers will want to know, also assess their positions in the organization reviewing your proposal. You will have more than one reader because proposals usually require more than one level of review and approval. Each will assess the proposal from the perspective of his or her responsibilities in the organization.

- *Executives* and other high-level decision makers, for example, will want to know the long-term benefits of what you propose, as well as the amount of money, the number of personnel, and the timetable that your plan requires.
- *Managers* will need to evaluate your credibility and consider how they would put your plan into action. They would be responsible for site preparation, staff training and motivation, and the schedule to implement the project.
- *Technical staff* will need even more information on how to put your plan to work and will focus on the sections in your proposal that cover your previous experience and the proposed detailed solution, including the work plan, schedule, blueprints, and diagrams. They will also evaluate the résumés of the staff assigned to the project to ensure that their professional credentials and experience are adequate.

CONSIDERING AUDIENCE AND PURPOSE

Writing Proposals

- Is your audience a manager within your organization (for an internal proposal) or a potential customer outside your organization (for an external proposal)?
- Does your proposal answer clearly the following questions?
  - What do you propose to do?
  - What benefits does your proposed plan offer?
  - How will you implement your plan?
  - Do you have the resources to do it?
  - How much do you estimate your plan will cost?
  - When will you begin and how long will it take?
- Does your proposal address the functional needs of those who must evaluate it by including
  - A summary in nontechnical language for decision makers?
  - A description of the proposed solution, budget, schedule, and training requirements for managers?
  - Technical details and visuals of the proposed solution for the specialists who must assess your degree of expertise to perform the work?
- Is the language professional and respectful?
- Is the proposal written, organized, and submitted exactly as specified in the request for proposals?
- Have you carefully revised repurposed material from other relevant workplace sources to fit seamlessly into the proposal?

Project Management

Companies that depend on the work generated by proposals are frequently faced with the need to prepare high-quality, persuasive proposals under tight deadlines. To meet these aims, companies assemble proposal-writing teams. Collaborative teams like these are usually headed by a project leader to guide the process, organize the content, and ensure that the deadline is met. Proposal management software is popular for companies that manage frequent and extensive proposal writing projects. Such software allows businesses to automate the more routine tasks while easily tracking multiple versions.

WRITER'S CHECKLIST

Leading a Collaborative Team

✔ Hold a planning meeting with the proposal team to assign work and establish due dates for all tasks.

✔ Assign a team member to each section to ensure that it is complete, consistent, and complies with the requirements of the request for proposals.

✔ Set priorities so that the most important sections of the proposal receive adequate attention and are on schedule.

- ✔ Delegate work to ensure that subject-area experts are available within the schedule established and that those team members best able to conduct interviews are available to do so.
- ✔ Schedule the project so that work begins on the sections that will take the longest, encouraging team members to work on as many sections as possible simultaneously.
- ✔ Repurpose existing content as extensively as possible, being careful to adapt it to the prospective customer.
- ✔ Schedule periodic meetings, videoconferences, or draft exchanges with other team members to allow for reviews.
- ✔ Select the best medium to communicate among proposal team members.
- ✔ Track the status of each part of the proposal carefully, sending periodic reminders about upcoming deadlines.

◆ *For a detailed overview of the collaborative writing process, see Chapter 5, Collaborating on a Document.*

For additional guidance on preparing a proposal on a tight schedule, see Meeting the Deadline: The Time-Sensitive Proposal on pages 464–465.

Repurposing Content

Repurposing is the copying or converting of existing content, such as written text and visuals, from one document into another for a different purpose. In the workplace, this process saves time and resources because content that often requires substantial effort to develop need not be re-created for each new use.

Repurposing may be as simple as copying and pasting content from one document to another. Note, however, that content can be repurposed exactly as it is written only if it fits the scope, audience, and purpose of the new document. If not, adapt the content to fit its new context. If you are writing a sales proposal, for example, and you need to describe the specifications of a product, you may be able to use the same specifications posted at your company's website. For narrative content, however, you may need to adapt the verb tense, voice, tone, and point of view to fit the context of a proposal aimed to persuade a potential customer.[1] Discuss sources of existing material useful to your proposal in team planning meetings and store them in electronic folders, on network drives, or on internal websites for sharing with other team members. If your organization relies on a content management system to house its written materials, consider using it as a source for content relevant to your proposal before writing your proposal. A content management system quickly enables various boilerplate snippets to be easily integrated into multiple media and transmittal methods.

ETHICS NOTE: Repurpose Workplace-Created Content Freely In the workplace, repurposing content within an organization does not violate copyright because the organization owns the information it creates and can share it freely across the company. Likewise, a writer in an organization may use and repurpose material in the public domain and, with limitations, content that is licensed under Creative

[1]The reuse of standard texts or content in workplace publications is often referred to as "single-source publishing" or simply "single sourcing." Traditionally, such reuse of standard content has been referred to as "boilerplate."

Commons, as described at http://creativecommons.org/about. Be sure to credit the source for public domain or Creative Commons content, however.

In the classroom, of course, the use of content or someone else's unique ideas without acknowledgment, or the use of someone else's exact words without quotation marks and appropriate credit, is plagiarism.

See pages 177–184 in Chapter 6, Conducting Research for a Document.

Organization

Any proposal—whether it is internal or external or whether it is short and uncomplicated or long and complex—should be planned and organized carefully. The organization of internal proposals varies according to topic and scope of coverage. Figures 13–1 through 13–5 on pages 429–435 illustrate two typical examples. For external or grant proposals, follow guidance in the request for proposals exactly when organizing the proposal. (See Requests for Proposals on pages 465–468.)

Many organizations now have internal document repositories that keep samples of previously written proposals on file. Consider reviewing these as you research and organize materials to write your own proposal. In addition, many websites also provide excellent examples of successful proposals useful to reference in your preparation phase. The samples throughout this chapter are representative of proposals used in a variety of workplace settings.

Persuasive Writing

Persuasive proposal writing means convincing writing, so how you present your ideas is as important as the ideas themselves. Avoid ambiguity; do not wander from your main point; and, above all, never make false claims. Support your appeal with relevant facts, statistics, and examples. Your supporting evidence must lead logically, even inevitably, to your conclusions and your proposed solution—that is, begin with the most important evidence and end with valid but secondary evidence. Finally, cite the relevant sources of information used to support your position. Doing so gives your arguments strong credibility.

For a detailed overview of researching and citing evidence and supporting information, see Chapter 6, Conducting Research for a Document.

ETHICS NOTE: Address Conflicting Opinions and Evidence Candidly As you develop your proposal, acknowledge any contradictory evidence or potentially conflicting opinions; doing so allows you to anticipate and overcome objections to your proposal and even helps you to support your argument. By acknowledging negative details or opposing views, you not only gain credibility but also demonstrate ethical responsibility.

The tone of your proposal should be positive, confident, and tactful. The following example, addressed to the Qualtron Corporation, is inappropriate because of its condescending tone:

> The Qualtron Corporation needs to consider the potential problem of not having backup equipment available when a commercial power failure occurs. The corporation would also be wise indeed to give a great deal more consideration to the volume of output expected per machine.

The following version of the same passage is positive, confident, and tactful:

> To prevent damage to essential Qualtron equipment in the event of a commercial power failure, we recommend a system redesign to upgrade Qualtron's existing backup power supply. The backup configuration proposed is based on a technical analysis of the output of each machine and takes into account future system growth. For example, . . .

WRITER'S CHECKLIST

Writing Persuasive Proposals

- ✔ Analyze your audience carefully to determine how to best meet their needs or requirements. If you are responding to a request for proposals, be sure to meet each of the written requirements or suggested points of response.
- ✔ Write a concise purpose statement to clarify your proposal's goals.
- ✔ Emphasize the proposal's benefits and anticipate reader questions or objections.
- ✔ Incorporate evidence to support the claims of your proposal, being careful to cite your sources.
- ✔ Review the descriptions of proposal sections and their uses in this chapter.
- ✔ Unless the request for proposals requires an electronic submission via specific software or templates, select an appropriate, visually appealing format (see Chapter 7, Designing Documents and Visuals).
- ✔ Use a confident, positive tone throughout the proposal.

Internal Proposals

◆ *The telecommuting proposal by Christine Thomas (see Figure 1–7 on page 23) is an example of an internal proposal.*

The purpose of an internal proposal is to recommend a change or an improvement within an organization. Often transmitted electronically, it is sent to a superior within the organization who has the authority to accept or reject the proposal. Internal proposals are typically reviewed by one or more departments for cost, practicality, and potential benefits. Two common types of internal proposals — routine and formal — are often distinguished from each other by the frequency with which they are written and by the degree of change proposed.

Routine Internal Proposals

Routine internal proposals typically include requests for permission to hire new employees or to recommend current employees for an award or a bonus and requests to attend conferences or purchase new equipment. In writing routine proposals, highlight any key benefits to be realized.

Figure 13–1 shows a typical internal proposal. It was written as a memo by a plant safety officer to the plant superintendent and recommends changes in specific safety practices at the company.

Formal Internal Proposals

Formal internal proposals could involve requests to expand or reorganize a business, to implement a companywide program, and the like. These proposals often involve committing large sums of money. They are usually organized into sections that describe

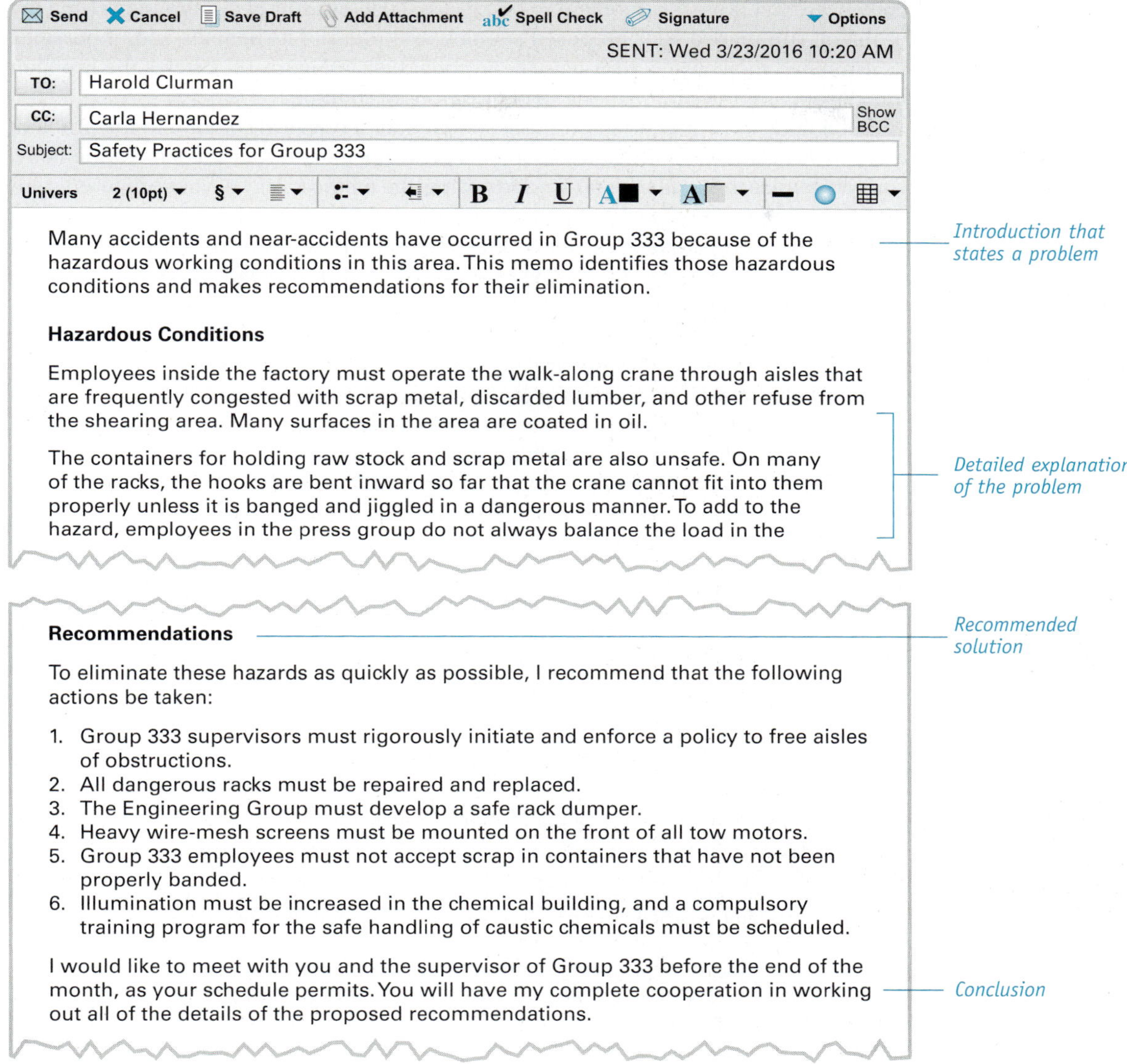
Send Cancel Save Draft Add Attachment Spell Check Signature Options

SENT: Wed 3/23/2016 10:20 AM

TO: Harold Clurman

CC: Carla Hernandez

Subject: Safety Practices for Group 333

Many accidents and near-accidents have occurred in Group 333 because of the hazardous working conditions in this area. This memo identifies those hazardous conditions and makes recommendations for their elimination.

Hazardous Conditions

Employees inside the factory must operate the walk-along crane through aisles that are frequently congested with scrap metal, discarded lumber, and other refuse from the shearing area. Many surfaces in the area are coated in oil.

The containers for holding raw stock and scrap metal are also unsafe. On many of the racks, the hooks are bent inward so far that the crane cannot fit into them properly unless it is banged and jiggled in a dangerous manner. To add to the hazard, employees in the press group do not always balance the load in the

Recommendations

To eliminate these hazards as quickly as possible, I recommend that the following actions be taken:

1. Group 333 supervisors must rigorously initiate and enforce a policy to free aisles of obstructions.
2. All dangerous racks must be repaired and replaced.
3. The Engineering Group must develop a safe rack dumper.
4. Heavy wire-mesh screens must be mounted on the front of all tow motors.
5. Group 333 employees must not accept scrap in containers that have not been properly banded.
6. Illumination must be increased in the chemical building, and a compulsory training program for the safe handling of caustic chemicals must be scheduled.

I would like to meet with you and the supervisor of Group 333 before the end of the month, as your schedule permits. You will have my complete cooperation in working out all of the details of the proposed recommendations.

Figure 13–1 Routine Internal Proposal

a problem, propose one or more solutions, recommend one solution, and offer to implement the recommendation. The body, in turn, is further divided into sections to reflect the subject matter. The proposal may begin with a section describing the background or history of an issue and go on to discuss options for addressing the issue in separate sections.

The introduction of your internal proposal should establish that a problem exists and needs a solution. This section is sometimes called a "problem statement." (Internal proposals are sometimes referred to as *problem-solution memos*.) If the audience is not convinced that there is a problem, your proposal will not succeed. After identifying the problem, summarize your proposed solution and indicate its benefits and, if possible, its estimated total cost. Notice how the introduction in Figure 13–2 states the problem directly and then summarizes the writer's proposed solution.

The body of your internal proposal should offer a practical solution to the problem and provide the details necessary to inform and to persuade your readers. In the body, you will itemize the problem you are addressing; the methodology of your proposed solution; information about equipment, materials, and staff; cost breakdowns; and a detailed schedule. Figure 13–3 shows the body of the internal proposal introduced in Figure 13–2.

The conclusion of your internal proposal should tie everything together, restate your recommendation, and close with a spirit of cooperation (offering to set up a meeting, supply additional information, or provide any other assistance that might be needed). Keep your conclusion brief, as in Figure 13–4 on page 434.

◆ *For guidance on researching and citing background information, see Chapter 6, Conducting Research for a Document.*

If your proposal cites information that you obtained through research, such as published reports, government statistics, or interviews, follow the conclusion with a references list that provides complete publication information for each source, as in Figure 13–5 on page 435.

ABO, Inc.
Memo

To: Joan Marlow, Director, Human Resources Division
From: Leslie Galusha, Chief, Employee Benefits Department
Sent: October 14, 2016
Subject: Employee Fitness and Health-Care Costs Proposal

Introduction clearly states problem

Health-care and worker's compensation insurance costs at ABO, Inc., have risen 100 percent over the last four years. In 2011, costs were $5,675 per employee per year; in 2015, they reached $11,560 per employee per year. This doubling of costs mirrors a national trend in which health-care costs are anticipated to rise at the same rate for the next ten years. Controlling these escalating expenses will be essential. They are eating into ABO's profit margin because the company currently pays 70 percent of the costs for employee coverage.

Introduction summarizes proposal solution

Healthy employees bring direct financial benefits to companies in the form of lower employee insurance costs, lower absenteeism rates, and reduced turnover. Regular physical exercise promotes fit, healthy people by reducing the risk of coronary heart disease, diabetes, osteoporosis, hypertension, and stress-related problems. I propose that to promote regular, vigorous physical exercise for our employees, ABO implement a health-care program that focuses on employee fitness. . . .

Figure 13–2 Formal Internal Proposal, Introduction (Transmittal Memo Excerpt)

Joan Marlow 2 Employee Fitness Proposal

Problem of Health-Care Costs

The U.S. Department of Health and Human Services recently estimated that health-care costs in the United States will triple by the year 2020. Corporate expenses for health care are rising at such a fast rate that, if unchecked, in eight years they will significantly erode corporate profits.

Information explaining extent of problem

According to Health and Human Services, people who do not participate in a regular and vigorous exercise program incur double the health-care costs and are hospitalized 30 percent more days than people who exercise regularly. Nonexercisers are also 41 percent more likely to submit medical claims over $10,000 at some point during their careers than are those who exercise regularly (U.S. Department of Health and Human Services, 2010).

These figures are further supported by data from independent studies. A model created by the National Institutes of Health (NIH) estimates that the average white-collar company could save $596,000 annually in medical costs (per 1,000 employees) just by promoting wellness. NIH researchers estimated that for every $1 a firm invests in a health-care program, it saves up to $3.75 in health-care costs (Goetzel, Jacobson, Aldana, Vardell, & Yee, 1998, p. 342). In an overview of studies that evaluated the benefits of company wellness programs, the Public Health & Health Policy Institute of Wisconsin reported that "an unhealthy lifestyle or modifiable risk factors . . . account for at least 25 percent of employee health-care expenditures" (Zank & Friedsam, p. 1).

Information explaining extent of problem

Citations identify sources of information in APA style

Proposed Solutions for ABO

The benefits of regular, vigorous physical activity for employees and companies are compelling. To achieve these benefits at ABO, I propose that we choose from one of two possible options: build in-house fitness centers at our warehouse facilities or offer employees several options for membership at a national fitness club.

In-House Fitness Center

Building in-house fitness centers would require that ABO modify existing space in its five warehouses and designate an area outside for walking and running. To accommodate the weight-lifting and cardiovascular equipment and an aerobics area would require a minimum of 4,000 square feet. Lockers and shower stalls would also have to be built adjacent to the men's and women's bathrooms.

Explanation of proposed solution

Figure 13–3 Formal Internal Proposal, Body

Joan Marlow 3 Employee Fitness Proposal

The costs to equip each facility are as follows:

Required equipment and materials

Breakdown of costs

1	Challenger 3.0 Treadmill	$4,395
3	Ross Futura exercise bicycles @ $750 each	$2,250
1	CalGym S-370 inner thigh machine	$2,250
1	CalGym S-325 outer thigh machine	$2,250
1	CalGym S-260 lat pull-down machine	$2,290
1	CalGym S-360 leg-extension, combo-curl	$1,900
1	CalGym S-390 arm-curl machine	$2,235
1	CalGym S-410 side-lat machine	$1,950
1	CalGym S-430 pullover machine	$2,110
1	CalGym S-440 abdominal machine	$2,250
1	CalGym S-460 back machine	$2,250
1	CalGym S-290 chest press	$2,000
1	CalGym S-310 pectoral developer	$1,950
10	5710321 3-wide lockers @ $81 each	$810
4	5713000 benches and pedestals @ $81 each	$324
	Carpeting for workout area	$3,000
3	showers each, men's/women's locker room	$15,000
	Men's and women's locker-room expansion	$15,000
	Remodeling expenses	$450,000
	Total per ABO site	$514,214
	Grand Total	**$2,571,070**

Required staff

At headquarters and at the regional offices, our current Employee Assistance Program staff would need to be available several hours each workday to provide instructions for the use of exercise equipment. Aerobics instructors can be hired locally on a monthly basis for classes. The Buildings and Maintenance Department staff would clean and maintain the facilities.

Fitness-Club Membership

Explanation of proposed solution

Offering a complimentary membership to a national fitness club for all employees can also help reduce company health-care costs. AeroFitness Clubs, Inc., offers the best option for ABO's needs. They operate in over 45 major markets, with over 300 clubs nationwide. Most important, AeroFitness Clubs are located here in Bartlesville and in all four cities where our regional warehouses are located.

AeroFitness staff are trained and certified in exercise physiology and will design individualized fitness programs for our employees. They offer aerobics classes for all levels, taught by certified instructors. Each club also features the latest in resistance exercise equipment from Nautilus, Universal, Paramount, and Life Fitness. Most AeroFitness facilities provide competition-size swimming pools, cushioned indoor running tracks, saunas, whirlpools, steam rooms, and racquetball courts.

Figure 13–3 Formal Internal Proposal, Body *(continued)*

AeroFitness offers a full range of membership programs that include corporate discounts. The basic membership of $600 per year includes the following:

- Unlimited use of exercise equipment
- Unlimited aerobics classes
- Unlimited use of racquetball, sauna, and whirlpool facilities
- Free initial consultation with an exercise physiologist for exercise and nutrition programs
- Free child care during daytime working hours

The club offers a full range of membership programs for companies. ABO may choose to pay all or part of employee membership costs. Three membership program options are available with AeroFitness:

- *Corporate purchase.* ABO buys and owns the memberships. With 10 or more memberships, ABO receives a 35 percent discount.

  ABO costs: $600 per employee × 1,200 employees − 35% discount = $468,000 per year.*

- *Corporate subsidy.* Employees purchase memberships at a discount and own them. With 10 or more memberships, employees and the company each pay one-half of annual membership dues and receive a 30 percent discount off annual dues. The corporation also pays a one-time $50 enrollment fee per employee.

  ABO costs: $300 per employee × 1,200 employees − 30% discount = $252,000 per year. The one-time enrollment fee of $50 per employee adds $60,000 to first-year costs.*

- *Employee purchase.* Employees purchase memberships on their own. With five or more memberships, employees receive 25 percent off regular rates. Club sales representatives conduct an on-site open-enrollment meeting. Employees own memberships.

  ABO costs: None.

Breakdown of costs

*Assumes that all employees will enroll.

Figure 13–3 Formal Internal Proposal, Body *(continued)*

Conclusion restates recommendation

Conclusion closes with spirit of cooperation

Joan Marlow 5 Employee Fitness Proposal

Conclusion and Recommendation

I recommend that ABO, Inc., participate in the corporate membership program at AeroFitness Clubs, Inc., by subsidizing employee memberships. By subsidizing memberships, ABO shows its commitment to the importance of a fit workforce. Club membership allows employees at all five ABO warehouses to participate in the program. The more employees who participate, the greater the long-term savings in ABO's health-care costs. Building and equipping fitness centers at all five warehouse sites would require an initial investment of over $2.5 million. These facilities would also occupy valuable floor space — on average, 4,000 square feet at each warehouse. Therefore, this option would be very costly.

Enrolling employees in the corporate program at AeroFitness would allow them to attend on a trial basis. Those interested in continuing could then join the club and pay half of the membership cost, less a 30 percent discount on the $600 yearly fee. The other half of the membership fee ($300) would be paid for by ABO. If an employee leaves the company, he or she would have the option of purchasing ABO's share of the membership to continue at AeroFitness or selling their half of the membership to another ABO employee wishing to join AeroFitness.

Implementing this program will help ABO, Inc., reduce its health-care costs while building stronger employee relations by offering employees a desirable benefit. If this proposal is adopted, I have some additional thoughts about publicizing the program to encourage employee participation. I look forward to discussing the details of this proposal (including the implementation schedule for each option) with you and answering any questions you may have.

Figure 13–4 Formal Internal Proposal, Conclusion

Joan Marlow 6 Employee Fitness Proposal

References

Centers for Medicare & Medicaid Services. (2014). *National health expenditure projections 2012–2022*. Retrieved from https://www.cms.gov

Goetzel, R. Z., Jacobson, B. H., Aldana, S. G., Vardell, K., & Yee, L. (1998). Health care costs of worksite health promotion participants and nonparticipants. *Journal of Occupational and Environmental Medicine, 40*(4), 341–346. Retrieved from http://www.ncbi.nlm.nih.gov/pubmed/9571525

U.S. Department of Health and Human Services, Office of the Assistant Secretary for Planning and Evaluation. (2010). *Physical activity fundamental to preventing disease*. Retrieved from http://www.hhs.gov

Zank, D., & Friedsam, D. (2010, September). Employee health promotion programs: What is the return on investment? (Issue Brief No. 12). Retrieved from the Wisconsin Public Health & Health Policy Institute website, http://instituteforwihealth.org

References section lists research sources in APA style

Figure 13–5 References Section in a Formal Internal Proposal

WRITER'S CHECKLIST

Creating Internal Proposals

- ✔ Prepare your proposal for someone in your organization with the power to act on it.
- ✔ Describe the problem clearly, providing any essential technical or historical background to clarify why the problem exists.
- ✔ Offer your solution in sufficient detail so that a decision maker can evaluate your approach.
- ✔ Note any resource requirements necessary for a solution (personnel, equipment, materials).
- ✔ Provide a schedule for implementing the solution.
- ✔ Specify the benefits expected to result from your solution.

External Proposals

External proposals are prepared for clients and customers outside your company. They are either submitted in response to a request for goods and services from another organization (a solicited proposal) or sent to them without a prior request (an unsolicited proposal). Research and grant proposals, a type of external proposal, are usually submitted to nonprofit organizations, which include medical and research institutions, as well as to local, state, and federal government agencies, to request funding in support of research or development that could benefit the funding organization.

Solicited Proposals

To find the best method of doing a job and the most qualified company to do it, procuring organizations commonly issue a request for proposal (RFP) or an invitation for bids (IFB) that asks competing companies such as yours to bid for a job. An RFP may be rigid in specifying how the proposal should be organized and what it should contain, but it is normally quite flexible about the approaches that bidding firms may propose. Ordinarily, the RFP simply defines the basic work that the procuring organization needs and leaves it up to the proposers to put forth their method of performing the work economically and within their stated schedule. An IFB, however, is restrictive, binding the bidder to produce an item or a service that meets the exact requirements of the agency or company. (For guidance in preparing RFPs, see Requests for Proposals on pages 465–468.)

When you respond to an RFP or IFB, pay close attention to any specifications in the request governing the preparation of the proposal and follow them carefully. Such specifications usually state how the proposal should be organized, the kind of technical expertise required, the basis for calculating cost estimates, the location of the work site, and the like. Also, if the RFP or IFB provides a scoring method that the requesting organization will use to rank proposals it receives, ensure that your work complies with that scoring methodology. Figure 13–6 shows an example of a real-world proposal — excerpted by the LS Group — that presents a comprehensive plan for evaluating a state-supported housing program. Notice how the introduction establishes the credentials of the LS Group and its partners, outlines the scope of the evaluation, and provides an overview of the proposal's structure. On the second page, you can see that the proposal's work plan is formatted as a table and itemizes in detail each task of the work being proposed. It assigns target due dates, describes the involvement of all parties, projects outcomes, and identifies deliverables (or products) for each task listed. Figure 13–7 on page 439 shows a short solicited sales proposal that responds to a property-management company's IFB on a landscaping project.

Unsolicited Proposals

Unsolicited proposals are those submitted to a company without a prior request and are not as unusual as they may sound: Companies often operate for years with a problem they have never recognized (unnecessarily high maintenance costs, for example, or poor inventory-control methods). You might prepare an unsolicited proposal for such a company if you were convinced that the potential customer could realize substantial benefits by adopting your solution to a problem. You could also propose that a company purchase your services if the company does not provide them (Figure 13–8 on pages 440–441). Of course, you would need to convince the customer of the need for what you are proposing and that your solution would be the best one. Many unsolicited proposals are preceded by a letter of inquiry that specifies the problem or unmet need to determine whether there is any potential interest. If you receive a positive response, you would conduct a detailed study of the prospective client's needs to determine whether you can be of help and, if so, exactly how. You would then prepare a formal proposal on the basis of your study.

PROPOSAL TO CONDUCT A MULTIYEAR EVALUATION OF PERMANENT SUPPORTIVE HOUSING IN LOWELL COUNTY

LS Group is pleased to partner with Barton Consulting, LLC, to provide the Supportive Housing Initiative (SHI) with a proposal to evaluate State-Financed Permanent Supportive Housing (PSH) in Lowell County. LS Group's national research and technical assistance experience in homelessness, housing, and community development, complemented by Barton's expertise in housing development, finance, and operations, provides an exceptional foundation on which to help SHI and its partners execute groundbreaking research on the long-term sustainability of PSH and its effectiveness over time for the tenants housed in various PSH settings. We are very excited about this study and believe the results have the opportunity to shape state policy, local practice, and national understanding of PSH and its ongoing impact and role.

Opens by establishing the consulting firm's credentials

LS Group and Barton offer SHI a ***"full-service" research team***, with the breadth of staff and project skills necessary to complete ***all three components*** of the proposed study: program and cost effectiveness, community and neighborhood impact, and project stability and quality. This comprehensive approach allows us to achieve economies of scale across the three evaluation components, enabling us to propose richer analysis and more frequent interim reports than might otherwise be feasible. Most important, the technical approach is sufficiently rigorous to yield results that can guide important decision-making about the future of PSH in Lowell County.

Highlights the firm's enthusiasm about and staff expertise for the project

Our proposal is organized as follows: In Section 1, we discuss the key elements of our technical approach and design considerations, including challenges that may be encountered and strategies to mitigate these challenges, and our plan for reporting and dissemination. Section 2 details the work plan and overall project time line. Section 3 describes our management plan and organizational and staff qualifications related to this study. Appendix A presents résumés for project staff, and Appendix B contains our references. Our budget and budget narrative and writing samples are included in separate documents.

Describes the proposal's scope and organization

Figure 13–6 Research Consulting Proposal

Section 2. Work Plan

This section presents our proposed work plan for designing and completing the required study tasks. The LS Group/Barton team has extensive experience researching and providing technical assistance on homelessness, housing development, and neighborhood redevelopment. Our technical approach and work plan is based on these perspectives, as well as on extensive experience analyzing administrative data, designing and conducting site-visit interviews and cost data collection. Time lines are noted to convey the general time frames for the proposed work; however, these dates may be able to be adjusted depending on data availability. For instance, from our experience negotiating access to mainstream data on other projects, we have allotted a significant period of time to obtain mainstream data. If these data are available sooner, this work can be completed and delivered earlier. In addition, the schedule can be resequenced or adapted in other ways to better meet SHI and state legislative or programmatic deadlines.

Project work plan in table format with a time line and detailed task descriptions

	Properties and Neighborhoods	**Tenants, PSH Involvement, PSH Outcomes**	**Mainstream System Use and Outcomes**	**Project Planning, Management, and Deliverables**
Year 1				
May 2016	Assess data on properties and costs	Assess data on tenants, PSH occupancy and service use, and outcomes	Assess mainstream system data availability and access	Opening meeting
June 2016	Analyze inventory and prepare description of properties Select Samples A, B, and C	Work with SHI on a strategy to obtain data (SHI will assume lead role in data acquisition)	Agree upon target data sets and plan for obtaining data	Develop work plan based on assessment of data types and availability Draft and deliver work plan
July 2016	Develop/refine cost templates and cost specs related to development cost data Use GIS to analyze neighborhood characteristics and appropriateness	Develop protocols for assessing tenant satisfaction Define specifications for data needs re: tenants, service use, and outcomes	Develop data-use agreement template and mainstream table shells to inform mainstream data request(s)	Prepare data collection and analysis plan (DCAP) Deliver DCAP

Figure 13–6 Research Consulting Proposal *(continued)*

Jerwalted Nurseries

Ronald Malcomson, President

12 Rogers Highway West
St. Louis, MO 63101
jerwaltednurseries.com
Ph. 1-800-212-1212
Fax (314) 999-1111

February 1, 2016

Ms. Tricia Olivera, Vice President
Watford Valve Corporation
1600 Swanson Avenue
St. Louis, MO 63121

Dear Ms. Olivera:

Jerwalted Nurseries, Inc., proposes to landscape the new corporate headquarters of the Watford Valve Corporation, on 1600 Swanson Avenue, at a total cost of $14,871. The lot to be landscaped is approximately 600 feet wide and 700 feet deep. Landscaping will begin no later than April 30, 2016, and will be completed by May 31.

Introduction states purpose and scope of proposal and indicates when project can be started and completed

The following trees and plants will be planted, in the quantities given and at the prices specified.

4	maple trees	@ $110 each	$440
41	birch trees	@ $135 each	$5,535
2	spruce trees	@ $175 each	$350
20	juniper plants	@ $15 each	$300
60	hedges	@ $12 each	$720
200	potted plants	@ $12 each	$2,400
		Total Cost of Plants =	$9,745
		Labor =	$5,126
		Total Cost =	$14,871

Body lists products to be provided and cost per item

All trees and plants will be guaranteed against defect or disease for a period of 90 days, the warranty period to begin June 1, 2016.

The prices quoted in this proposal will be valid until June 28, 2016.

Thank you for the opportunity to submit this proposal. Jerwalted Nurseries has been in the landscaping and nursery business in the St. Louis area for 30 years, and our landscaping has won several awards and commendations, including a citation from the National Association of Architects. We are eager to put our skills and knowledge to work for you, and we are confident that you will be pleased with our work. If we can provide any additional information or assistance, please call us at the number listed above.

Conclusion specifies time limit of proposal, expresses confidence, and looks forward to working with prospective customer

Sincerely,

Ronald Malcomson
RLM@jerwaltednurseries.com

Figure 13–7 Short Solicited Sales Proposal

Longo's Shoe Repair

1211 Erie Street
Hobard, OH 44425

longoshooz.com
Phone: (331) 467-0333

Introduction states purpose of the proposal and establishes the company's reputation

Dear Mr. Rice:

Longo's Shoe Repair Shop congratulates you on the grand opening of JK Sports! We would like to offer you our services as the area's leading repair shop for baseball and softball gloves. We currently hold five-year contracts with the Locker Room and the S & S Baseball Express store. We also value your time and offer the convenience of pickup and delivery on all orders.

Repair Procedures

We evaluate each glove and estimate the cost of repair based on the degree of damage and the estimated time of repair. If the actual cost exceeds the estimated cost by more than $5, we will call you to discuss the reason for the additional cost and will proceed only upon your approval. Most repairs will be confined to the section damaged, but if the glove is old and the strings appear weak, we will re-string the glove to ensure its fitness for continued use.

Once a glove has been repaired, we fully condition it. The inside of the glove will be treated with Dr. Glove's Foam System, which helps protect against the sweat and dirt that crack leather and cause increased wear. The outside of the glove is then treated with Easton Oil, which keeps the glove soft, pliant, and resistant to dirt. We also provide instructions to the glove owner to keep the glove oiled throughout the playing season and to oil it again for off-season storage.

Cost Guidelines and Equipment

Body details the product line, prices, and specific features

We charge an initial $21 for each repair job and $12 per hour after the initial hour. We also include the cost of supplies in the total bill. Supplies are priced as follows:

- 2-foot 10-gauge string $2.50
- 3½-foot 10-gauge string $3.75
- 2-foot 12-gauge string $3.25
- 3½-foot 12-gauge string $4.10
- 2 x 4 leather patch $3.00
- 3 x 5 leather patch $3.75
- Waxed thread $0.16 per inch

The string gauge used depends on the glove manufacturer and location of the repair. Repairs to the Web area always require 12-gauge string.

Figure 13–8 Short Unsolicited Sales Proposal

Mr. Harry Rice 2 March 15, 2016

We also feature special rates for bulk orders — for repair orders of 10 or more gloves, we fix the tenth glove free! And remember, we value your time, so we offer free pickup and delivery on all orders.

Recommendation and Qualifications

We hope that our reputation for top-quality services encourages you to consider our company as your first choice for glove repairs. Our 40 years of experience and our equipment, tools, and staff expertise account for our reputation as the premier shop for the fine-detailed work that goes into every glove we repair. The added glove conditioning and break-in services we believe enhance this reputation.

Persuasive conclusion showcases company's skill and experience and extends an offer to follow up with more information

We welcome your review of this offer and look forward to establishing good working relations with you, your staff, and your customers. I would be pleased to meet with you or send any additional information you request. Please contact me at the shop during business hours, Monday through Friday, 8 a.m. until 5 p.m., or by e-mail at vlongo@longoshooz.com.

Vincent Longo

Vincent Longo, Proprietor
vlongo@longoshooz.com

Figure 13–8 Short Unsolicited Sales Proposal *(continued)*

PROFESSIONALISM NOTE: Remember That Sales Proposals Are Legally Binding Keep in mind that, once submitted, a sales proposal is a legally binding document that promises to offer goods or services within a specified time and for a specified price. Many sales proposals also note that the offer is valid for a limited time period, which often depends on the product. For example, printing proposals are usually good for 30 days—a short time period attributed to the often fluctuating costs of paper and ink.

Grant and Research Proposals

Grant and research proposals are written to nonprofit organizations to request the approval of and funding for projects that solve a problem or fulfill a need. For example, a professor of education might submit a research proposal to the state or federal

Department of Education to request funding for research on the relationship of class size to educational performance; similarly, a community center might submit a grant proposal to obtain funding from a local government agency for an after-school job-training program.

Many government agencies, private foundations, and other nonprofit groups solicit research and grant proposals. Granting organizations typically post opportunities, along with detailed application guidelines, on their websites. They usually specify their requirements for the format and content of proposals, as shown in the RFP from Purdue University's College of Education, Figure 13–9. Always research the grant-making organization first to familiarize yourself with its areas of interest and its purpose in granting the funding. If your organization pursues multiple grants, be careful to tailor your grant or research proposal to each specific audience by carefully following the guidelines provided by the granting agency. In addition, remember that proposals must always be persuasive: Explain your project's goals, your plan for achieving those goals, and your qualifications to perform the project.

Although application guidelines may differ from one organization to another, grant proposals generally require the following sections at a minimum:

- Cover letter
- Title page
- Application form
- Introduction/summary/abstract
- Literature review
- Project narrative
- Project description
- Project outcomes
- Budget narrative
- Schedule
- Organization description
- Conclusion
- Attachments

Cover Letter Usually a page long, the cover letter should identify who you are and your affiliation. It should specify the grant for which you are applying, summarize the proposed project, and include the amount of funding you are requesting. Be sure to include any credentials you feel reinforce your organization's ability to complete the project successfully. End the letter by expressing your appreciation for the opportunity to submit the proposal and include information about how you can be reached. The letter should include a subject line with the grant title in addition to the address of the recipient, date of submission, salutation (Dear . . .), and complimentary close (Sincerely), as in Figure 13–10 on page 444.

Title Page The title page is the grant-proposal cover. On a single page, show the title of the project, names of team members and their affiliations, date submitted, and name of the recipient's organization, as shown in Figure 13–11 on page 445.

Application Form Especially in online grant applications, an application form may replace the cover letter and title page. This form may be one or more pages and may require you to check boxes, fill in blanks, or insert brief descriptions or other information into text boxes or blank spaces. A word or character limit (typically 250–400 words)

Request for "Launch the Future" Incentive Grant Proposals

College of Education
Office of the Dean

Deadline:
March 2, 2016; funds available July 1, 2016

Purpose and Vision

The College of Education will support initiatives designed to foster the development of human potential through discovery, learning, and engagement and will prioritize initiatives which are focused on the grand challenges of STEM education and social justice. The "Launch the Future" incentive grant program is intended to accelerate progress toward this strategic goal. The intent of this program is to provide resources to assist faculty in preparing to develop large-scale, collaborative, interdisciplinary projects.

General purpose

Eligibility

The Principal Investigator (PI) must be a voting faculty member in the College of Education, Purdue–West Lafayette and approved by Sponsored Program Services to serve as a PI to an outside agency. The project team may include personnel from other units.

Proposal Submission Process

Proposals should be submitted electronically as a single PDF file. The document should be set for 8 1/2-by-11-inch paper, margins no less than one inch all around, and a font no smaller than 11 point. The body of the proposal may be single-spaced. The specific components of the proposal should be included as outlined below.

Cover page, including:

- Proposal title
- Principal Investigator(s), with signature(s)
- PI's department head, with signature
- Total budget request
- Project period

Project plan, limited to five pages, single-spaced, one-inch margins, no smaller than 11-point font. The project plan must include:

- Introduction to the project/rationale with supporting literature
- Project goals: identify both long-term goals and specific achievable project goals
- Key elements: describe how the proposed project addresses the required characteristics of the "Launch the Future" program
- Project plan: summarize the approaches to be used in the proposed project
- Sustainability: discuss how the proposed project will be sustained after funding ends

Additional requirements:

- References cited in APA format
- Two-page biographical sketch for each PI/Co-PI
- Budget

Format guidelines

The deadline for receipt of proposals in March 2, 2016. Proposals should be submitted as a single PDF file attachment to an e-mail message (subject: Launch the Future Proposal) addressed to discovery@education.purdue.edu.

Figure 13–9 Request for Grant-Proposal Format Specifications Reprinted by permission of Purdue University.

October 7, 2016

Ms. Joan Atwater
Executive Director
ABC Foundation
13 Hill Street
Boston, MA 02116

Subject: Read to Succeed! Program

Dear Ms. Atwater:

Orchard Middle School is pleased to present this proposal for your review. We look forward to partnering with you to provide a reading intervention program for our students with poor reading skills called Read to Succeed! Orchard Middle School has more than 50 students who are at risk with a reading performance of at least two years behind their current grade level. The objective of the Read to Succeed! program is to help all students with poor reading skills learn to read at grade level and increase their reading speed, comprehension, and reading attention span.

Summary of program and objective

Last year, we ran a pilot Read to Succeed! program with a small group of students with poor reading skills and have seen dramatic improvements, with most of the students increasing their reading ability by one or two grade levels. . . .

We have seen measurable success, and we are now seeking to expand our Read to Succeed! program to address the needs of all at-risk students in Orchard Middle School. Our proposal requests $16,504 in funding to obtain the software, hardware, and training necessary to equip the Orchard Middle School resource room with five assistive reading systems, each including a computer, a scanner, and assistive reading software.

Funding request

We appreciate ABC Foundation taking an interest in helping our students develop their reading skills through our new reading program! Please call me at (888) 555-1212, ext. 342, or e-mail me at JMH@orchardmiddleschool.edu if you require any further information or have any questions concerning this proposal.

Contact information

Thank you.

Sincerely,

Jennifer Hazelton

Jennifer Hazelton
JMH@orchardmiddleschool.edu
Special Education Coordinator
Orchard Middle School
387 Pine Hill Road
Orchard, VT 02331

Figure 13–10 Grant-Proposal Cover Letter Copyright © Kurweil Educational Systems. Cambium Learning Group, Inc. Reprinted by permission.

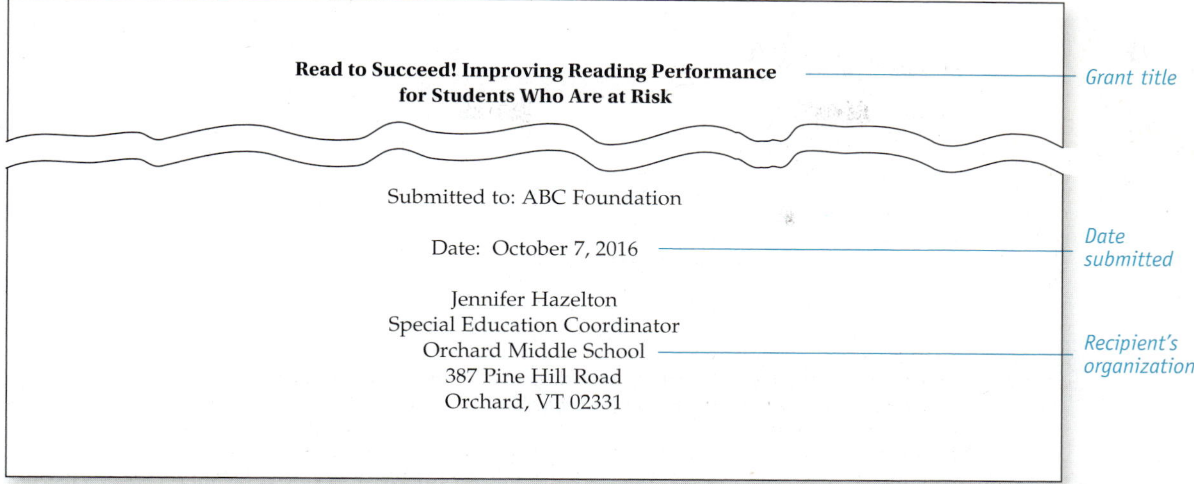
Read to Succeed! Improving Reading Performance
for Students Who Are at Risk

Submitted to: ABC Foundation

Date: October 7, 2016

Jennifer Hazelton
Special Education Coordinator
Orchard Middle School
387 Pine Hill Road
Orchard, VT 02331

Figure 13–11 Grant-Proposal Title Page Copyright © Kurweil Educational Systems. Cambium Learning Group, Inc. Reprinted by permission.

may be imposed or enforced. An official signature (or its electronic equivalent) is often required. This section may request detailed information about the applicant organization, such as staff or board of directors' demographic composition or its human resources policies.

Introduction/Summary/Abstract The introduction, also called the summary or abstract, is your proposal at a glance. It briefly describes in a page the problem to be solved in the language used in the request for proposals, as in Figure 13–12. Most important, your introduction should sketch the expected outcomes of your grant proposal, answering the question: What will you achieve? For a research proposal, you may also describe your

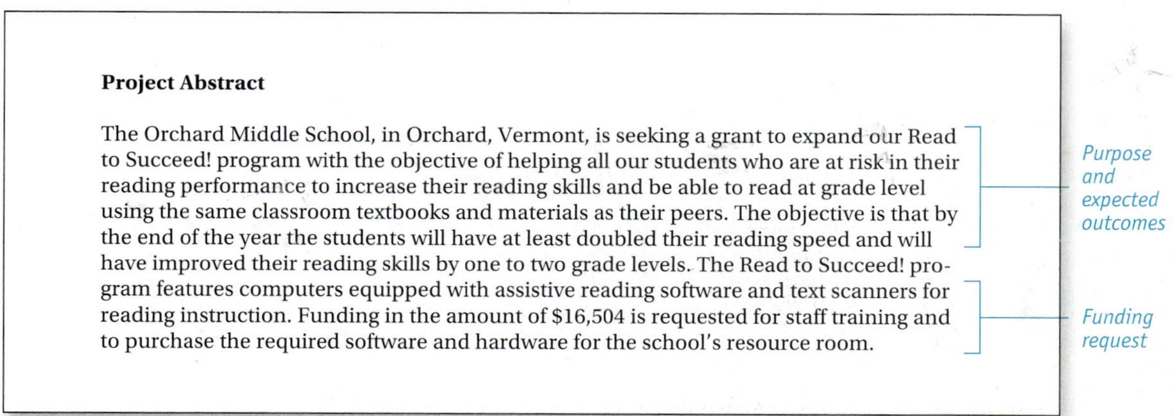
Project Abstract

The Orchard Middle School, in Orchard, Vermont, is seeking a grant to expand our Read to Succeed! program with the objective of helping all our students who are at risk in their reading performance to increase their reading skills and be able to read at grade level using the same classroom textbooks and materials as their peers. The objective is that by the end of the year the students will have at least doubled their reading speed and will have improved their reading skills by one to two grade levels. The Read to Succeed! program features computers equipped with assistive reading software and text scanners for reading instruction. Funding in the amount of $16,504 is requested for staff training and to purchase the required software and hardware for the school's resource room.

Figure 13–12 Grant-Proposal Introduction Copyright © Kurweil Educational Systems. Cambium Learning Group, Inc. Reprinted by permission.

Selective program research sources in APA format

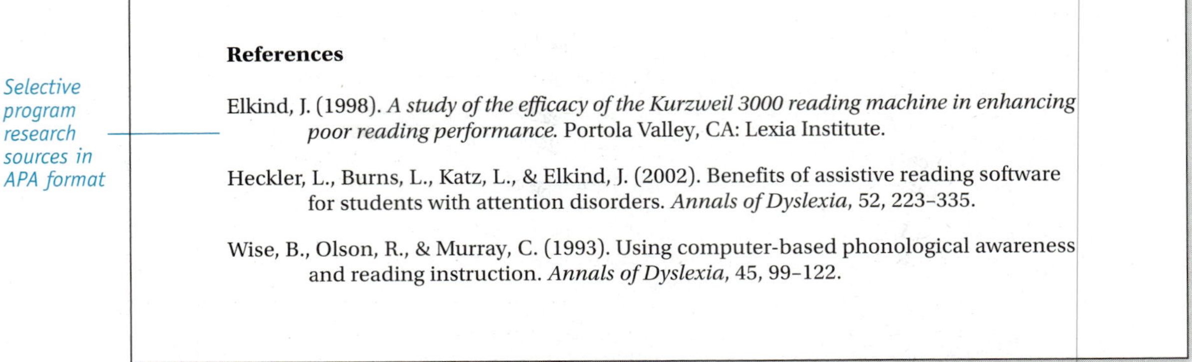

References

Elkind, J. (1998). *A study of the efficacy of the Kurzweil 3000 reading machine in enhancing poor reading performance.* Portola Valley, CA: Lexia Institute.

Heckler, L., Burns, L., Katz, L., & Elkind, J. (2002). Benefits of assistive reading software for students with attention disorders. *Annals of Dyslexia*, 52, 223–335.

Wise, B., Olson, R., & Murray, C. (1993). Using computer-based phonological awareness and reading instruction. *Annals of Dyslexia*, 45, 99–122.

Figure 13–13 Grant-Proposal References Section (Excerpt) Copyright © Kurweil Educational Systems. Cambium Learning Group, Inc. Reprinted by permission.

proposed research methods in a separate paragraph: interviews, questionnaires, videotapes, observations, and so on.

Literature Review The literature review allows reviewers of your proposal to assess your familiarity with current research in the field, as shown in Figure 13–13. Is your research up to date? thorough? pertinent? Be selective in listing sources, which may include journal articles, books, and websites, as well as interviews, podcasts, blogs, and other sources. A literature review will also reveal whether conclusive research has already been done in an area or whether competing programs have successfully addressed the same problem. Some or all of the sources may be annotated to establish their scope and pertinence.

Project Narrative The project narrative or statement of need is the heart of the proposal. It's where you describe in detail the scope of the work, expected outcomes, list of tasks, schedule from start to finish, and proposed cost. The detailed statement of need must be specific and thorough. The excerpt shown in Figure 13–14 from a grant proposal states the problem and includes pertinent data.

Scope of proposal

Statement of Need

Orchard Middle School has 276 students, 59 of whom have been determined to be at risk in their reading performance for a variety of reasons, including learning disabilities, such as attention deficit disorder (ADD) and dyslexia, or other language difficulties based on economic status. Orchard Middle School is eligible for Title 1 funds, and if these students are not given an opportunity to improve their reading skills, they are, as studies show, more likely to be truant and drop out of school.

Figure 13–14 Grant-Proposal Statement of Need Copyright © Kurweil Educational Systems. Cambium Learning Group, Inc. Reprinted by permission.

Program Description

The Orchard Read to Succeed! program will enable students who are at risk in their reading performance to improve their reading skills through the use of five computers equipped with scanners and assistive reading software. Students using this innovative reading system will be able to use all their classroom materials, including textbooks, providing them access to the general curriculum. The students will increase their reading speed and comprehension, which will help them obtain classroom subject proficiency. Included in the Read to Succeed! program will be a day of training for the reading specialist and classroom teachers on the features and use of the Kurzweil 3000 software.

Specific program details

Figure 13–15 Grant-Proposal Program Description Copyright © Kurweil Educational Systems. Cambium Learning Group, Inc. Reprinted by permission.

Project Description The project-narrative section usually includes details of how the research will be conducted (the methodology), as in the excerpt shown in Figure 13–15 from the reading-performance proposal. In nonresearch proposals, include a succinct *statement of need*—also called a *case statement*—that presents the facts and evidence that support the need for the project. The information presented can come from authorities in the field, as well as from your agency's own experience or research. A logical and persuasive statement of need demonstrates that your company or nonprofit organization sufficiently understands the situation and is therefore capable of addressing it satisfactorily. Clearly indicate why or how your solution improves on existing or previous ones, and cite evidence to support this. Emphasize the benefits of the proposed activities for the grant maker's intended constituency or target population and why your solution to the problem or plan to fulfill the need should be approved. Most RFPs and grant-maker guidelines provide a list of specific questions for applicants to answer or required topics that must be persuasively addressed in this section.

Project Outcomes Having discussed the preparation for the program and how the participants will be evaluated, the grant must describe the outcomes, or deliverables, of the proposal. It must describe what results the organization can expect based on the time, labor, and funding it has invested in the program. In this case, the outcomes are stated as quantifiable objectives, as in Figure 13–16. This section is also called "objectives."[2]

Budget Narrative Include a budget narrative section that provides a detailed listing of costs for personnel, equipment, building renovations, and other grant-related expenses. This information must be clear and accurate. List costs in a format easily grasped by those evaluating the data, as shown in Figure 13–17. If your proposal is approved, you are being entrusted with funds belonging to someone else, and you are

[2]Many grant writers find the system called SMART useful. The SMART system assists writers in setting feasible performance goals and means of measuring success. It is described at www.yale.edu/hronline/focus/goal.html and www.ala.org/acrl/aboutacrl/directoryofleadership/sections/is/iswebsite/projpubs/smartobjectives.

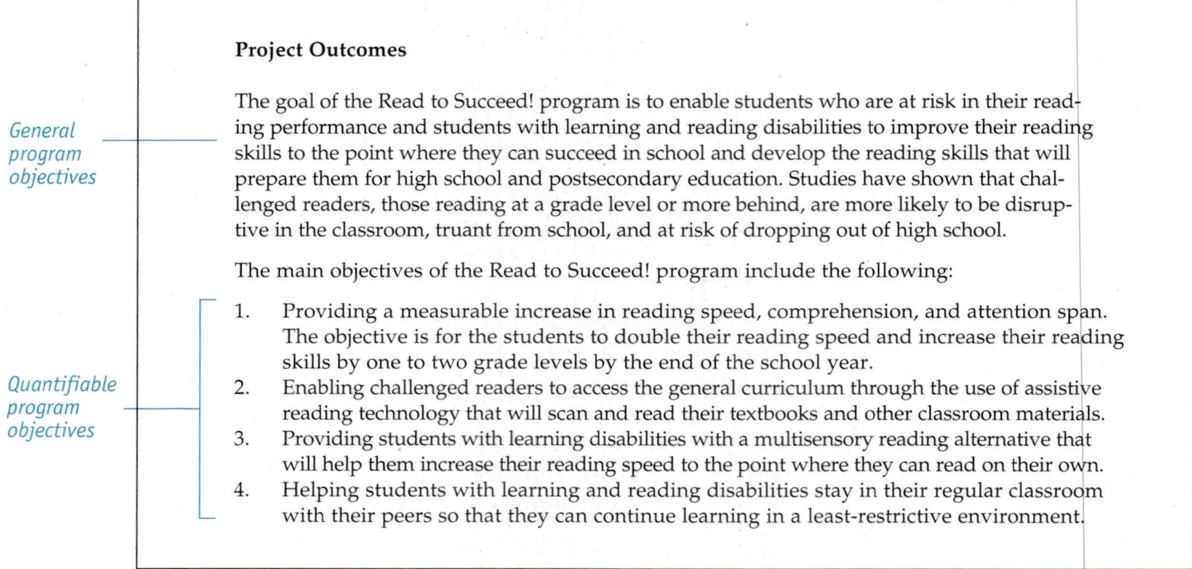

Project Outcomes

The goal of the Read to Succeed! program is to enable students who are at risk in their reading performance and students with learning and reading disabilities to improve their reading skills to the point where they can succeed in school and develop the reading skills that will prepare them for high school and postsecondary education. Studies have shown that challenged readers, those reading at a grade level or more behind, are more likely to be disruptive in the classroom, truant from school, and at risk of dropping out of high school.

The main objectives of the Read to Succeed! program include the following:

1. Providing a measurable increase in reading speed, comprehension, and attention span. The objective is for the students to double their reading speed and increase their reading skills by one to two grade levels by the end of the school year.
2. Enabling challenged readers to access the general curriculum through the use of assistive reading technology that will scan and read their textbooks and other classroom materials.
3. Providing students with learning disabilities with a multisensory reading alternative that will help them increase their reading speed to the point where they can read on their own.
4. Helping students with learning and reading disabilities stay in their regular classroom with their peers so that they can continue learning in a least-restrictive environment.

Figure 13–16 Grant-Proposal Project Outcomes Copyright © Kurweil Educational Systems. Cambium Learning Group, Inc. Reprinted by permission.

Budget

The budget includes funds for a Lab Pack containing five copies of Kurzweil Educational System's Scan/Read Color software, along with five computers and scanners. They will provide five independent assistive reading workstations. This combination will give students the greatest flexibility in using their textbooks and other classroom materials.

Detailed list of program requirements

	Price	*Quantity*	*Total*
Kurzweil Scan/Read Lab Pack (Color) 5-Pack	$7,095	1 (5-Pack)	$ 7,095
Software Maintenance Agreement (SMA)	$ 709	1 (5-Pack)	$ 709
Epson 300 Scanner	$ 300	5	$ 1,500
Dell PC with Monitor	$1,200	5	$ 6,000
Training	$1,200	1 day	$ 1,200
Total			**$16,504**

Figure 13–17 Grant-Proposal Budget Narrative Copyright © Kurweil Educational Systems. Cambium Learning Group, Inc. Reprinted by permission.

accountable for them. Your cost estimates may also be subject to changes over which you have no control, such as price increases for equipment, software, or consulting assistance. The project may also require ongoing funding following completion of the grant's tasks. Either estimate such costs or note that they will appear in a Future Funding section.

Schedule Prepare a schedule of tasks that need to be performed to complete the project. Arrange them as bulleted points in sequence from first to last with due dates for each. Schedules can also be presented in table format, as shown in Figure 13–18, or in a Gantt chart, as described in Chapter 7, page 233.

Organization Description The organization description may follow the introduction or it may be placed just prior to the conclusion, depending on RFP requirements or the granting organization's guidelines. Describe the applicant organization briefly in terms of mission, history, qualifications, and credibility (significant, related accomplishments), taking care to include all information requested in the RFP or grant guidelines. Granting organizations consider not only the merits of the proposed program or research but also your organization's standing in the community and similar advantages.

Conclusion The conclusion is a brief wrap-up section that emphasizes the benefits or advantages of your project. This section gives you one more opportunity to give the funding organization a reason why your proposal merits its approval. This is also the place to express your appreciation for the opportunity to submit the proposal.

Activity	Date
Submit grant proposal	October 2016
Expected grant notification	December 2016
Obtain hardware and software	January 2017
Set up Kurzweil 3000 program	January 2017
Training session for teachers	February 2017
Student introduction	February 2017
Test initial reading speed	February 2017
Begin first 12-week phase	March–May 2017
Test reading improvement	June 2017
Prepare project results report	July 2017

Program time line and dates

Figure 13–18 Grant-Proposal Schedule Copyright © Kurweil Educational Systems. Cambium Learning Group, Inc. Reprinted by permission.

Finally, note the time frame during which the proposal is valid and close with a statement of your willingness to provide further information. Because proposals are legally binding in some industries, be sure that your proposal is reviewed by legal counsel, if applicable.

Attachments Funding organizations request supporting information, such as nonprofit-status documentation, copies of legal documents (for example, articles of incorporation or bylaws), or lists of information that you may need to design and compose yourself. Provide a comprehensive list of attachments and clearly label each item to guide the grant reviewer in evaluating the proposal package.

DIGITAL TIP: Using Grant Software

Grants.gov provides a simple, unified electronic storefront for interactions between grant applicants and the federal agencies that manage grant funds. There are 26 federal grant-making agencies and more than 900 individual grant programs. The grant community, including state, local, and tribal governments; academia and research institutions; and not-for-profits, need visit only one website. You can also sign up at the Grants.gov website to get automatic e-mail alerts about grant opportunities that are of interest to your organization.

Sales Proposals

The sales proposal, a major marketing tool for business and industry, is a company's offer to provide specific goods or services to a potential buyer within a specified period of time and for a specified price. The primary purpose of a sales proposal is to demonstrate that the seller's products or services will meet the prospective customer's requirements to solve a problem, improve operations, or offer other benefits.

Sales proposals vary greatly in length and sophistication. Some are a page or two written by one person, others are many pages written collaboratively by several people, and still others are hundreds of pages written by a proposal-writing team. A short sales proposal might bid for painting the outside of a single-family home, a sales proposal of moderate length might bid for the installation of a network operating system for a small company, and a very long sales proposal might bid for the construction of a multimillion-dollar shopping center or sports complex. Short sales proposals are often written on standardized forms that are available within word-processing programs under Forms Templates, as well as on the Web from business-form template sites. They are also available from office-supply and stationery stores.

Your first task in writing a sales proposal is to find out exactly what your prospective customer needs. Then determine whether your organization can satisfy that customer's needs. If appropriate, compare your company's strengths with those of competing firms, determine your advantages over them, and emphasize those advantages in your proposal. For example, say a small biotechnology company is bidding for the contract to supply several types of medical test kits to a hospital. The proposal writer who believes that the company has a better-qualified staff than its competitors might include the résumés of the key people who would be involved in the project as a way of emphasizing that advantage.

Although simple sales proposals are often written on standardized forms, the long sales proposal contains more parts to accommodate the requirements set out in a request for proposal. The long sales proposal may include some or all of the following sections:

- Cover, or transmittal, letter (Figure 13–19 on page 452)
- Title page
- Executive or project summary (Figure 13–20 on page 454)
- General description of products (Figure 13–21 on page 455)
- Detailed solution or rationale (Figure 13–22 on page 456)
- Cost analysis (Figure 13–23 on page 457)
- Delivery schedule or work plan (Figure 13–23 on page 458)
- Site-preparation description (Figure 13–24 on page 459)
- Training requirements (Figure 13–25 on page 460)
- Statement of responsibilities (Figure 13–26 on page 461)
- Description of vendor (Figure 13–27 on page 462)
- Organizational sales pitch (optional) (Figure 13–27 on page 462)
- Conclusion (optional) (Figure 13–28 on page 463)
- Appendixes (optional)

Optional sections may be included at the discretion of the proposal-writing team. A conclusion, for example, may be added to a very long proposal as a convenience to the reader, but it is not mandatory. A site-preparation section, however, is essential if the work proposed requires construction, remodeling, or such preparatory work as facility rewiring before equipment can be installed.

Transmittal A long sales proposal begins with a cover letter — sometimes called a *transmittal letter* — that expresses your appreciation for the opportunity to submit your proposal and for any assistance you may have received in studying the customer's requirements. The letter should acknowledge any previous positive association with the customer. Then it should summarize the recommendations offered in the proposal and express your confidence that they will satisfy the customer's needs. Figure 13–19 shows the cover letter for the proposal illustrated in Figures 13–20 through 13–28 — a proposal that the Waters Corporation of Tampa provide a computer system for the Cookson's chain of retail stores.

◆ *For additional guidance on writing cover letters and transmittals, see page 300 in Chapter 9, Writing Routine and Sensitive Messages, and page 363 in Chapter 11, Writing Formal Reports.*

Opening expresses appreciation for chance to bid on the project and stresses success of past working relationship

Body describes purpose of work proposed and belief in its success in meeting the customer's need

Ending assures customer of company's commitment to success

The Waters Corporation

17 North Waterloo Blvd., Tampa, FL 33607
Phone: (813) 919-1213 Fax: (813) 919-4411
waterscorp.com

September 2, 2016

Mr. John Yeung, General Manager
Cookson's Retail Stores, Inc.
101 Longuer Street
Savannah, GA 31399

Dear Mr. Yeung:

The Waters Corporation appreciates the opportunity to respond to Cookson's Request for Proposal dated July 26, 2016. We would like to thank Mr. Becklight, Director of your Management Information Systems Department, for his invaluable contributions to the study of your operations before we prepared our proposal. Waters's close working relationship with Cookson's has resulted in a clear understanding of your corporate strategy and needs.

Our proposal describes a Waters Interactive Terminal/Retail Processor System designed to meet Cookson's network and processing needs. It will provide all of your required capabilities, from the point-of-sale operational requirements at the store terminals to the host processor. The system is easily installed without extensive customer reprogramming and is compatible with much of Cookson's present equipment. It will provide the flexibility to add new features and products in the future. The system's unique hardware modularity, microprocessor design, and flexible programming capability greatly reduce the risk of obsolescence.

Thank you for the opportunity to present this proposal. We will use all the resources available to the Waters Corporation to ensure the successful implementation of the new system.

Sincerely yours,

Janet A. Curtain

Janet A. Curtain
Executive Account Manager
General Merchandise Systems
jcurtain@waters.com

Enclosure: Cookson's Proposal

Figure 13–19 Cover Letter for a Sales Proposal

Title Page The title page contains the title of the proposal, the date of submission, the company to which it is being submitted, your company's name, and any symbol or logo that identifies your company.

◆ *For more advice on preparing a title page, see pages 363–364 in Chapter 11, Writing Formal Reports.*

◆ *For a discussion of executive summaries, see pages 370–374 in Chapter 11, Writing Formal Reports.*

Executive Summary The executive summary—sometimes called a *project summary*—is addressed to the executive who will ultimately accept or reject the proposal and should summarize in nontechnical language how you plan to approach the work. Figure 13-20 on page 454 shows the executive summary of the Waters Corporation proposal.

Product Description If your proposal offers products as well as services, it should include a general description of the products, as shown in Figure 13-21 on page 455. In many cases, product descriptions will already exist in other company publications; be sure to check your company's files or server before drafting a description from scratch.

Rationale Following the executive summary and the general description, explain exactly how you plan to do what you are proposing. This section, called the *detailed solution, or rationale,* will be read by specialists who can understand and evaluate your plan, so you can feel free to use technical language and discuss complicated concepts. Figure 13-22 on page 456 shows one part of the detailed solution appearing in the Waters Corporation proposal, which included several other applications in addition to the payroll application. Notice that the detailed solution, like the discussion in an unsolicited sales proposal, begins with a statement of the customer's problem, follows with a statement of the solution, and concludes with a statement of the benefits to the customer. In some proposals, the headings "Problem" and "Solution" are used for this section.

Cost Analysis The cost analysis, or budget, itemizes the estimated cost of all the products and services that you are offering.

Work Plan The delivery schedule—also called a *work plan*—commits you to a specific timetable for providing those products and services. Figure 13-23 on page 457 shows the cost analysis and delivery schedule of the Waters Corporation proposal.

Site-Preparation Description If your recommendations include modifying your customer's physical facilities, you would include a site-preparation description that details the modifications required. In some proposals, the headings "Facilities" and "Equipment" are used for this section. Figure 13-24 shows the site-preparation section.

Training Requirements If the products and services you are proposing require training the customer's employees, your proposal should specify the required training

The Waters Proposal September 2, 2016

EXECUTIVE SUMMARY

Opens with overview of the proposed system

The Waters 319 Interactive Terminal/615 Retail Processor System will provide your management with the tools necessary to manage people and equipment more profitably with procedures that will yield more cost-effective business controls for Cookson's.

The equipment and applications proposed for Cookson's were selected through the combined effort of Waters and Cookson's Management Information Systems Director, Mr. Becklight. The architecture of the system will respond to your current requirements and allow for future expansion.

Summarizes scope of system proposed

The features and hardware in the system were determined from data acquired through the comprehensive survey we conducted at your stores in February of this year. The total of 71 Interactive Terminals proposed to service your four store locations is based on the number of terminals currently in use and on the average number of transactions processed during normal and peak periods. The planned remodeling of all four stores was also considered, and the suggested terminal placement has been incorporated into the working floor plan. The proposed equipment configuration and software applications have been simulated to determine system performance based on the volumes and anticipated growth rates of the Cookson's stores.

Ends with projected cost savings of interest to the executive reader

The information from the survey was also used in the cost justification, which was checked and verified by your controller, Mr. Deitering. The cost effectiveness of the Waters 319 Interactive Terminal/615 Retail Processor System is apparent. Expected savings, such as the projected 46 percent reduction in sales audit expenses, are realistic projections based on Waters's experience with other installations of this type.

-1-

Figure 13–20 Executive Summary of a Sales Proposal

The Waters Proposal September 2, 2016

GENERAL SYSTEM DESCRIPTION

The point-of-sale system that Waters is proposing for Cookson's includes two primary Waters products. These are the 319 Interactive Terminal and the 615 Retail Processor.

Waters 319 Interactive Terminal

The primary component in the proposed retail system is the 319 Interactive Terminal. It contains a full microprocessor, which gives it the flexibility that Cookson's has been looking for.

The 319 Interactive Terminal provides you with freedom in sequencing a transaction to suit your needs rather than limiting you to a preset list of available steps or transactions. The terminal program can be adapted to provide unique transaction sets, each designed with a logical sequence of entry and processing to accomplish required tasks. The 319 Interactive Terminal also functions as a credit-authorization device, either by using its own floor limits or by transmitting a credit inquiry to the 615 Retail Processor for authorization.

Data-collection formats have been simplified so that transaction editing and formatting are much more easily accomplished. The information systems manager has already been provided with documentation on these formats and has outlined all data-processing efforts that will be necessary to transmit the data to your current systems. These projections have been considered in the cost justification.

Waters 615 Retail Processor

The Waters 615 Retail Processor is a server-based system designed to support the Waters family of retail terminals. The processor will reside in your data center in Jacksonville. Operators already on your staff will be trained to initiate and monitor its activities.

Detailed breakdown of system components and functions essential for technical readers

Software

The Retail III software used with the system has been thoroughly tested and is operational in many Waters customer installations. The software provides the complete processing of the transaction, from the interaction with the operator on the sales floor through the data capture on disk in stores and in your data center.

Retail III provides a menu of modular applications for your selection. Parameters condition each of them to your hardware environment and operating requirements. The selection of hardware will be closely related to the selection of the software applications.

Additional system details for technical specialists

-2-

Figure 13–21 General-Description-of-Products Section of a Sales Proposal

A primary system feature described in problem-solution form

Supporting cost analysis illustrates company savings

The Waters Proposal September 2, 2016

PAYROLL APPLICATION

Current Procedure

Your current system of reporting time requires each hourly employee to sign a time sheet; the time sheet is reviewed by the department manager and sent to the Payroll Department on Friday evening. Because the week ends on Saturday, the employee must show the scheduled hours for Saturday and not the actual hours; therefore, the department manager must adjust the reported hours on the time sheet for employees who do not report on the scheduled Saturday or who do not work the number of hours scheduled.

The Payroll Department employs a supervisor and three full-time clerks. To meet deadlines caused by an unbalanced work flow, an additional part-time clerk is used for 20 to 30 hours per week. The average wage for this clerk is $10.31 per hour.

Advantage of the Waters System

The 319 Interactive Terminal can be programmed for entry of payroll data for each employee on Monday mornings by department managers, with the data reflecting actual hours worked. This system would eliminate the need for manual batching, controlling, and data input. The Payroll Department estimates conservatively that this work consumes 30 hours per week.

Hours per week	30
Average wage (part-time clerk)	×10.31
Weekly payroll cost	$309.30
Annual Savings	$16,083.60

Elimination of the manual tasks of tabulating, batching, and controlling can save 0.25 hourly unit. Improved work flow resulting from timely data in the system without data-input processing will allow more efficient use of clerical hours. This would reduce payroll by the 0.50 hourly unit currently required to meet weekly check disbursement.

Eliminate manual tasks	0.25
Improve work flow	0.50
40-hour unit reduction	1.00
Hours per week	40
Average wage (full-time clerk)	12.62
Savings per week	$509.80
Annual Savings	$26,509.60
TOTAL ANNUAL SAVINGS:	**$42,593.20**

-3-

Figure 13–22 Detailed Solution of a Sales Proposal

The Waters Proposal — September 2, 2016

COST ANALYSIS

This section of our proposal provides detailed cost information for the Waters 319 Interactive Terminal and the Waters 615 Retail Processor. It then multiplies these major elements by the quantities required at each of your four locations.

319 Interactive Terminal

	Price	Maintenance (1 year)
Terminal	$2,895	$167
Journal Printer	425	38
Receipt Printer	425	38
Forms Printer	525	38
Software	220	—
Totals	**$4,490**	**$281**

The following breakdown itemizes the cost per store:

Store No. 1

Description	Quantity	Price	Maintenance (1 year)
Terminals	16	$68,400	$4,496
Backup Memory Pack	1	350	147
Laser Printer	1	2,490	332
Software	16	3,520	—
Totals		**$74,760**	**$4,975**

Breakdown of hardware, software, and maintenance costs

-4-

Figure 13–23 Cost Analysis and Delivery Schedule of a Sales Proposal

Further cost breakdown and delivery schedule

The Waters Proposal September 2, 2016

The following summarizes all costs:

Location	Hardware	Maintenance (1 year)	Software
Store No. 1	$ 74,760	$ 4,975	$ 3,520
Store No. 2	89,190	6,099	4,400
Store No. 3	76,380	5,256	3,740
Store No. 4	80,650	5,537	3,960
Data Center	63,360	6,679	12,480
Subtotals	$ 384,340	$28,546	$28,100
Total	**$440,986**		

DELIVERY SCHEDULE

Waters is normally able to deliver 319 Interactive Terminals and 615 Retail Processors within 90 days of the date of the contract. This can vary depending on the rate and size of incoming orders.

All the software recommended in this proposal is available for immediate delivery. We do not anticipate any difficulty in meeting your tentative delivery schedule.

-5-

Figure 13–23 Cost Analysis and Delivery Schedule of a Sales Proposal *(continued)*

and its cost. Figure 13–25 on page 460 shows the training-requirements section of the Waters proposal.

Statement of Responsibilities To prevent misunderstandings about what you and your customer's responsibilities will be, you should draw up a statement of responsibilities (Figure 13–26 on page 461), which usually appears toward the end of the proposal.

Description of Vendor Also toward the end of the proposal is a description of the vendor, which gives a profile of your company, its history, and its present position in

The Waters Proposal September 2, 2016

SITE PREPARATION

Waters will work closely with Cookson's to ensure that each site is properly prepared prior to system installation. You will receive a copy of Waters's installation and wiring-procedures manual, which lists the physical dimensions, service clearance, and weight of the system components in addition to the power and environmental requirements. Cookson's is responsible for all building alterations and electrical facility changes, including the purchase and installation of communication cables, connecting blocks, and receptacles.

Details of system requirements and division of responsibilities for the work

Wiring

For the purpose of future site considerations, Waters's in-house wiring specifications for the system call for two twisted-pair wires and 22 shielded gauges. The length of communications wires must not exceed 2,500 feet.

-6-

Figure 13–24 Site-Preparation Section of a Sales Proposal

the industry. The description-of-the-vendor section typically includes a list of people or subcontractors and the duties they will perform. The résumés of key personnel may also be placed here or in an appendix.

Organizational Sales Pitch Following this description, many proposals add what is known as an organizational sales pitch. To this point, the proposal has attempted to sell specific goods and services. The sales pitch, striking a somewhat different chord, is designed to sell the company and its general capability in the field. The sales pitch promotes the company and concludes the proposal on an upbeat note. Figure 13–27 on page 462 shows the vendor-description and sales-pitch sections of the Waters proposal.

The Waters Proposal September 2, 2016

TRAINING

To ensure a successful installation, Waters offers the following training course for your operators.

Interactive Terminal/Retail Processor Operations

Employee training costs and length

Course number: 8256
Length: three days
Tuition: $500.00

This course provides the student with the skills, knowledge, and practice required to operate an Interactive Terminal/Retail Processor System. Online, clustered, and stand-alone environments are covered.

We recommend that students have a department-store background and that they have some knowledge of the system configuration with which they will be working.

-7-

Figure 13–25 Training-Requirements Section of a Sales Proposal

The Waters Proposal September 2, 2016

RESPONSIBILITIES

Based on its years of experience in installing information-processing systems, Waters believes that a successful installation requires a clear understanding of certain responsibilities.

Waters's Responsibilities

Generally, it is Waters's responsibility to provide its users with needed assistance during the installation so that live processing can begin as soon thereafter as is practical.

- Provide operations documentation for each application that you acquire from Waters.
- Provide forms and other supplies as ordered.
- Provide specifications and technical guidance for proper site planning and installation.
- Provide adviser assistance in the conversion from your present system to the new system.

Customer's Responsibilities

Cookson's will be responsible for the suggested improvements described earlier, as well as the following:

- Identify an installation coordinator and a system operator.
- Provide supervisors and clerical personnel to perform conversion to the system.
- Establish reasonable time schedules for implementation.
- Ensure that the physical site requirements are met.
- Provide personnel to be trained as operators and ensure that other employees are trained as necessary.
- Assume the responsibility for implementing and operating the system.

-8-

Division of tasks between customer and vendor

Figure 13–26 Statement-of-Responsibilities Section of a Sales Proposal

Statements of the vendor's history and commitment to its core business to highlight its experience and reputation

The Waters Proposal September 2, 2016

DESCRIPTION OF VENDOR

The Waters Corporation develops, manufactures, markets, installs, and services total business information-processing systems for selected markets. These markets are primarily in the retail, financial, commercial, industrial, health-care, education, and government sectors.

The Waters total-system concept encompasses one of the broadest hardware and software product lines in the industry. Waters computers range from small business systems to powerful general-purpose processors. Waters computers are supported by a complete spectrum of terminals, peripherals, and data-communication networks, as well as an extensive library of software products. Supplemental services and products include data centers, field service, systems engineering, and educational centers.

The Waters Corporation was founded in 1934 and presently has approximately 26,500 employees. The Waters headquarters is located at 17 North Waterloo Boulevard, Tampa, Florida, with district offices throughout the United States and Canada. For a comprehensive listing of Waters products and services, visit our website at waterscorp.com.

WHY WATERS?

Corporate Commitment to the Retail Industry

Waters's commitment to the retail industry is stronger than ever. We are continually striving to provide leadership in the design and implementation of new retail systems and applications that will ensure our users of a logical growth pattern.

Research and Development

Over the years, Waters has spent increasingly large sums on research-and-development efforts to ensure the availability of products and systems for the future. In 2012, our research-and-development expenditures for advanced-systems design and technological innovations reached the $70 million level.

Leading Point-of-Sale Vendor

Waters is a leading point-of-sale vendor, having installed over 150,000 units. The knowledge and experience that Waters has gained over the years from these installations ensure well-coordinated and effective systems implementations.

-9-

Figure 13–27 Description-of-Vendor and Sales-Pitch Sections of a Sales Proposal

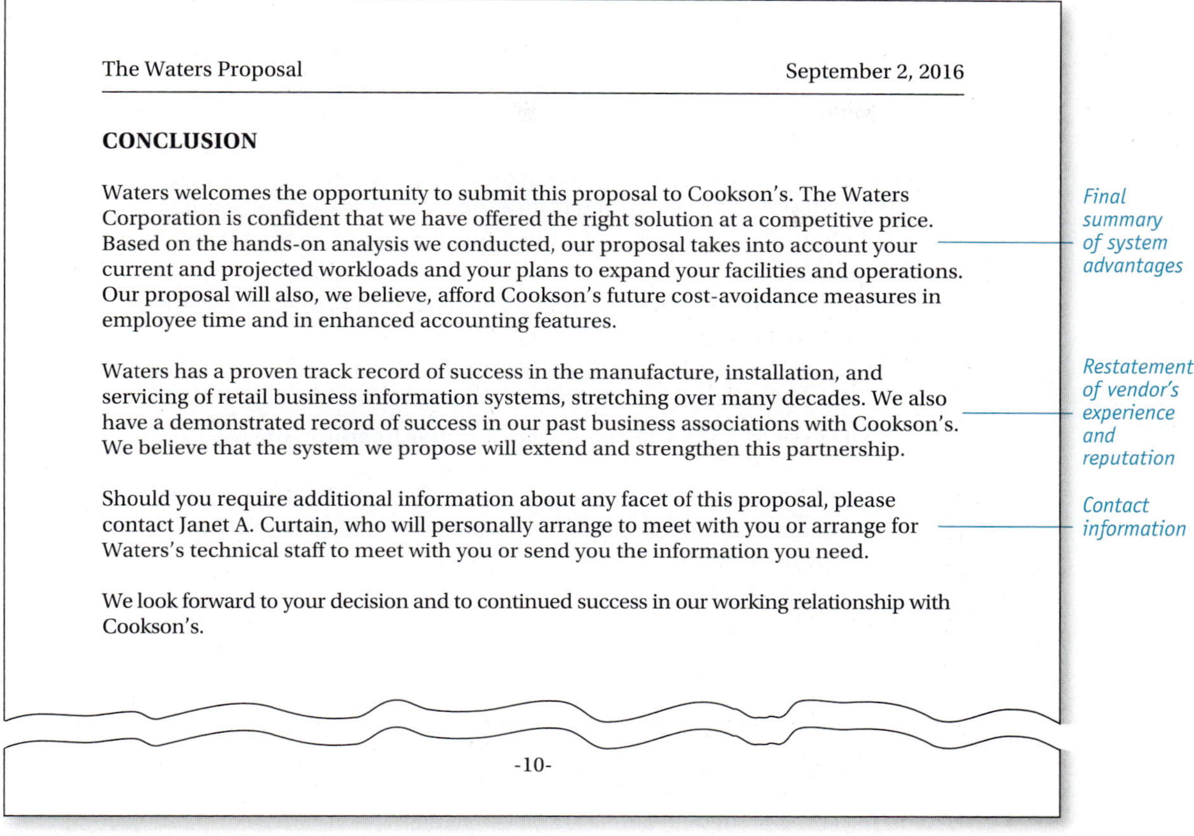
The Waters Proposal September 2, 2016

CONCLUSION

Waters welcomes the opportunity to submit this proposal to Cookson's. The Waters Corporation is confident that we have offered the right solution at a competitive price. Based on the hands-on analysis we conducted, our proposal takes into account your current and projected workloads and your plans to expand your facilities and operations. Our proposal will also, we believe, afford Cookson's future cost-avoidance measures in employee time and in enhanced accounting features.

Waters has a proven track record of success in the manufacture, installation, and servicing of retail business information systems, stretching over many decades. We also have a demonstrated record of success in our past business associations with Cookson's. We believe that the system we propose will extend and strengthen this partnership.

Should you require additional information about any facet of this proposal, please contact Janet A. Curtain, who will personally arrange to meet with you or arrange for Waters's technical staff to meet with you or send you the information you need.

We look forward to your decision and to continued success in our working relationship with Cookson's.

-10-

Figure 13–28 Conclusion of a Sales Proposal

Conclusion Some long sales proposals include a conclusion section that summarizes the proposal's salient points, stresses your company's strengths, and includes information about whom the potential client can contact for further information. It may also end with a request for the date the work will begin should the proposal be accepted. Figure 13–28 shows the conclusion of the Waters proposal.

Appendixes Depending on length and technical complexity, some proposals include appendixes made up of statistical analyses, maps, charts, tables, and résumés of the principal staff assigned to the project. Appendixes to proposals should contain only supplemental information; the primary information should appear in the body of the proposal.

MEETING THE DEADLINE: The Time-Sensitive Proposal

Proposal writers must give top priority to meeting the procuring organization's deadline, while also producing a high-quality, persuasive proposal likely to receive favorable evaluations. Late proposals are hardly ever accepted, and if your organization is relying on funding from granting institutions, a missed deadline could have devastating consequences. The following time-management strategies can help toward meeting these goals.

1. *Hold an initial planning session.* Hold a planning meeting to introduce the project team members, set priorities, determine and delegate tasks, set milestone deadlines for each task, and decide the most effective way to create and exchange drafts: e-mail, wikis (collaborative-project websites), faxing, and the like.
2. *Assign coordinators.* Choose a writing coordinator to organize the creation and production of text and graphics, and a compiler (often an administrative assistant) to integrate all sections and elements of the final proposal and to make sure that those sections and elements adhere to the potential customer's requirements in the request for proposal (RFP).
3. *Set priorities.* Give the most attention to the sections or features likely to weigh most heavily during the prospective customer's evaluation of the proposal. These are likely to be the sections describing how you plan to fulfill the requirements in the RFP and the cost analysis.
4. *Delegate tasks.* Assign more than one person to work on each section, and allow them to work out a way to collaborate efficiently to meet the deadline for submitting their section. This strategy works best when the contributors have diverse schedules and areas of specialization. Often, two or three subject experts coauthor parts of a single section, and the writing coordinator edits the resulting draft for clarity and coherence.
5. *Work out a schedule.* Determine how much time each task is likely to require. Start work immediately on tasks likely to take longer to complete, but also begin to collect other important pieces, such as résumés, biographies, and project descriptions. Decide which tasks can be done simultaneously and which tasks must precede others. When establishing a schedule, work backward from the proposal deadline. If the RFP specifies that the proposal be submitted to a website or an e-mail address by a certain date, work backward from that date. If the RFP requests a paper copy, leave at least a day for the proposal to reach its destination by express delivery, half a day before that for collecting company signatures and making multiple copies of the proposal, and half a day before that for last-minute edits and proofreading.
6. *Use repurposed material.* When possible, import into the proposal standard content from previous proposals, such as résumés, descriptions of past projects, and company goals and accomplishments.

7. *Track progress and deadlines.* Use e-mail or your proposal-management software to periodically send out reminders about deadlines or to prompt someone to deliver material that you need right away. Hold interim meetings if doing so will speed up your work. If interim task deadlines are missed, ask everyone on the project team to devote full-time and extra hours to the proposal so that you can meet the final deadline.
8. *Hold a lessons-learned meeting, if necessary.* After sending the proposal, or once you have received an answer to your proposal, hold a debriefing session to identify any problems and plan strategies for avoiding them when planning and writing future proposals.

Requests for Proposals

When a company or another organization needs a task performed or a service provided outside its staff expertise or capabilities, it seeks help from vendors that can provide the expertise or capabilities needed. The company seeking help usually makes its requirements known to potential vendors by issuing a request for proposals. The RFP details the company's requirements so that vendors can evaluate whether to bid on the project.

The details provided in an RFP permit vendors to understand your needs and enable you to determine from their responses which vendor to select to meet your requirements. Although RFPs lay out your requirements, they usually do not specify how these requirements are to be met. Potential vendors prepare proposals to describe their solutions for meeting your requirements; you then choose from among them the one that best suits your needs, budget, and schedule.[3]

DIGITAL TIP: RFP Site Search Software

The federal government lists RFPs at Federal Business Opportunities (fbo.gov), and many state, county, and municipal governments list their RFPs at Bid Net (bidbet.com). Both sites aggregate RFPs from agencies throughout the United States and categorize them by type of work required (construction, security, transportation, etc.) and geographic location. Because of their size and complexity, the sites also provide detailed guidance on their features and functionality for site searches. The guidance includes videos, user guides, Webinars, and FAQs.

Note that businesses and nonprofit organizations often distribute RFPs directly to approved vendor lists, so they are less likely to appear at aggregator sites or to be posted at their websites.

[3]A related document is an invitation for bids. An IFB strictly defines the quantity, type, and specifications for an item that an organization, such as a government agency, intends to purchase.

RFP Structure

Like proposals, RFPs vary in length, formality, and structure. Some are a page or two, and others run to hundreds of pages. The scope of information included and even the terminology used to describe specific sections vary with the type of task or service being solicited. For example, RFPs involving computer systems usually include a "Technical Requirements" section, specifying site-preparation requirements and describing the current technical infrastructure at the company issuing the RFP. The purpose and context of RFPs also vary. Each RFP involves unique legal, budgetary, confidentiality, and administrative considerations. The following sections describe typical components for RFPs.

Information About Your Company

In a separate section, the organization issuing the RFP should describe its mission, goals, size, facility locations, position in the marketplace, and possibly a brief company history. It should also provide contact information. This section parallels the "Description of Vendor" section in proposals (see Figure 13–27 on page 462).

Project Description

Another section, sometimes called "Scope of Work" or "Workscope Description," describes the deliverable (the product or service) you need, with a detailed list of requirements. For example, an RFP prepared by a pharmaceutical company soliciting training for its sales representatives about a new drug divided the project description into three sections:

- Target audience (members of sales staff and their technical background and computer experience)
- Content (specific curriculum and length of training)
- Deliverable (in-person training, online or virtual training by Webinar, website, or video)

Vendors responding to this RFP would organize their proposals in line with these requirements. For some projects, requirements can be described in a summary statement, as shown in the following examples.

▶ The project deliverable will be a questionnaire to be mailed to approximately 400 adults regarding their consumer experiences with various health-care providers.

▶ The deliverable will be a networked online-forms package for approximately 1,200 employees, permitting information to be completed online, stored in a database, routed by e-mail, and printed on paper. The package shall be integrated into the company's current network environment at its headquarters facility.

The project description may also indicate whether the deliverable must be created new or can be obtained commercially and adapted to the project's needs. For example, if the project involves software development, the description may state whether the requesting company prefers commercially available software or expects the vendor to develop unique software for the project. The project-description section can also specify other details such as a project-management plan and any warranty or liability requirements.

Delivery Schedule

For complex projects lasting a month or longer, specify the time allotted for the project and a proposed schedule of tasks.

Proposal Description

Many RFPs provide format requirements for proposals, such as how the proposal should be organized; the number of copies expected; whether an electronic file is required; where, the date by which, and to whom the proposal should be e-mailed or sent; and how the proposal should be sent (registered mail, courier service, etc.). Many companies now provide an online proposal template for vendors to follow.

Vendor Qualifications

Most RFPs request information about the vendor as well — a summary of the vendor's experience, professional certifications, number of employees, years in business, quality-control procedures, awards and honors, and the like. An RFP may require references from recent customers as well as financial references. The RFPs usually require that vendors submit the résumés of the principal employees who would be assigned to the project.

Proposal-Evaluation Criteria

The proposal-evaluation section informs vendors of the criteria your company or organization will use to select the vendor to work for you. Will you decide solely on cost? a combination of cost and vendor past performance? technical expertise? Many companies organize the criteria by importance or weight while others grade proposals with a point system and include a table of criteria, each of which is given a point value on a scale of either 100 or 1,000 total points, as in the following sample:

▶ Proposal-Evaluation Criteria

CRITERIA	**POINTS**
Administrative	50
Technical	700
Management	100
Price	100
Presentation and demonstration	50
Total	**1,000**

Appendixes

Some RFPs include one or more appendixes or "Attachments." These may include sample forms and questionnaires, a sample contract, technical information about a company's server and workstation configurations, workflow-analysis diagrams, dates and times when vendors can visit the work site before finalizing their proposals, and other essentials too detailed for the body of the RFP.

ETHICS NOTE: Protect Company-confidential Information If your RFP contains any company-confidential information, you could include a legally binding nondisclosure statement for vendors to sign before you send the full RFP. Many companies also include a guarantee not to open proposals before the due date and never to disclose information in one vendor's proposal to a competing vendor.

CHAPTER 13 SUMMARY: WRITING PROPOSALS

A proposal

- Is written to persuade the potential customer to purchase your service or product.
- Is written from the perspective and needs of the audience for the proposal.
- Is produced by a collaborative team of specialists when the proposal is complex.
- Consists of the following parts (and may include additional parts, based on the needs of your topic and specifications of the request for proposals):
  - The problem you propose to solve and your solution to it
  - The benefits of your solution, product, or service that persuade the reader to take action
  - The dates on which you propose to begin and complete work
  - The total cost of the project
  - Any previous positive association between your company and the potential customer (if a sales proposal)
  - How the job will be done
  - The procedures you propose to use to perform the work
  - The materials you will use (if applicable)
  - The schedule for each stage of the project
  - Your confidence in your ability—or, if a sales proposal, in your company's ability—to carry out the project
  - Your willingness to provide further information
  - The advantages of your company over its competitors
  - Your appreciation for the opportunity to submit the proposal
  - The time period during which the proposal is valid
  - A list or description of any supplemental materials

An internal proposal

- Is written to a manager within your organization.
- Is usually written to persuade management to make a change or an improvement or to fund a project that you would like to launch.

An external proposal

- Is written to a potential client outside your organization.
- May be solicited or unsolicited.
- Might be written to persuade a potential customer to purchase your company's products or services.
- May be short or long, depending on the complexity of the topic.
- Is often time sensitive and must be produced by a collaborative writing team under the pressure of a tight deadline.

A grant proposal

- Is written to a nonprofit organization—local, state, or federal government agency, educational or research institution, or private foundation.
- Is solicited in a grant request for proposals that specifies exactly how the grant proposal should be organized and what it should contain.
- May offer assistance with a project that requires an investigation or research into an issue.
- May be required to explain the expected outcomes of the project—"What will you achieve?"
- Is always required to be submitted by a specified date.

A request for proposals

- Is written by an organization to solicit proposals from outside vendors for a service or product.
- Describes its requirements and expected deliverables in sufficient detail for vendors to respond with realistic solutions.
- Provides format requirements on what the proposal should include and how it should be organized.
- Includes evaluation criteria to inform vendors of the organization's selection criteria for their proposals.

Exercises

1. Address an internal proposal to your supervisor, recommending that your company begin a tuition-refund plan or specific technology-training program. Propose at least three major advantages to having either of these educational programs, and present them in decreasing order of importance.
2. You are a landscaping contractor and would like to respond to the following RFP, which appears in your local newspaper:

   - Lawn-mowing agreement for the Town of Augusta, Oregon. Weekly mowing of 5 miles of Route 24 median and sidings, 10 acres in Willoughby Park, and 23 acres at Augusta Memorial Golf Course, May 30 through September 30. Proposals are due April 30.

   Write a proposal in which you estimate the number of labor-hours the contract would require, what you would charge, the ability of your staff and equipment to do the job, your firm's experience and qualifications, and the weekly schedule that you propose to follow.

3. Write a proposal letter to change a specific rule or regulation of an organization to which you belong, such as your school, religious organization, professional association, or fitness club. List the current rule or regulation, then present your proposed changes and explain the advantages of your new rule. Address your short proposal to the president or head of the organization.

4. Imagine that you work as a proposal writer for an electronics company that makes specialized equipment for the U.S. Navy. You have been informed that should your company win a contract next year, a record will be kept of your performance assessments and evaluations. Both positive and negative information will be recorded, such as quality reviews, overbudget cost reports, user comments, and technical successes and failures (see http://posts.same.org/kentuckiana/SB2007/ACASS%20Presentation%20-%20Gilbertson.pdf for detailed information on the Navy's Contractor Performance Assessment Reporting System). Draft an internal proposal to your boss detailing this new information and suggesting procedures and processes that could be put into place so that your company's performance assessments and evaluations will be positive.

5. As a human resources coordinator of a large company, you've noticed an increase in the number of employee medical emergencies, some serious, over the past two years. Write an internal-proposal memo to your supervisor, offering plans that would (1) contribute to employees' good health and (2) help employees respond to medical emergencies. Plans for improving employees' health could include a more comprehensive medical-benefits package, on-site health screening, stress-management and nutrition counseling, and corporate memberships to fitness centers. Plans for helping employees handle medical emergencies could include on-site CPR and first-aid training. Explain the benefits of each solution you propose.

6. Imagine that you run your own business and want to expand your client base. First, choose a small-business concept that interests you and identify a service or product that such a business might provide. Prepare a one-page cost analysis for a sales proposal that you would submit to a prospective client. Your cost analysis should be clearly written and well formatted, and it should include the following breakdown for the project:

   - Cost of personnel or labor
   - Cost of overhead
   - Cost of new equipment
   - Total cost of project

   Submit any amounts you wish in these categories and change the category titles as needed. Each category except total cost must contain at least four different line items. For example, cost of personnel or labor might include the hourly rate for the time the company president will spend on this project and the cost of other staff specialists required on the project. Overhead might include the cost of support staff, supplies, company vehicles, and so forth. The cost of new equipment would include the cost of items purchased solely for the client. Although you may use any numbers you wish in the line items, all subtotals should equal the total cost when added together.

7. Imagine that you were a consultant hired by a company that creates security systems for the average homeowner. Although its new wireless surveillance camera was supposed

to work in low light and transmit pictures up to 100 meters, your tests revealed that the camera's picture and sound quality were negatively impacted by the interference of other electrical equipment in the house, such as baby monitors, microwave ovens, and cordless phones. Static noises and jumping lines made it nearly impossible to understand the sound and picture.

Now, imagine that you are the head of the security systems company's development team. Write an internal proposal to the head of the company detailing the test results and requesting funds to hire an electronics consultant who specializes in solving such problems.

8. Identify a problem that you feel needs to be solved either at work or at school. For example, the increasing number of students and limited number of parking spaces are causing a major parking problem. Or sealed windows in your office building are creating sick-building syndrome, and many employees are getting ill more frequently and for longer periods of time. Your assignment is to write a proposal offering a solution to the problem. (Your instructor may want to approve your topic selection.) Assume that your proposal is internal, and include the following in your proposal:

   a. Transmittal letter
   b. Executive summary
   c. Introduction, body, and conclusion
   d. Cost analysis (you may invent the numbers)
   e. Time line or schedule of delivery
   f. Description of vendor

   Your completed proposal will be seven to ten pages long, with the executive summary less than one page, single-spaced. Your introduction, body, and conclusion will be approximately three pages of text, 1½-spaced. Insert at least two visuals within the text.

Collaborative Classroom Projects

1. In teams of three to five members, review the description of the vendor included in Figure 13–27 on page 462 and develop and design an organizational sales pitch. Referring back to this chapter, develop a rough draft, including an original layout and design created by your team. Set priorities for the information to be included and be creative in the manner you choose to present the information. Take 45 minutes to one hour to complete this assignment.
2. In teams of five to seven members, develop an internal proposal asking the dean's office to upgrade or expand a facility, technology, or course offering (or another topic approved by your instructor). Your proposal is due in three weeks. Spend 45 minutes developing a plan for completing your group's proposal. Refer to Meeting the Deadline: The Time-Sensitive Proposal on pages 464–465.
   a. Your team will need to assign a project manager, a writing coordinator, a compiler, and a budget specialist.
   b. Once chosen, the project manager will begin the session by introducing team members, setting priorities, and determining and delegating tasks.
   c. In a collective effort, make a list of the tasks that will need to be completed.

d. Decide what sections will be included in the proposal.
e. Develop a time line, including scheduling and sequencing of the tasks. Include any other details you feel are relevant as you develop your plan.

As directed by your instructor, present your plan for how your team will meet the deadline orally to the class or submit the plan in writing to your instructor. Submit the finished proposal to your instructor.

Research Projects

1. Many government and research proposals have very specific instructions on the format and content of each proposal. For example, a proposal's instructions may specify the number of characters per inch allowed in the text, and the size of the margins and number of lines allowed per page. Assume that you and three other classmates are interested in pursuing a career as professional grant writers for medical and educational institutions. Research at least six specific grants dealing with medical or educational products or research. Create a report of your findings (review Chapter 10, Writing Informal Reports) that gives many examples of the instructions you found and also explains why agencies that fund research projects would be so specific about such seemingly inconsequential details.
2. For Exercise 2 in Chapter 10, you wrote an investigative report detailing back injuries and workers' compensation claims at a large online retailer. Research warehouse equipment companies and manufacturers of safety equipment and use your findings to create an internal proposal that comments on such issues as the design of warehouse equipment, especially the kind that transports heavy boxes, and makes suggestions for the purchase of new equipment that would help the warehouse workers prevent injuries.
3. Your high-tech company is interested in changing its security procedures to include biometric verification technology. Employees' fingerprints or retina patterns (or both) would now be scanned before they could enter top-secret areas. You have been asked to investigate at least three websites of companies that provide this kind of technology. Write a proposal letter to your boss that details how the technology works, the cost, and the advantages over traditional security methods.
4. Assume that you run the Adult Basic Education (ABE) program at your local county jail. Your job is to offer instructional and support services that will help incarcerated adult students improve their literacy and English-speaking skills through the high school level, to the point that they are ready, upon their release, to continue and succeed in postsecondary education. Search the Web for educational grants that might help you meet your goals. You may apply for funds to address potential courses in ABE, literacy, pre-adult secondary education, English for speakers of other languages (ESOL), preliteracy ESOL, and adult diploma classes, among others.
   a. Begin by searching the website of your state's Department of Education, then move to the federal agencies. Create a report of at least three sources of funding available, what they give money for, and the requirements for applying for the funding. (These may include required forms, like letters of intent and budget details.) Also note all of the deadlines.

b. Draft a proposal to your state's Department of Education that answers the questions in Considering Audience and Purpose: Writing Proposals on page 425.

c. Now rework your proposal draft according to the Writing Persuasive Proposals checklist on page 428. Remember that you are arguing that your program has the greatest need and offers the most for its students, so persuasive writing is essential. (You won't be rewriting the proposal in a specific format for a specific funding source unless you wish to but rather reworking the existing draft.)

14 Giving Presentations and Conducting Meetings

Contents

Although most of this book covers the principles of writing that work in business and industry, much workplace information is communicated orally during presentations and meetings. Central to the success of both is effective listening. This chapter offers practical guidelines for the following:

Writing and presentations have much in common. Both must be logically organized and are most effective when clear and succinct. However, much is different between writing and presentations, and this chapter explores those elements unique to oral communication. Oral communication is most widely used in the workplace for giving presentations and in conducting meetings.

Preparing and Delivering Presentations

The steps required to prepare an effective presentation parallel the steps you follow to write other workplace information: (1) Determine your purpose and analyze your audience, (2) find and gather the data to support your point of view and proposal, and (3) logically organize your information. However, because presentations are intended for listeners, not readers, your manner of delivery, the way you organize the material, and your supporting visual aids require as much attention as your content.

Determining Your Purpose

Every presentation is given for a purpose — to share information, to urge an audience to take action, to analyze data, to present solutions to a problem. To determine the purpose of your presentation, use these questions as a guide: What do I want my audience to know? What do I want my audience to believe? What do I want my audience to do when I have finished the presentation? Based on the answers to these questions, write a purpose statement that answers the questions *what* and *why.*

▶ The purpose of my presentation is to explain to my classmates the various tasks I performed last semester as a part-time volunteer at the Maplewood Adult Day Care Center [*what*] so that other members of the class will consider becoming volunteers at Maplewood [*why*].

▶ The purpose of my presentation is to convince my company's chief information officer of the need to hire a full-time coordinator for our company's social-media sites [*what*] so that she will include additional funds in the budget for this position next fiscal year [*why*].

Keep in mind that the context of the presentation will affect your purpose and your audience's reaction to it. Will your audience be expecting you to address an existing companywide or industrywide issue important to them? Will your organization's goals, expectations, or even jargon be appropriate when you address outside groups? Will your gestures and use of eye contact be appropriate for your audience's background or cultural frame of reference? These and other matters make up the context affecting the success of your presentations.

◆ ***For a fuller discussion of determining purpose, analyzing an audience, considering your context, and gathering information, see pages 5–8 in Chapter 1, Understanding the Workplace Writing Context: A Case Study.***

Analyzing Your Audience

Once you determine the desired end result of the presentation, answer the following five questions about your audience:

1. What is their level of experience or knowledge about your topic?
2. What is their general educational level and age?
3. What is their attitude toward the topic you are speaking about, and — based on that attitude — what interests, concerns, fears, or objections might they have?
4. Are there subgroups among them that might have different concerns or needs?
5. What questions might they ask about this topic?

Sales representatives listening to a briefing on a new product line will likely be positive and enthusiastic. But townspeople being briefed at a public meeting about cleanup options for a toxic-waste site near their town will be wary or even frightened. Tailor your presentation accordingly.

Gathering Information

Once you have focused the presentation, find the information that supports your point of view or the action you propose. Give the audience only the information necessary to accomplish your goals; too much information will overwhelm them and too little information will leave them either with a sketchy understanding of your topic or with the feeling that they need more information to support the course of action you wish them to take. And what kind of information will be most persuasive? Will the audience expect data-centered information, like specific facts, figures, and statistics? Or will quotations from subject experts or even anecdotes be more convincing? Your topic will affect the information you present, but so will the makeup of your audience. Graphs, tables, and equations, for example, will be of limited value to an audience unfamiliar with these analytical tools.

Structuring Your Presentation

Structure your presentation for listeners. They remember openings and closings best because they are freshest at the outset and refocus their attention as you wrap up your remarks. Take advantage of this pattern. Give your audience a brief overview of your presentation at the beginning, use the body to develop your ideas, and end with a summary of what you covered and, if appropriate, a call to action.

Introduction

The introduction to your presentation may include an opening — something designed to catch and focus the audience's attention. The following opening *defines a problem*:

> ▶ You're an information technology specialist working on your annual program plans and budgets. Your budget pot is shrinking and your personnel and hardware costs are rising. Your three-year equipment and software replacement cycle may have to stretch to four years and your need for more data-storage capacity keeps increasing. Short of a financial windfall, you're in a bind. Have I got a solution for you!

Notice how this opening appeals to the audience member, addressing him or her directly, and describes a common work-related problem. Once it captures the audience's attention, it leads into the body of the presentation (the "solution").

You could also use any of the following types of openings:

- *An attention-getting statement:* As many as 26 million Americans have some form of diabetes.
- *A rhetorical question:* Would you be interested in a full-size computer keyboard that is waterproof, is noiseless, and can be rolled up like a rubber mat?

- *A personal experience:* On a recent business trip, my rental van's navigation system not only had me on the wrong highway — it had me in the wrong state! Suspecting that the van's onboard computer had been hacked, I parked the van and started to make some calls. Here's what happened next.
- *An appropriate quotation:* According to researchers at the Massachusetts Institute of Technology, "Garlic and its cousin the onion confer major health benefits — including fighting cancer, infections, and heart disease."
- *A video or other visual demonstration:* Please direct your attention to this short video segment on the release of our new tablet.

Following your opening, set the stage for your audience by giving an overview of the presentation. The overview may include general or background information that your audience will need to understand the more detailed information in the body of your presentation. It may also be an overview of how you've organized the material.

> This presentation explains the options available to you, the employees of Acme Corporation, for making payroll contributions to a long-term retirement plan that will enhance the income you will receive from Social Security and pension benefits.

> This presentation will answer your questions about the following:
> - How much can I save?
> - How much does Acme contribute to the plan?
> - What are my investment options?

For additional examples of openings, see pages 87–89 in Chapter 3, Drafting a Document.

Body

In the body of your presentation, persuade your audience of the validity of your conclusion. If you are addressing a problem, demonstrate that the problem exists and offer a solution or range of possible solutions. If your introduction stated that the problem was low profits, high costs, outdated technology, or high employee absenteeism, for example, you might use the following approach:

1. Offer a solution.
   a. Increase profits by lowering production costs.
   b. Cut overhead to reduce costs.
   c. Upgrade existing technology to improve productivity.
   d. Offer employees more flexibility in their work schedules or other incentives.
2. Prove your point.
   a. Gather the facts and data you need.
   b. Present the facts and data using easy-to-understand visual aids. (The next section, Using Visual Aids, discusses this topic in more detail.)
3. Call for action.
   a. Convince your audience to agree, to change their minds, or to do something.
4. Anticipate questions ("How much will it cost?") and objections ("We're too busy now. When will we have time to learn the new software?"), and be ready for them.

Transitions

Transitions, which may be no longer than a sentence or two, let the audience know that you are moving from one topic to the next. If your presentation involves visuals, tell your audience what they are and explain their purpose. Transitions also prevent a choppy, disjointed presentation and provide you, the speaker, with assurance that you know where you are going and how you will get there. They should appear between the introduction and the body, between the points in the body, and between the body and the closing.

▶ Before getting into the specifics of the mutual fund families available to you, I'd like to describe the investment goals and strategies of each. That information will provide you with the background you'll need to compare the differences among them to make an informed decision about what works best for you: If you'll direct your attention to the screen, you'll see a brief description of Plan A. . . .

It is a good idea to pause for a moment after you've delivered a transitional line between topics to let the audience members shift gears with you. Remember, they don't know where you're headed and—unlike in a written report—they cannot flip ahead to see what's coming next. If you are using presentation software in conjunction with your speech, be sure to time the transition of your visuals so that they coincide with verbal transitions. Audiences tend to focus on visual over verbal cues; if you're still speaking on a topic, but your slide has already skipped ahead, your audience is likely to tune you out and focus on the new material on-screen. For more guidelines on the use of visuals, consult the next section, Using Visual Aids.

Figure 14–1 illustrates the typical pattern of a workplace presentation, although the number of slides and their content will vary, depending on the speaker's topic. The complete presentation for the savings and investment program is shown in Figure 14–3 on page 481. Note the conciseness and layout of the language and visuals.

WRITER'S CHECKLIST

Organizing a Presentation

- ✔ When preparing a presentation, follow the same guidelines that you follow for writing.
- ✔ Use a logical structure that includes an introduction, a body, and a conclusion.
- ✔ Be clear, direct, and precise.
- ✔ Support your presentation with specific examples, both verbally and visually.
- ✔ Use transitions between subtopics to help your listeners understand how the parts are related.

Closing

Your closing should achieve the goals of your presentation. If your purpose is to motivate the members of your audience to take action, ask them to do what you want them to do; if your purpose is to get your audience to think about something, summarize

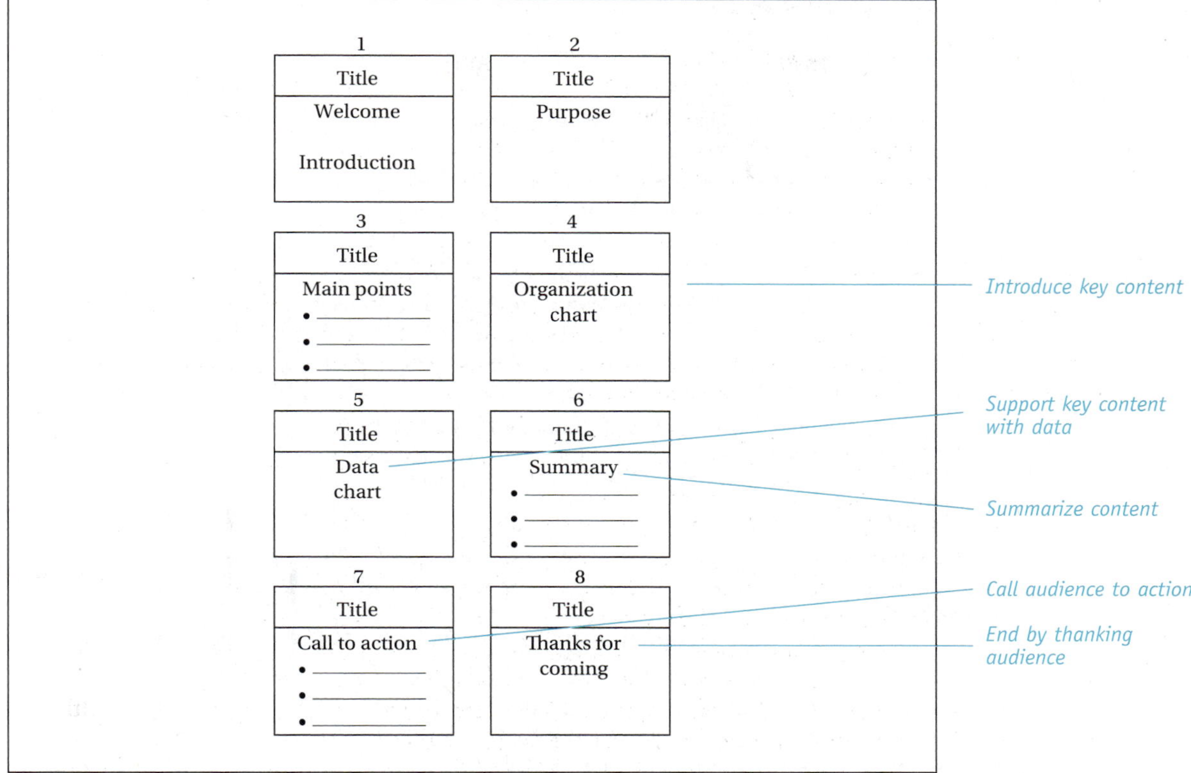

Figure 14–1 Pattern for a Typical Slide Presentation

what you want them to think about. Many presenters make the mistake of not actually closing — they simply quit talking, shuffle papers around, and then walk away.

Because your closing is what your audience is most likely to remember, it is the time to be strong and persuasive. Returning to the retirement savings-plan example on page 478, consider the following possible closing:

▶ This is the first step toward your future security.

- Decide how much you can save each month.
- Note that taxes are deferred on your contributions until you begin to make withdrawals.
- Remember Acme's contribution.
- Choose the investment options that best fit your needs.
- ENROLL NEXT WEEK!

This closing brings the presentation full circle and asks the audience to act on the information provided in the presentation — exactly what a closing should do. And it is courteous to end by thanking the members of the audience for their time and attention.

Using Visual Aids

Well-planned visual aids can clarify and simplify your message because they communicate clearly, quickly, and vividly. They are also attention-getting devices that help retain audience interest. Charts, graphs, and illustrations greatly increase audience understanding and retention of the information, especially for complex issues and technical information that could otherwise be misunderstood or glossed over by your audience. A bar graph, pie chart, diagram, or concise summary of key points can eliminate misunderstanding and save many words. Note the impact of the transformation of data in Figure 14–2 from a text-based (left) to a graphics-based (right) format. The graphic depiction makes the percentages easier to compare and to retain for future reference.

Keep visuals as simple as possible for presentations by including only essential information. Bear in mind that presentation audiences have less time to absorb complex visuals than readers do. Tables, for example, are ideal for showing detailed data (budget expenditures, production output, staff hours worked) but are poor at showing trends and overviews of these data. Instead, use a chart or graph to show the data and discuss important details orally.

Use text sparingly on slides. Instead of blocks of text, use bulleted or numbered lists, keeping them parallel in meaning and grammatical form. Use numbered lists if sequence matters or bulleted lists if it does not. And limit bulleted or numbered lists to five or six items per slide.

The slide should contain no more than 40 to 45 words. Any more will clutter the slide and force you to use a smaller type size, which could impair the audience's ability to read the information. The slide should list only the key points you wish to cover. You can tell the audience about any additional background and context for what's on the slide — it is an oral presentation, after all.

◆ ***Use the guidelines for preparing visuals discussed in Chapter 7, Designing Documents and Visuals.***

You can create and present your visual aids in a variety of media. Although most presentations now rely on digital slides and videos, other visual media include whiteboards, handouts, and, less frequently, flip charts and chalkboards. Note that visuals in presentations require titles; however, they generally do not need figure numbers because you will refer to them in the proper sequence during the presentation.

Data in graphics format

Data in text-based format

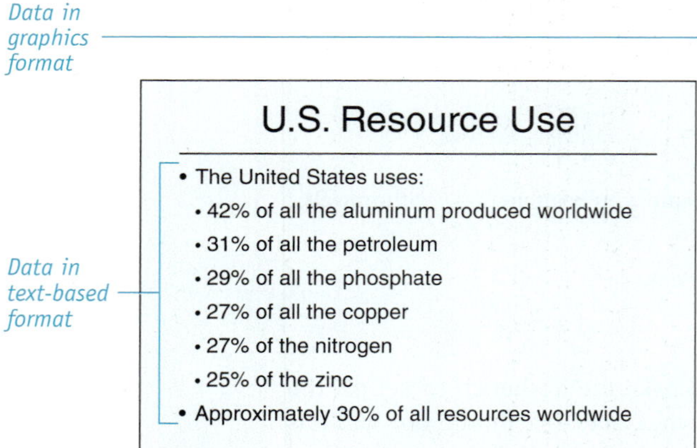

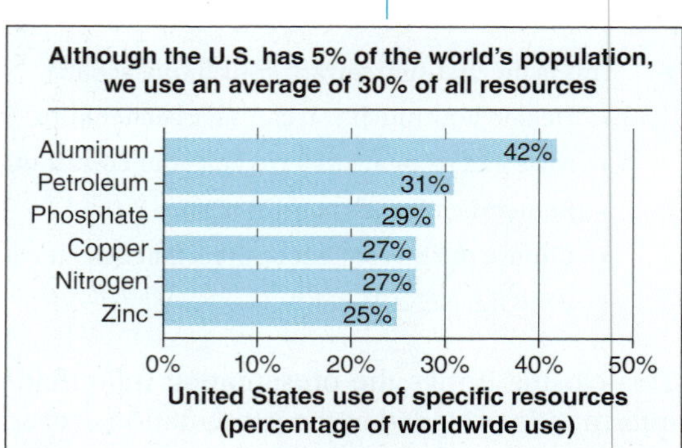

Figure 14–2 Data Transformed from Traditional Text-Based Format to Graphics Format Reprinted by permission of Madeline Schreiber (Virginia Tech College of Engineering).

EMPLOYEE BENEFITS

Acme Corporation

Presented by Laura Phelps

Office of Human Resources

June 2016

Cover slide for presentation information — who, what, when

Acme Corporation
Savings and Investment Program

Are You Saving Enough for Your Future?

This program will enhance your retirement security above the level of your pension and Social Security benefits.

This presentation explains our options for contributing to the plan through payroll deductions.

-1-

Introductory slide with overview of topic and attention-getting statement

Acme Corporation
Savings and Investment Program

Questions to Ask Yourself

- How much can I save?
- How much does Acme Corporation contribute?
- What are my investment options?
- Are there tax advantages?

-2-

Rhetorical questions to pique audience interest and announce organization of information

Figure 14–3 Sample Slide Presentation

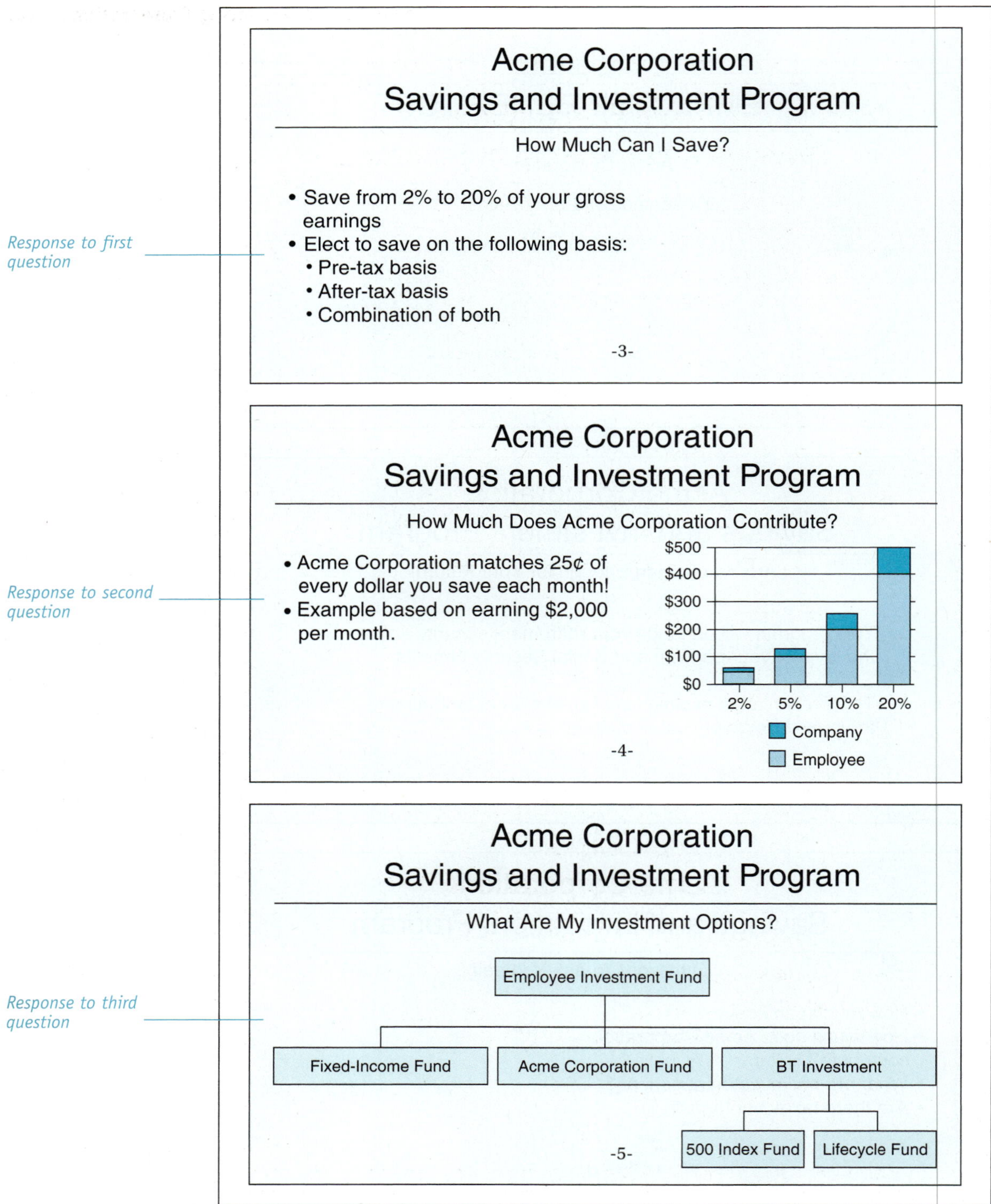

Figure 14–3 Sample Slide Presentation *(continued)*

Acme Corporation
Savings and Investment Program
Are There Tax Advantages to the Program?
• No income taxes on contributions or earnings until withdrawn
• Reduces current taxable income
• Defers taxes until you take distributions
• Earnings tax free on contributions
• Maximizes the compounding value of contributions
• Increases your retirement income
Pre-Tax Deferral Example
Annual compensation $50,000
Annual deferral $ 8,500
Annual taxable income $41,500
-6-
Response to fourth question
Acme Corporation
Savings and Investment Program
The Next Step to Your Future Security
• Decide how much you can save each month.
• Remember Acme's contribution.
• Choose the investment options that best fit your needs.
• ENROLL NEXT WEEK!
-7-
Call to action
Acme Corporation
Thank You for Coming
Your Future Is Important to Us
• Consider your options.
• Enroll next week.
• Questions? Call or e-mail the Benefits Office:
• (301) 990-1200, extension 03
• E-mail: benefits@acme/internal.com
-8-
Instructions for response to call to action

Figure 14–3 Sample Slide Presentation (*continued*)

ETHICS NOTE: Acknowledge Print and Online Information Sources in Presentations Be sure to provide credit for any visual taken from a print or an online source. You can include a citation either on an individual visual (such as a slide), at the end of a video presentation, or in a list of references or works cited that you distribute to your audience with your handouts.

Using Presentation Software

Visual information in workplace presentations is most frequently displayed on computer monitors, for a small audience, or by projectors connected to a laptop computer, for larger audiences (Figure 14–4). Computers have largely replaced projectors that rely on transparencies and 35-mm slides; however, both transparencies and 35-mm slides can be scanned for digital use.

Presentation software, such as PowerPoint, Corel Presentations, Apple Keynote, Prezi, and open-source products, helps you simultaneously create your slides as you prepare your presentation. You can import text, charts, and graphs from other files, and you can use standard templates and other aids that help you design effective visuals. Possible enhancements include a selection of layouts, typefaces, background textures and colors, as well as clip-art images, audio (including music), and video (such

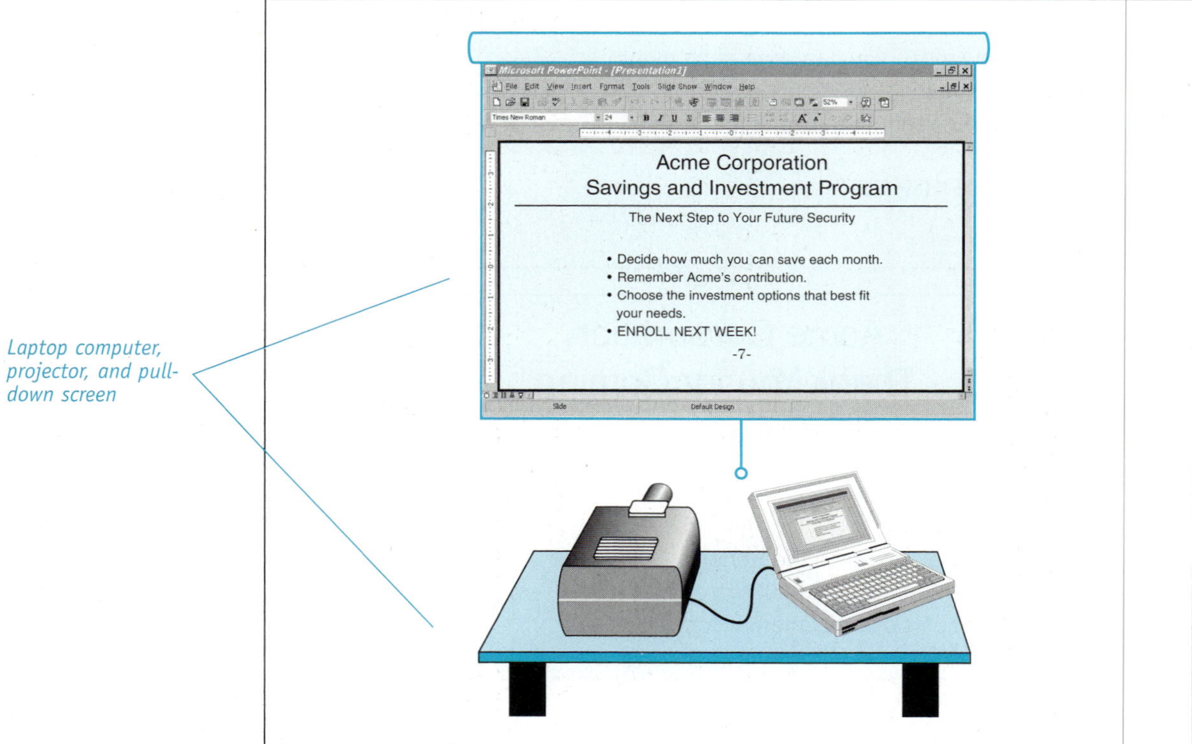

Figure 14–4 Computer-Presentation Setup

as animation) from outside sources, such as the Internet. Presentation software also allows you to link your slides to the Internet, which is useful for presentations on subjects such as product demonstrations or website evaluations. Avoid using too many enhancements, however, because they could distract viewers from your message. In addition, unless warranted by your audience and purpose, avoid using images, music, or other items that do not directly promote your purpose. (Figure 14–5 shows a slide that uses a bulleted list and clip art.)

Presentation software also makes it possible to convert a presentation to Web format and post it to your company's intranet site, a feature that makes your slides accessible to your colleagues during or after your presentation. For interested outside audiences, you can post the presentation slides on your blog or website. You could even post a video of yourself making the presentation and responding to questions on your company's intranet or public website or even with a shared video service, such as YouTube.

WRITER'S CHECKLIST

Using Visuals in a Presentation

- ✔ Limit each visual to a number of words that can be quickly read by your audience.
- ✔ Use a font size readable to audience members at the back of the room. (Type should be no smaller than 30 point and bold. For headings, 45 or 50 point is better.)

Plain-Language Award of the Month

What Are the Criteria for the Award?

Use "Plain-Language Principles," such as

- Common, everyday words
- Short sentences
- Active voice
- "You" and other pronouns (as appropriate)
- Logical organization
- Easy-to-read design features (lists and tables)

Figure 14–5 Presentation Slide with Bulleted List and Clip Art

- ✔ Limit the number of bulleted or numbered items in lists to no more than five or six per visual, and use numbers if sequence is important and bullets if not.
- ✔ Keep lists in parallel structure and balanced in content.
- ✔ Make your visuals consistent in font style, size, and spacing.
- ✔ Consider the contrast between your text and the background to ensure the text and images are clear to those in the audience.
- ✔ Use only one or two illustrations per visual (or slide) to avoid clutter and confusion.
- ✔ Use graphs, charts, and infographics to show data trends.
- ✔ Avoid overloading your presentation with so many visuals that you distract or tax the audience's concentration: One visual for every two minutes is a common guideline.
- ✔ Avoid using sound or visual effects in presentation software that distract from the content or may seem unprofessional.
- ✔ Do not read the text on your visual word for word. Your audience can read the visuals; they look to you to provide the key points in detail.
- ✔ Match your delivery of the content to your visuals. Do not put one visual on the screen and talk about the previous visual or, even worse, the next one.

Using Flip Charts, Whiteboards, and Chalkboards

Flip charts, whiteboards, and chalkboards are ideal media for brainstorming sessions and short presentations for small groups in a conference or classroom. Flip charts are large sheets of white paper bound like a tablet and fastened to the top of an easel (Figure 14–6). The presenter writes on the sheets with colored felt-tip pens, often during the presentation.

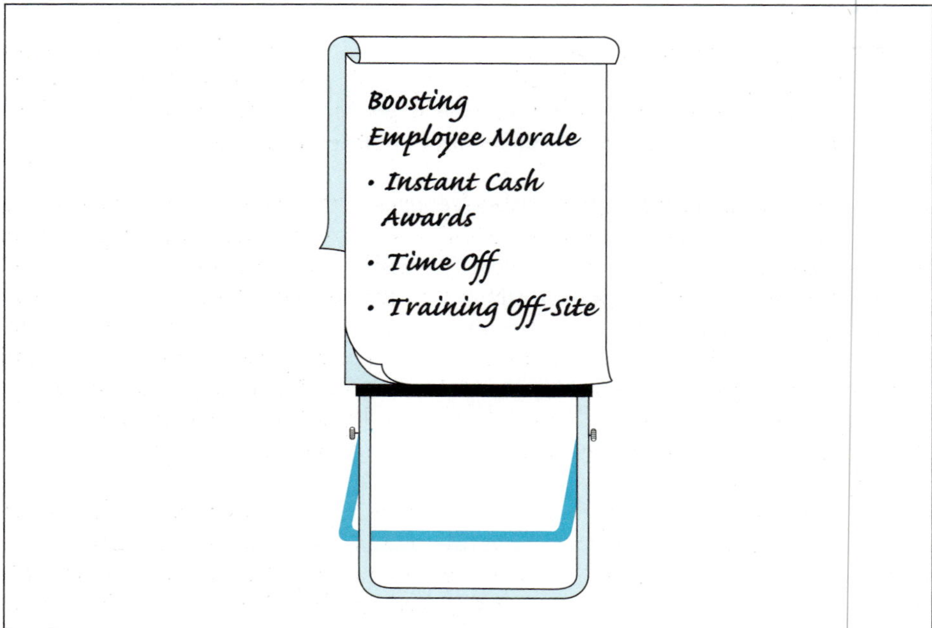

Figure 14–6 Flip Chart

To avoid distracting your audience by writing as you speak, prepare text and sketches ahead of time on a series of sheets and flip through them during your presentation. Flip charts are also an ideal medium for brainstorming with your audience. You can fill sheet after sheet with ideas, tape them on the walls for everyone to see, and use a clean sheet or sheets to organize the ideas into an outline for follow-up work. Some organizations have moved to digital flip charts, allowing these brainstorming sessions to be conducted via pen and digital tablet and projected on a large screen for the entire audience.

Whiteboards and chalkboards, common to classrooms, are convenient for creating impromptu sketches and for jotting notes during your presentation. If your presentation requires extensive notes or complex drawings, create them before the presentation to minimize audience impatience. Ensure before the presentation that you have ample chalk or marking pens and an eraser. If you need to keep ideas that will be erased because you're running out of space, assign someone in the audience to record them for future reference. Some organizations now offer digital whiteboard technology that allows for digital copies or photos of whiteboard contents to be saved and made available to the audience.

Using Handouts

Handouts typically are paper copies of your presentation slides, although they may be a summary of key points; supporting data in tables, charts, and graphs; or other supplementary information. They benefit you and your audience by reinforcing what is said and by permitting your listeners to take notes and retain the material for future reference. They are usually distributed before the presentation for your audience to review.

Practicing Your Presentation

Once you have outlined and drafted your presentation and prepared your visuals, you are ready to practice your delivery. Familiarize yourself with the sequence of the material — major topics, notes, and visuals — in your outline. Once you feel comfortable with the content, you're ready to practice the presentation itself.

Practice on your feet and out loud. Try to practice in the room where you'll give the presentation to learn the idiosyncrasies of the space: acoustics, lighting, how the chairs will most likely be arranged, where the electrical outlets and switches are located, and so forth. Practicing out loud is more effective than just rehearsing mentally because you process the information in your mind many times faster than you can possibly speak it. Rehearsing out loud will make clear exactly how long your presentation will take and will highlight any problems, such as awkward transitions. Rehearsing also helps you to eliminate or reduce verbal tics, such as "um," "you know," and "like," as well as helps you to determine how loudly you need to speak based on the size of the room.

Practice with your visuals. Integrate your slides, transparencies, or other visuals into your practice sessions. This will help your presentation go more smoothly. Operate the equipment (computer, slide projector, or overhead projector) until you're comfortable with it. Decide if you want to use a remote control or wireless mouse or if you want to have someone else advance your slides. Even if things go wrong, being prepared and practiced will give you the confidence and poise to continue.

PROFESSIONALISM NOTE: Rehearse Your Presentation Rehearse your presentation using your electronic slides and practice your transitions from slide to slide. Also practice loading your presentation and anticipate any technical difficulties that might arise. Should you encounter a technical snag during the presentation, stay calm and give yourself time to solve the problem. If you cannot solve the problem, move on without the technology. As a backup, carry a printout of your electronic presentation as well as an extra electronic copy on a storage medium.

Videotape or have someone observe your practice session. Videotape is a very effective and sometimes embarrassing way to catch what you are doing wrong. The tape will reveal how you present your material from the audience's perspective. If you do not have access to a video recorder, consider using the recording options on a mobile phone or, at the very least, use an audio recorder to evaluate your vocal presentation. Another effective technique is to ask a friend or colleague to watch you rehearse and comment on your delivery.

Delivery Techniques that Work

Your delivery is both aural and visual. In addition to your words and message, your nonverbal communication affects your audience. Be animated—your words have impact and staying power when they are delivered with physical and vocal animation. If you want listeners to share your point of view, show enthusiasm for your topic. The most common delivery techniques include making eye contact; using movement and gestures; and varying voice inflection, projection, and pace.

Eye Contact The best way to establish rapport with your audience is through eye contact. In a large audience, directly address those people who seem most responsive to you in different parts of the room. Doing that helps you establish rapport with your listeners by holding their attention and gives you important visual cues that let you know how your message is being received. Do the listeners seem engaged and actively listening? Based on your observations, you may need to adjust the volume or tone of your voice or the speed of your presentation.

Movement Animate the presentation with physical movement. Take a step or two to one side after you have been talking for a minute or so. That type of movement is most effective at transitional points in your presentation between major topics or after pauses or emphases. Too much movement, however, can be distracting, so try not to pace. Another way to integrate movement into your presentation is to walk to the screen and point to the visual as you discuss it. Touch the screen with the pointer and then turn back to the audience before beginning to speak (remember the three t's: touch, turn, and talk).

Gestures Gestures both animate your presentation and help communicate your message. Most people gesture naturally when they talk; nervousness, however, can inhibit gesturing during a presentation. Keep one hand free and use that hand to gesture.

Voice Your voice can be an effective tool in communicating your sincerity, enthusiasm, and command of your topic. Use it to your advantage to project your credibility.

Vocal inflection is the rise and fall of your voice at different times, such as the way your voice naturally rises at the end of a question ("You want it *when*?"). Conversational delivery and eye contact promote the feeling among audience members that you are addressing them directly. Use vocal inflection to highlight differences between key and subordinate points in your presentation.

Projection Most presenters think they are speaking louder than they are. Remember that your presentation is ineffective for anyone in the audience who cannot hear you. If listeners must strain to hear you, they may give up trying to listen. Correct projection problems by practicing out loud with someone listening from the back of the room.

Pace Be aware of the speed at which you deliver your presentation. If you speak too fast, your words will run together, making it difficult for your audience to follow. If you speak too slowly, your listeners will become impatient and distracted.

WRITER'S CHECKLIST

Practicing Your Presentation

✔ Practice out loud and, if possible, in the room where you'll deliver the presentation.

✔ Incorporate your visuals as you practice, using the computer, projector, or remote control.

✔ Videotape or audiotape your practice session and evaluate it critically, or have a colleague or classmate observe and comment.

✔ Because the meaning of gestures differs greatly from culture to culture, carefully choose and rehearse those that you will use during your presentation.

✔ Practice your presentation in front of colleagues or friends and have them watch for any gestures that could be misinterpreted by your audience.

CONSIDERING AUDIENCE AND PURPOSE

Engaging Your Audience When Speaking

- Establish rapport and trust by looking into the eyes of as many audience members as possible.
- Use your voice to communicate sincerity and enthusiasm, and, above all, do not speak in a monotone. Project your voice so that you're heard by everyone, and pace your delivery so that your words don't run together.
- Be animated, moving to the screen to emphasize points and gesturing naturally.
- Hold the interest of your audience by looking at your notes as little as possible. Never read directly from your notes.
- Deliver your talk from a prepared outline on slides rather than memorizing it word for word. This way, your delivery
    - Sounds more natural and less monotonous.
    - Enhances audience attention and comprehension.
    - Enables more eye contact with your audience, which helps convey your interest in and enthusiasm for the topic.

Dealing with Presentation Anxiety

Everyone experiences nervousness before a presentation. Survey after survey reveals that dread of speaking in front of others ranks among the top five fears for most people. Typical reactions to this stress include shortness of breath, a racing heartbeat, trembling, and perspiration. Instead of letting this stress inhibit you, focus on channeling your nervous energy into a helpful stimulant. That is, if you can't eliminate your stress entirely, manage it. The best way to master this feeling is to know your topic thoroughly. If you know what you are going to say and how you are going to say it, you will gain confidence and reduce anxiety as you become immersed in your subject.

Rehearsing your presentation will help. Do so alone or, if possible, in front of one or more listeners. If you're anxious because you may forget something or get lost during your delivery, you may find it helpful to write out the presentation in full, put it aside, and rehearse using only brief notes. If you falter, refer to your written version. After a practice session, imagine yourself in front of your audience delivering your material point by point. Begin by saying to yourself, "My subject is important. I am ready. My listeners are here to listen to what I have to say." If you cannot remember every point you wish to make during the practice presentation, review your notes or visuals. These will trigger your memory both as you imagine the presentation and when you're actually giving it.

You can use several techniques to quell the butterflies immediately before a presentation. Fill your lungs with a deep breath — feel your chest (not your belly!) expand — and hold it for a count of ten. Then exhale and repeat, doing so several times or until you feel your body begin to relax. Tensing and relaxing muscles is another effective stress reducer. Clench both fists tightly and count to ten while inhaling and then exhale. Repeat several times until your stress begins to diminish.

During the presentation, do not be upset if you use the wrong word, refer to the wrong visual, or otherwise do something unplanned. Simply take a deep breath, correct your mistake, and move forward. Do not refer to your mistake unless you must — chances are that the audience will think you are moving according to plan.

Reaching Global Audiences

The prevalence of multinational corporations and multinational trade agreements, the increasing diversity of the U.S. workforce, and even increases in immigration have made the ability to reach audiences with varied cultural backgrounds an essential skill. The multicultural audiences for your presentations may include clients, business partners, colleagues, and current and potential employees and customers of varied backgrounds.

Presentations to global audiences involve special challenges. As with all materials intended for these readers and listeners, keep your language simple and consistent. Don't call something a "ratio" in one place and a "rate" in another. Puns and wordplay may entertain a U.S. audience but will likely confuse foreign listeners. State the main points of your presentation often and in the identical language each time. Follow these guidelines whether you are addressing an audience for whom English is a second language or speaking through an interpreter. As you deliver your presentation, speak slowly and deliberately, enunciating clearly and pausing often. Keep in mind the following additional points about delivering presentations:

CONSIDERING AUDIENCE AND PURPOSE

Evaluating Your Presentation

- Have you analyzed the purpose of your presentation so that it focuses on what you want your audience to know, to believe, or to do when they leave?
- Do you know the makeup of your audience so that your presentation accommodates their level of knowledge of, experience with, and attitude toward your topic?
- Is your presentation structured in the best sequence for an audience of listeners?
- Are your presentation's visual aids concise, informative, and visible to everyone in the room?
- Have you practiced your presentation so that your delivery is animated, shows mastery of the topic, can be heard by everyone, and is not rushed?
- For international audiences, is your presentation free of U.S.-centered idioms, references, and jargon?

- Clean is better than colorful. Avoid idioms ("dog and pony show," "barking up the wrong tree"), jargon ("emoticons," "debugging"), and acronyms. They will put an unnecessary impediment between you and your audience. Avoid U.S.-centered examples of business, political, or sports figures unless they are essential to your discussion. They will not be understood and, worse, they will suggest to your audience that your perspective about the world is narrowly focused on the United States.
- Do not use the trite sports metaphors that are all too common in American speech ("slam dunk," "touchdown," "home run"). They will puzzle the members of your international audience and could leave them thinking that you are insensitive about their culture and customs.
- Jokes can backfire even with U.S. audiences, so they are especially tricky with international listeners. If you think that humor is important to your message, try it out on someone familiar with the languages and cultures of your audience beforehand and revise accordingly.
- With U.S. audiences, maintaining eye contact enhances the speaker's credibility and connectedness with the audience. In some cultures, however, making direct eye contact is seen as an invasion of privacy. For these listeners, try instead to sweep your gaze across the room rather than looking at anyone too long.

For additional information and tips on communicating with multicultural audiences, see page 74 in Chapter 3, Drafting a Document; pages 251–257 in Chapter 7, Designing Documents and Visuals; and pages 320–326 in Chapter 9, Writing Routine and Sensitive Messages.

MEETING THE DEADLINE: The Time-Sensitive Presentation

When you need to prepare a presentation under a tight deadline, it helps to follow a structured approach — one that will enable you to work efficiently, reduce anxiety, and feel confident in what you have to say. Use the following guidelines to help you plan, create, practice, and deliver a presentation that will satisfy you and your audience while meeting your deadline.

Part I: Planning Your Presentation (45 Minutes)

1. *Know the purpose of your presentation.* Write a purpose statement based on what you want your audience to know, to believe, or to do as a result of your presentation. Then define the scope of your presentation and jot down what you plan to cover. After you draft your purpose statement, decide how to introduce your topic, select the key points that will explain your topic, and choose a closing take-away message that your audience will remember.
2. *Analyze your audience.* Concentrate on the key decision makers in your audience and gear your presentation toward them. Based on your audience, decide how technical your presentation needs to be, use language suitable to your listeners' level of expertise, and avoid *unnecessary* jargon. Select a medium that suits the audience, the purpose, and the venue in which the presentation is being delivered.
3. *Gather your information.* Use only what's essential. If your presentation covers a topic you have already written about in a proposal or report, organize all relevant information on your topic into one electronic or hard-copy file. For a new topic, brainstorm with colleagues more knowledgeable than you about the topic and review relevant in-house information.
4. *Plan your delivery time frame.* As you plan and develop your presentation, remember that you will need to get your points across within a set time period. Whether your presentation is scheduled for five minutes or an hour, think of your main points in relation to your time frame.
5. *Structure the content of your presentation.* Structure the points you want to make in an outline. Plan how many slides or transparencies you will need to convey your message. For a five-minute presentation, you will need no more than five to ten slides. If you decide to work with five slides, plan to discuss these for about a minute each. If you have ten slides, plan to discuss each for about 30 seconds. Some slides — those covering key points and benefits — will require more time than, say, an introductory slide. Consider the following structure:

Slide 1	Introduce yourself.
Slide 2	Introduce your topic.
Slide 3	State your purpose.
Slides 4–6	State and explain your key points — points that will inform or persuade your audience.
Slides 7 & 8	Explain how what you propose will benefit your listeners.
Slide 9	Close by reviewing the parts of your presentation that you want your listeners to remember most.
Slide 10	Thank your listeners for their attention. Credit outside sources, if necessary, and include your contact information.

Part II: Creating Your Presentation (90 Minutes)

- Work with one of your presentation software's basic templates to create your slides.

- To add notes for yourself about each slide, use the software's "insert notes" feature.
- Cover no more than five to seven ideas or "bullet points" for each slide.
- Keep your slides uncluttered and easy to read, even from the back of the room.
- Import existing charts and graphs to your presentation, but don't spend time creating and designing new ones. If time permits, add complementary images where appropriate or a neutral background color (use light background colors to ensure a contrast between the type and the background). If not, focus on the clear presentation of your content. (*Note:* For visuals you are unable to import but that are important, bring printouts to hand out to your audience.)
- Once your slides are complete, work within the presentation software's "insert notes" feature to write the text of your presentation. You can later print out your notes for practice or for reference if you need them when delivering your presentation. See Figure 14–7.

What Are the Benefits to Employees?

- Access The Sports Center for $20/month—includes all athletic facilities, whirlpool, and sauna.
- Support of personal trainers or massage therapists, for an additional $15/month.
- Free cholesterol and blood-pressure screening.
- Free nutrition and weight-management counseling.
- Employee incentive "wellness points" that earn discounts on fitness gear and clothing at The Sports Center Shop.

-2-

This slide appears on-screen for the audience

The Healthy Life Program offers your employees one of the best and most affordable wellness packages available nationwide. For modest monthly fees, your employees can become members of The Sports Center and Day Spa, a facility that won the "Best of Chicago" award in 2015, and that was recently rated #1 by Shape Magazine. Here they can enjoy numerous benefits that include not only a generous offering of classes such as aerobics, spinning, kickboxing, Pilates, and yoga, all taught by top-notch instructors — but they will also enjoy the support of the highly qualified personal trainers, nutrition counselors, and health-care professionals on staff. We do all we can to make sure our members approach exercise, diet, and lifestyle change safely and sensibly.

The Notes pages give you a space in which to expand the ideas of your slide with concrete details; they do not appear on-screen

Figure 14–7 Notes Page of a PowerPoint Presentation

The Slide-Sorter view allows you to evaluate the structure of your presentation

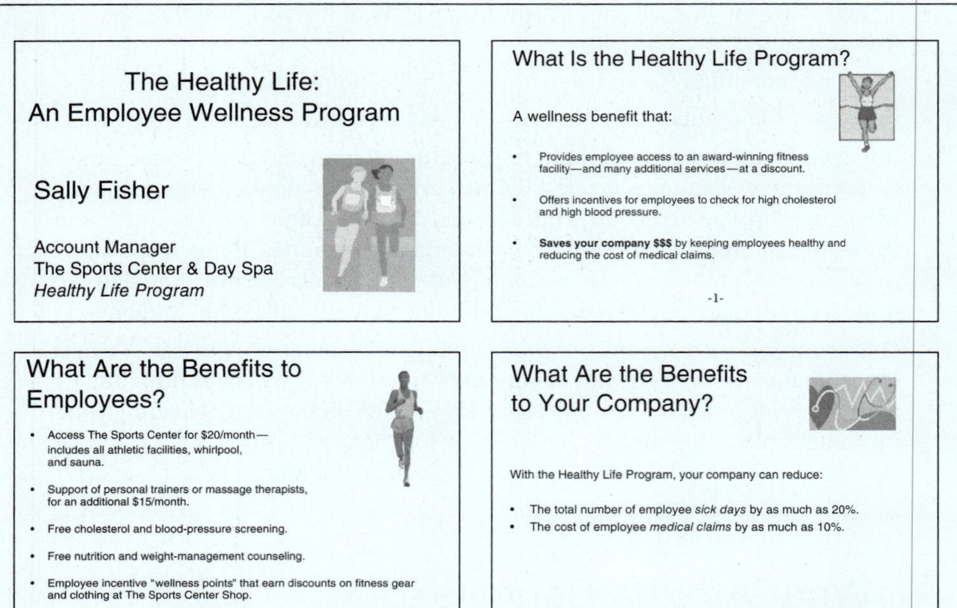

Figure 14–8 Slide-Sorter View of a PowerPoint Presentation

- Evaluate your slides in the presentation software's preview feature and edit, rearrange, delete, or add to them as needed. See Figure 14–8.

Part III: Practicing Your Presentation (45 Minutes)

- Practice your delivery at least three times.
- Time yourself and make any necessary adjustments. If you edit your presentation at this point, practice it again at least twice.
- Use your time constructively. If you find yourself worrying, practice again or mentally run through your slides and key points.
- Avoid memorizing your presentation. A spontaneous delivery will be more credible and engaging to your audience.
- Try to visit the room where you will be presenting a day ahead of time. If this is not possible, arrive at least 45 minutes before your presentation. Check out the presentation equipment — making sure it is in good working order and that you know how to operate it. Evaluate the setup of the room, the location of electrical outlets, and the lighting and temperature conditions. Make any necessary adjustments.

Part IV: Delivering Your Presentation (Allotted Time)

- Speak energetically. Your enthusiasm will energize your listeners, keep their attention, and incline them to consider what you propose.
- Refer to your slides during your presentation, but don't read them word for word — what you say should provide detail and depth to what appears on the screen.
- Know what you want to say about each slide. If necessary, refer to the notes you created when you developed your slides. Tape notes for each slide onto index cards for a less-intrusive way to check them during the presentation.
- Use vocal inflection to emphasize key points; a monotone voice will put your audience to sleep.
- Breathe deeply. Bringing oxygen to the brain keeps you composed and mentally sharp and helps you to speak slowly and more clearly.

Listening

An equally important counterpart to a good presentation is active listening. Active listening enables you to understand an instructor's directions, a speaker's presentation, a manager's goals, and a customer's needs and wants. Above all, it lays the foundation for cooperation when both the speaker and the listener focus clearly on the content of the message and attempt to eliminate as much as possible that impedes the communication.

Fallacies About Listening

Most people assume that because they can hear, they know how to listen. In fact, *hearing* is passive and *listening* is active. Hearing voices in a crowd or a ringing telephone requires no analysis and no active involvement. We hear such sounds without choosing to listen to them — we have no choice but to hear them. Listening, however, requires taking action, interpreting the message, and assessing its worth. Listening also requires that you consider the context of messages and the differences in meaning that may be the result of differences in the speaker's and the listener's occupation, education, culture, language, sex, ethnicity, or other factors. The more carefully you listen, the better you will communicate with managers, colleagues, and clients in all settings, whether in a phone conversation, face-to-face, in a meeting, or during a presentation.

Steps to More Effective Listening

To listen more effectively, (1) make a conscious decision to listen actively, (2) think about your purpose for listening, (3) take specific actions to listen more efficiently, and (4) adapt to the situation.

Make a Conscious Decision

The first step to effective listening is simply making up your mind to do so. This step requires conscious effort, something that does not come naturally. To listen actively, the well-known precept is true: "Seek first to understand and then to be understood."[1] If you follow this rule, you may find it easier to take the steps or the time required to ensure that you are indeed exerting a conscious effort to listen effectively.

Define Your Purpose

Know *why* you are listening. Focusing on your purpose will help minimize the most common problems people have with listening: drifting attention, formulating a response while the speaker is still talking, and interrupting the speaker. To practice active listening, take the time to focus on the following questions:

- What kind of information do I hope to get from this conversation or meeting and how will I use it?
- What kind of message do I want to send while I'm listening? Is it understanding? determination? flexibility? competence? patience?
- Do I foresee any problems, such as boredom, wandering attention, anger, or impatience?
- How can I keep these problems from preventing me from listening effectively?

Take Specific Actions

In conversations with others, become a responder rather than a reactor. A *responder* is a listener who slows down the communication to be certain that he or she is accurately interpreting the speaker. A *reactor* simply says the first thing that comes to mind, regardless of whether he or she understands the message. Take the following actions to help you become a responder and not a reactor.

- Aim to be impartial when evaluating a message. Do not dismiss a message because you dislike the speaker or are distracted by the speaker's appearance, mannerisms, or accent.
- Slow down the communication by asking for more information or by paraphrasing the message before you offer your thoughts. Paraphrasing lets the speaker know that you are listening, gives the speaker an opportunity to clear up any misunderstanding, keeps you focused, and helps you remember the discussion.
- Listen with empathy by putting yourself in the speaker's position or by looking at things from the speaker's perspective. Try to understand the speaker's feelings, wants, and needs — appreciate his or her point of view. When people feel they are being listened to, they tend to respond with appreciation and cooperation.
- For briefings and lectures, take notes while you are listening. Note-taking provides several benefits. It helps you stay focused on what the speaker is saying, especially during a presentation or lecture. It helps you remember what you've heard

---

[1]Steven R. Covey, *The 7 Habits of Highly Effective People: Powerful Lessons in Personal Change*, 15th ed. (New York: Free Press, 2004).

because you reinforce the message by writing it. (You can also check the notes at a later date, when you need to recall what was said.)

Adapt to the Situation

Listening at peak efficiency at all times is not necessary. For a casual conversation, you may legitimately listen without giving it your full attention. Even during a lecture, you may be listening for specific information only. However, if you are on a team project where the success of the project depends on everyone's contribution, pay close attention. Doing so enables you to gather information important to the project as well as to recognize other nuances, such as the ongoing relationships among team members.

PROFESSIONALISM NOTE: Be a Courteous Listener As a listener, extend the presenter or other speaker the same degree of courtesy that you would wish extended to you as a speaker. Do not chat, text message, or otherwise divert your attention, so turn off all mobile devices and close your computer. You would appreciate your audience doing the same for you.

CONSIDERING AUDIENCE AND PURPOSE

Listening Effectively for Workplace Presentations

To get the most out of a presentation, keep the following guidelines in mind:

- Be prepared.
  - Before the presentation, review any handouts—note the topic and how it is organized.
    - What kind of information do you want or need from the presentation?
    - How will you use the information?
  - Search online for an overview of a topic unfamiliar to you, time permitting.
  - For a technical presentation, review one or two of the speaker's publications to become familiar with his or her areas of interest.
- Be an active listener.
  - Focus on what is said and shown.
  - Listen for the main points: the key concepts and ideas.
  - Be alert for organizational patterns and transitions between primary and secondary topics.
  - Avoid distractions, such as checking for e-mails, text messages, or phone calls.
- Take notes.
  - Take notes: doing so forces you to concentrate on the topic.
  - Use shorthand when possible to keep pace with the speaker.
  - Annotate any handouts to expand or clarify the content for future reference.
- Ask questions appropriately.
  - Be tactful rather than challenging.
  - Confine questions to the topic of the presentation.
  - Save open-ended or multipart questions until after the presentation.

Conducting Productive Meetings

Meetings are often a fact of workplace life. At best, they are opportunities to efficiently disseminate information, delegate tasks, work through problems, brainstorm solutions, and solidify collaboration in a group, across a department, or with a client. At worst, they can be time-consuming and even stressful if the topic is contentious or if there are personality conflicts among participants. The suggestions in this section will help you minimize these concerns and make the most out of your meetings.

In basic terms, a meeting is a face-to-face exchange among a group of people who have come together for a common purpose. Meetings allow people to share information and collaborate in ways that are often more productive than exchanges of multiple messages or conversations. A meeting requires planning and preparation, just as writing and oral presentations do.

Planning a Meeting

For a meeting to be successful, determine the focus of the meeting, decide who should attend, and choose the best time and place to hold it. Prepare an agenda for the meeting and, if a record of decisions is necessary, determine who should take the meeting minutes.

What Is the Purpose of the Meeting?

Focus on your desired outcome. Ask yourself what you want those attending to know, to believe, or to do as a result of attending the meeting.

Suppose you called a meeting of your sales staff to design a sales campaign to launch a new tablet successfully. In response to the questions in the previous paragraph, you could jot down the following answers:

▶ As a result of this meeting:

- I want the salespeople *to know* how this tablet can increase their sales considerably.
- I want the salespeople *to believe* that this is the most revolutionary tablet on the market and that their customers will want it.
- I want the salespeople *to offer* their ideas for the sales campaign.

Once you focus on your desired outcome, use the information to write a purpose statement for the meeting that answers the questions *what* and *why*.

▶ The purpose of this meeting is to gather ideas from the sales force [*what*] that will create an effective sales campaign for our new tablet [*why*].

Who Should Attend?

Invite to the meeting only those who can contribute to fulfilling your planned outcome. If a meeting must be held without some key participants, send or e-mail the agenda to them prior to the meeting and ask for any contributions they would like to make. If employees from regional offices or other geographic locations need to participate, they can do so by speakerphone, Skype, or other videoconferencing application. Circulate the meeting minutes to everyone, including those who could not attend, following the meeting.

When Should the Meeting Be Held?

Schedule a meeting when all or most of the key people can be present. The time of day and the length of the meeting can affect its outcome. Consider the following when planning your meeting:

- Be mindful that people need Monday morning to focus on the upcoming week.
- Note that often people need Friday afternoon to focus on completing the current week's tasks.
- Avoid the hour following lunch because some people feel sleepy or lethargic then.
- Avoid early morning meetings because attendees may be delayed by traffic and everyone likes a few minutes in the morning to check e-mails, get a cup of coffee, and so on.
- Include adequate breaks in meetings scheduled to last longer than two hours so that attendees can check their messages, make important phone calls, or use the restroom.
- Avoid meetings during the last 15 minutes of the day. You can be assured of a quick meeting, but it is likely that no one will remember what went on.
- Schedule meetings at a time convenient to those participating remotely by phone or videoconference in different time zones. To correlate the times for meetings, teleconferences, and other events for attendees in other time zones, go to timezoneconverter.com.

DIGITAL TIP: Scheduling Meetings Online

You can simplify the process of scheduling meetings by using the advanced features of your organization's calendar application or using one of several free online scheduling tools.

Where Should the Meeting Be Held?

If the meeting involves in-house personnel only, hold the meeting in the office of the most senior member, or in a conference room, if you need more space. For meetings with clients, vendors, or other outside personnel, having a meeting in your office or conference room can give you an advantage. You feel more comfortable, and your guests' newness to the surroundings may give you an edge. Agreeing to hold the meeting at their location, however, signals your cooperation. For balance, especially for first-time gatherings, meet at a neutral site, such as at an off-site conference center. That way, no one has a distinct advantage and attendees often feel freer to participate. Meetings away from the office also afford fewer distractions and interruptions.

For meetings with clients, vendors, or outside personnel who are not in close geographic proximity, consider using a videoconferencing or Webinar site, program, or device. Such services allow for participants who are located far apart to "meet" in a virtual space, see each other, and conduct the next best thing to a face-to-face meeting.

What's on the Agenda?

A tool for focusing participant attention, the agenda is an outline of the issues the meeting will address. Never begin a meeting without an agenda, even if that agenda is only a handwritten list of topics you want to cover. Distribute the agenda a day or two before the meeting so that those attending have time to prepare or gather the necessary materials. For a longer meeting in which participants will make a presentation or need to be prepared to discuss an issue in detail, try to distribute the agenda a week or more in advance. If you have no time to distribute the agenda early, however, be sure to distribute it at the beginning of the meeting.

The agenda should cover only a few major items: the topics to be discussed, the time and place of the meeting, and the names of attendees. If people are presenting material, note the amount of time allotted for each speaker. Finally, the agenda should give the start and stop times for the meeting so that participants can plan the rest of their day. Figure 14–9 shows a sample agenda.

If distributed in advance of the meeting, the agenda should be accompanied by a memo or an e-mail message that invites people to the meeting. The message should include the following:

- The purpose of the meeting. Everyone should know not only exactly why this meeting is being held but also what you hope to accomplish.

Sales Meeting Agenda

What, where, when, who details

Purpose: To Get Input for a Sales Campaign for the New Tablet
Date: May 9, 2016
Place: Conference Room 14-C
Time: 9:30 a.m.–11 a.m.
Attendees: Advertising Manager, Sales Manager and Reps, Customer Service Manager

Topics of meeting, presenters, and periods scheduled

Topic	Presenter	Time
The Tablet	Bob Arbuckle	9:30–9:45
The Sales Strategy	Mary Winifred	9:45–10:00
The Campaign	Maria Lopez	10:00–10:15
Discussion	Led by Dave Grimes	10:15–11:00

Figure 14–9 Meeting Agenda

- The meeting start and stop times. People need this information so that they will know how to budget their time. A word of warning: When you announce an ending time for the meeting, end it on time unless everyone agrees to extend the meeting beyond the stated stop time.
- The date and place.
- The names of the people invited. Add these as a courtesy for those who do not know the other attendees or their organizational affiliations.
- Instructions on how to prepare for the meeting. Indicate who will be expected to give a briefing or be prepared to answer questions about their project.

Figure 14–10 shows an e-mail message transmitting a meeting agenda.

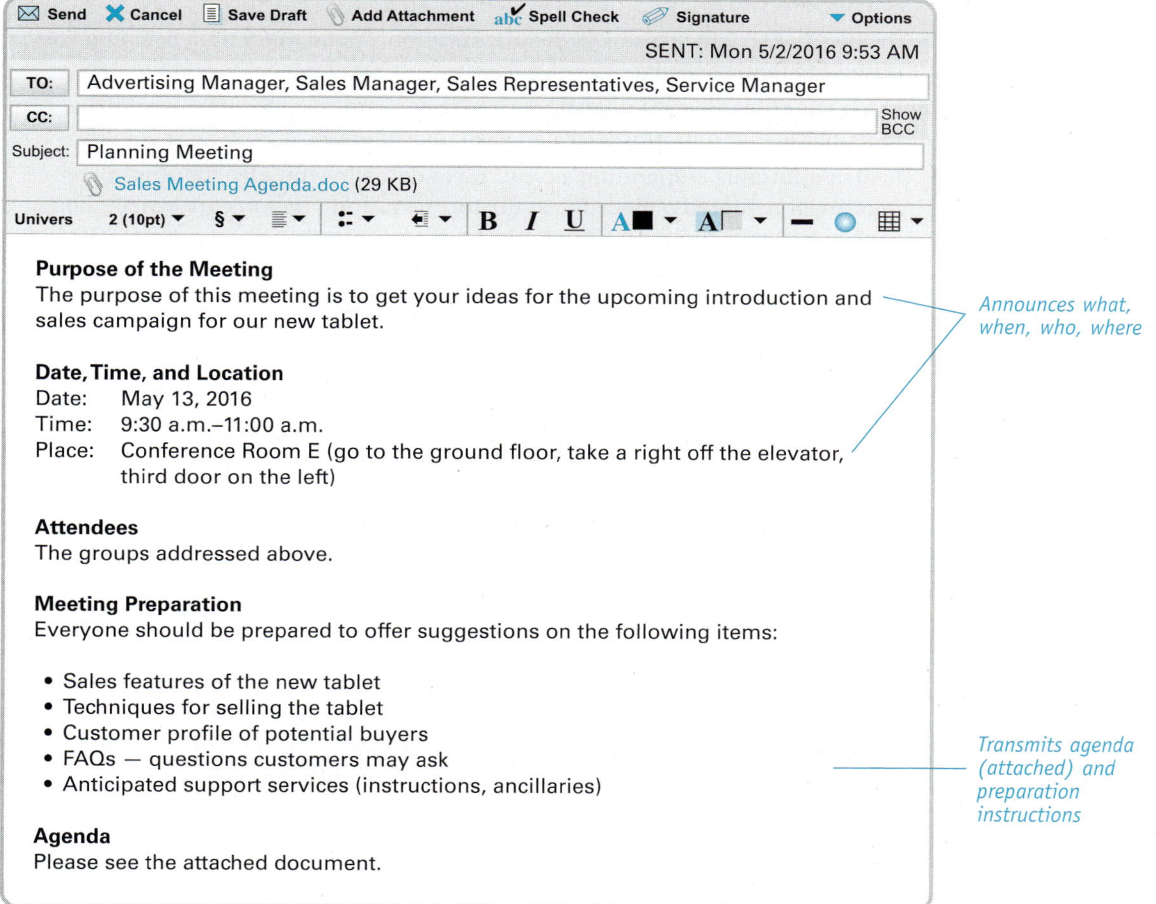

Figure 14–10 E-mail Message Announcing a Meeting and Transmitting an Agenda

DIGITAL TIP: Conducting Online Meetings

When participants cannot meet face to face, consider holding an online videoconference. In such meetings, the participants use an application on their computers to connect with other computers running the same application. Many of these applications are free or inexpensive, but all participants will need computers with high-speed Internet connections and webcams.

PROFESSIONALISM NOTE: Participate Tactfully, Attentively, and Openly

To make meetings as productive as possible, be mindful of the following guidelines:

- Be punctual. When attending a meeting, always arrive several minutes early. Being aware of time shows that you acknowledge the value of other attendees' schedules.
- Be attentive. If you are new to the organization, spend more time listening and observing than speaking.
- Share your ideas even if they differ from those expressed by other attendees; meetings are an opportunity for an exchange of ideas.
- Feel comfortable responding as your ideas come to you. Also, because meetings are considered a place for brainstorming, don't be too concerned about expressing your thoughts in complete sentences or in perfect grammatical form.

Chairing a Meeting

To lead a successful meeting, follow your agenda — the topics that must be covered and the outcomes that you wish — and ensure that you have invited the right people with the necessary information. Equally important, keep in mind how the personalities of those attending a meeting may affect its success. Most of the time you need only be tactful and diplomatic in your dealings with everyone and the meeting will go well. Set an example for the group by listening carefully and by encouraging participants to listen to each other. (Review the section on listening on pages 495–497 in this chapter.)

1. Consider the feelings, thoughts, ideas, and needs of others; don't ignore other points of view.
2. Help others feel valued and respected by listening and responding to them.
3. Respond positively to the comments of others whenever possible.
4. Try to adapt to communication styles and approaches different from your own, particularly those of people from other cultures.

Despite your best efforts, you will encounter people whose personalities hinder effective communication during the meeting. The following guidelines should help you to deal with these potential impediments and keep the group's focus on successfully working through the agenda.

- *The interruptive person.* An interruptive person rarely lets anyone finish a sentence and can intimidate the group's quieter members. Tell that person in a firm but nonhostile tone to let the others finish what they are saying in the interest of getting everyone's best thinking.
- *The negative person.* A negative person generally has difficulty accepting change and will often oppose a new idea or project. If left unchecked, this attitude can demoralize the group as a whole. Of course, not all negative views are invalid. As long as the negative person is making valid points, ask the group for its suggestions as to how to remedy the issues being raised. When these issues are outside the agenda of the meeting in progress, let everyone know that you will schedule a separate meeting to discuss these issues. Then move to the next item on the agenda.
- *The rambling person.* The rambling person cannot collect his or her thoughts quickly enough to state them succinctly. Even so, their thoughts may be of value. Help by restating or clarifying their ideas. If the person nods in agreement, move on. Try to strike a balance between providing your own interpretation and drawing out the person's intended meaning.
- *The quiet or nonparticipating person.* This person may be reluctant to speak in a group setting or may be simply deep in thought. Ask for this person's thoughts, being tactful so as not to cause embarrassment. In some cases, ask such a person *before the meeting* to jot down his or her thoughts on the meeting agenda for use during the meeting.
- *The territorial person.* The territorial person fiercely defends his or her group against all threats — real and perceived — and may fail to cooperate with members of other departments or companies. To deal with this situation, point out that although the individual's territorial concerns may be valid, everyone is working for the same organization and its overall goals take precedence.

Dealing with Conflict

Despite your best efforts, conflict is inevitable. Keep in mind, however, that conflict is also potentially valuable; when managed positively, it can stimulate creative thinking by challenging complacency and showing ways to achieve goals more efficiently or economically.

Try to deal with conflict so that its benefits are retained and its negative effects are minimized. First, be sure that those involved in the conflict are aware of any areas of agreement, and emphasize these areas to establish common ground. Then identify any differences and ask why they exist. If facts seem to be at issue, determine which are correct. If goals differ, encourage each party to try to look at the problem from the other person's point of view. You can take any of a number of approaches to resolve a conflict, including the following:

- *Noncombative tactics.* Avoid accusations, threats, or disparaging comments, and emphasize common interests and mutual goals. Praise conciliatory acts and express a desire for harmonious relations. This can have a very disarming effect on an aggressive person.

- *Persuasion*. Try to convince the other party to accept your point of view. How successful this is likely to be will depend on your credibility and on the other person's willingness to consider your views. Provide facts or previous practices to support your position. Point out how your position benefits the other person (if true). Show how your position is consistent with precedent, prevailing norms, or accepted standards. Tactfully point out any overlooked costs, any disadvantages, or any errors in logic in the other party's point of view.
- *Bargaining*. Exchange concessions until a compromise is reached. Compromising means settling for half a victory rather than risking an all-out win-or-lose struggle. A compromise must provide each side with enough benefits to satisfy minimal needs.
- *Collaborating*. Each side accepts the other's goal as well as its own, and works to achieve the best outcome for both. For such a win-win approach to succeed, each side must understand the other's point of view and discover the needs that must be satisfied. A flexible, exploratory attitude is a prerequisite for collaboration. Trust must be high, but collaborating to resolve conflict often leads to creative results. Define the problem, then define alternative solutions, and then select the one that provides both sides with the most benefits.

Making a Record of Decisions and Assignments

Organizations and committees that keep official records of their meetings refer to such records as *minutes*. If you are facilitating the meeting, delegate the minute-taking to someone else in advance. The minute taker then writes and distributes the minutes before the next meeting, at which point attendees vote to accept the minutes from the previous meeting as prepared or to revise or clarify them.

Not all meetings require formal notes, but it can be helpful to record major decisions made, tasks assigned, or information needed to complete a discussion at a later date. For a standing committee, either rotate responsibility for taking minutes or assign someone permanently to the task.

Keep minutes brief and to the point. Except for recording formally presented motions, which must be transcribed word for word, summarize what occurs and paraphrase discussions.

As an alternative, Web-based conferencing services host and, importantly, record meeting audio, video, and desktop content. Once recorded, the content can be listened to by anyone who missed the meeting and reviewed by attendees who want to jog their memories or clarify their meeting notes. To keep the minutes concise, follow a set format and use headings for each major topic. Keep abstractions and generalities to a minimum and, most important, be specific. Following a set format, such as that shown in Figure 14–11, will help you to keep the minutes organized and concise.

In addition to the minute taker, meeting participants must also record decisions and assignments in the course of the meeting that pertain to them. Someone may be assigned for the group to record decisions on flip charts for this purpose (see Figure 14–6 on page 486). Information on the charts can be revised for clarity later and distributed

WARETON MEDICAL CENTER
DEPARTMENT OF MEDICINE

Minutes of the Monthly Meeting of the Credentials Committee

DATE: April 22, 2016

PRESENT: M. Valden (Chairperson), R. Baron, M. Frank, J. Guern, L. Kingston, L. Kinslow (Secretary), S. Perry, B. Roman, J. Sorder, F. Sugihana

Meeting attendees

Dr. Mary Valden called the meeting to order at 8:40 p.m. The minutes of the previous meeting were unanimously approved, with the following correction: the secretary of the Department of Medicine is to be changed from Dr. Juanita Alvarez to Dr. Barbara Golden.

Meeting opening time, a correction and acceptance of previous minutes

Old Business

None.

New Business

The request by Dr. Henry Russell for staff privileges in the Department of Medicine was discussed. Dr. James Guern made a motion that Dr. Russell be granted staff privileges. Dr. Martin Frank seconded the motion, which passed unanimously.

Terse coverage of topics and decisions

Similar requests by Dr. Ernest Hiram and Dr. Helen Redlands were discussed. Dr. Fred Sugihana made a motion that both physicians be granted all staff privileges except respiratory-care privileges because the two physicians had not had a sufficient number of respiratory cases. Dr. Steven Perry seconded the motion, which passed unanimously.

Dr. John Sorder and Dr. Barry Roman asked for a clarification of general duties for active staff members with respiratory-care privileges. Dr. Richard Baron stated that he would present a clarification at the next scheduled staff meeting, on May 20.

Dr. Baron asked for a volunteer to fill the existing vacancy for Emergency Room duty. Dr. Guern volunteered. He and Dr. Baron will arrange a duty schedule.

There being no further business, the meeting was adjourned at 9:15 p.m. The next regular meeting is scheduled for May 20, at 8:40 p.m.

Meeting adjournment time

Respectfully submitted,

Leslie Kinslow | MARY VALDEN

Leslie Kinslow
Medical Staff Secretary

Mary Valden, M.D.
Chairperson

Signatures of minute taker and committee chairperson

Figure 14–11 Minutes of a Monthly Meeting

to those who attended. Another option is to use a laptop computer to record decisions and assignments and to have these notes projected on a screen so that participants can see what is being recorded. The resulting file can be revised for clarity and distributed to all attendees by e-mail. It can also serve as the basis for official meeting minutes.

CONSIDERING AUDIENCE AND PURPOSE

Planning and Conducting Meetings

- Develop a purpose statement to focus your thoughts.
- Invite only those essential to fulfilling the purpose of the meeting.
- Select a meeting time and place convenient to all attendees.
- Create an agenda and distribute it a day or two before the meeting.
- Assign someone to take notes or to arrange for the meeting to be recorded. Make clear to the note-taker what the notes should include: assignments; their due dates; and, if necessary, the date, time, and location of a follow-up meeting.
- Follow the agenda to keep everyone focused on the purpose of the meeting and the time available.
- Be respectful of the views of others and their ways of expressing those views.
- Review the strategies in this chapter for dealing with attendees whose style of expression in some way prevents you from getting everyone's best thinking.
- Deal with conflict positively to maximize its benefits.
- Close the meeting by reviewing aloud all decisions and assignments.

ETHICS NOTE: Ensure That Meeting Minutes Are Accurate and Complete Because minutes can be used to settle disputes, they must be accurate, complete, and clear. When approved, minutes become the official record of decisions made at the meeting and can be used as evidence in legal proceedings.

Remember that meeting minutes may be used in the future by a lawyer, judge, or jury who probably won't be familiar with the situation you are describing—and that you may not be available to explain what you wrote or you may not remember any of the details of the situation. After all, the reason for taking minutes is to create a permanent record that will be available should it be needed.

The minutes must list all meeting attendees, so, unless you know everyone there, circulate a lined sheet of paper at the beginning of the meeting so that people can write their names and titles or organizations for you to incorporate into the minutes. Request e-mail addresses, too, for distribution of the minutes. Be specific when you refer to people. Instead of using titles ("the Chief of the Marketing Division"), use names and titles ("Florence Johnson, Chief of the Marketing Division"). If a member of the committee is to report to the committee at its next meeting, state the member's name and the topic so that there is no uncertainty about the assignment and who is responsible for it. Be consistent in the way you refer to people. Do not use a title when referring to one person

(Mr. Jarrell) and first and last name when referring to another (Janet Wilson). It may be unintentional, but a lack of consistency in titles or names may imply deference to one person at the expense of another. Minutes should always be objective and impartial.

When you have been assigned to take the meeting minutes, go adequately prepared. A laptop or tablet computer is an ideal tool for this task. Bring the minutes of the previous meeting and any other necessary material. Take memory-jogging notes during the meeting and then expand them with the appropriate details immediately after the meeting. Remember that minutes are primarily a record of specific actions taken, although you may sometimes need to summarize what was said or state the essential ideas in your own words.

Closing the Meeting

Set aside five or ten minutes before closing the meeting to review all decisions and assignments by having the minute taker read them aloud. Doing so helps the group focus on what they have collectively agreed to do. This period also allows for any questions to be raised or misunderstandings to be clarified and promotes everyone's agreement about the group's decisions. Set a date by which everyone at the meeting can expect to receive the minutes. Finally, thank everyone for their participation and close the meeting on a positive note.

WRITER'S CHECKLIST

Writing Minutes of Meetings

Include the following information in meeting minutes:

- ✔ The name of the group or committee holding the meeting
- ✔ The topic of the meeting
- ✔ The kind of meeting (a regular meeting or a special meeting called to discuss a specific subject or problem)
- ✔ Names of attendees and their titles or organizations
- ✔ The place, time, and date of the meeting
- ✔ A statement that the chair and the secretary were present or the names of any substitutes
- ✔ For standing committees, a statement that the minutes of the previous meeting were approved or revised
- ✔ A list of any reports that were read and approved
- ✔ All the main motions that were made, with statements as to whether they were carried, defeated, or tabled (vote postponed), and the names of those who made and seconded the motions (motions that were withdrawn are not mentioned)
- ✔ A full description of resolutions that were adopted and a simple statement of any that were rejected
- ✔ A record of all ballots with the number of votes cast for and against resolutions
- ✔ The time the meeting was adjourned (officially ended) and the place, time, and date of the next meeting, if any
- ✔ The recording secretary's signature and typed name, and, if desired, the signature of the chairperson

CHAPTER 14 SUMMARY: GIVING PRESENTATIONS AND CONDUCTING MEETINGS

In planning a presentation, ask the following questions:

- What is my purpose?
- Who is my audience?
- What amount of information should I prepare to adequately cover the topic for my audience in the time available?
- What is the best medium for my purpose, audience, and venue?

In preparing the presentation:

- Gather the needed information.
- Decide how to organize the information.
- Structure the presentation around this organization.
- Decide on the types of visuals you will need.

In rehearsing your presentation:

- Practice on your feet, out loud, and with your visuals.
- Videotape your practice sessions, if possible, and review the video for posture, gestures, and voice, as well as for content.
- Try to rehearse in the room where the presentation will take place to familiarize yourself with its layout.

When delivering the presentation:

- Remember that nervousness before a presentation is normal.
- Show enthusiasm for your topic through the effective use of movement, eye contact, gestures, and your voice.

To maximize your effectiveness as a listener:

- Adapt your level of concentration to the situation.
- Take the time to understand what the speaker is saying before speaking yourself.
- Define what you need or hope to take away from listening to someone else.
- Consciously work to control yourself from letting boredom, distractions, anger, or other impediments affect you.

In conducting effective meetings:

- Determine the purpose of the meeting.
- Decide who should be invited.
- Determine the best time and place for the meeting.
- Create and distribute an agenda before the meeting.
- Select someone to take minutes.
- Manage different types of people tactfully to achieve the best outcome for the group.
- Deal with conflict positively by adopting noncombative tactics, persuasion, bargaining, or collaborating.
- Review all decisions made and assignments to participants at the close of the meeting.

To record the minutes of a meeting:

- Be prepared to record the proceedings — a laptop or tablet is ideal. Also bring minutes from the previous meeting and any other necessary materials, like handouts.
- Be accurate, complete, and clear because minutes of a meeting may be used to settle disputes or as evidence in legal proceedings. Follow a set format for taking notes.

- Be concise and avoid generalities.
- Be specific and consistent when referring to people, places, and events.
- Be objective and impartial, avoiding adjectives and adverbs that suggest either good or bad qualities.
- Record tasks and the names of attendees who will perform these tasks.
- Expand your notes immediately after the meeting, adding appropriate details, if necessary.

Exercises

1. Select a topic for a presentation and write a purpose statement that is based on your answers to the three questions discussed on page 475: (1) What do I want my audience to know? (2) What do I want my audience to believe? and (3) What do I want my audience to do? Possible topics include the following:
   - Should Congress censor content on the Internet?
   - What policy would you like to see changed or what initiative would you like to see implemented on your campus? (Examples include more parking spaces; additional campus-safety measures, such as more emergency call boxes; more focus on hands-on health care for introductory nursing classes; on-campus voting polls for local and national elections; and ecologically friendly laundry facilities in dormitories.)
   - Are printed books a thing of the past?
   - What responsibility do businesses have toward the public?
   - Should local, state, and federal governments tax Internet purchases?
   - Should K–12 school cafeterias ban hamburgers, hot dogs, pizza, and soft drinks?
   - Would you and one or more partners stand a better chance of business success if you opened a coffee kiosk (in a hospital lobby, in a shopping mall, or on a busy street corner, for example) or if you invested in and ran a coffee shop for a coffee-chain franchise (Seattle's Best, Starbucks, Cosi, and so on)?
2. Complete the following statements about the audience for the presentation topic you selected for Exercise 1:
   a. The experience or level of knowledge that my audience currently has about my subject is ______________________________. Based on their existing knowledge, I should ______________________________.
   b. The general educational level of my audience is ____________________. Based on their general educational level, I'll need to ____________________.
   c. The type of information I should provide this audience to achieve my objective is ______________________________.
   d. Some of the questions that the audience may have throughout the presentation include the following:
      - ______________________________
      - ______________________________
      - ______________________________
3. Continuing with the presentation topic you used in Exercises 1 and 2, prepare an introduction for your presentation that includes the following:
   - An interesting opening
   - A statement of purpose
   - An explanation of how you are going to present the topic (method of development)

4. Using the same presentation topic and materials from Exercises 1, 2, and 3, create a closing for your presentation that asks your audience to take a specific action or that summarizes the main points and restates the purpose of your presentation.

5. Prepare an outline for the presentation you've been working on in the previous four exercises. Use at least four headings and three subheadings under each heading. Include an opening, an introduction, a body, and a closing. Next, prepare at least six slides using bulleted statements and keywords that will help keep the audience focused during your presentation. For this assignment, concentrate on using effective text and images, if desired, when preparing each slide. Add two of the following to the set of visuals you prepared: table, chart, graph, map, or pictorial other than clip art. You will discover that your finished product serves not only as an aid to your presentation but as an outline for you to follow during the presentation, possibly eliminating the need for notes.

6. Write a brief explanation of the impact that the audience has on any presentation you might prepare. Consider the following:
   - How does the education or reading level of the audience guide your choices in what information to include and how you will convey it?
   - If the audience shares your field or major, how will that affect your choices in what information to include and how you will present it?
   - How might your understanding of your audience affect the purpose of your presentation? How do your purpose and understanding of your audience affect the way that you organize your presentation? (It may be helpful to review pages 37–40 in Chapter 2, Planning a Document.)

7. A popular expression used to describe ineffective presentations is "death by PowerPoint." Whether the problem lies with the presentation or the presenter, examples include pointlessly long presentations, presenters who read each slide word for word, slides that are cluttered and printed in a tiny font, and presentations that are either too plain and boring or too filled with distracting text animations. Using at least three of the presentation exercises or projects that are offered in this chapter, write a memo to the class cautioning your classmates against "death by PowerPoint" and suggesting how to avoid it. Give specific examples of where the slide presentation creator could go wrong in each instance.

8. Attend a lecture on campus given by a speaker with whom you are likely to disagree (you may also choose to attend a lecture on a topic about which you have a strong opinion). Take to the presentation the list of points about listening on pages 495–497. As you listen to the presentation, make brief notes of your reactions; for example, note when you are tempted to be distracted by the speaker's appearance, mannerisms, or accent. Immediately after the presentation, expand your notes and review this chapter for advice on listening. Turn your observations of your own use of listening techniques into a brief report (length as specified by your instructor) on how using those techniques can help others listen better.

Collaborative Classroom Projects

1. During a presentation, verbal, visual, and nonverbal communications affect your audience. To make a positive impression on your audience and to keep their attention, you must convey your genuine enthusiasm for your topic. With this principle in mind, take turns in front of the class introducing yourselves and explaining what you plan to accomplish in

your career. Speak for no more than three minutes, and pay attention to the nonverbal communication signals that you and your classmates use. Do some students seem more excited about their future careers than others? Do some seem bored? Think about which gestures and expressions work well and which should be avoided while speaking.

2. Plan a meeting to take place outside class in order to organize a particular class activity or trip; to decide on a specific policy; or to vote on a specific campus, national, or international issue. The meeting will require the participation of everyone in your class. As a group, determine what you expect to achieve at the meeting and prepare a short agenda. Appoint a meeting facilitator to keep the meeting focused and a meeting secretary to record the minutes. At the meeting, maintain an atmosphere in which students listen to each other. When the meeting is concluded and decisions have been made or actions decided, write a brief analysis of the interaction that occurred during the session. What, if anything, could have been improved? Did the environment encourage participation?

Research Projects

1. PowerPoint has been heralded and criticized by many business people and visual experts. Prepare a five-minute presentation in which you give the history of PowerPoint and describe the reasons people support and denigrate the tool. Be sure to both paraphrase and directly cite each of the experts you use as a source. Structure your presentation so that the introduction has an attention-getting opening, a body that presents your research, and a closing that summarizes major points and asks your audience to ponder some of the major issues with PowerPoint.
2. Research cataracts, the most popular surgeries used to correct them, and the costs and benefits associated with each surgery. Create a visual presentation that could be used by an ophthalmologist to inform new cataract patients about their surgical options. Assume these patients have vision problems already and adjust the slides accordingly.
3. Imagine that you are the chief executive officer for a national property group interested in building a shopping mall in your state. You have several national and international chain stores interested in opening stores in your mall, so you want to establish your mall in a county where customers of various economic and racial demographics reside. Begin by going to the U.S. Census Bureau website at www.census.gov and selecting your state under "Quick Facts." Look at the demographics for your state and explore the data from several local counties. Narrow your choice to two counties that offer the best customer base for the type of mall you are considering. Prepare a table, graph, or chart using presentation software of your choice, comparing relevant information regarding the two counties and listing the U.S. Census Bureau as your source. The visuals should be simple, with a font large enough for an audience to read it from a distance. Be ready to share the visuals and your recommendation with the class.
4. Imagine that you work with several other college students at a carpet-cleaning company that puts coupons in local fliers and newspapers to solicit business. Potential customers often call to discuss their carpets and schedule a free consultation. Employees take turns answering the phones when the receptionist is on break, but Lee and Janice let the phone ring four or five times before picking it up because they like to finish what

they're doing before beginning what could be a long discussion. If another employee accidentally transfers a call to Lee, he bounces it back to the front desk or transfers it to Janice so that he can focus on something else. Because Janice is on the phone all day, she often has to eat at her desk, and occasionally answers the phone mid-chew. Sometimes Janice stops by Lee's desk to ask him about orders; Lee usually puts his hand over the receiver before answering her. Because Lee, Janice, and others like them will soon be fired unless they improve their telephone skills, you have decided to hold a meeting to address the problem.

a. Determine what the purpose of your meeting is and who should attend it.
b. Search the Web for at least three sites that describe proper phone etiquette, then make a list of what employees should be doing to create a good impression to potential customers.
c. Use your list to prepare an agenda for the meeting.
d. Keeping in mind that employees are sensitive to criticism and that you want to maintain a positive attitude among the staff—but that you also want to solve the phone-etiquette problem—write a transmittal memo that will be distributed with the meeting agenda.

15 Writing Résumés and Cover Letters

Contents

The search for a job can be logically divided into six steps, each of which is covered in this chapter:

You have enviable advantages as you look for a job. You've prepared for the world of work with an education, training, and experience. You have desirable skills to offer — some directly applicable to a specific job, others more general that are applicable regardless of the job. (The writing skills acquired in this and other classes are also applicable across a broad range of occupations.) Your awards, honors, extracurricular activities, and life experiences all demonstrate these broadly applicable abilities, as does your willingness to take on challenging work — in an office, a laboratory, a hospital, a community clinic, an industrial site, a wilderness area, or other location.

Whether you are applying for your first professional job, changing jobs, or returning to the job market after an absence, you'll need to be systematic and persistent in your job search. Occasionally a desirable job comes your way without much effort, but the odds are against that happening. As well prepared as you may be, you need to plan your job search carefully. The detailed guidance in this chapter will increase your chances of translating your skills into a successful job search.

Before you begin your search for a job, do some serious thinking about your future. What would you most like to be doing now? two years from now? five years from now? Once you have established your goals, you can begin your job hunt with greater confidence because you'll have a better idea of what kind of position you are looking for and in what companies or other organizations you are most likely to find that position.

Determining the Best Job for You

◆ *Brainstorming is discussed on pages 8–10 in Chapter 1, Understanding the Workplace Writing Context: A Case Study.*

Begin by assessing your skills, interests, and abilities. Next, consider your career goals and values. Ask yourself questions like the following: What courses have I most enjoyed? Does helping others interest me? How important are career stability and a certain standard of living? Where do I want to live? Do I prefer working independently or collaboratively?[1]

Once you've reflected on and brainstormed about the type of work that's right for you, a number of sources can help you locate the job you want:

- Networking and recruiters
- Campus career services
- Strategic Web searches and job boards
- Job advertisements
- Trade and professional journal listings
- Employment agencies (private, temporary, and government)
- Internships
- Direct queries and informational interviews

Finding the job that's right for you may take many months. If you face unemployment during this period, consider working for a temporary employment agency, as described on page 520.

PROFESSIONALISM NOTE: Establish and Promote Your Personal Brand *Personal branding* is a concept that has increasingly gained in popularity. Businesses work to establish a positive reputation and image for high-quality products and the successful execution of their services. Personal branding is the idea of marketing a positive image or reputation of yourself. For example, if you are a consultant who sells your services, the consistently professional and successful execution of that service will be remembered as a core part of your brand. By learning how to influence other people's perceptions of your brand, you gain an important advantage over the competition. For additional information, see www.fastcompany.com/28905/brand-called-you.

Many components of the job search in this chapter can help you establish a strong personal brand. As you evaluate the opportunities of networking, social

---

[1]A good source for stimulating your thinking is the most recent edition of *What Color Is Your Parachute? A Practical Manual for Job-Hunters & Career Changers* by Richard Nelson Bolles, published by Ten Speed Press and updated annually. Online resources, such as those available at the "Career Planning" section of About.com and those offered by Monster.com, can also help you choose a career.

media, and internships, for example, keep in mind the core message you would like to send about yourself. Every interaction provides opportunities to enhance your visibility through a full suite of job-search materials. These materials may include a video résumé, business cards, a narrative biography, LinkedIn and other social-media profiles, a personal website, a portfolio, reference letters, and testimonials. As you prepare these materials, project a consistent and unified branding message across all media outlets.

Networking

Career development experts agree that many open positions are filled through networking. Networking is communicating with people who might provide useful advice about your intended career or connect you with potential employers. They may be people already working in your chosen field, contacts in professional organizations and volunteer groups, professors and former employers, family members, friends, or neighbors; any of them might direct you to exactly the job lead you need. Use your closest colleagues to expand your network of contacts. Consider that many open positions are filled through networking. Networking frequently takes place online too, through e-mail, discussion groups, and social-networking websites such as LinkedIn. See the section Strategic Web Searches below for more information.

Campus Career Services

Visiting your school's career center — and working with a counselor who understands your strengths and interests — is a great way to begin your job search. Career centers often hold job fairs and workshops on such topics as preparing your résumé for your particular field and doing well in an interview; they also offer other job-finding resources on their websites. Career counselors can help you in the brainstorming phase of your career selection as well as put you in touch with the best, most current resources— identifying where to begin your search and saving you time. Some even provide links to graduate-only job opportunities through an internal job board or e-mail list. In addition, recruiters from business, industry, and government often visit college job-placement offices to interview prospective employees. Recruiters also keep your school's career counselors aware of current employment needs, trends, and job openings.

Strategic Web Searches

The Web provides a wealth of sites that give advice about careers, job seeking, and résumé preparation; some sites make it possible to search job listings, post your résumé, and apply for positions confidentially. Social-networking sites are also growing in importance for job-search and career-networking opportunities; although many students regularly use social-networking sites for friendships and casual communication, don't overlook their value during the job search. The following sites include job-search and career-networking guidance as well as job listings.

- CareerOne Stop (www.careeronestop.org)
  Sponsored by the U.S. Department of Labor, America's Job Bank is a comprehensive listing of job postings categorized by state. It also contains such information as salary and demographic employment profiles for job seekers interested in relocating to another region.
- Monster (www.monster.com)
  One of the best-known sites for job seekers, Monster.com contains such information as career advice and job postings (including international listings). Specialized pages cater to the interests of occupational groups. The site also posts articles on preparing résumés and cover letters as well as information about preparing for job interviews.
- CareerBuilder (www.careerbuilder.com)
  An increasingly popular site, CareerBuilder.com posts job openings by job categories, company, and city and state location. The site also includes an Advice and Resources section covering a broad range of job-search information: personal branding, networking, negotiation, résumés, interviewing, and more. The site also highlights the job postings of ten companies each week.
- CollegeGrad.com (www.collegegrad.com)
  CollegeGrad.com is a site for the entry-level job seeker. It has user-friendly design links to sections on résumés, cover letters, interviews, and negotiations; explains what to do when you get an offer; and posts an E-Zine for job hunters.
- Riley Guide: Employment Opportunities and Job Resources on the Internet (www.rileyguide.com)
  The Riley Guide contains introductions and annotated links to resources by career field, employer type, and location. It also has sections on résumé preparation and online recruiting.
- What Color Is Your Parachute? JobHuntersBible.com (www.jobhuntersbible.com)
  What Color Is Your Parachute? is a site for job seekers and career changers based on the best-selling book of the same name by Richard N. Bolles. It provides such resources as an interactive test for career counseling, tips for using the Internet, tips for preparing an effective résumé, and links to job postings and other useful sites.
- LinkedIn (www.linkedin.com)
  This site combines job-search and business networking opportunities for professionals. Site users can post a professional profile of accomplishments that can be accessed by potential employers, clients, and service providers. The profile forms the hub of a network of trusted contacts that, in turn, bring their own trusted connections so that profiles may be linked to hundreds of contacts with shared career interests and needs. LinkedIn also circulates job-opening announcements to members based on their professional profiles. Such social-networking sites allow users to expand their contact base considerably, perhaps connecting with colleagues or friends of friends in a chosen field of interest. The site also posts job listings and hosts blogs by members who wish to post information about their job-related experiences and accomplishments.

- Facebook (www.facebook.com)
  Perhaps the most popular social-networking platform, Facebook provides a convenient way to job network with people who already know you. Although Facebook was primarily designed to be a social-networking rather than a business-networking platform, many businesses host Facebook pages and those with job openings use their sites to recruit employees. Of course, you must search the sites of those firms of interest to you.

  Although many professionals use LinkedIn for its job-search opportunities, you could also create a Facebook page for professional networking separate from your social Facebook page. The page should include your professional profile with a summary of your work experience, an occupational status update, and a flattering head-shot photograph of yourself. Be sure to adjust the site's privacy settings to share your information solely with those of your choosing. (For additional guidance on establishing your online identity, see the Professionalism Note on personal branding on page 514.)

  You can also participate in Facebook Groups, a feature that allows users with similar career interests to connect. To find a group relevant to your job search, enter the appropriate keywords into the Facebook search box — "nursing groups," "accounting groups," "school security groups," and the like — and filter by result type: groups. Evaluate the search results for the groups that best fit your purposes, join them, and begin by posting an introduction that sketches your professional background. Be sure to note your interest in finding a job.

In addition to these resources, always visit the websites of companies you are interested in. Not only do they help you learn about the company's background and current activities, but most corporate websites also list job openings, provide instructions for applicants, and offer other information, such as descriptions of employee benefits. Knowing about the company allows you to tailor your job-application materials to that specific organization, as well as to prepare for an interview later. Many websites include an option that allows you to e-mail your cover letter and résumé directly to the appropriate department or person.

Also consider exploring Internet discussion groups and blogs that relate to your career interests. These sites can provide a useful way to keep up with the trends in your profession and with general employment conditions over time — and some also post job openings that may be appropriate for you. One resource for finding professional discussion groups is Google Groups, organized by subject and available at http://groups.google.com.

◆ *See also pages 168–172 in Chapter 6, Conducting Research for a Document.*

Finally, consider posting your résumé on your personal website, as shown in Figure 15–1. The site displays the author's résumé in HTML format with links to other relevant content, like a portfolio of his work. The site also includes a link to a PDF version of his résumé for ease of printing. Although posting your résumé on an employment database will undoubtedly attract more potential employers, and often be targeted for a specific job, including your résumé on your own site has benefits. For example, you might provide a link to your site in e-mail correspondence or provide your website's URL in an inquiry letter to a prospective employer. If you use a personal website, however, it should contain only material that would be of interest to prospective employers, such as examples of your work, awards, and other professional items.

◆ *Before you create your own website, see the introductory material on pages 578–583 in Appendix A, Writing in an Online Environment.*

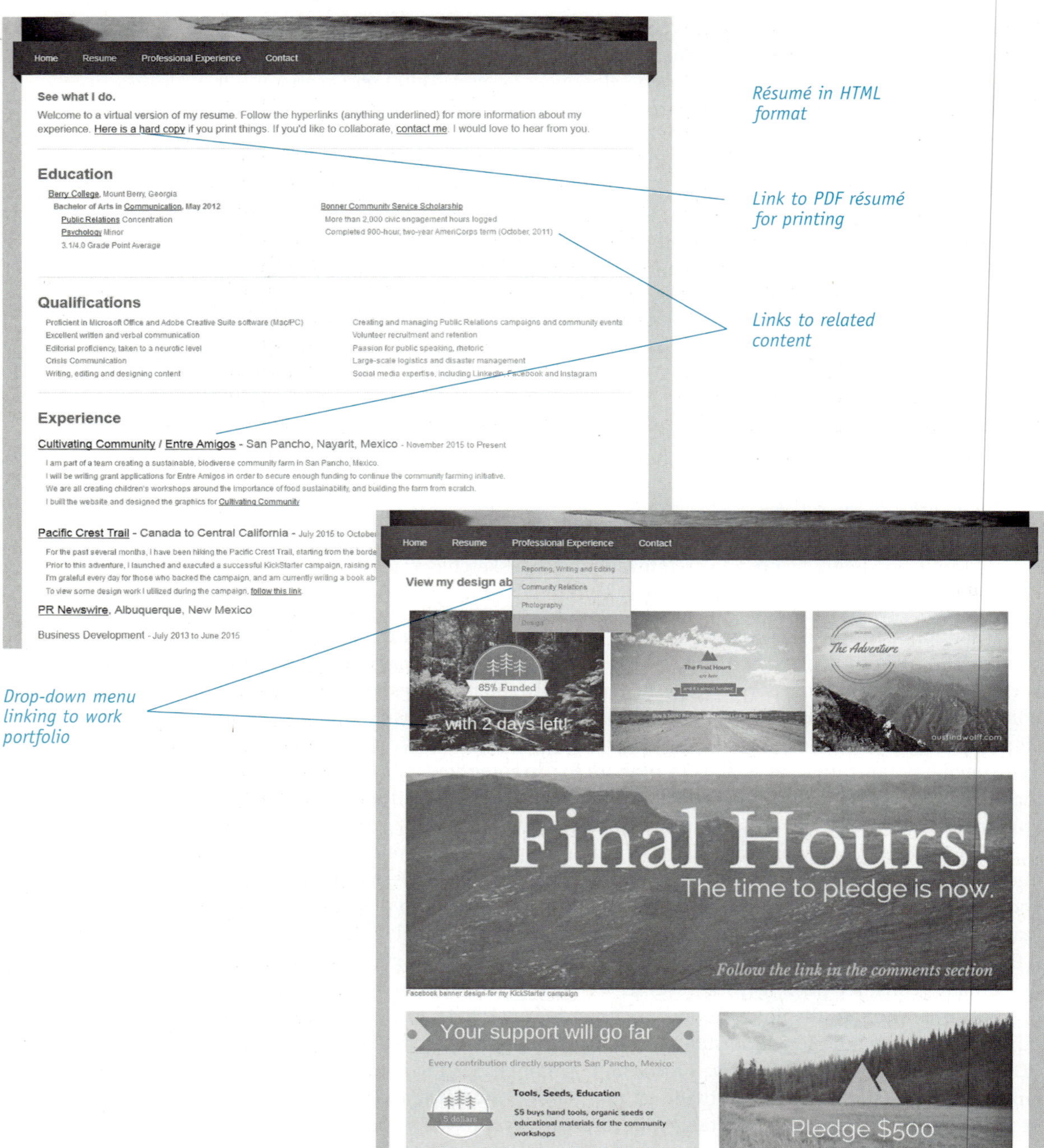

Figure 15–1 Résumé Posted on a Personal Website Courtesy of Austin Wolff.

Before posting your résumé on the Web, review the guidance on Web résumés on pages 536–538.

PROFESSIONALISM NOTE: Manage Your Online Presence Look yourself up as you prepare to do a job search. Be aware of how you present yourself in online public spaces. Employers and employment recruiters now routinely check the Web (including personal sites, blogs, and social-networking sites such as LinkedIn, Twitter, Facebook, and YouTube) for materials posted by and about job candidates and current employees. Remember that your Web presence is available for anybody to see, so maintain a professional demeanor when searching for a job. To see how your Facebook or LinkedIn page looks to others, use the "View As" feature (as opposed to your "edit" view) to see your profile from that perspective. Do not post any comments, photographs, videos, or links that a potential employer may find objectionable or inappropriate. Even seemingly harmless materials, such as pictures from a party or expressions of support for a particular sports team or political candidate, could compromise your chances of being considered for employment. Regularly update the privacy settings for sites you use to protect your content from unwanted access.

Advertisements

Many employers advertise job openings on their websites, job boards, social-media sites, and, in some cases, the classified sections of print and online newspapers. Occasionally, newspapers print special supplements that provide valuable information on résumé preparation, job fairs, and other facets of the job market. Check the Sunday editions or help-wanted Web pages of major newspapers for the widest selection of employment listings. Keep in mind that a position may be listed under various classifications. A clinical medical technologist seeking a job, for example, might find the specialty listed under "Medical Technologist," "Clinical Medical Technologist," "Laboratory Technologist," or simply grouped under "Medical Field" listings. Depending on a hospital's or a pathologist's needs, the listing could be even more specific, such as "Blood Bank Technologist" or "Hematology Technologist." Try to read or search all areas that may be pertinent to your interests.

Job alerts on job-aggregator sites, such as indeed.com and simplyhired.com, scour job boards, company websites, and newspaper listings for jobs that meet your criteria and send you e-mail notifications.

As you read the ads, take notes on such things as salary ranges, job locations, job duties and responsibilities, and even the terminology used in the ads to describe the work. A knowledge of the words and expressions used to describe a particular type of work can help when you prepare your résumé and letters of application. Using the appropriate terminology is especially important for résumés that you submit electronically. (See the section Digital Formats and Media Résumés on pages 535–538.)

Trade and Professional Journal Listings

See also pages 168–172 in Chapter 6, Conducting Research for a Document.

In many industries, trade and professional associations publish periodicals of interest to people working in specific occupations. Such periodicals (print and online) often contain job listings. If you were seeking a job in forestry, for example, you could check the job listings in the *Journal of Forestry*, published by the Society of American Foresters. To learn about the trade or professional associations for your occupation, consult resources on the web, such as Google's *Directory of Professional Organizations*, or online resources offered by your library or campus career office. You may also consult the following references at a library: *Encyclopedia of Associations*, *Encyclopedia of Business Information Sources*, and *National Directory of Employment Services*.

Private, Temporary, and Government Employment Agencies

Private employment agencies are organizations in business to help people find jobs — for a fee. Reputable agencies provide you with job leads, help you organize your job search, and supply information on companies doing the hiring.

Choose a private employment agency carefully, preferably through a personal recommendation. Some are very well established and reputable; others are not. Check with your local Better Business Bureau and with friends, acquaintances, or your school's career office before you sign an agreement with a private employment agency. Before signing a contract, be sure you understand who is paying the agency's fee. Often the employer pays the agency's fee; however, if you have to pay, make sure you know exactly how much. As with any written agreement, read the fine print carefully.

If you are interested in — but not certain about — a professional area, consider working in that area as a temporary or part-time employee. A temporary placement agency could match you with temporary paid employment in your field, lasting anywhere from a few days to six months or longer. Even as a short-term member of a support staff, you can gain valuable experience that can help you decide whether a particular profession is right for you. Temporary work in a professional area will also build your network of contacts while you continue your job search. Finally, temporary work may lead to a permanent position; if you prove to your manager and colleagues that you are serious about the industry and an asset to their department, you may be in a good position if a permanent job opens up.

Local, state, and federal government agencies also offer many employment services. Locate local government agencies in web or telephone directories under the name of your city, county, or state. For information on occupational trends of more than 250 occupations, see the most recent edition of the *Occupational Outlook Handbook*, published by the U.S. Department of Labor at www.bls.gov/oco. For information on jobs with the federal government, contact the U.S. Office of Personnel Management at www.opm.gov, or USAJOBS, the federal government's official jobs site at www.usajobs.gov.

Internships

As you evaluate job options, consider taking an internship. An entry-level position lasting anywhere from six weeks to an entire semester (and in some cases longer), an internship provides you with the opportunity to gain experience in a field of your choice. These positions offer you a variety of career benefits by allowing you to do the following:

- Try a position without making a permanent commitment.
- Explore a field to clarify your career goals while getting on-the-job experience.

- Develop skills and gain experience in a new field or industry.
- Evaluate a prospective employer or firm.
- Acquire a mentor in the workplace.
- Benefit from networking contacts for future job opportunities.
- Gain access to professional references.
- Be eligible for a job offer based on the employer's satisfaction with your work.

Almost all types of workplace organizations have internship programs: companies; law firms; nonprofit organizations (such as educational institutions, public interest groups, museums, foundations, political parties, think tanks, and research facilities); local, state, and federal government agencies; and more. The experience you gain will depend on the type of organization you join. Small organizations may expose you to a great variety of tasks; larger organizations may rotate participants through several departments or positions.

Ask If the Internship Is Paid

Although many firms offer salaries or stipends, some, like nonprofit organizations, may not. In many cases, the experience and the potential for course credit might make an internship valuable even if the salary is low.

Ask if the internship is paid or unpaid during your interview. If not, find out how the internship will benefit you based on U.S. Department of Labor (DOL) criteria for unpaid internships. Under recent DOL guidelines,[2] for-profit employers are required to pay interns at least the minimum wage unless the following six duties apply:

1. The internship, even though it includes actual operation of facilities of the employer, is similar to training that would be given in an educational environment.
2. The internship experience is for the benefit of the intern.
3. The intern does not displace regular employees, but works under close supervision of existing staff.
4. The employer that provides the training derives no immediate advantage from the activities of the intern; and on occasion its operations may actually be impeded.
5. The intern is not necessarily entitled to a job at the conclusion of the internship.
6. The employer and the intern understand that the intern is not entitled to wages for the time spent in the internship.

Locate Internship Opportunities

To locate internship opportunities, begin with your career office on campus, which often posts such opportunities on its website. If geographic location is important, the listings will yield the most positions in the vicinity of your campus. Otherwise, check the online job/

[2]See U.S. Department of Labor, Wage and Hour Division, at www.dol.gov/whd/regs/compliance /whdfs71.htm.

internship listings of local newspapers. Finally, go to www.internships.com. This site lists positions by type of employer (profit, nonprofit, government), specific employer (Microsoft, Disney), geographic region (city, state, county), ideal radius (20 miles), type of compensation (paid, unpaid), schedule (full-time, part-time), and more. The site also offers interview tips.

Keep a Record of Your Accomplishments

During your internship, keep a journal of tasks performed and job responsibilities that you can include in your résumé or portfolio. You may have created a brochure, designed or posted content to a website, created a poster, input data to a spreadsheet or database, used your computer skills to troubleshoot problems for the office, tracked and reported on industry trends, or organized a conference. Whatever the task, take note of it and, if it could be appropriate for your résumé or portfolio, ask your employer if you could use it for that purpose. These accomplishments are of interest to prospective employers.

Direct Queries and Informational Interviews

If you would like to work for a particular company, e-mail or write and ask whether it has any openings for people with your qualifications. If you are considering an internship, ask about those. Normally, you should send the query either to the director of human resources or to the department head; for a small company, however, you may write directly to the head of the company. Your e-mail or letter should present a general summary of your employment background or training. (See Writing an Effective Letter of Application on pages 551–557.)

In your request, ask if you can meet with someone for an informational interview and whether you may bring your résumé with you. Some organizations welcome the opportunity to talk with prospective employees, even when they have no immediate job openings. It's a way for them to assess fresh talent, promote their company, and expand their file of eligible prospects. You could also request an informational interview from one of your networking contacts. Although the interview is informal, dress appropriately and do some homework beforehand: What is the company's core business or mission and its size? Does it plan to expand? (Review the list of topics discussed in Doing Well in the Interview on pages 561–565.) Use the interview as an opportunity to practice your interview skills, to learn about accepted workplace standards, and to gain insight into the organization's expectations for prospective employees.

A related strategy is to prepare a job-proposal letter — a highly targeted cover letter that outlines why your skills and credentials would be valuable to the employer. Before writing the letter, research the employer to find out about any upcoming plans, goals, and even obstacles to the company's success. Your job-proposal letter can show that you understand the challenges that the employer is facing and you are part of the solution. Describe what you expect to accomplish, both short- and long-term, if given the opportunity.

Job-Search Record Keeping

As you pursue a job, keep an electronic or a paper record of your search to track your progress. Include copies of job ads, the dates they were published, the period during which applications will be accepted, copies of application letters, versions of your résumé (if you revised it for specific jobs), notes requesting interviews, and the names of important contacts. Keep the contact information for interviews and the dates they were held: who, what, when, and where. Also note salient facts about interviews, such as type of work, salary offers, promotion potential, benefits, and assistance with student loans. Use these records to compare job options and as a reminder for any follow-up questions.

Preparing an Effective Résumé

A résumé is a summary of your qualifications and your main tool for finding a job.[3] Generally limited to one page (or two if you have a great deal of experience), your résumé itemizes the qualifications that you can summarize in your application letter. The information in your résumé is key to helping employers decide whether to contact you for a personal interview. It can also serve as the source for specific questions asked during an interview.

Because résumés form the basis for a potential employer's first impression, make sure that yours is well organized, carefully designed, consistently formatted, easy to read, and free of errors. Keep the following guidelines in mind.

- Organize the information to highlight your goals, as suggested by the examples shown in this chapter.
- Experiment with the headings, fonts, and other design elements that make your résumé easy to scan for content.
- Be consistent. Use, for example, the same date formats (5/2016 or May 2016), punctuation, and spacing throughout.
- Proofread carefully, verify the accuracy of the information, and have at least one other person — preferably your instructor or someone in your professional field — review it.
- Use a high-quality printer and high-grade paper.
- For electronic résumés, use an accessible file format like a PDF.

◆ *See also pages 211–216 in Chapter 7, Designing Documents and Visuals, and pages 115–117 in Chapter 4, Revising a Document.*

Analyzing Your Background

In preparing to write your résumé, determine what kind of job you are seeking. Then ask yourself what information about you and your background would be most important to a prospective employer in the field you have chosen. On the basis of your answers, decide what details to include in your résumé and how you can most effectively present

[3]A detailed résumé for someone in academic and scientific fields is often called a *curriculum vitae* (also *vita* or *c.v.*). It may include education, publications, projects, grants, and awards, as well as a full work history. Outside the United States, the term "curriculum vitae" is often used as a synonym for the word *résumé*.

your qualifications. Brainstorm about yourself and your background, answering the following questions:

- What college or colleges did you attend? What degree(s) do you hold? What was your major field of study? What was your grade point average? What academic honors have you been awarded? What particular academic projects reflect your best work? Have you earned continuing education credits? attended relevant conferences or seminars?
- What internships or jobs have you held? What were your principal and secondary duties in each of them? When and for how long did you hold each job? Have you been promoted? Be sure to list any work-study, summer, or volunteer jobs as well.
- What skills have you developed that potential employers value and seek in ideal job candidates? What projects or accomplishments reflect your important contributions? What language and computer skills do you have?
- What other experiences and activities would be of value in the kind of job you are seeking? Consider extracurricular activities that have contributed to your learning experience; leadership, interpersonal, and communication skills you have developed; or any collaborative work you have performed.
- Have you served in the military? What were your principal duties? Were you promoted to a leadership position? Can you translate your military occupational specialty into comparable skills for the civilian workplace?

Use your answers as a starting point and let one question lead to another. Because you are brainstorming, don't censor your answers; record all of your experiences and accomplishments. As you organize your résumé, you can winnow items that are less relevant or outdated. Moreover, try to be specific, including quantifiable answers. *How many* projects did you handle per year? *How much* money did you raise? *What percentage* of new business did you bring in?

Returning Job Seekers

If you are returning to the workplace after an absence, most career experts say that it is important to acknowledge the gap in your career rather than try to hide it. That is particularly true if, for example, you are reentering the workforce because you have devoted a full-time period to care for children or dependent adults. Do not undervalue such work. Although unpaid, it often provides experience that develops important time-management, problem-solving, organizational, and interpersonal skills. Figure 15–2 illustrates how you might reflect such experiences in a résumé.

If you have done volunteer work during such a period, list that experience as well. Volunteer work often results in the same experience as full-time, paid work, a fact that your résumé should reflect, as in Figure 15–3. As with a paid job, be specific about what you accomplished in the position.

Primary Child-Care Provider, 2013 to 2016
Furnished full-time care to three preschool children at home. Instructed in beginning scholastic skills, time management, basics of nutrition, arts, and swimming. Organized activities, managed household, and served as neighborhood-watch captain.

Home Caregiver, 2012 to 2013
Provided 60 hours per week in-home care to Alzheimer's patient. Coordinated medical care, developed exercise programs, completed and processed complex medical forms, administered medications, organized budget, and managed home environment.

Highlights the organizational and time-management responsibilities of unpaid home care

Figure 15–2 Unpaid Experience Included in a Résumé

School Association Coordinator, 2013 to 2016
Managed special activities of the Briarwood Elementary School Parent-Teacher Association. Planned and coordinated meetings, scheduled events, and supervised fund-drive operations. Raised $70,000 toward refurbishing the school auditorium.

Emphasizes the coordination, organizational, and funds-management skills of volunteer tasks

Figure 15–3 Volunteer Experience Included in a Résumé

Organizing Your Résumé

A number of different organizational patterns can be used effectively. The following categories are typical—the one you choose should depend on your experience and goals, the employer's needs, and any standard practices in your profession.

Heading (name and contact information)
Job objective (also called Profile) (optional)
Qualifications summary (Professional Profile, Key Attributes)
Education (Academic and Professional Certifications)
Employment experience (Career History and Chronology)
Related skills and abilities (Professional Affiliations, Volunteer Work, Networking Assets)
Honors and activities (Awards, Recognition, Notable Contributions, Publications, Promotions)
References
Portfolio (optional)

Whether you place education or employment experience first depends on the job you are seeking and which credentials would strengthen your résumé more. If you are a recent graduate without much work experience, you would list education first. If you have years of job experience, including jobs directly related to the kind of position you are seeking, you would list employment experience first. In your education and employment sections, list the most recent experience first, the next most recent experience second, and so on. This is known as reverse chronological order.

The Heading

At the top of your résumé, include your name, telephone number (home or cell), e-mail address, and links to social-media sites where you have a professional presence. Make sure that your name stands out on the page. A centered heading usually works best (Figure 15–4). If you are in transition and have both a school address and a permanent home address, place your school address on the left side of the page and your permanent home address on the right side of the page. Place both underneath your name, as shown in Figure 15–5. You can omit street addresses but include city, state, and zip codes.

PROFESSIONALISM NOTE: Use Appropriate E-mail Addresses for Employment Correspondence Do not use an unprofessional e-mail address in employment correspondence (beerlover@xxx.com). E-mail addresses based on your last name work best.

CONSUELA B. SANDOVAL
Somerville, MA 02144
(617) 635-1552
cbsand@cpu.fairview.edu
LinkedIn.com/in/cbsandoval

Figure 15–4 Centered Résumé Heading

VIKRAM L. MATHUR

SCHOOL	HOME (AFTER JUNE 2013)
Bloomington, IN 47405	Nashville, TN 37204
(812) 652-4781	(615) 343-0406
mathur2@iu.edu	vlmathur@yahoo.com

Figure 15–5 Résumé Heading for a Student with Two Addresses

Job Objective vs. Job Title and Tagline

Job objectives versus job titles and taglines introduce the material in a résumé and help the reader quickly understand your goal. The differences between these two are slight but should be considered when organizing your résumé. A tagline is a brief quotation that summarizes your vision in seeking a particular employment opportunity. Although your personal objective may not provoke interest in the reviewer or meet the needs of a potential employer, a job title, tagline, or combination of both will immediately reveal your goal. Weigh the benefits of using a job title and tagline versus stating your objective. The following examples illustrate the differences:

Sample Objective Statements

- A full-time computer-science position aimed at solving online computer vulnerabilities.
- A position that meets the concerns of women, such as family planning, career counseling, or crisis management.
- A programming internship position requiring software-development and software-debugging skills.

Sample Job-Title and Tagline Combinations

- FINANCIAL SERVICES / BANKING PROFESSIONAL
  "Ensuring the Financial Success of Customers, Clients, and Communities"
- MECHANICAL ENGINEER
  "Developing Innovative, Efficient, Environmentally Friendly Energy Solutions"
- FIREFIGHTER / EMT
  "Prevention, Mitigation, Response" or "Protecting Life, Property, and the Environment"

Keep in mind that the objective or tagline section is optional. Although some potential employers prefer to see a clear employment objective in résumés, many employment specialists counsel against them because they can have the unintended consequence of limiting your options. If you are responding to a specific advertisement or job posting, stating the objective or creating a tagline can be useful in showing employers that your skills and experiences can meet their needs; however, if you are sending out a résumé blindly, consider leaving this feature off.

PROFESSIONALISM NOTE: Use an Appropriate Job Objective If you include an objective on your résumé, avoid using clichés, such as "seeking a challenging opportunity with potential for advancement" and other overused statements.

Qualifications Summary

Include a brief summary of your qualifications to persuade hiring managers to select you for an interview. Sometimes called a *professional profile, summary statement,* or *career summary,* a qualifications summary can include skills, achievements, experience, or personal qualities that make you especially well suited to a position. You can simply call this section "Qualifications." To capture a prospective employer's attention, you may use a headline, such as "Award-Winning Financial Analyst," as shown in Figure 15–16 on page 546.

Education

List the college(s) you have attended, the degrees you received and the dates you received them, your major field(s) of study, and any academic honors you have earned (Figure 15-6). Include your grade point average only if it is 3.0 or higher — or include your average in your major if that is more impressive. Omit your GPA if you earned your degree long ago and are focusing on experience rather than education. List courses or independent work only if they are relevant to the job you seek. Mention your high school only if you want to call attention to special high school achievements, awards, projects, programs, internships, or study abroad.

Employment Experience

The two most common ways to organize employment experience are in reverse chronological order and by category of professional experience, although both approaches may be combined if the job history warrants it. Using reverse chronological order, begin with your most-recent job and work backward under a single major heading

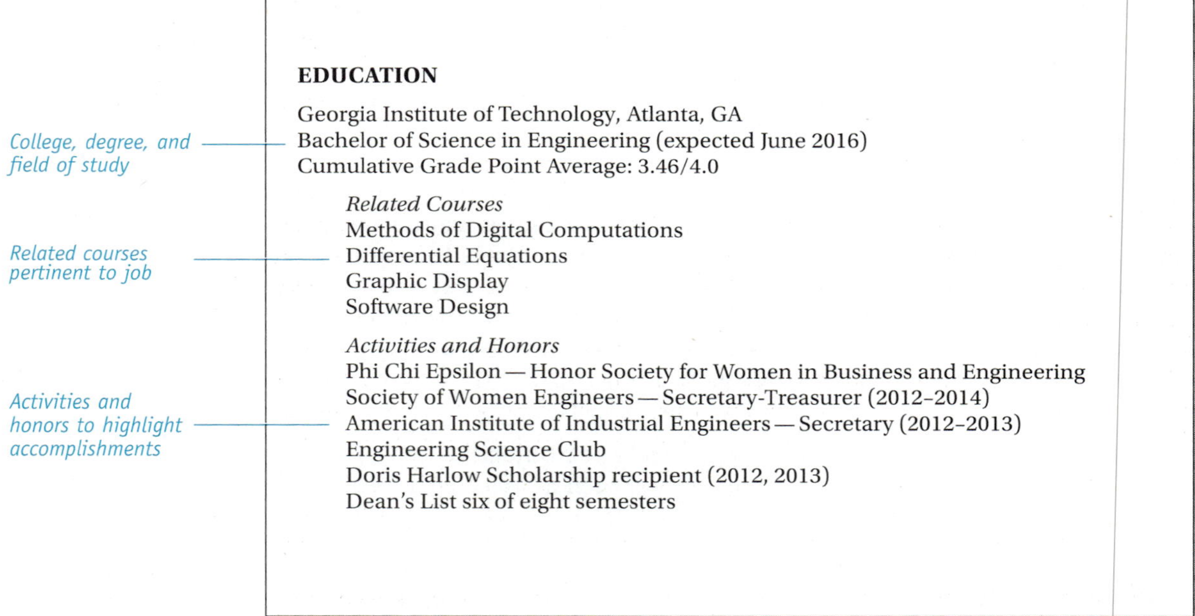

EDUCATION

Georgia Institute of Technology, Atlanta, GA
Bachelor of Science in Engineering (expected June 2016)
Cumulative Grade Point Average: 3.46/4.0

Related Courses
Methods of Digital Computations
Differential Equations
Graphic Display
Software Design

Activities and Honors
Phi Chi Epsilon — Honor Society for Women in Business and Engineering
Society of Women Engineers — Secretary-Treasurer (2012–2014)
American Institute of Industrial Engineers — Secretary (2012–2013)
Engineering Science Club
Doris Harlow Scholarship recipient (2012, 2013)
Dean's List six of eight semesters

Figure 15–6 Education Section of a Résumé

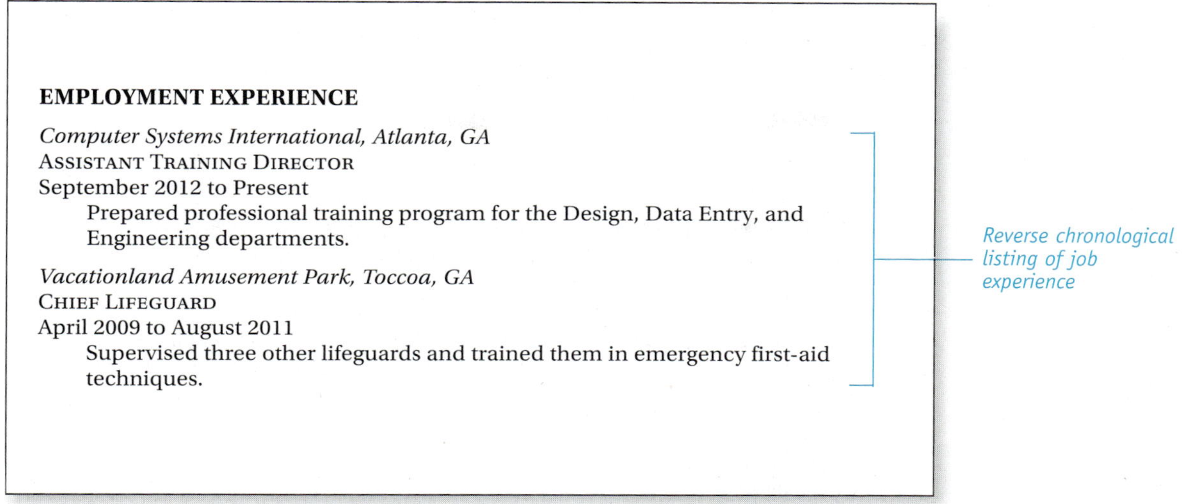
EMPLOYMENT EXPERIENCE

Computer Systems International, Atlanta, GA
ASSISTANT TRAINING DIRECTOR
September 2012 to Present
Prepared professional training program for the Design, Data Entry, and Engineering departments.

Vacationland Amusement Park, Toccoa, GA
CHIEF LIFEGUARD
April 2009 to August 2011
Supervised three other lifeguards and trained them in emergency first-aid techniques.

Figure 15–7 Employment Experience Organized in Reverse Chronological Order

called "Employment Experience," "Employment," "Professional Experience," or the like (Figure 15–7). You could, alternatively, organize your experience functionally by clustering similar types of jobs or experience into one or several sections with specific headings such as "Management Experience," "Major Accomplishments," or "Summary of Qualifications" (Figure 15–8).

One type of arrangement might be more persuasive than the other, depending on the situation. For example, if you are applying for an accounting job but have a limited background in accounting, you would probably do best to list past and present jobs in chronological order, from most to least recent. If you are applying for a supervisory position and have had three supervisory jobs in addition to two nonsupervisory positions, you might choose to create a single section called "Supervisory Experience" and list only your three supervisory jobs. Or, you could create two sections — "Supervisory Experience" and "Other Experience" — and include the three supervisory jobs in the first section and your nonsupervisory jobs in the second section.

The functional résumé groups work experience by types of workplace activities or skills rather than by jobs in chronological order. Organization by function is useful for applicants who want to stress certain skills important to the prospective employer or industry or who have been employed at only one job and want to demonstrate the diversity of their experience in that position. Functional arrangement is also useful if you are changing careers and want to highlight transferable skills. However, many employers are suspicious of functional résumés because they can be used to hide a questionable work history, such as excessive job hopping or extended gaps in employment. Functional elements can be combined with a chronological arrangement by using a qualifications summary or skills category, as shown in Figure 15–8.

Opens with qualifications and career accomplishments

Uses active verbs to describe experiences

Lists job history and volunteer work following qualifications and accomplishments

SUMMARY OF QUALIFICATIONS

SPANISH-LANGUAGE SKILLS
- Fluent speaking, reading, and writing in Spanish (native language is English)
- Judged highly proficient in medical vocabulary and interpreting by Harvard Pilgrim Health Care
- Write and report in Spanish for *Siglo 21*, a newspaper based in Lawrence, MA
- Translate newspaper articles from English to Spanish

INTERPERSONAL SKILLS
- Conduct culturally appropriate bilingual interviews under stressful conditions
- Trained to remain calm and focused when talking to people at the scene of fires, crimes, and in the wake of family tragedies
- Bicultural as well as bilingual

COMMUNICATION SKILLS
- Relay speakers' words and ideas to others with accuracy and speed
- Write press releases for the largest immigrant advocacy group in Massachusetts

EMPLOYMENT HISTORY

Freelance reporter and copy editor, Boston, MA	2013–present
Reporter, *News & Record*, Greensboro, NC	2011–2013
Reporter, *Gaston Gazette*, Gastonia, NC	2009–2011
Reporter, *Press & Standard*, Walterboro, SC	2007–2009

VOLUNTEER WORK

Writer, Massachusetts Immigrant and Refugee Advocacy Coalition, Boston, MA	2013–present
Interpreter, blood drives and United Way campaigns, Greensboro, NC	2011–2013
Intake worker, El Vínculo Hispano, Siler City, NC	2009–2011
English as a Second Language teacher, Walterboro, SC	2010–2012

Figure 15–8 Employment Experience Organized Functionally

ETHICS NOTE: Keep It Truthful: Employers Reject Candidates with Inaccurate or Embellished Résumés Be truthful. The consequences of giving false information in your résumé could result in your employment being terminated long after you were hired. The truthfulness of your résumé reflects not only your personal ethics but also the integrity with which you would represent an employer. Keep in mind that many employers use outside agencies to check references and experience; they automatically reject applicants with inaccuracies or embellished résumés.

In general, follow these conventions when working on the "Experience" section of your résumé. Use the brainstorming list you created earlier, deciding which work experiences and skills are relevant for the specific job or organization to which you are applying.

- Include jobs or internships when they relate directly to the position you are seeking. Although some applicants omit internships and temporary or part-time jobs, including them can make a résumé more accurate and impressive if they have helped you develop specific, relevant skills.
- Include volunteer experiences, such as taking on a leadership position in a college organization or directing a community-service project, if they demonstrate skills valued by potential employers. Such skills might include supervisory roles, entrepreneurial positions, or fund-raising experience.
- List military service as a job; give the dates served, the duty specialty, and the rank at discharge. Describe military duties if they relate to the job you are seeking by translating military terminology into language understandable to hiring managers.
- For each job or experience, list both the job title and company name. Begin consistently with either the job or the company, depending on which will likely be more impressive to potential employers.
- Under each job or experience, provide a concise description of your primary and secondary duties. If a job is not directly relevant, provide only a job title and a brief description of duties that helped you develop skills valued in the position you are seeking. For example, if you were a lifeguard now seeking an entry-level management position, focus on supervisory experience or even experience in averting disaster to highlight your management, decision-making, and crisis-control skills.
- Use action verbs (for example, "managed" rather than "as the manager") and state ideas succinctly, as shown in Figure 15–8 on page 530. Even though the résumé is about you, do not use "I" (for example, instead of "I was promoted to Section Leader," use "Promoted to Section Leader").
- Focus as much as possible on your achievements in your work history. Employers want to hire doers and achievers. Note the difference between the résumé in Figure 15–9, that mixes accomplishments with routine duties, and the résumé in Figure 15–9 on page 533, that was revised to better focus on high-order job responsibilities and tangible accomplishments. The first version, showing comments from a colleague's review, overwhelms what the employee achieved with explanations of how the work was done. Save these details for your job interviews. A busy employer scanning résumés will grasp the essentials of the revised résumé much more quickly than those in the original version.

Related Skills and Abilities

Employers are interested in hiring applicants with a variety of skills or the ability to learn new ones fairly quickly. Depending on the position, you might list items such as fluency in a foreign language; writing and editing abilities; specialized technical knowledge;

[Reviewer Comments]

PROFESSIONAL PLANNING EXPERIENCE

Planner, XYZ County Regional Planning Commission, State 2013–Present

- ~~As program manager~~ Secured and administered a $1 million U.S. EPA Brownfield Coalition assessment Grant. ~~This effort included securing access agreements, using Excel to monitor grant progress, creating a project financial tracking system, completing reporting documents, invoice reviews, editing of reports, consultant supervision as well as working with assigned USEPA grant project officer.~~ ~~This~~The grant resulted in:
  - Approximately 40 environmental reports leveraged to secure some $1.6 million in state assessment and cleanup funds as well as $5 million in private redevelopment monies.
  - 100 local jobs created at brownfield sites, as well as an estimated 100 to follow. ~~created at Brownfield sites~~.
  - An XYZ County Brownfield Recognition Award for leadership and commitment from U.S. EPA Region 5 in 2015.
- ~~Lead the grant writing effort in obtaining~~Obtained $715,000 from the state Housing Finance Agency to fund demolitions of blighted properties in XYZ County.
- ~~This undertaking included playing~~Played an instrumental role in establishing the XYZ County **land bank**, ~~writing and editing grant sections,~~ using **ArcGIS 10x** to create maps of the affected properties., ~~as well as coordinating the work of others in the application process~~.
- Co-managed ~~with a consultant~~ a grant application that secured approximately $300,000 in Clean State grant funding for soil and water sampling at a brownfield site. ~~Wrote resolutions of support for this application that were adopted by XYZ county, a township and a city. Coordinated the grant application public notice and hearing~~. Researched potential property re-use along with other support documentation.
- Developed XYZ County's first Land Use Plan. ~~Gathering data and u~~Used **ArcGIS 10x** to create 28 maps covering such topics as steep slopes, floodplains, road networks, pipelines, and waterlines. ~~Did~~ Conducted extensive research to inventory the county's physical plant assets~~:~~ and ~~Made certain key planning concepts such as development constraints were incorporated into the final document. C~~coordinated Land Use committee public meetings~~: and supervised the county's land use consultant. by reviewing and editing land use plan chapters. Facilitated land use plan adoption by county commissioners.~~
- ~~Has~~ Oversee day-to-day responsibility for the county's floodplain regulations. ~~This process includes working with the public to a~~Advise ~~them~~ the public on floodplain issues as well as review~~ing~~ **FEMA FIRM** maps, site plans, other project permits for compliance with county regulations. Assist~~ed~~ the state **Department of Transportation** and the state EPA with floodplain permitting in the county. Coordinate amending the penalty portion of the county's floodplain regulations ~~Work~~ with the state **Department of Natural Resources** and the XYZ County commissioners. ~~to amend the penalty portion of the county's floodplain regulations.~~
- Assist with **CDBG** grant applications to create ~~This involves creating~~ community and area maps using **ArcGIS 10x** and write ~~as well as writing~~ project net effect statements that encompass census and other data in support of the county CDBG applications.
- ~~Has given some~~ Routinely make ~~40~~ **public presentations** to members of XYZ County Regional Planning Commission and . ~~As a part of this process~~ produce a monthly planner's report detailing progress on each assigned project.

Important to spell out acronyms

Need to use imperative voice

Too many overlapping details

Comment [ABC1]: Spell out EPA.

Comment [ABC2]: Focus on accomplishments and key responsibilities rather than on the day-to-day means by which they were achieved.

Comment [ABC3]: Use consistent imperative voice to begin each bullet.

Comment [ABC4]: Make this a new accomplishment.

Comment [ABC5]: These are routine grant-proposal tasks but the property re-use effort is central to the grant's success, so retain it.

Comment [ABC6]: Some detail OK here to support plan implementation.

Comment [ABC7]: Spell out these acronyms.

Comment [ABC8]: Spell out CDBG.

Figure 15–9 Résumé That Obscures Accomplishments with Description of Routine Duties

[Revised]

PROFESSIONAL PLANNING EXPERIENCE

Planner, XYZ County Regional Planning Commission, State **2013–Present**

- Secured and administered a $1 million U.S. Environmental Protection Agency (EPA) Brownfield Coalition Assessment Grant. The grant resulted in:
    - Approximately 40 environmental reports leveraged to secure some $1.6 million in state assessment and cleanup funds as well as $5 million in private redevelopment monies.
    - Creation of 100 local jobs at brownfield sites, as well as an estimated 100 to follow.
    - A County Brownfield Recognition Award for leadership and commitment from U.S. EPA, Region 5 in 2015.
- Obtained $715,000 from the state Housing Finance Agency to fund demolitions of blighted properties in XYZ County.
- Played an instrumental role in establishing the XYZ County land bank, using ArcGIS 10x to create maps of the affected properties.
- Co-managed a grant application that secured approximately $300,000 in Clean State grant funding for soil and water sampling at a brownfield site. Researched potential property re-use along with other support documentation.
- Developed XYZ County's first Land Use Plan. Used ArcGIS 10x to create 28 maps covering such topics as steep slopes, floodplains, road networks, pipelines, and waterlines. Conducted extensive research to inventory the county's physical plant assets and coordinated Land Use committee public meetings.
- Oversee day-to-day responsibility for the county's floodplain regulations. Advise the public on floodplain issues as well as review of Federal Emergency Management Agency (FEMA) Flood Insurance Rate maps, site plans, other project permits for compliance with county regulations. Assist the state Department of Transportation and the state EPA with floodplain permitting in the county. Coordinate amending the penalty portion of the county's floodplain regulations with the state Department of Natural Resources and the XYZ County commissioners.
- Assist with Community Development Block Grant (CDBG) applications to create community and area maps using ArcGIS 10x and write project net effect statements that encompass census and other data in support of the county CDBG applications.
- Routinely make public presentations to members of XYZ County Regional Planning Commission and produce a monthly planner's report detailing progress on each assigned project.

Concise descriptions better highlight accomplishments:

- *money saved*
- *jobs created*
- *awards and recognition*
- *leadership*

Figure 15–9 Professional Experience Draft Revised to Highlight Achievements and Responsibilities *(continued)*

Announces student's official job title

Identifies supervisory roles

Uses active verbs

Emphasizes student's achievements and quantifies her contributions to the organization

Vague, Lackluster Résumé

Student Volunteer Council

I helped sign up new members for community volunteer projects.

Baker Library

I worked in the archives.

Concise, Active Résumé

Vice president, Student Volunteer Council

Organized recruitment drive for more than 30 different community-service projects; raised campuswide participation by 25%.

Research fellow, Baker Library

Catalogued and photographed new collection of historical documents for university archives.

Figure 15–10 Vague Job Description Revised for Clarity

equipment or mechanical training; or computer skills, including knowledge of specific languages, software, and hardware, as well as websites created. Also include relevant online social-networking activities (hobby, school club, volunteer work), such as blogs, podcasts, and Facebook or LinkedIn profiles; these activities can highlight your technical and writing skills as well as your interests; just be sure they portray you in a professional light.

Honors and Activities

List honors and unique activities near the end of your résumé. Include student or community activities, professional or club memberships, awards received, and works published. Be selective; do not duplicate information given in other categories, and include only information that supports your employment objective. Depending on which skills or activities you want to emphasize, use a heading such as "Activities," "Honors," "Professional Affiliations," or "Publications and Memberships."

References

Avoid listing references unless that is standard practice in your profession or your résumé is sparse. Instead, use the phrase "References available upon request" to signal the end of a long résumé, or write "Available upon request" after the heading "References" as a design element to balance a page. In any case, you should have a separate list of references to give to prospective employers after interviews; your list should include the main heading "References for [your name]" and the names, affiliations, titles, and contact information for each of your references. Do not give anyone as a reference without first obtaining his or her permission.

Portfolios

The résumé may also state that a "Portfolio is available upon request." A portfolio is a collection of samples in a binder or at a website of your most impressive work and accomplishments. Portfolios have traditionally been used by artists and writers to illustrate their work. However, a portfolio also may provide samples of your most impressive written work (reports, proposals, presentations), copies of letters of praise, certificates that attest to special abilities, newspaper clippings, or a link to a website or other multimedia project you created, and other items that visually display your accomplishments and potential contributions to a prospective employer. If you create a Web résumé, you can post your portfolio with it. For an interview, it is best to bring a portfolio containing ten items or fewer.

PROFESSIONALISM NOTE: Avoid Listing Salary Requirement in a Résumé
Avoid listing the salary you desire in your résumé. On the one hand, you may price yourself out of a job you want if the salary you list is higher than a potential employer is willing to pay. On the other hand, if you list a low salary, you may not get the best possible offer. (See Salary Negotiations on page 565.)

Digital Formats and Media Résumés

Consider adapting your résumé for multiple media and digital formats. Increasingly, employers request electronic résumés. They can be posted on a website or submitted through e-mail to be included in an organization's database of job candidates. Remain current with the forms and protocols that employers prefer by reviewing popular job-search sites, such as Career Builder at www.careerbuilder.com and Monster.com at www.monster.com. As you apply for jobs electronically, be prepared to fill out online versions of your résumé many times by cutting and pasting details into forms and fields on various websites.

E-mail–Attached Résumés

An employer may request or you may prefer to submit a résumé as an e-mail attachment to be printed out by the employer. If a file format preference is not stated, send the résumé in Adobe PDF or Microsoft Word format. The PDF file format will preserve the fonts, images, graphics, and layout of your résumé. In either case, your e-mail message can serve as your application letter.

See also Digital Tip: Using PDF Files on page 590 in Appendix A.

Applicant Tracking System Résumés

When you submit your résumé via e-mail or to an employer's website, it may be added to an electronic applicant tracking system (ATS). These systems parse, store, manage, and rank résumés based on criteria specified by the hiring manager. Although these systems vary, some guidelines are standardized:

- Avoid fancy graphics and icons because they will be unreadable to the ATS.
- Choose common titles for headers, such as "Professional Experience" and "Education."
- Incorporate keywords that are relevant to your career field in descriptions, but avoid a separate "Keyword" section that wastes valuable space.
- Use a consistent format in the placement of employer names and job titles.

Plain-Text Résumés

Some employers request ASCII[4] or plain-text résumés via e-mail, which they can add directly to their résumé database without scanning. ASCII résumés also allow employers to read the file regardless of the type of software they are using. You can copy and paste such a résumé directly into the body of the e-mail message. To create an ASCII résumé, look for an option to "Save as" plain text in your word-processing program. After you save it as text file with a .txt extension, reopen the file in a text editor (such as Notepad for Windows-based computers or TextEdit for Macs) and clean up the file as needed. For more information, visit resumepower.com/ascii-resumes.html.

Scannable Résumés

A scannable résumé format is a paper document that you mail to an employer. After it is received, the résumé is scanned into an automated program and downloaded into the company's searchable database. For scanned résumés, avoid decorative, uncommon, or otherwise fancy typefaces; use simple font styles (a sans serif font such as Arial) and sizes for text and headings between 10 and 14 points. Use white space generously because scanners use it to recognize where one topic has ended and another has begun. Although a paper résumé is best kept to one page, you need not limit an electronic résumé to a single page. However, keep the résumé as simple, clear, and concise as possible. Use white or off-white paper and do not fold it for mailing because a scanner can misread a folded line.

Web Résumés

Another option is to post your résumé on your own website, as shown in Figure 15–1. Doing so makes it available to potential employers at their convenience — then you need only send potential employers your Web address. A Web résumé can also be updated as often as necessary without the need to mail updates to everyone. Perhaps the chief advantage of a Web résumé is that it allows you to create an electronic portfolio linked to samples of your work — reports, articles, graphics projects, presentations, and the like. An interactive résumé with links to the portfolio will work only if you create an HTML (hypertext markup language) version of your work. If you wish to post a résumé and portfolio without hyperlinks, you could use a plain-text version or PDF image file instead. If you plan to post your résumé on your own website, keep the following points in mind:

- Follow the general advice for writing for the Web, outlined in Appendix A, Writing in an Online Environment.
- Just below your name, provide a series of internal links to such important categories as "Experience" and "Education" and external links to the social-media sites where you have a professional presence, such as LinkedIn.

---

[4]ASCII (pronounced as´-kēy) is an acronym for American Standard Code for Information Interchange and is the most basic format for transferring files between different programs. In word-processing terms, it can be thought of as unformatted text.

- Consider building a multipage site for displaying a work portfolio, publications, reference letters, and the like.
- To protect your privacy, include an e-mail link ("mailto") at the top of the résumé rather than your home address and phone number.
- View your résumé on several browsers to see how it looks.
- Post copies of your résumé in several file formats so that employers can select the best format for their needs.

DESIGNING YOUR DOCUMENT

Formatting the Résumé

Make your first impression count. To do so, use the following guidelines for designing an easy-to-read résumé — online and in print — that will highlight your qualifications and get you noticed.

At-a-Glance Look

- Ensure that each section is balanced proportionally on the page with the other sections.
- In addition to 1-inch margins, use ample white space consistently to prevent a cluttered look:
  - Separate each section with sufficient white space so that it stands out from the elements above and below it.
  - Single-space within sections.
  - Double-space or, if space permits, triple-space between sections.
  - Indent the second line within a section when it continues the previous line.

Font Size and Design

- Use no more than two font styles.
- Select fonts to identify different levels of information.
- Use sans serif fonts for headings and serif fonts for text.
- Use **boldface**, *italics*, underlining, and ALL CAPITALS sparingly for emphasis; do not overdesign.
- Use font sizes to differentiate headings from text: 10 to 13 points for text and 14 to 20 points for headings.
- Use bullets to signal a new topic within each section and to emphasize individual items, such as each job responsibility, accomplishment, college course, or internship position.
- Be consistent and uniform throughout:
  - Use fonts and design features consistently — bullets, indentions, text boxes, capital and lowercase letters, and other elements.
  - Show headings, date formats, punctuation, and spacing consistently, as well.
- Consider alternative methods of creating the résumé:
  - Use a résumé template in your word-processing package.
  - Have a professional graphic designer create your résumé.

DIGITAL TIP: Creating a Résumé Using a Template

Many word-processing programs offer templates for a variety of résumé styles.

- Select from a variety of templates to organize and present the content:
  - Entry level
  - Chronological
  - Functional
- Adapt the template to your needs or preferences by applying an array of design features:
  - Add lines (rules) across the page.
  - Change fonts.
  - Standardize headings.
- Spell-check before printing. Proofread carefully.
- Be flexible and change the template based on your needs, such as your professional branding profile, and the discussion in this book. Many employers have seen the templates available in most word-processing programs, so consider using such a template as a starting point and adapt it to suit your professional branding profile.

Keep in mind that using a personal website for job searches is less effective than using commercial services that attract recruiters with their large databases of candidates.

PROFESSIONALISM NOTE: Use Suitable Content and Style in Résumés for U.S. Government Positions When applying for a position with the U.S. government, make sure your résumé's content and style are suitable for a federal application. The format for your federal résumé will vary depending on the specific agency you are targeting, but your résumé must address how your qualifications match the requirements outlined in the vacancy announcement. Kathryn Troutman provides excellent resources for preparing federal résumés and hosts a companion blog on federal résumé writing (http://www.resume-place.com/fedresblog/federal-resume-writing/).

Sample Résumés

The sample résumés in this section are provided to stimulate your thinking about how to tailor your résumé to your own job search. Before you design and write your résumé, look at as many samples as possible, and then organize and format your own to best suit your previous experience and your professional goals and to make the most persuasive case to your target employers.

- Figure 15–11 presents a conventional résumé in which a recent college graduate is seeking an entry-level position. Notice that education is listed first.
- Figure 15–12 on page 541 shows a résumé with a variation in the design and placement of conventional headings to highlight professional credentials.
- Figure 15–13 on page 542 depicts a résumé that incorporates a tagline and focuses on the applicant's management experience. A tagline is a short quotation summarizing your reasons for seeking a certain position. (Taglines are described in more detail on page 527.)
- Figure 15–14 on page 544 reflects the résumé of a candidate seeking to switch career fields. It uses a job title and immediately states a goal, followed by credentials.
- Figure 15–15 on page 545 focuses on how the applicant advanced and was promoted within a single company.
- Figure 15–16 on page 546 illustrates how an applicant can organize a résumé by combining functional and chronological elements.

During your job search, apply for as many positions as possible that are acceptable to you and for which you qualify. However, be careful to adapt your core résumé to the specific requirements of each job listing before you submit it. Note how the applicant, Joshua Goodman, tailors the two résumés in Figures 15–17 and 15–18 on pages 549–550 in response to two different job listings for a graphic designer. Both résumés are formatted in an unconventional style to highlight his graphic-design skills. The ABC Services listing (Figure 15–19 on page 551) describes a candidate who can use graphics and desktop-publishing software to produce printed products ("ads, brochures, signs, flyers, etc."). Joshua's résumé (Figure 15–18 on page 550) focuses on his experience with this work under Graphic-Design Experience. Note that this focus for the listing in Figure 15–20 on page 551 gives equal coverage to his graphic- and Web-design capabilities in response to the XYZ Group's listing for someone with both skills. He specifically inserts a new section (Web-Design Experience) for this purpose. And to highlight the Web-design experience, he changes the reverse chronological order of the résumé in Figure 15–17 on page 549. If he's interviewed by ABC Services and asked about Web design, he can discuss his background then.

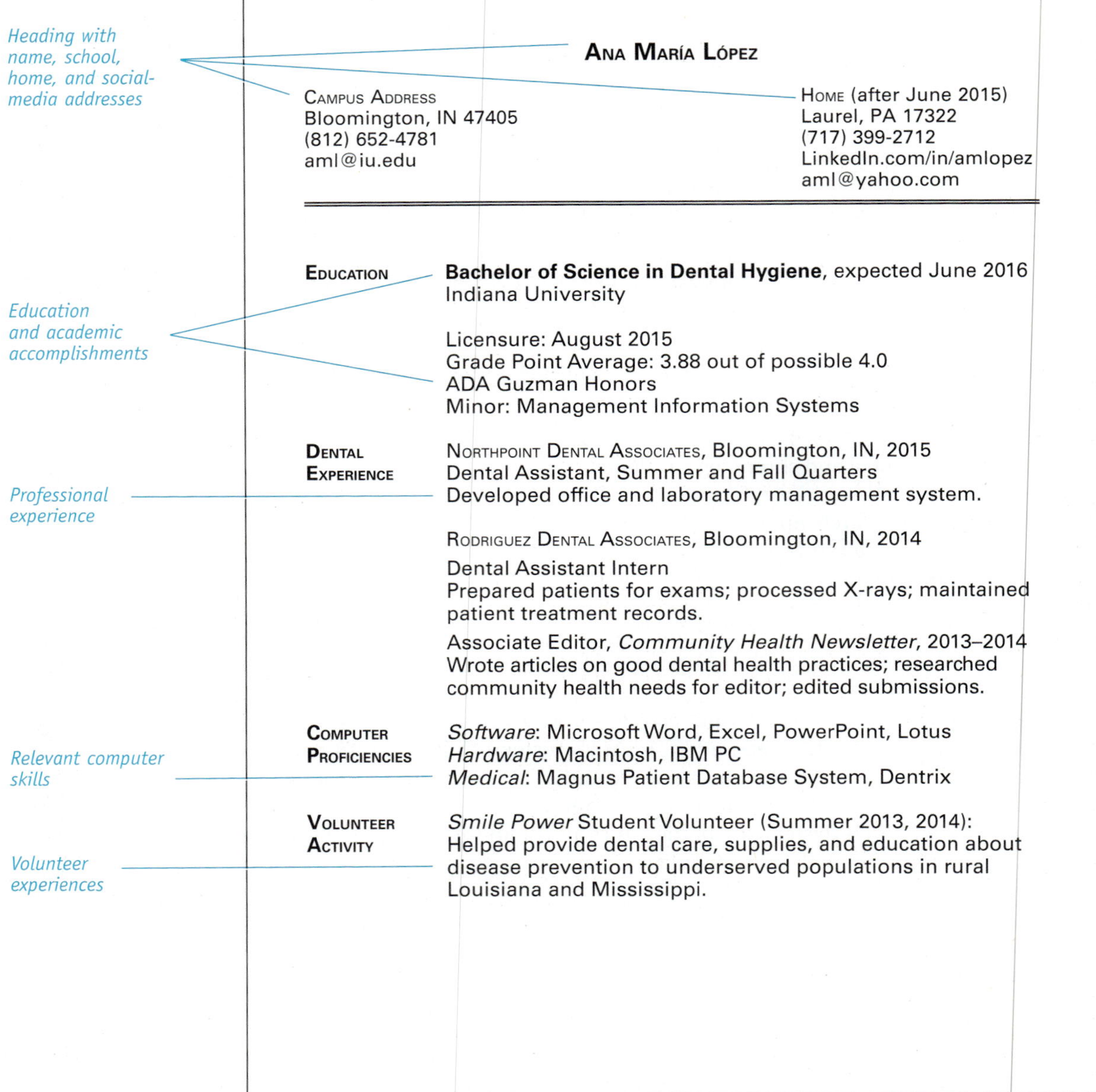

ANA MARÍA LÓPEZ

CAMPUS ADDRESS
Bloomington, IN 47405
(812) 652-4781
aml@iu.edu

HOME (after June 2015)
Laurel, PA 17322
(717) 399-2712
LinkedIn.com/in/amlopez
aml@yahoo.com

EDUCATION

Bachelor of Science in Dental Hygiene, expected June 2016
Indiana University

Licensure: August 2015
Grade Point Average: 3.88 out of possible 4.0
ADA Guzman Honors
Minor: Management Information Systems

DENTAL EXPERIENCE

NORTHPOINT DENTAL ASSOCIATES, Bloomington, IN, 2015
Dental Assistant, Summer and Fall Quarters
Developed office and laboratory management system.

RODRIGUEZ DENTAL ASSOCIATES, Bloomington, IN, 2014
Dental Assistant Intern
Prepared patients for exams; processed X-rays; maintained patient treatment records.

Associate Editor, *Community Health Newsletter*, 2013–2014
Wrote articles on good dental health practices; researched community health needs for editor; edited submissions.

COMPUTER PROFICIENCIES

Software: Microsoft Word, Excel, PowerPoint, Lotus
Hardware: Macintosh, IBM PC
Medical: Magnus Patient Database System, Dentrix

VOLUNTEER ACTIVITY

Smile Power Student Volunteer (Summer 2013, 2014): Helped provide dental care, supplies, and education about disease prevention to underserved populations in rural Louisiana and Mississippi.

Figure 15–11. Student Résumé (for an Entry-Level Position)

CHRIS RENAULT, RN, ACLS, BSN

LinkedIn.com/in/chrisrenaultrn
Phoenix, AZ 67903 • (555) 555-5555 • chrisrenault@somedomain.com

Heading with name and contact information

Reliable, compassionate, and competent RN seeking medical-surgical position

Dedicated Registered Nurse routinely praised for strengths in patient relations; clinical knowledge; collaboration with interdisciplinary health-care teams; chart accuracy; and ability to treat assorted illnesses, injuries, and medical emergencies.

Highlights professional credentials

Education & Nursing Credentials

UNIVERSITY OF PHOENIX – Phoenix, AZ

Bachelor of Science in Nursing (BSN), 2015 — Graduated summa cum laude (GPA: 3.9)

Associate Degree in Nursing (AN), 2012 — Graduated cum laude (GPA: 3.5)

LICENSURE & CERTIFICATIONS

RN License (AZ), 4/2013 • **ACLS**, 1/2014 • **IV Practice**, 8/2014 • **CPR**, 8/2014

AFFILIATIONS

ANA (Arizona Nurses Association) • **ANA** (American Nurses Association)

Education and licenses related to job objective

Professional Experience–Clinical Rotations

- Earned excellent marks on evaluations throughout clinical rotations in diverse practice areas. Participated in activities including patient assessment, treatment, medication disbursement, and surgical preparation as a member of the health-care team.
- Preceptor Comments: "*Chris has an excellent ability to interact with patients and their families, showing a high degree of empathy, medical knowledge, and concern for quality and continuity of patient care.*"

Relevant professional experience

ROTATIONS SUMMARY

Surgery/Internal Medicine	ABC Hospital: Core Telemetry/Medical-Surgical
Emergency Medicine	ABC Hospital: Emergency Department
Cardiology	GHI Medical Center: Cardiac Telemetry
Oncology	ABC General Hospital: Oncology Department
Long-Term Care	XYZ Skilled-Care Unit
Orthopedics	ABC Hospital: Orthopedic Center
Pediatrics	DEF Hospital: Pediatrics Unit
Rehabilitative Medicine	ABC Hospital: Health Rehabilitation Center

Volunteerism

Active Volunteer, The American Cancer Society, Scottsdale, AZ Chapter, 2012 to Present
Participant, *Making Strides Against Breast Cancer* walks, 2014, 2015

Volunteer experience

Figure 15–12. Résumé (Highlighting Professional Credentials)

ROBERT MANDILLO
Dayton, OH 45424 • 555.555.1212 • mandillo@somedomain.com
Connect on LinkedIn: LinkedIn.com/in/robertmandillomba
Design Portfolio: www.robertmandillomba.com

QUALIFICATIONS SUMMARY

Tagline

Quality-driven mechanical engineering manager whose tenure with Exhibit Design Lab has been distinguished by exemplary-rated performance and proven results. Developer of next-generation exhibit design solutions that have led to increased leads and sales. Qualifications reinforced by strong aptitudes in reliability engineering, system troubleshooting, and Lean Six Sigma principles.

EXPERIENCE

Begins with job experience relevant to prospective employers

MANAGER, EXHIBIT DESIGN LAB—May 2008–Present
Wright-Patterson Air Force Base, Dayton, OH

- Managed production of 1,200+ exhibit designs throughout tenure, supervising a team of 11 technicians in support of engineering exhibit design and production.
- Coordinate all phases of exhibit installations from initial concept and development of technical drawings to construction, installation, and fabrication of models.
- Ensure the attainment of manufacturing goals and compliance with safety standards.
- Negotiate with vendors and procure materials and supplies for exhibit design support.

SUPERVISOR, GRAPHICS ILLUSTRATORS—June 2005–April 2008
Henderson Advertising Agency, Cincinnati, OH

- Led team to create original design themes, layouts, and graphics for marketing materials, television commercials, videos, and website.
- Recruited, trained, and supervised a team of five illustrators and four drafting mechanics.
- Established strong vendor-partner relationships, competitive rates, and detailed schedules that elevated quality and decreased turnaround time.

Figure 15–13. Résumé (Applicant with Management Experience)

EDUCATION

MASTER OF BUSINESS ADMINISTRATION (MBA), 2014
University of Dayton (Dayton, OH)

BACHELOR OF SCIENCE IN MECHANICAL ENGINEERING (BSME), 2005
Edison State College (Wooster, OH)

AFFILIATIONS

American Society of Mechanical Engineers (ASME)
National Society of Professional Engineers (NSPE)

SKILLS

Rapid Prototyping • SolidWorks • Product Development • Machining • Product Design • CAD Manufacturing • Engineering • Simulations • Plastics • Sheet Metal • LabVIEW Procurement & Supply-Chain Management • Pressure Vessel Internals • R&D

Education and affiliations emphasize rigorous preparation in field and continuing professional interests

Figure 15–13. Résumé (Applicant with Management Experience) (*continued*)

LINDA H. GRANGER

lhg.granger@gmail.com
(206) 577-8869 / (206) 656-3324

Sun Valley Heights, VA 20109
LinkedIn.com/ni/lhgranger

INFORMATION TECHNOLOGY / SECURITY SPECIALIST

Signals goal of switching careers

Seeking to build an exciting career in law enforcement with a focus on the application of Information Technology (IT) / Information Security (INFOSEC).

- Application Design / System Analysis
- Testing / Implementation / Integration
- Program / Project Development
- Business Policies / Procedures
- Customer / Client Service
- Dynamic Team Building / Leadership

EDUCATION

BACHELOR OF SCIENCE – INFORMATION TECHNOLOGY
Sun Valley University, VA, May 2014

INTERNSHIP / PROFESSIONAL EXPERIENCE

Federal Law Enforcement Training Center (FLETC), Arlington, VA *June–Sept. 2014*
Volunteer – Computer, Financial, Intelligence Division

- Accepted into highly selective, competitive FLETC College Intern Summer Program
- Analyzed, evaluated, assessed performance or operating methodology of forensic software
- Assisted law-enforcement staff and instructors with office support in efforts to advance the mission of the FLETC
- Participated in and observed basic-training classes and activities designed to develop and promote the growth of future law-enforcement candidates

Board of Education, Forrest Hills, VA *Sept. 2012–June 2014*
Instructor / Substitute Teacher

- Provided an educational foundation designed to enable K–12 students to develop confidence, self-direction, and a lifelong interest in learning
- Fostered the development of communication, citizenship, and personal growth

AWARD / RECOGNITION

SUPERB ADMINISTRATIVE SUPPORT – FORENSIC DATA HUB
Federal Law Enforcement Training Center

Figure 15–14 Résumé (Experienced Applicant Seeking Career Change)

CAROL ANN WALKER
Laurel, PA 17322
(717) 399-2712
caw@yahoo.com • LinkedIn.com/in/cawalker

FINANCIAL EXPERIENCE

Kerfheimer Corporation, Philadelphia, PA

Senior Financial Analyst, June 2012–Present
Report to Senior Vice President for Corporate Financial Planning. Develop manufacturing cost estimates totaling $30 million annually for mining and construction equipment with Department of Defense.

Financial Analyst, November 2004–June 2007
Developed $50 million funding estimates for major Department of Defense contracts for troop carriers and digging and earth-moving machines. Researched funding options, resulting in savings of $1.2 million.

Job-experience opening highlights promotion

First Bank, Inc., Bloomington, IN

Planning Analyst, September 2011–November 2012
Developed successful computer models for short- and long-range planning.

EDUCATION

Ph.D. in Finance: expected, June 2016
The Wharton School of the University of Pennsylvania

M.S. in Business Administration, 2012
University of Wisconsin–Milwaukee
"Executive Curriculum" for employees identified as promising by their employers.

B.S. in Business Administration (*magna cum laude*), 2010
Indiana University
Emphasis: Finance Minor: Professional Writing

PUBLISHING AND MEMBERSHIP

"Developing Computer Models for Financial Planning," *Midwest Finance Journal* 34.2 (2009): 126–36.

Association for Corporate Financial Planning, Senior Member.

REFERENCES

References and a portfolio of financial plans are available upon request.

Figure 15–15 Advanced Résumé, Showing Promotion Within a Single Company

CAROL ANN WALKER

Sometown, PA 55555 • (555) 555-5555
caw@somedomain.com • LI: Linkedin.com/in/carolannwalker
Twitter Handle: @carolannwalker

Award-Winning Financial Analyst

Opens by highlighting career accomplishments

- Senior financial analyst offering proven success enhancing P&L scenarios by millions of dollars.
- Excellent analytical capabilities, with an expert foundation in statistics, financial modeling, and complex financial/business/variance analysis.
- Backed by solid credentials, industry honors, and a history of delivering goal-surpassing results.

Financial Analyst of the Year, 2014

Recipient of national award from the Association for Investment Management and Research (AIMR)

Showcases functional areas of expertise

Expertise

- Financial Analysis & Planning
- Forecasting & Trend Projection
- Trend/Variance Analysis
- Comparative Analysis
- Asset-Capacity Planning
- Economic Profit/EVA
- Business Valuation/Due Diligence
- SEC & Financial Reporting
- Risk Assessment
- Auditing/Accounting

Continues with chronological history that features accomplishments

Professional Experience

KERFHEIMER CORPORATION, Sometown, PA 2005 to Present

Senior Financial Analyst, 12/2008 to Present
Financial Analyst, 11/2005 to 12/2008

Promoted to lead team of 15 analysts in the management of financial/SEC reporting and analysis for publicly traded, $2.3 billion company and its four subsidiary entities. Develop financial/statistical models used to project and maximize corporate financial performance; provide ad-hoc financial analysis; and support nationwide sales team by providing financial metrics, trends, and forecasts.

Key Accomplishments

- Developed long-range funding requirements crucial to firm's subsequent capture of $52 million in government and military contracts.
- Secured more than $100 million through private and government research grants.

Figure 15–16 Advanced Résumé (Combining Functional and Chronological Elements)

CAROL ANN WALKER

Résumé • Page Two

Sometown, PA 00000 • (555) 555-5555
caw@somedomain.com • LI: LinkedIn.com/in/carolannwalker
Twitter Handle: @carolannwalker

Professional Experience (*continued*)

- Facilitated a 15 percent decrease in company's long-term debt during several major building expansions by developing computer models for capital acquisition.
- Designed model that saved 65 percent in proposal-preparation time. Cited by executive VP of sales for efforts that shortened the sales cycle, which helped displace the competition.
- Partnered with department managers to provide budget planning and profitability/cost-per-unit (CPU) analysis, including income, balance sheet, and cash-flow statements.
- Jointly led large-scale systems conversion to Hyperion, including personal upload of database in Essbase. Completed initiative on time and with no interruptions to business operations.

FIRST BANK, INC., Sometown, PA 2000 to 2005

Planning Analyst, 9/2000 to 11/2005

Compiled and distributed weekly, monthly, quarterly, and annual closings/financial reports. Prepared depreciation forecasts, actual-vs.-projected financial statements, key-matrix reports, tax-reporting packages, auditor packages, and balance-sheet reviews.

Key Accomplishments

- Devised strategies to secure $6.2 million credit line at 2 percent below market rate.
- Positioned bank for continued growth by conducting business-unit analysis and cost/benefit studies to determine optimal investment strategies.
- Analyzed financial performance for consistency to plans and forecasts, investigated trends and variances, and alerted senior management to areas requiring action.
- Prepared and presented financial analysis on impacts of foreign currencies, inflationary factors, product-mix changes, merger and acquisition (M&A) activity, and capacity/fixed-cost structures.
- Achieved an average 14 percent return on all investments. Applied critical thinking and sound financial and strategic analysis in all funding options research.

Figure 15–16 Advanced Résumé (Combining Functional and Chronological Elements) (*continued*)

CAROL ANN WALKER

Résumé • Page Three

Sometown, PA 55555 • (555) 555-5555
caw@somedomain.com • LI: LinkedIn.com/in/carolannwalker
Twitter Handle: @carolannwalker

Education

THE WHARTON SCHOOL OF THE UNIVERSITY OF PENNSYLVANIA, Philadelphia, PA

Ph.D. in Finance, 5/2013

UNIVERSITY OF WISCONSIN, Milwaukee, WI

M.S. in Business Administration ("Executive Curriculum"), 5/2000

INDIANA UNIVERSITY, Bloomington, IN

B.S. in Business Administration, Emphasis in Finance, 5/1998

Affiliations

- Association for Investment Management and Research (AIMR), Member, 2000 to Present
- Association for Corporate Financial Planning (ACFP), Senior Member, 2002 to Present

Portfolio of Financial Plans Available on Request

Figure 15–16 Advanced Résumé (Combining Functional and Chronological Elements) *(continued)*

Layout and design of résumé reflect candidate's graphic-design skills

JG

Joshua S. Goodman
Pittsburgh, PA 15212
(878) 111-1234
www.goodmandesign.com
LinkedIn.com/in/joshuagoodman

OBJECTIVE

A position as a graphic designer with responsibilities in information design, packaging, and media presentations.

EMPLOYMENT EXPERIENCE

Job experience highlights qualifications for position described in Figure 15–19

Assistant Designer • Dyer/Khan
Los Angeles, California
Summer 2014, Summer 2015
Assistant Designer in a versatile design studio. Responsible for design, layout, comps, mechanicals, pre-press production for four-color posters, booklets, brochures, etc.
Clients: Paramount Pictures, Mattel Electronics, and Motown Records.

Highlights publications experience from design through the print-production cycle

Graphic Designer • Barton & Barton
Los Angeles, California
Summer 2013
Graphic Designer for advertising firm. Designed websites and created templates for two corporate clients. Created interactive banners and screen interfaces to facilitate online advertising for three corporate clients.

Features graphic-design background

Production Assistant • Grafis
Los Angeles, California
Summer 2012
Production assistant at fast-paced design firm. Assisted with comps, mechanicals, and miscellaneous studio work.
Clients: ABC Television, A&M Records, and Ortho Products Division.

EDUCATION

Carnegie Mellon University, Pittsburgh, Pennsylvania
BFA in Graphic Design — May 2016

Graphic Design
Corporate Identity
Industrial Design
Graphic Imaging Processes
Color Theory
Computer Graphics
Typography
Serigraphy
Photography
Video Production

Relevant course work

SKILLS

Adobe Creative Cloud and Creative Suite (esp. Photoshop, Illustrator, and InDesign), JavaScript, QuarkXPress, MapEdit (Image Mapping), Micromedia Dreamweaver, Adobe Flash Professional, Microsoft Access/ Excel, XML, HTML, iGrafx, CorelDRAW

ACTIVITIES

Member, Pittsburgh Graphic Design Society; Member, The Design Group

Figure 15–17 Résumé Tailored to a Job Listing for a Traditional Graphic Designer (for ABC Services, see Figure 15–19 on page 551)

Joshua S. Goodman
Pittsburgh, PA 15212
(878) 111-1234
www.goodmandesign.com
LinkedIn.com/in/joshuagoodman

OBJECTIVE

A position as a graphic designer with responsibilities in web and document design, packaging, and media presentations.

WEB-DESIGN EXPERIENCE

Revised version of résumé targets job listing requiring Web-design skills and experience

Separate Web section calls attention to key experience, even though not most recent chronologically

Graphic Designer • Barton & Barton
Los Angeles, California
Summer 2014
Planned major revision of advertising firm's corporate website. Designed websites and created templates for two corporate clients. Created interactive banners and screen interfaces to facilitate online advertising.

GRAPHIC-DESIGN EXPERIENCE

Assistant Designer • Dyer/Khan
Los Angeles, California
Summer 2014, Summer 2015
Assistant designer in a versatile design studio. Responsible for design, layout, comps, mechanicals, and project management.
Clients: Paramount Pictures, Mattel Electronics, and Motown Records.

Production Assistant • Grafis
Los Angeles, California
Summer 2012
Production assistant at fast-paced design firm. Assisted with comps, mechanicals, and miscellaneous studio work.
Clients: ABC Television, A&M Records, and Ortho Products Division.

EDUCATION

Carnegie Mellon University, Pittsburgh, Pennsylvania
BFA in Graphic Design — May 2016

Relevant course work as recent graduate

Web Design
Computer Graphics
Graphic Design
Corporate Identity
Industrial Design
Graphic Imaging Processes
Color Theory
Typography
Serigraphy
Photography
Video Production

SKILLS

Adobe Creative Cloud and Creative Suits (esp. Photoshop, Illustrator, and InDesign), JavaScript, QuarkXPress, MapEdit (Image Mapping), Micromedia Dreamweaver, Adobe Flash Professional, Microsoft Access/Excel, XML, HTML, iGrafx, CorelDRAW

Highlights Web-software capabilities

ACTIVITIES

Member, Pittsburgh Graphic Design Society; Member, The Design Group.

Figure 15–18 Résumé Tailored to a Job Listing for a Graphic Designer with Web-Development Experience (for XYZ Group, see Figure 15–20 on page 551)

Graphic Designer
ABC Services, Inc., a hospitality management company located in Anywhere, USA, is in search of a full-time graphic designer able to multitask and proficient in Adobe PageMaker, Illustrator, Photoshop, Acrobat, and Word to create ads, brochures, signs, flyers, etc. Must be familiar with print process and IBM platforms. ABC offers great benefits, competitive salary, and flexible work environment. Please send résumé and salary requirements to ABC Group, etc.

Figure 15–19 Job Listing for a Traditional Graphic Designer (ABC Services)

Graphic Designer

Description The XYZ Group, a prestigious scientific organization located in Anyplace, USA, seeks a graphic designer. Position requires an experienced and creative graphic designer with strong concept and design skills to work on a wide range of projects, including logos, brochures, posters, annual reports, and website design. Candidate must be able to manage many projects simultaneously and work with minimal supervision on all aspects of projects from start to finish. Must have good interpersonal skills for interaction with a wide variety of staff and volunteers to ensure timely production of all projects.

Requirements Candidates must have expert-level knowledge of InDesign, Photoshop, and Illustrator in the Windows environment and Adobe Dreamweaver (current release). Must have previous print-buying experience. Web-page development experience, good proofreading skills, and scanner experience are essential. Bachelor's degree in graphic design, fine arts, communications, or related field with a minimum 3–5 years recent experience using all required skills. Send cover letter and résumé, including salary history, to XYZ Group, etc.

Figure 15–20 Job Listing for a Graphic Designer with Web-Development Experience (XYZ Group)

Writing an Effective Letter of Application

When applying for a job, you almost always need to submit an application or a cover letter, even if it is a brief e-mail (or e-note), with your résumé. The application cover letter is essentially a sales letter in which you market your skills, abilities, and knowledge as they pertain to the position for which you are applying. The successful application letter accomplishes four tasks: (1) it serves as your personal introduction, provoking

◆ *For a discussion of sales letters, see pages 304–309 in Chapter 9, Writing Routine and Sensitive Messages.*

interest in recruiters by describing how your skills can contribute to the organization; (2) it explains to a particular employer which job interests you and why; (3) it convinces the reader that you are a viable candidate by highlighting specific qualifications in your résumé; and (4) it provides the opportunity to request a job interview.

Opening Paragraph

In the opening paragraph, provide context and show your enthusiasm.

1. Indicate how you heard about the opening. If you have been referred to a company by an employee, a career counselor, a professor, or someone else, be sure to mention this even before you state your job objective ("I recently learned from Ms. Jodi Hammel of an opening in your firm").
2. State your job objective and mention the specific job title ("I am writing to apply for the position of district manager"). Those who make hiring decisions review many application letters. To save them time while also calling attention to your strengths as a candidate, state your job objective directly in your first paragraph.
3. Explain why you are interested in the job and demonstrate your initiative as well as your knowledge of the organization by relating your interest to some facet of the organization. ("This position interests me greatly not only because your firm is number one in the region but also because I am impressed with Advertising Media's Employee Development Program.")

Note how the following opening paragraph cites where the position was advertised, states the position title, and expresses interest in line with a career objective.

▶ Dear Mr. Lupert:

In the February 24, 2016, issue of the *Butler Gazette*, I learned that you have summer technical training internships available. This opportunity interests me because I have the professional and educational background necessary to make positive contributions to your firm.

Body Paragraphs

In the second paragraph (and third, if necessary), show through examples how you are qualified for the job. Limit each of these paragraphs to just one basic point that is clearly stated in the topic sentence. For example, your second paragraph might focus on work experience and your third paragraph on educational achievements. Don't just *tell* readers that you're qualified — *show* them by including examples and details. Come across as proud of your achievements and refer to your enclosed résumé, but do not simply summarize your résumé. Indicate how (with your talents) you can make valuable contributions to the company you are interested in, such as "I was the national winner of TI's 'Outstanding Customer Service Award' for 2013, 2014, and 2015. I have strong contacts with key buyers at all the major firms in our industry."

Note how the following two paragraphs from the application letter for an internship position give specific examples of project experience, provide information on course work and degree goals, reference the enclosed résumé, and emphasize how these experiences can contribute to the company.

> My professional experiences are representative of my abilities. My current project, a computer tutoring system that teaches LISP (an artificial intelligence programming language), is the first of its kind and is now being sold across the country to corporations and universities. I work with a team to test and revise our work until we have solved each problem. I have also developed leadership and collaborative skills that I could contribute to a summer position at Applied Sciences. As a cofounder of a project to target and tutor high school students with learning disabilities, I organized and implemented many of the training and tutoring sessions. My ability to take the initiative on challenging projects would be a valuable asset to your company.
>
> Pursuing degrees in industrial management and computer science has prepared me well to make valuable contributions to your goal of successfully implementing new software. Through varied courses, described in my résumé, I have the ability to learn new skills and to interact effectively in a technical environment. I look forward to applying all these abilities at Applied Sciences, Inc.

Closing Paragraph

In the final paragraph, request an interview. Let the reader know how to reach you by including your phone number or e-mail address. End with a statement of goodwill, even if it is only "thank you." (Note that if you submit your résumé as an e-mail attachment, the transmittal message serves as your application letter. Your transmittal heading will include your e-mail address, so you need not include it at the end of the message.)

> I would appreciate the opportunity to interview with you at your earliest convenience. If you have questions or would like additional information, contact me at (435) 228-3490 any Tuesday or Thursday after 10 a.m. or e-mail me at sennett@excepr.com.
>
> Molly Sennet
>
> Enclosure: Résumé

Proofreading and Follow-up

Proofread your letter carefully. Research indicates that if employers notice even one spelling, grammatical, or mechanical error, they often eliminate the candidate from consideration immediately. Such errors give employers the impression that you lack writing skills or that you are generally sloppy and careless in the way you present yourself professionally.

See also pages 115–117 in Chapter 4, Revising a Document.

After a reasonable period, consider following up with a reminder. ("I wrote to you a week ago about the job opening you advertised, and I wonder if that position is still available.") Your initiative will portray your sincere interest in the opportunity. This approach may also provoke a need for action by the reviewer — for example, the need to pass this application to the hiring authority.

WRITER'S CHECKLIST
Writing a Letter of Application

✔ In the opening paragraph:
- Indicate how you heard about the opening.
- State your job objective and interest in the job.
- Mention the job title.

✔ In the body of the letter:
- Cite project and previous employment experiences that demonstrate your qualifications for the job.
- Indicate how college course work, your degree, and pertinent training add to your qualifications for the job.
- Refer to your enclosed résumé.
- Explain how your qualifications and achievements can contribute to the prospective employer.

✔ In the closing paragraph:
- Request an interview.
- Provide your phone number and e-mail address so that you can be contacted.
- End with a goodwill statement.

Sample Letters

The sample application letters shown in Figures 15–21 through 15–23 follow the application-letter structure described in this section. Each is adapted according to emphasis, tone, and style to fit its particular audience.

- In Figure 15–21 on page 555, a college student seeks an internship in a retail business.
- In Figure 15–22 on page 556, a recent college graduate applies for a job in graphic design.
- In Figure 15–23 on page 557, a person with many years of work experience applies for a job as a district manager.

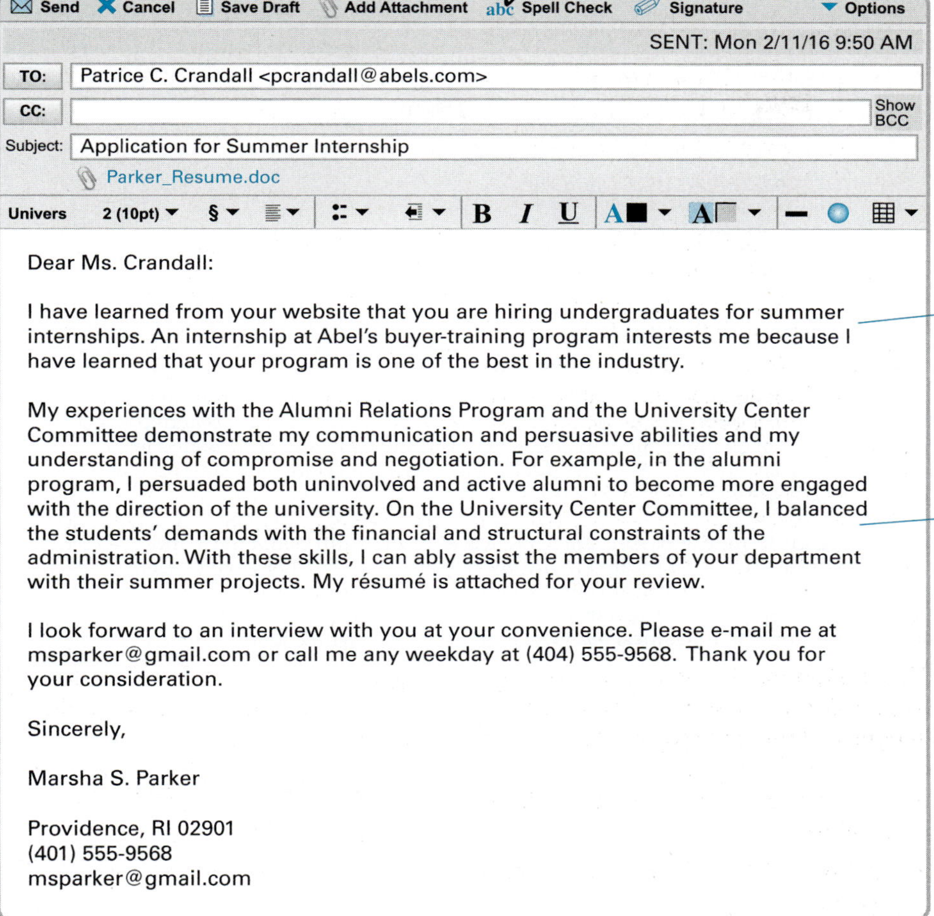
Send Cancel Save Draft Add Attachment Spell Check Signature Options

SENT: Mon 2/11/16 9:50 AM

TO: Patrice C. Crandall <pcrandall@abels.com>

CC:

Subject: Application for Summer Internship

Parker_Resume.doc

Dear Ms. Crandall:

I have learned from your website that you are hiring undergraduates for summer internships. An internship at Abel's buyer-training program interests me because I have learned that your program is one of the best in the industry.

My experiences with the Alumni Relations Program and the University Center Committee demonstrate my communication and persuasive abilities and my understanding of compromise and negotiation. For example, in the alumni program, I persuaded both uninvolved and active alumni to become more engaged with the direction of the university. On the University Center Committee, I balanced the students' demands with the financial and structural constraints of the administration. With these skills, I can ably assist the members of your department with their summer projects. My résumé is attached for your review.

I look forward to an interview with you at your convenience. Please e-mail me at msparker@gmail.com or call me any weekday at (404) 555-9568. Thank you for your consideration.

Sincerely,

Marsha S. Parker

Providence, RI 02901
(401) 555-9568
msparker@gmail.com

Opens by demonstrating initiative in researching the company, locating the program, and noting its value to the applicant's career

Continues by linking the applicant's personal characteristics to tangible accomplishments

Figure 15–21 Application Letter Sent as an E-mail from a College Student Applying for an Internship

222 Morewood Ave.
Pittsburgh, PA 15212
April 16, 2016

Ms. Judith Castro
Director, Human Resources
Natural History Museum
1201 S. Figueroa Street
Los Angeles, CA 90015

Dear Ms. Castro:

Opens by referencing a personal contact at the firm

A graphic designer at Dyer/Khan, Jodi Hammel, informed me that you are recruiting for a graphic designer in your Marketing Department. Your position interests me greatly because it offers me an opportunity both to fulfill my career goals and to promote the work of an internationally respected institution. Having participated in substantial volunteer activities at a local public museum, I am aware of the importance of your work.

Continues with a strong emphasis on recent experience and accomplishments

I bring strong up-to-date academic and practical skills in multimedia tools and graphic arts production, as indicated in my enclosed résumé. Further, I have recent project-management experience at Dyer/Khan, where I was responsible for the development of client brochures, newsletters, and posters. As project manager, I coordinated the project time lines, budgets, and production with clients, staff, and vendors.

Refers to enclosed résumé

My experience and contacts in the Los Angeles area media and entertainment community should help me make use of state-of-the-art design expertise. As you will see on my résumé, I have worked with the leading motion picture, television, and music companies; that experience should help me develop exciting marketing tools museum visitors and patrons will find attractive. For example, I helped design an upgrade of the CGI logo for Paramount Pictures and was formally commended by the Director of Marketing.

Could we schedule a meeting at your convenience to discuss this position further? Call me any weekday morning at 412-555-1212 (cell) or e-mail me at jgoodman@goodmandesign.com. Thank you for your consideration.

Sincerely,

Joshua S. Goodman

Joshua S. Goodman

Enclosure: Résumé
Portfolio: www.goodmandesign.com

Figure 15–22 Application Letter from a Recent Graduate Applying for a Graphic-Design Job

522 Beethoven Drive
Roanoke, VA 24016
November 15, 2016

Ms. Cecilia Smathers
Vice President, Dealer Sales
Hamilton Office Machines, Inc.
6194 Main Street
Hampton, VA 23661

Dear Ms. Smathers:

During the recent NOMAD convention in Washington, one of your sales representatives, Karen Jarrett, informed me of a possible opening for a district manager in your Dealer Sales Division. My extensive background in the office-systems industry makes me an ideal candidate for the position.

Opens by referencing a personal contact at the firm

I was with Technology, Inc., Dealer Division from its formation in 2000 until TI's merger and reorganization last year. During that period, I was involved in all areas of dealer sales, both within Technology, Inc., and through personal contact with a number of independent dealers. From 2008 to 2013, I served as Dealer Sales Manager and Special Representative. As described in the enclosed résumé, I was the national winner of TI's "Outstanding Customer Service Award" for 2011, 2014, and 2015. I have strong contacts with key buyers at all the major firms in our industry.

Continues with a concise career summary

I would be happy to discuss my qualifications in an interview at your convenience. Please telephone me at (804) 449-6743 or e-mail me at gm302.476@sys.com.

Closes with contact information

Sincerely,

Gregory Mindukakis

Gregory Mindukakis

Enclosure: Résumé

Encloses a résumé

Figure 15–23 Application Letter from an Applicant with Many Years of Experience

Completing a Job or an Internship Application

The job application can be a key element to securing a job or an internship and provides you with an additional opportunity to portray personal assets that meet a specific job's requirements and to provide employers with a clear picture of your background and skill set. Job applications typically reflect the standard candidate information companies require in order to consider you for a position. Forms used by employers, recruiters, institutions, and job-search sites can be found at the actual place of business or online at the company website. Some employers only require that you complete the job application and submit a résumé and application cover letter. Employers may also ask you to complete an application online or download it for completion and send it back to the employer by mail, fax, or attached to an e-mail.

When filling out a job application, follow all directions carefully and complete every blank; if a particular area does not apply to you, indicate it is nonapplicable by writing *N/A* in the empty space. This strategy signifies to the employer that you have thoroughly read the form and taken note of every requirement. Do not volunteer more information than the employer is asking for on the application. If you do not complete all entries or if you miss the application deadline, it is likely you will not be considered for the position. See Figure 15–24, Sections from a Job-Application Form, for guidance.

WRITER'S CHECKLIST

Completing a Job Application

- ✔ Read the entire application before you begin to fill it out.
- ✔ Follow all directions carefully. (This includes adhering to small details like date format, as these indicate how well you follow directions.)
- ✔ Copy and paste responses to online applications from your word-processing program.
- ✔ Always list a job title for the "Position Seeking" entry. A busy employer rarely has time to determine where you will best fit into the organization; applications with entries such as "any" or "open" will receive less consideration.
- ✔ Provide all requested information and complete irrelevant entries with *N/A*.
- ✔ Proofread the job application for errors or blank entries before turning it in.
- ✔ List the most recent information (employer or education) first, working backward in time.
- ✔ When the application asks for your salary requirements, indicate "open," "negotiable," or a range commensurate with the industry and region.
- ✔ Use positive phrases if the application asks why you left a previous employer: "relocation," "seeking new challenge," or "career advancement." You can address direct inquiries about a situation during the interview. See also Doing Well in the Interview on pages 561–565.
- ✔ List references (with their permission) who can speak to your professionalism, character, or work ethic.
- ✔ Write legibly for paper applications.
- ✔ Sign, date, and submit the application by the deadline.
- ✔ Save a copy or screen capture of the completed application for your records.

Employment Application

Employer Name: *ACME Tech Support–Internship Department* **Announcement / Job Number:** *ATS-11096*

Position Title: *Computer Support Technician Candidate* **Current Date:** *JAN/03/2016*

PERSONAL INFORMATION **Social Security Number:** *404-25-0776*

Name (Last, First, Middle)		Cell Phone Number
Duffy, John W.		*404-522-7765*
Home Address	**Mailing Address**	**Home Phone Number**

EMPLOYMENT HISTORY / WORK EXPERIENCE—Begin with Most Recent Employer

Dates From–To (MMM/DD/YYYY)	Company Name	Address, City, State, Zip
JUL/02/2014 – DEC/20/2015	*Computer Service Mart*	*1234 E. HWY 1, Atlanta, GA 30301*

Job Title and Responsibilities, Skills, Attributes — *Customer Service Representative. Received more than 150 incoming calls daily, and responded to more than 100 online contacts; documented customer concerns; routed calls to appropriate department (over 15 in-house, and 10 corporate); established rapport with customers and department representatives; used five different automated data-management systems to track service initiatives; supervised and trained four employees; promoted twice in a nine-month period; filled Computer Tech position when required.*

Reason for Leaving:	Salary or Hourly Wage:	Supervisor's Name	Telephone Number
Relocation	*$29,550 per year*	*Mr. Alfred Smith*	*404-506-1298*

Dates From–To (MMM/DD/YYYY)	Company Name	Address, City, State, Zip

LEGAL

Have you ever filed for bankruptcy? ☐ YES ☒ NO

MILITARY HISTORY—Complete a Separate Entry for Each Branch of Service

Dates From–To (MMM/DD/YYYY)	Branch of Service	Last Duty Station
MAY/03/2006 – MAY/18/2014	*U.S. Army*	*Ft. Army, SC*

Occupational Skill, Description of Responsibilities — *Communications Specialist. Sustained communication assets and provided continuity in phone service, Internet service, and secure satellite connections to organizations in both tactical and garrison operating environments. Supervised and trained 10 subordinates, prepared performance evaluations and scheduled continuing education, compiled weekly/monthly equipment status reports, traveled worldwide supporting unit operations in three different continents and more than 10 countries.*

Figure 15–24 Sections from a Job-Application Form

EDUCATION / TRAINING—Include Technical/Academic Achievements/Correspondence and Military Courses

Have you obtained a high school diploma or GED certificate? ☒ YES ☐ NO

Type School	Institution Name & Location	Diploma/ Degree	Major	Date/Year	GPA
College/University	*University of Maryland, College Park, MD*	*B.S.*	*Bus Mgmt*	*Projected 2016*	*3.4*

PROFESSIONAL CERTIFICATIONS / LICENSES

Type of License or Certificate	Awarded by:	Registration or Certificate No.	Expiration Date (MMM/DD/YYYY)
Commercial Driver's License	*State of Maryland*	*S87233597*	*NOV/07/2017*
Type of License or Certificate	**Awarded by:**	**Registration or Certificate No.**	**Expiration Date (MMM/DD/YYYY)**
Notary Public	*State of Georgia*	*752-09-330027*	*N/A*

OTHER SPECIAL SKILLS—List Other Specific Skills You Have to Offer for This Job Opening

Web Page Design and Hosting (Summer Internship, Programming Department, IBM, 2012).
Computer Maintenance / Repair Technician (Freelance Consultant, Community Research Department, 2012–2014).
Unit Communications / Networking Technician (Additional Duty, U.S. Army, 2010).
Typing Evaluation (Department of Labor Skills Assessment Division, 2012).
Bilingual (Fluent; Speak, read, and write Spanish and English).
Culturally Diverse (Traveled to three continents and visited more than 10 countries; firsthand experience in overcoming communication barriers).

REFERENCES—Provide Three Professional References (Persons Not Related to You)

Name, Job Title	Mailing Address	E-mail Address	Day Telephone	May We Contact?
Dr. J. R. Howard, Professor	*222 Hartford Street Atlanta, GA 30201*	*j.r.howard@gnet.com*	*404-522-9732*	☒ YES ☐ NO

I, *John Duffy*, certify that the information provided on this application is true and accurate to the best of
(printed name)
my knowledge.

Signature *John Duffy* Date *1/3/16*

Figure 15–24 Sections from a Job-Application Form (*continued*)

Doing Well in the Interview

Preparing a professional résumé, writing an effective letter of application, and, in some cases, submitting a job-application form are essential to obtaining a job interview; that preparation helps you understand your strengths as a potential employee and articulate your career objectives. Nevertheless, the interview is often the most difficult part of the job search because it is so pivotal in the hiring process. A job interview may last for 30 minutes, or it may take several hours; it may be conducted by one person or by several, either at one time or in a series of interviews, in person, by phone, or by teleconference or videoconference. Because it is impossible to know exactly what to expect, be as prepared as possible. If you are interviewed by phone, set aside a time and place where you won't be interrupted, and have your résumé and note-taking tools (notepad, computer) available.

Before the Interview

The interview is not a one-way communication. It presents you with an opportunity to ask questions of your potential employer and to demonstrate your knowledge of the position and the organization itself. In preparation, learn everything you can about the company before the interview by answering the questions listed in the Learning About Employers checklist on pages 563–564. You can obtain information from the company's website, current employees, company literature, and the business section of local and national newspapers, such as the *New York Times*, the *Los Angeles Times*, the *Wall Street Journal*, and the *Washington Post* (available online and in the library). You can also use other Web resources, such as a company's Twitter or Facebook accounts, or information provided on other websites about the company you are researching. For many larger or publicly traded companies and for many nonprofits, you may be able to learn about the company's size, sales volume, product line, credit rating, branch locations, subsidiary companies, new products and services, building programs, and other such information from its annual reports; publications such as *Moody's Industrials* at www.moodys.com, *Dun & Bradstreet* at www.dnb.com, *Standard & Poor's* at www.standardandpoors.com, and *Thomas' Register* at www.thomasnet.com; and other business reference sources a librarian might suggest. What you cannot find through your own research, ask your interviewer. Now is your chance to make certain that you

ETHICS NOTE: Respond Carefully to Sensitive or Illegal Questions When you are faced with questions that are sensitive or illegal (such as age, sex, disabilities, health, marital status, children, race, and criminal activity), you must carefully consider your response. If the question does not seem to raise a problem, you can choose to answer it. If you feel the question is inappropriate on an application form, you can respond with N/A or another response (such as a line through the blank) to indicate that you read the content. Understanding that many employers conduct background checks on candidates to protect their interests will help you determine the validity of a question. For example, a banking institution might be very concerned about a candidate's credit history, current debts, or bankruptcy status, or a government organization might be concerned about citizenship or ties to foreign countries.

are considering a healthy and growing company. It is also your chance to show your interest in the company and to find out as much as possible about company-employee relations, including opportunities for career growth. You may also want to ask your interviewer some or all of the following questions:

- Is there a probationary period for new employees?
- How often are employees formally evaluated on their performance?
- Does the company require training or certification?
- Does the company fund career-related training and outside education?
- Does the position I'm applying for have promotion potential?

Finally, as a way of gaining insight into how the company operates, you could ask your interviewer how he or she started at the company—if time permits.

Try to anticipate the questions your interviewer might ask, and prepare your answers in advance. Be sure you understand a question before answering it, and avoid responding too quickly with a rehearsed answer—try to answer in a natural and relaxed manner. Interviewers typically ask the following questions:

- Why do you want to work here?
- What are your short-term and long-term occupational goals?
- Where do you see yourself five years from now?
- What are your major strengths and weaknesses?
- Do you work better with others or alone?
- What academic or career accomplishments are you particularly proud of? (Describe one that stands out.)
- Why are you leaving your current job?
- May we contact your previous employer?
- What salary and benefits do you expect?

Some of these questions are difficult. Give them careful thought, try to be as concrete as possible by offering examples when appropriate, and remember that there is no one correct answer. Be prepared, though, for questions that are broader, that seem designed to throw you off, or that present situations and ask for your reaction. Demonstrate how well you can think on your feet by taking the time necessary to compose a response and by presenting that response clearly.

- Whom do you most admire, and why?
- Can you describe a job environment in which you would not thrive?
- In your last employee review, what areas for improvement were identified?

Many employers use behavioral interviews. Rather than traditional, straightforward questions, the behavioral interview focuses on asking the candidate to provide examples or respond to hypothetical situations. Interviewers who use behavior-based questions are looking for specific examples from your experience. Prepare for the behavioral interview by recollecting challenging situations or problems that were successfully resolved. Examples of behavior-based questions include the following:

- Can you tell me about a time when you experienced conflict on a team?
- If I were your boss and you disagreed with a decision I made, what would you do?
- How have you used your leadership skills to bring about change?
- Can you tell me about a time when you failed and what you have learned from the experience?

The interviewer may also ask pointed questions about your job history:

- Have you ever been laid off or fired?
- Why did you stay with previous employers on average for just a year?
- Why do you have such a large employment gap between [dates]?

Your best strategy is to be truthful. If your career is just under way, changing jobs — for professional or personal reasons — is not unusual. Nor is it unusual to be laid off in uncertain economic periods. If you have been fired, you may have been in the wrong position for your qualifications or for another understandable reason. Again, be truthful.

PROFESSIONALISM NOTE: Be Prepared for the Interview Arrive at or before the appointed time. In fact, it is usually a good idea to arrive early because you may be asked to fill out an application before you meet your interviewer. Read the application form before filling it out, and proofread your answers when you are finished. Not only does the application form provide the company with a record for its files, but it also gives the company an opportunity to see how closely you follow directions, how thoroughly you complete a task, and how well you express your ideas in writing. Always bring extra copies of your résumé and samples of your work (if applicable) and a list of references with contact information. Some of the people you meet may not have a copy of your résumé, and it contains much of the same information the application asks for: personal data, work experience, and education. Turn off all electronic devices before the interview. Bring a laptop or tablet only if you need to access a portfolio of your work. Otherwise, typing with your head down during the interview creates a barrier between you and your interviewer.

WRITER'S CHECKLIST

Learning About Employers

As you search for information about potential employers, use these questions as a guide:

- ✔ What kind of organization is it? Is it for profit? nonprofit? governmental? educational?
- ✔ Does it provide a service or product? If so, what kind?
- ✔ How diversified are its products, services, or goals?

- ✔ How large is the business? How large are its assets? How many employees work there?
- ✔ Is it locally owned? Is it a subsidiary of a larger organization? Is it expanding?
- ✔ How long has it been in business?
- ✔ Where will you fit in?

During the Interview

The interview actually begins before you are seated: What you wear and how you act make a first impression. In general, dress simply and conservatively, avoid extremes in fragrance and cosmetics, be well groomed, and never chew gum. Be mindful that even for a video interview, such as on Skype, your upper half is visible.

PROFESSIONALISM NOTE: Present an Appropriate Office Appearance Be aware that visible tattoos and body piercings are not acceptable in many white-collar and service-industry positions. Employers are within their legal rights to maintain such a policy. Find out before applying or interviewing for a position about the corporate policy. If tattoos and piercings are acceptable, fine. If not, act prudently if you want to work there. Cover tattoos and remove piercings. (You do not want your piercings to set off an entrance metal detector on your way to the interview!) If you are hired, be honest with your employer about the best way to adapt if your tattoos or piercings could later create a conflict.

Behavior

First, thank the interviewer for his or her time, express your pleasure at meeting him or her, and remain standing until you are offered a seat. Then sit up straight (good posture suggests self-assurance), look directly at the interviewer, and try to appear relaxed and confident. If you feel nervous during the interview, use that nervous energy to your advantage by channeling it into alertness. Listen carefully and record important information in your memory. Jot down a few facts and figures as needed, but do not attempt to take extensive notes. Use a laptop or notebook computer only if you need to showcase a portfolio. Be sure to get the names and titles of your interviewers. They are crucial to any follow-up contacts.

◆ *See also the discussion on listening on pages 495–497 in Chapter 14, Giving Presentations and Conducting Meetings.*

Responses

When answering questions, don't ramble or stray from the subject. Say only what you must to answer each question properly and then stop, but avoid giving just yes or no answers — they usually don't permit the interviewer to learn enough about you. Some interviewers allow a silence to fall just to see how you will react. The burden of conducting the interview is the interviewer's, not yours — and he or she may interpret your rush to fill a void in the conversation as a sign of insecurity. If such a silence makes you uncomfortable, be ready to ask pertinent questions about the company from your prepared list. If the interviewer overlooks important points, such as the probationary period or promotion potential, bring them up.

Interviewers look for a degree of self-confidence and understanding of the field in which the applicant is applying for a job, as well as genuine interest in the field, the company, and the job. Less is expected of a beginner, but even a newcomer must show some self-confidence and command of the subject. One way to communicate your interest in the job and company is to ask specific and well-researched questions. Interviewers respond favorably to applicants who can communicate and present themselves well.

Salary Negotiations

Although it is better to negotiate salary after you have a job offer or certainly late in the interview, you may be asked, "What are your salary requirements?" You cannot answer such a question without solid preparation. To determine salary ranges in your field, check websites such as salary.com, payscale.com, and glassdoor.com.

First, your goal should be to work toward a win-win situation for you and your prospective employer. Avoid overemphasizing money because it tends to make your potential loyalty to an organization suspect. The issue is not simply one of dollar amounts but of your own job satisfaction and what value you can bring to your employer.

Remember that you are negotiating a package and not just a starting salary. Some employers have excellent benefits packages that can balance a lower base salary, as the following possibilities suggest:

- Tuition reimbursement for continued education
- Payment for relocation costs
- Paid personal leave or paid vacations
- Retirement and pension plans
- Profit sharing: investment or stock options
- Bonuses or cost-of-living adjustments
- Overtime potential and compensation
- Flexible hours and work-from-home options
- Health, dental, optical, and disability benefits
- Commuting or parking-lot reimbursement
- Family leave or elder-care benefits

If you do not wish to provide a specific salary requirement during a job interview, you can respond with a salary range reasonable for someone at your level in your line of work in that region of the country. You could say, "I would hope for a salary somewhere between $35,000 and $40,000, but of course this is negotiable." Throughout this process, focus on what is most important to you. Remember, it's always acceptable to say to a prospective employer that you would like to think about an offer.

Conclusion

At the conclusion of the interview, thank your interviewer for his or her time. Indicate that you are interested in the job (if true), and try to get an idea of when you can expect to hear from the company (do not press too hard). Reaffirm friendly contact with a firm handshake.

Sending Follow-up Correspondence

After you leave the interview, review your notes for accuracy and fill in any gaps while the information is fresh — it may be helpful in comparing job offers. As soon as possible after the interview (no later than two days), send the interviewer a note of thanks in a brief letter or handwritten card. If the interviewer invited e-mail follow-up inquiries, consider using e-mail for the note of thanks. Such notes often include the following:

- Your thanks for the interview and to individuals or groups that gave you special help or attention during the interview
- The name of the specific job for which you interviewed
- Your impression that the job is attractive, if true
- Your confidence that you can perform the job well
- An offer to provide further information or answer additional questions

Figure 15–25 shows a typical example of follow-up correspondence. If you have not heard back from the company about the status of your application in two weeks,

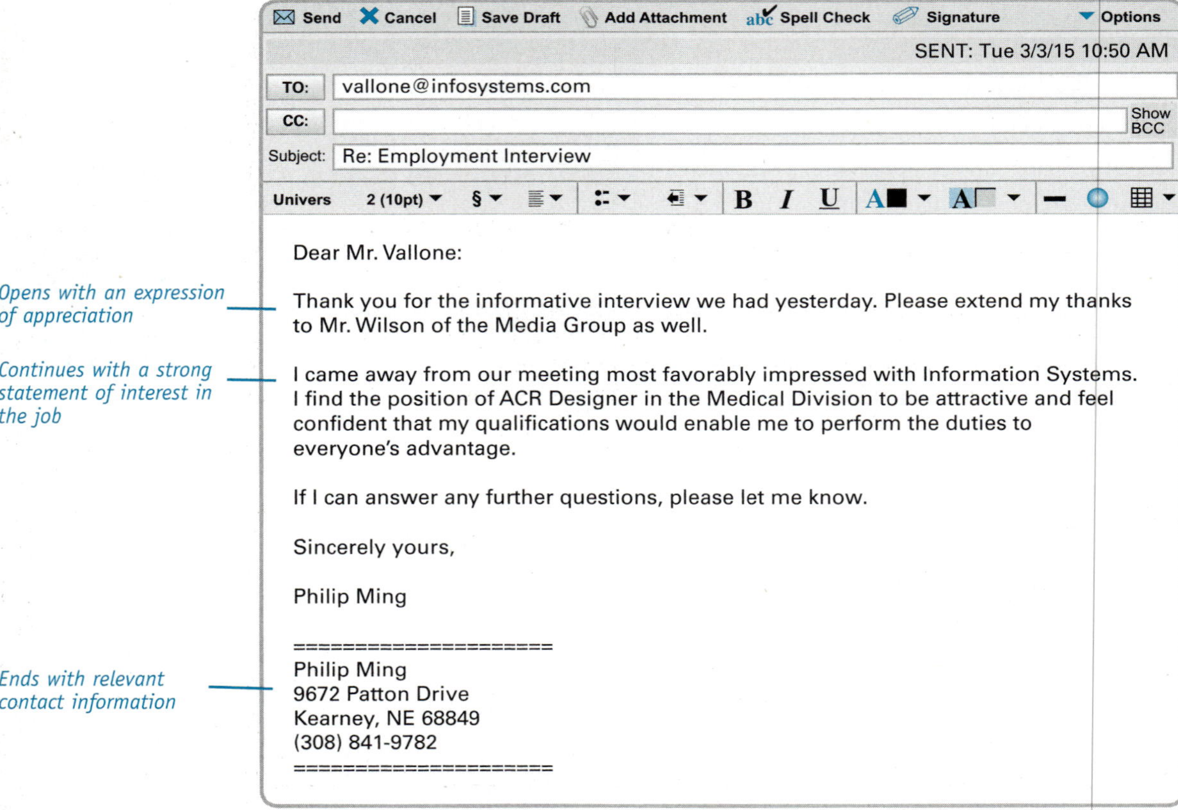

Figure 15–25 Follow-up E-mail Thanking the Interviewer

send another brief and courteous letter or e-mail message. Beyond that period, it is the responsibility of the company to contact you.

If you are offered a job you want, accept the offer verbally and write a brief letter of acceptance as soon as possible — certainly within a day or two. The organization of such a message is simple. Begin by accepting the job you have been offered. Identify the job by title and state the exact salary so that there will be no confusion on these two important points. The second paragraph might go into detail about moving dates and the time for reporting to work. The details will vary, depending on the nature of the job offer. Conclude with a statement that you are looking forward to working for your new employer, as in the acceptance letter written by a college student in Figure 15–26.

9672 Patton Drive
Kearney, NE 68849
(308) 841-9782
June 11, 2016

Mr. F. E. Vallone
Manager of Human Resources
Information Systems, Inc.
3275 Commercial Park Drive
Raleigh, NE 68501

Dear Mr. Vallone:

I am pleased to accept your offer of $45,500 per year as a junior ACR designer in the Medical Group.

Opens by accepting the job and verifying the salary, title, and organizational unit

After graduation, I plan to leave Kearney on Tuesday, June 19. I should be able to make suitable living arrangements within a few days and be ready to report for work on the following Monday, June 25. Please let me know if this date is satisfactory to you.

Continues with near-term schedule and start date

I look forward to working with the design team at Information Systems.

Ends with goodwill statement

Very truly yours,

Philip Ming

Philip Ming

Figure 15–26 Acceptance Letter Written by a College Student

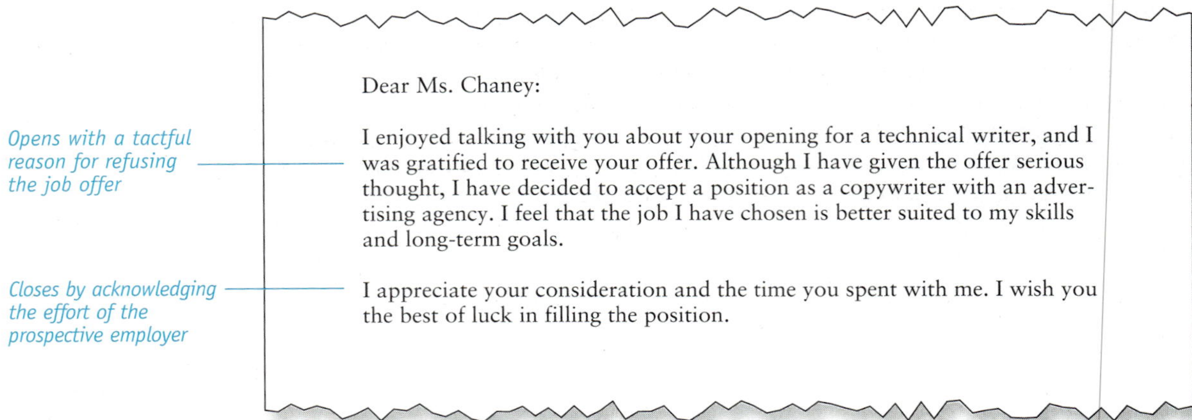
Dear Ms. Chaney:

I enjoyed talking with you about your opening for a technical writer, and I was gratified to receive your offer. Although I have given the offer serious thought, I have decided to accept a position as a copywriter with an advertising agency. I feel that the job I have chosen is better suited to my skills and long-term goals.

I appreciate your consideration and the time you spent with me. I wish you the best of luck in filling the position.

Figure 15–27 Letter of Refusal

◆ *For additional advice on writing refusal letters, see pages 270–274 in Chapter 8, Writing E-mails, Memos, and Letters, and pages 309–312 in Chapter 9, Writing Routine and Sensitive Messages.*

Because you will probably have applied to more than one company or organization, you will need to write a letter of refusal if you receive more than one job offer. Be especially tactful and courteous because the employer you are refusing has spent time and effort interviewing you and may have counted on your accepting the job. It is also possible that you may apply for another job at this company in the future. Figure 15-27 is an example of a job-refusal letter. It acknowledges the consideration given the applicant, offers a logical reason for refusal of the offer, and then concludes on a pleasant note.

Sending a Resignation Letter or Memo

When you are planning to leave a job, for any reason, you usually write a resignation letter or memo to your supervisor or to an appropriate person in the Human Resources Department.

◆ *For strategies concerning negative messages, see pages 269–276 in Chapter 8, Writing E-mails, Memos, and Letters.*

- Start on a positive note, regardless of the circumstances under which you are leaving.
- Consider pointing out how you have benefited from working for the company or say something complimentary about the company.
- Comment on something positive about the people with whom you have been associated.
- Explain why you are leaving in an objective, factual tone.
- Avoid angry recriminations because your resignation will remain on file with the company and could haunt you in the future when you need references.

Your memo should give enough notice to allow your employer time to find a replacement. It might be no more than two weeks, or it might be enough time to put your files in order and train your replacement. Some organizations may ask for a notice equivalent to the number of weeks of vacation you receive. Check the policy of your employer before you begin your letter. The sample resignation letter in Figure 15–28 is from an employee who is leaving to take a job offering greater opportunities. The resignation memo in Figure 15–29 is written by an employee who is leaving under unhappy circumstances; notice that it opens and closes positively and that the reason for the resignation is stated without apparent anger or bitterness.

227 Kenwood Drive
Austin, TX 78719
January 4, 2016

R. W. Johnson
Director of Metallurgy
Hannibal Laboratories
1914 East 6th Street
Austin, TX 78702

Dear Mr. Johnson:

My three years at Hannibal Laboratories have been an invaluable period of learning and professional development. I arrived as a novice, and I believe that today I am a professional—primarily as a result of the personal attention and tutoring I have received from my superiors and the fine example set by both my superiors and my peers.

Positive opening

I believe, however, that the time has come for me to join a firm that provides expanded job opportunities for my professional development. Therefore, I have accepted a position with Procter & Gamble, where I am scheduled to begin on January 28. Thus, my last day at Hannibal will be January 18. I will be happy to train my replacement during the next two weeks.

Reason for leaving

Many thanks for the experience I have gained and best wishes for the future.

Positive closing

Sincerely,

J. L. Washburne

J. L. Washburne
jlwashburne@gmail.com

Figure 15–28 Resignation Letter to Accept a Better Position

MEMORANDUM

To: T. W. Haney, Vice President, Administration
From: L. R. Rupp, Executive Assistant *LR*
Date: February 9, 2016
Subject: Resignation from Winterhaven, effective March 1, 2016

Positive opening — My five-year stay with the Winterhaven Company has been a very pleasant experience, and I believe that it has been mutually beneficial.

Reason for leaving — Because the recent restructuring of my job leaves no career path open to me, I have accepted a position with another company that I feel will offer me greater advancement opportunities. I am, therefore, submitting my resignation, to be effective on March 1, 2016.

Positive closing — I have enjoyed working with my coworkers at Winterhaven and wish the company success in the future.

Figure 15–29 Resignation Memo Under Negative Conditions

CHAPTER 15 SUMMARY: WRITING RÉSUMÉS AND COVER LETTERS

Follow these six steps for finding a job:

- Determine the best job for you.
- Prepare an effective résumé.
- Write an effective letter of application.
- Complete a job or internship application if required.
- Conduct yourself professionally during the interview.
- Send a follow-up message after the interview.

Research the following sources of information and options for locating jobs:

- Campus career center
- Web resources
- Tips from family, friends, and acquaintances
- Letters of inquiry
- Informational interviews
- Advertisements in newspapers
- Advertisements in trade and professional journals
- Private and temporary employment services

- Internships
- Local, state, and federal agencies

Plan your résumé carefully.

- Determine the type of job you seek and compile a list of prospective employers.
- Consider the type of information about you and your background of most importance to potential employers.
- Determine, based on this information, the details that should be included and the most effective way to present them.

Write an effective letter of application.

- Catch the reader's attention.
- Create the desire for your services.
- Include a brief summary of your qualifications for the specific job for which you are applying.
- State when and where you can be reached.

Follow these steps to prepare for a job interview:

- Learn everything you can about your prospective employer.
- Arrive on time.
- Highlight those strengths most useful to the job for which you are applying.
- Demonstrate your knowledge of your field.
- Send the interviewer a brief note of thanks after the interview.

When you receive a job offer, write one of the following letters:

- If you plan to accept the offer, send a letter of acceptance as soon as possible after you receive the offer.
- If you plan to refuse, send a letter as soon as possible refusing the offer but expressing your appreciation for the organization's time and effort in considering you.

Follow these guidelines in preparing a letter or memo of resignation:

- Begin and end the message on a positive note.
- Explain the reason for your departure factually and objectively.
- Give at least two weeks' notice (and preferably longer) to allow your employer time to prepare for your departure.

Exercises

1. Write a letter or an e-mail message to a past or present teacher, employer, or other appropriate person, asking permission to use him or her as a job reference. Be prepared to explain in class why you think this person is especially well qualified to comment on your job qualifications.
2. Obtain a sample résumé at your school's career-development center or local copy center. Annotate and write a brief critical analysis of the résumé for your instructor, pointing out its strong points and how it might be improved in content, organization, or design.
3. List five specific features a company or other employer would need to have to make you interested in working for it. Next, list what you would want to gain from your

work experience, such as learning more about a specific technology or other field that interests you.

4. Following the guidelines on pages 535–538, create a résumé to send in response to an online posting advertising a summer position in your field of study. Submit your résumé as an e-mail attachment to your instructor.
5. Using the guidelines in this chapter, write a letter of application and a résumé in response to an advertisement for a job you will be qualified for when you graduate. Use high-quality white bond paper and make sure the letter and résumé are error- and blemish-free.
6. Assume that you have been interviewed for the job in Exercise 5. Write a follow-up letter expressing thanks for the interview.
7. If your current résumé is organized by job chronology, prepare a second functional résumé that not only organizes work experience by type but also helps you identify important skills, abilities, or experiences. Follow the guidelines on pages 525–535. Your instructor may ask you to submit your chronological résumé with your functional résumé.
8. Review your existing résumé to make sure that the verbs and nouns in your job descriptions are consistent and parallel in structure. (See pages 104–105 in Chapter 4, Revising a Document.) Then modify your résumé to apply for two very different jobs.
9. Create an ASCII, or a plain-text, résumé that you could send via e-mail or upload to your website.

Collaborative Classroom Projects

1. Divide into groups of four to six classmates who share your major area (or a similar area) of study. Appoint a group leader and a recorder. For the first 30 minutes, brainstorm a list of action words that could be used to describe your collective skills, abilities, and experiences and that could work well in a résumé to be used to apply for a job in your field. During the next 15 minutes, brainstorm a list of positions that you could apply for when you graduate. Be ready to share your information with your classmates.
2. Working in pairs, spend 20 minutes during which you play the role of the job interviewer, while your partner plays the role of the interviewee. Then switch roles for the next 20 minutes. Begin by referring to the interview section of this chapter, and decide the name and type of company where you are interviewing, the position, and other details about the job. Include the following questions in the interview:
    - What are your short-term and long-term professional goals?
    - What are your major strengths and weaknesses?
    - Why do you want to work for our company?
    - What accomplishment are you particularly proud of? Describe it.
    - Why should I hire you?

    In conclusion, consider what answers you would change in preparation for your next interview.

Research Projects

1. Research three major employers in your field and, in an outline format, answer the following questions about each:
   a. What kind of an organization is it?
   b. Is it a for-profit, nonprofit, or governmental organization?
   c. Does it provide a service or services? If so, what kind(s)?
   d. What does its mission statement reveal?
   e. How large is the business? How large are its assets?
   f. Is it locally owned? Is it a subsidiary of a larger operation? Is it expanding?
   g. How long has it been in business?
   h. If it is government employment, at what level or in what sector is it?
   i. Where would you fit in?

   You can obtain information from the Internet, current employees, company literature such as employee publications, and the business section of back issues of local and national newspapers (available in the library and on the Web).

2. Imagine that you work for a large consulting company that has been hired to give a presentation in several European countries on how to seek employment in the United States. You've received several samples of would-be applicants' résumés and have noticed many differences between the structure of their résumés and what is expected in the United States. Research job-hunting and résumé-writing strategies used in two other countries of your choice, then create a presentation on American-style résumé writing for job seekers from those countries (review Chapter 14, Giving Presentations and Conducting Meetings). Be sure to address the following issues:
   - The use of the title "motivation letter" instead of "cover letter"
   - The inclusion of an applicant's date of birth, marital status, and children on résumés
   - Personal photographs
   - Chronological order versus reverse chronological order
   - Spelling
   - College-level education described as "tertiary" education
   - Paper size (can your printer accommodate, say, European Union correspondence?)

3. Review the websites of at least three online college or university placement centers, including the one hosted by your school. These centers offer links and general job-search information and can be helpful as you plan your own specific job search. Begin with the Center for Career Opportunities at Purdue University at www.cco.purdue.edu. Write a brief analysis of at least three career-planning sites you reviewed (include the URLs). Be ready to share your results with the class.

4. Find information about the future employment potential of graduates in your major field of study by using at least five Web sources. In a brief memo to your instructor, answer the following questions about your major field:
   a. Based on current indicators, what are the job projections in your field in this country?
   b. Is there a worldwide demand for people in your field?
   c. Do employees in your field have an opportunity to advance?
   d. In your field, is there a wide range in salary expectations based on geographic location?
   e. What other relevant information can you provide?

PART 4
Appendixes

Appendix A

Writing in an Online Environment

This appendix offers guidance to help you write and organize online content. It emphasizes the importance of collaborating closely with designers, developers, and media strategists to optimize content for speed and accessibility.[1] From corporate Web pages to social-media sites to intranet and document-management systems, nowadays you need not only produce content but also tailor that content to the expectations and protocols of the type of technology where your writing appears. You may be asked to create a blog for customer relations, post messages to a company's Twitter feed, develop answers for an FAQ page, write a product description for inclusion in a company catalog, update and expand a company's social-media presence, and more. Writing for the Web is very much like writing for print: You need to understand your purpose and your audience, carefully research your subject, organize your thoughts, use plain language, and make your text free of typographical or grammatical errors. Writing online, however, also includes the need to familiarize yourself with the type of technology you use to distribute your content as well as with the media's existing overall design and content areas. Be sure to review recently published material at the site to get a sense of the site's purpose and audience and how your content works in relationship to both. Also be sure that the content complies with organizational policies and legal standards.

[1]In the workplace, Web masters or site designers maintain site-wide technical and design standards; media coordinators play the same role for other online media. On campus, your instructor or the campus computer support staff can guide you on standards for posting content.

Despite their overlapping similarities, writing online content is different from writing for print—and more challenging—because your online audience is scanning a screen and expects to get information quickly and efficiently, with competing sources of information only a click away. Moreover, you may have a global audience that requires special communications awareness. For these reasons, ease of access to your content will be affected by how it is written and organized, the speed at which it loads to your readers' screens, the technology that's available and used to transmit your content, and even the language-translation options available at your site.

Crafting Content for Rapid Consumption

People read text on websites differently than they read text on paper. Few people read online content word for word. Most—up to 80 percent—scan the screen for what interests them or for what they need. "The average user spends less than a minute" on a page before leaving.[2] And although motivated readers slow down to read medical, financial, or how-to information, for example, most people scan and read rapidly. Given the reader's brief attention span and other features unique to websites, you must plan and organize your information to promote ease of use and comprehension, as well as select the outlet or transmittal method that best displays your information to readers scanning your content.

Whether you plan to write original content for a website or repurpose content from an existing source, use the following guidelines to plan and organize your text and graphics.

Using the Inverted Pyramid

Begin with the bottom line—your conclusions—by using the inverted-pyramid method traditionally used by journalists to organize your writing. State your most important points before providing the detailed background information—facts, data, and logic—to support them. As the data shows, most Web readers skim content and may not scroll to the end of your content, so placing the most important information first allows readers to grasp its significance or "take-away" message quickly. Of course, you still need to provide essential background details, explanations, documentation, and other information for readers wishing for the additional level of detail. You can also reduce the amount of background information on a page by linking to second- or third-level content elsewhere. (This technique is described in detail on pages 586–589.) Placing your most important ideas first also optimizes your content for Web searches because search engines scan the first several paragraphs of a Web page, in addition to other relevant site information, like paragraph headings. Figure A-1 depicts this method in principle, and Figure A-2 shows how it works in practice.

◆ ***The inverted-pyramid method is also described as decreasing order of importance on pages 50–51 in Chapter 2, Planning a Document.***

[2]Neilson Norman Group, "How Long Do Users Stay on Web Pages?," http://www.nngroup.com/articles/how-long-do-users-stay-on-web-pages/.

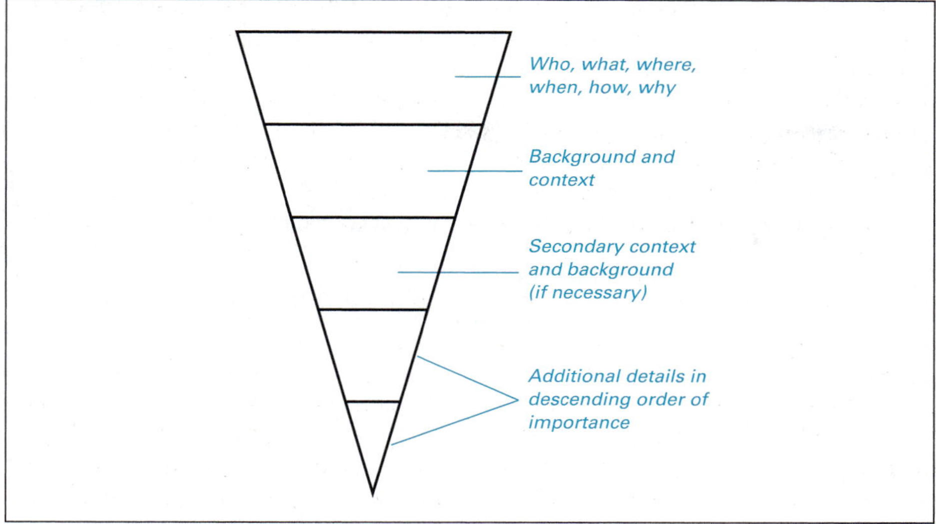

Figure A–1 The Inverted-Pyramid Method of Organizing Information

Using a Simple Style and an Appropriate Tone

If you want your ideas to make an impact on the Web, your writing style must be plain, honest, and to the point. Web users are looking for information, not unsupported claims—whether you are describing a product (such as a smart phone) or a public policy idea (such as charter schools). To this end, avoid promotional language that inflates the claims of the product or idea but provides no corroborating information to support those claims, as in the first example.

UNSUPPORTED CLAIM	Amco's All-in-One Mini Sound System is the best product in its class on the Internet! Buy one today!
SUPPORTED CLAIM	Amco's All-in-One Mini Sound System is a proven leader in compact systems based on industry tests and was voted the #1 mini sound system for 2016 by *Audio Magazine*.

Note that the improved version links directly to the source of the evidence (*industry tests* and *Audio Magazine*) that supports the company's claims about the product.

Remember that regardless of the technology used to reach your reader, your words and tone represent your company or project. Eliminate any biased or sexist language and resist the temptation to insert unnecessary and inappropriate humor in any writing—Web or otherwise—intended for the public. Also avoid puns, which suggest too much informality and can confuse your international readers. This guidance applies equally to the language of the captions and callouts for graphics or other design elements, such as videos or the inclusion of live data from other sites.

◆ ***For comprehensive guidance on style, tone, and the avoidance of biased language, see Chapter 4, Revising a Document.***

Press Release

Tetra Tech Wins $30 Million NIST Engineering Services Contract

Who, what, where, and when

PASADENA, Calif.–(BUSINESS WIRE)– Sep. 29, 2014–Tetra Tech, Inc. (NASDAQ: TTEK) announced today it has been awarded a five-year Indefinite Delivery-Indefinite Quantity, $30 million contract with the National Institute of Standards and Technology (NIST) to provide engineering services for the NIST Center for Neutron Research (NCNR).

Scope of activity

Tetra Tech will support the NCNR by providing world-class engineering services, including conceptual design/requirements analysis, and systems design and integration services to support upgrades for scientific instrumentation, procedures, and other NCNR components. In addition, Tetra Tech will develop new tools and systems to support the research objectives at the NCNR.

Background information about company

The NCNR includes a heavy water cooled and moderated nuclear test reactor licensed by the Nuclear Regulatory Commission that provides neutrons for cutting-edge research in biology, materials science, chemistry, and physics. www.ncnr.nist.gov.

About Tetra Tech (www.tetratech.com)

Tetra Tech is a leading provider of consulting, engineering, program management, construction management, and technical services. The Company supports government and commercial clients by providing innovative solutions to complex problems focused on water, environment, energy, infrastructure, and natural resources. With 14,000 employees worldwide, Tetra Tech's capabilities span the entire project life cycle.

Disclaimer statement

Any statements made in this release that are not based on historical fact are forward-looking statements. Any forward-looking statements made in this release represent management's best judgment as to what may occur in the future. However, Tetra Tech's actual outcome and results are not guaranteed and are subject to certain risks, uncertainties and assumptions ("Future Factors"), and may differ materially from what is expressed. For a description of Future Factors that could cause actual results to differ materially from such forward-looking statements, see the discussion under the section "Risk Factors" included in the Company's Form 10-K and 10-Q filings with the Securities and Exchange Commission.

Contact information

Tetra Tech, Inc.
Jim Wu, Investor Relations
Charlie MacPherson, Media & Public Relations
626-470-2844

Figure A–2 Press Release at a Website, Using Inverted-Pyramid Organization
Source: Tetra Tech, Inc.

Writing Concisely

Readers looking for useful content in a hurry value conciseness. The following guidelines will help you achieve conciseness:

- Cover one idea in each paragraph.
- Begin each paragraph with a topic sentence.
- Try to limit each paragraph to three or four sentences.
- Aim for short sentences with simple sentence structure; use concrete nouns and active verbs.
- Use plain language.

If the medium you use has text limitations or styles that are different from these guidelines, still strive for conciseness. Doing so is especially important when users access your Web content on mobile devices. For example, for postings to a Twitter page, use the 140-character limitation to your advantage by employing plain and concrete language.

PROFESSIONALISM NOTE: Condense Online Content for Ease of Scanning Writing concisely requires critical thinking to sort essential from "nice to have" but nonessential content. As you condense content, do not omit essential terms and phrases like articles (a, *an*, *the*), pronouns (*I*, *we*, *them*, etc.), conjunctions (*or*, *nor*, *and*), and transitional terms (*however*, *therefore*, *nevertheless*). These terms enhance clarity and coherence; their omission can cause ambiguity and create misunderstanding. For Twitter postings, the character limitations make abbreviated writing tempting, especially for personal messages. In the workplace, however, check your employer's policy for use of shortened terminology before using it.

Figure A–3 depicts a page on the website of the U.S. Small Business Administration (SBA), which explains how to start and manage a home-based business. Because it provides how-to information, the language must be detailed and accurate. Even so, it can be made concise and organized for ease of reading. The page is effective because each paragraph is introduced by a pertinent heading, opens with a topic sentence, and covers one facet of the subject in plain language. The page integrates an engaging visual as well.

Chunking Content

Another way to focus reader attention is to break up dense blocks of text by dividing them into short paragraphs so that they stand out and can be quickly scanned and absorbed. Each chunked passage should coherently focus on one facet of your topic. Identify such passages with captions or headings that announce the topic and help the reader decide at a glance whether to read the material. Include links for more detailed secondary or background information to avoid slowing readers not interested in that level of information. Use the inverted-pyramid principle shown in Figure A–1 to organize these passages.

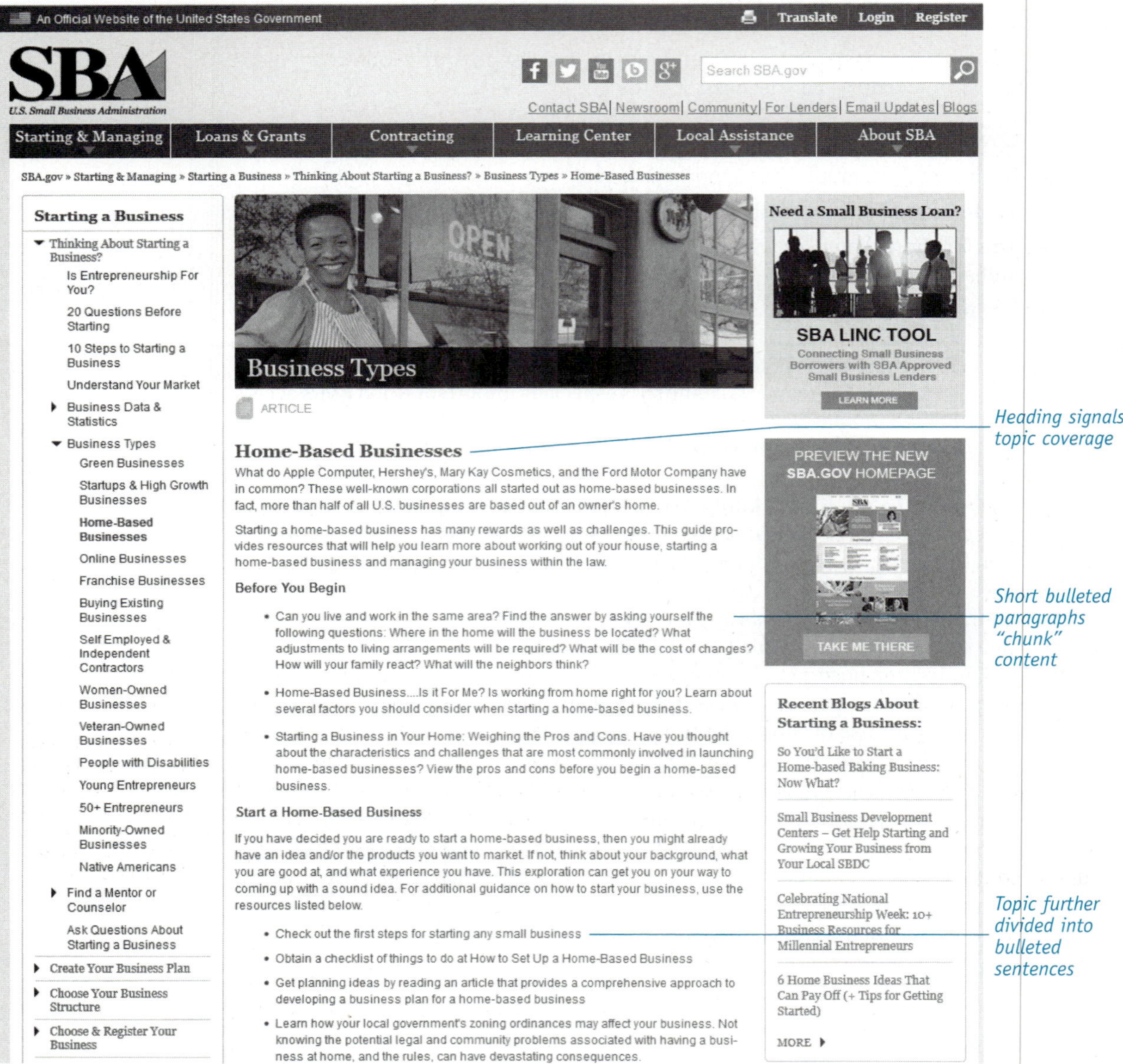

Figure A–3 Web Page Featuring Chunked Content

Source: https:/www.sba.gov/content/home-based-businesses.

◆ *For additional guidelines on using topic sentences, achieving conciseness, and using plain language, see Chapter 4, Revising a Document.*

The Web pages shown in Figures A–2 and A–3 both effectively divide their content into short paragraphs and include links to additional material. Each paragraph in Figure A–2 focuses on one point and, for ease of access, is set off from the others by white space. The use of headings and bulleted lists in Figure A–3 makes the information even easier to scan. The passages in both figures are grouped in a logical sequence for the information covered.

WRITER'S CHECKLIST

Crafting Content for the Web

- ✔ Organize content from the top down—begin with your most important point, adding supporting details and background information in descending order of importance.
- ✔ Present ideas as concisely as possible and express them in plain language.
- ✔ Support all claims with relevant data.
- ✔ Chunk dense blocks of text into shorter passages that stand out for ease of reading and introduce them with informative headings.
- ✔ Create hyperlinks to additional information to reduce content on your page and to enrich coverage of your topic.
- ✔ Review hyperlinks periodically to ensure that their content continues to be relevant to your purposes.

Highlighting Information

Writing and organizing text for rapid consumption are essential first steps to promoting ease of access to your content. You can further augment access through a variety of highlighting techniques, some common to printed text and some unique to online content.

Using Headings and Subheadings

Headings reduce the complexity of text by highlighting structure and showing organization. They also signal breaks in coverage from one topic to the next. Readers use them to scan rapidly for meaningful information on-screen as well as in printed documents. Set off headings in boldface or another text attribute, such as color, on a separate line either directly above or in the left margin directly across from the text they describe. Figure A–3 on page 582 uses headings effectively to introduce and divide content.

◆ ***For additional guidance about the use of headings to highlight content, see pages 216 in Chapter 7, Designing Documents and Visuals, and pages 377–382 in Chapter 11, Writing Formal Reports.***

Using Bulleted and Numbered Lists

Like headings, bulleted and numbered lists break up dense paragraphs. They also reduce text length and highlight relevant content instead of embedding it within paragraphs. Bulleted lists show readers that the items displayed are parallel in importance. Numbered lists inform readers immediately that the sequence of your information is crucial. Regardless of the form the list takes, make all items in it grammatically parallel.

Note that not all text passages should be broken into bulleted lists. Doing so would make your pages look like a PowerPoint presentation but without a speaker to fill in the context for the bulleted points. Lists without supporting explanatory text lack coherence. The bulleted items in Figure A–3 are effective because they focus reader attention on specific issues to consider before starting a home-based business, including some of the pros and cons.

◆ ***For more information about creating numbered and bulleted lists, see pages 105–106 in Chapter 4, Revising a Document.***

Giving Directional Cues

Avoid navigational cues that make sense on the printed page but not on a screen, such as "as shown in the example below" or "in the graph at the top of this page." Phrases like these can be confusing when there is no real reference for "above" and "below" and no "top" or "bottom" of the document. Instead, position links so that they are tied directly to the content to which they pertain. (See the sample Back to Top link on page 587.)

The terms "next" and "previous" can also cause confusion. Use these terms only when you know users accessed your page from an immediately preceding page. These terms are, however, used appropriately to navigate through PDF files.

Providing Keywords for Content Retrieval

One challenge of writing for the Web is making sure that your desired audience can find your page. To increase the odds that Web search engines will locate your site, use keywords to describe your important content.

NO KEYWORDS

Remembering Our Founder
We are proud to introduce a new commemorative coin honoring our company's founder and president. The item will be available on this website after December 1, 2016, which is the 100th anniversary of our first sale.

WITH KEYWORDS

Reynolds Commemorative Coin on Sale
The new *Reynolds* commemorative coin features a portrait of *George G. Reynolds*, the founder and president of *Reynolds Corporation*. The *coin* can be purchased on our website (www.reynoldswidgetcorp.com/coin.htm) after December 1, 2016, in honor of the 100th anniversary of the sale of the first *Reynolds widget*.

By using such words in the text and heading as "Reynolds," "George G. Reynolds," and "coin" instead of "our company's," "our founder," and "item," you will give the search engines specific information that they, in turn, can give to users. The revised paragraph also includes a link to the company's website for ease of access to those wishing to purchase the coin. To learn more about search-engine optimization (SEO), Google Ad Words, and Internet marketing tools, visit http://moz.com/beginners-guide-to-SEO.

Using Graphics and Typography

The way your content looks on-screen when published will be affected by the site's existing design and by the standards in place at your organization or imposed by the transmittal method that you choose. On your company's website, the page will likely display a banner at the top, featuring the organization or company name; navigational toolbars at the top, bottom, or left side of the screen; links to other content areas; and other elements. The site's design standards may affect the line length of your text (such as single or double columns); the standardized type sizes and styles in use at the site;

and the preferred format for graphics files, color, and a variety of other features. On social-media platforms, however, the way your content looks is predetermined and limited, so you must consider how to adapt content for your audience and purpose into the existing site limitations. (See the Professionalism Note on page 581 about using concise language.)

Graphics

As with print publications, your audience and purpose should determine *why* graphics are important to your content. At times, graphic elements — photographs, line drawings, animations, or videos — provide visual relief from dense text and are appealing and motivational, as in Figure A-3 on page 582. For the most part, however, use only images that illustrate essential information. Because users depend on the site for accessible and visually clear information, use graphics that load as quickly as possible and be mindful that some international site users may not have high-speed Internet access. Large or high-resolution graphics, like color photographs or animated images, can cause long delays as they download in some systems. For high-resolution graphics that are essential, use thumbnails — images reduced to 10 to 15 percent of the original file size — for quick access. Work with the site's Web master to optimize all graphics for speed of access. Ask about the preferred file-compression format — JPEG, GIF, or other — for visuals you submit. Unless the graphic is meant to be downloaded or printed, a higher dpi makes the document slower to load. Also consider giving visitors a graphics-free option for quicker access to your content. Doing so also makes your information accessible to individuals with disabilities who use screen-reader technology.

Font Size and Style

Font sizes and styles affect screen legibility. Computer screens display fonts at lower resolutions than in most printed text. If your company has a standard font preference, use it. Otherwise, review the text of your content on an internal browser for legibility before posting it for public access. Be aware, however, that even with your best efforts to ensure legibility, the user's browser, operating system, and font preferences can affect how your text looks on the user's screen.

◆ ***For more information about type sizes and styles, see pages 214–215 in Chapter 7, Designing Documents and Visuals.***

Line Length

Line length also affects legibility. Short line lengths reduce the amount of eye movement necessary to scan text. For websites, the optimal line length is approximately half the width of the screen.[3] To achieve this length, draft text that's between 50 and 70 characters, or 10 to 12 words to a line. Longer lines make it difficult for readers to locate the next line of text at the left margin, particularly for single-spaced paragraphs. Finally, as with printed material, do not use all-capital letters or boldface type for blocks of text. They slow reader speed and comprehension.

---

[3]Patrick L. Lynch and Sara Horton, *Web Style Guide: Basic Design Principles for Creating Web Sites*, 3rd ed. (New Haven, CT: Yale University Press, 2009), 192, 215. See also www.webstyleguide.com.

Special Font Characters

For content that contains special or international characters, consult with the Web master about the best way to submit the files for HTML coding. Special font characters include, among others, bullets, dashes, and asterisks; symbols for chemical and mathematical equations; and fonts and accent marks for non-English languages. Consult your site's standards for converting these characters to HTML before submitting your files for posting or before posting them yourself.

DESIGNING YOUR CONTENT

Highlighting Information

- Use headings and subheadings to introduce text passages, to signal changes in topics, and to provide visual breaks on the page.
- Use bulleted lists to display text in an easy-to-scan format when the ideas are parallel in meaning.
- Use numbered lists to display content when the sequence or hierarchy of the information matters.
- Make all bulleted and numbered lists grammatically parallel.
- Provide hyperlinks to additional content rather than written directions for finding it elsewhere on the site.
- Use keywords to describe important content so that Web search engines will find your page.
- Select graphics that are essential to your audience and purpose.
- Optimize graphics files so that they download quickly.
- If you cannot avoid large file sizes, use thumbnails of the graphics on your page that link to the original-size images.
- Use appropriate font styles, type sizes, and line lengths to enhance the legibility of your content.

Linking to Internal Content

Use internal *hyperlinks* as additional access points to your information. These links work best to provide facts, data, charts, glossaries, or documentation to support or expand coverage of information on the screen, such as a link to a research article or an illustration. Internal links can also connect your writing with other company applications, such as access to digital repair manuals, ordering systems, or "live help" messaging systems. They give site users quick access to material and save them the trouble of having to scroll through screen after screen to locate content.

If your coverage on a single page stretches beyond two or three screens, as for a short report, booklet, or pamphlet, create a table of contents for it at the top of the Web page. Create a hyperlink for each heading in the table of contents to the same heading further down the page. Make sure these links are visible on the first screen so that readers need not scroll down to see them but can access a specific section quickly and easily as shown in Figure A–4. Depending on the overall site design, the complete document may even be located at a different part of the site, such as in a collection of similar documents, thus eliminating the need for the reader to scroll down a single screen to review it.

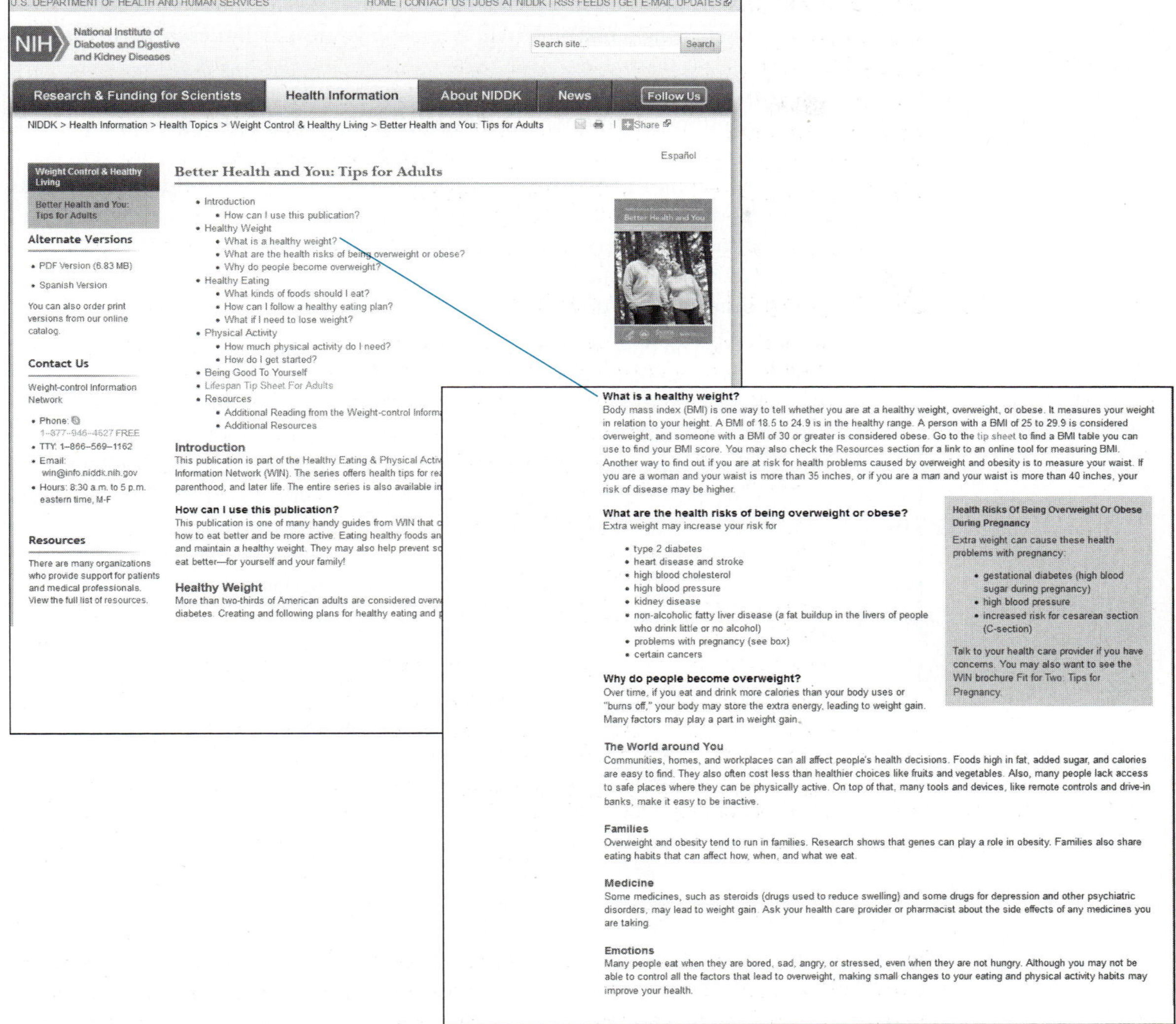

Figure A–4 Table of Contents Linking to Content on Same Web Page

Source: http://www.niddk.nih.gov/health-information/health-topics/weight-control/better-health/Pages/better-health-and-you-tips-for-adults.aspx#r.

Likewise, you can link site users to smaller related "chunks" of content on a given topic (such as technical specifications, price lists, or engineering drawings) that are located in a content management system for company product information.

In addition to informational links, Web pages also include navigational links that move visitors through a document and site. For lengthy content on a single page, include directional cues, such as links at convenient breaks so that users can get to the top of the page without having to scroll.

▲
Back to Top

These links are placed between text passages where they do not interrupt readers. Most sites use standardized navigational links whose meanings are usually described at the site's Help page.

Use links to focus user attention, not to distract it. Keep hyperlinks *within* text paragraphs to a minimum. Otherwise, they are visually distracting (underlined or colored) and make scanning the text difficult. Embedded links also tempt readers to leave the page before reaching the end of your content. Rather than embedding hyperlinks throughout the body of your text, combine them into short, well-organized lists that are introduced with explanatory text. Be sure to inform readers where the link will take them. In some cases, the title of the link is self-explanatory: Glossary or For Additional Information. At other times, you need to add a brief explanatory passage:

- Refer to the section on Plug-ins, Viewers, and Other Tools for information on icons associated with document formats, such as PDFs, used at this site.

You can place lists of hyperlinks periodically throughout your document to break up large blocks of text or you can place a list of links at the end of your document, as you would with footnotes. Finally, avoid cuing readers with the phrase "Click Here." The phrase offers no useful information and is considered a Web cliché.

AVOID	To learn more about our company, Click Here.
BETTER	Learn more about the XYZ Corporation.

Linking to External Content

Links to external (or outside) sites can be an invaluable way of expanding your content. However, be sure to review such sites and their content carefully before linking to them. Is the site's author or sponsoring organization reputable? Is the content accurate and current? Does the site date-stamp its content (such as "This page was last updated on January 12, 2016")? Is the information unbiased?

Some websites request that you ask their permission before linking to them. To determine a site's policy in this regard, review its Terms of Use page, usually accessible from the home page. Although linking to another site is easily done, your organization may have a policy of asking permission of outside sites before linking to them. Your organization may also require a "you are leaving our site" warning or that external links open in a new browser window, so learn your company's requirements before adding external links. To ask permission, e-mail a request to the site's Web master and check with your site's Web administrator to find out if standardized language exists for making such requests. Finally, remember that you have no control over the site to which you are linking, so keep in mind that the content on that site could change dramatically at any time. Although workplace websites usually have software that identifies nonworking links, you still need to check links that are working to ensure that their content continues to meet your requirements.

Link directly to the page or specific area of an external site that is relevant to your users and be sure that your writing provides a clear context for why you're sending your readers there and what they will find. The following passage appears at the Web site for the Nuclear Regulatory Commission (NRC). It directs users to a non-NRC site to obtain automatic updates about business opportunities with the agency.

> **How to Identify Potential Contract Opportunities**
>
> NRC publicizes and posts proposed business opportunities valued at greater than $25,000 on the FedBizOpps EXIT Web site. Once at this site, select "Vendors," select "NRC" from the pull-down menu, and select "Posted Dates," which takes you into NRC business opportunities. From here, select the posted opportunity you are interested in. You may also register at FedBizOpps EXIT to receive any further notifications about that specific opportunity by selecting "Register to Receive Notification." Enter your e-mail address, Solicitation Number, and select the "Subscribe to Mailing List" button at the bottom of the page. By registering with FedBizOpps, your company can be notified via e-mail of procurement opportunities the day they are posted.

Note the EXIT label in this passage. Many sites place an icon or a text label next to links to external sites to inform users that they are leaving the host site. Other sites show pop-up text, saying, "You are now leaving the XYZ Corporation site. Continue or stay?" A site's Help page may explain the purpose of the practice, such as the following passage:

> **Exit** EXIT
>
> The Exit icon is placed directly after an external link to let you know that the link is going to take you away from the XYZ Corp. site. These links are provided as a service and do not imply any official endorsement of or responsibility for the opinions, ideas, data, or products presented at these locations or guarantee the validity of the information provided. (For more information, refer to the Site Disclaimer.)

Check with your Web master or site administrator about site policy for these notices if your content includes links to external sites.

For guidance evaluating research sources, including websites, see the Writer's Checklist, pages 175–176 of Chapter 6, Conducting Research for a Document.

Once you link to another site, you are responsible for checking periodically to ensure that the content remains accurate and current—or that it hasn't disappeared. Many corporate or organizational sites post a disclaimer, such as the following, to inform users that information at external sites is not under their control and may at times be erroneous.

> *Disclaimer:* The XYZ Corporation cannot guarantee the accuracy, completeness, or reliability of all information on non-XYZ servers and websites to which the XYZ site links.

Repurposing Existing Content

You may be asked to submit existing content to a website. It may be a report, user manual, or parts of a policy-and-procedure handbook. In its original form, the content will be organized to be read in the sequence written for paper publication. If the document is lengthy, it makes sense to retain the document's original sequence and page layout. If you shorten or revise your original document for posting on the Web, footnote or otherwise mark the Web content accordingly, as in the following example, so that readers will know that it differs from the original.

> *The data in Appendix A of this report are updated monthly and vary from the data in the printed report, which is published each February.

Documents posted on the Web are frequently converted to PDF files to display the pages on-screen exactly as they appear in print. Readers can read the PDF version online, download it to a hard drive, or print it in whole or in part. Converting an important document to a PDF file also protects the content from being tampered with. PDF files can be formatted to prevent the viewer from being able to make changes to the document or from easily copying, pasting, or editing the document in a word processor. Regardless of the format or version you use, do the following before you prepare existing print documents for public availability on a website:

- Review the document for compliance with your organization's publishing policies:
  - Is it appropriate for public access?
  - Is it consistent with current policies and practices for the organization's products and services?
  - Does it contain proprietary and privacy information that must be protected or deleted?
- Obtain permission for Web publication if the document contains copyrighted text, tables, or images. (Some copyright holders require separate permissions for printed and Web publication of their content.)
- Contact the site Web staff about the preferred electronic-file format in which to submit the document for coding and posting: Microsoft Word, PageMaker, PDF, FrameMaker, or other format.
- Ask the Web master to optimize any slow-loading graphics files for quick access.
- Review the coded document on an internal website *before* it is posted to the public site to ensure that it is the correct version, that no information is missing, and that all links work and go to the right places.

If your document is long, assume that users will print it to read offline. Consult your site's Web master about creating a single-file version of the document to optimize printing.

DIGITAL TIP: Digitally Enhancing Repurposed Content

Many organizations publish repurposed content, like formal reports, as PDF files or Web documents. By taking advantage of these digital media, you can add functionality to the content. Digital versions of formal reports can, for example, offer tables of contents that link directly to the individual sections within a report. You can add hyperlinks or mouse-over elements that add definitions of specialized terms or links to supplemental information. Further enhancements could include interactive components, such as forms and graphics that readers can manipulate.

Documenting Sources of Information

As with print publications, you must document and acknowledge outside sources of information or of help received — text, images, streaming video, and other multimedia material. If any of this source material is copyrighted, you must seek approval from the copyright holder before using it. Likewise, you may use material in the public domain and, with some limitations, content that is licensed under Creative Commons, as described at http://creativecommons.org/about. Documenting sources at your site has at least two major advantages: (1) It discloses where you obtained your information, thereby bolstering the site's credibility, and (2) it allows users to locate that source, if necessary. The site should also document information in the public domain, such as publications and websites of the federal government.

Site credibility is further enhanced by acknowledging help received in the creation or review of content at the site. Note the passage in the third paragraph of the Weight-control Information Network of NIH's website, shown in Figure A–5. These acknowledgments attest to the accuracy, quality, and objectivity of the information provided. However, text created by company employees, information repurposed from one medium to another, or research internal to a company is considered authored by the company and does not require citation.

◆ *For guidance on the use and documentation of source material, including electronic information, see Chapter 6, Conducting Research for a Document.*

ETHICS NOTE: Document Sources of Online Content in a Citation or by Linking to Them Keep a record of how and where you find content online, be it text, images, tables, streaming video, or other material. Seek prior approval from the copyright holder before using any such information. Documenting your sources not only is required legally and ethically but also bolsters the credibility of your site. To document your sources, either provide links to your source or use a citation, as described in Chapter 6, Conducting Research for a Document.

Protecting User Privacy

Most Internet users wish to have information about themselves — name, residential and e-mail addresses, phone number, personal opinions, and the like — kept confidential. In response to this concern, all reputable websites post a privacy notice. Usually a link on the home page, the notice informs users about how the website intends to handle solicited and unsolicited information from individuals received at the site and includes its policy on the use of cookies.[4] If you plan to collect such information on your page or if your page has a Contact Us link, ask the site Web master to put a link on your page to the site-wide privacy statement. Note that the privacy notice in Figure A–6, excerpted from the Amazon.com website, appears on its home page (www.amazon.com) and other locations throughout the site.

---

[4]Cookies are small files that are downloaded to your computer when you browse certain Web pages. Cookies hold information, such as language and selections that you've made, so you do not need to render those selections each time you visit the site.

Weight-control Information Network

1 WIN Way
Bethesda, MD 20892-3665
Phone: (202) 828-1025
Toll-free number: 1-877-946-4627 Fax: (202) 828-1028
Email: WIN@info.niddk.nih.gov
Internet: *http://www.win.niddk.nih.gov*

The Weight-control Information Network (WIN) is a national information service of the National Institute of Diabetes and Digestive and Kidney Diseases (NIDDK) of the National Institutes of Health (NIH), which is the Federal Government's lead agency responsible for biomedical research on nutrition and obesity. Authorized by Congress (Public Law 103-43), WIN provides the general public, health professionals, the media, and Congress with up-to-date, science-based information on weight control, obesity, physical activity, and related nutritional issues.

Detailed listing of content reviewers

Publications produced by WIN are reviewed by both NIDDK scientists and outside experts. This fact sheet was also reviewed by Rick Troiano, Ph.D., National Cancer Institute; Cynthia Ogden, Ph.D., National Center for Health Statistics (NCHS), CDC; and Katherine Flegal, Ph.D., Senior Research Scientist, NCHS, CDC.

This publication is not copyrighted. WIN encourages users of this fact sheet to duplicate and distribute as many copies as desired. This fact sheet is also available at *http://www.win.niddk.nih.gov*.

NIH Publication Number 04-4158
Updated February 2010

Toll free: 1-877-946-4627; Fax: 202-828-1028; Email: win@info.niddik.nih.gov
Weight-control Information Network, 1 WIN Way, Bethesda, MD 20892-3665

Figure A–5 Page Acknowledging Expert Review of Content
Source: National Institute of Health, http://www.niddk.nih.gov/health-information/health-topics/weight-control/better-health/Pages/better-health-and-you-tips-for-adults.aspx#r%20/%20http://www.win.niddk.nih.gov.

Some corporate privacy statements describe their policy for sharing user information, such as subscriber lists, with third parties for marketing purposes. Informing users of this practice is both candid and ethical. These sites often give users the opportunity to refuse permission to use their addresses for marketing.

Although important to keep confidential, user information (search patterns, content feedback, questions about goods and services) is a valuable source of information about the public's use of a site. The Web server, for example, can log data on site usage (number of users accessing a page, duration of their stay, etc.). This and other kinds of feedback are collected and compiled anonymously and can be used to make helpful revisions to your content.

CONSIDERING AUDIENCE AND PURPOSE

Protecting the Privacy of Your Users

- Provide users with a link to the site's privacy statement, particularly if you solicit comments or provide an e-mail link for unsolicited comments.
- Inform users if you intend to use their information for marketing or if you intend to share their information with third parties.
- Give visitors the option of refusing permission to have their information used for marketing.

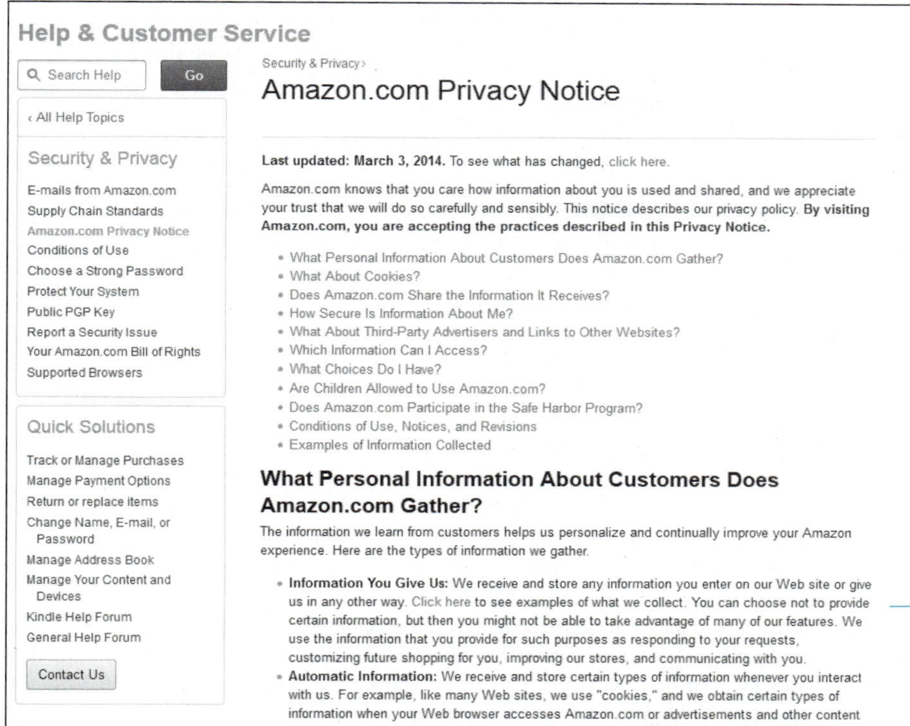

Help & Customer Service

Search Help Go

‹ All Help Topics

Security & Privacy

E-mails from Amazon.com
Supply Chain Standards
Amazon.com Privacy Notice
Conditions of Use
Choose a Strong Password
Protect Your System
Public PGP Key
Report a Security Issue
Your Amazon.com Bill of Rights
Supported Browsers

Quick Solutions

Track or Manage Purchases
Manage Payment Options
Return or replace items
Change Name, E-mail, or Password
Manage Address Book
Manage Your Content and Devices
Kindle Help Forum
General Help Forum

Contact Us

Security & Privacy ›

Amazon.com Privacy Notice

Last updated: March 3, 2014. To see what has changed, click here.

Amazon.com knows that you care how information about you is used and shared, and we appreciate your trust that we will do so carefully and sensibly. This notice describes our privacy policy. **By visiting Amazon.com, you are accepting the practices described in this Privacy Notice.**

- What Personal Information About Customers Does Amazon.com Gather?
- What About Cookies?
- Does Amazon.com Share the Information It Receives?
- How Secure Is Information About Me?
- What About Third-Party Advertisers and Links to Other Websites?
- Which Information Can I Access?
- What Choices Do I Have?
- Are Children Allowed to Use Amazon.com?
- Does Amazon.com Participate in the Safe Harbor Program?
- Conditions of Use, Notices, and Revisions
- Examples of Information Collected

What Personal Information About Customers Does Amazon.com Gather?

The information we learn from customers helps us personalize and continually improve your Amazon experience. Here are the types of information we gather.

- **Information You Give Us:** We receive and store any information you enter on our Web site or give us in any other way. Click here to see examples of what we collect. You can choose not to provide certain information, but then you might not be able to take advantage of many of our features. We use the information that you provide for such purposes as responding to your requests, customizing future shopping for you, improving our stores, and communicating with you.
- **Automatic Information:** We receive and store certain types of information whenever you interact with us. For example, like many Web sites, we use "cookies," and we obtain certain types of information when your Web browser accesses Amazon.com or advertisements and other content served by or on behalf of Amazon.com on other Web sites. Click here to see examples of the information we receive.
- **Mobile:** When you download or use apps created by Amazon or our subsidiaries, we may receive information about your location and your mobile device, including a unique identifier for your device. We may use this information to provide you with location-based services, such as advertising, search results, and other personalized content. Most mobile devices allow you to turn off location services. For more information about how to do this,click here.
- **E-mail Communications:** To help us make e-mails more useful and interesting, we often receive a confirmation when you open e-mail from Amazon.com if your computer supports such capabilities. We also compare our customer list to lists received from other companies, in an effort to avoid sending unnecessary messages to our customers. If you do not want to receive e-mail or other mail from us, please adjust your Customer Communication Preferences .
- **Information from Other Sources:** We might receive information about you from other sources and add it to our account information. Click here to see examples of the information we receive.

Opt-out choice

Figure A–6 Privacy Notice (Excerpt)

Enhancing Access to Content

The techniques discussed in the previous sections will help you organize and present text and graphics for the Web that are easy for your audience to understand. This section describes your responsibility as a content provider to ensure that your information is accessible to people with disabilities and that it meets the needs of international users.

Ensuring Access for People with Disabilities

Many of the advantages of websites include colorful graphics, animation, and streaming video and audio. However, these design elements can be barriers to people with impaired vision or hearing or those who are color blind. To overcome these barriers to your content, discuss the following strategies with your site-accessibility specialist or review relevant sections of the Americans with Disabilities Act (ADA), which requires accessible writing. Visit ada.gov for more information.

- Avoid frames, complex tables, animation, JavaScript, and other design elements that are incompatible with text-only browsers and adaptive technologies, such as screen readers or large-print software.[5] Work with available Web designers or work to develop an understanding of cascading style sheets to ensure that they are used properly to make the site easily accessible.
- Include closed captions for audiovisual files or text-equivalent captions that describe the graphic elements of your content (for example, "Photograph of Harriet V. Sullivan, President, HVS Accounting Services"). Also, learn about and implement "alt" and "label" tags that help accessibility programs successfully navigate many Web pages.
- Design for the reader who is color blind; use captions and other text to make meaning independent of color (Green, labeled *G*, means *All Safe*).

Implementing these measures requires the expertise of a Web-technology specialist. However, as the content provider, you will be expected to write text captions for all graphics and sound features. You may also want to offer different options for site visitors, such as full-graphics, light-graphics, and text-only versions of your content. Discuss these options with the developer or learn about the automatic tools in many content management systems that allow for the creation of separate versions of a page.

Finally, arrange with the site developer to have your content tested for accessibility. A complete list of Web-accessibility evaluation tools is located at www.w3.org/WAI/ER/tools/complete.

[5]Adaptive technologies, such as screen readers, use software to activate a voice synthesizer that reads aloud the text and captions for nontext elements (e.g., graphics) on a computer screen.

CONSIDERING AUDIENCE AND PURPOSE

Enhancing Access to Content

- Work with your site's Web master or accessibility specialist to provide content — text, graphics, audio — that is compatible with adaptive technologies used by people with disabilities.
- Create text captions used by screen-reader technology that accurately describe the graphics and audio features of your content.
- Describe color-coded content so that its meaning can be understood independent of color.
- Test your content for accessibility using an appropriate site listed at www.w3.org/WAI/ER/tools/complete.
- Create text, graphics, and units of measurement to accommodate international readers.

Considering International Users

Consider the needs of international readers if they are part of your target audience. You need not write simplistic prose to do so, nor do you need to write separate versions of your content for domestic and international readers. As with other writing aimed at readers of English as a second language, review your text to eliminate expressions and references that make sense only to someone very familiar with American English. Avoid expressions such as "throw in the towel," "a no-brainer," and "slam dunk." Likewise, when appropriate, express dates, clock times, and measurements consistent with international practices.

Choose visual content carefully, too. Opt for symbols and icons, colors, representations of human beings, and captions that can be easily understood. And use graphics (including video files) that load quickly for users without high-speed Internet access. (See Using Graphics and Typography, pages 584–586, for additional information.)

Finally, consider providing links to online translation sites for your international users. Your site Web master will likely provide information about online translation tools. If not, a selective listing of free translation sites is available at http://websearch.about.com/od/internetresearch/a/translate.htm.

◆ *For more information about international use of dates, times, and measurements, see page 323 in Chapter 9, Writing Routine and Sensitive Messages.*

◆ *For additional guidance on communicating with international audiences, see the following:*

- *Writing for an International Audience, page 74 in Chapter 3.*
- *Using Visuals to Communicate Internationally, pages 251–257 in Chapter 7*
- *Writing International Correspondence, pages 320–323 in Chapter 9.*
- *Reaching Global Audiences, pages 490–491 in Chapter 14.*

WRITER'S CHECKLIST

Thinking Globally

- ✔ Avoid slang — it's the least translatable content.
- ✔ For online sales sites, specify the currency you're using and add a link to a currency converter.
- ✔ Identify size or measurement units and add a link to a unit-conversion site.
- ✔ Specify the region and country to which you're referring. (There's a Kensington in Maryland as well as in England.)
- ✔ Note whether your company ships products to multiple countries or only domestically.

Social and Collaborative Media in the Workplace

A growing number of Web genres have become the focus of social and workplace interaction for the public and special-interest users. They include distinct Web genres, like blogs and other social-media sites that encourage the exchange of ideas and opinions among users interested in consumer goods, politics, technology, job opportunities, sports, and much more. They also include Web-based platforms, like wikis, that enable writers to collaborate on a writing project. The best-known example of a wiki is the online encyclopedia Wikipedia. Frequently asked questions (FAQs), although not unique to Web writing, have become a popular feature of corporate and organizational websites. By highlighting the information most commonly sought by users of an organization's products and services, FAQs save time and frustration for site users. Podcasting, a Web-based multimedia genre, is another important means of distributing a variety of workplace, educational, medical, and leisure-pursuit information to interested audiences.

Blogs and Forums

A blog (short for "Web log") is a Web-based journal for posting opinions, information, and responses to other bloggers on subjects of mutual interest to them. Blog sites may also include links to relevant websites or may contain documents and audiovisual files. The usefulness of a blog stems in large part from the immediate interactivity it offers target audiences. That is, anyone can submit a comment or question to a blog and have the organizational sponsor or other interested bloggers respond to it. All these postings are displayed and become part of an ongoing "conversation" about a topic. Blog entries are displayed in reverse chronological order, with the most recent post first. Blogs also allow the writer to offer timely and evolving information about a topic — such as a company's development of new products — while getting user feedback via conversations about the topic. And because it is an ongoing activity, readers who follow blogs expect the postings to be useful and to appear routinely. So posting blog entries and keeping them current requires a substantial commitment of time and effort. Sporadic postings and dated information will hurt you and your organization's credibility. As you plan a blog, survey such popular blogging platforms as WordPress (www.wordpress.com) and consult with your IT and marketing staff on how a blog might contribute to your organization.

Although blogs may allow readers to post comments, a *forum* typically fosters a wider "conversation" in which site visitors can not only respond to the posts of others but also begin new topics or discussion threads. Organizations often use forums for customer or technical support. If your website features a forum, you must promote it, contribute content, and solicit content from users or the forum will quickly lose its usefulness and fade.

Organizational Uses

Companies, local governments, and nonprofit organizations create blogs to help meet such goals as attracting and retaining clients or customers; promoting and obtaining feedback on their products and services; and even developing a sense of community among their customers, employees, citizens, and others. Unlike websites, which usually present a formal perspective on an organization, blogs provide an informal and interactive forum for organizations to communicate directly with a target audience. Organizations can create both external and internal blogs and forums.

External sites are publicly available on the Internet both for an organization's customers or clients and for executives, spokespeople, or employees to share their views. Blogs help build credibility for an organization because customers know they can "chat" with an organization's representative and exchange current information instead of relying on information in published documents and on websites. Google, for example, has an external blog where company marketing and engineering officials present information about their new products, changes in policies and features, and the reasoning behind some decisions. Broad in scope, the blog lists topics covered under the heading "Labels" in the right margin. Figure A–7 shows the first screen for Google's nonprofit organizational policies and practices blog. The open dialogue box lists the links to the blog archive for that topic.

Internal blogs are usually created for employees and can be accessed only through the organization's intranet site. Such internal blogs may serve as newsletters and help achieve the following organizational goals:

- Provide opportunities for employees to discuss issues or concerns.
- Encourage employee participation in upcoming events or initiatives.
- Share employee and community news, such as promotions, wedding and birth announcements, community outreach activities, and more.

Writing for Organizational Blogs and Forums

Write blog or forum entries in an informal, conversational style that uses contractions, first person, and active voice.

BLOG POSTING Check out the latest concept for our new 2016 Toyota Camry dashboard — we've added enough space to hold your coffee and a digital device by moving the air ducts to. . . . Tell us what you think.

FORUM POSTING I'm new to this thread, but I'm surprised no one's discussed the issue of confidentiality. My experience has been Facebook's recent change in privacy settings is just confusing. Have I missed something?

Keep your sentences and paragraphs concise. Use bulleted lists, italics, and other layout and design elements, such as boldface and white space if possible. Doing so can help readers scan the postings or text to find information that is interesting or relevant to them. Keep headlines short and direct to catch attention and increase the visual appeal and readability. Where helpful, provide links to other sites and resources that participants might find useful. When blogs expand or forums become popular, you may need to organize them using *categories* (links to discussion topics) or *tags* (keywords for searching the site's postings).

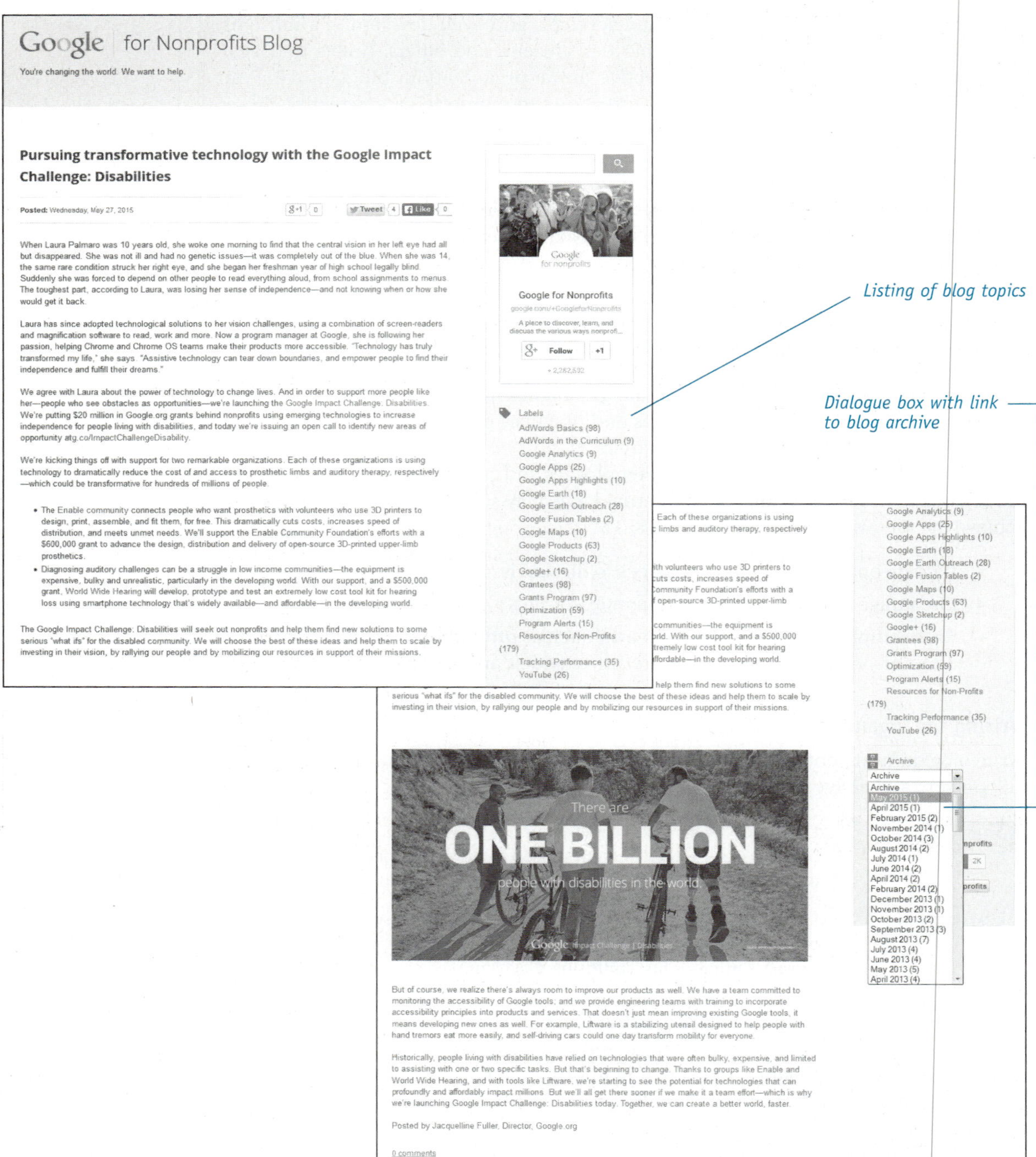

Google | for Nonprofits Blog

You're changing the world. We want to help.

Pursuing transformative technology with the Google Impact Challenge: Disabilities

Posted: Wednesday, May 27, 2015

When Laura Palmaro was 10 years old, she woke one morning to find that the central vision in her left eye had all but disappeared. She was not ill and had no genetic issues—it was completely out of the blue. When she was 14, the same rare condition struck her right eye, and she began her freshman year of high school legally blind. Suddenly she was forced to depend on other people to read everything aloud, from school assignments to menus. The toughest part, according to Laura, was losing her sense of independence—and not knowing when or how she would get it back.

Laura has since adopted technological solutions to her vision challenges, using a combination of screen-readers and magnification software to read, work and more. Now a program manager at Google, she is following her passion, helping Chrome and Chrome OS teams make their products more accessible. "Technology has truly transformed my life," she says. "Assistive technology can tear down boundaries, and empower people to find their independence and fulfill their dreams."

We agree with Laura about the power of technology to change lives. And in order to support more people like her—people who see obstacles as opportunities—we're launching the Google Impact Challenge: Disabilities. We're putting $20 million in Google.org grants behind nonprofits using emerging technologies to increase independence for people living with disabilities, and today we're issuing an open call to identify new areas of opportunity atg.co/ImpactChallengeDisability.

We're kicking things off with support for two remarkable organizations. Each of these organizations is using technology to dramatically reduce the cost of and access to prosthetic limbs and auditory therapy, respectively—which could be transformative for hundreds of millions of people.

- The Enable community connects people who want prosthetics with volunteers who use 3D printers to design, print, assemble, and fit them, for free. This dramatically cuts costs, increases speed of distribution, and meets unmet needs. We'll support the Enable Community Foundation's efforts with a $600,000 grant to advance the design, distribution and delivery of open-source 3D-printed upper-limb prosthetics.
- Diagnosing auditory challenges can be a struggle in low income communities—the equipment is expensive, bulky and unrealistic, particularly in the developing world. With our support, and a $500,000 grant, World Wide Hearing will develop, prototype and test an extremely low cost tool kit for hearing loss using smartphone technology that's widely available—and affordable—in the developing world.

The Google Impact Challenge: Disabilities will seek out nonprofits and help them find new solutions to some serious "what ifs" for the disabled community. We will choose the best of these ideas and help them to scale by investing in their vision, by rallying our people and by mobilizing our resources in support of their missions.

Google for Nonprofits

google.com/+GoogleforNonprofits

A place to discover, learn, and discuss the various ways nonprofi...

Follow +1

+ 2,282,532

Labels

AdWords Basics (98)
AdWords in the Curriculum (9)
Google Analytics (9)
Google Apps (25)
Google Apps Highlights (10)
Google Earth (18)
Google Earth Outreach (28)
Google Fusion Tables (2)
Google Maps (10)
Google Products (63)
Google Sketchup (2)
Google+ (16)
Grantees (98)
Grants Program (97)
Optimization (59)
Program Alerts (15)
Resources for Non-Profits (179)
Tracking Performance (35)
YouTube (26)

There are ONE BILLION people with disabilities in the world

Google Impact Challenge | Disabilities

But of course, we realize there's always room to improve our products as well. We have a team committed to monitoring the accessibility of Google tools, and we provide engineering teams with training to incorporate accessibility principles into products and services. That doesn't just mean improving existing Google tools, it means developing new ones as well. For example, Liftware is a stabilizing utensil designed to help people with hand tremors eat more easily, and self-driving cars could one day transform mobility for everyone.

Historically, people living with disabilities have relied on technologies that were often bulky, expensive, and limited to assisting with one or two specific tasks. But that's beginning to change. Thanks to groups like Enable and World Wide Hearing, and with tools like Liftware, we're starting to see the potential for technologies that can profoundly and affordably impact millions. But we'll all get there sooner if we make it a team effort—which is why we're launching Google Impact Challenge: Disabilities today. Together, we can create a better world, faster.

Posted by Jacquelline Fuller, Director, Google.org

0 comments

Archive

Archive
May 2015 (1)
April 2015 (1)
February 2015 (2)
November 2014 (1)
October 2014 (3)
August 2014 (2)
July 2014 (1)
June 2014 (2)
April 2014 (2)
February 2014 (2)
December 2013 (1)
November 2013 (1)
October 2013 (2)
September 2013 (3)
August 2013 (7)
July 2013 (4)
June 2013 (4)
May 2013 (5)
April 2013 (4)

Figure A–7 Corporate Blog

ETHICS NOTE: Ensure That Content Posted to Your Employer's Blog Reflects Its Policies and Values Because organizations expect employees to assume full responsibility for the content they post on a company blog or forum, you must maintain high ethical standards.

- Do not post information that is confidential, proprietary, or sensitive to your employer.
- Do not attack competitors or use abusive language toward other participants while making strong points on topics — be respectful.
- Do not post content that is profane, libelous, or harassing or that violates the privacy of others.
- Be aware that everything that you post becomes permanently accessible to a wide, public audience, especially for external sites.
- Obtain permission before using any material that is protected by copyright, and identify sources for quotations.

Tagging Postings

Consider using "tags" at your site. Tags are keywords that identify the subject of each blog post. They are usually listed following each post and link to all other posts on that topic. The tags listed in Figure A–8 indicate popular topics for postings at a blog site discussing how to find a niche business to work at from home.

Tags are important for two reasons. (1) They permit users to retrieve by topic the postings not visible on the home page. Older postings are usually filed so that only recent posts appear on the home page. (2) Tags can be picked up by search engines and social-networking bookmarking sites such as delicious.com. Tagging allows your site to become "visible" to external users seeking information discussed at your site's blog.

Many blogs and forums allow users to add tags. Called a "folksonomy," user-generated tags can broaden the site's keywords and benefit both routine visitors and search-engine effectiveness. The disadvantages of user-generated tags, however, include misspelled words and arbitrary terms that can reduce the site's "visibility" to search engines and make it difficult for other users to locate specific sites.

Wikis

Wikis are websites that host collaborative writing projects. They allow users to collaborate on a writing project by editing or commenting on its content and organization. Wikis may be used for public-access collaborative reference works or for Internet-only sites maintained by a company. Users become Web authors by using the system's writing and editing software to post comments or questions to drafts of existing documents. These features are especially useful for a group of collaborators developing a report or proposal. Wiki sites also track all edits so that users can see who revised what. Wikis differ from blogs in that they permit all users to both change and comment on content (like Wikipedia), whereas blogs permit users only to comment on the content posted by the site's author.

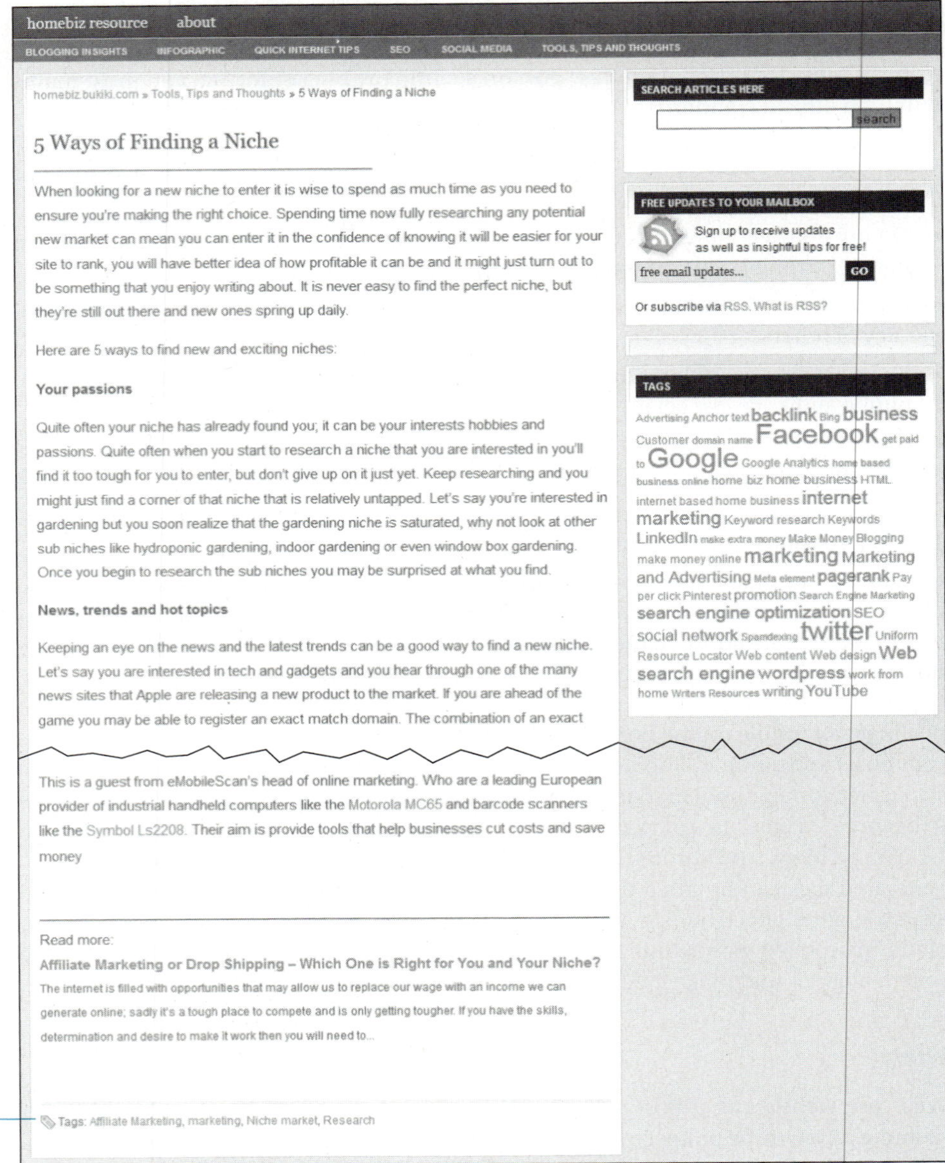
homebiz resource about
BLOGGING INSIGHTS INFOGRAPHIC QUICK INTERNET TIPS SEO SOCIAL MEDIA TOOLS, TIPS AND THOUGHTS

homebiz.bukiki.com » Tools, Tips and Thoughts » 5 Ways of Finding a Niche

5 Ways of Finding a Niche

When looking for a new niche to enter it is wise to spend as much time as you need to ensure you're making the right choice. Spending time now fully researching any potential new market can mean you can enter it in the confidence of knowing it will be easier for your site to rank, you will have better idea of how profitable it can be and it might just turn out to be something that you enjoy writing about. It is never easy to find the perfect niche, but they're still out there and new ones spring up daily.

Here are 5 ways to find new and exciting niches:

Your passions

Quite often your niche has already found you; it can be your interests hobbies and passions. Quite often when you start to research a niche that you are interested in you'll find it too tough for you to enter, but don't give up on it just yet. Keep researching and you might just find a corner of that niche that is relatively untapped. Let's say you're interested in gardening but you soon realize that the gardening niche is saturated, why not look at other sub niches like hydroponic gardening, indoor gardening or even window box gardening. Once you begin to research the sub niches you may be surprised at what you find.

News, trends and hot topics

Keeping an eye on the news and the latest trends can be a good way to find a new niche. Let's say you are interested in tech and gadgets and you hear through one of the many news sites that Apple are releasing a new product to the market. If you are ahead of the game you may be able to register an exact match domain. The combination of an exact

This is a guest from eMobileScan's head of online marketing. Who are a leading European provider of industrial handheld computers like the Motorola MC65 and barcode scanners like the Symbol Ls2208. Their aim is provide tools that help businesses cut costs and save money

Read more:

Affiliate Marketing or Drop Shipping – Which One is Right for You and Your Niche?

The internet is filled with opportunities that may allow us to replace our wage with an income we can generate online; sadly it's a tough place to compete and is only getting tougher. If you have the skills, determination and desire to make it work then you will need to...

Tags: Affiliate Marketing, marketing, Niche market, Research

SEARCH ARTICLES HERE
search

FREE UPDATES TO YOUR MAILBOX
Sign up to receive updates as well as insightful tips for free!
free email updates... GO
Or subscribe via RSS. What is RSS?

TAGS
Advertising Anchor text backlink Bing business Customer domain name Facebook get paid to Google Google Analytics home based business online home biz home business HTML internet based home business internet marketing Keyword research Keywords LinkedIn make extra money Make Money Blogging make money online marketing Marketing and Advertising Meta element pagerank Pay per click Pinterest promotion Search Engine Marketing search engine optimization SEO social network Spamdexing twitter Uniform Resource Locator Web content Web design Web search engine wordpress work from home Writers Resources writing YouTube

Tags link to other blog posts on that topic

Figure A–8 Blog Post Showing Keyword Tags

In the workplace, wikis can be used for a variety of purposes, including co-authoring and co-editing documents, sharing and distributing information, managing projects, and providing communication spaces for clients and customers. They are especially helpful when collaborators are geographically separated, and they simplify the process of tracking multiple versions of a draft because the system displays all changes to it by author and date.

◆ *For additional information about using wikis for collaborative writing, see pages 132–133 in Chapter 5, Collaborating on a Document.*

Podcasts

Podcasts are audio files about a specific topic that are created in .mp3 format for distribution over the Internet. They can be downloaded for listening onto a computer, an MP3 player, or an iPod. One main advantage of podcasts is that the audience can play them when and where they wish — on their home or office computer or on an MP3 player anywhere else. Video podcasts, possible with some MP3 players, are also becoming an ideal means of distributing how-to information.

Podcasts support many valuable functions in educational and workplace settings. Educators use them to distribute lectures, class assignments, foreign-language lessons, and demonstrations. Students in turn can create podcast presentations, class diaries, and interviews, to cite a few examples of their use. Audio podcasts can be augmented with such visual elements as presentation slides and videos.

With their flexible audiovisual capability and their portability, podcasts are an increasingly popular workplace medium to distribute product information to customers and clients as well as technical how-to information to employees at remote work sites.

When you create a podcast, use some of the same techniques important to a successful presentation. Begin by preparing the script: Analyze the audience; gather and organize the information; and note where to integrate visuals, including videos. Rehearse your delivery, recording it for playback and analysis. Is your voice clear? Is your tone enthusiastic? sincere? credible? Then record the audio for posting.

◆ *For detailed guidance in preparing and delivering a presentation, see pages 475–495. in Chapter 14, Giving Presentations.*

FAQs (Frequently Asked Questions)

A list of frequently asked questions and their answers provides information that readers would likely ask about a company's products or services, for example, and is usually located on a website or in customer-oriented brochures or instructions. Presenting commonly sought information in one place, FAQs save readers from searching through an entire website or document to find what they need.

A well-planned FAQ list helps a company or an organization spend less time answering phone calls and e-mail questions. It can also help create a positive impression with customers because it acknowledges that their time is valuable.

ETHICS NOTE: Do Not Use FAQs to Evade Product or Service Problems
If customers are experiencing numerous problems because of a faulty product design or programming flaw, you need to work with the company's product developers to correct the problem rather than try to skirt it with an FAQ list. However, even in this situation, FAQs can be used to help customers until an update is released.

Questions to Include

Develop the list of questions and their answers by brainstorming with colleagues regularly in contact with customers. They are in the best position to know what customers ask. Study other FAQ lists your customers might review for products or services. If customers often ask about company stock information and request annual reports, for example, your FAQ could include the question "How do I obtain a copy of your latest annual report?" The question can be followed by a brief answer that includes the Web address from which the report can be downloaded or the name, phone number, and e-mail address of the person who distributes annual reports.

Organization

Organize the questions so that readers can find the information they need quickly and easily. List your questions in decreasing order of importance so that readers can locate the most frequently asked questions first. If you have a number of questions that are related to a specific topic, such as investor relations, product returns, or online sales, group them into categories and identify each category with a heading, such as "Investor Relations," "Shipping," and "Sales." You may also want to create a table of contents at the top of the FAQ page so that readers can quickly find the topics relevant to their interests.

Study other FAQ lists for products or services similar to yours. Analyze them for their approach and organization: Can you find answers quickly, or do you need to scroll through many pages to find them? Are the questions with their answers separated into logical categories or listed in random order? Is it easy to differentiate the question from the answer? Do the answers provide too little or too much information? Does the FAQ list offer specialized search tools to help readers find information for longer FAQs?

Placement

On websites, FAQ pages are usually linked from the home page. In small printed documents, such as brochures, FAQs are usually highlighted and placed after the standard information in the body of the document.

WRITER'S CHECKLIST
Developing FAQs

- ✔ *Focus on your reader.* Write your questions and answers from a "you" point of view and use a positive, conversational tone.
- ✔ *Divide long FAQ lists.* Group related questions under topic headings. For long online FAQ lists, consider including only questions with links to separate pages, each containing an individual question and answer.
- ✔ *Distinguish questions from answers.* Use boldface for questions and use white space to separate questions from answers. Minimize use of multiple colors, italics, or other formatting styles that can make the list difficult to read at a glance.
- ✔ *Keep questions and answers concise.* If a question has a long answer, add a link to a separate Web page or refer to an appropriate page number in a printed document.
- ✔ *Keep the list updated.* Review and update FAQ lists at least monthly—or more frequently if your content changes often. Make it possible for your customers to submit questions they would like to see added to the FAQ list.

- ✔ *Give readers the opportunity to respond.* Provide an e-mail link for existing and future customers to submit questions they would like to see added to the FAQ list.
- ✔ *Consider available tools for automating the process.* Many content-management systems, for example, have built-in FAQ-writing software.

Social Media

Social media refers to websites—such as Facebook, LinkedIn, Twitter, and YouTube—that allow the creation of online communities through which individuals and organizations with common interests can create content, interact, and share information. Accessed primarily through Web browsers or mobile devices, social-media platforms often incorporate instant messaging and e-mail components, and many have blogs and forums that allow for comments, links to other websites, and the collection of information that is of interest to its community.

Organizations use social media to connect with their clients, share information about their products, and reach new customers. Social media can help organizations promote goodwill, resolve problems, and obtain near-instant feedback on their products and services through the conversation of online communities. For those who are self-employed or beginning a job search, social media can both act as a networking tool and provide a way to learn about an organization and its community of users.

Choosing the Appropriate Platform

When choosing which social-media platform to join, consider what you or your organization hopes to accomplish and which community reaches more of the organization's target customers or contacts. A manufacturing company might seek out a platform that focuses on users of products similar to its own products, while a service-oriented company might select a platform that allows users to request and receive immediate assistance. An independent contractor might choose several platforms for different purposes, advertising on one used by many clients while participating in another that allows the contractor to build a professional network.

Two main components of such platforms are the most useful in the workplace: status updates and networking connections. *Status updates* allow individuals or organizations to post brief announcements and responses to questions and have those posts immediately disseminated and responded to by others. *Networking connections* allow one individual or organization to link the company and its products to another individual or organization. By doing so, the two entities become "connected" in the social-media community, allowing their posts to intertwine into a type of ongoing conversation. The table in Figure A–9 provides an overview of three popular social-media platforms of interest to businesses and professionals and shows how each uses status updates and networking connections to support its community.

Before selecting a specific social-media platform, understand that conversations within social media are impossible to control or pause. You must be willing to respond to the inquiries and comments, positive and negative, of other community members. Consider as well the time commitment that your selection may demand—users of many social-media platforms have expectations of quick and ongoing responses and

LinkedIn	Offers individuals opportunities to connect with others and to create a professional network or community.
	Provides a profile page that acts much like a résumé by highlighting an individual's work, education, skills, and experiences.
	Allows community members to participate in profession-specific discussion boards, as well as post and respond to employment ads.
	Allows people to "follow" specific businesses and organizations.
	Circulates job-opening announcements to members based on their profiles.
Facebook	Enables businesses to broaden their brand recognition and to interact with current and new customers.
	Provides insight about potential employees, vendors, and business associates.
	Assigns each individual or business a "wall" that can be used to post status updates, pictures, videos, or links to other websites.
	Allows users to "friend" or "like" other users, connecting the accounts and allowing interaction between each user.
Twitter	Allows users to "follow" a company or individual who can keep clients and others aware of an organization's or individual's activities.
	Limits every message or status update to 140 characters; businesses and individuals can post timely updates or critical announcements.
	Allows organizations to enter near-synchronous conversations with their clients and customers.

Figure A–9 Comparison of Social-Media Platforms

updates. Finally, before joining a social-media platform, understand that your communications within that platform might have a wider audience than you intend.

Writing Style and Privacy Considerations

For writing style, follow both the practices of your organization and the requirements of the selected social-media platform. Some organizations have very strict guidelines for who can contribute to social-media-based conversations and how those contributions must be designed and worded. Pay close attention to the context, purpose, and audience of your message, ensuring that your message is clear, precise, and free of grammatical errors.

Posts in a social-media platform are immediately and often widely shared among other community participants and potentially on other unassociated websites. For this reason, consider both the benefit of your post to your immediate audience and the potential implications of that post to those outside the membership in your social-media community. While many platforms are considered "informal" and used primarily for personal communications, the ability of writing to be shared throughout a given network demands that you consider how your contributions represent you professionally. Most organizations review the social-media platforms of job candidates as part of the employment process. Other organizations employ services to monitor what is said about them online. Many organizations have policies that prohibit employees from discussing the workplace even within a personal social-media account. Consider also the information in the Ethics Note on page 599 as you compose your message.

WRITER'S CHECKLIST: Judicious Use of Social Media

✔ *Always consider the purpose and suitability of your contributions.* Avoid contributions that publicly discuss topics better suited for one-on-one communication or that are considered divisive. Consider whether your contribution provides information that your audience would find appropriate and useful.

✔ *Understand the availability of your social-media contributions.* Consider your posts to be available to everyone and how someone, such as your employer or school, might view your status update or shared picture.

✔ *Follow your employer's policies regarding social media.* Attempting to circumnavigate policies by using a mobile device to access a blocked site, for example, could result in severe penalties or even termination.

✔ *Never use personal social-media accounts while at work or in a class.* Remember that most contributions are recorded with the date and time of the post, allowing others to know when you were using the site.

✔ *Never comment about a job, employer, or instructor.* Consider everything that you contribute to a social-media platform as available to the organization or individuals that you might be writing about. Avoid comments on workplace relationships.

✔ *Carefully consider "friend" requests.* Before establishing a connection, consider your organization's policy, your professional relationship, and any potential current or future conflicts of interest.

✔ *Monitor what is said or shared about you.* Be aware of posts about you and work with your connections to maintain a public persona that best represents you in a positive light.

◆ *For additional guidance on the need to be careful about what you post at these sites, see the Professionalism Note on page 519 of Chapter 15, Writing Résumés and Cover Letters.*

APPENDIX A SUMMARY: WRITING IN AN ONLINE ENVIRONMENT

Use the following revision checklist to make sure that content you develop or adapt for the Web and related media is crafted for ease of reading by site visitors and is accessible to people with disabilities as well as to international users.

- Plan, organize, and write content that can be grasped quickly:
  - Use the inverted-pyramid method to organize content top down so that key points and conclusions appear first.
  - Develop content that is accurate, backed by supporting evidence, and expressed in a tone appropriate for your audience.

- Write concisely and use plain-language principles consistent with your content.
- Break up dense blocks of text into smaller paragraph-length passages that are sequenced by the inverted-pyramid method.
- Expand access to your information by hyperlinking it to content at your website or other websites or media locations.

- Augment access to your content using the following highlighting techniques:
  - Introduce topics with headings and subheadings to signal the shift from one topic to another.
  - Use bulleted and numbered lists to further break up dense blocks of text and focus reader attention on relevant points.
  - Use directional cues appropriate to a screen and avoid those that make sense only in printed material.
  - Highlight introductory passages with key terms and concepts that allow search engines to locate your content.
  - Select graphics pertinent to your audience and purpose, and optimize them for quick access.
  - Choose type sizes and fonts to enhance legibility.
  - Limit line length to promote ease of scanning.
- Submit a previously published document to a website according to the following guidelines:
  - Convert the document into the most suitable file format for the site.
  - Inform site users if the online version is abridged or otherwise differs from the printed version.
  - Obtain prior permission to publish works that contain copyrighted text or graphics.
  - Examine the document on an internal Web server for accuracy and effectiveness before it is posted for public access.
  - For a long document, post a single file version for users wishing to print the document.
  - Add functionality to such content with digital enhancements.
- Give credit to outside sources of content at your site, including approval to use copyrighted material.
- Inform site users of how or whether their privacy is protected if they submit solicited or unsolicited information to you.
- Provide for the special needs of people with disabilities and international site visitors by adhering to the following guidelines:
  - Create content compatible with adaptive technologies.
  - Use language, units of measurement, and graphics that are consistent with the practices of international and U.S. site visitors.
  - Be mindful of users without high-speed Internet access and work with the site Web staff to tailor graphic and audiovisual content accordingly.

When creating a blog or forum, adhere to the following guidelines:

- Write in a conversational tone.
- Keep entries short and focused on the topic.
- Link to important topic-related information.
- Identify information sources to enhance site credibility.
- Tag blog and forum postings to enhance user and search-engine access to topical content.

- Ensure that organizational postings are in line with the organization's norms, values, and policies.

Consider using a wiki for a collaborative project in the following situations:

- There are several content providers or reviewers.
- Some or all collaborators are geographically separated.
- Tracking multiple versions of a document draft is important.

Consider creating a podcast in the following situations:

- The information is suitable to audio or audiovisual treatment.
- The information is intended for an audience in need of a how-to presentation in a portable format.

Use the following guidelines when creating and posting an FAQ list:

- Develop questions based on customer and client concerns.
- Organize questions in a pattern logical to the topic, putting the most important concerns before secondary concerns.

When creating content for or communicating with customers and clients at workplace social-media sites:

- Adhere to your employer's policies and procedures for what is acceptable professional content and conduct.
- Be prepared to commit the time necessary to respond to all questions and comments.
- Separate personal from professional social-media accounts.
- Be mindful of the needs of people with disabilities and international users.
- Acknowledge sources of information.
- Write in plain language that is clear, concise, and free of grammatical and spelling errors.
- Be wary of sharing personal information or opinions.

Exercises

1. Bring in a report, a research paper, or an essay written for another course and rework it so that it is chunked for online reading. Use appropriate captions and headings. Then, rework it again for use on a blog.
2. Review the reworked research paper or essay that you prepared for Exercise 1 and note places where you could link elements in your text to existing websites. Find websites to link to and list them on a separate page.
3. As your instructor directs, post a report, a research paper, an essay, or another text you have already written to your personal or class website. (Review Repurposing Existing Content on pages 589–590 before you begin.) You can also use your text from Exercise 1.
4. Using this textbook (or a textbook from another class that you are taking) as a model, analyze the use of headings, subheadings, white space, models and examples, visuals, and so on. Note the consistency in the use of these and other textual elements. Do they invite the reader to continue to read from section to section and chapter to chapter? Present your findings to the class.

5. Imagine that you are a writer who wants to publish an online book because it is much less expensive to present your book in a PDF file and let readers print the pages than it is to print a hard-copy book yourself. Create an idea for your book, and then create the specifications for the design of the pages, including font sizes, heading styles, line width, and so on. Use your findings from Exercise 4 to help in your design choices.
6. For Collaborative Classroom Project 2 in Chapter 8, you created an information sheet that explained to donors how to deduct a car donation to a local nonprofit organization on their taxes. Revise this information sheet into content to be posted on the nonprofit organization's website. Remember that tax information is often very wordy and difficult to follow, so you will need to be strategic about presenting it online. Review the Highlighting Information checklist on page 586 before you begin.
7. Many companies have intranets that they use to share information with employees as well as with selected vendors and clients. For Exercise 7 in Chapter 12, you were asked to write a set of instructions to help supermarket managers assist customers who use self-checkout systems. Rework those instructions for uploading to the system manufacturer's intranet site. Consider adding links as well as highlighting techniques, like directional cues.
8. For Research Project 4 in Chapter 13, you were asked to research and apply for a grant to fund an Adult Basic Education program at your local county jail. Assume that your organization received the grant. Using the example of the press release in this chapter as a model (Figure A–2 on page 580), write a press release that announces your organization's success in obtaining the grant and telling readers how the funds will be used to further the organization's mission. Use the inverted-pyramid structure explained on page 578.

Collaborative Classroom Projects

1. In groups of three or four students who share your major, bring to class information from three websites that you might use to research a career of your choice. Print out relevant pages from each site and together review the guidelines in this chapter for documenting sources of information. Draft a list of questions to consider when evaluating online text as a research resource specific to your field. Evaluate and compare each of the sites that your group members have found and decide which sites would be the most reliable for career research. Write a brief group summary of your findings to share with the class.
2. Assume that you and two other students are consultants who work with various groups that represent people with special needs. One of your tasks is to write letters to companies with Web or social-media sites that do not adhere to Web-accessibility standards, explaining that because customers with special needs cannot use their sites, the companies are losing potential business.

   Before the next class, decide on a type of company to investigate (for example, insurance companies, professional sports teams, movie theaters, grocery stores, community banks, and so on), then run several of the companies' websites through a Web-accessibility tool at www.w3.org/WAI/ER/tools/complete (you will need to know their URLs). Print the results and bring them to class. As a group, analyze your findings, looking closely at quality and accessibility. Which of these companies would you write to in order to explain website accessibility? What changes would you suggest be made to the site, and why?

Research Projects

1. For your major department's website, write an online article that describes five databases to which your college library has access that are pertinent to your field of study.
2. For Exercise 2 in Chapter 10 and Research Project 2 in Chapter 13, you prepared reports about back injuries and workers' compensation at the warehouse of a large online retailer and proposed ways to improve employee safety. Now assume that you work for the Human Resources Department of this company and you want to create a page for the company intranet to explain safe-lifting procedures.
   a. Begin by researching ways to safely lift heavy objects. Remember that you will need to cite your sources. (You may use any research you've already completed as a starting point.) You also want to consider what sources (if any) you might link to from your page.
   b. Consider your audience for this page: Do they speak English as a second language or have low literacy skills, for example? It may be prudent to use more graphics than text. (Review Using Visuals to Communicate Internationally on pages 251–257 in Chapter 7, Designing Documents and Visuals.) Remember that many graphics on the Web are copyrighted: Be sure to determine if you need permission before cutting and pasting any images into your document. (For this exercise, you need not seek copyright permission, but you must cite the sources of your content.)
   c. Draft your page either in hard copy (through thumbnail sketches) or in a website design program if you have access to one. Then, with a classmate, conduct a usability test (see Chapter 12, Writing Instructions) of your instructions. Take any comments regarding the page layout into consideration as well.
   d. Finish your page.
3. On the Web, you can find several sites that explain how things work. (One excellent resource is www.howstuffworks.com.) Review the guidelines in this chapter for creating documents and integrating visuals, then do the following:
   a. Choose an electronic object, such as a cell phone, digital camera, notebook computer, or other device, and explore how it works. Print the explanation of how the object works and evaluate both the explanation and the Web page, according to the criteria described in this chapter.
   b. Mark up the Web-page layout and the explanation, indicating any changes you would make to improve its design. You may focus on one aspect of the explanation, such as its use of chunking, or many aspects. Feel free to sketch out your ideas.
   c. Write a memo to your instructor in which you explain what does and does not work for the original design of the Web page and the explanation, supporting your ideas with information in this appendix. Specify how your changes would improve the document's design. Attach to your memo the marked-up printout of the explanation and any sketches you've created.

4. Many local convention and visitors-bureau sites describe local attractions, provide listings of educational institutions in the area, recommend shopping and art areas, and so on. Go to such a website or social-media site (Facebook, YouTube) and analyze the material already on the site. Then get the name and e-mail address of the site's social-media coordinator and write an e-mail to that person with ideas for stories on colorful characters or events or places in the city that might be of interest to visitors of their site.

Appendix B

Revision Guide: Sentences, Punctuation, and Mechanics

MARK/SYMBOL	MEANING	EXAMPLE	CORRECTED TYPE
	Delete	the ~~manager's~~ report	the report
^	Insert	the^report (manager's)	the manager's report
stet	Let stand	the manager's report	the manager's report
≡ cap	Capitalize	the monday meeting	the Monday meeting
/ lc	Lowercase	the Monday Meeting	the Monday meeting
tr	Transpose	the cover lettre	the cover letter
	Close space	a loud speaker	a loudspeaker
#	Insert space	a loudspeaker	a loud speaker
¶	Paragraph	...report. The meeting...	...report. The meeting...
	Run in with previous line or paragraph	...report. The meeting...	...report. The meeting...
— ital	Italicize	the New York Times	the *New York Times*
bf	Boldface	Use boldface sparingly.	Use **boldface** sparingly.
⊙	Insert period	I wrote the e-mail	I wrote the e-mail.
	Insert comma	However we cannot...	However, we cannot...
=	Insert hyphen	clear cut decision	clear-cut decision
m	Insert em dash	Our goal productivity	Our goal—productivity
or :|	Insert colon	We need the following	We need the following:
or ;|	Insert semicolon	we finished we achieved	we finished; we achieved
	Insert quotation marks	He said, I agree.	He said, "I agree."
	Insert apostrophe	the managers report	the manager's report

Handwritten Proofreaders' Marks, Their Meaning and Size

Sentences

A sentence is the most fundamental and versatile tool available to writers, but sentence faults and issues with pronouns, adjectives, adverbs, and verbs can cause difficulties for your readers. To help you avoid these problems, this section describes common sentence errors and how to correct them.

Sentence Faults

Sentence-level errors can make your meaning hard to determine or, worse, alter the meaning entirely. Grammatically, the most serious sentence problems are run-on sentences, comma splices, sentence fragments, and dangling and misplaced modifiers.

Run-on Sentences and Comma Splices

An independent clause expresses a complete thought by itself. It may be part of a larger sentence or stand alone as a separate sentence:

- The training division will offer three new courses.
- Interested employees should sign up by Wednesday.

Two independent clauses joined without any punctuation result in a *run-on*, or *fused*, *sentence*. Two independent clauses joined with only a comma results in a *comma splice* or *comma fault*. Correct either problem by (1) making two sentences, (2) joining the two clauses with a semicolon (if they are closely related and balanced in meaning), (3) joining the two clauses with a comma and a coordinating conjunction, or (4) subordinating one clause to the other.

◆ ***For tips on subordinating clauses effectively, see pages 103–104 in Chapter 4, Revising a Document.***

RUN-ON	The training division will offer three new courses interested employees should sign up by Wednesday.
COMMA SPLICE	The training division will offer three new courses, interested employees should sign up by Wednesday.
CORRECT	The training division will offer three new courses. Interested employees should sign up by Wednesday. [two sentences]
CORRECT	The training division will offer three new courses; interested employees should sign up by Wednesday. [semicolon]
CORRECT	The training division will offer three new courses, so interested employees should sign up by Wednesday. [comma plus coordinating conjunction]
CORRECT	*When* the training division offers the new courses, interested employees should sign up for them. [one clause subordinated to the other]

Sentence Fragments

A sentence fragment is an incomplete grammatical unit that is punctuated as a sentence.

FRAGMENT And quit his job.

SENTENCE He quit his job.

A sentence must contain a main, or finite, verb; verbals (gerunds, participles, and infinitives) cannot function as verbs. The following examples are sentence fragments because they lack main verbs.

FRAGMENT *Providing* all employees with disability insurance.

SENTENCE The company *provides* all employees with disability insurance.

FRAGMENT *To work* a 40-hour week.

SENTENCE Most of our employees *work* a 40-hour week.

Explanatory phrases beginning with *such as, for example, because,* and similar terms may lead to sentence fragments.

, such as
- The staff wants additional benefits~~. For example,~~ the use of company cars.

Dangling and Misplaced Modifiers

Phrases that do not clearly and logically refer to the correct noun or pronoun are called *dangling modifiers.* Correct this problem by adding the appropriate noun or pronoun for the phrase to modify or by rewriting the phrase as a clause.

I was
- While visiting the work site, the auxiliary generator malfunctioned.

we relaxed at dinner.
- After finishing the negotiations, ~~dinner was relaxing.~~

A *misplaced modifier* refers, or appears to refer, to the wrong word or phrase. Avoid this problem by placing modifiers as close as possible to the words they modify. Position each modifier carefully so that it says what you mean.

just
- We ~~just~~ bought the property for expansion.
- Our copier was used to duplicate materials ~~for other departments~~ that needed to be
for other departments
reduced.

A *squinting modifier* is located between two sentence elements and might refer to either one. To eliminate the ambiguity, move the modifier or revise the sentence.

During the next week, the
- ~~The~~ union agreed ~~during the next week~~ to return to work.

to return to work

- The union agreed ^ during the next week ~~to return to work~~.

Nouns

Nouns are people, places, things, concepts, or qualities.

Count and Mass Nouns

Count nouns refer to things that can be counted (tables, pencils, projects, reports). *Mass nouns* (also called *noncount nouns*) identify things that cannot be counted (electricity, water, air, loyalty, information). This distinction can be confusing with words like *electricity* and *water*. Although we can count kilowatt-hours of electricity and bottles of water, counting becomes inappropriate when we use the words in a general sense, as in "*Water* is an essential resource." Count nouns have plural forms; mass nouns do not. Following is a list of common mass nouns.

acid
advice
air
anger
biology
business
clothing
coffee
education
electricity
equipment
furniture
health
honesty
information
knowledge
loyalty
machinery
money
news
oil
precision
research
technology
transportation
waste
weather
work

This distinction between whether something can or cannot be counted determines the form of the noun to use (singular or plural), the kind of article that precedes it (*a, an, the,* or no article), and the kind of comparative adjective it requires (*fewer* or *less, many* or *much,* and so on).

Articles

This discussion of articles applies only to common nouns (not to proper nouns, such as the names of people) because count and mass nouns are always common nouns.

The general rule is that every count noun must be preceded by an article (*a, an, the*), a demonstrative adjective (*this, that, these, those*), a possessive adjective (*my, your, her, his, its, their*), or some expression of quantity (such as *one, two, several, many, a few, a lot of, some, no*). The article, adjective, or expression of quantity appears either directly in front of the noun or in front of the whole noun phrase.

- Beth read *a* report last week. [article]
- *Those* reports Beth read were long. [demonstrative adjective]
- *Their* report was long. [possessive adjective]
- *Some* reports Beth read were long. [indefinite adjective]

The articles *a* and *an* are used with count nouns that refer to one item of the whole class of like items.

- Matthew has *a* pen. [Matthew could have *any* pen.]

The article *the* is used with nouns that refer to a specific item that both the reader and the writer can identify.

- Matthew has *the* pen. [Matthew has a *specific* pen that is known to both the reader and the writer.]

The article *the* is used with the superlative form of adjectives and adverbs.

- His analysis was ^*the* best the board had ever read.

Do not use *the* with the comparative form.

- Which of these two restaurants is ~~the~~ better?

When making generalizations with count nouns, writers can either use *a* or *an* with a singular count noun or use no article with a plural count noun. Consider the following generalization using an article.

- *An* egg is a good source of protein. [any egg, all eggs, eggs in general]

However, the following generalization uses a plural count noun with no article.

- Eggs are good sources of protein. [any egg, all eggs, eggs in general]

When you are making a generalization with a mass noun, do not use an article in front of the noun.

- Sugar is bad for your teeth.

Prepositions

Prepositions are words that help connect nouns or pronouns to other parts of a sentence. They help to specify a relationship between items.

The word *on* is used with days of the week.

- We have staff meetings *on* Mondays.

At is used with hours of the day and with noon, night, and dawn.

- We leave work *at* 5:00 p.m.
- Lunch will be served *at* noon.

In is used with other parts of the day and with months, years, and seasons.

- I check my e-mail *in* the morning.
- I started to work for the firm *in* May.

The word *on* indicates a surface on which something rests.

- The files are *on* the desk.

At refers to an area or to a place.

- My assistant is *at* her desk.

In indicates a place that is inside an enclosure.

- The documents are *in* the file folder.

Pronouns

A *pronoun* is used as a substitute for a noun (the noun for which a pronoun substitutes is called the *antecedent*). An unclear link between a pronoun and its antecedent can cause confusion.

Pronoun Case

The case of a pronoun is always determined by how it functions in a phrase, clause, or sentence. If it functions as the subject, it is in the subjective case; if it functions as an object, it is in the objective case; if it reflects possession or ownership and modifies a noun, it is in the possessive case. The subjective case can indicate the person or thing acting (*He* sued the vendor), the person or thing acted on (*He* was sued by the vendor), or the topic of description (*He* is the vendor). The objective case can indicate the thing acted on (The vendor sued *him*) or the person or thing acting but in the objective position (The vendor was sued by *him*). The possessive case indicates the person or thing owning or possessing something (It was *his* company).

Singular	**Subjective**	**Objective**	**Possessive**
First person	I	me	my, mine
Second person	you	you	your, yours
Third person	he, she, it	him, her, it	his, her, hers, its
Plural	**Subjective**	**Objective**	**Possessive**
First person	we	us	our, ours
Second person	you	you	your, yours
Third person	they	them	their, theirs

Determining Case

One test to determine the proper case of a pronoun is to try using it with a transitive verb that requires a direct object — a person or thing to receive the action expressed by the verb. *Hit* is a useful verb for this test. If the pronoun would logically precede the verb, use the subjective case; if it would logically follow the verb, use the objective case.

- *She* hit the volleyball. [subjective case]
- The volleyball hit *her*. [objective case]

An *appositive* is a noun or noun phrase that follows and amplifies another noun or noun phrase. A pronoun appositive takes the case of its antecedent.

- Two systems analysts, *Joe and I*, were selected to represent the company.

  [*Joe and I* is in apposition to the subject, *systems analysts*, and therefore must be in the subjective case.]
- The systems analysts selected two members of our department—*Joe and me*.

  [*Joe and me* is in apposition to *two members*, the object of the verb *selected*, and therefore must be in the objective case.]

The reverse situation can also present problems. To test for the proper case when the pronouns *we* and *us* are followed by an appositive noun that defines them, try the sentence without the noun.

SENTENCE	(*We/us*) pilots fly our own airplanes.
INCORRECT	*Us* fly our own airplanes. [The incorrect usage sounds wrong.]
CORRECT	*We* fly our own airplanes. [The correct usage sounds right.]

To determine the case of a pronoun that follows *as* or *than*, mentally add the words that are omitted but understood.

- The other sales representative is not paid as well as *she* [is paid].

  [You would not write, "*her* is paid."]
- His partner was better informed than *he* [was informed].

  [You would not write, "*him* was informed."]

If pronouns in compound constructions cause problems, try using them singly to determine the proper case.

- In his report, Jamel thanked Sam and (*me/I*).
- In his report, Jamel thanked *Sam*.
- In his report, Jamel thanked *me*.

Using *Who* or *Whom*

Who is the subjective case form, whereas *whom* is the objective case form. When in doubt about which form to use, substitute a personal pronoun to see which one fits. If *he*, *she*, or *they* fits, use *who*.

- Who is the training coordinator? [You would say, "*She* is the training coordinator."]

If *him*, *her*, or *them* fits, use *whom*.

- It depends on *whom*? [You would say, "It depends on *them*."]

Pronoun Reference

A pronoun should refer clearly to a specific antecedent. Avoid vague and uncertain references.

, which is worth $1.5 million,
- We got the account ^ after we wrote the proposal. ~~It was a big one.~~

For coherence, place pronouns as close as possible to their antecedents.

, praised for its design, is
- The office building ^ next to City Hall ~~was praised for its design~~.

A general (or broad) reference or one that has no real antecedent is a problem that often occurs when the word *this* is used by itself.

experience
- He deals with personnel problems in his work. This ^ helps him in his personal life.

Another problem is a hidden reference, which has only an implied antecedent.

the formation of ketone bodies.
- A high-lipid, low-carbohydrate diet is "ketogenic" because it favors ^ ~~their formation.~~

Do not repeat an antecedent in parentheses following the pronoun. If you feel you must identify the pronoun's antecedent in this way, rewrite the sentence.

AWKWARD	The senior partner first met Bob Evans when he (Evans) was a trainee.
IMPROVED	Bob Evans was a trainee when the senior partner first met him.

Pronoun-Antecedent Agreement

A pronoun must agree, or correspond in form, with its antecedent in person, gender, and number.

Person

For a pronoun to agree with its antecedent in person, use either the third person or the second person. Don't mix them.

INCORRECT	*Employees* must sign the logbook when *you* enter a restricted area.
CORRECT	*Employees* must sign the logbook when *they* enter a restricted area.
CORRECT	*You* must sign the logbook when *you* enter a restricted area.

Gender

A pronoun must agree in gender with its antecedent.

- Isabel was wearing *her* identification badge, but *Tom* had to clip *his* on before they could pass the security guard.

Traditionally, a masculine pronoun was used to agree with antecedents that include both sexes, such as *everybody, nobody, one, person, someone*, or *student*.

To avoid the implied sexual bias in such usage, use *he or she* or the plural form of the pronoun *they*.

GENDER BIAS	*Everybody* completed *his* report on time.
FREE OF BIAS	*Everybody* completed *his or her* report on time.
FREE OF BIAS	*Everybody* completed their report on time.

Often, the best solution is to rewrite the sentence in the plural; but be sure to make all related objects plural, too. Do not, however, use a plural pronoun when the antecedent is singular.

◆ *See also page 112 in Chapter 4, Revising a Document.*

INCORRECT	*Everybody* completed *their* reports on time.
	[The antecedent, *Everybody*, is singular, but the pronoun, *their*, is plural.]
CORRECT	The *employees* completed *their* reports on time.
	[The antecedent, *employees*, is plural; the pronoun, *their*, is also plural.]

In many languages, possessive pronouns agree in number and gender with the nouns they modify. In English, however, possessive pronouns agree in number and gender with their antecedents. Check your writing carefully for agreement between a possessive pronoun and the word, phrase, or clause to which it refers.

- The *woman* bought *her* brother lunch.
- *Robert* sent *his* mother flowers on Mother's Day.

Number

Number is a frequent problem with only a few indefinite pronouns (*each, either, neither*, and those ending with *-body* or *-one*, such as *anybody, anyone, everybody, everyone, nobody, no one, somebody, someone*) that are normally singular and so require singular verbs and are referred to as singular pronouns.

- As *each member arrives* for the meeting, please hand *him or her* a copy of the confidential report. *Everyone* must return the copy before *he or she* leaves. *Everybody* on the committee *understands* that *neither* of our major competitors *is* aware of the new process we have developed.

Adjectives and Adverbs

An adjective modifies or describes a noun or pronoun. An adverb modifies the action or condition expressed by a verb. An adverb may also modify an adjective, another adverb, or a clause.

Comparatives and Superlatives

The three degrees of comparison are called the *positive* (the basic form of the adjective or adverb), the *comparative* (showing comparison with one other item), and the *superlative* (showing comparison with two or more other items): *long, longer, longest.*

Many two-syllable adjectives and most three-syllable adjectives are preceded by the word *more* or *most* to form the comparative or the superlative.

- The new Media Center is *more* impressive than the old one. It is the *most* impressive in the state.

Most adverbs with two or more syllables end in *-ly,* and most adverbs ending in *-ly* are compared by inserting the comparative *more* or *less* or the superlative *most* or *least* in front of them.

- Her sales rose *more quickly* last quarter than those of any other company's sales representative.

A few adjectives have irregular forms of comparison (*much, more, most; little, less, least*). A few irregular adverbs require a change in form to indicate comparison (*well, better, best; worse, worst; far, farther, farthest*).

Absolute words (such as *unique, perfect, exact,* and *infinite*) are not logically subject to comparison, especially in workplace writing, where accuracy and precision are often crucial.

- We modified our mission statement to more ~~exactly~~ *closely* reflect our long-term goals.

Use adverbs sparingly in workplace writing. Because they are often subjective (*hot/cold, hard/soft, long/short*), provide specific figures or descriptions that quantify them or provide context. How hot? (Give the temperature.) How fast? (State the speed or rate.) How short or long? (State the length.) How cautiously or carefully? (State why caution is necessary or the consequences of not being careful.)

Placement

Within a sentence, adjectives may appear before or after the nouns they modify.

- We negotiated a *bigger* contract than our competitor did.
  [attributive position]
- We negotiated a contract *bigger* than our competitor's.
  [predicative position]

An adjective is called a predicate adjective when it follows a linking verb, such as a form of the verb *to be.* By completing the meaning of a linking verb, a predicate adjective describes, or limits, the subject of the verb.

- The job is *easy.*
- The manager was very *demanding.*

An adjective also can follow a transitive verb and modify its direct object (the person or thing that receives the action of the verb).

- They painted the office *white.*

An adverb may appear almost anywhere in a sentence, but its position can affect meaning. Avoid placing an adverb between two verb forms where it will be ambiguous because it can be read as modifying either.

AMBIGUOUS The man making the calculations *hastily* e-mailed the results to the engineering staff.

[Did the man calculate hastily or e-mail the results hastily?]

IMPROVED The man making the calculations then *hastily* e-mailed the results to the engineering staff.

IMPROVED The man *hastily* making the calculations then e-mailed the results to the engineering staff.

Usage

In English, unlike many other languages, adjectives have only one form. Do not add *-s* or *-es* to an adjective to make it plural.

- the *long* letter
- the *long* letters

Likewise, adjectives in English do not change to show gender.

- The *tall* man (masculine noun)
- The *tall* woman (feminine noun)
- The *tall* building (neuter noun)

Capitalize adjectives of origin (city, state, nation, continent).

- the *Venetian* canals
- the *Texas* legislature
- the *French* government
- the *African* continent

In English, verbs of feeling (for example, *bore, interest, surprise*) have two adjectival forms: the present participle (*-ing*) and the past participle (*-ed*). Use the present participle to describe what causes the feeling. Use the past participle to describe the person who experiences the feeling.

- We heard the *surprising* election results.

  [The *election results* cause the feeling of surprise.]
- The *surprised* candidate found out she had lost the election.

  [The *candidate* experienced the feeling of surprise.]

Adjectives follow nouns in English in only two cases: when the adjective functions as a subjective complement, as in:

- That project is not *finished*.

and when an adjective phrase or clause modifies the noun, as in:

- The project *that was suspended temporarily* has a new deadline.

Adjective Clauses

Because of the variety of ways adjective clauses are constructed in different languages, they can be particularly troublesome for nonnative writers of English. The following guidelines will help you form adjective clauses correctly.

Place an adjective clause directly after the noun it modifies.

- *who is standing across the room*
  The tall woman ^ is a vice president of the company ^ ~~who is standing across the room.~~ .

The adjective clause *who is standing across the room* modifies *woman*, not *company*, and thus comes directly after *woman*.

Avoid using a relative pronoun with another pronoun in an adjective clause.

- The man who ~~he~~ sits at that desk is my boss.

In all other cases, adjectives are placed before the noun.

When there are multiple adjectives, the order illustrated in the following example would apply in most circumstances, with some exceptions. (Normally, do not use a phrase with so many stacked modifiers.)

The six extra-large rectangular brown cardboard takeout containers . . .

determiner (The), *number* (six), *comment* (extra-), *size* (large), *shape* (rectangular), *color* (brown), *material* (cardboard), *qualifier* (takeout), *noun* (containers)

Verbs

A verb is a word or group of words that describes an action (The copier *jammed* at the beginning of the job), states the way in which something or someone is affected by an action (He *was disappointed* that the proposal was rejected), or affirms a state of existence (She *is* a district manager now). This section focuses on those areas of verb usage that can cause inexperienced writers problems.

Subject-Verb Agreement

Agreement, grammatically, means the correspondence in form between different elements of a sentence. A verb must agree with its subject in person and number.

- *I am* going to approve his promotion.

  [The first-person singular subject, *I*, requires the first-person singular form of the verb, *am*.]

- His *colleagues are* supportive.

  [The third-person plural subject, *colleagues*, requires the third-person plural form of the verb, *are*.]

Intervening Words

Subject-verb agreement is not affected by intervening phrases and clauses.

- *One* in 20 hard drives we receive from our suppliers *is* faulty.

  [The verb, *is*, must agree in number with the subject, *one*, not *hard drives* or *suppliers*.]

The same is true when nouns fall between a subject and its verb.

- Only *one* of the emergency lights *was* functioning.

  [The subject of the verb is *one*, not *lights*.]

- *Each* of the managers *supervises* a statewide region.

  [The subject of the verb is *each*, not *managers*.]

Note that *one* and *each* are normally singular.

Modifying phrases can obscure a single subject.

- The *endorsement* of two engineers, one lawyer, and three executives *was* necessary before the CEO approved the proposal.

  [The subject of the sentence, *endorsement*, requires the single verb, *was*.]

Inverted Word Order

Inverted word order can confuse agreement between subject and verb.

- From this work *have come* several important *improvements*.

  [The subject of the verb is *improvements*, not *work*.]

Collective Subjects

Subjects expressing measurement, weight, mass, or total often take singular verbs even though the subject word is plural. Such subjects are treated as a unit.

- *Four years is* the normal duration of the apprenticeship program.

However, when such subjects refer to the individual items that make up the unit, a plural verb is required.

- *Three hematology technicians are* necessary to staff the blood bank on Sundays.

Similarly, collective subjects take singular verbs when the group is thought of as a unit. They take plural verbs when the individuals are thought of separately.

- The *committee is* holding its meeting on Thursday.
- The *majority were* opposed to adjourning the meeting early.

Compound Subjects

A compound subject is composed of two or more elements joined by a conjunction such as *and, or, nor, either . . . or,* or *neither . . . nor.* Usually, when the elements are connected by *and,* the subject is plural and requires a plural verb.

- *Courses in inorganic and organic chemistry are* prerequisites for a forensic-science degree.

If the elements connected by *and* form a unit or refer to the same person, however, the subject is regarded as singular and takes a singular verb.

- His accountant and business partner *prepares* the tax forms.

  [His accountant is also his business partner.]

A compound subject joined by *or* or *nor* requires a singular verb with two singular elements and a plural verb with two plural elements.

- Neither the doctor nor the nurse practitioner *is* on duty.
- Neither the doctors nor the nurse practitioners *are* on duty.

A compound subject with a singular and a plural element joined by *or* or *nor* requires that the verb agree with the element closer to it.

- Neither the office manager nor the *accountants were* there.
- Neither the accountants nor the *office manager was* there.

Indefinite Pronouns

Indefinite pronouns such as *some, none, all, more,* and *most* may be singular or plural, depending on whether they are used with a mass noun (*Most* of the heating oil *has* been used) or with a count noun (*Most* of the drivers *know* why they are here). Mass nouns are singular, and count nouns are plural. Other words, such as *type, part, series,* and *portion,* take singular verbs even when they precede a phrase containing a plural noun.

See also page 615.

- A *series* of meetings *was* held about the best way to market the new product.
- A large *portion* of most annual reports *is* devoted to promoting the corporate image.

Relative Pronouns

A relative pronoun (*who, which, that*) may take either a singular or a plural verb, depending on whether its antecedent is singular or plural.

- He is an *auditor* who *works* from home two days a week.
- He is one of the *auditors* who *work* from home two days a week.

Singular Nouns Ending in *-s*

Some abstract nouns are singular in meaning though plural in form; examples include *mathematics, news, physics,* and *economics.*

- *Textiles is* an industry in need of import quotas.
- *Statistics is* a branch of mathematics that analyzes and interprets data based on samples and populations.

Some words, such as the plural *jeans* and *scissors*, cause special problems.

- The *scissors were* ordered last week.

  [The subject is the plural *scissors.*]
- A *pair* of scissors *is* on order.

  [The subject is the singular *pair.*]

Book Titles

A book with a plural title requires a singular verb.

- *Monetary Theories is* a useful text.

Subject Complements

A *subject complement* is a noun or an adjective in the predicate of a sentence following a linking verb. The number of a subject complement does not affect the number of the verb — the verb must always agree with the subject.

- The topic of his report *was* weather data derivatives.

  [The subject is *topic*, not *derivatives.*]

Voice

In grammar, *voice* indicates the relation of the subject to the action of the verb. When the verb is in the *active voice*, the subject acts; when it is in the *passive voice*, the subject is acted on. Because the active voice is generally more direct, more concise, and easier for readers to understand, use the active voice in most cases.

- *The agency*
  ~~"It was"~~ reported ~~by the agency~~ that the new model recharger is defective.

Whether you use the active or the passive voice, be careful not to shift voices in a sentence.

◆ ***For additional guidance on choosing between active and passive voice, see pages 102–103 in Chapter 4, Revising a Document.***

- *identified it*
  David Cohen corrected the inaccuracy as soon as ~~it was identified by~~ the editor.
- *he does not permit them*
  The captain permits his crew to go ashore, but ~~they are not permitted~~ to go downtown.

Mood

Mood in grammar indicates whether a verb is intended to make a statement or ask a question, give a command, or express a hypothetical possibility.

The *indicative mood* states a fact, gives an opinion, or asks a question.

- The setting *is* correct.
- *Is* the setting correct?

The *imperative mood* expresses a command, suggestion, request, or plea. In the imperative mood, the implied subject *you* is not expressed.

- *Install* the wiring today.
- Please *let* me know if I can help.

The *subjunctive mood* expresses something that is contrary to fact, conditional, hypothetical, or purely imaginative; it can also express a wish, a doubt, or a possibility. In the subjunctive mood, *were* is used instead of *was* in clauses that speculate about the present or future, and the base form (*be*) is used following certain verbs, such as *propose*, *request*, or *insist*.

- If we *were* to close the sale today, we would meet our monthly quota.
- The senior partner insisted that she *be* in charge of the project.

The most common use of the subjunctive mood is to express clearly that the writer considers a condition to be contrary to fact. If the condition is factual, use the indicative mood.

SUBJUNCTIVE If I *were* president of the firm, I would change several hiring policies.

INDICATIVE Although I *am* president of the firm, I don't control every aspect of its policies.

Do not shift haphazardly from one mood to another within a sentence; to do so makes the sentence unbalanced as well as ungrammatical.

INCORRECT *Reboot* the computer first [imperative]; then you *should empty* the cache [indicative].

CORRECT *Reboot* the computer first [imperative]; then *empty* the cache [imperative].

There is an increasing tendency to use the indicative mood where the subjunctive traditionally has been used. Note the differences between traditional and contemporary usage in these examples:

Traditional (Formal) Use of the Subjunctive Mood

- I wish he were here now.
- If I were going to the conference, I would travel with him.
- I requested that she show up on time.

Contemporary (Informal) Use of the Indicative Mood

- I wish he was here now.
- If I was going to the conference, I would travel with him.
- I requested that she shows up on time.

You are faced with a choice: Do you use the subjunctive and, with some groups of people, sound sophisticated or intellectual? Or, do you use the indicative and, with other groups, sound uneducated? The answer might be to master both uses and be able to move freely between the different groups. In business and technical writing, however, it is better to use the more traditional expressions.

Tense

Tense is the grammatical term for verb forms that indicate time distinctions. To determine which verb tense to use, consider the time in which the action you are describing occurs in relation to other actions. English has six simple tenses, each of which has a corresponding progressive form.

Tense	Basic Form	Progressive Form
Present	I start	I am starting
Present perfect	I have started	I have been starting
Past	I started	I was starting
Past perfect	I had started	I had been starting
Future	I will start	I will be starting
Future perfect	I will have started	I will have been starting

Use the *simple present tense* to represent action occurring in the present, without any indication of time duration (I *ride* the subway to work); to present actions or conditions that have no time restrictions (Water *boils* at 212°F); or to indicate habitual action (I *pass* the coffee shop every day). A general truth is always expressed in the present tense (Time *heals* all wounds). In addition, the present tense can be used as a "historical present" to make things that occurred in the past more vivid (Dow Jones *Reaches* a Record High).

Use the *present perfect tense* to describe something from the recent past that has a bearing on the present — a period of time before the present but after the simple past. The present perfect tense is formed by combining the present tense of the helping verb *have* with the past participle of the main verb (We *have finished* the draft and can now circulate it for review).

Because it is so closely related to the past tense, the present perfect tense remains one of the most problematic of all tenses. In general, use the present perfect tense to refer to events completed in the past that have some implication for the present.

PRESENT PERFECT She *has revised* that report three times.

[She might revise it again.]

When a specific time is mentioned, however, use the simple past.

SIMPLE PAST I *wrote* the letter yesterday morning.

[The action, *wrote*, does not affect the present.]

Use the present perfect with a *since* or *for* phrase to describe actions that began in the past and will continue in the present.

- This company *has been* in business *for* 17 years.
- This company *has been* in business *since* I was a child.

To indicate an action that took place entirely in the past, use the *simple past tense.* The past tense is usually formed by adding *-d* or *-ed* to the root form of the verb (We *circulated* the draft for review).

To indicate that one past event preceded another, use the *past perfect tense*, which is formed by combining the helping verb *had* with the past participle of the main verb (He *had finished* the project early).

Use the *simple future tense* to indicate a time that will occur after the present. The helping verb *will* (or *shall*) is used along with the main verb (I *will finish* the review tomorrow). Do not, however, use the future tense needlessly; doing so merely adds complexity.

- This system ~~will be~~ is explained on page 3.
- When you press this button, the feeder ~~will move~~ moves the paper into position.

Use the *future perfect tense* to indicate an action that will be completed at the time of or before another future action. It is formed by linking the helping verbs *will have* to the past participle of the main verb (The courier *will have driven* 400 miles by the time he returns).

Be consistent in your use of tense. The only legitimate shift in tense records a real change in time. Illogical shifts in tense will only confuse your readers.

- Before he attended the appropriations briefing, the manager ~~meets~~ met with his budget analyst.

English uses the progressive form, particularly the present progressive, more frequently than other languages do. The progressive form of the verb is composed of two features: a form of the helping verb *be* and the *-ing* form of the base verb.

PRESENT PROGRESSIVE	I *am updating* the blog.
PAST PROGRESSIVE	I *was updating* the blog last week.
FUTURE PROGRESSIVE	I *will be updating* the blog regularly.

The present progressive tense is used to describe some action or condition that is ongoing (or in progress) in the present and may continue into the future, where the simple present tense more often relates to habitual actions. The present progressive is used in three ways:

1. To refer to an action that is in progress at the moment of speaking or writing
    - My assistant *is taking* the meeting minutes.
2. To highlight that a state or an action is not permanent
    - The office temp *is helping* us for a few weeks.
3. To express future plans
    - The summer intern *is leaving* to return to school this Friday.

PRESENT PROGRESSIVE I *am searching* for an error in the software.

[The search is occurring now and may continue.]

SIMPLE PRESENT	I *search* for errors when there's a software glitch.
	[I regularly search for errors, but I am not necessarily searching at this moment.]

The past progressive is used to refer to a continuing action or condition in the past, usually with specified limits.

- I *was failing* calculus until I got a tutor.

The future progressive is used to refer to a continuous action or condition in the future.

- We *will be monitoring* his condition all night.

Verbs that express mental activity or the senses of sight, smell, touch, sound, and taste are generally not used in the progressive.

- I *believe* the defendant's testimony.

Helping Verbs

In English, 23 helping verbs (forms of *have, be,* and *do*) may also function as main verbs. In addition, nine modal verbs (*can, could, may, might, must, shall, should, will, would*) function only as helping verbs. *Have, be,* and *do* change form to indicate tense; the nine modals do not.

The following guidelines will help you determine the proper use of modals. One-word modals do not change form to show a change in subject.

- I *could* quit. She *could* quit.

Most two- and three-word modals do change form, like other helping verbs.

- I *have to* finish the project. She *has to* finish the project.

Never use *to* between a one-word modal and the main verb.

- I can ~~to~~ type.

  [Most of the two- and three-word modals include *to,* as in *ought to drive.*]

Never use two one-word modals together.

- I might ~~could~~ work tomorrow.

Conditional Sentences

In *conditional sentences,* clauses that follow the words *if, when,* and *unless* show whether the result is possible or real, depending on other circumstances. Conditional sentences have two parts: a subordinate clause that begins with *if, when,* and *unless,* and a main clause that expresses a result.

A *prediction* foretells something based on conditional circumstances. Use a present-tense verb within the *if* clause. The clause that expresses the result is formed with a modal helping verb (usually *will*) and the base form of the verb.

- *If* you treat employees fairly, they *will be* more productive.

A *fact* explains a factual relationship between two or more occurrences. Use the same verb tense in both the conditional clause and the result clause.

- When it *snows*, I *leave* for work an hour earlier.
- When the chairperson *started* the meeting, he *welcomed* all new employees.

A *hypothetical sentence* explains that a result is impossible, did not happen, or is unlikely to happen. Use a past-tense verb within the *if* clause, and *would, could,* or *might* in the result clause.

- *If* I were CEO, I *would take* three months' vacation every year.

Gerunds and Infinitives

Nonnative writers are often puzzled by which form of a verbal (a verb used as another part of speech) to use when it functions as the direct object of a verb—or a complement. No structural rule exists for distinguishing between the use of an infinitive or a gerund as an object of a verb. Any specific verb may take an infinitive as its object, others may take a gerund, and yet others take either an infinitive or a gerund. At times, even the base form of the verb is used.

- He enjoys *working.* [gerund as a complement]
- She promised *to fulfill* her part of the contract. [infinitive as a complement]
- The president had the manager *assign* her staff to another project. [basic verb form as a complement]

Punctuation

Punctuation is a system of symbols that helps the reader understand the intention of a sentence and the structural relationships within it. Punctuation may link, separate, enclose, terminate, classify, and indicate omissions from sentences. Most of the 13 punctuation marks in English can perform more than one function. Their use is determined by grammatical conventions and by the writer's intention.

Commas

◆ ***See also Semicolons, page 637.***

The *comma* (,) is used more frequently than any other mark of punctuation because it can link, enclose, and separate sentence elements.

Linking Independent Clauses

Use a comma before a coordinating conjunction (*and, but, or, nor,* and sometimes *so, yet,* and *for*) that links independent clauses.

- The microwave disinfection system was delivered, *but* the installation will require an additional week.

However, if two independent clauses are short and closely related — and there is no danger of confusing the reader — the comma may be omitted. Both of the following examples are correct.

- The cable snapped and the power failed.
- The cable snapped, and the power failed.

Introducing Elements

Clauses and Phrases

Generally, place a comma after an introductory clause or phrase, especially if it is long, to identify where the introductory element ends and where the main part of the sentence begins.

- *Because of limited vaccine production capacity for this year's strain of influenza,* we are urging that high-risk patients be given priority for available vaccine supplies.

A long modifying phrase that precedes the main clause should always be followed by a comma.

- *During the first series of field-performance tests at our Colorado proving ground,* the new engine failed to meet our expectations.

When an introductory phrase is short and closely related to the main clause, the comma may be omitted.

- *In two seconds* a 5°C temperature rise occurs in the test tube.

A comma should always follow an absolute phrase. (An absolute phrase is made up of a noun or pronoun and a participle that modifies the whole sentence rather than a specific word.)

- *The tests completed,* we organized the data for the final report.

Words

Certain types of introductory words are followed by a comma. One example is a transitional word or phrase (*however, in addition*) that connects the preceding clause or sentence with the thought that follows.

- *Furthermore,* steel can withstand a humidity of 99 percent, provided there is no chloride or sulfur dioxide in the atmosphere.
- *For example,* this product line will make us more competitive in urban markets.

When adverbs closely modify the verb or entire sentence, they should not be followed by a comma.

- *Perhaps* we can still solve the high turnover problem. *Certainly* we should try.

A proper noun used in an introductory direct address is followed by a comma, as is an interjection (such as *oh, well, why, indeed, yes,* and *no*).

- *Nancy,* enclosed is the article you asked me to review. [direct address]
- *Yes,* I will ensure that your request is forwarded. [interjection]

Quotations

Use a comma to separate a direct quotation from its introduction.

- Morton and Lucia White said, "People live in cities but dream of the countryside."

Do not use a comma when giving an indirect quotation.

- Morton and Lucia White said that people dream about country life, even though they live in cities.

◆ ***See also Quotation Marks, pages 643–644, and Quoting from Your Sources, pages 177–179.***

Enclosing Elements

Use commas to enclose nonrestrictive and parenthetical sentence elements. Nonrestrictive elements add subordinate information about the things they modify; parenthetical elements also insert extra information into the sentence. Each is set off by commas to show its loose relationship with the rest of the sentence.

- Our refurbished Detroit factory, *which began operations last month*, should add 25 percent to total output capacity. [nonrestrictive clause]
- We can, *of course*, expect their lawyer to call us. [parenthetical element]

Similarly, enclose a nonrestrictive participial phrase (any form of a verb used as an adjective) within commas.

- The lathe operator, *working quickly and efficiently*, finished early.

In contrast, restrictive elements — as their name implies — restrict the meaning of the words to which they apply and cannot be set off with commas.

- The patient *in room 22A* has peripheral neuropathy. [restrictive]
- The patient, *who has peripheral neuropathy*, is in room 22A. [nonrestrictive]

In the first sentence, *in room 22A* is essential to the sentence: The phrase identifies the patient by location. In the second sentence, the relative clause *who has peripheral neuropathy* is incidental to the patient's location: The main idea can be communicated without it.

An appositive phrase (which identifies another noun or pronoun phrase in the sentence) is enclosed in commas.

- The food industry, highly regulated and capital-intensive, is rarely rich soil for entrepreneurs.

Separating Elements

Items in a Series

Although the comma before the last item in a series is sometimes omitted, it is generally clearer to include it.

- Random House, Bantam, Doubleday, and Dell were individual publishing companies before the industry's restructuring.

  [Without the final comma, *Doubleday and Dell* could refer to one company or two.]

Phrases and clauses in coordinate series are also punctuated with commas.

- Plants absorb noxious gases, act as receptors of dirt particles, and cleanse the air of other impurities.

When phrases or clauses in a series contain commas, separate those phrases or clauses with semicolons.

- Our product line includes amitriptyline, which has sold very well; dipyridamole, which has not sold well; and cholestyramine, which was just introduced.

Adjectives

When adjectives modifying the same noun can be reversed and make sense, or when they can be separated by *and* or *or*, they should be separated by commas.

- The drawing was of a *modern, sleek, swept-wing* airplane.

When an adjective modifies a phrase, no comma is required.

- She was investigating the *damaged inventory-control system.*

  [The adjective *damaged* modifies the phrase *inventory-control system.*]

Never separate a final adjective from its noun.

- He is a conscientious, honest, reliable/worker. [omit comma]

Dates

A full date that is written in the month-day-year format uses a comma preceding and following the year.

◆ ***See also page 323 in Chapter 9, Writing Routine and Sensitive Messages.***

- Note that November 30, 2025, is the payoff date for the bond.

Do not use commas for dates in the day-month-year format, which is used in many parts of the world and by the U.S. military.

- Note that 30 November 2025 is the payoff date for the bond.

Do not use commas if only the day or the year is included.

- The target date of May 2017 is optimistic, so I would like to meet on March 4 to discuss our options.

Numbers

Use commas to separate the elements of Arabic numbers.

- 1,528,200 feet

However, because many countries use the comma as the decimal marker, use periods or spaces rather than commas in international documents.

- 1.528.200 feet *or* 1 528 200 feet

Addresses

Commas are conventionally used to separate the elements of an address written on the same line (but they are not inserted between the state and the zip code).

- Kristen James, 4119 Mill Road, Dayton, OH 45401

Use commas to separate elements of geographic names.

- Toronto, Ontario, Canada

Names

Use a comma to separate names that are reversed or that are followed by an abbreviation of an earned title, such as Ph.D., M.D., and C.P.A.

- Smith, Alvin
- Jane Alverez, Ph.D.

In current usage, however, no comma is necessary before abbreviations of personal and corporate names (such as Jr., Sr., and Inc.).

- Ray Aragon Jr.
- Grace Inc.

Using Commas with Other Punctuation

When a comma should follow a phrase or clause that ends with words in parentheses, the comma always appears outside the closing parenthesis.

- Although we left late (at 6:30 p.m.), we arrived in time for the keynote address.

Commas always go inside quotation marks.

- The operator placed the discharge bypass switch at "normal," which triggered a second discharge.

A comma should not be used with a dash, an exclamation mark, a period, or a question mark.

- "Have you finished the project?," I asked. [omit comma]

Avoiding Unnecessary Commas

Writers often add commas where they do not belong because they assume that a pause should be indicated by a comma. It is true that commas usually signal pauses, but it is not true that pauses *necessarily* call for commas.

Be careful not to place a comma between a subject and its verb or between a verb and its object.

- The wet weather across the region, makes spring planting difficult. [omit comma]
- The firm employs, four writers, two artists, and one photographer. [omit comma]

Do not use a comma between the elements of a compound subject or a compound predicate consisting of only two elements.

- The board chair, and the president prepared the press release. [omit comma]
- The manager revised the schedules, and improved morale. [omit comma]

Placing a comma after a coordinating conjunction (*and, but, for, nor, or, so, yet*) is an especially common error.

- We doubled our sales, but, we still did not dominate the market. [omit comma]

Do not place a comma before the first item or after the last item of a series.

- We purchased new office furniture, including/desks, chairs, and tables. [omit comma]

Semicolons

The *semicolon* (;) links independent clauses or other sentence elements that are of equal weight and grammatical rank. The semicolon indicates a longer pause than a comma would but not so long a pause as a period would.

Two closely related independent clauses can be linked by a semicolon.

- No one applied for the position; its responsibilities were too vaguely defined.

The relationship between the two statements should be so clear that a reader will understand why they are linked without further explanation. Often, such clauses balance or contrast with each other.

- Our last supervisor allowed only one long break; our new supervisor allows two short ones.

Use a semicolon between two main clauses connected by a coordinating conjunction (*and, but, for, or, nor, yet, so*) if the clauses are long and contain other punctuation.

- In most cases these individuals are corporate executives, bankers, or Wall Street lawyers; but they do not, as the economic determinists seem to believe, simply push the button of their economic power to affect fields remote from economics.

A semicolon should be used before conjunctive adverbs (such as *therefore, moreover, furthermore, indeed, in fact, however*) that connect independent clauses. Commas follow conjunctive adverbs.

- I won't finish today; moreover, I doubt that I will finish this week.

Do not use a semicolon between a dependent clause and its main clause. Elements joined by semicolons must be of equal grammatical rank or weight.

- No one applied for the position, even though it was heavily advertised.

Colons

The *colon* (:) is a mark of anticipation and introduction that alerts the reader to the close connection between the first statement and the one following.

- We carry four brands of watches: Timex, Swiss Army, Seiko, and Omega.

Do not, however, place a colon between a verb and its objects.

- The three fluids for cleaning pipettes are: water, alcohol, and acetone. [omit colon]

Do not use a colon between a preposition and its object.

- I would like to be transferred to: Tucson, Boston, or Miami. [omit colon]

A colon can link one statement to another that develops, explains, amplifies, or illustrates the first, including two independent clauses.

- Any large organization must confront two separate, though related, information problems: It must maintain an effective internal and external communication system.

Occasionally, a colon may be used to link an appositive phrase to its related statement if special emphasis is needed.

- Only one thing will satisfy Mr. Sturgess: our finished report.

Colons separate bibliographic citation elements and time designations.

- 3:144 [refers to page 144 of volume 3]
- Sowell, T. (2011). *Basic economics: A common sense guide to the economy* (4th ed.). New York, NY: Basic Books. [separates location and name of publisher]
- *The Black Swan: The Impact of the Highly Improbable* [separates a book's title and subtitle]
- 9:30 a.m. [9 hours and 30 minutes]

In a ratio, the colon indicates the proportion of one amount to another and replaces *to*.

- The cement is mixed with the water and sand at a ratio of 5:3:1. [the colon is read as the word *to*]

A colon follows the salutation in business correspondence, even when the salutation refers to a person by first name.

- Dear Ms. Jeffers:
- Dear Frank:

The first word after a colon may be capitalized if it begins a complete sentence, a formal resolution or question, or a direct quotation.

- The conference attendance was low: We did not advertise widely enough.

Begin a subordinate element following a colon with a lowercase letter.

- We have only one way to stay within our present budget: to reduce expenditures for research and development.

Apostrophes

An *apostrophe* (') is used to show possession; to mark the omission of letters; and sometimes to indicate the plural of numbers, letters, and acronyms.

Showing Possession

Possession is generally expressed with *'s* (the *report's* title), with a prepositional phrase using *of* (the title *of the report*), or with the possessive form of a pronoun (*our* report). Practices vary for some possessive forms, but the following guidelines are widely used in business writing.

◆ *See also Pronoun Case, pages 617–618.*

Use *'s* with personal names, personal nouns, collective nouns, and animals. (Use just an apostrophe for plural nouns that end with *s*.)

- *Joan's* class
- the *receptionist's* lunch hour
- the state *government's* pension plan
- the *employees'* stock portfolios

You can also use *'s* (or just an apostrophe) with some inanimate nouns: geographical and institutional names, nouns that refer to time, and nouns of special interest to human activity.

- *the company's* investors
- *today's* agenda
- a *week's* rest
- *business'* influence on politics

Use *of* with inanimate objects and measurements.

- the title *of* the monthly report
- a cup *of* coffee
- the length *of* the memo

Singular Nouns

Most singular nouns indicate possession with *'s*.

- the *manager's* office
- the *company's* stock value
- the *witness's* testimony
- the *bus's* schedule

When pronunciation is difficult or when a multisyllable noun ends in a *z* sound, you may use only an apostrophe.

- *New Orleans'* levee reconstruction plans

Plural Nouns

Plural nouns that end in *-s* or *-es* show the possessive case with only an apostrophe.

- the *managers'* reports
- the *companies'* joint project
- the *witnesses'* testimony
- the *buses'* schedules

Plural nouns that do not end in *-s* or *-es* show the possession with *'s*.

- *children's* clothing/*women's* resources/*men's* locker room

Compound Nouns

Compound nouns form the possessive with *'s* following the final letter.

- the *vice president's* proposal/the *editor-in-chief's* desk

Plurals of some compound expressions are often best expressed with a prepositional phrase (presentations of the *editors-in-chief*).

Coordinate Nouns

Coordinate nouns show joint possession with *'s* following the last noun.

- *Fischer and Goulet's* partnership was the foundation of their business.

Coordinate nouns show individual possession with *'s* following each noun.

- The difference between *Barker's* and *Washburne's* test results was statistically insignificant.

Possessive Pronouns

The possessive pronouns (*yours, its, his, her, ours, whose, theirs*) do not require apostrophes. (Even good systems have *their* flaws.) *Its* is a possessive pronoun and does not use an apostrophe; *it's* is a contraction of *it is* and does not show possession.

- *It's* important that the sales department meet *its* quota.

Indicating Omission

An apostrophe is used to mark the omission of letters or numbers in a contraction or a date (*can't, I'm, I'll;* the class of *'18,* the crash of *'29*). This usage is not wrong, but it is less formal than the longer forms and should be used sparingly in business and professional writing.

Forming Plurals

An apostrophe can be used in forming the plurals of letters, words, or lowercase abbreviations if confusion might result from using *s* alone.

- The search program does not find *a*'s and *i*'s.
- *I*'s need to be distinguished from the number 1.
- Industrywide *COLA*'s averaged 1.2 percent last year.

Generally, however, add only *s* (in Roman type) when referring to words as words or to capital letters (which should be set in italics).

- Five *and*s appear in the first sentence.
- The applicants received *A*s and *B*s in their courses.

Do not use an apostrophe for plurals of abbreviations with all-capital letters (DVDs) or a final capital letter (ten Ph.D.s) or for plurals of numbers (7s, the late 1990s).

Quotation Marks

Quotation marks (" ") are used to enclose direct repetition of spoken or written words. Quotation marks have other special uses, but they should not be used for emphasis.

- "exceptional" *not* „exceptional" or «exceptional»

Identifying Quotations

Enclose in quotation marks anything that is quoted word for word (a direct quotation) from speech or written material.

◆ *For tips on achieving emphasis, see pages 102–107 in Chapter 4, Revising a Document.*

- She said at this morning's staff meeting, "I want the progress report by three o'clock."

Do not enclose indirect quotations — usually introduced by the word *that* — in quotation marks. Indirect quotations paraphrase a speaker's words or ideas.

- She said that she wanted a copy of the progress report by three this afternoon.

Material quoted directly and enclosed in quotation marks cannot be changed from the original unless you show the change in brackets.

◆ *See also Paraphrasing, pages 179–180 in Chapter 6, Conducting Research for a Document.*

Use single quotation marks (' ') to enclose a quotation that appears within another quotation.

- John said, "Jane told me that she was going to 'stay with the project if it takes all year.'"

◆ *For further information on incorporating quoted material and inserting comments, see Avoiding Plagiarism and Other Intellectual Property Violations, pages 181–184; Quoting from Your Sources, pages 177–180; Parentheses and Brackets, pages 644–645; and Ellipses, pages 647–648.*

Setting Off Words, Phrases, and Titles

Words and Phrases

Use quotation marks to set off special words or terms only to point out that the term is used in context for a unique or special purpose (that is, in the sense of the term *so-called*).

- A remarkable chain of events caused the sinking of the "unsinkable" *Titanic* on its maiden voyage.

Slang, colloquial expressions, and attempts at humor, although infrequent in workplace writing, should not be set off by quotation marks unless they indicate a direct quote.

- Our first six months in the new office amounted to little more than a "shakedown cruise" for what lay ahead. [omit quotation marks]

Titles of Works

◆ See also Italics, pages 655–656.

Use quotation marks to enclose titles of short stories, articles, essays, chapters of books, episodes of radio and television programs, and songs. However, do not use quotation marks for titles of books and periodicals, which should appear in italics.

- Did you see the article "No-Fault Insurance and Your Motorcycle" in last Friday's *Wall Street Journal*?

Using Quotation Marks with Other Punctuation

Commas and periods always go inside closing quotation marks.

- "We hope," said Ms. Abrams, "that the merger will be announced this week."
- "as a last resort," *not* "as a last resort",
- "to the bitter end." *not* "to the bitter end".

Semicolons and colons always go outside closing quotation marks.

- He said, "I will pay the asking price"; this was a real surprise to us.
- "there is no doubt"; *not* "there is no doubt;"

◆ See also use of quotation marks with question marks, page 643.

All other punctuation follows the logic of the context: If the punctuation is part of the material quoted, it goes inside the quotation marks; if the punctuation is not part of the material quoted, it goes outside the quotation marks.

Periods

A *period* (.) usually indicates the end of a declarative or an imperative sentence. Periods may also end questions that are actually polite requests and questions to which an affirmative response is assumed. ("Will you please send me the financial statement.")

Use a comma, not a period, after a declarative sentence that is quoted in the context of another sentence.

- "The project has every chance of success." she stated.

◆ See also Quotation Marks, pages 641–642, and Quoting from Your Sources, pages 177–180.

A period is, by convention, placed inside quotation marks.

- He stated clearly, "My vote is yes."

If a sentence ends with an item in parentheses, the period should follow the end parenthesis.

- The institute was founded by Harry Denman (1931–2002).

When a complete sentence within parentheses stands independently, however, the end punctuation goes inside the final parenthesis.

- The project director listed the problems her staff faced. (This was the third time she had complained to the board.)

When a sentence ends with an abbreviation that ends with a period, do not add another period.

- Please meet me at 3:30 p.m.

Question Marks

The *question mark* (?) most often ends a sentence that is a direct question or request.

- Where did you put the tax report? [direct question]
- Will you e-mail me if your shipment does not arrive by June 10? [request]

Use a question mark to end a statement that has an interrogative meaning—a statement that is declarative in form but asks a question. (The tax report is finished? [question in declarative form])

Question marks may follow a series of separate items within an interrogative sentence.

- Do you remember the date of the contract? its terms? whether you signed it?

Use a question mark to end an interrogative clause within a declarative sentence.

- It was not until July (or was it August?) that we voted to veto the proposal.

Retain the question mark in a title that is being cited, even if the sentence in which it appears has not ended.

- *Can Investments Be Protected?* is now in its third edition.

Never use a question mark to end a sentence that is an indirect question.

- He asked me where I put the tax report?.

◆ *See also Periods, pages 642–643.*

When used with quotations, the placement of the question mark is important. If the writer is asking a question, the question mark belongs outside the quotation marks.

- Did she say, "I don't think the project should continue"?

◆ *See also Quoting from Your Sources, pages 177–179 in Chapter 6, Conducting Research for a Document.*

If the quotation itself is a question, the question mark goes inside the quotation marks.

- She asked, "Do we have enough funding?"

If both cases apply — the writer is asking a question and the quotation itself is a question — use a single question mark inside the quotation marks.

- Did she ask, "Do we have enough funding?"

Exclamation Marks

The *exclamation mark* (!) indicates strong feeling, urgency, elation, or surprise (*Hurry! Great! Wow!*). However, it cannot make an argument more convincing, lend force to a weak statement, or call attention to an intended irony.

An exclamation mark can be used after a whole sentence or an element of a sentence.

- This meeting — please note it well! — concerns our budget deficit.

When used with quotation marks, the exclamation mark goes outside, unless what is quoted is an exclamation.

- The paramedics shouted, "Don't touch the victim!" The bystander, according to a witness, "jumped like a kangaroo"!

In instructional and signage writing, the exclamation mark is often used in cautions and warnings (*Danger! Stop!*).

Parentheses and Brackets

Parentheses (( )) and *brackets* ([ ]) are used to enclose explanatory or digressive words, phrases, or sentences.

Material in parentheses often clarifies or defines the preceding text without altering its meaning.

- She severely bruised her shin bone (or *tibia*) in the accident.

Parentheses are also used to enclose numerals or letters that indicate sequence.

- The following sections deal with (1) preparation, (2) research, (3) organization, (4) writing, and (5) revision.

The primary use of brackets is to enclose a word or words inserted by the writer or an editor into a quotation.

- The text stated, "Hypertext systems can be categorized as either modest [not modifiable] or robust [modifiable]."

Use brackets to set off a parenthetical item that is already within parentheses.

- We should be sure to give Randolph Chaney (and his brother Scott [1912–1982]) credit for his part in founding the institute.

Parenthetical material does not affect the punctuation of a sentence. If a parenthesis or bracket appears at the end of a sentence, the ending punctuation should appear after the parenthesis or bracket. Likewise, a comma following a parenthetical word, phrase, or clause appears outside the closing parenthesis or bracket.

- She severely bruised her shin bone (or *tibia*), and he tore the cartilage (or *meniscus*) in his knee.

When a complete sentence within parentheses stands independently, however, the ending punctuation goes inside the final parenthesis.

- The project director listed the problems her staff faced. (This was the third time she had complained to the board.)

Hyphens

The *hyphen* (-) serves both to link and to separate words. The hyphen joins compound words (able-bodied, self-contained, self-esteem), forms compound numbers from twenty-one through ninety-nine, and divides fractions when they are written out (three-quarters).

Dashes, similar in appearance but different in function from hyphens, are discussed beginning on page 647.

Linking Modifiers

Two- and three-word modifiers that express a single thought are hyphenated when they precede a noun.

- It was a *well-researched* report.

However, a modifying phrase is not hyphenated when it follows the noun it modifies.

- The report was *well researched.*

If each of the words can modify the noun without the aid of the other modifying word or words, do not use a hyphen.

- a *new digital* copier

If the first word is an adverb ending in *-ly*, do not use a hyphen.

- a *privately* held company/a *thoroughly* researched analysis

A hyphen is always used as part of a letter or number modifier.

- 22-inch screen, A-frame structure

In a series of unit modifiers that all have the same term following the hyphen, the term following the hyphen need not be repeated throughout the series; for greater smoothness and brevity, use the term only at the end of the series.

- The third-, fourth-, and fifth-floor offices were recently re-carpeted.

Separating Prefixes and Suffixes

When a prefix precedes a proper noun, use a hyphen to connect the two.

- pre-Internet
- anti-Americanism
- post-Newtonian

A hyphen may (but does not have to) be used when the prefix ends and the root word begins with the same vowel. When the repeated vowel is *i*, a hyphen is almost always used.

- re-elect
- re-enter
- anti-inflationary

A hyphen is used when *ex-* means "former."

- ex-partners
- ex-wife

The suffix *-elect* is connected to the word it follows with a hyphen.

- president-elect

Hyphens identify prefixes, suffixes, or syllables written as such.

- *Re-*, *-ism*, and *ex-* are word parts that can cause spelling problems.

Other Uses

Hyphens separate letters showing spelling (or misspelling).

- In his e-mail, he misspelled "believed" b-e-l-e-i-v-e-d.

To avoid confusion, some words and modifiers should always be hyphenated. *Re-cover* does not mean the same thing as *recover*, for example; the same is true of *re-sent* and *resent*, *re-form* and *reform*, *re-sign* and *resign*.

A hyphen can stand for *to* or *through* between letters, numbers, and locations.

- pp. 44-46
- The Detroit-Toledo Expressway
- A-L and M-Z

Hyphens are also used to divide words at the end of a line. Avoid dividing words if possible; however, if you must divide them, consult a dictionary about where to place the hyphen.

Dashes

The *dash* (—) is a versatile, yet limited, mark of punctuation. It is versatile because it can perform all the functions of punctuation (to link, to separate, to enclose, and to show omission). It is limited because it is especially emphatic and easily overused. Use the dash cautiously, therefore, to indicate more informality, emphasis, or abruptness than the conventional marks would show.

A dash can indicate a sharp turn in thought.

- The project will end October 30 — unless we receive additional funds.

A dash can indicate an emphatic pause.

- The project will begin — after we are under contract.

Sometimes, to emphasize contrast, a dash is also used with *but.*

- We completed the survey quickly — but the results were not representative.

A dash can be used before a final summarizing statement or before repetition that has the effect of an afterthought.

- It was hot near the annealing ovens — unbearably hot.

A dash can be used to set off an explanatory or appositive series.

- Three of the applicants — John Evans, Rosalita Fontiana, and Kyong-Shik Choi — seem well qualified for the job.

Dashes set off parenthetical elements more sharply and emphatically than commas or parentheses.

- Only one person — the president — can authorize such activity.
- Only one person, the president, can authorize such activity.
- Only one person (the president) can authorize such activity.

Use dashes for clarity when commas appear within a parenthetical element.

- Retinal images are patterns in the eye — made up of light and dark shapes, in addition to areas of color — but we do not see patterns; we see objects.

The first word after a dash is never capitalized unless it is a proper noun. When keying in the dash, use two consecutive hyphens (--), with no spaces before or after the hyphens.

Ellipses

An *ellipsis* indicates the omission of words from quoted material; it is indicated by three spaced periods called *ellipsis points* (. . .). When you use ellipsis points, omit marks of internal punctuation at the point of omission, unless they are necessary for clarity or the omitted material comes at the end of a quoted sentence.

ORIGINAL TEXT	Promotional material is sometimes charged for, particularly in high volume distribution to schools, although prices for these publications are much lower than the development costs when all factors are considered.
WITH OMISSION AND ELLIPSIS POINTS	Promotional material is sometimes charged for . . . although prices for these publications are much lower than the development costs. . . .

Notice that the final period is retained and what remains of the quotation is grammatically complete. When the omitted part of the quotation is preceded by a period, retain the period and add the three ellipsis points after it, as in the following example.

ORIGINAL TEXT	Of the 172 major ethics cases reported, 57 percent were found to involve unsubstantiated concerns. Misinformation was the cause of unfounded concerns of misconduct in 72 cases.
WITH OMISSION AND ELLIPSIS POINTS	Of the 172 major ethics cases reported, 57 percent were found to involve unsubstantiated concerns. . . .

◆ *See also Quoting from Your Sources, pages 177–179 in Chapter 6, Conducting Research for a Document.*

Do not use ellipsis points when the beginning of a quoted sentence is omitted.

- The ethics report states that "26 percent of the total cases reported involved incidents partly substantiated by ethics officers as serious misconduct."

Slashes

The *slash* (/) — called a variety of names, including *slant line*, *diagonal*, *virgule*, *bar*, and *solidus* — both separates and shows omission.

The slash can indicate alternatives or combinations.

- David's telephone numbers are (333) 549-2278/2235.
- The on/off switch is located at the bottom left of the front panel.

The slash often indicates omitted words and letters.

- miles/hour (miles per hour) / w/o (without)

In fractions and mathematical expressions, the slash separates the numerator from the denominator (3/4 for three-fourths; x/y for x over y).

Although the slash is used informally with dates (5/11/16), do not use this form in international communications because many countries in Europe reverse the month-day order using this system. Thus, in Europe 5/11/16 would mean November 5, 2016, rather than May 11, 2016.

The forward slash (/) is often used to separate items in the URL (uniform resource locator) addresses for sites on the Internet (macmillanhighered.com/professionalwriting1e). The backward slash (\) is used to separate parts of computer file names (c:\myfiles\reports\annual10.doc).

Mechanics

Certain writing conventions tend to confound workplace writers. Should a number be written as a word or figure? How are acronyms used? Should a date be stated day-month-year or month-day-year? Should I capitalize certain titles and events? This section will help you answer such perplexing questions.

Capitalization

The use of capital, or uppercase, letters is determined by custom. Capitals are used to call attention to certain words, such as proper nouns and the first word of a sentence. Use them carefully, especially when they affect a word's meaning (march/March, china/China, turkey/Turkey).

Proper Nouns

Proper nouns name specific persons, places, things, concepts, or qualities and are capitalized (Business Writing 205, Microsoft, Pat Wilde, Peru).

Common Nouns

Common nouns name general classes or categories of people, places, things, concepts, or qualities rather than specific ones and are not capitalized (business writing, company, person, country).

First Words

The first letter of the first word in a sentence is always capitalized, as is the first word after a colon when the colon introduces an independent clause or a complete sentence.

- The meeting will address only one issue: What is the firm's role in environmental protection?

If a subordinate element follows the colon or if the thought is closely related, use a lowercase letter after the colon.

- We kept working for one reason: the approaching deadline.

The first word of a complete sentence in quotation marks is capitalized.

- Peter Drucker said, "The most important thing in communication is to hear what isn't being said."

The first word of a complete sentence enclosed in dashes, brackets, or parentheses is not capitalized when it appears as part of another sentence.

- We must make an extra effort in safety this year (accidents last year were up 10 percent).

In correspondence, the first word in the salutation (Dear Ms. Markels,) and complimentary close (Sincerely yours,) are capitalized, as are the names of recipients.

Specific Groups

Capitalize the names of ethnic groups, religions, and nationalities (Native American, Christianity, Mongolian). Do not capitalize the names of social and economic groups (middle class, working class, unemployed).

Specific Places

Capitalize the names of all political (Ward Six, Chicago, Cook County, Illinois) and geographic (Europe, Asia, North America, the Middle East) divisions. Do not capitalize geographic features unless they are part of a proper name.

- The mountains in some areas, such as the *Great Smoky Mountains*, make cell-phone reception difficult.

The words *north*, *south*, *east*, and *west* are capitalized when they refer to sections of the United States. They are not capitalized when they refer to directions.

- I traveled south on Interstate 81 for 30 miles./I was raised in the South.

Specific Institutions, Events, and Concepts

Capitalize the names of institutions, organizations, and associations (U.S. Department of Health and Human Services). An organization usually capitalizes the names of its internal divisions and departments (Aeronautics Division, Human Resources Department). Types of organizations are not capitalized unless they are part of an official name (a business communication association; Association for Business Communication). Capitalize historic events (the Great Depression of the 1930s). Capitalize words that designate holidays, specific eras, months, or days of the week (Labor Day, the Renaissance, January, Monday). Do not capitalize seasons of the year (spring, autumn, winter, summer).

Titles of Works

Capitalize the initial letters of the first and last words of the title of a book, an article, a play, or a film, as well as all major words in the title. Do not capitalize articles (*a*, *an*, *the*) or coordinating conjunctions (*and*, *but*, *for*, *or*, *nor*, *yet*, *so*), unless they begin or end the title (*The Lives of a Cell*). Capitalize prepositions within titles only when they contain more than four letters (*Between*, *Within*, *Until*, *After*), unless you are following a style that recommends otherwise. The same rules apply to the subject line of an e-mail message or a memo.

Professional and Personal Titles

Titles preceding proper names are capitalized (Ms. Berger, Senator McCain). Appositives following proper names normally are not capitalized (John McCain, *senator* from Arizona). However, the word *President* is capitalized when it refers to the chief executive of a national government.

Though dependent on the style manual and conventions used by your industry, generally job titles used with personal names are capitalized (Ho-shik Kim, *Division Manager*). Job titles used without personal names are not capitalized (The *division manager* will meet us tomorrow).

Use capital letters to designate family relationships only when they occur before a name (my *uncle*; *Uncle* Fred).

Abbreviations, Letters, and Units

Capitalize abbreviations if the words they stand for would be capitalized, such as M.B.A. (Master of Business Administration). Also capitalize the following:

- Letters that serve as names or indicate shapes (vitamin B, T-square, U-turn, I-beam)
- Certain units, such as parts and chapters of books and rooms in buildings, when specifically identified by number (Chapter 5, Ch. 5; Room 72, Rm. 72)

Minor divisions within such units are not capitalized unless they begin a sentence (page 11, verse 14, seat 12).

Numbers

The standards for how to express numbers in workplace writing vary; however, unless you are following an organizational or a professional style manual, observe the following guidelines.

Words or Numerals

Write numbers from zero through ten as words, and write numbers above ten as numerals.

- I rehearsed my presentation *three* times.
- The meeting was attended by *150* people.

Do not follow a word representing a number with a numeral in parentheses that represents the same number. Doing so is redundant.

- Send five ~~(5)~~ copies of the report.

Spell out numbers that begin a sentence, even if they would otherwise be written as numerals. If spelling out such a number seems awkward, rewrite the sentence so that the number does not appear at the beginning.

- *Last month, 273* ~~Two hundred seventy three~~ defective products were returned ~~last month.~~ .

Spell out approximate and round numbers.

- We've had *over a thousand* requests this month.

In most writing, spell out ordinal numbers, which express degree or sequence (first, second; but 27th, 42nd), when they are single words (our *third* draft) or when they modify a century (the *twenty-first* century). However, avoid ordinal numbers in dates on correspondence (use March 30 or 30 March, not March 30th).

When several numbers appear in the same sentence or paragraph, write them the same way, regardless of other rules and guidelines.

- The company employs *271* people, leases *7* warehouses, and owns *150* trucks.

Plurals

Indicate the plurals of numerals by adding *-s* (7s, the late 1990s). Form the plural of a written number (like any noun) by adding *-s* or *-es* or by dropping *-y* and adding *-ies* (elevens, sixes, twenties).

Money

In general, use numerals to express exact amounts of money. (We charge $28.95 per unit.) Use words to express indefinite amounts of money. (The printing system may cost several thousand dollars.) Use numerals and words for rounded amounts of money over one million dollars; use numerals alone for more complex or exact amounts.

- The contract is worth $6.8 million.
- The corporation paid $2,452,500 in taxes last year.

Measurements

Express units of measurement as numerals (3 miles, 45 cubic feet, 9 meters). When numbers run together in the same phrase, write one as a numeral and the other as a word.

- The order was for *twelve* ~~12~~ 6-inch pipes.

Generally give percentages as numerals and write out the word *percent*. (Approximately *85 percent* of the land has been sold.) However, in a visual, like a figure or table, use a numeral followed by a percent symbol (*85%*).

Express fractions as numerals when they are combined with whole numbers (27 1/2 inches, 4 1/4 miles). Spell out fractions when they are expressed without a whole number (one-fourth, seven-eighths). Always write decimal numbers as numerals (5.21 meters).

Time and Dates

Divide hours and minutes with colons when a.m. or p.m. follows (11:30 a.m., 7:30 p.m.). Do not use colons with the 24-hour system (0730, 2330). Spell out time that is not followed by a.m. or p.m. (four o'clock in the afternoon).

In the United States, dates are usually written in a month-day-year sequence (August 11, 2016). Never use the strictly numerical form for dates (8/11/16) in business writing because the date is not always immediately clear, especially in international correspondence (in which the day-month-year sequence is more frequently employed).

Addresses

Spell out numbered streets from one to ten unless space is at a premium (East Tenth Street). Write building numbers as numerals. The only exception is the building number *one* (4862 East Monument Street; One East Monument Street). Write highway numbers as numerals (U.S. 40, Ohio 271, I-94).

Punctuation

Some rules for punctuating numbers in American English are summarized as follows.

Use a comma to separate numbers with four or more digits into groups of three, starting from the right.

- 2,500
- 57,890 cubic feet
- $187,291

Do not use a comma in years, house numbers, zip codes, and page numbers.

- June 2010
- 92401 East Alameda Drive
- The zip code is 91601
- Page 1204

Use a period to represent the decimal point (4.2 percent; $3,742,097.43).

Documents

In manuscripts, page numbers are written as numerals, but chapter and volume numbers may appear as numerals or as words (page 37, Chapter 2 or Chapter Two, Volume 1 or Volume One). Express figure and table numbers as numerals (Figure 4 and Table 3).

Abbreviations

Abbreviations are shortened versions of words or combinations of the first letters of words (Corp./Corporation, URL/*u*niform *r*esource *l*ocator). Those that combine the first letter or letters of several words — and can be pronounced as words — are called *acronyms* (PIN/*p*ersonal *i*dentification *n*umber, laser/*l*ight *a*mplification by *s*timulated *e*mission of *r*adiation). Abbreviations and acronyms, if used appropriately, can be convenient for both the writer and the reader. Like symbols, abbreviations can be important space savers in workplace writing.

Abbreviations and acronyms are useful only when your readers understand them. Some abbreviations, for example, can have several different meanings (NEA stands for both the National Education Association and the National Endowment for the Arts in the United States; British readers would associate it with the Nuclear Energy Association). When in doubt, spell it out.

Names of Organizations

A company may include in its name a term such as *Brothers, Incorporated, Corporation,* or *Company*. If the term is abbreviated in the official company name that appears on letterhead stationery or on its website, use the abbreviated form: *Bros., Inc., Corp.*, or *Co*. If the term is not abbreviated in the official name, spell it out in writing, except with addresses, footnotes, bibliographies, and lists where abbreviations may be used. Likewise, use an ampersand (&) only if it appears in the official company name. For names of divisions within organizations, terms such as *Department* and *Division* should be abbreviated (*Dept., Div.*) only when space is limited.

Measurements

Except for abbreviations that may be confused with words (*in.* for *inch* and *gal.* for *gallon*), abbreviations of measurement do not require periods (*yd* for *yard* and *qt* for *quart*). Abbreviations of units of measure are identical in the singular and plural: 1 *cm* and 15 *cm* (*not* 15 *cms*). Some abbreviations can be used in combination with other symbols (°*F* for *degrees Fahrenheit* and *ft*² for *square feet*).

The following list includes abbreviations for the basic units of the International System of Units (SI), the metric system. This system not only is standard in science but also is used in international commerce and trade.

Measurement	**Unit**	**Abbreviation**
length	meter	m
mass	kilogram	kg
time	second	s
electric current	ampere	A
thermodynamic temperature	kelvin	K
amount of substance	mole	mol
luminous intensity	candela	cd

Personal Names and Titles

Personal names generally should not be abbreviated: Thomas (*not* Thos.) and William (*not* Wm.). An academic, civil, religious, or military title should be spelled out and in lowercase when it does not precede a name. (The *captain* ordered the inspection.) When they precede names, some titles are customarily abbreviated (*Dr.* Smith, *Mr.* Mills, *Mrs.* Katz).

An abbreviation of a title may follow the name; however, be certain that it does not duplicate a title before the name (Angeline Martinez, Ph.D. *or* Dr. Angeline Martinez, *not* Dr. Angeline Martinez, Ph.D.). When you are addressing correspondence and including names in other documents, spell out titles (The Honorable Mary J. Holt; Professor Charles Martin). Traditionally, periods are used with academic degrees, although they are sometimes omitted (M.A./MA, M.B.A./MBA, Ph.D./PhD).

Italics

Italics is a style of type used to denote emphasis and to distinguish foreign expressions, book titles, and certain other elements. *This sentence is printed in italics.* Italic type is signaled by underlining in a manuscript submitted for publication or where italic font may not be available, such as in text messages. Italicize words that require special emphasis in a sentence. (Contrary to projections, sales have *not* improved.) Do not overuse italics for emphasis, however. (*This* will hurt *you* more than *me.*)

◆ ***For more-effective ways to achieve emphasis, see pages 102–107 in Chapter 4, Revising a Document.***

Foreign Words and Phrases

Foreign words and phrases that have not been assimilated into the English language are italicized (*sine qua non, coup de grâce, in re, in camera*). Foreign words that have been fully assimilated into the language need not be italicized. A word may be considered assimilated if it appears in most standard dictionaries and is familiar to most readers (cliché, etiquette, vis-à-vis, de facto, siesta).

Titles

Italicize the titles of separately published documents, such as books, periodicals, newspapers, pamphlets, brochures, and legal cases, as well as movies and radio and television series.

- *Turning Workplace Conflict into Collaboration* [book] by Joyce Richards was reviewed in the *New York Times* [newspaper].

Italicize the titles of compact discs, DVDs, plays, long poems, paintings, sculptures, and musical works.

CD-ROM	*Computer Security Tutorial on CD-ROM*
PLAY	Arthur Miller's *Death of a Salesman*

LONG POEM	T. S. Eliot's *The Waste Land*
MUSICAL WORK	Gershwin's *Porgy and Bess*

Some titles are not set off by italics, quotation marks, or underlining, although they are capitalized.

- Professional Writing [college course title], the Constitution, the Bible, Lincoln's Gettysburg Address, the Lands' End Catalog.

◆ *See also Quotation Marks, pages 641–642.*

Do not italicize the titles of holy books and legislative documents (New Testament, U.S. Constitution).

Use quotation marks for parts of publications, such as chapters of books, and sections of larger works.

- *Small Business Trends* (smallbiztrends.com/) [blog] posted "Microbusiness Economic Trends: Into the Future." [article]

Proper Names

The names of ships, trains, and aircraft (but not the companies or governments that own them) are italicized (U.S. Aircraft Carrier *Independence*; Amtrak's passenger train *Coast Starlight*). Craft that are known by model or serial designations are not italicized (DC-7; Boeing 747).

Words, Letters, and Numerals

Words, letters, and numerals discussed as such are italicized.

- The word *inflammable* is often misinterpreted.
- The *S* and *6* keys on my keyboard do not work.

Subheads

◆ *For guidance on using italics as a design element, see page 216 in Chapter 7, Designing Documents and Visuals.*

Subheads in a report are sometimes italicized.

- *Training managers.* We are leading the way in developing first-line managers who not only are professionally competent but . . .

Index